ENCYCLOPEDIA OF WOMEN IN TODAY'S WORLD

ENCYCLOPEDIA OF WOMEN IN TODAY'S WORLD

3

EDITORS

MARY ZEISS STANGE
Skidmore College

CAROL K. OYSTER
University of Wisconsin, LaCrosse

JANE E. SLOAN
Rutgers University

®SAGE | reference

Los Angeles | London | New Delhi
Singapore | Washington DC

Los Angeles | London | New Delhi
Singapore | Washington DC

FOR INFORMATION:

SAGE Publications, Inc.
2455 Teller Road
Thousand Oaks, California 91320
E-mail: order@sagepub.com

SAGE Publications India Pvt. Ltd.
B 1/I 1 Mohan Cooperative Industrial Area
Mathura Road, New Delhi 110 044
India

SAGE Publications Ltd.
1 Oliver's Yard
55 City Road
London EC1Y 1SP
United Kingdom

SAGE Publications Asia-Pacific Pte. Ltd.
33 Pekin Street #02-01
Far East Square
Singapore 048763

Vice President and Publisher: Rolf A. Janke
Senior Editor: Jim Brace-Thompson
Project Editor: Tracy Buyan
Cover Designer: Janet Kiesel
Editorial Assistant: Michele Thompson
Reference Systems Manager: Leticia Gutierrez
Reference Systems Coordinator: Laura Notton

Golson Media
President and Editor: J. Geoffrey Golson
Director, Author Management: Susan Moskowitz
Senior Layout Editor: Mary Jo Scibetta
Layout Editors: Kenneth Heller, Lois Rainwater,
    Mary Sudal
Copy Editors: Anne Hicks, Laura Liebeck,
    James Mammarella, Mary Miller, Barbara Paris
Proofreaders: Joyce Li, Mary Beth Curran
Indexer: J S Editorial

Printed in the United States of America

Library of Congress Cataloging-in-Publication Data

Encyclopedia of women in today's world / Mary Zeiss Stange, general editor, Carol K. Oyster, general editor, Jane E. Sloan, multimedia editor.
    p. cm.
    Includes bibliographical references and index.
ISBN 978-1-4129-7685-5 (hardback)
    1. Women--Encyclopedias. 2. Women--Social conditions--21st century--Encyclopedias. I. Stange, Mary Zeiss. II. Oyster, Carol K. III. Sloan, Jane, 1946-
    HQ1115.E55 2011
    305.403--dc22   2010049272

11 12 13 14 15 10 9 8 7 6 5 4 3 2 1

Contents

List of Articles

N

Namibia

Despite the postindependence efforts to improve the social, political, and economic position of Namibian women, there continue to be considerable discrepancies in the situations of men and women. The government of the Republic of Namibia has developed a substantial Gender Machinery (a system embodied by governmental institutions aimed at the promotion of gender equality) and counts on a significant number of associations working on women's issues. Yet, customary law still has a great influence in women's daily lives at all levels.

Women in Namibia constitute 51 percent of the population. Female life expectancy is 62 years. Literacy ratio for women compared with men is 0.96. These differences increase when talking about income ratio, as women's salaries are almost half of those of men (0.57), despite the fact that women's participation in the labor force is 46 percent. There are 30 percent of women in decision-making positions: 55 percent are female professionals and specialized workers. Since 2005, parliament seats are 27 percent women.

The National Gender Machinery is composed of a Ministry of Gender Equality and Child Welfare, as well as gender focal points in any other ministry, all of which are used to coordinate gender mainstreaming. However, there are no governmental gender structures locally yet. The government of Namibia is linked to supranational organizations, with specific gender units within them at the regional and the continental levels.

The numerous women's associations of Namibia are working on legal reforms; on raising awareness on the position of Namibian women; at lobbying on legal, medical, and emotional issues; on offering support to female victims of gender-based violence; on creating resource and research centers; and so on. In terms of health, many Nigerian women are human immunodeficiency virus (HIV)-positive.

The legal system includes the following: the Constitution of Namibia, which recognizes the significance of gender differences, enshrines the principle of equality, and prohibits gender-based discrimination, among other forms; the 1996 Married Persons Equality Act, which grants men and women equal access to property beyond land and allows that right to each spouse without his or her partner's consent; the 1997 National Gender Policy, which increases female participation in politics and decision making at all levels; the 2003 Anti-Rape Law, which broadens the definition of rape and punishes perpetrators of spousal rape; and Article 5 of the 2007 Labour Law, which prohibits sexual discrimination at the workplace.

Namibian legislation guarantees women's civil rights, but discriminatory traditions widely persist. Although the constitution enshrines gender equality, the daily lives of a vast majority of women continue to be determined by customary and common law in a population setting in which 80 percent of the inhabitants are Christian. Legislation has had little effect on changing attitudes and practices that are embedded within culture and tradition.

See Also: Gender Roles, Cross-Cultural; HIV/AIDS: Africa; Rape, Cross-Culturally Defined.

Further Readings

LeBeau, D. "The Changing Status of Women in Namibia and Its Impact on Violence Against Women." In Ingolf Diener and Olivier Graefe, eds., *Contemporary Namibia: The First Landmarks of a Post-Apartheid Society.* Windhoek, Namibia: Gamsberg Macmillan, 2001.

Zuckerman, Elaine and Marcia Greenberg. "The Gender Dimensions of Post-Conflict Reconstruction: An Analytical Framework for Policymakers." *Gender and Development*, v.12/3 (2004).

Juan Rodríguez-Medela
University of Granada

Nannies

The term *nanny* popularly evokes images of Mary Poppins or Supernanny Jo Frost—a woman with a British accent who, through magic or management, solves all problems. Then there are the headline nannies whose exploits with celebrity employers are the stuff of tabloid titillation.

The reality in the 21st century is that a nanny may be a college-educated professional on the lists of some pricey agency or, more likely, a woman who has emigrated from the Philippines, Central America, or the Caribbean. She—nannies are predominantly female—is employed on either a live-in or live-out, part-time or full-time basis to care for children within the home, typically working from 40 to 60 hours per week. According to a 2006 survey by the International Nanny Association, a nanny's salary ranges from $300 to $1,000 per week. As Western women have entered previously male-dominated jobs in business, politics, and other professions, the need for a nanny has grown proportionally. In the United States, two-thirds of women with children provide the primary source of family income or an essential supplementary income. More than half of

mothers with children younger than 6 years work outside the home. Of the childcare options available to these women, the preferred choice for those who can afford to do so is to hire a nanny.

The need for childcare within the home has been filled to a high degree by millions of women from poor countries immigrating to wealthy nations. Since the 1960s, women have accounted for international migration in ever-increasing numbers; in 2008, they made up almost 50 percent of emigrants worldwide. Unknown numbers of these women end up working as nannies. Some lack formal education and employable skills. Others, who have been educated for a profession, lack the credentials that will allow them to work in their fields. All possess the domestic skills almost universally defined as "women's work," and for some their only choice is between working as a nanny, a housekeeper, or a maid and prostitution.

In many cases, these women leave their own children in their native land, often in the care of a grandmother, with months or even years between visits. They send home a large portion of their earnings, hoping to provide a better life for their families. Their earnings are important not only for the families they left but also for the economies of their countries. In the Philippines, for example, overseas employment is considered a major component in the national economy. According to the Philippine Central Bank, for 11 sequential months in 2006–07, deposits from overseas employment remained above the $1 billion mark. Given the importance of their salaries, it is unsurprising that when visas, usually given for only a few months, expire, women continue in their jobs as undocumented workers—a situation some employers are willing to exploit because it allows them to avoid paying the "nanny tax," Social Security, and Medicare taxes.

The most fortunate of the nannies are well paid, well treated, and able to forge a better future for themselves and their families, but some are victims of many kinds of abuse, from low wages to sexual harassment and even rape. Even in the best of situations, they are vulnerable to indignities and insecurities. Lucy Kaylin, executive editor of *Marie Claire* and author of *The Perfect Stranger: The Truth About Mothers and Nannies*, describes a "status hierarchy" that allots higher salaries to white nannies than to nannies who are women of color. Nannies also lack job security. Even long employment ends when a child reaches the age when a nanny's care is no longer required. Changing circumstances may render a nanny redundant, as many found in the economic crunch of the early 21st century, when layoffs and downsizing made nannies dispensable.

Without citizenship, and often without legal documentation, the emigrants who work as nannies have little recourse when they are mistreated. Domestic workers are not covered under the National Labor Relations Act. Unlike men who immigrate and find employment as construction workers or cab drivers, nannies are isolated from one another and are nearly invisible to the outside world. They lack the information that is passed to the more experienced about rights and protections, and activists have discovered that traditional strategies are ineffective.

Efforts to win some protection for nannies and other domestic workers in Houston failed, although campaigns in San Francisco, Los Angeles, New York, and Washington, D.C., have fared somewhat better. The Coalition for Humane Immigrant Rights of Los Angeles worked for years to win overtime pay for nannies and saw the bill pass the state legislature in 2006, only to have it vetoed by Governor Arnold Schwarzenegger, who claimed it would not benefit the nanny business. New York has proposed a Bill of Rights, drafted by Domestic Workers United, an organization of Caribbean, Latina, and African domestic workers, that would guarantee nannies and other domestic workers overtime pay, vacation and sick days, protection from discrimination, and notice before termination.

See Also: Childcare; Domestic Workers; Philippines; Professions by Gender.

Further Readings

Ehrenreich, Barbara and Arlie Russell Hochschild, eds. *Global Woman: Nannies, Maids, and Sex Workers in the New Economy.* New York: Metropolitan Books, 2003.
Kaylin, Lucy. *The Perfect Stranger: The Truth About Mothers and Nannies.* New York: Bloomsbury, 2007.
Liebelt, Claudia. "On Sentimental Orientalists, Christian Zionists, and Working Class Cosmopolitans." *Critical Asian Studies*, v.40/4 (2008).

Wylene Rholetter
Auburn University

NARAL

NARAL Pro-Choice America is one of the leading organizations in the United States seeking to advance and protect reproductive rights. It works to elect pro-choice candidates to public office, organizes individuals throughout the country to advocate on behalf of reproductive rights and defend against antichoice efforts, lobbies members of Congress, and conducts research and analysis on relevant legislation and judicial decisions at the federal and state levels. NARAL Pro-Choice America consists of three branches that fulfill different roles: NARAL Pro-Choice Inc., NARAL Pro-Choice America Foundation, and NARAL Pro-Choice America PAC. The organization also has 22 state affiliates that operate independently to engage with state politics and policy.

History and Structure

In 1969, a group of activists established the National Association for the Repeal of Abortion Laws (NARAL). Four years later, following the Supreme Court's *Roe v. Wade* decision legalizing abortion, the organization kept the acronym but changed its name to the National Abortion Rights Action League. In 1993, it again kept the acronym and revised its name to the National Abortion and Reproductive Rights Action League, prior to changing its name to NARAL Pro-Choice America.

NARAL Pro-Choice America, Inc., is a 501(c)(4) organization, holding a tax-exempt status that allows it to conduct lobbying activities and participate in legislative processes. NARAL Pro-Choice America Foundation has 501(c)(3) tax-exempt status that enables it to receive tax-deductible donations but restricts the type of political activity in which it may engage. NARAL Pro-Choice America PAC is a political action committee that contributes financially to pro-choice political candidates and further engages in electoral politics. Established in 1978, NARAL Pro-Choice America PAC is the largest nonpartisan pro-choice political action committee in the United States.

NARAL Pro-Choice America, Inc., the 501(c)(4) organization, advocates for comprehensive reproductive health policies and reproductive choice. It uses the political and legislative systems, engaging members across the country and lobbying legislators. Excluding electoral activities that the foundation are prohibited from being involved with NARAL Pro-

Choice America, Inc., and the foundation are largely intertwined. Sharing office space and staff, together they conduct strategic planning and implement advocacy and public education campaigns. The authority to endorse political candidates, however, lies solely with NARAL Pro-Choice America PAC.

Much of NARAL Pro-Choice America's work between 2000 and 2008 was oriented toward defeating antichoice legislation, judicial appointments, ballot measures, and corporate policy, while mobilizing grassroots efforts to elect pro-choice candidates, support pro-choice elected officials, and expand women's access to reproductive healthcare. For example, the organization helped increase women's access to emergency contraception by acting to persuade Walmart and Kroger to carry it. It also helped prevent President George W. Bush's antichoice nominee from receiving a lifetime appointment as a U.S. district court judge.

In 2004, the organization cosponsored the March for Women's Lives that included between 500,000 and 1.15 million participants, making it one of the largest demonstrations in U.S. history. In May 2008, three months before the conclusion of the Democratic presidential primary campaign, NARAL Pro-Choice America PAC made the controversial decision to endorse Democratic candidate Barack Obama for president. NARAL Pro-Choice America President Nancy Keenan explained that both Senator Obama and his opponent, Senator Hillary Clinton, were equally pro-choice, but Senator Obama was likely to win the primary.

In 2009, with a Democratic president and congressional majority, the organization worked to increase low-income women's access to abortion, reduce obstacles to comprehensive sexual education, and increase funding for family-planning programs in the United States and abroad. It added more than 160,000 email activists, who participated in campaigns sending 340,000 e-mails to legislators on behalf of reproductive rights. In early 2010, NARAL Pro-Choice America focused on health insurance reform, organizing and lobbying against the inclusion of antichoice proposals. Ultimately, the organization did not endorse the bill because of its restrictions on abortion coverage, but it also did not call for its defeat, as the bill's other reproductive health provisions were worthwhile. The organization also called for President Obama to nominate, and Congress to confirm, a pro-choice Supreme Court Justice to replace retiring Justice John Paul Stevens.

Leadership and Staff

NARAL Pro-Choice America, Inc., and NARAL Pro-Choice America Foundation have separate boards of directors made up of from 21 to 30 members and no more than 21 members, respectively. All serve three-year terms. NARAL Pro-Choice America, Inc., board members may also be elected to serve on the PAC. Annually, NARAL Pro-Choice America, Inc., has three board meetings, and the foundation has at least two. Board members also participate in conference calls and committee meetings. Board members include civic leaders, former elected officials, and healthcare experts. To protect the safety of its staff, NARAL Pro-Choice America is housed in a secure building and does not publish the names of staff members or board members.

NARAL Pro-Choice America relies on members for financial support and, critically, for activism toward shared goals. As of 2010, NARAL Pro-Choice America has 1 million members, or "member activists," who are located in every state.

NARAL Pro-Choice America partners with a number of pro-choice organizations, including the Planned Parenthood Federation of America, the National Latina Institute for Reproductive Health, the National Asian Pacific American Forum, SisterSong, the National Partnership for Women and Families, and the National Abortion Federation. In partnership with organizations that specifically represent women of color, NARAL Pro-Choice America collaborates on lobbying efforts, cosponsors SisterSong's annual conference, and consults with the organizations' leaders on increasing engagement with diverse communities. On issues such as judicial nominations, NARAL Pro-Choice America partners with groups in the broader progressive community, such as the Human Rights Campaign, Leadership Conference on Civil Rights, the Alliance for Justice, and People for the American Way.

See Also: Abortion, Access to; Abortion Laws, United States; Planned Parenthood; Reproductive and Sexual Health Rights; *Roe v. Wade*.

Further Readings

Hayden, S. "Revitalizing the Debate between Life and Choice: The 2004 March for Women's Lives." *Communication and Critical/Cultural Studies*, v.6/2 (2009).

Keenan, N. "Why NARAL Pro-Choice America Endorsed Barack Obama." *The Huffington Post* (May 2008). http://www.huffingtonpost.com/nancy-keenan/why-naral-pro-choice-amer_b_101708.html (accessed April 2010).

NARAL Pro-Choice America. http://www.prochoiceamerica.org (accessed June 2010).

Shin, Y. "Constituency Opinion and PAC Contributions: A Case of the National Abortion and Reproductive Rights Action League." *Public Choice*, v.118/1/2 (2004).

Perrin L. Elkind
University of California, Berkeley

National Museum of Women in the Arts

The National Museum of Women in the Arts is the only art museum in the United States that is dedicated to the work of women artists. Wilhelmina Cole Holladay founded the museum in 1981 after her good friend Nancy Hanks, the first female chair of the National Endowment of the Arts, jokingly suggested that Holladay and her spouse, Wallace F. Holladay, start a museum with their collection of approximately 500 works by women artists that they had acquired over a 20-year period. Today the collection includes more than 3,000 works by more than 800 women artists, dating from the 16th century to the present, and represents a broad range of media, styles, and nationalities. For example, the collection includes works by 16th-century Italian painter Lavinia Fontana, 19th-century French sculptor Camille Claudel, and 20th-century Mexican photographer Lola Álvarez Bravo.

The mission of the museum is to bring recognition to the achievements of women artists of all periods and nationalities. The museum supports this mission by preserving and acquiring artworks in the permanent collection, holding special exhibitions, offering approximately 80 educational and outreach programs annually to the community and educators, and maintaining a library and research center

The interior of the National Museum of Women in the Arts in Washington, D.C. The museum's mission is to display and bring recognition to the achievements of women artists of all periods and nationalities.

that includes files on more than 18,000 women artists and more than 18,500 books and catalogues. The museum also publishes a quarterly magazine for museum members, *Women in the Arts*, and books on women artists.

According to Wilhelmina Cole Holladay, her interest in collecting art by women artists began when she and her husband were traveling in Europe in the early 1970s and saw works by 17th-century Flemish painter Clara Peeters in museums in Austria and Spain. On their return to the United States, they discovered that there was no mention of Peeters, or of any other woman artist, in art history reference books. The Holladays began collecting artworks, focusing on the contributions of women artists.

The museum began as tours of the Holladays' collection in their home in 1981. The collection was relocated to a historic building near the White House in 1983, and in 1987 it was moved to its present location at 1250 New York Avenue NE in Washington, D.C. The museum has more than 200,000 members and has hosted 1.2 million visitors since opening. One of the museum's growth goals is to expand its network of 28 U.S. state and three international committees that help support the museum. The National Museum of Women in the Arts has promoted a greater recognition of women artists and their contributions to the history of art.

In 1986, *Janson's History of Art*, an authoritative text on art history, included women artists for the first time since its initial publication in 1962. In 2006, Holladay was awarded both the National Medal of Arts from the U.S. government and the Legion of Honor from the French government for her services to the arts. She serves as chair of the museum board of trustees.

See Also: Art Criticism: Gender Issues; Arts, Women in the (21st Century Overview); Studio Arts, Women in.

Further Readings

Cole Holladay, Wilhelmina. *A Museum of Their Own: National Museum of Women in the Arts.* New York: Abbeville, 2008.

National Museum of Women in the Arts. http://www .nmwa.org (accessed December 2009).

Smart Woman. "A Museum of Their Own: Founder of the National Museum of Women in the Arts." http://smart womanonline.com/feature/2009/01/a-museum-of -their-own (accessed December 2009).

Deborah R. Bassett
University of Washington

National Organization for Women

The National Organization for Women, commonly called NOW, is currently the largest nonprofit membership organization in the United States working to advance women's civil rights. The history of this activist organization began with its formation in 1966 and includes significant examples of public demonstrations for women's equality in all aspects of women's lives. As a contemporary organization, NOW has been publically advocating for six priority issues: advocating constitutional equality, ending violence against women, supporting abortion rights and other reproductive issues, promoting diversity and ending racism, forwarding lesbian rights, and ensuring economic justice for women.

The organization was formed in 1966 by several feminist activists who were advocating the enforcement of Title VII of the Civil Rights Act of 1964, which prohibited sex discrimination in employment. Founding members included a large circle of feminist activists and academics, including Betty Friedan, author of *The Feminine Mystique*; Dr. Pauli Murray, activist and attorney; and Aileen Hernandez, an Equal Employment Opportunity Commissioner. Other founding members active in the early leadership of NOW include Richard Graham, Caroline Davis, Inka O'hanrahan, Rosalind Loring, Mary Eastwood, and Kay Clarenbach.

The organizing conference was held in October 1966, with 30 attendees representing approximately 300 charter members. At the conference, NOW founding members wrote a Statement of Purpose for the organization, which was formed to bring women closer to the goals of equality and partnership with men. In order to achieve this goal, target areas were formed for equal opportunity of employment, legal and political rights, education, women in poverty, the family, the image of women, and religion.

The first elected president of NOW was Betty Friedan, who served in this role between 1966 and 1970. As president, she brought the spotlight of celebrity to the organization due to the success of her best-selling book, *The Feminine Mystique*, attracting greater numbers of members. During her tenure, the organization also continued to become more politically and publically active. For example, NOW members initiated a persuasive boycott against Colgate-Palmolive products in protest of rules that barred women from certain company positions. In another example, NOW members organized large public demonstrations outside the offices of the Equal Employment Opportunity Commission in every large city in the United States to decry the use of sex-specific job advertisements in newspapers, a practice that continued despite the passage of the Civil Rights Act of 1964. Both efforts resulted in more public awareness and an end to these discriminatory practices. Finally, NOW also became the first national organization to officially support the legalization of abortion while under Friedan's leadership.

Throughout the 1970s, NOW experienced continued growth in membership and more success in lobbying and activist activities. In 1970, NOW organized the "Women's Strike for Equality" event in cities throughout the United States to celebrate the 50th anniversary of the Nineteenth Amendment that gave women the right to vote: in New York City, an estimated 50,000 women participated in the walk down Fifth Avenue. In 1972, NOW organized a campaign to recognize girls as equal to boys in all facets of education and celebrated when Congress passed the Education Amendments of 1972, which included the Title IX protections that guarantee equal education opportunities, including sports, to girls and boys. In the mid-1970s, organizers from NOW aided the movement to redefine rape as a crime of violence, and they helped plan the first "Take Back the Night" rally to protest violence against women in 1975. Later in the 1970s, NOW's platform expanded to specifically include the rights and interests of battered women and lesbians.

Nearly from its inception, NOW provided public support of the passage of the Equal Rights Amendment (ERA), which was a proposed amendment to the U.S. Constitution that would affirm the equality of men and women. After significant lobbying efforts by NOW and other feminist organizations, the ERA was passed by overwhelming majorities in the U.S. House and Senate in 1972. As is required by the Constitution, the Congress then sent the proposed amendment to the individual state legislatures, seeking the required three-quarters approval within seven years. By 1977, 35 of the required 38 states had voted to ratify the ERA, and when the deadline approached in 1979, NOW organized a march of 100,000 women down Constitution Avenue to the U.S. Capitol in Washington, D.C., to push Congress for an extension. Although the extension was ultimately granted, the ERA failed in 1982 when no additional states moved for ratification. NOW continues to support the amendment, and it has been reintroduced into the Senate every subsequent year by legislators such as Edward Kennedy (former D-MA) and Carolyn B. Maloney (D-NY).

Although the ERA failed to become an amendment to the Constitution, NOW has continued to advocate for women's rights and has been successful in attracting media attention to these issues, often with large public rallies in Washington, D.C., and other cities. For example, NOW sponsored a massive public demonstration in 1992 called the "March for Women's Lives" that involved 500,000 demonstrators who gathered on the mall in Washington to advocate for women's reproductive rights. In 1995, NOW organized another demonstration at the capitol that was designed to draw attention to violence against women, and more than 250,000 attended. In 2004, NOW drew 1.15 million demonstrators to the nation's capitol to advocate women's reproductive health rights.

NOW Foundation

In 1986, The NOW Foundation was formed to specifically engage in litigation, education, and advocacy for women's rights in all aspects of their personal and professional lives. Unlike NOW, which is a political organization, the NOW Foundation is registered as a 501(c)(3) tax-exempt organization. The NOW Foundation is closely allied with NOW, and the two organizations share office space and support staff.

The foundation uses litigation to protect reproductive health options, including abortions. In a famous example, NOW used federal antitrust laws to sue Joe Scheidler and other antiabortion activists, claiming that Schiedler and the others had conspired to close women's health clinics. The case was highly contested and was in litigation for 20 years, eventually being heard by the U.S. Supreme Court. When the court ruled against NOW on February 20, 2006, NOW publically stated that such a ruling could make safe access to reproductive choices even more difficult for women, and it vowed to continue to protect a woman's right to choices in reproductive health.

The NOW Foundation also uses education and advocacy to promote the goals of equality for women through the planning and implementation of conferences, seminars, and training sessions. One example of this work is the Love Your Body Campaign. Started in 1998, the Campaign's focus is to promote healthy, positive body images for women in the face of the negative and unrealistic messages about women's bodies popular in the media. The Love Your Body Campaign involves educational events at many college campuses and a poster contest with a cash prize. The NOW Foundation also promotes voter-empowerment programs, encouraging women to vote and to become and remain politically active.

Contemporary Issues

Currently, NOW focuses its activism on the six priority issues of advocating constitutional equality, ending violence against women, supporting abortion rights and other reproductive issues, promoting diversity and ending racism, forwarding lesbian rights, and ensuring economic justice for women.

The issue of constitutional equality is an issue that continues to retain central importance to members of NOW, despite the 1982 failure of the ERA. NOW argues that any progress in women's equality in job opportunities and pay, politics, and education will always risk erosion until they are protected by a constitutional amendment that guarantees equality between women and men.

A second key issue of NOW's agenda is to end violence against women. This focus has been a central tenet since the founding of the organization, and NOW continues to fight all forms of violence against women, including domestic violence, sexual assault, sexual harassment, violence at abortion clinics, and hate crimes related to gender and sexual identity. Special campaigns constructed to address violence have focused on sexual assault specifically on college campuses and in the branches of the U.S. Military.

Supporting abortion rights and other reproductive concerns is the third key issue for NOW, which fully supports a woman's right to a legal abortion. Since the 1973 *Roe v. Wade* Supreme Court decision that upheld a woman's legal right to abortion, NOW has rallied against the erosion of abortion rights in state and federal legislation. NOW also campaigns for effective birth control and emergency contraception. The organization is particularly concerned that women retain the right to receive reproductive education in schools and in health clinics.

A fourth priority for NOW is the promotion of diversity and the ending of racism. As a civil rights organization, NOW has consistently maintained a position against racism and has publically supported every civil rights bill that has been considered by federal legislators since its inception. NOW also has a specific campaign for the concerns faced by undocumented, immigrant women and supports immigration reform that would recognize the basic rights of undocumented individuals.

Lesbian rights is the fifth key issue in NOW's current platform and has been an official part of NOW's focus since 1971. By 1973, NOW organized the Task Force on Sexuality and Lesbianism and resolved to introduce and support civil rights legislation to end discrimination based on sexual orientation. More recently, NOW has applauded the passage of the Matthew Shepard and James Byrd, Jr. Hate Crimes Prevention Act, which expanded federal hate crime laws to include crimes based on gender or sexual identity or orientation. NOW has supported the repeal of the the "Don't Ask, Don't Tell" policy currently enforced by all branches of the U.S. Armed Forces that requires gay and lesbian service people to hide their sexual preference to retain their positions. In March 2010, the U.S. House of Representatives approved a proposal to repeal the law, and government leaders, including President Obama, remained hopeful that the policy will be overturned. NOW also supports the equal rights of marriage for all, including gay and lesbian couples.

Finally, the sixth priority issue promoted by NOW is economic justice for women, and the organization continues to rally for equal pay for women and men in comparable positions, a goal that has not yet been achieved. NOW is also committed to other economic issues impacting women, including welfare reform, job discrimination, livable wages, housing discrimination, and social security and pension reform. Toward these ends, NOW began the Women-Friendly Workplace and Campus Campaign that publicizes the concerns of sexual harassment and discrimination in the workplace through consumer pledges of support for women-friendly organizations, employer pledges of minimum standards for women in the workplace, and direct action and consumer campaigns targeted against the merchants who have poor track records in discrimination and equality in the workplace.

NOW continues to promote advocacy work and education to promote equality for women. NOW maintains an active Website that serves as a clearinghouse for news and events of interest to NOW members at http://www.now.org.

See Also: Equal Rights Amendment; Feminism, American; Gay and Lesbian Advocacy; Reproductive and Sexual Health Rights; Sex Education, Comprehensive.

Further Readings

Barasko, Maryann. *Governing NOW: Grassroots Activism In The National Organization For Women.* Ithaca, NY: Cornell University Press, 2004.
Commire, Anne. *Live From The Dorothy Chandler Pavilion: NOW's 20th Anniversary* [VHS Recording]. Peg Yorkin Productions, 1986.
National Organization for Women. "History of N.O.W." http://www.now.org/history/index.html (accessed December 2009).

Jennifer Adams
DePauw University

National Women's Political Caucus

The National Women's Political Caucus (NWPC) was founded in 1971 by Bella Abzug, Gloria Steinem, Shirley Chisholm, and Betty Friedan. Originally the group was organized as a response to the lack of women both in public office and as political appointees. The NWPC started out as a local grassroots organization focused on getting women elected to public office at every level. In 1973, the NWPC became one of the first organizations to open a Washington, D.C., office with the idea of lobbying Congress and promoting the election of women. Initial lobbying efforts focused on the Equal Rights Amendment. Subsequently, the group began to focus on other women's issues.

The NWPC defined its objectives early on when it decided not to endorse Shirley Chisholm in 1972 for president. Instead, NWPC founders such as Bella Abzug believed the caucus needed to focus on statewide caucuses and to gain political representation for women at local and national political conventions. The NWPC continued to believe that getting women into public office, from the local level up to Congress, was a top priority.

The NWPC pressured the political parties to be more inclusive of women. Even though the group was only established in 1971, it worked with other interest groups to increase female representation at the 1972 political conventions. NWPC leadership called for proportional representation of delegates at the 1972 Democratic National Convention. As a result, the number of women delegates was increased at the 1972 convention compared with the 1968 convention.

During the 1980s, the NWPC worked to reduce sexism in the federal code and to improve insurance and pension legislation. The NWPC emphasized the mobilization of voters over advocating the forms of protest commonly used in the 1970s and 1980s. Following the confirmation of Justice Clarence Thomas, the NWPC ran an advertisement in the *New York Times* pointing to the Senate Judiciary Committee's all-male membership. As part of the campaign, NWPC President Harriett Woods went to New York to pressure magazines to write articles calling 1992 "The Year of the Woman." The NWPC's political action committee played a significant role in funding women's campaigns during this election cycle.

In 1994, the NWPC commissioned an oft-cited study uncovering the fact that men and women in traditionally political occupations perceived running for public office differently. They found that half of the women believed they were not qualified to run for public office.

Reductions in membership during the 1980s and 1990s forced NWPC to reduce the size of its staff, and today it only has one full-time employee. Still, at this time, the NWPC belongs to a number of active lobbying coalitions and uses its political action committee to focus government attention on concerns such as pay equity and family-planning issues. Local chapters in 38 states continue to work on getting women elected to public office and to raise awareness for national women's issues. To help women get elected to public office, the NWPC offers training literature and provides local and national training to women seeking public office at the local and national levels. Its workshops focus on encouraging women to run for public office and teaching women how to develop winning campaign strategies.

See Also: EMILY'S List; Equal Rights Amendment; League of Women Voters; Government, Women in; Representation of Women in Government, U.S.; Social Justice Activism; Steinem, Gloria.

Further Readings

Boles, Janet K. "Form Follows Function: The Evolution of Feminist Strategies." *Annals of the American Academy of Political and Social Science*, v.515 (1991).

Darcy, R., et al. *Women, Elections, and Representations.* Omaha: University of Nebraska Press, 1994.

Freeman, J. "Women at the 1988 Democratic Convention." *PS: Political Science and Politics*, v.21/4 (1988).

Sawyers, Traci M. and David S. Meyer. "Missed Opportunities: Social Movement Abeyance and Public Policy." *Social Problems*, v.46/2 (1999).

Angela L. Bos
Alexander Lans
College of Wooster

National Women's Studies Association

The National Women's Studies Association (NWSA) is a professional organization meant to lead the fields of Women's Studies and gender studies, both educationally and socially. The organization believes that Women's Studies is vital to education and is comparative, global, intersectional, and interdisciplinary. Scholarship, activism, and teaching are not mutually exclusive for members of the NWSA but, rather, inseparable elements of academic life.

The first convention of the NWSA was held at the University of San Francisco on January 13–16, 1977. A founding preamble to the NWSA Constitution was adopted at this meeting, which outlined the mission and goals of the NWSA and also credited the movement for the liberation of women via the existence of women's studies. The preamble was revised in 1982 to incorporate more inclusive language. The original document cited the need to eradicate sexism and racism; the revised edition builds on that need, adding the abolition of class and ethnic bias; anti-Semitism, as directed against both Arabs and Jews; ageism; and heterosexual bias.

NWSA membership is composed of approximately 2,000 faculty, staff, and students from educational institutions of all levels, employees of women's centers, and community scholars. The organization is led by a president, who serves as the intellectual leader for NWSA and also spearheads the programming for the annual conference, and a full-time executive director, as well as a director of media and technology, a deputy director, a national administrator, and a member services and operations coordinator. The staff aids the NWSA in its mission to further the social, political, and professional development of its members through publications, conferences, workshops, job listings, scholarships, and supporting scholarship that transforms the knowledge of women and puts that knowledge into practice.

The major publication of the organization, the *NWSA Journal*, is currently published triennially by Johns Hopkins University Press. Although it is independently incorporated, the *NWSA Journal*, similar to its flagship organization, is committed to publishing feminist research and creating space for dialogue among feminist scholars. As of January 1, 2010, the journal will be published at the University of Minnesota under the name *Feminist Formations*. It has been published previously at the Ohio State University, University of New Hampshire, Appalachian State University, Iowa State University, and Louisiana State University. Along with the *NWSA Journal*, the NWSA has produced numerous publications to further scholarship and curriculum development in women's studies and gender studies such as *Liberal Learning and the Women's Studies Major*; *Guide to Graduate Work In Women's/Gender Studies*; *Bridges of Power: Women's Multicultural Alliances*; *The Courage to Question:*

Women's Studies and Student Learning; and *Students at the Center: A Feminist Assessment.*

The NWSA hosts a conference in a different location annually that brings together feminist scholars and activists from around the globe. The president of the NWSA leads the planning for the annual gatherings. Each conference celebrates a particular theme pertinent to the field of women's studies and includes plenary sessions that celebrate the diverse work of leading feminist scholars and activists, panels and workshops proposed by NWSA members, and feminist cultural events and entertainment. Proposals for conference papers and posters are accepted from students, faculty, community members, and representatives from women's centers. One hundred registration and travel scholarships are available for each conference for students, activists, and community members who are presenting and demonstrate financial need.

The NWSA has a strong commitment to providing support and resources to women's studies and gender studies scholars. Each year the organization recognizes excellence in the field of women's studies with scholarships and monetary prizes. The Sara A. Whaley Book Prize honors members for exceptional books on the topic of women and labor. The Gloria Anzaldúa Book Prize is awarded for groundbreaking women's studies scholarship, with a specific focus on multicultural and transnational issues for women of color. The NWSA offers a distinguished fellowship each year to a feminist scholar who has demonstrated a longstanding commitment to women's studies. The recipient spends a summer, semester, or full academic year in residence at the NWSA office in College Park, Maryland, working on a research project dedicated to the promotion and development of Women's Studies scholarship.

The NWSA also offers several scholarships for eligible graduate students. The NWSA Graduate Scholarship Award is granted to a student who will be writing a master's thesis or doctoral dissertation in the fall of the year the award is granted; the Lesbian Caucus Scholarship is given to the graduate student whose master's thesis or doctoral dissertation project emphasizes the goals of the NWSA and the Lesbian Caucus; and four awards are given by the Women of Color Caucus to graduate students of African descent; Latina descent; Asian/Asian American/Pacific Islander/Arab/Middle Eastern descent;

and African Native American, American Indian, and Alaskan Native descent.

The history of the NWSA has been controversial at times. The annual conference at the University of Akron in 1990 was a watershed moment for the members and leaders of the NWSA, as attendees argued over the future goals of the association. It was decided, however, that the NWSA is needed to foster interdisciplinary scholarship; to promote feminist theory, pedagogy, and practice; to establish the professional identities of women's studies scholars; and to mentor graduate students in women's studies.

See Also: College and University Faculty; Education, Women in; "Femininity," Social Construction of; Feminism, American; Feminist Publishing; Social Justice Activism; Women's Studies.

Further Readings
McFadden, Margaret, ed. "25 Years of NWSA: Vision, Controversy, Transformation." *NWSA Journal*, v.14/1 (2002).
National Women's Studies Association. http://www.nwsa.org (accessed November 2009).

Katie M. White
University of Maryland, College Park

Native American Religion

At the beginning of European contact with the Western Hemisphere in the 16th century, there were literally hundreds of small-scale traditional or tribal religions throughout the Americas. At the core of many of those religions were expressions of the creative power as a goddess who grew from the power of women and the feminine. Many new religious movements among Native Americans over the centuries of contact grew from both Native traditions and unique interpretations of Christian teachings, which also focused on the role of women in bringing God or the gods to life on Earth.

By the start of the 20th century, many tribal religions, especially in North America, had diminished or disappeared due to violence, disease, missionization, and a systematic persecution of Native American religious traditions. As women's rights became an issue in industrialized nations and women gained the right to vote in many parts of the world, restrictions against traditional religious practice among Native Americans began to ease and a resurgence of interest in the preservation of traditional philosophies among tribal nations emerged.

In Native American religions, as in most religions, the first contact with the sacred is through our mothers. Membership in a tribal religion is through birth from a woman, affiliation with a clan with its requisite clan mothers, or membership in a tribe where women were the head of the family, the clan, or recognized as the chief or head of the tribe. Birth is a sacred event and is marked by Native religious practice as something more than a woman having a baby. The tribe has a new citizen and at birth becomes a son or daughter, grandchild, niece or nephew, and the responsibility of the entire tribal community. A name for the newborn is given from or through the ancestors or spirits associated with the tribal religion, and family, clan, and tribe realizes the promise of new life and a continuation of the ancestral ways.

For every child, puberty signals another time of ceremony to celebrate the acquisition of more responsibility and status: in Native American religions, the puberty ceremony for the transition of girls to women is more marked than it is for boys. A girl's menarche, or first menses, engenders an intense time of teaching about her fecundity and potential contribution to the future of the entire tribe. The ceremonies of menarche are often four days of fasting, sweating, instruction on the role of women in the tribe, and the acquisition of power through the changes in her body. She is a new woman, and as such can attract good or bad intentions from other tribal members or even outsiders who might exploit her power for their own selfish ends.

Throughout the life of each Native American, these transitions are noted by contact with women of the tribe; mother, grandmother, wife, daughter, and grandchildren, as well a recognition of the power of the feminine at the heart of those rites of passage. Women give birth to boys and girls, marry men, heal and mourn the dead men or women-and replace the dead with their power to give birth.

Just as many religions in the world rely on men or women to worship and celebrate a male creator, most Native American religions lay out paths for their believers to find their way to the sacred feminine.

Central American Catholicism centers around the worship of the Virgin de Guadalupe, and millions of recent immigrants of predominantly Central American Indian ancestry have brought those religious ideas to the United States. Even though tribal religions in North America accouns for only few million, the addition of Native American Catholics, whose spiritual path takes them to the feet of the "brown virgin," should be counted as followers of Native American religions as well.

Contemporary Native American Religious Expression

Native American religious ideas have also found their way into contemporary religious expressions through the New Age religious movements, not only in America, but also in Western Europe. Worship of the goddess or goddesses of creation, celebration of the earth and its cycles (which harmonize with women and their cycles), the use of the sweat lodge as a method purification and rebirth, and a recognition of women and the feminine as core beliefs are shared by both Native American religions and most New Age religious sects.

Language and culture revitalization efforts by tribes in the United States have found their greatest success through the development of programs that focus on teaching young women of chil-bearing age. In reverse of church and government policies of the 19th and early 20th century, which took children, especially girls, from the homes of Native Americans for instruction and "civilization" in white culture, Native American leaders recognize the role of women as first and primary teachers of new generations of tribal citizens.

There are more than 560 federally recognized tribes in the United States, and overo200 groups that have applied for federal recognition since applications were opened in the late 1970s. Once women in the dominant society gained voting rights and began to get elected in significant numbers to leadership positions, women leaders were also allowed to emerge among Native American tribes.

Ada Deer, a Menominee, led the movement to reestablish the Menominee reservation in Wisconsin in the 1970s, and went on to become the first woman to lead the Bureau of Indian Affairs (1993–97). The late Wilma Mankiller was elected to lead the largest Native

American tribe, the Cherokee Nation of Oklahoma. All across the United States, women are being elected to tribal councils and as chiefs, governors, and chairpersons of tribes which a hundred years earlier, faced the end of their religious and cultural identity. Native American tribes are undergoing a resurgence of their traditional religions. Women and expressions of the feminine are at the core of that revival. Languages once forgotten are being taught to mothers, who teach their children and grandchildren, and the circle of traditional teaching centered on the family is once again being embraced by Native American women.

See Also: Indigenous Religions; LaDuke, Winona; Mankiller, Wilma; Religion, Women in; Virgin of Guadelupe.

Further Readings
Allen, Paul Gunn. *The Sacred Hoop: Recovering the Feminine in American Indian Traditions.* Boston: Beacon Press. 1992.
LaDuke, Winona. *Recovering the Sacred: The Power of Naming and Claiming.* Cambridge, MA: South End Press. 2005
Mankiller, Wilma. *Every Day Is a Good Day: Reflections by Contemporary Indigenous Women.* Golden, CO: Fulcrum Publishing, 2004.

Johnny P. Flynn
Indiana University–Purdue University, Indianapolis

Nauru

After years of foreign occupation by Australia and other nations and a period as a League of Nations mandate, the Pacific island of Nauru achieved independence in 1968, becoming the world's smallest independent republic in 1999. By 2008, the entire island had become urbanized. Ethnically, 58 percent of the population is Nauruan, and 27 percent is Pacific Islanders. The island is religiously divided among Nauru Congregationalists (35.4 percent), Roman Catholics (33.2 percent), and Nauru Independent Church (10.4 percent). Suffrage is compulsory for all Nauruans aged 20 years and older, but few women participate in politics. Reports indicate that many women have been intimidated when trying to cast ballots. There are no women in parliament. Feminist scholars have attributed this fact to cultural prejudice that prevents women from taking an active role in either politics or religion. Although no specific data exist on incidences of domestic violence, evidence suggests most families deal with the issue on their own.

Economically, Nauru is struggling for survival. When it became clear that phosphate supplies on which Nauru's economy depended were being exhausted, the government established a trust fund to prepare for a transition economy. However, those funds were used for other purposes, plunging the government into virtual bankruptcy. Subsequently, wages were frozen, and government staffs were cut. By the early 21st century, Nauru had a per capita income of $5,000 and an unemployment rate of 90 percent.

The median age for Nauruan females is 22.2 years. With an infant mortality rate of 9.25 deaths per 1,000 live births, Nauru ranks 155th in the world. From the beginning of life, female infants (6.8 deaths per 1,000 live births) have a survival advantage over boys (11.58 deaths per 1,000 live births). This advantage continues throughout life, resulting in a female life expectancy of 68 years compared with that of men (61 years). Nauruan women have an average fertility rate of 2.85 children per woman. Nauruan women generally attend school for nine years—a year longer than men.

In response to international pressure following the Beijing Women's Conference in 1995, the government of Nauru launched a conscious effort to improve the life of women on the island. In 1997, a Women's Office was created at the national level to monitor women's rights and promote professional opportunities for women. A new national plan identified the following areas in which women's issues needed to be addressed: health, education and training, violence, human rights, decision making, economics, media, the environment, culture, and agriculture and fisheries.

See Also: Australia; Educational Opportunities/Access; Environmental Issues, Women and; Health, Mental and Physical; Indigenous Women's Issues.

Further Readings
Central Intelligence Agency. "The World Factbook: Nauru." https://www.cia.gov/library/publications/the-world-factbook/geos/nr.html (accessed February 2010).

Republic of Nauru. "Response to the United Nations Questionnaire on the Implementation of the Beijing Platform for Action and the Outcome of the Twenty-Third Special Session of the General Assembly, August 2009." http://www.unescap.org/ESID/GAD/Issues /Beijing+15/Responds_to_Questionnaire/Nauru.pdf (accessed February 2010).

U.S. Department of State. "2008 Human Rights Report: Nauru." http://www.state.gov/g/drl/rls/hrrpt/2008 /eap/119050.htm (accessed February 2010).

Elizabeth Rholetter Purdy
Independent Scholar

Navdanya

Navdanya is a women-centered network of seed keepers and organic producers in India. Created in 1987 by scientist and environmentalist Vandana Shiva to ensure the protection of both biological and cultural diversity, the organization endeavors to create awareness of the dangers of genetic engineering, to safeguard indigenous knowledge from biopiracy, and to guarantee food rights in the face of economic

Navdanya was created by scientist and environmentalist Vandana Shiva to protect biological and cultural diversity.

globalization and climate change. Spread across 16 states in India, Navdanya has been instrumental in the creation of 54 community seed banks and the largest direct-marketing, fair trade organic network in the country. Over the past two decades, Navdanya has trained more than 500,000 farmers in seed sovereignty, food sovereignty, and sustainable agriculture.

An outgrowth of the Research Foundation for Science, Technology and Ecology, a public interest research organization founded by Dr. Shiva to counter dominant paradigms in science and technology, Navdanya (the word refers to the nine crops that represent India's collective source of food security) began as a biodiversity conservation program to support local farmers and to rescue crops and plants that were being pushed to extinction—to conserve them and make them available through direct marketing. In the years following its inception, the network launched several campaigns, including a challenge to the patenting of the neem seed (an important ingredient in skin care creams and a natural insect repellent) and of basmati rice, and has protested against the Monsanto Corporation's creation of GMO Bt. Cotton (because of what they perceive as an effort by multinational companies to control Indian agriculture and its markets). More recently, the organization has allied itself with Slow Food International, the Center for Food Safety, the Waterkeepers Alliance, and the Dalai Lama, as well as a plethora of other organizations to, disseminate the Navdanya vision and philosophy more widely throughout the world.

A concrete manifestation of Dr. Shiva's philosophical commitment to the creation of what she has termed Earth Democracy (a living democracy committed to the defense of the rights of nature and human rights), the network's mission is to promote peace, justice, and sustainability through the conservation and renewal of nature's gifts of biodiversity to maintain them as a commons for all humanity. Members of Navdanya believe that seeds, biodiversity, and traditional knowledge must be kept in the hands of the people to generate livelihoods and provide basic needs to eradicate poverty. To that end, they advocate that the world community respect seed sovereignty (*bija swaraj*), food sovereignty (*anna swaraj*), and water sovereignty/democracy (*jal swaraj*). They are also committed to changing the rules of trade that they say are forced on small peasants through the

World Trade Organization Agreement on Agriculture—an accord they claim is leading many farmers into debt, destitution, and suicide.

Recipient of a Slow Food Award in 2001, Navdanya hosts interns from across India and around the world at Bija Vidyapeeth (Earth University), an educational partnership with Schumacher College in the United Kingdom that is designed to promote environmental and economic solutions rooted in deep ecology and the principles of democracy.

See Also: Ecofeminism; Environmental Activism, Grassroots; Environmental Issues, Women and; Environmental Justice; Fair Trade; Nongovermental Organizations Worldwide; Shiva, Vandana; Social Justice Activism; Women in Farm Economy; Women's Environment and Development Organization; Women's Thrift Cooperatives.

Further Readings

Navdanya. http://www.navdanya.org/home (accessed April 20, 2010).

Shiva, Vandana. *Earth Democracy: Justice, Sustainability, and Peace.* Cambridge, MA: South End, 2005.

Shiva, Vandana, ed. *Manifestos on the Future of Food and Seed.* Cambridge, MA: South End, 2007.

Shiva, Vandana. *Soil Not Oil.* Cambridge, MA: South End, 2008.

Danielle Roth-Johnson
University of Nevada, Las Vegas

Nepal

Despite its small size, Nepal contains an impressive diversity of ethnic and caste groups: more than 100 groups and 90 languages are represented. Prior to 2008, Nepal was the world's only Hindu kingdom. Eighty-one percent of the population is Hindu, 11 percent is Buddhist, and 4 percent is Muslim. In 2008, the monarchy was overthrown and the country became the Republic of Nepal.

One of the biggest challenges to development in Nepal is the creation and maintenance of adequate physical infrastructure to support healthcare and education in rural, remote areas. The violence and

Women in Nepal harvesting lemongrass for use in perfume and cosmetics, helping them earn an income in their rural town.

destruction perpetrated by an insurgent group with general communist aims called *Maowadi,* or Maoists, along with the Security Forces seeking to eliminate them, was a major impediment to improving country indicators between 1995 and 2006. However, a more enduring challenge is the range of Himalayan mountains that stretch across the northern two-thirds of the country. Nepal is home to some of the highest mountains in the world, including Mount Everest.

The quality of life for Nepali women has improved on a few fronts. In 2002, a bill was passed allowing daughters to inherit property from their parents. Previously only an unmarried daughter over 35 years of age had the right to inherit ancestral property. Life expectancy at birth for women has surpassed that of men, at 64 and 63 respectively. While advances have been made in terms of the percentage of girls attending primary school, the percentage of adult women who attended secondary or higher education was 13 in 2001 and 21 in 2006. The literacy rate for adult females is 47 percent and 73 percent for adult males. Trafficking of women and girls into the sex trade remains a rampant problem. Maternal mortality rates remain high; in response the government is offering free maternal health services as of January 2009.

These statistics reflect the overall poverty of the country, the fact that approximately 80 percent of the people of Nepal live in rural areas, and the negative effects of being involved in an armed conflict for a decade. However, they have not precluded Nepali women from achieving international recognition as leaders in literature, journalism, art, politics, law, medicine, and humanitarian work. And the constitution, still under construction as of 2010, has the potential to bring about a more equitable society.

When the Constituent Assembly formed in 2008, women filled one-third of the seats. Also in 2008, the Supreme Court awarded rights and protection to Nepal's lesbian, gay, bisexual, transgender, and intersex population. Many challenges lie ahead as Nepalis grapple with the difficulties of forming a stable government and a new constitution.

See Also: Hinduism; Kumari: The Living Goddess of Nepal; Maternal Mortaility; Reproductive Cancers; Tamang, Stella.

Further Readings

Amnesty International. "Human Rights in Federal Democratic Republic of Nepal: Report 2009." http://www.amnesty.org/en/region/nepal/report-2009 (accessed January 2010).

World Bank. "Unequal Citizens: Gender, Caste, and Ethnic Exclusion in Nepal." (2006). http://siteresources.worldbank.org/INTRANETSOCIALDEVELOPMENT/Resources/Bennett.rev.pdf (accessed June 2010).

Jan Brunson
Bowdoin College

Netherlands

In the first decade of the 21st century, the Netherlands finds itself in a paradoxical situation when it comes to gender equality. The self-image of Dutch society as tolerant—based on its welfare state, the legalization of soft drugs and prostitution, and openness toward homosexuality—needs to be further examined. First, tolerance is on the decline because of the growing popularity of anti-immigration forces in politics. Second, the schism between a high degree of gender mainstreaming and a low degree of gender equality, called the "Dutch Case," still exists. This produces a Third Wave feminist attempt to bridge the gap between women from different generations and ethnic groups.

Dutch Second Wave feminism has been very successful in its "long march through the institutions." As early as the late 1960s, the feminist group Man Vrouw Maatschappij (Man Woman Society) worked closely with policy makers and parliament in order to instigate change. However, institutionalizing feminism has resulted in a paradox. What is meant by the "Dutch Case" is a schism between the successful governmental implementation of the feminist struggle and the actual state of affairs in Dutch society. Despite the wide range of gender mainstreaming policies and organizations on the governmental, provincial, and municipal levels, the facts concerning "gender" issues in Dutch society are striking. First, in 2007, only 9 percent of women with children under 18 had a full-time job. Twenty-six percent of them did not work at all, whereas another 26 percent only worked 20–27 hours a week. In the Netherlands, women are victims of a prevalent "one and a half earners" model. Another striking figure is that in 2009, only 12 percent of Dutch professors were female. This is an incredibly low figure in comparison to other European countries and on a worldwide basis.

Women's and Gender Studies

The "Dutch Case" has been extensively studied by women's and gender studies scholars. This topic of women's issues has a long history in the Netherlands. The first women's studies departments were set up in the late 1970s, and in the 1980s and 1990s, women's studies were present in all Dutch universities. In the wake of the restructuring of Dutch higher education instigated by the European Union–wide "Bologna process," which sought to create a unified European higher education system, this situation has changed.

Women's and gender studies are still prominent at the universities of Amsterdam, Nijmegen, and Utrecht. In Amsterdam, the focus is on the social sciences, and in Nijmegen and Utrecht, on the humanities. The Netherlands Research School for Women's Studies, based in Utrecht, offers interdisciplinary Ph.D. courses. Utrecht is a center for European women's and gender studies as well, hosting academic and professional networks such as ATHENA and ATGENDER. Several professors in women's and gender studies based in the Netherlands have gained international fame, in particular Rosi Braidotti.

Third Wave Feminism and the Decline of Tolerance

Third Wave feminism in the Netherlands finds itself affected by the "Dutch Case" and the decline of women's and gender studies. It also has to deal with the current political climate characterized by, apart from the sexualization of the Dutch media landscape, a decline of tolerance. After the political murders of right-wing politician Pim Fortuijn in 2002 and the outspoken filmmaker Theo van Gogh in 2004, a strong anti-immigration climate has begun in the country, voiced by politicians like Geert Wilders and Ayaan Hirsi Ali. This backlash is accompanied by an abuse of feminism and sexual freedom: it is argued that the Netherlands is a feminist country, whereas many have seen that this is an overstatement, and it is presupposed that migrants from Muslim countries affect "our" gay rights negatively. Dutch Third Wave feminists like Stine Jensen address the need to bring together women from different ethnic groups.

A Third Wave feminist who has a particular impact is Sunny Bergman. Her 2007 documentary *Beperkt Houdbaar* (Over the Hill) generated [inter]national media attention. Bergman addresses the beauty myths that Dutch girls are influenced by and published a manifesto that was supported by a wide range of Dutch (Second Wave) feminists. Treating women's issues internationally and placing feminism in a transgenerational and transnational frame, her feminism is also based on bridging gaps, and helps define Third Wave Dutch feminism.

See Also: Feminism on College Campuses; Gomperts, Rebecca; Social Justice Activism; Women's Studies.

Further Readings

Bosch, Mineke. "Women in Science: A Dutch Case?" *Science in Context,* v.5/2 (2002).
Buikema, Rosemarie and Iris van der Tuin. *Doing Gender in Media, Art and Culture.* London: Routledge, 2009.
Davis, Kathy and Marianne Grünell. "The Dutch Case: An Interview With Margo Brouns." *European Journal of Women's Studies,* v.1/1 (1994).
Statistics Netherlands. http://www.cbs.nl (accessed March 2010).

Iris van der Tuin
Utrecht University

New Age Religion

The expression *New Age,* which alludes to an upcoming age of peace and harmony, indicates a "postmodern" (as Paul Heelas defines it) religious or spiritual movement whose beliefs and practices are highly variable. The New Age shifting of the locus of religious authority from established, and historically male-dominated, religious hierarchies to the individual seems to have offered a unique chance to women traditionally marginalized by such structures. However, Monica Sjoo has criticized the movement as antifeminist and patriarchal. The New Age holds the idea of an evolutionary "quantum leap" in consciousness that awaits the human species; each individual "seeker" collaborates to the arising of the global consciousness of the living planet Earth (Gaia) through an inner journey of self-understanding and a spiritual quest in search of harmony, healing, and happiness.

As scholars have noted, the New Age arises from a process of detraditionalization that took place in the past century and that allows practitioners to freely borrow beliefs and practices from Eastern and native religions, from previous religious movements (Spiritualism), and also from genre literature and cinema. Thus the New Age adopts concepts such as that of synchronicity; karma or the cycle of birth-death-rebirth; and a set of practices such as channeling, palm and crystal healing, divination systems, massage, visualization, yoga exercises, and "[neo]shamanic" practices. As New Agers have a holistic view of mind, body, and soul, such practices aim at bringing together mental focus, physical wholeness, and spiritual harmony.

Academic studies on the New Age agree on the complexity and diversity of its beliefs, rooted in modern esotericism, the Enlightenment, Romanticism, and several spiritual 19th-century movements. The New Age has been defined as self-religion, as its focus is on the self and inner life; all authority rests on the individual, who is able to decode "occult teachings" because of the divine spark hidden within each human being. The divine can be conceived as a personal god or in a pantheistic way, as in the New Age coexisting diverging views on the divine.

Scholarly criticism of the New Age has focused on its antimodernist attitude; on its beliefs on healing, which contrast with official medicine, on its millenaristic tendencies; and on its idea of a teleological development of human history. Several scholars read the New Age as the religious expression of consumerist capitalism, offering ready-made and rapidly changing spiritual teachings that avoid dealing with structural social issues (such as inequality, racism, and exclusion).

The absence of hierarchies and dogmatism, as well as the stress on self-improvement and alternative healing techniques, has been appealing for women, especially those belonging to the middle class. Some well-known spokespersons for the New Age have indeed been women—for example, Marilyn Ferguson or Shirley MacLaine.

See Also: Health, Mental and Physical; Native American Religion; Religion, Women in; Yoga.

Further Readings

Hanegraaf, Wouter J. *New Age Religion and Western Culture.* Leiden, Netherlands: Brill, 1997.

Heelas, Paul. *The New Age Movement.* Oxford, UK: Blackwell, 1996.

Lewis, J. R. and J. G. Melton, eds. *Perspectives on the New Age.* Albany: State University of New York Press, 1992.

Possamai, Adam. "Alternative Spiritualities and the Cultural Logic of Late Capitalism." *Culture and Religion*, v.4/1 (2003).

Sjoo, Monica. "New Age and Patriarchy." *Journal of Contemporary Religion*, v.9/3 (1994).

York, Michael. *The Emerging Network: A Sociology of the New Age and Neo-Pagan Movements.* Lanham, MD: Rowman & Littlefield, 1995.

Maria Beatrice Bittarello
Independent Scholar

New Zealand

New Zealand is an island nation in the South Pacific Ocean that became an independent dominion of Great Britain in 1907. The population of 4.2 million is primarily of people of European descent (69.8 percent), with large minorities of Maoris (native New Zealanders; 7.9 percent), Asians (5.7 percent), and Pacific Islanders (4.4 percent). The largest religious denominations are Anglican (14.9 percent) and Roman Catholic (12.4 percent), and about a quarter of the population does not indicate a religion.

New Zealand enjoys a high standard of living comparable with many European countries, with a per capita gross domestic product (GDP) of $27,700 in 2009. Life expectancy is among the highest in the world, with an average of 78.43 years for men and 83.20 years for women.

Gender equality is among the highest in the world—the World Economic Forum ranked New Zealand 5th of 134 countries in 2009. On a scale in which 0 indicates inequality and 1 perfect equality, New Zealand had an overall score of 0.788, ranking behind only Iceland, Finland, Norway, and Sweden. On educational attainment, New Zealand got a score of 1.000 (best in the world), on health and survival 0.974 (72nd), in economic participation 0.784 (7th), and on political empowerment 0.393 (7th). Despite efforts to integrate the Maori population into a society that sprung from what was formerly a British colony, Maoris have poorer health and lower educational and economic attainment and are more likely to be victims of domestic violence than the national average.

Women in New Zealand constitute almost 50 percent of the labor force and hold a disproportionate share of technical positions, although they earn about 77 percent of the average wage paid to men for comparable work. Literacy is 100 percent for both men and women, and substantially more women than men are enrolled in tertiary education. About one-third of the New Zealand Parliament is female, and women hold a comparable percentage of ministerial positions. Helen Clark served as the prime minister of New Zealand for three terms (1999–2008) and is currently head of the United Nations Development Programme. Margaret Wilson has served as speaker of the House of Representatives, and several women have served as governor-general, most recently Dame

Sian Elias (who has also served as chief justice) and Dame Sylvia Cartwright.

New Zealand women enjoy a high standard of maternal and child care. Ninety-five percent of births are attended by skilled personnel, and infant and maternal mortality are quite low, at 5 per 1,000 live births and 4 per 100,000 live births, respectively. Abortion is available on several grounds, including fetal deformity, rape, and to preserve the mother's life or mental or physical health, and almost three quarters of married women report using contraceptives. Save the Children ranks New Zealand 5th on its Mother's Index, 6th on the Womens' Index, and 19th on the Children's Index.

See Also: Abortion, Access to; Abortion Laws, International; Representation of Women in Government, International.

Further Readings

Central Intelligence Agency. "The World Factbook: New Zealand." https://www.cia.gov/library/publications/the-world-factbook/geos/nz.html (accessed July 2010).

Montgomerie, Deborah. *The Women's War: New Zealand Women 1939–45*. Auckland, New Zealand: Auckland University Press, 2001.

Zschokke, Magdalena. *Delayed Paradise*. Port Orchard, WA: Windstorm Creative, 2007.

Sarah Boslaugh
Washington University School of Medicine

Nicaragua

The Republic of Nicaragua is the largest country in Central America, with a high population growth rate, young population, and low population density. The majority of the population is mestizo or indigenous, Hispanic is the dominant culture, and Roman Catholicism is the dominant religion. Gender roles are shaped by traditional Hispanic values and the concepts of machismo and marianismo, although women have made business and political advancements, including the election of a female president in the 1990s. Nicaragua ranked 49th out of 134 countries in the World Economic Forum's 2009 Global Gender Gap Report.

The predominant Roman Catholic culture places a strong emphasis on church marriages, although there are also numerous common law marriages. The average age of marriage is in the early 20s. The 2009 fertility rate was 2.8 births per woman. Skilled healthcare practitioners attend 67 percent of births. The 2009 infant mortality rate was 29 per 1,000 live births, and the maternal mortality rate was 170 per 100,000 live births. The state social security system provides women with 12 weeks of paid maternity leave at 60 percent of their wages. About 72 percent of married women use contraceptives. Large families are common and highly valued, with women usually bearing most of the responsibility for childcare and rearing. Many couples live with their parents due to poverty and an affordable housing shortage.

Issues Facing Disadvantaged Groups

The 1980s struggles that brought the Sandinistas to power also brought attention to issues facing traditionally disadvantaged groups such as women and the poor. Public education is free and compulsory from age 7 to 12 but lacks adequate funding, and many children do not attend due to agricultural needs. Female school attendance rates stand at 96 percent at the primary level, 49 percent at the secondary level, and 19 percent at the tertiary level. Literacy rates are almost equal, at 81 percent for women and 79 percent for men. Access to healthcare is improving. Other problems include political instability, poverty, unemployment, inadequate water and sewage systems, and disease. Life expectancy is age 63 for women and age 60 for men.

Nicaraguan women have entered the workforce in significant numbers since the 1980s, many due to high poverty rates. Currently, 40 percent of women participate in the workforce. Women make up 43 percent of the paid nonagricultural workforce and 52 percent of professional and technical workers. Key employment includes seasonal migrant agriculture, manufacturing, industry, and education. Some women supplement family incomes through laundry or street food vending. A gender gap still exists in average estimated earned salary of $1,182 for women and $3,703 for men, and unemployment rates, which stand at 4.9 percent for women and 5.4 percent for men. Women have the right to vote. Women hold 19 percent of parliamentary seats and 33 percent of ministerial positions. Violeta Barrios de Chamorro served as president of the country from 1990 to 1996.

See Also: Gender Roles, Cross-Cultural; Heads of State, Female; Machismo/Marianismo; Migrant Workers; Roman Catholic Church.

Further Readings

Dore, Elizabeth and Maxine Molyneux. *Hidden Histories of Gender and the State in Latin America*. Durham, NC: Duke University Press, 2000.

Hausman, Ricardo, Laura D. Tyson, and Saadia Zahidi. *The Global Gender Gap Report 2009*. Geneva: World Economic Forum, 2009. http://www.weforum.org /en/Communities/Women%20Leaders%20and%20 Gender%20Parity/GenderGapNetwork/index.htm (accessed February 2010).

Hepburn, Stephanie and Rita J. Simon. *Women's Roles and Statuses the World Over*. Lanham, MD: Lexington Books, 2006.

Marcella Bush Trevino
Independent Scholar

Nicks, Stevie

One of the most recognizable figures of 1970s rock music, Stevie Nicks is still spotted running errands in her custom designed six-inch high platform boots, shawls, and gypsy girl apparel. Journalists have commented that her mystical, uniquely bohemian ensembles have made her an archetype of personal style.

Born in 1948 in Phoenix, Arizona, Stephanie Lynn Nicks is one the most notable female singers, songwriters, mentors, and producers of music in the 20th century. Although most often recognized as a member of legendary group Fleetwood Mac, Nicks has also had a successful career as a solo artist. Her passion for music and dance began in high school, when she joined Changing Times, a tribute band to Bob Dylan, and became influenced by the harmonies of the Mamas and the Papas. Her experience in this group eventually led Nicks to partner with Lindsey Buckingham, and the two produced their *Buckingham Nicks* album in 1973. *Buckingham Nicks* caught the attention of Mick Fleetwood of Fleetwood Mac, a successful English blues band, and a collaboration soon followed. Throughout her career with Fleetwood Mac, the band was plagued with turmoil and breakups that eventually manifested in one of their most popular hits, "Go Your Own Way." In press interviews, Stevie accused her male rocker companions of chauvinism, arguing that she should be taken seriously as a writer. In 1977, she met Paul Fishkin, and the two co-founded Modern Records in 1980 with Danny Goldberg. By 2000, with seven solo releases on that label, Nicks sold over 15 million albums. She did, in fact, "go her own way" and produced 12 solo albums by 2009, including a Japanese edition of her 1994 collection, *Street Angel*.

The pressures of multiplatinum selling albums and tumultuous relationships with bandmates and other rock icons took a toll on Nicks, and she developed issues with cocaine and alcohol abuse. After successful rehabilitation at the Betty Ford Center in 1986, Stevie returned to the music world to continue her life's passion. Since that time, she has appeared on the cover of *Rolling Stone* six times, and has performed on numerous albums, with artists such as B. B. King, Tom Petty, and Sheryl Crow, and in movie soundtracks of such films as *Boys on the Side* and *School of Rock*.

Nicks also performs charitable concerts to support research at the Arizona Heart Foundation, a cause of personal importance given her family's relationship to the foundation. Nicks and other members of Fleetwood Mac dined with wounded veterans at Walter Reed Memorial Hospital and participated in benefit concerts for Special Olympics and other charities. In 2009, Nicks reunited with Fleetwood Mac for another world tour and has no plans to retire from performing or producing in the near future. Nicks has also become something of a fashion icon for women "of a certain age." Designers Izaac Mizrahi and Anna Sui claim to have taken inspiration from her California look.

See Also: Celebrity Women; Madonna; Rock Music, Women in.

Further Readings

Bruni, Frank. "After the Show With: STEVIE NICKS; Going Her Own Way, But Slowly This Time." *New York Times* (November 25, 1997). http://www.nytimes.com /1997/11/25/arts/after-the-show-with-stevie-nicks

-going-her-own-way-but-slowly-this-time.html?page
wanted=1 (accessed July 2010).

La Ferla, Ruth. "Still Dressing for Stevie." *New York Times* (April 8, 2009). http://www.nytimes.com/2009/04/09 /fashion/09STEVIE.html (accessed July 2010).

The Nicks Fix. http://www.nicksfix.com (accessed November 2009).

Erika Cornelius Smith
Purdue University

Niger

A Sahelian country with few resources, Niger has the second-poorest living standards in the world. However, a recent change in government has given hope that the extreme poverty may be alleviated. Little progress has been made in promoting women's rights, particularly because traditional practices, including the use of family or traditional courts, still regulate living conditions for most women. Nevertheless, Niger's women's activism has hesitantly grown.

The Republic of Niger has ratified numerous international conventions on gender equality and human rights, but the ratification of legal and political public instruments does not guarantee their effective and systematic implementation, with particular consequences for women. Negative gender stereotypes have persisted and continued to legitimize harmful traditional practices, such as early and forced marriages, female genital mutilation, domestic violence, woman trafficking, and wife repudiation. Islam and consuetudinary law, despite numerous public reforms working toward gender equality, dilute the fight against discrimination and inequality. In addition, women often have little or no knowledge of their rights.

Niger has no discriminatory family code against women and did ratify the Convention on the Elimination of All Forms of Discrimination Against Women (CEDAW), with certain reservations; in fact, the National Assembly rejected the Protocol on African Women's Rights of the African Union in June 2006. Nevertheless, diverse legal reforms on gender equality have been passed in Niger, such as law 2000-008, which set quotas on women in main decision-making offices, where government and public administration must

have a minimum of 25 percent women and 10 percent of elected officials be female. In 2004, revisions of the penal law included the banning of female genital mutilation and slavery. A health law in 2006 has also started to regulate reproductive health rights for women.

Statistics from the Human Development Report (2007–08) and the United Nations provide a clear picture of women's position in Niger. Women make up more than half the population of the country; their life expectancy at birth is 52 years; and their literacy rate is 16 percent, whereas it is 44 percent for men. Only 37 percent of girls are enrolled in primary school.

Large differences are experienced, depending on individual family rules, but the minimum marriage age is 15 for women and 18 for men; 61.9 percent of women between 15 and 19 years old are married, whereas only 4.2 percent of men that age are married. The number of women dying as a result of pregnancy, delivery, or postpartum complications is 1,800 per 100,000 live births. Women in Niger have between seven and eight children each, and only 5 percent of women use modern contraception.

At the national level, gender issues are developing, such as by the Ministry for Women Promotion and Infant Protection. Created by law in December 1999, the ministry serves to promote, coordinate, and support gender equality policies statewide. Women's associations, nongovernmental organizations, and women's groups, all quite aware of their role in working toward equality and of their growing effect on developing civil society, have increasingly supported these efforts.

See Also: Domestic Violence; Reproductive and Sexual Health Rights; Stereotypes of Women; Trafficking, Women and Children.

Further Readings
Alidou, Ousseina D. *Engaging Modernity: Muslim Women and the Politics of Agency in Postcolonial Niger.* Madison: University of Wisconsin Press, 2005.

Dunbar, Roberta A. "Islamic Values the State and the 'Development of Women': The Case of Niger." In Catherine Coles and Beverly Mack, eds., *Hausa Women in the 20th Century.* Madison: University of Wisconsin Press, 1999.

M. Dolores Ochoa-Rodríguez
University of Granada

Nigeria

Because the almost 70 million women of the Federal Republic of Nigeria make up 49 percent of the population, African feminist and women's movements are extremely important in this western region of Africa. Nigerian women contribute considerably to improving gender equality both at the international and the national levels. Their activism and activities have focused on different aspects of their lives, such as health, education, work, family, marriage, rights and laws, and so on. In fact, the national gender machinery has been put into place to gradually and eventually provoke significant economic, political, and cultural changes in the country.

According to the 2006 census, Nigeria's population has reached 140 million, making it the most populous of any African country. Most estimates have shown that more than 40 percent of Nigeria's population is younger than 15 years. Life expectancy is 46.6 years. Nigeria is a multiethnic country with over 250 ethnic groups, 10 of which account for 80 percent of the total population: the Hausa and Fulani (both located in the north), Yoruba (mainly in the southwest), and Ibo (in the east). Most Nigerians speak languages that belong to these groups, although English is the official language. Religious affiliations are divided as follows: Muslims, 50 percent; Christians, 40 percent; and indigenous religions, 10 percent.

After Nigeria gained independence from British rule in 1960, the country went through turbulent political periods and frequent forceful governmental change by several military dictatorships. Indeed, a movement against intellectuals by military rulers persists, particularly against intellectual women. The transition to democracy became effective in May 1999, and at this time, the country is divided into 36 states.

The Constitution of Nigeria acknowledges gender equality. Women political representation and female participation in decision-making processes remain very low compared with other African countries, such as Rwanda or Mozambique, with hardly 6.1 percent of representatives in parliament being women and 3.7 percent of the senate. In spite of this, there are very important political and civil organizations fighting for the advancement of women's rights.

The Federal Ministry of Women Affairs and Youth Development, currently named the Federal Ministry of Women Affairs and Social Development, was created in 1999. This ministry is responsible for the design of equal gender policies, gendered planning and implementation, and the provision of specialized services for Nigerian women and children, as well as coordinating and supervising those policies in other ministries (education, health, and so on). Nevertheless, the national gender machinery and its new political order offer some negative aspects, such as the First Lady Syndrome, or Femocracy, which refers to women who end up being prone to bureaucratic corruption. In fact, Nigerian women are conscious that to have women in high offices and with access to decision making does not guarantee gender equality, as some women may use their power, and manage their political relationships in government, toward other goals. Many femocrats have not only accumulated

Two Nigerian women in an outdoor food preparation area, pounding grain with a large mortar and pestle.

enormous wealth through illegal means but also have wielded tremendous political influence.

The National Council of Women's Societies was founded in Nigeria as early as 1958. The women's movement of Nigeria also uses research, lobbying, advocacy, and activism and has done so formally since 1983. The women's movement of Nigeria aims to transform the conditions that women suffer under as members of a subordinate class and as women in general. Market women's associations, the Federation of Women Lawyers, and numerous civil society organizations are all parts of the women's movement of Nigeria.

Although Nigeria can boast of being the first African country to organize a women's conference in 1960, the path toward gender equality really gained speed as a result of the United Nations Women Conference in Beijing (1995). In fact, the Beijing Platform promoted national policies such as state sections of the Federal Ministry of Women Affairs and Social Development being extended to the 36 states of the federation and a Women's Department being created in the Federal Capital Territory, Abuja. Those state ministries, in conjunction with the Federal Ministry of Women Affairs and Social Development, implement the Beijing Plan of Action in coordination with international agencies, such as the United Nations Development Fund for Women; the United Nations Children's Fund; the United Nations Educational, Scientific and Cultural Organization; and the International Labor Organization, among others.

Social awareness about the predicament of Nigerian women and their need for empowerment is growing. Significant social transformations are taking place regarding urbanization, education (very much influenced by Western values), marriage (monogamy has become more common among the younger generation and the elite), modern economies, and the local and foreign media (and its enormous influence in gender ideology).

See Also: Mozambique; Niger; Property Rights; Rwanda; United Nations Conferences on Women United Nations Development Fund for Women; .

Further Readings

Maduganu, Bene E. "The Nigerian Feminist Movement: Lessons From Women in Nigeria, WIN." *Review of African Political Economy*, v.35/118 (2008).
Mama, Amina. "Khaki in the Family: Gender Discourses and Militarism in Nigeria." *African Studies Review*, v.41/2 (1998).
Para-Mallam, Oluwafunmilayo J. *Nigerian Women Speak—A Gender Analysis of Government Policy on Women*. Saarbrücken, Germany: VDM, 2007.

Marian del Moral-Garrido
University of Granada

9to5

9to5, the National Association of Working Women, began as a local organization in the early 1970s and grew to become the largest nonprofit organization of working women in the United States. 9to5 supports research, advocacy, and policy reform leadership in areas of concern to American working women and their families. The organization seeks to overturn the gender discrimination they believe exists within the American workplace. Issues of interest include equal pay, sexual harassment, the glass ceiling, job retention, workplace discrimination, pregnancy discrimination, civil rights, health and safety laws, family leave, and welfare policies. The organization has achieved considerable political influence and success.

9to5 began on a grassroots level in 1972, when Boston female office workers such as Karen Nussbaum gathered to discuss issues of interest to women workers, such as pay inequalities, sexual harassment, and the difficulties of balancing work and family responsibilities. It first published the newsletter *9to5 News* and then formed a collective. The group grew to become a national nonprofit organization headquartered in Milwaukee, Wisconsin, with a number of local chapters and members in every state. Its main constituents are women who work for low wages in traditionally female occupations or who have experienced workplace gender discrimination.

9to5 also seeks to educate working women and their employers on workplace and family issues—a key component in the organization's efforts to end workplace discrimination. Guidebooks published by 9to5 include *The Job/Family Challenge: A 9to5 Guide*; *9to5 Guide to Combating Sexual Harassment*; *The Job Family Challenge: Not for Women Only*; and

What Do I Do if I'm Experiencing Race Discrimination? It also publishes fact sheets and newsletters, sends Action Alerts to local chapters and members, maintains the toll-free Job Survival Hotline, provides a Speak Out program so women can voice their individual experiences, maintains a Speakers Bureau for public presentations and diversity training, and runs the Job Retention Project to aid office workers in enhancing their skills.

One of 9to5's main goals is to publicize, advocate, and provide research and leadership for the fight to gain favorable legislation and oppose unfavorable legislation on the federal, state, local, and workplace levels. It emphasizes nonpartisan voter registration and education and has served on state and local task forces and provided expert testimony to U.S. Congress. It also monitors equal-opportunity enforcement agencies to ensure adherence to the laws.

9to5 helped ensure passage of the federal Family and Medical Leave Act and Civil Rights legislation changes. At all levels, 9to5 has worked for paid sick days, programs to expand Family and Medical Leave Act benefits, the maintenance of equal-opportunity programs, health and safety laws, living wages and equal pay, antidiscrimination legislation, more funding for child care and healthcare for working families, and job training. It has actively opposed welfare reform, which it argues enforces a punitive approach to welfare; the privatization of Social Security, which could cut benefits to working families; and the religious and political right wing, which it argues threatens women's rights, abortion access, and affirmative action programs.

See Also: Affirmative Action/Equal Opportunity; Business, Women in; Equal Pay; Glass Ceiling; Sexual Harassment; Working Mothers.

Further Readings

O'Toole, James and Edward E. Lawler. *The New American Workplace.* New York: Palgrave Macmillan, 2006.

U.S. Department of Labor. "Federal Glass Ceiling Commission Executive Summary Report." (1995). www.dol.gov/oasam/programs/history/reich/reports/ceiling1.pdf (accessed December 2009).

Marcella Bush Trevino
Barry University

No Child Left Behind

The legislation known as the No Child Left Behind Act of 2001 (NCLB) is a piece of U.S. federal legislation designed to reform kindergarten through 12th-grade education based on standards. A majority of both the U.S. House of Representatives and Senate voted in favor of the legislation, and it was signed into law by President George W. Bush. Although NCLB is often perceived to be a brand-new law, it is actually the latest reauthorization of the Elementary and Secondary Education Act of 1965, which is best known for the creation of titles (such as Title I, a federal program for low-income children, and Title 9, a mandate for gender equity in education). The Elementary and Secondary Education Act is reauthorized every few years; similarly, NCLB will need to be reauthorized—an issue that Congress is currently considering.

The foundation of NCLB is standards-based education—the theory that combining high standards with intermittent checkpoints is the most effective way to improve individual educational outcomes. Although NCLB is federal legislation, it does not mandate standards for individual states; instead, it mandates that individual states set standards and then implement a series of standardized assessments to evaluate student progress on those standards. The assessment program is a prerequisite for obtaining federal funding for public schools in a given state.

The broad measurement of a school's success in educating students is called Adequate Yearly Progress (AYP). AYP was designed as a tool that schools could use to help students know where they were ineffective in producing positive student outcomes. AYP is composed of testing scores in the areas of language arts and mathematics and a measure of graduation (for high schools and districts overall) or attendance rates (for elementary and middle schools). Schools and districts must show a higher percentage of achievement from one year to the next. If schools or districts do not increase their percentage of achievement, they have not met AYP. The consequences of not meeting AYP increase progressively for each year AYP is not met; they include offering tutoring to students, state takeover, reconstitution, and opening the school as a charter.

Supporters of NCLB argue that the legislation is having positive effects. National Assessment of

Education Progress (NAEP) results demonstrate increased average levels of achievement over scores recorded before 2001. In addition, NAEP results indicate that at least some achievement gaps have narrowed. Supporters also argue that mandating that teachers meet particular content-area mastery requirements results in a more professional and effective teacher workforce. Finally, supporters argue that the requirement that schools implement "scientifically based research practices" increases curriculum effectiveness for all students.

Critics of NCLB argue that increased test scores do not necessarily transfer to real-world learning, as the test questions themselves may reflect a narrow set of skills rather than broad understandings. In addition, critics argue that teachers may be pressured to teach specific skills that they know are tested rather than teaching higher-order thinking skills or nontested concepts or even content areas. Critics also argue that the emphasis on low-performing students may harm gifted and talented students. Finally, critics are concerned that the specificity of the legislation limits what schools may choose to teach while simultaneously limiting local control.

One challenge presented by NCLB, regardless of an individual's perspective on the legislation, is the issue of funding. NCLB places demands on school districts that require financing to implement. For example, increased professional development and standardized test preparation are both additional costs that school districts must bear. However, the funding provided through NCLB does not equal the increased cost associated with its implementation. The funding associated with NCLB has increased each year since its passage.

As NCLB comes up for reauthorization, a number of reforms have been proposed. One theme among these reform proposals is a move away from sanctioning individual failing schools to working for system-wide changes. Another theme is to move from skills-based standardized tests to more holistic outcome measures. Finally, another theme among reforms is to increase funding to those schools and districts working with high-need student populations.

It can be argued that the implementation of NCLB falls to women disproportionately. Estimates differ; however, according to the U.S. Census, approximately 70 percent of teachers are women. In addi-

tion, according to the National Center for Educational Statistics, approximately 50 percent of school principals are women. Thus, a majority of those responsible for implementation of NCLB's mandates in schools are women.

See Also: Education, Women in; Educational Administrators, Elementary and High School; "Girl-Friendly" Schools.

Further Readings

Cochran-Smith, M. "No Child Left Behind: Three Years and Counting." *Journal of Teacher Education*, v.56/2 (2005).

Fusarelli, L. D. "The Potential Impact of the No Child Left Behind Act on Equity and Diversity in American Education." *Educational Policy*, v.18/1 (2004).

Hess, F. M. and M. J. Petrilli. *No Child Left Behind*. New York: Peter Lang, 2006.

Brandelyn Tosolt
Northern Kentucky University

Nongovernmental Organizations Worldwide

Nongovernmental Organizations (NGOs) worldwide have grown tremendously in the last several decades and play an increasing role in international politics. Through the consultative status granted to NGOs at the United Nations (UN), and through the UN global conferences beginning in the 1970s, more NGOs were created. By the turn of the century, NGOs had begun to use the strategy of forming coalitions, increasingly influencing international politics and women's lives.

NGOs are not a homogenous group. They can be local, national, or international; international NGOs are often referred to as INGOs. While the term *NGOs* is sometimes used interchangeably with "grassroots organizations," "social movements," and "civil society," NGOs differ from these. Grassroots organizations are generally locally organized groups of individuals that have spring up to empower their members and take action on particular issues of concern to them. Some NGOs are grassroots organizations, but many are not. Social movements are broader and more diffuse than organizations; a social movement encompasses a broad segment of society that is interested in fomenting or resisting social change in some particular issue area, such as disarmament, environmental, civil rights, or women's movements. A social movement may include NGOs and grassroots organizations. Finally, the term *civil society* became popularized at the end of the Cold War to describe what appeared to have been missing in state-dominated societies: broad societal participation in and concern for governance, but not necessarily government. Civil society is thought to be the necessary ingredient for democratic governance to arise. NGOs are one part of civil society.

The long list of acronyms that has accumulated around NGOs illustrates their diversity. People speak of NGOs, INGOs (international NGOs), BINGOs (business international NGOs), RINGOs (religious international NGOs), ENGOs (environmental NGOs), WINGOs (women's international NGOs), GONGOs (government-operated NGOs—which may have been set up by governments to look like NGOs in order to qualify for outside aid), QUANGOs (quasi-nongovernmental organizations—that is, those that are at least partially created or supported by states), and many others.

While some other groups are nongovernmental, and are generally included as nonstate actors, they are not usually included under the term *NGO*. The term usually explicitly excludes for-profit corporations, and private contractors, and multinational corporations (MNCs), although associations formed by MNCs, such as the International Chamber of Commerce, are considered NGOs. Similarly, political parties, liberation movements, and terrorist organizations are not usually considered NGOs. Recently, however, some from outside the field of international organization, especially military writers, have begun to refer to terrorist movements as NGOs, some would say in order to discredit NGOs. Peter Willetts, an authority on NGOs, argues in defining NGOs that a commitment not to use violence is a basic characteristic.

NGOs in International Politics

Nongovernmental organizations have existed for centuries, but there was a sizable rise in their numbers following World War II, and especially in the 1990s. Both the number of nongovernmental organizations and their involvement in national and international policy making increased tremendously. With the advent of the UN global conferences in the 1970s, NGO interest in the UN began to skyrocket. According to the *Yearbook of International Organizations*, at the time of the foundation of the United Nations in 1945 there were 2,865 international nongovernmental organizations (NGOs); by 2004 that number had increased to roughly 63,000. More importantly, by the 1990s, the importance of the NGO role began to be recognized. NGOs began to be recognized for their role in influencing public policy at the UN and on the ground in nation-states in human rights, including women's rights, development, environment, and even disarmament.

NGOs follow many strategies to influence international politics. The United Nations has played an important role with this. The 1945 San Francisco Conference provided for the establishment of a relationship between the Economic and Social Council (ECOSOC) and nongovernmental organizations, formalizing the League of Nations practice of consultation with NGOs. Thus Article 71 of the United Nations Charter came to read: "the Economic and Social Council may make suitable arrangements for consultation with nongovernmental organizations which are concerned with matters within its competence. Such arrangements may be made with international organizations and, where appropriate, with national organizations after consultation with the Member of the United Nations concerned."

ECOSOC's current policy on arrangements for consultation with nongovernmental organizations was updated in Resolution 1996/31. Similar to previous resolutions, it provides for general consultative status (organizations concerned with most of the activities of the council and broadly representative of populations in a large number of countries), special consultative status (internationally known organizations with special competence in a few of the fields of activity of the council), and roster status (other useful organizations), and allocates different rights to them in attending meetings, speaking, and receiving documents, and so forth. As of September 2009, there were 3,413 NGOs in consultative status, with 138 general, 2,166 special, and 983 roster status organizations. Women's NGOs are represented in all three categories, with 2,328 NGOs indicating gender issues and the advancement of women as one of their fields of activity.

ECOSOC, along with the General Assembly and the Secretary-General, wrestled with the question of NGO involvement in the UN system throughout the 1990s and early 2000s. Following the passage of ECOSOC 1996/31, the Conference of Non-Governmental Organizations in Consultative Status with ECOSOC (CONGO) proposed that similar arrangements be extended to the General Assembly. In June 2004, the Secretary-General's Panel of Eminent Persons on Civil Society and UN Relationships suggested a single NGO accreditation process under the General Assembly. While the proposal has had some support from states and NGOs, it has thus far not been furthered.

Historical Development of Women's NGOs

Women's NGOs developed along with the feminist movement, with early women's NGOs concerned both with the issue of woman suffrage as well as with issues of prohibition, slavery, and peace. Among the earliest women's NGOs, which in 2010 continue to have ECOSOC consultative status, were the Women's Christian Temperance Union (WCTU), created in 1874, International Council of Women (1888), Young Women's Christian Association (1894), International Council of Women (1904), International Federation of University Women (1919), Zonta International (1919), All India Women's Conference (1926), Pan Pacific and Southeast Asia Women's Association (1928), Associated Country Women of the World (1930), and the International Federation of Business and Professional Women (1930). Early women's NGOs had, and continue to have, relatively broad both reformist and revolutionary agendas.

NGOs and the UN Global Women's Conferences

NGOs were both influential in the development of the UN global women's conferences that began in the 1970s and repeated through the 1990s, with review conferences held in 2005 and 2010, and the conferences in turn were influential in the expansion of NGOs and the NGO role in international politics. Women's NGOs were the actual initiators of the UN women's conferences. In 1972, a group of NGOs, under the leadership of a representative of the International Federation of Business and Professional Women, asked ECOSOC's Commission on the Status of Women (CSW) to call for an International Women's Year. At the 1972 session of the CSW, 10 NGOs

signed a statement calling for such a year (E/CN.6/NGO/244). The Women's International Democratic Federation (WIDF), in particular, used its consultative status to get Romania to introduce this resolution in the CSW. It was the work of women's NGOs, particularly the International Council of Women and WIDF, consistently lobbying governments on the subject, which insured that the proposal did not get dropped at any stage.

The General Assembly subsequently declared 1975 International Women's Year (IWY) and held the IWY Conference in Mexico City. Women's organizations continued to contribute significantly to the series of large ad hoc or mega-conferences which would be repeated in the 1980s and 1990s, especially the women's conferences: the 1980 Copenhagen Mid-Decade Review, at which the Convention on the Elimination of all Forms of Discrimination Against Women was opened for signature, the 1985 Nairobi Review and Appraisal of the UN Decade for Women, the 1995 Beijing Fourth World Conference on Women, and the review sessions in 2005 and 2010. They worked with states, foundations, and UN agencies, both to run the forums and to impact the intergovernmental policy-making at the official conferences. At the Commission on the Status of Women's 10-year review of Beijing in 2005, 536 NGOs attended; at the 15 year review in 2010, 463 attended.

The International Women's Tribune Center, set up in 1976 to facilitate communication among women's groups following the 1975 conference, continues to help sustain north–south linkages between women's NGOs. Women's World Banking, generated by ideas presented at the IWY, was created in 1979. DAWN, or Development Alternatives with Women for a New Era, grew from a meeting in August 1984 in Bangalore, India, and presented a southern feminist critique of development that was widely acclaimed at the Nairobi Conference. DAWN's Website (http://www.dawnnet.org) describes it as a network of feminist scholars and activists from the global south working for economic and gender justice and sustainable and democratic development.

Other key NGOs include the Green Belt Movement, founded in 1977 under the auspices of the National Council of Women of Kenya by Wangari Maathi (who won the 2004 Nobel Peace Prize for her work), and utilizing tree-planting to link its goals of environmental conservation and community empowerment (especially for women), and highly visible internationally since the 1985 Nairobi Women's Conference. The Women's Environment and Development Organization (WEDO), cofounded by Bella Abzug and Mim Kelber in 1991 to link the issues of women and environment and influence the 1992 "Earth Summit," brought together over 1,500 women from 83 countries to work on a strategy. The international group became the leading NGO in developing strategies for the 1995 Beijing Conference on Women and its Forum, the largest meeting of women's NGOs held thus far, and in the 2005 and 2010 reviews.

NGOs and the Millennium Development Goals

When world leaders at the United Nations adopted the Millennium Development Goals (MDGs) in 2000, they set 2015 as the date by which broad goals were to be accomplished in reducing poverty and hunger, increasing the number of children in school, improving gender equality, reducing child and maternal mortality, combating human immunodeficiency virus and acquired immune deficiency syndrome (HIV/AIDS), improving environmental sustainability, and furthering a partnership for development. At the UN Summit meeting on the MDGs September 20–22, 2010, NGOs partnered with UN agencies to present roughly 80 events toward meeting the goals. Informal interactive hearings with NGOs were organized by the UN General Assembly from June 14–15, 2010, but many NGOs expressed disappointment with the lack of specifics in the final outcome document. Some NGOs took advantage of the presence of so many world leaders to argue for stronger action. The Global Leaders Council for Reproductive Health took out a full page ad in the *New York Times* on September 22, 2010 to state: "We believe that a nation's security, prosperity and progress are linked to the reproductive health of its women and men." To bring attention to maternal death rates, Amnesty International installed a Maternal Death Clock in Times Square, New York, during the high-level UN meeting.

In connection with the goals of maternal and child health, NGOs continue to work to promote breastfeeding and counter the marketing of infant formula: two organizations are most significant. The International Baby Food Action Network (IBFAN), an organization begun in 1979 and present in 67 countries,

works to reduce child morbidity and mortality and improve the health of babies, mothers and families through support of breastfeeding (http://www.ibfan.org). The World Alliance for Breastfeeding Action, a global network formed in February 1991 to promote breastfeeding worldwide in the framework of the 1990 and 2005 Innocenti Declarations, and the Global Strategy for Infant and Young Child Feeding work closely with the United Nations Children's Fund (UNICEF).

Women's NGOs and the Nobel Peace Prize

Women winners of the Nobel Peace Prize have formed NGOs that foster women's work on peace. The first two women winners of the Nobel Peace Prize, Jane Addams in 1931, and Emily Greene Balch in 1946, were active in the development of the Women's International League for Peace and Freedom (WILPF), founded in 1815, which has become significant in the development of new policy in the 21st century, continuing its work for peace and justice and challenging the root causes of oppression, especially in the development of UN Security Council Resolution 1325 in 2000.

The Nobel Women's Initiative was established in 2006 by six out of the only 12 women ever awarded the Nobel Peace Prize: Jody Williams, Shirin Ebadi, Wangari Maathai, Rigoberta Menchú Tum, Betty Williams and Mairead Corrigan Maguire. They believe that ". . . peace is much more than the absence of armed conflict. Peace is the commitment to equality and justice; a democratic world free of physical, economic, cultural, political, religious, sexual and environmental violence and the constant threat of these forms of violence against women—indeed against all of humanity." The group holds meetings of women every two years in different regions of the world. Its Website supports action, in cooperation with other organizations, on disarmament and on women's rights and justice in Iran, Israel-Palestine, Sudan and elsewhere, and urges support of Aung San Suu Kyi (another Nobel Prize winner unable to join them) and resistance to the military regime in Burma.

NGO Networks and Coalitions and Their Accomplishments

Nongovernmental organizations have, particularly since the mid-1990s, worked successfully in transnational advocacy networks to influence and sometimes even create international policy and new international regimes. Among the better known initiatives are the work of Canada and the like-minded countries in coordination with the International Campaign to Ban Landmines (ICBL), in which the Ottawa Process produced the Land Mines Convention. It was signed in December 1997 and put into force in record time in March 1999, and won the ICBL and its leader Jody Williams the 1997 Nobel Peace Prize. Other important transnational advocacy networks have included the Coalition for an International Criminal Court, which helped to develop support for the ICC, signed in 1998 and in force in 2002, as well as the International Action Network on Small Arms (IANSA), launched at the May 1999 Hague Appeal for Peace and successful in promoting the development of the UN's 2001 Programme of Action on Small Arms and Light Weapons. The Coalition to Stop the Use of Child Soldiers (CSC), founded in June 1998, worked successfully for adoption of the Optional Protocol on the Involvement of Children in Armed Conflict to the Convention on the Rights of the Child, which came into force February 12, 2002.

The movement toward the establishment of the International Criminal Court represents a unique collaboration between nongovernmental organizations and the like-minded group of states, largely small and middle powers, with the strong support of the UN Office of Legal Affairs. Following years of negotiations, the UN General Assembly established a Prep-Com in 1995, and authorized a diplomatic conference from June 15 to July 17, 1998, in Italy to finalize and adopt the treaty. Six NGOs in fall 1994, recognizing their inability to influence negotiations, came together to form the NGO Coalition for an International Criminal Court (CICC). Founded primarily by human rights NGOs and organized by Bill Pace of the World Federalist Movement, the CICC worked to support the like-minded group, both by attempting to influence governments at home and, more directly, negotiations at the UN. Among the NGOs prominent in the CICC were Amnesty International, Human Rights Watch, the Lawyers' Committee for Human Rights, the European Law Students Association, and the No Peace Without Justice/Transnational Radical Party. The CICC, which began with 30 members, expanded to include 800 NGOs from all regions, including humanitarian, parliamentary, religious, and women's groups, with the more prominent groups producing expert documents that influenced the negotiations and others disseminating information and building coalitions.

The coalition itself did not take positions, but groups within it, such as the women's caucus for gender justice, the victims' working group, the faith-based working group, and the children's group did. The Women's Caucus for Gender Justice, formed in February 1997, grew to over 300 organizations by the time of the final conference. Most of their aims were achieved, including the inclusion of their language in a subparagraph on gender specific crimes, to include "rape, sexual slavery, forced prostitution, forced pregnancy, forced sterilization and other sexual or gender violence or abuse." Once the court came into being in 2002, the caucus turned its concern to gender parity in the 2003 election of the 18 judges on the court; with nominations of 10 women and 33 men, the elections finally resulted on February 7, 2003, after 33 rounds of voting, in seven female and 11 male judges. The Women's Caucus for Gender Justice concluded its work in March 2003.

Recognizing the need for continued advocacy for and the monitoring of gender justice in the ICC, Women's Initiatives for Gender Justice was formed in January 2004, based in the Hague. It works for gender-inclusive justice, especially in connection with the work of the International Criminal Court and promotes the rights of female survivors of armed conflict. Together with the Nobel Women's Initiative, it organized the International Gender Justice Dialogue held in Puerto Vallarta, Mexico April 19–21, 2010, to promote accountability for gender-based crimes.

NGOs Working Toward Peace and Nonviolence

Among the many organizations that have been created to continue work on issues such as violence against women is the Coalition for Women's Human Rights in Conflict Situations, created originally by roughly 60 organizations in 1996 to introduce a gender perspective into the work of the International Criminal Tribunal on Rwanda. Consisting of lawyers, legal scholars, women's rights activists, and NGOs on gender justice, its mandate is to promote the prosecution of perpetrators of crimes of gender violence in conflict situations, especially in Africa.

The Women's International League for Peace and Freedom (WILPF) and other women's NGOs worked closely with Bangladesh, and later Namibia, to get the Security Council to pass Resolution 1325 on Women,

Peace and Security in October 2000 the first time the Council had taken up this linkage.

NGOs have continued their work with the support of UN Security Council Resolution 1820 (June 19, 2008), which explicitly recognizes a relationship between sexual violence and international peace and security, and follow-up resolutions 1888 (September 30, 2009), and 1889 (October 5, 2009). PeaceWomen, a project of WILPF, began the Security Council Monitor in 2006 to analyze and make the content on women, peace and security in all Security Council resolutions, debates, and reports available to advocates.

While it is often argued that NGOs are the voice of the people, representing grassroots democracy, a counter argument is made that NGOs have tended to reinforce rather than counter existing power structures, having members and headquarters that are primarily in the wealthy northern countries. While this may have been true earlier, since the decade of the UN global women's conferences, there has been a rise in the numbers of southern NGOs. There has also been a rise in networks and coalitions of NGOs and their influence. Some believe that NGO decision-making provides for responsible, democratic representation or accountability; others do not. What is clear, however, is that NGOs provide different voices, and these voices have been able to change global policy in a number of areas significant for women's lives.

See Also: Green Belt Movement; International Action Network on Small Arms; Transnational Feminist Networks; Women's Environment and Development Organization; Women's International League for Peace and Freedom.

Further Readings

Foster, Catherine. *Women for All Seasons: the Story of the Women's International League for Peace and Freedom.* Athens: University of Georgia Press, 1989.

Hill, Felicity, et al. "Nongovernmental Organizations' Role in the Buildup and Implementation of Security Council Resolution 1325." *Signs,* v.28/4 (2003).

PeaceWomen. "Translation Initiative: Call for Translation of Security Council Resolution 1325." http://www.peace women.org/translation_initiative/ (accessed May 2010).

Schiff, B. N. *Building the International Criminal Court.* Cambridge, UK: Cambridge University Press, 2008.

Stephenson, C. M. "Women's' International Nongovernmental Organizations at the United Nations." In A. Winslow. ed., *Women, Politics, and the United Nations.* Westport, CT.: Greenwood Press, 1995.

United Nations Economic and Social Council. "List of Nongovernmental Organizations in Consultative Status With the Economic and Social Council as of September 1, 2009." http://esango.un.org/paperless/content /E2009INF4.pdf (accessed October 2010).

Women's Initiatives for Gender Justice. http://www.icc women.org (accessed October 2010).

Carolyn M. Stephenson
University of Hawaii at Manoa

Nontraditional Careers, U.S.

A person can be considered employed in a nontraditional career if his or her gender only represents about 25 percent of the staff. The U.S. Department of Labor lists examples of nontraditional jobs held by women as architects, computer programmers, computer software and hardware engineers, detectives, chefs, barbers, clergy, engineers, computer and office machine repairers, construction and building inspectors (and other jobs in the construction field), railroad conductors, machinists, truck drivers, firefighters, and aircraft pilots.

Throughout history, men have taken on roles in skilled trades and labor-oriented jobs like construction, agriculture, manufacture, transport, and communication, while women have performed housework, care giving, teaching, and clerical duties. A woman's role was defined by society as being the primary care giver for her family, and men were considered the wage earners. Since at least the middle of the 20th century, women have pursued professional careers and employment requiring physical labor. Although the distribution of occupations has changed since the 1970s, and women have entered administrative and service occupations, men still hold a greater number of managerial, professional, and government positions worldwide. A woman choosing a nontraditional career may receive a higher entry-level wage, however, it may be difficult to find suitable mentors. Women in male-dominated occupations may face difficulties with ill feelings from their coworkers and the perception that they are not physically or mentally suited to the position—obstacles that faced many early female firefighters.

Statistics from the 2008 report "Quick Stats on Women Workers" reveal that 59.5 percent of women are employed or are looking for jobs. Women make up 46.5 percent of the total U.S. labor force, 75 percent working in full-time jobs and 25 percent working part time. Thirty-nine percent work in management, 33 percent work in sales, and 21 percent work in service-related work, while 6 percent work in productions, construction and maintenance. Interestingly, 46 percent of employed Asians and 41 percent of caucasian women work in management, professional, or related occupations. Thirty-two percent of African American women and 33 percent of Hispanic women are employed in sales and administrative jobs. Overall, women account for 51 percent of all workers in high-paying management, professional, and related occupations.

Statistics show that men work 59 percent of the total U.S. working hours and make up 52 percent of the total workforce, working for an average of 38 years compared to women, who work for an average of 32 years.

According to the National Council for Research on Women, 45 percent of the U.S. workforce is composed of women, of which only 12 percent occupy science and engineering jobs in business and industry. The Federal Aviation Administration reported that less than 6 percent of the people who became pilots in the year 2000 were women. The American Association of University Women (AAUW) states that only 20 percent of information technology professionals are women. According to the U.S. Bureau of Labor Statistics, fewer than 33 percent of girls are involved in computer-related activities and that nearly 75 percent of future jobs are projected to require an extensive use of computers. Research shows that girls demonstrate "computer reticence," partially because society has traditionally steered women away from working with machines.

The U.S. Department of Labor, Women's Bureau, reported that the share of women in the labor force increased from 46 percent to 48 percent from 2007 to 2008. A large increase was projected for Latin and Asian American women—49 percent among Latinas, 46 percent among Asian American women—with increases projected of 21 percent among African American women and 13 percent among Caucasian women. Women earning a bachelor's degree in the computer science field decreased from 37 percent to 28 percent since 1984. Only 9 percent of women were recipients of bachelor's degrees in engineering. Out of 54 percent of women who took the SAT I test in the year 1999, only 19 percent planned to go into engineering, and 23 percent of those who planned to go into computer science were young women.

Women still continue to concentrate in some degree in fields that have been historically dominated by women. In 1996, women earned 75 percent of education degrees, the same rate as in 1970. Per the National Center for Education Statistics, women in engineering grew from less than 1 percent in 1970 to 16 percent in 1996. In 1999, 55 percent of young men took AP calculus, while 45 percent of women took the course. Fifty-seven percent of young men versus 43 percent of young women took AP chemistry. Forty-three percent young men versus 57 percent of young women took AP biology. Around 70 to 80 percent of the test takers were male in AP physics, according to the College Board in 1999, indicating the largest gap in gender disparity. Girls tend to be more successful in mathematics and science programs with cooperative, hands-on approaches than in programs that focus on competition and person-to-person learning.

Traditionally, women are most likely to work in the education and health industries and remain underrepresented in mining, construction, science, engineering, and technology fields. Conversely, women in nontraditional industries are often overrepresented in lower-level positions and/or underrepresented in leadership positions. They concentrate more on clerical and service occupations, and in comparison to male coworkers, female professional scientists tend to stagnate at lower hierarchy levels. Hence there continues to be a gap between male and female pay rates. One of the causes of gender pay inequity is occupational segregation. Despite the fact that their skills and experience are often comparable, male industries generally pay higher wages than female-dominated industries.

See Also: Equal Pay; Mathematics; Science, Women in; Science Education for Girls; Stereotypes of Women.

Further Readings

American Association of University Women. "Tech-Savvy: Educating Girls in the New Computer Age." (2000). http://www.aauw.org/learn/research/upload/Tech Savvy.pdf (accessed July 2010).

Hartigan, R. "Girls Byte Back." *Teacher Magazine* (April 1999).

Thom, Mary. *Balancing the Equation: Where Are Women & Girls in Science, Engineering & Technology?* New York: National Council for Research on Women, 2001.

U.S. Department of Labor. "Quick Stats on Women Workers." http://www.dol.gov/wb/stats/main.htm (accessed July 2010).

Judy Jamal
Columbia University

Indra Nooyi, chairperson and chief executive officer of PepsiCo., was named one of Time*'s 100 most influential people.*

Nooyi, Indra

Indra Krishnamoorthy Nooyi is the chairperson and chief executive officer of PepsiCo, a global beverage, food, and snack company. Nooyi has been lauded for breaking the invisible glass ceiling and becoming the 11th woman to be at the top position in a Fortune 500 company. She made it to the number three position, following German Chancellor Angela Merkel and the former–British prime minister's wife Cheryl Blair, in the *Forbes* list of 100 most powerful women in the world in 2009. She was also part of *Time*'s list of 100 most influential people.

Nooyi was born on October 28, 1955, in Chennai, India, to a bank officer and a stay-at-home mother. She attended the Christian College in Madras and has a master's degree in business management from the Indian Institute of Management Calcutta, as well as from Yale University—two highly ranked institutions of learning located in India and the United States.

Nooyi has been heralded for displaying exemplary business acumen and sophisticated strategy by expanding the scope and focus of Pepsi's beverages beyond U.S. territories and for making forays into the Chinese market. Her work experience includes positions with Johnson & Johnson, where she was instrumental in the launch of Stayfree sanitary napkins for women. She has also been a part of prestigious institutions, such as the Boston Consulting Group. Her credo for her company is to deliver "performance with purpose."

Nominated the 2009 CEO of the Year by the Global Supply Chain Leaders Group, Nooyi has been forthright about her commitment to socially responsible corporate leadership. She has expanded the PepsiCo product line with healthy drinks and food products, such as the Quaker Oats division and health-oriented beverages. Nooyi is considered the motivating force for the company's health-conscious decisions, such as removing trans fats from their products.

Drawing a salary of more than $13 million annually, Nooyi is known to be an active philanthropist. Nooyi exemplifies an ideal for maintaining a balance between work and building a globally recognized identity as an individual.

Nooyi is also a wife and the mother of two girls. She has managed to remain involved in her children's lives and gives credit to her partner for taking the supporting role that has helped her stay focused on her career. She is currently the chairperson of the U.S.–India Business Council. She has also been a champion of women's rights and is frequently invited to speak on the topic. In her keynote address at Cornell University, Nooyi said "If women don't speak out on women's issues, whether it be women in the workplace or maternal mortality or little girls in Africa who are abandoned, if women don't speak out on those issues, I don't know who's going to speak out on them."

She envisions a future in Washington, D.C., working alongside the political powers and devoting time to social good and social policy. If Indra Nooyi's list of accomplishments, innate leadership skills, single-minded dedication, and professional competence are any indication, making it to Washington, D.C., should not be too difficult a task for this accomplished individual.

See Also: Chief Executive Officers, Female; India; International Women's Day; Working Mothers.

Further Readings
Cohen, Ed and Tom Rath. *Leadership Without Borders: Successful Strategies From World-Class Leaders.* Hoboken, NJ: Wiley, 2007.
Sellers, Patricia. "The Queen of Pop." *Fortune International (Europe),* v.160/5 (2009).

Shweta Singh
Loyola University Chicago

North Korea

The Democratic People's Republic of Korea, more familiarly known as North Korea, is located in eastern Asia, bordering on Korea Bay and the Sea of Japan. Early in the 20th century, Korea lost its independence to Japan as a result of the Russo-Japanese War. After World War II, the country split, and the northern section came under the sponsorship of Soviet communists. Early in the following decade, the United States became instrumental in foiling North Korea's attempt to annex South Korea. Subsequently, the government adopted a policy of diplomatic and economic self-reliance. The following decades were characterized by economic mismanagement and ill-founded resource allocation.

Much of the country's economic resources were directed at building up its military and gaining nuclear capability, which has aroused considerable global concern. Because the communist government tightly controls information released to international organizations, accurate details on the status of women is difficult to obtain. According to the official government position, women have continued to make considerable gains since the 1940s. However, outsiders remain convinced that women are vulnerable to incidences of violence and human trafficking that go unreported by the North Korean government. Civil libertarians contend that North Korean women continue to be discriminated against by laws that ban them from participating in activities that are deemed "improper." Such activities include smoking, driving, and cycling. In some areas, women also are banned from wearing trousers.

Religion and Reproduction Rights
By the 21st century, 63 percent of the population lived in urban areas. Except for small groups of Chinese and Japanese, North Korea is ethnically homogeneous. The same is true of religion. Most North Koreans are Buddhist and Confucianists. A small number have endorsed either Christianity or *Chondogyo* (the Religion of the Heavenly Way). In reality, North Koreans have almost no religious freedom.

Until the early 20th century when the Chosn Dynasty came to an end, Korean women had only limited access to social, economic, political, and educational opportunities. Reproduction was considered to be the primary role for women, who were seen only as extensions of males. In a society that honored male heirs, female children were considered undesirable. By some reports, this practice continues in some families, even though it is no longer a government-sanctioned policy. In 1945, under the communist government of North Korea, females were granted constitutional equality. North Korea passed the Law on Sex Equality in 1946 and declared that marriage should be based on free will and mutual consent. In reality, many women continue to marry only with the approval of their parents. According to information released by Radio Free Asia, the average age North Korean women marry is 28, compared to age 30 for men. Legally, wives have equal rights to property and inheritance. In divorce settlements, mothers usually win custody of children under age three, but custody of older children may be awarded to fathers.

According to social indicators, the median age for North Korean females is 34.9 years. With an overall infant mortality rate of 51.34 deaths per 1,000 live births, North Korea ranks 49th in the world. Female infants (43.6 percent of births) have a considerably higher survival rate than male infants (58.64 percent). Female life expectancy is 66.53 years, which continues to surpass that of males, at 61.23 years. North Korean women bear 1.96 children, and the country ranks 138th in the world in this area. Both males and females have a reported literacy rate of 99 percent.

Women in Elected Office

Politically, North Korean women have made significant gains in recent decades since quota regulations have increased the presence of women in elected office. However, feminists have questioned the ability of quota women to act independently. Despite the increased number of women in the work place, women are still expected to perform traditional roles assigned to Korean females.

See Also: Divorce; Domestic Violence; United Nations Development Fund for Women.

Further Readings

Central Intelligence Agency. "The World Factbook: North Korea." https://www.cia.gov/library/publications/the-world-fact-book/geos/kn.html (accessed February 2010).

Fleshenberg, A. "The Path to Political Empowerment? Electoral Gender Quotas in South Asia." *Pakistan Journal of Women's Studies*, v.14/2 (2007).

Elizabeth Rholetter Purdy
Independent Scholar

Norway

Following centuries of reluctant unions with Denmark and Sweden, Norway, which borders both the North Sea and the northern Atlantic Ocean, achieved independence in 1905. Norway is often considered to have the most favorable climate for women of any nation in the world. Some scholars believe this preference for equality dates back to Viking invasions, which were common before the acceptance of Christianity in 994 C.E.

The discovery of extensive oil and gas in the 1960s led to an economic boom and further development of the social welfare state. The country is highly homogeneous, and 94.4 percent of the population is Norwegian. Religiously, 85.7 percent identify with the Church of Norway. In the 21st century, Norway ranks first on the United Nations Development Programme's list of countries with Very High Human Development. Some 77 percent of the population is urbanized. Despite setbacks that have resulted from global economic woes, Norway has the fifth highest per capita income ($59,300) in the world. Norwegian feminism has a long history, which dates to the publication of Henrik Ibsen's feminist play, *A Doll House*, in 1880. Norway passed the Equal Status Act in 1978, and equal pay for equal work is mandated by law. However, women still earn 10 to 15 percent less than men in wages and benefits. Within the Office of Equality and Antidiscrimination, the ombudsman is responsible for monitoring gender equality. Despite its commitment to equal rights, Norway has some of the same problems that plague countries around the world, including violence against women and human trafficking.

Norway has an infant mortality rate of 3.33 deaths per 1,000 live births for girls and 3.92 deaths per 1,000 live births for boys. Women have a life expectancy of 82.74 years compared with 77.29 years for men. Norwegians have a fertility rate of 1.78 children per woman. The median age for Norwegian women is 40.2 years. Literacy is universal, and Norway ranks 20th in the world in educational spending. Women have an 18-year school life expectancy, as opposed to 17 years for men.

By 1991, Gro Harlem Brundtland was serving her third term as prime minister of Norway. At her insistence, the Labour Party began stipulating that at least 40 percent of party nominees be women, and other parties followed suit. In 2006, gender equality was expanded to the business community, and all publicly traded firms were required to report at least 40 percent representations on all boards by 2008 or be shut down. They complied. By 2008, 64 of 169 parliament members were women; nine of 19 ministers were women; and seven women sat on the 19-member Supreme Court. Norway recognizes the economic value of homemakers by assuming that both household and income are shared, and Norway has allowed women in combat since 1984.

Rape, including spousal rape, is illegal. Despite strict enforcement of laws, incidences have continued to rise, and many more cases go unreported, partly because of the male-dominated justice system. Incidences of domestic violence also continue to rise. The government has established support programs for victims, and each of the 27 police districts funds a domestic violence coordinator. The government and nongovernmental organizations work together to fund shelters and manage crisis hot lines. Since January 2009, it has been illegal in Norway to purchase sexual services, but it is not illegal to provide them. Most Norwegian prostitutes are foreign-born, and many of them are trafficked into the country from Africa, Eastern Europe, Eastern Asia, and South America. Sexual harassment carries both fines and prison terms in Norway.

See Also: Domestic Violence; Sex Workers; Trafficking, Women and Children.

Further Readings

Breneman, Anne R. and Rebecca A. Mbuh. *Women in the New Millennium: The Global Revolution.* Lanham, MD: Hamilton Books, 2006.

Burk, Martha. "The 40-Percent Rule." *Ms.*, v.16/3 (2006).

Central Intelligence Agency. "The World Factbook: Norway." https://www.cia.gov/library/publications/the -world-factbook/geos/no.html (accessed June 2010).

Naft, Naomi and Ann D. Levine. *Where Women Stand: An International Report on the Status of Women in 140 Countries, 1997–1998.* New York: Random House, 1998.

U.S. State Department. "2008 Human Rights Report: Norway." http://www.state.gov/g/drl/rls/hrrpt/2008 /eur/119097.htm (accessed June 2010).

Weise, Beth Reba. "Feminism in Scandinavia." *Off Our Backs*, v.30/3 (1990).

WIN News. "Reports From Around the World: Europe." *WIN News*, v.17/3 (1991).

Elizabeth Rholetter Purdy
Independent Scholar

Novelists, Female

The novel has often been the province of men, but there have always been female counterparts to challenge the domination of the novel by male writers. Some critics, such as Franco Moretti, suggest that literary history usually oscillates between domination of the novel form by either women or men. The success or failure of women writers has often depended on the popularity of particular genres. Fewer women writers have been published in eras in which the most popular genres are traditionally masculine novels with a military, nautical, or historical slant. In comparison, female novelists have sometimes been confined to writing about the domestic, provincial, and sensational. One of the challenges for women writers has been how to redefine or break out of conventional female genres.

When exactly women began writing in the novel form is impossible to say, though most critics define the 18th century as a crucial period for the development of European women novelists. Beyond the 18th century, the feminist critic, Elaine Showalter, defines three significant periods in the development of women novelists: the feminine novel (1840–80), the feminist novel (1880–1920), and the female novel (1920 onward). These stages represent the development of a stronger identity for women novelists and a growing sense of their project as opposed to that of men.

The late 20th and early 21st centuries, however, have been defined by a new generation of powerful world writing, often originating from writers with hyphenated origins or in a postcolonial setting. There has been new recognition for this world women's writing in the form of prizes for female novelists.

Early Female Novelists, Pre-1840

Before the 19th century, female novelists did not have a sense of a female tradition, and often they were trailblazers—unique in their style and approach to the novel. One such writer is Aphra Behn, whose novels are some of the earliest ever written. Returning destitute after working as a spy for Charles II, Behn turned to writing to make a living, producing poetry, drama, and a number of novels. Behn's novels explored the popular forms of the day, including the epistolary novel in *Love-Letters Between a Nobleman and His Sister* (1684–87) and narratives about foreign places and peoples in *Oroonoko; or the Royal Slave* (1688).

As more women began to write, early female novelists often presented themselves through the stereotype of helpless femininity—a tactic that worked to protect them from the scrutiny of male reviewers. Novels by women in this period usually presented wry social commentary on the experiences of women and the education of young women. For example, the British writer Fanny Burney depicts "the History of a Young Lady's Entrance into the World" in her novel *Evelina* (1778), whereas the Anglo-Irish Maria Edgeworth portrays the social progress of her heroine *Belinda* (1801), describing her many suitors and her quest for a good marriage.

The other genre dominated by women in this period was the Gothic Romance. Female novelists combined foreignness, the supernatural, and romance to define this genre—a typical example being Anne Radcliffe's *The Mysteries of Udolpho* (1794). The Gothic Romance was also put to political use by feminist writers such as Mary Wollstonecraft, so that the genre's sinister preoccupations were combined with a critique of patriarchy. Wollstonecraft's *Maria: or, The Wrongs of Woman* (1792) presents a loveless marriage in which the wife-heroine is eventually condemned to an insane asylum by her own husband.

One of the most eponymous writers of this period was Jane Austen, whose development of a free, indirect style complemented her critique of modern socialization. Similar to other female novelists of this period, Austen was interested in writing novels about the education and development of young women, as well as the quest for a suitable marriage. This is most obvious in *Pride and Prejudice* (1813), which begins with the famous dictum that every wealthy young man "must be in want of a wife." Austen, however, also pays homage to the Gothic Romance in *Northanger Abbey* (1818), in which Austen describes her heroine Catherine as having read Radcliffe's *The Mysteries of Udolpho*. Austen successfully parodies the classic Gothic themes but is always ultimately a novelist of female education and development.

The Feminine Novel, 1840–80

By 1840, more female novelists were encouraged to write, though sometimes they adopted a male pseudonym. For example the Brontë sisters, Charlotte, Emily, and Anne, adopted the pen names Currer, Ellis, and Acton Bell, and George Eliot's real name was Mary-Anne Evans. This period represents a moment when women wanted to become the intellectual equals of men.

Showalter defines this period as the era of the "feminine novel," not because the writers are any more feminine than their counterparts in other historical periods but because to be a woman in Victorian society was to be bound to the rules of 19th-century femininity. As a consequence, women novelists were often stereotyped as vain and narcissistic, and they also had to defend themselves from charges of being prurient or "unwomanly" when writing on more controversial subject matters. Critics of the time, such as John Stuart Mill and G.

H. Lewes, suggested that women would never match men's artistry and genius in the writing of the novel.

In spite of such discouragement, this era marked the rise of the bourgeois woman, and female novelists engaged with the key genres of the day. The Brontë sisters brought their unique vision to the Gothic Romance, especially in Charlotte Brontë's *Jane Eyre* (1847), Emily Brontë's *Wuthering Heights* (1847), and Anne Brontë's *The Tenant of Wildfell Hall* (1848). Meanwhile, novelists like Elizabeth Gaskell (1810–65) brought a woman's perspective to the Industrial Novel, offering a working-class viewpoint in *Mary Barton* (1848) and a middle-class heroine in *North and South* (1854–55). The social realism of George Eliot in novels such as *Silas Marner* (1861), and especially *Middlemarch* (1871–72), proved as well that women writers could construct a complex masterpiece of a novel that illuminated the lives of both women and men.

The Feminist Novel, 1880–1920

The feminist period of women's novel writing occurred at a time of suffrage and radicalism—the first wave of the feminist movement. This was also an era when the English novel was giving way to new world writing, and the novels produced by women often represented the New Woman, a figure that demanded sexual autonomy and independence. The South African Oliver Schreiner presents this New Woman in her novel *The Story of an African Farm* (1883), in which the heroine Lyndall describes herself as Napoleon in a woman's body. The Irish novelist Sarah Grand considers the hypocrisy of differing attitudes to men's and women's promiscuity in *The Heavenly Twins* (1893), and the American Elizabeth Robins presents a subversive model of womanhood in reworking her adventures in the Alaska wilderness for the novel *The Magnetic North* (1904). Altogether, the period of the New Woman represented the beginning of a more rigorous sexual critique, which would be performed by women writing all over the world.

The Female Novel, 1920 Onward

From 1920 onward, women's experience was not only the source of women's novels but also inspired the techniques and forms used. Virginia Woolf's recommendation of an androgynous writing sensibility did not detract from her powerful, modernist representations of women's interiority, such as the portrayal of

Mrs. Dalloway (1925) or Mrs. Ramsay in *To the Light-house* (1927). Dorothy Richardson was the first writer to use the stream-of-consciousness narrative technique, using it to illuminate the viewpoint of her heroine, Miriam, in the *Pilgrimage* sequence of 13 novels (1915–67). Similarly, in Jean Rhys's *Good Morning, Midnight* (1939) and the late *Wide Sargasso Sea* (1966), disjointed narrative flashbacks offered a stark critique of power relations between men and women.

Post–World War II

With the rise of Second Wave Feminism after World War II, female novelists rigorously explored the repression of women in their everyday and domestic lives. In *The Prime of Miss Jean Brodie* (1961), Muriel Sparks uses the technique of prolepsis (flash-forward) to show that though the teacher, Jean Brodie, is now in her prime, her sexual adventures will soon be betrayed by one of her own students. Other important works that explored the repression of women include Doris Lessing's *The Golden Notebook* (1962), Sylvia Plath's *The Bell Jar* (1963), A. S. Byatt's *Shadow of the Sun* (1964), and Angela Carter's *The Magic Toyshop* (1967). What these novels share is a commitment to working through the disjointed identities of women and challenging or undermining figures of patriarchy.

The 1960s, however, was also an era that ushered in a new sexual freedom, which was the inspiration for many female novelists of the time. The Irish-born Iris Murdoch wrote in *The Bell* (1958) about the sexual intrigues of a group of people living in and around Imber Court, a lay religious community, and in Margaret Drabble's *The Millstone* (1965), the heroine becomes a pregnant, single mother after a brief and casual sexual encounter. Joyce Carol Oates also writes about sex, the pressure to marry, and illegitimacy in her novel *them* (1969), though she sets it in the context of the American working class and urban life. The sexual revolution of the 1960s meant that women could write more honestly and openly about relationships, and by the 1980s, the technique of studying the intricacies of human relationships was available to gay writers too, as in Jeanette Winterson's portrayal of lesbian lovers in *Sexing the Cherry* (1989).

Hyphenated Origins

The strength of the American novel in the 20th century created possibilities for communities within the United States to write their stories. Particularly successful is the African American novel, which had long been championed by women writers from the time of Harriet Beecher Stowe's *Uncle Tom's Cabin* (1852). Toni Morrison is significant in portraying the experience of black women, from her realism in *The Bluest Eye* (1970) to the more Gothic sensibility of her eponymous novel *Beloved* (1987). Alice Walker also gained acclaim for her portrait of the double-repression of African American women in *The Color Purple* (1982), and Octavia Butler's *Kindred* (1979) employs analepsis (a flashback) to send her confident, modern African American heroine back to the time of slavery.

Perhaps following on from the African American remaking of the novel, other groups with hyphenated origins within the United States have reclaimed the novel. Chicana writing is growing, its best-known female novelist perhaps being Sandra Cisneros, whose book *The House on Mango Street* (1984) presents vignettes from the lives of Chicana teenagers. In *The Joy-Luck Club* (1989), Amy Tan, an American writer of Chinese descent, presents a moving portrait of a mother–daughter relationship and the reconciliation of Chinese American identity. The Haitian American Edwidge Danticat writes in *Breath, Eyes, Memory* (1994) of the difficulty of life in the United States for Haitian immigrants traumatized by war and suffering. These writers bring a fresh perspective to the form of the novel and offer fascinating explorations of national and female identity.

Postcolonial Women Novelists

The 20th century has also seen the rise of the postcolonial novel, in which English-speaking colonies "write back" against the literary canon. The role of women in writing the postcolonial novel is particularly significant, because all too often in colonial and postcolonial discourse, women's bodies are used in intellectual exchanges about the ownership of culture and the rape of the land. In the same year, 1982, postcolonial women writers Anita Desai and Isabel Allende published portraits of families living through the aftermath of colonialism, though at different ends of the world: Desai's portrait of family struggles in India titled *The Village by the Sea* and Allende's family saga of violence, *The House of the Spirits*. Women writers from all over the postcolonial world have used the novel to convey women's experience of the violence and the wrongs of colonialism, from Jamaica Kincaid in Antigua to Yvonne Vera in Zimbabwe.

In 1996, a new award for women's writing, the Orange Prize for Fiction, was established in the United Kingdom. In addition, the Nobel Prize for Literature has been awarded to a woman on 12 occasions, including to novelists such as Doris Lessing, Nadine Gordimer, and Toni Morrison, and the Pulitzer Prize and Man Booker Prize are now more regularly awarded to women novelists.

See Also: Arts, Women in the (21st Century Overview); Lessing, Doris; Morrison, Toni; Oates, Joyce Carol; Showalter, Elaine.

Further Readings

Lane, Richard J. *The Postcolonial Novel*, Cambridge, MA: Polity, 2006.

Moretti, Franco. *Graphs, Maps, Trees: Abstract Models for Literary History*. London: Verso, 2007.

Showalter, Elaine. *A Jury of Her Peers: American Women Writers From Anne Bradstreet to Annie Proulx*. London: Virago, 2009.

Showalter, Elaine. *A Literature of Their Own: British Women Novelists From Brontë to Lessing*. London: Virago, 1977 (reprinted 1984).

Zoe Brigley Thompson
University of Northampton

Nuns, Buddhist

The order of the Buddhist nuns, also known as *theris*, established by the Buddha is a landmark in women's history as the first and the only women's order to strive toward the most noble kind of freedom. It was in the 6th century B.C.E. when Buddhist nuns established an ideal of sisterhood, becoming the first feminist order. Buddha's mother, Mahapajapati Gotami, was the first Buddhist nun ordained into the *Dhamma*, after much reluctance on Buddha's part. It was at the insistence of Gotami that Buddha gave his consent to the *bhikkuni* order.

Buddha prescribed eight special rules (*gurudhamma*) that the *bhikkunis* had to agree to before they were ordained. Compiled in *Bhikkuni Vinaya*,

these rules establish male superiority over female if examined by modern standards. However, judging by the contemporary standards, these nuns were the champions of the feminist cause for their time, because the *bhikkuni* order brought Buddhism closer to the ideals that were later to be known as feminist. The order had on the one hand Sumeda and Sela, who were of royal lineage, and on the other the slave girl Punnika. There were former courtesans like Ambapali and Vimala and daughters of noble families like Bhadda, Kundalkesa, and Sujata.

The Brahminical religion of the Buddha's time did not grant any parity to women. In such times, the order of the *bhikkunis* may be seen as a progressive step against the engendered norms of patriarchy. The nuns' order received its orientation from the monks initially, but when the monks' resentment and reluctance was sensed, it was felt that the nuns' order needed to be redefined. Greater autonomy was granted to the *bhikkunis*, and they were allowed to teach their own disciples. Ordination of the nuns has

Girls train to become Buddhist nuns in Thailand. Most faiths will not let women under 18 take their vows.

three levels: *sramanerika* (novice); *siksamana* (probationary); and *bhikkuni* (full ordination), and it is received at a slow, steady pace to acclimatize the nuns with the *Sangha,* or spiritual community.

The actual number of *theris* is not known, but the *Khuddaka Nikaya* has 73 poems, organized into 16 chapters written by Dhamma, Ubbiri, Patacara, Kisa Gotami, Mittakkali, Samana, Mutta, and many more. This is known as *Therigatha,* or "Verses of the Elder Nuns." *Therigatha* is a record of the position of nuns in the order and its verses reaffirm the equal position accorded to women in terms of religious attainment. Author Kathryn R. Blackstone looks upon these verses as "liberation manuals." Through not only their verses but also their lives, the nuns proved that women are equal and also that even without rebellion, women can choose not only their own path but also guide others to a path of discipline that leads to knowledge and freedom from all suffering.

The nuns' order flourished in India for some time, and in the 3rd century B.C.E. spread to Sri Lanka. After a century, the order expanded to China and Korea as well. After almost 500 years of Buddhism, there was a bifurcation seen in the Mahayana and the Theravada streams. Although the Theravada *bhikkuni* order has still not been completely revived, in countries like Sri Lanka the Theravada *bhikkuni* survives to this today.

In the Mahayana sect, the *bhikkuni* order is being nurtured by educated, active nuns. Today, however, the term *nun* in Buddhism refers to women called *dasasilamatas,* who undertake the 10 precepts and wear a white robe. In 1998, at Saranath in India, 11 *dasasilamatas* were ordained as *bhikkunis,* who in turn ordained 23 more *dasasilamatas,* and in this way the lineage is growing in Theravada countries. In July 2007, Buddhist leaders and scholars of all traditions met at the International Congress on Buddhist Women's Role in the Sangha in Hamburg, Germany, to work toward a worldwide consensus on the reestablishment of *bhikkuni* ordination.

See Also: Buddhism; Nuns, Roman Catholic; Religion, Women in.

Further Readings

Blackstone, K. R. *Women in the Footsteps of the Buddha: Struggle for Liberation in the Therigatha.* Surrey, UK: Curzon, 1998.

Brown, S. *The Journey of One Buddhist Nun.* Albany: State University of New York Press, 2001.

Gutschow, K. *The Struggle for Enlightenment in the Himalayas.* Cambridge, MA: Harvard University Press, 2004.

Asha Choubey
M .J. P. Rohilkhand University

Nuns, Roman Catholic

The word *nun* is commonly used to refer to a woman who has made a visible commitment to religious life. The Latin *nonna,* or "tutor," came to denote a woman under monastic vows. The Latin *moniale* and the Old English *nunne* are later versions of the same. In modern usage, the terms *nun* and *sister* are used interchangeably in popular speech, yet under church (canon) law there is a distinction between the two groups. Nuns profess solemn vows and generally maintain a contemplative life, while sisters profess simple vows and have an active apostolate often involving education or charitable work. Both solemn and simple vows are made publicly, accepted by a superior, and binding. The definition of nun and the precise form of life that nuns lived has changed dramatically throughout the past two millennia; however, the commitment and desire of religious women to participate in the ministry, mission, and life of the Catholic Church has not.

When Anthony, the father of western monasticism, became a hermit, he left his sister in the care of "pious nuns." His biography, written in the mid-4th century, provides a witness to communities of nuns in the early church. Although evidence for communities at this time is fragmented, it appears that nuns were women living in enclosed contemplative communities who chose to separate themselves from the world and dedicate themselves to the Lord. Idealization of enclosure is apparent among early religious communities. The earliest rule for women, written about 534 C.E. by Caesarius of Arles, placed particular emphasis on enclosure. Similar sentiments are echoed in other early rules, and enclosure continued to be emphasized throughout the Middle Ages.

Social changes between the 12th and 14th centuries resulted in increased emphasis on enclosure, as well as more rigid rules governing canonical requirements for recognition as a nun. The fourth Lateran Council of 1215 asked that emerging religious groups adopt and approve rules. Despite resistance to innovation, new communities developed. Groups that were inspired by Clare of Assisi or some early Cistercian women created patterns of religious life that accepted enclosure and were otherwise compatible with the religious climate of the time. In 1298, the growing emphasis on enclosure culminated in Boniface VIII issuing the decree *Periculoso,* which made enclosure mandatory for all nuns.

The church's support for strict enclosure of nuns was reaffirmed by the Council of Trent and by three subsequent papal proclamations in the 16th century. However, strict enclosure was to prove difficult to regulate and to enforce. The canonical situation was complicated by the many irregular groups of religious women, including beguines and tertiary groups of Franciscans and Dominicans, which developed throughout the 13th century.

The status of non-enclosed religious women was resolved canonically until Leo XIII's bull *Conditae a Christo* in 1900. At this time, congregations of sisters who were under simple vows and groups of non-cloistered women were given full papal recognition.

Active ministry continued to cause problems in both the early modern and modern worlds. Women in what began as secular institutes or congregations with a specific charitable focus were both supported and disdained in the church and in society. The Institute of the Blessed Virgin Mary, founded by Mary Ward (1585–1645), was dedicated to education and justice. Ward was dedicated to Ignatian spirituality and is now recognized as a visionary champion for religious women. However, during her life, Ward was a controversial figure who was imprisoned by the church and whose convents and schools were suppressed. It was not until more than two centuries after Ward's death that her community was able to honour her as foundress.

Feminist Spirit

The radical, even feminist, spirit of early modern women was to continue. In the 19th century, nuns and sisters participated in acts of public service. These women involved themselves in tasks as diverse as working with prostitutes to help them become

more economically independent to nursing victims of cholera and pox.

Through the work done by these women and by more recent scholars of women's history, it is evident that nuns, sisters, and religious women can be considered precursors of feminism. In an age where women were seldom active in public life, religious women founded and administered hospitals, charities, and houses of education. Many communities of Catholic women have continued to be on the forefront of the women's movement.

The decree, *Perfectae Caritatis* (1965), issued by the Second Vatican Council, asked religious orders to return to the original intentions of their founder or foundress. After this time, many congregations of nuns and sisters began to explore questions of identity more fully. Nuns and sisters who were trained as historians began to explore the early public and social roles of their orders. By investigating the feminist past of their congregations, these women radically altered the official histories of their religious communities.

Today, and throughout history, communities of nuns and sisters belong to a particular order and community. Each order has particular characteristics and work and has many communities. Each community has an individual superior, who is ultimately responsible to the governing body of her order. Nuns like the Poor Clares and the Carmelites still observe strict enclosure and live lives of contemplative prayer. Benedictine nuns do not maintain the same degree of strict enclosure. Other orders, such as the Franciscans, are often involved in ministry in the world but still maintain lives of shared prayer. Congregations of nuns and sisters can often be identified by their religious habits; however, many elect to dress in clothing that is virtually indistinguishable from that worn by the laity.

Lives of Service

Many congregations of nuns and sisters have returned to lives of radical service. Religious women run hospices for victims of human immunodeficiency virus and acquired immune deficiency syndrome (HIV/AIDS), work with political refugees and with victims of human trafficking. Sisters such as the American Sister of St. Joseph, Helen Préjean, have caused controversy by ministering to prisoners who have been condemned to death. As Catholic nuns and sisters work with the marginalized, they often show greater openness to social problems than the institutional church. It is not uncommon for nuns and sisters to work in areas wracked by conflict. Groups of sisters often work with individuals on both sides of a conflict, often with disastrous results. A Franciscan Missionary of Mary, Maria Teresalina, died while working in Kashmir in 1947. Both this order and many others still maintain schools and hospitals in this area.

Nuns and sisters maintain a connection to community, both in their order and to the universal church. Although there are no limitations on the type of employment that religious women can seek, the roles that nuns and sisters play are generally discerned by community needs. The careers of nuns and sisters range from counseling and medicine to working as professors in universities.

The feminist roots of nuns and sisters often manifest themselves in issues concerning women in the church. This is particularly true with regards to women in ministry. In many areas, the decline in vocations has meant a shortage of priests. This leaves nuns and sisters to run liturgies and communion services. Although the vocation of nuns and sisters is often service rather than liturgy, there are some who wish for greater participation in the liturgy. Notably, the Benedictine nun Joan Chittester has expressed controversial views on women's ordination and women's participation in liturgy.

The church remains committed to the religious life of enclosed and contemplative nuns. The 1999 Vatican document on enclosed life, *Verbi Sponsa* states that "enclosure, for nuns, is a recognition of the specific character of the wholly contemplative life in its feminine form" and that "separation from the world, silence and solitude, express and protect the integrity and identity of the wholly contemplative life." Enclosed nuns can be found throughout the world. They often maintain close ties with houses of religious men, who provide for both their spiritual and practical needs.

Since the mid-20th century, the church has seen a decline in vocations to the religious life. Religious women have commented on the need for religious expressions that are suited for the modern age. The 21st century has seen a growth in semireligious communities composed of nuns, sisters, and even lay women. Like the early communities of sisters, such women tend to be involved in social justice.

In his Apostolic Exhortation *Vita Consecrata*, John Paul II stated that consecrated life for both men and women was "to be sought in the special relationship which Jesus, in his earthly life, established with some of his disciples" (c. 1, par. 14). A vocation to the consecrated life takes many different forms, each of which is recognized as making a unique contribution to the church. Since the earliest days of the church, women have been involved in its spiritual life and mission. Although their characteristics have changed and evolved over time, the importance of their contribution has not diminished.

See Also: Italy; Nuns, Buddhist; Religion, Women in; Roman Catholic Church.

Further Readings

John Paul II. *Mulieris Dignitatem: On Dignity and Vocation of Women.* London: CTS, 2002.

John Paul II. *Vita Consecrata: The Consecrated Life.* Vatican City: St. Paul's Publications, 1996.

McNamara, JoAnn. *Sisters in Arms: Catholic Women through Two Millennia of Christianity.* Cambridge, MA: Harvard University Press, 1998.

The Teachings of the Second Vatican Council: The Complete Text of the Constitutions, Decrees and Declarations. Westminster, UK: The Newman Press, 1966.

Verbi Sponsa: Instruction on the Consecrated Life and the Enclosure of Nuns. Vatican City: Liberia Editrice Vaticana, 1999.

Alison More
St. Bonaventure University

Nurses

Nursing may be the most familiar health professional group in the world, second only to physicians. Nurses far outnumber all other groups of health workers, with an estimated 12 million nurses working worldwide. Women constitute the overwhelming majority of nurses, with estimates ranging from 89 to 97 percent in countries of the global north. According to the 2003 American Nurses Association Social Policy Statement, "nursing is the protection, promotion, and optimization of health and abilities, prevention of illness and injury, alleviation of suffering through the diagnosis and treatment of human response, and advocacy in the care of individuals, families, communities, and population."

To achieve this range of activities, nurses operate in four domains: clinical or bedside practice (the work most commonly associated with nursing in the public imagination), nursing management, nursing education, and nursing research. Nurses work in a variety of hospital-based and community settings and in many capacities: in clinics as nurse practitioners, in colleges and universities as faculty educators and researchers, in government as policy makers, in schools as public health nurses, in hospitals as administrators and clinical nurse specialists, and in the home caring for a child with a disability or a senior recovering from a stroke.

Nurses are highly educated, skilled practitioners of the art and science of nursing who contribute to individual and community health and well being, the domestic economy, and the reproduction of community values. Despite this, nurses continue to be variously misrepresented in the popular media and on the Internet as angels of mercy, doctors' handmaidens, glorified waitresses, and "naughty girls." Nursing as care work and individual and collective identity illustrate well the gendered, classed, and raced meanings of women's lives.

History of Nursing

Nursing dates to the mid-1800s, although women's work as healers, herbalists, and midwives predates the professionalization of care work. Florence Nightingale, who was born into a wealthy British family, wrote about being "called" to nursing. Known as the "Lady with the Lamp" in recognition of her service to injured and dying soldiers during the Crimean War and elsewhere, she established the first professional nursing school in London in 1860.

Mary Seacole was a Jamaican-born woman of color who, like Florence Nightingale, traveled widely to care for populations hard hit by cholera and other epidemics and to serve for three years during the Crimean War. Unlike Nightingale, Seacole's contributions to nursing practice were largely forgotten. Some historians and feminists claim she fell into obscurity because race and class prejudice made Seacole a less fitting role model during the Victorian era. When Seacole's contributions were rediscovered, she became a sym-

bol for minoritized nurses and the civil rights movement.

Until the mid-1950s, women learned the knowledge and skills that prepared them to be a nurse through apprenticeship. Their training typically occurred in a hospital setting under the watchful eye of a physician or senior nurse. The naturalness of these expectations was reinforced by educational institutions and religious-based hospitals, that trained nurses. Schools of nursing operated by Catholic and Mormon churches, for instance, reinforced women's role in health and healing at work and at home. Nursing has been considered a "calling" for which an individual is chosen to serve God's plan in a unique or special way.

Historically, individual ambition, self-fulfillment, and sexual desires were constrained by the strict dictates and moral codes of behavior, the demand for faithfulness and self-sacrifice in the service of the greater needs of the sick and injured, and the good of the hospital or organization. Today, many nursing students are introduced to Nel Nodding's ethics of care, which emphasize that the caring and moral nurse is empathetic, concerned, gentle, kind, warm, compassionate, good humored, authentic, and engaged.

Education and Credentialing of Nurses

Over time and in response to health-sector demands, the scope of nurses' work increased, as has the knowledge and skills required to competently fulfill those duties. Today, nurses operate on many rungs of the professional ladder. Each step requires additional educational preparation beyond the minimum entry to practice, which in turn qualifies a nurse to engage in a wider scope of practice and in a wider variety of practice settings. Along with this added responsibility and accountability come greater autonomy and control over work and decision making; improved wages and career mobility; and greater social, economic, and political power. Depending on the country or state, a practical nurse or nursing assistant may require a few months to two years of preparation in an approved program to acquire the basic knowledge and skills deemed necessary to perform competently.

Minimum entry to practice for a nurse has increased from two years of college preparation to four years of university preparation. The clinical nurse specialist, nurse anesthetist, nurse midwife, and nurse practitioner require several years of advanced training to develop the expertise to practice in these specialist roles. Nurses may be prepared at the master's and doctoral levels to assume work in senior administration, education, and research.

The International Council of Nurses unites more than 130 national nursing associations from around the world. The goal of the federation is to promote quality nursing care by sharing information about health and social issues from a range of international perspectives and by informing health practice and policies that contribute to health and healthcare globally. One initiative is to provide credentialing services and products. Credentialing is a mechanism for ensuring that an individual has met a set of standards of professional practice set by a regulatory body, professional association, government agency, or other organization created to accredit education programs and healthcare facilities. Typically, nurses are expected to renew their credentials periodically as a way of communicating to their employers and the public that they are maintaining their knowledge and skill competencies.

Minimum standards for competent practice vary from country to country, and the array of credentialing activities and services provided by credentialing associations also varies. For decades, this has meant that nurses trained in the Caribbean or the Pacific Islands, for example, did not have their credentials recognized as equivalent when they emigrated to work in Canada and the United States. This policy decision had material consequences for these immigrant nurses of color, who tended to be concentrated in less prestigious, less autonomous nursing positions as compared to their white, locally trained counterparts. The current international nursing shortage is providing the impetus for streamlining credentialing standards and practices to facilitate the international movement of nurses.

Nursing as Care Work

Nursing has long been considered an appropriate vocation for young women and was promoted as a normal and natural extension of women's domestic role. The classic image of the nurse is a woman performing in a hospital, a clinic, or a community setting. Although caring is considered a fundamentally human quality, care work is typically undertaken by women and girls. Women are believed to be well suited to perform the instrumental, emotional, moral, and relational labor of nursing. Nursing literature has long debated whether nursing is an art, a science, or both. That debate about nursing as practice or discipline reflects the long-standing tension about the valuation of nursing labor as subordinate to the biomedical structure in which the discipline of nursing operates.

The work of nurses is physically and emotionally demanding, oftentimes unrewarded, undervalued, or unrecognized, and has been associated with poor health, low levels of satisfaction, unhappiness, and depression. Nurses are expected to meet the demands of work through selfless devotion to those in their charge. However, nurses typically have divided allegiances, serving the interests of one group that is vulnerable (patients and children), while at the same time reporting to and negotiating with another group that represents their financial and social security (senior nurses and doctors).

The everyday work of nursing varies significantly within each group, mirroring the social hierarchies of race, class, and gender. Some nurses (those working part-time, in settings with less social cache, or those with training outside North America, for example) have far less latitude in negotiating their work practices. Nurses are subject to direct and indirect surveillance in the performance of their duties by their clients, families, colleagues, supervisors, and their professional association.

Nursing Identity

The identity of nurses as individuals and as a collective is forged by institutional expectations and the care work they perform. Feminine identity as a natural caregiver is accorded varying degrees of social value, and a poorly circumscribed but wide-ranging set of caring practices. Historically, women were believed to be subject to their capacity as reproducers, and therefore, the natural guardians of virtue, morals, and values. By contrast, men were freed of their biology by rationality. Men exercised their power through politics, education, and culture; women exercised their power through womanly arts of human and social reproduction. Thus, nurses' identity as caregiver came to be regarded as women's domain and inextricably linked to her biological, reproductive capacity, while physicians' identity became institutionalized as men's domain.

At times, there are calls for a revaluation of the paid and underpaid work done by nurses, work that is simultaneously invisible yet subject to surveillance, valorized yet culturally devalued. Nursing as a social institution reproduces and reflects family and community values and structures and is regulated directly and indirectly by legal, political, and sociocultural expectations.

Pay equity—equal pay for work of equal value—continues to be the most serious gender issues in the area of equal opportunity. Female-dominated professions such as nursing tend to be less valued socially and financially than traditionally male-dominated professions such as medicine. Although women make up the vast majority (93 percent of staff positions in the United Kingdom [UK], for example), men tend to accept a disproportionate amount (45 percent in the UK) of advanced educational opportunities and senior management positions. Gender discrimination may be addressed by developing bias-free job evaluations; enforcing equal opportunity legislation; and tackling systemic barriers, such access to 24-hour licensed childcare facilities.

Representation of Nurses

The physician-dominated healthcare model in which nurses operate is reproduced in the media. Dramas about physicians and medicine have been much more prevalent over the last 50 years than dramas about nurses and nursing practice. *Dr. Kildare* (played by TV heartthrob Richard Chamberlain) and *Ben Casey* (played by Vince Edwards) were the physician leads in TV dramas of the 1960s. These shows ran for 190 and 153 episodes respectively. More recent popular and long-running TV medical shows (*St. Elsewhere, M*A*S*H, ER, House, Grey's Anatomy, Private Practice*) also starred physicians with nurses featured in less central storylines.

By comparison, there have been relatively few programs featuring nurses in lead roles. *Julia* was the first program to feature a black actress, Diahann Carroll, in the lead, playing a widowed nurse. First airing in 1968, it ran for 86 episodes. While exceptional for this reason, it was criticized for being an unrealistic and apolitical portrayal of nursing practice and African American families. Two other notable series are *Nurse Jackie,* which first aired in 2009 and features an emergency room nurse struggling with substance abuse and an extramarital affair, and *Scrubs,* which first aired in 2001 and features a caring and competent Latina nurse character in the one of the lead roles. While all these shows may have artistic merit, organizations such as the Centre for Nursing Advocacy, which is concerned with promoting public understanding of nursing practice, are less enthusiastic about the portrayal of nurses.

The focus tends to be on physicians' professional hierarchy and advancement rather than on nurses' autonomy and expertise. Nurses are seldom represented as knowledgeable, ethical, and skilled practitioners. In other arenas, such as advertising, pornography, and the apparently benign creation of Halloween costumes, sexualized images of nurses continue to appear.

Nursing Shortage

The supply of nurses has not kept up with worldwide demand. This has negative implications for population health, with poorer health outcomes expected among the most disadvantaged populations. This shortage translates into increased mortality, postoperative complications, and infection rates for the poorest of the poor. A report published by the International Council of Nurses reported that the projected shortage of nurses is more acute in some regions than in others. Rural and remote regions have been historically underserved, although urban areas are now experiencing shortages as well. Third World countries tend to have more acute shortages than Europe, North America, and Australia. For example, there are 1,000 nurses per 100,000 population in Norway, compared with 10 nurses per 100,000 population in Uganda.

Four challenges have been identified. First, the global population is aging, which affects both supply and demand for nursing. Supply is affected because the existing workforce, which is disproportionately composed of baby boomers, is reaching retirement age. Shift work and the physical and emotional demands of nursing labor are more challenging for the aging worker. This means that nurses are working fewer hours or leaving direct patient care positions. At the same time, the demand for nurses is increasing because the general population is living longer and requiring care for both normal conditions and chronic diseases associated with aging.

The second challenge is that nurses are relocating within and beyond their national borders in search of more professional autonomy, more opportunity for advancement, a fairer wage commensurate with their educational preparation, and higher levels of public respect and social status. In the Gulf nations, for example, local nurses constitute only a fraction of the workforce, with many sourced from the Philippines and other Pacific Island countries. This example illustrates two points: the international movement of nurses that addresses the shortage of the host country results in a shortage in the home country; and nurses tend to move from low income to higher income countries, resulting in a loss of human resources and economic instability in an already poor nation.

The third challenge is the need for organizational restructuring and health-sector reform. Although the issues may be more acute in some countries than others, gender, race, and class politics play a significant role in educational inequalities and wage disparities within and beyond the health sector and even among categories of nurses in the same locale. Collectively, these problems impact negatively on the recruitment and retention of nurses, the attractiveness of nursing as a career, and the likelihood of attracting women and men into the profession.

For instance, in some parts of Africa and South America, there are persistent staffing shortages, inefficient or inadequate infrastructure, unreliable or inadequate supply of basic health supplies and medications, and gender discrimination and workplace violence. In countries such as Canada and the United States, nurses are leaving the profession earlier because of work-related stress, injury, and discontent.

The fourth cause of the nursing shortage worldwide is the enormous demand of the human immunodeficiency virus and acquired immune deficiency syndrome (HIV/AIDS) epidemic in sub-Saharan Africa. War, political unrest, and environmental disasters, such as the earthquakes that hit Haiti and central Chile in 2010, also affect the adequacy and efficiency of the health sector and increase the demand for nurses to care for the sick, injured, and dying.

See Also: Advertising, Portrayal of Women in; Affirmative Action/Equal Opportunity; Equal Pay; Midwifery; Professional Education; Representation of Women; Stereotypes of Women.

Further Readings
Buchan, Jim and Lynn Calman. "The Global Shortage of Registered Nurses: An Overview of Issues and Actions." Geneva: International Council of Nurses, 2004.
D'Antonio, Patricia. "Nurses–Wives and Mothers: Women and the Latter-day Saints Training School's Class of 1919." *Journal of Women's History*, v.19/3 (2007).
Ehrenreich, Barbara and Deirdre English. *Witches, Midwives, and Nurses: A History of Women Healers.* 2nd Ed. New York: The Feminist Press at City University of New York, 2010.
Ingall, Athena Harris. "Professional Nurse Caring: A Review of the Literature." *St Vincent's Health Care Campus Nursing Monograph* (2001).
McPherson, Kathryn. *Bedside Matters: The Transformation of Canadian Nursing, 1900–1990.* Oxford, UK: Oxford University Press, 1996.
Nodding, Nel. *Caring: A Feminine Approach to Ethics and Moral Education.* Berkeley: University of California Press, 1984.

Diana L. Gustafson
St. John's, Canada

Nutrition

Nutrition can be defined as the process of absorbing nutrients from food and processing them in the body for growth, replacement of tissues, and maintenance of good health. Historically, women have been responsible for cooking and providing meals for their families. Often, that food was grown in the family garden or local community. The women may not have had much formal education, but they seemed to know, almost instinctively, what was good for their families. Life was less complex earlier in time, and fewer food choices existed.

The evolution of technology and modern farming techniques has caused a great deal of change in the quality of our food. Water, soil, and air pollution are depleting our soil of vitamins essential for good health, and an increase in the amounts of food additives, chemicals, sugar, and unhealthy fats in our foods has contributed to the increase in chronic diseases present in society. Therefore, it is critical that women learn as much as they can about their nutritional needs and the connection between their diet and their health.

Although nutritional guidelines exist for the general population, there are some suggested practices specific to the health and wellness of women. Women's bodies are unique in how they respond to the six basic nutrients: carbohydrates, fats, proteins, minerals, vitamins, and water. These nutrients are needed for various different body functions in varying amounts. Poor health can result from a lack of one of these essential nutrients or, in some cases, an excessive amount of them. Diseases linked to an improper diet include anemia, cardiovascular disease, hypertension, osteoporosis, type 2 diabetes, and obesity. These illnesses will be discussed in more detail later.

Good Nutrition for Women

Eating a variety of foods and appropriate amounts of the six nutrients can boost energy, improve mood, control weight, prevent disease, and improve overall health. Nutritional tips for women of all ages include the following:

- Eat predominately plant-based foods and avoid processed foods. Choose a variety of fruits and vegetables.
- Eat foods rich in calcium to support bone health, such as dairy products and leafy green vegetables. Choose fat-free or low-fat milk products.
- Eat lean protein. Excessive amounts of protein can cause calcium loss, which can lead to osteoporosis.
- Eat foods rich in iron. Iron is especially important during menstruation.
- Limit alcohol and caffeine. Caffeine can interfere with hormone levels and increase the loss of calcium.
- Eat whole grains. Whole grains contain the entire kernel and can aid in the prevention of some chronic diseases.

Women's bodies are especially sensitive to nutritional requirements because of hormonal fluctuations that occur during a woman's life. These fluctuations take place during a woman's monthly cycle as well as throughout her life as she moves through adolescence, puberty, reproduction, and menopause.

Puberty

Federal guidelines indicate that dietary recommendations are essentially the same until puberty. The age at which girls enter puberty has dropped over the years, which has been attributed to nutritional factors connected to childhood obesity. Girls with a lower intake of protein and dietary fiber have been associated with a slower onset of puberty. During puberty, there is an increased need for iron, as the girls will begin menstruating during this time. Good sources of iron include lean meat, fish, poultry, spinach, beans, and lentils. Women build bone into their 20s and need to eat a calcium-rich diet. Good sources of calcium are low-fat milk, cheese, yogurt, broccoli, spinach, kale, and oranges.

Reproduction

Women of reproductive age who are pregnant or are considering being pregnant have additional nutritional needs. The nutritional habits of the woman before, during, and after pregnancy greatly affect the fetus and developing child. Overweight and obese women are at risk for infertility problems, as well as gestational diabetes and preeclampsia throughout the pregnancy. One nutrient that is essential for women in this stage of life is folic acid. Folic acid is used to aid the body in producing extra blood needed for pregnancy and helps prevent neural defects in the developing baby, such as spina bifida and anencephaly. Folic acid is often taken as a dietary supplement but can also be found in foods such as spinach, citrus fruits, and beans. Calcium is also important for women in this age group to support bone health.

Menopause

As mentioned in both the previous sections, calcium continues to be an important nutrient for women going through menopause. Vitamin D is also important in the absorption of calcium. However, it is controversial at high doses because of the link to kidney stones and constipation. In addition to calcium, women in this phase of life should eat foods low in saturated fat and cholesterol to lower the risk of heart disease. Foods high in fiber are important to prevent colon cancer, and foods high in salt should be limited or avoided to help prevent high blood pressure. In addition, foods with an excessive amount of sugar should be avoided because they contain empty calories with no nutritional value.

Diseases Associated With Poor Nutrition

Many of the leading causes of death are directly related to poor nutrition. Diseases linked to an improper diet include anemia, cardiovascular disease, hypertension, osteoporosis, type 2 diabetes, and obesity.

Anemia is caused by a deficiency in iron and affects more than 30 percent of the world's population and 12 percent of women in the United States. Symptoms may include fatigue, headaches, general weakness, and irregular or increased heart rate. Pregnant women with anemia and their fetuses are at risk of premature birth, low birth weight, and maternal death. To prevent anemia, one should eat iron-rich foods such as lean red meats, chicken, fish, chickpeas, soybean, kidney beans, and lentils.

Cardiovascular disease—the leading cause of death in women—is directly linked to poor nutrition. Risks for heart disease include being overweight or obese; consuming too much fatty foods, salt, sugar, and alcohol; smoking cigarettes; and not exercising regularly. Heart-healthy foods include fruits, vegetables, whole grains, low-fat dairy, and lean proteins.

Hypertension is blood pressure that remains elevated above a safe level. Blood pressure levels of 140/90 or higher are considered unsafe. Over time, arteries become thicker and less elastic, resulting in arteriosclerosis, which increases the risk for heart disease and stroke. This condition, affecting approximately one in three adults in the United States, can be prevented by maintaining a healthy weight and reducing salt.

Diabetes, a condition that affects how the body uses energy from food, creates a high level of glucose in the blood. Causes include the body not accepting or using the insulin it produces, the pancreas creating too little insulin, or a combination of both. Type 2 diabetes, also called adult-onset diabetes, develops slowly and usually occurs in adulthood as a result of poor diet and obesity. Approximately 10 percent of women age 20 years or older have diabetes. However, this disease is becoming more prevalent in children and teenagers as a result of increases in obesity among these groups. Although diabetes cannot be cured, it can be managed with a healthy diet, proper exercise, and medication when necessary. Diabetes also creates an increased risk of heart disease and stroke.

Obesity, defined as having a body mass index greater than 30 kg/m^2, is the result of having too much fat in your body. In the United States, approximately two-thirds of adults and one-fifth of children are overweight or obese. Obesity increases risk for cardiovascular disease, diabetes, cancers, and hypertension. Prevention includes a healthy, well-balanced diet and physical activity.

Osteoporosis, affecting approximately 30 million U.S. women, is characterized by fragile bones that may fracture or break easily. To prevent osteoporosis, a bone-building diet at any age rich in calcium and vitamin D is important to form new bone cells. Foods rich in calcium include dairy products (milk, cheese, yogurt), dark green leafy vegetables, and almonds. With less than half of adolescent males and one-fifth of adolescent females consuming enough calcium, half of women and one-fourth of men older than 50 years will experience an osteoporosis-related bone fracture. For those not able to eat foods containing calcium or drink milk, calcium supplements are available.

Other diseases related to poor nutrition include certain cancers, scurvy (which results from a vitamin C deficiency), rickets from a vitamin D deficiency, blindness from a vitamin A deficiency, goiter (enlarged thyroid glands) from an iodine deficiency, nerve disorders and appetite disorders from a vitamin B and/or iron deficiency, and bleeding disorders from a vitamin K deficiency.

See Also: Cancer, Women and; Diabetes; Diet and Weight Control; Heart Disease; Nutrition in Pregnancy; Puberty; Reproductive and Sexual Health Rights.

Further Readings

Alexander, L. L., et al. *New Dimensions in Women's Health*, 5th Ed. Boston: Jones and Bartlett, 2010.

American Dietetic Association. "Disease Management and Prevention." http://www.eatright.org/Public (accessed April 2010).

Centers for Disease Control and Prevention. "Nutrition for Everyone." http://www.cdc.gov/nutrition/everyone /index.html (accessed April 2010).

U.S. Department of Agriculture. "Life Stages." http://www .nutrition.gov/nal_display/index.php?info_center=11& tax_level=2&tax_subject=395&topic_id=1690& placement_default=0 (accessed April 2010).

Jennifer J. Kane
Elissa M. Barr
University of North Florida

Nutrition in Pregnancy

For optimal fetal growth and development and good maternal outcomes, a healthy balanced diet is of great importance before conceiving, as well as throughout the pregnancy. There are a number of key nutrients of importance in pregnancy and a number of food safety issues that need to be considered before and during pregnancy.

Prepregnancy and Nutrition

The nutritional status of the mother at the time of conception is an important determinant of fetal growth and development. Being a healthy weight before conception (body mass index [BMI], 18.5–24.9 kg/m^2) is of great importance, and being underweight (BMI, less than 18.5kg/m^2) or overweight (BMI, more than 25kg/m^2) can affect both fertility and birth outcome. There is now evidence to confirm that folic acid, found in many foods such as green leafy vegetables, fortified cereals, and bread, is of great importance during the period from before conception to early pregnancy and can reduce the risk of neural tube defects. Women planning a pregnancy are advised to take 400 grams a day of folic acid supplement before and up to the 12th week of pregnancy to ensure that they meet this recommendation.

Nutritional Requirements and Weight Management During Pregnancy

Nutritional requirements are increased during pregnancy. Additional maternal stores of energy and nutrients are required for fetal development, as well as for lactation postpregnancy. During pregnancy, women have large variations in fat deposition, energy expenditure, and physical activity; this reflects the wide variation in energy requirements in women. For women with a normal prepregnancy BMI, only a small amount of additional energy is required. This is because in pregnancy, the body adapts to the increased energy requirements and becomes more energy efficient through reduced physical activity and a lowered metabolic rate. It is only during the last trimester of pregnancy that there are increased energy requirements of an additional 200 kcal/day. However, underweight women or women who remain active and do not reduce their activity levels may require more energy.

Studies have shown that women with a healthy prepregnancy BMI have a weight gain on average of around 12 kg (10–14 kg), which is associated with the lowest risk of complications in pregnancy and labor, and a lowered risk of having a low-birth-weight (LBW) baby (birth weight, less than 2.5 kg). Other risk factors associated with a LBW baby are smoking and use of alcohol or drugs during pregnancy. LBW is associated with increased infant morbidity and mortality, as well as an increased risk of diseases in later life, such as cardiovascular disease and type 2 diabetes.

The "Barker" hypothesis states that impaired intrauterine growth and development may be the root cause of many degenerative diseases of later life through the mechanism of fetal programming, in which a stimulus or insult at a critical period in early life development has a permanent effect on the structure, physiology, or function of different organs and tissues. A review by the World Health Organization showed that a birth weight of 3.1–3.6 kg is considered in the normal range and is associated with positive fetal outcomes for a baby born full term. Excessive weight gain during pregnancy can increase the risk of complications such as high blood pressure, and in the long term it can lead to overweight and obesity in the mother postpartum.

Key Nutrients of Importance in Pregnancy

The main recommendation for pregnant women is to follow a varied, healthy, balanced diet. Nutrients for which there is evidence of increased requirements during pregnancy include protein, energy, and certain micronutrients such as thiamine, riboflavin, folate, and vitamin D.

During pregnancy there are physiological adaptations thought to help meet the increased demand for certain minerals; for example, iron and calcium absorption increases during pregnancy. However, women of childbearing age are at risk of developing anemia because of poor iron stores and are therefore advised to consume iron-rich foods such as red meat, pulses, bread, green vegetables, and fortified breakfast cereals during pregnancy, and in some cases, a supplement may be required. Calcium is an important nutrient particularly during teenage pregnancy, as a rapid increase in bone mass occurs in adolescence. Pregnant teenagers have higher requirements of calcium because the maternal skeleton is still developing. Vitamin D, found in a small number of foods but mainly obtained from summer sunlight, is important for calcium absorption. A daily vitamin D supplement of 10 g/day is recommended throughout pregnancy. In addition to the recommendation regarding the importance of folic acid in reducing the risk of neural tube defects, there is also an increased requirement of folate during pregnancy to prevent megaloblastic anemia.

Food Safety Issues During Pregnancy

It is important during pregnancy to avoid eating foods that could increase the risk of exposure to harmful pathogens that may be harmful for the fetus, such salmonella, found in raw eggs, mayonnaise, and undercooked meat; listeria, found in mold-ripened and blue-veined cheeses; and toxoplasmosis, found in raw or undercooked meat.

Pregnant women are advised to avoid excessive intakes of vitamin A (retinol), which is present in high levels in liver and liver products and in some multivitamin supplements. Excessive intakes of retinol are toxic to the developing fetus and may cause birth defects. Alcohol consumption is shown to influence fertility and can increase the risk of fetal alcohol syndrome, characterized by LBW and a variety of congenital abnormalities. In the United States and other countries, it has been recommended that alcohol be avoided during pregnancy.

A number of studies have shown that caffeine is associated with LBW and spontaneous abortion. It is recommended that caffeine intake should be limited to within the current guidelines of no more than 300 mg/day, which is roughly equivalent to four cups of instant coffee (190 mL/cup), six cups of tea (190 mL/cup), eight cans of cola (330 mL), or six bars of plain chocolate (50 g).

Studies have shown that oily fish is a rich source of long-chain n-3 fatty acids, which are important for optimal fetal brain and nervous system development. Epidemiologic studies show protective associations of maternal fish intake during pregnancy on atopic or allergic outcomes in infants/children. The recommendation is now limited to two portions of oily fish per week for pregnant women (and those who may become pregnant). This is to avoid the risk of exposure to environmental contaminants such as polychlorinated biphenyls and dioxins. It is also impor-

tant for pregnant women to avoid swordfish, shark, and marlin and to limit consumption of tuna during pregnancy. These types of fish have high levels of methylmercury, which are harmful for the developing nervous system of the fetus.

Women with allergies or a strong family history of allergies (hay fever, asthma, eczema, or other allergies) are advised to avoid peanuts and food containing peanut products while pregnant and breast-feeding.

Diet-Related Complications During Pregnancy

Preeclampsia (hypertension) is a condition that can occur toward the end of pregnancy in some women. Evidence shows that obesity is a common risk factor, but further research is required to confirm whether supplementation with calcium or certain vitamins during pregnancy may help prevent this condition.

Symptoms of morning sickness, nausea, and vomiting are commonly reported in pregnancy. Changes in appetite and taste can cause aversion to some foods. These changes are unlikely to have any adverse effect on the nutritional status. Some women experience pica (cravings for certain nonfood substances such as chalk) in pregnancy, but the reasons for this are unclear. Constipation during pregnancy can be common. Increasing fiber intake, drinking plenty of fluids, and taking gentle exercise like walking can be helpful to alleviate the problem.

Food hygiene is important to prevent food poisoning during pregnancy, as well as avoidance of certain at-risk foods that contain harmful pathogens such as listeria. It is important to consume oil-rich fish (two portions per week) but to avoid certain fish (e.g., shark, marlin) to prevent exposure to environmental contaminants harmful for the developing nervous system of the fetus.

See Also: Diet and Weight Control; Nutrition; Pregnancy; Prenatal Care.

Further Readings

Goldberg, G. "Nutrition in Pregnancy and Lactation." In P. Shetty, ed. *Nutrition Through the Life Cycle.* Leatherhead, UK: Leatherhead, 2002.
Hytten, F. E. "Nutritional Physiology During Pregnancy." In D. M. Campbell and D. G. Gillmer, eds., *Nutrition in Pregnancy.* London: Royal College of Gynaecologists, 1983.

Institute of Medicine, Food and Nutrition Board. *Nutrition During Pregnancy.* Washington, DC: National Academy Press, 1990.

Mozaffarian, D. and E. B. Rimm. "Fish Intake, Contaminants, and Human Health: Evaluating the Risks and the Benefits." *Journal of the American Medical Association*, v.18/296 (2006).

Mukherjee, R. A., et al. "Low Level Alcohol Consumption and the Fetus," *British Medical Journal*, v.330 (2005).

Picciano, M. F. "Pregnancy and Lactation." In E. E. Ziegler and L. J. Filer, eds. *Present Knowledge in Nutrition.* Washington, DC: ILSI, 1996.

World Health Organization. "Maternal Anthropometry and Pregnancy Outcomes. A WHO Collaborative Study." *World Health Organization Bulletin*, v.73 (1995).

Vasant Hirani
University College London

Oates, Joyce Carol

Joyce Carol Oates has been named the current Dark Lady of American Letters (after Mary McCarthy and Susan Sontag)—a designation given to an intellectual woman writer who challenges the categorization of "woman" writer.

Born on June 16, 1938, Oates was raised, along with two younger siblings, in the rural upstate New York town of Millersport. Oates's mother was a homemaker; her father a machinist. Her paternal grandmother lived with the family and was a key supporter of Oates's writing, giving her a portable typewriter for her 14th birthday. Oates received a scholarship to Syracuse University and earned a B.A. in 1960 as class valedictorian. While at Syracuse, she won a *Mademoiselle* writing prize (the same one Sylvia Plath had won a few years earlier). In 1961, she earned her M.A. from the University of Wisconsin–Madison and married Raymond Smith. In 1962, both Smith and Oates taught at the University of Detroit; from 1968 to 1978, the couple moved to the University of Windsor in Canada. In 1978, they settled in Princeton, New Jersey. Smith died in 2008. Oates is currently a Distinguished Professor in Humanities at Princeton University.

Since 1959, Oates has published hundreds of short stories and essays, nearly 60 novels, dozens of plays, and more than 15 collections of poetry, as well as books for children and young adults. Her novel *them* (1969) won the National Book Award, and three novels, *Black Water* (1992), *What I Lived For* (1994), and *Blonde* (2000), were nominated for the Pulitzer Prize. *We Were the Mulvaneys* (1996) was selected in 2001 by Oprah Winfrey for her book club.

Oates's early novels were set in Detroit: *them*, *Expensive People*, and *The Garden of Earthly Delights* (1967–69) each depict the emerging class consciousness of a young protagonist. The violent sexual awakening of another teen character is illustrated in her widely anthologized story, "Where Are You Going, Where Have You Been?" (1966). Several novels from the 1970s focus on characters with misguided worldviews (e.g., *Son of the Morning* [1978]). Other works have college campus settings (e.g., "In the Region of Ice" [1970]; *The Hungry Ghosts* [1974]; *Unholy Loves* [1979]; and *Marya: A Life* [1986]). In the early 1980s, Oates published three novels that depict the American dream (and failure) while also subverting the conventions of 19th-century domestic gothic and romance: *Bellefleur* (1980), *A Bloodsmoor Romance* (1984), and *Mysteries of Winterthurn* (1984).

Oates has also focused on the dualities within the female psyche, as depicted in two female characters (e.g., in *Solstice* [1985] and *You Must Remember This* [1987]) and as seen in twins, under the pseudonym Rosamond Smith (e.g., *Lives of the Twins* [1987] and *Soul/Mate* [1989]). Her favorite subjects, however, are the American family, the American dream, and the violence that seems to be inevitable in its pursuit (e.g., *American Appetites* [1989]; *Because It Is Bitter, and Because It is My Heart* [1990]; and *We Were The Mulvaneys* [1996]). In 2000, Oates' *Blonde*, a fictional account of the life of Marilyn Monroe, a woman not unlike many of Oates' characters, became a best seller. Oates also started writing young adult novels at this time, including *Big Mouth and Ugly Girl* (2002).

Oates's reception by the literary community has been mixed. In the early 1970s, Alfred Kazin complained that because her works were too heavily plotted with unlikeable characters, her novels were not high literary art. Yet he also criticized women who dismissed Oates's focus on working-class rather than feminist issues: he claimed that unlike many women writers, Oates was more sensitive to the violence of the American working-class experience. Harold Bloom has also hailed Oates as a major proletarian writer.

Oates's harshest critics are those who protest the violence in her work. In 1981, Oates responded to an essay in the *New York Times Book Review* called "Why Is Your Writing So Violent?" by noting that the question itself was sexist. Other critics have praised her for her violence, saying that she writes like a man. Many of Oates's male characters resort to violence out of frustration. When she was a child, Oates's father took her to boxing matches. *On Boxing* (1987) is a collection of essays on the topic: boxing, to Oates, explicitly reflects the drama of human struggle within one's self and with others. Oates justifies the violence and pessimism of late-20th-century fiction in general as simply realism. Tragic art, she notes, necessarily reflects moments of crisis and also shows how some individuals have the strength to overcome such moments.

Many feminist critics were slow to appreciate Oates's fiction, perhaps because of its depiction of both men and women equally constrained by gender roles. Oates has often chafed at being called a "woman" writer, grouped with other writers simply because of her sex, and has conceded that most of her mentors have been men. It was not until the 1980s, with her feminist trilogy exploring arranged marriages, rape, and sexual abuse during the 19th century, that Oates's work was admitted into the canon of feminist literature; an excerpt from *A Bloodsmore Romance* (1984) was published in *Ms.* magazine. Oates also expresses a feminist consciousness in her collection of essays *(Woman) Writer: Occasions and Opportunities* (1988), in which she explores the works of several women writers, though the bracketed "(Woman)" again reflects her questioning of a system that does not see male writers as a category.

Oates is rumored to have been shortlisted for the Nobel Prize in Literature since at least the 1980s.

See Also: Boxing; Feminism, American; *Ms.* Magazine.

Further Reading

"Celestial Timepiece: A Joyce Carol Oates Home Page." http://jco.usfca.edu/index.html (Accessed November 2009).

Creighton, Joanne V. Joyce Carol Oates: *Novels of the Middle Years.* New York: Twayne, 1992.

Johnson, Greg, ed. *Joyce Carol Oates Conversations 1970–2006.* Princeton, NJ: Ontario Review, 2006.

Stacey Lee Donohue
Central Oregon Community College

Obama, Michelle

Born in 1964, Michelle Robinson Obama is the first African American First Lady in U.S. history. She is married to President Barack Obama, who was sworn in as the 44th president on January 20, 2009. They have two daughters, Malia and Natasha (Sasha), born in 1999 and 2001, respectively.

Throughout her life, Obama has blazed trails and broken barriers. She has been praised for changing perceptions of African American women and of African American families. She has high approval ratings; in January 2010, 78 percent of Americans approved of the job she was doing as First Lady. Born in the South Side of Chicago six months after President Lyndon Johnson signed the landmark 1964 Civil Rights Act, Obama grew up in a home that stressed the value of education and hard work. Her father, Fraser Robinson, was a pump operator for the Chicago Water Department, living with multiple sclerosis.

Her mother, Marian Robinson, stayed home to raise Obama and her older brother, Craig. Obama attended Chicago's first magnet high school, where she was salutatorian, traveling two to three hours each day on public transportation to school.Obama

Michelle Robinson Obama, a lawyer by profession, is the first African American First Lady in U.S. history.

followed her brother to Princeton University, where she majored in sociology and minored in African American Studies, graduating cum laude in 1985. The national debate on affirmative action at the time influenced Obama's years at Princeton. In fact, she has written that it was at Princeton that she first felt self-conscious about her race. When Obama enrolled, there were only 94 African Americans (out of 1,100 students) in her class. She wrote a much-analyzed thesis titled "Princeton Educated Blacks and the Black Community" for which she surveyed African American alumni to determine whether they felt more comfortable with blacks or with whites at different times in their lives—before Princeton, at Princeton, and after Princeton.

Michelle Obama, after Princeton, attended Harvard Law School, from which she graduated in 1988.

At Harvard, she joined the Black Law Students Association and worked in the school's legal aid bureau, providing poor people with legal services.

She returned to Chicago to join the prominent national law firm Sidley Austin as an associate in the intellectual property group. It was there that she met Barack Obama in 1989, when he was a summer associate at Sidley and she was assigned to be his adviser. The Obamas began dating that summer and were married in 1992. In 1991, Obama left Sidley and her career focus shifted. She served as assistant commissioner of planning and development in Chicago's city government before becoming the founding executive director of the Chicago chapter of Public Allies, an AmeriCorps program that prepares youth for public service.

In 1996, Obama joined the University of Chicago, serving as associate dean of student services and vice president of community and external affairs for the University of Chicago Medical Center. Obama resisted her husband's entry into politics, chafing at the strain it placed on their family's life. After her husband's election to the U.S. Senate, she and their daughters continued to live in Chicago. When he decided to enter the race for president, she negotiated with him to quit smoking as a condition for his running.

Obama reduced her professional responsibilities by 80 percent to support his campaign. She was an effective surrogate, tasked with explaining his positions on issues, humanizing her husband, and often hosting events and fund-raisers solo. At first, she only worked on the campaign two days a week, but that steadily increased, and by February 2008, she attended 33 events in eight days.

Perceived as polarizing early in the campaign, she was sometimes labeled as an "angry black woman." But by summer 2008, perceptions of her had softened as she increased her focus on the hurdles facing the middle class and empathizing with those challenges.

As First Lady, Obama works to ensure that their daughters have as normal a life as possible. Her mother moved into the White House to assist with child care, and the two girls attend Sidwell Friends School.

She has focused her work on supporting military families, helping working women balance career and family, encouraging national service, promoting the arts and arts education, and fostering healthy eating.

Obama recently launched a campaign to tackle the challenge of childhood obesity, with the ambtious goal of solving the epidemic within a generation.

See Also: Attorneys, Female; Gardening; Nutrition; Political Ideologies.

Further Readings

Kantor, Jodi. "The Obamas' Marriage." *New York Times* (October 26, 2009).

Mundy, Liza. *Michelle: A Biography*. New York: Simon & Schuster, 2008.

Obama, Michelle and Susan A. Jones. *Michelle Obama in Her Own Words*. Self-published, CreateSpace, 2008.

Stephenie Foster
Independent Scholar

Obsessive Compulsive Disorder

Obsessive compulsive disorder (OCD) is an anxiety disorder that affects 2 to 3 percent of the U.S. population. OCD is characterized by consuming thoughts and beliefs that typically lead to the uncontrollable performance of behaviors. For a person to be diagnosed with OCD, his or her obsessions and/or compulsions must significantly negatively impact his or her life, such as an inability to work.

There are four types of OCD: (1) contamination/cleaning, characterized by overwhelming thoughts of filth and the need to remove the filth by cleaning; (2) obsessions/checking, characterized by a fanatical need to check on things (like making sure a stove is off or a door is locked); (3) symmetry/ordering, where a person visually requires items to be as symmetrical as possible and will arrange or rearrange things so that they are precisely and symmetrically ordered; and (4) hoarding, which is characterized by a compulsion to keep items that may be old, spoiled, out of date, or otherwise unused as a result of a fear that once discarded an item may be needed. Studies have found that each type is characterized by a unique distribution of symptoms. The most common obsession is fear of contamination and the most common compulsion is checking.

Symptoms that an OCD person may experience are severe anxiety, hyperventilation, sweating, accelerated heartbeat, and a tightening of the chest. OCD usually begins in late adolescence or early adulthood (33 percent of individuals experience symptoms before the age of 15) but can (rarely) develop at an earlier age. OCD affects U.S. adult men and women equally, but males develop OCD earlier than women (between 5 and 6 years of age compared to between 20 and 29 years of age, respectively). Women with OCD are more likely than men to be married with children and to have a past history of an eating disorder or major depression. Studies have found that OCD is comorbid with other psychiatric disorders; 67 percent of persons with OCD also have major depression, 25 percent also have social phobia, and 20 to 30 percent also suffer from tics.

Although OCD has a 2.5 percent lifetime prevalence rate in the United States, families that have one clinically diagnosed OCD person in them are 6.2 times more likely to have another OCD person. Studies have cited both a genetic component (using monozygotic and dizygotic twin studies, and parent and non-twin sibling samples) as well as a learned environmental component. Some researchers believe that children who grow up watching siblings or parents performing compulsive behaviors, and/or hearing obsessive thoughts spoken aloud, are more likely to have OCD symptoms because they learn the behavior as a normal course of daily life.

The presence of symptoms does not guarantee treatment for OCD. The average number of years between the onset of OCD and treatment is 17 years. Further, the median untreated rate is 59.5 percent for persons with OCD. Treatment plans depend on the type of OCD one is experiencing and the degree of impact on the individual's life. Selective serotonin reuptake inhibitors (SSRIs) are often prescribed to mediate the effects of the anxiety experienced and also to treat depression, social phobia, or other generalized anxiety that is present in persons with OCD.

Cognitive Behavioral Therapy (CBT) is also often initiated with an OCD person, where the individual is gradually exposed to increasing amounts of the situation that causes the obsessive thoughts but is taught new (preventative) methods by which to respond to the compulsions that follow to break the link between the obsession and compulsion. Research indicates that

SSRIs are most effective for individuals with later onset than if they were early onset. Desensitization (flooding) therapy has also been found effective, where persons with OCD are repeatedly exposed (sometimes over a long period of time) to their obsessive triggers to desensitize them to the anxiety produced and decrease the urge to perform the compulsive behaviors.

See Also: Anxiety Disorders; Depression; Health, Mental and Physical; Mental Illness, Incidence Rates of; Psychological Disorders by Gender, Rates of.

Further Readings

International OCD Foundation. http://www.ocfoundation .org (accessed November 2009).

Steketee, Gail and Teresa A. Pigott. *Obsessive Compulsive Disorder: The Latest Assessment and Treatment Strategies.* Sudbury, MA: Jones and Bartlett, 2006.

U.S. National Institute of Mental Health. "Obsessive-Compulsive Disorder, OCD." http://www.nimh.nih.gov /health/topics/obsessive-compulsive-disorder-ocd /index.shtml (accessed November 2009).

Valerie R. Stackman
Howard University

O'Connor, Sandra Day

Sandra Day O'Connor was the first woman to be appointed to the U.S. Supreme Court. She was nominated by President Ronald Reagan in 1981 and was confirmed by the U.S. Senate in a unanimous vote of 99–0. She was sworn into office on September 25, 1981, and served on the court for more than 25 years.

Justice O'Connor's appointment to the Supreme Court was not without controversy, as she drew criticism from both conservatives and liberals. Conservatives were concerned about her lack of knowledge of constitutional matters and lack of experience in the federal court system. Meanwhile, liberals were concerned about her failure to indicate explicit support for feminist issues. Justice O'Connor's tenure on the bench, however, alleviated some of the concerns on both sides. She gradually earned a reputation for being a moderate conservative, a free-thinker, and an effective compromiser. She became well-known for

Sandra Day O'Connor was the first woman to be appointed to the U.S. Supreme Court, at the time a controversial decision.

her commitment to careful analysis of the facts and issues presented in each of the cases that she heard.

Justice O'Connor's conservative values lay the foundation for her beliefs about the role of the courts. She made it clear that she believed the courts' role is to interpret the law, not legislate. She advocated for the exercise of judicial restraint, the primacy of state's rights, the safeguarding of personal freedoms, and incremental social change.

In 1982, her second year on the court, Justice O'Connor issued her first major opinion. In a sex discrimination case, she opined that male students could not be rejected from nursing school based on their gender. In her years on the bench, she shaped constitutional law in several areas, including affirmative action, voting rights, separation of church-and-state issues, the Fifth Amendment, states' rights, and abortion.

In fact, Justice O'Connor received the most attention for her opinions on cases related to abortion rights. In several cases, she was the deciding vote in upholding states' rights to regulate and limit abortion. Many conservatives had hoped that Justice O'Connor would take an even more active antiabortion position;

nevertheless, her opinions fell short of reversing the historic *Roe v. Wade* decision.

Though Justice O'Connor conceded the government some regulatory control over abortion, such as with regards to informed consent and parental approval provisions, her position upheld *Roe's* recognition of a personal freedom interest in a woman's right to choose. Therefore, her influence in preserving abortion rights in the United States is without question.

Justice O'Connor was born on March 26, 1930, in El Paso, Texas, and spent her early years on a ranch in Arizona. Later she attended school in El Paso under the care of her grandmother. She earned her undergraduate and law degrees from Stanford University, both with honors. In law school, she was an editor of the *Stanford Law Review*. She met her husband, John Jay O'Connor III, at Stanford, and the couple had three sons. Justice O'Connor's career took off in 1965, when she started to work part time for the Arizona attorney general's office. In 1969, she was appointed to the state senate and was subsequently reelected to that position. In 1973, she became the first woman to serve as the majority leader of a state senate. In 1974, she was elected to a position of trial judge for Maricopa County, and in 1979, she was appointed to the Arizona Court of Appeals. Then, in 1981, she was appointed to the Supreme Court and served until her retirement in 2006.

See Also: Abortion Laws, International; Cowgirls; Feminism, American; United States.

Further Readings
Biskupic, Joan. *Sandra Day O'Connor: How the First Woman on the Supreme Court Became Its Most Influential Member*. New York: HarperCollins, 2005.

McFeatters, Ann Carey. *Sandra Day O'Connor: Justice in the Balance*. Albuquerque: University of New Mexico Press, 2006.

O'Connor, Sandra Day. *The Majesty of the Law: Reflections of a Supreme Court Justice*. New York: Random House, 2003.

O'Connor, Sandra Day and Alan H. Day. *Lazy B: Growing Up on a Cattle Ranch in the American Southwest*. New York: Random House, 2002.

Julie Ahmad Siddique
City University of New York Graduate Center

Olympics, Summer

When considering the historic and current role of female athletes in the Summer Olympics, it is appropriate to begin with the modern Olympic Games, which began in 1894. The 1894 games marked the first modern Summer Olympic Games. The establishment of summer and winter Olympic Games as separate events with characteristically seasonal athletic activities did materialize until 1924.

Prior to the modern Olympic Games era, the ancient Olympic Games, which began in 676 B.C.E. in Greece, did not allow women as spectators, let alone as competitors. Some scholars believe that the inception of the modern Olympic era marks the commencement of the struggle for women and their athletic place in history.

Although the word *modern* describes the current era of Olympic Games, it is important to note that the general disposition among the men responsible for the development of the International Olympic Committee (IOC), which became and remains today the governing body of the Olympic games, was that women should not compete in the Olympic Games. Barron Pierre de Coubertin, the father of the modern Olympic Games and the first president of the IOC, was adamantly against female athletes' competition in the 1894 games, and thus, female competitors were banned from competition until 1900. Coubertin leaned on his Victorian ideals, in an attempt to justify excluding women as competitors, in the 1894 games and beyond. Coubertin defended his position by publicly rationalizing that female athletes were unattractive and indecent, and then expressed his "concern" that physical exertion may lead to injury. Although women competed in exhibition events in golf, tennis, and archery during the 1900, 1904, and 1908 games, 1912 marked the first year that women were able to participate in the Olympics as true competitors and that Olympic records about women were kept.

The Early Years
The early years of the modern Olympic Games continued to epitomize hegemonic thought that female athletic competition was unnatural. Despite the continued resistance during the early years of the female competitors as a part of the modern Olympic Games, signs of popularity and support for female competi-

tors began to cultivate throughout Europe and North America. The first female Olympic athletes came from white, socially privileged backgrounds, and these athletes initially competed in events that were a part of their social fabric, sports like golf and tennis. Beginning in 1912, swimming and diving as well as several track-and-field events were added to the women's competitive Olympic events.

The popularity of female athletes continued to grow throughout Western nations, and eventually, the IOC could no longer ignore or defend their position to exclude female athletes from competition without being challenged. Historical documentation denotes that a "last ditch effort" to ban women from Olympic competition occurred in 1925, when a medical paper titled "Women's Participation in Athletics" described the need to slow the advancement of female competition. The paper pointed out the physiological differences between the female and male body and, in particular, the biological and social "responsibilities" of the females and males. The report indicated that if women focused their efforts on competition and physical output, they may compromise their reproductive system and may impact the national welfare and moral. "Women's Participation in Athletics" aimed to reinforce the 19th-century conventional belief systems that women filled a particular social and cultural role, and it was not on an athletic field or in an arena. While the medical report did not fulfill its entire objective to ban women from competition due to their "natural" responsibilities, it did result in separate Olympic events for men and women.

Separate Competitive Spaces and Social Expectations

After Coubertin's retirement the preceding year, women were granted competitive access to the 1928 Olympic Games in event competitions separate from the male competitors. Separation of female and male Olympic events reinforced the notion of gender stereotyping, as female competitive events were constructed and governed by the IOC in a way that was deemed biologically and socially appropriate for women. Efforts to limit female participation to what was deemed biologically and socially appropriate seemed to overshadow the physical and competitive accomplishments of a few pioneering female athletes. Most female Olympic events adhered to rules that were

different from the male competitors. For example, the distance that women had to cover in certain track and field events was less than their male counterparts. In addition, the time that women were expected to compete in was longer than their male counterparts. Although women were marking their place in history as skillful and adapt movers and competitors, the rules and expectations of their physical performance was negotiated among the men at the IOC and was believed to be suitable for female competitors.

Continued Inequity

Male dominance in the sporting world has consistently been a barrier for female competitors in all realms. Even today, women are still less represented in Olympic completions than males are. At the 1984 Summer Olympics in Los Angeles, California, less than half of the competitors to represent the United States in their respective sport were female. Four years later, the imbalance seemed to have improved slightly. Throughout the past two decades, there has been an increase in the number of female Olympic athletes as well as the number of sports that these athletes compete in.

The summer games of 1996, held in Atlanta, Georgia, are commonly known as the "Summer of Women." It was the summer that Jackie Joyner-Kersee, ran her last Olympic track-and-field event. It was the summer that Kerri Strug and the U.S. Olympic Gymnastics team, often referred to as the "magnificent seven," won the gold medal, after Strug landed her dismount on a badly injured leg and ankle and was carried off the landing mat by her coach because she was unable to walk. It was the summer that the Women's Soccer team, led by Mia Hamm and Michelle Akers, won the first gold medal in U.S. women's soccer history. The U.S. Softball team experienced equal success and found their way to the top of the medal stand to receive their gold medals.

Standouts in the 2008 Summer Olympics in Beijing, China, include the U.S. women's basketball team, which won its fourth-consecutive gold medal, and the U.S. women's soccer team, which won its third gold medal in four Olympic Games. Jamaican Melaine Walker won a gold medal in the women's 400-meter hurdles and set an Olympic record, Ethiopian runner Tirunesh Dibaba won two gold medals, and Kenya's Pamela Jelimo won the gold medal in the 800-meter run, winning the first gold for Kenya in women's athletics. Female swimmers who won gold medals and set new records include Italian Federica Pellegrini, Rebecca Adlington of Great Britain, Kirsty Coventry of Zimbabwe, Rebecca Soni of the United States, and Germany's Britta Steffen. American Natalie Coughlin became the first U.S. female athlete in modern Olympic history to win six medals in a single Olympic competition, and the first woman to win a 100-meter backstroke gold for two consecutive Olympics.

As women continue to progress and continuously establish new social expectations for themselves and the female athletes who will follow in their footsteps, one thing remains constant regardless of social and biological expectations: women continue to defy the odds and continue to secure their place on their field and in the arena.

See Also: Greece; Olympics, Winter; Rhode, Kim; Sports, Women in; Stereotypes of Women; Swimming.

Further Readings

Borish, L. J. "Women at the Modern Olympic Games: An Interdisciplinary Look at American Culture." *QUEST*, v.48 (1996).

Hargreaves, J. "Olympic Women: A Struggle for Recognition." In J. O'Reilly and S. K. Cahn, eds., *Women and Sports in the United States: A Documentary Reader*. Lebanon, NH: Northeastern University Press, 2007.

Hargreaves, J. "Women and the Olympic Phenomenon." In Alan Tomlinson and Garry Whannel, eds., *The Five Ring Circus: Money, Power and Politics at the Olympic Games*. London: Pluto Press, 1984.

Remley, M. L. "Women in the Olympics." *The Journal of Physical Education, Recreation and Dance*, v.65/7 (1996).

Rintala, J. "Women in the Olympics-Making a Difference." *Journal of Physical Education, Recreation and Dance*, v.59/3 (1988).

Donna Duffy
University of North Carolina, Greensboro

Olympics, Winter

The current Olympic Games are considered to be a part of the modern Olympic era, which began in 1896. The Winter Olympic Games began as an exclusive competitive event in Chamonix, France, in 1924 and were originally referred to as the "International Winter Sports Week." Prior to 1924, the Winter Olympic Games were not held as an exclusive, seasonal event made up of characteristically cold weather sports. When figure skating made an appearance in the 1908 Olympic Games in London, England, the International Olympic Committee (IOC) began to contemplate the notion that two Olympic events consisting of sports that were seasonally appropriate should be held every four years. Although the IOC was experiencing progress in terms of establishing two separate—winter and summer—competitive events, women were not viewed as serious competitive athletes, and women's Olympic events were consistently not included in the competitive programming.

The IOC and its original founder and president, Pierre de Coubertin, believed that women were not able to compete at a high level and that competition would be detrimental to their health. Coubertin believed that a woman's worth should be measured by the number of children she could bear. Further, it was believed that including female athletes in the Olympic Games would upset the social structure and social expectations of women's roles. A commonly held belief endorsed by the male power structure that controlled the Olympic Games was that women who competed at high levels looked unattractive and therefore were not the best ambassadors for their country on the international stage.

The Early Years

Traditionally, the female athletes who participated in the Winter Olympic Games consistently struggled to be included and to be taken seriously as athletes. In 1922, the establishment of the Women's Olympic Games (WOG) became a reality. The WOG initially intended to challenge the ideological constraints that positioned women as "second-class citizens" in the Olympic community, and throughout the 1920s and 1930s, female athletes had their own competitive space in the women's Olympic movement. While these games are a part of Olympic history, scholars believe that through these games, female athletes made a significant contribution to the overall feminist movement. The WOG were developed and conceptualized by Alice Milliat, a female athlete from France, as a result of the IOC continuously failing to recognize female athletes as serious competitors.

The WOG games continued to gain momentum as a significant sporting event for women and experienced an increase in female athletic participation. In 1926, the WOG were held in Gothenburg, Sweden, and 10 countries participated. In 1934, the last WOG were held in London, England, and 19 countries participated. The WOG experienced an unprecedented number of spectators, and the IOC could no longer deny that female Olympic athletes were capable of attracting crowds. Although female athletes competed in Olympic events since the 1900 games, Milliat believed that the male power structure that governed the Olympic stage continually discredited female athletes; Milliat believed that female athletes should not have to justify their athletic prowess and ability to gain access again and again to the Olympic fields and arenas. Female athletes competed in their own Olympic Games until 1934, when the Olympics Games were slowly integrated, and year after year, more and more competitive Olympic events were added for women.

Social Reform and the Impact in the Winter Olympic Games

Coubertin and the members of the IOC committee did not anticipate the repercussions of the social reform movement and Western industrialization that immediately changed women's roles from passive to active. The change in women's roles extended beyond the home and workplace and slowly made its way to the sports fields and arenas. In 1937, female athletes who represented the United States experienced unforeseen challenges in most of their athletic competitions. Female athletes from the eastern European bloc nations and more mountainous countries were better prepared to compete in the Olympic Games. Therefore, the coaches and female athletes from the United States were forced to develop new training techniques for their Winter Olympics events.

Gender Stereotyping and the Events of the Winter Olympics

Women have been able to break into the events of the Winter Olympic Games based on the sports characteristics that are socially identified as "female" in nature. Female athletes have been granted access to sport and competitive events in the Winter Olympic Games that were modified from the men's structure and rules in an effort to maintain a sense of femininity.

There are some female Winter Olympics sporting events that draw more attention than others. Figure skating epitomizes femininity in sport; it is also the perfect example of how aggressively competitive attitudes, which are typically associated with male athletic competition, are present within the women's games. The off-ice attack on gold medal hopeful Nancy Kerrigan before the 1994 Lillehammer Winter Olympics is the perfect example of a "win at all costs" attitude gone amok. Kerrigan's U.S. teammate Tonya Harding was accused of planning an attack on Kerrigan with the help of then-husband Jeff Gillooly and a hit man. The attack on Kerrigan initiated conversations about the inside world of competitive figure skating and raised questions about the embodiment of grace and beauty in the sport.

Most recently, in the 2010 Winter Olympics in Vancouver, Canada, the women's ski-jumping event was still not included in the competitive events, even though Lindsey Van, an American ski jumper, holds the record among men and women for the longest ski jump. Female ski jumpers have petitioned to have ski jumping for female athletes included in the Winter Olympics Fames since the 1998 Nagano games. Today, ski jumping is the only Olympic event to remain "men only." While some argue that a lack of female ski jumpers is another obvious and current example of inequality in the Olympic Games, there is still a question about whether or not female ski jumpers will be included in the next Winter Olympic Games.

Contemporary discourse suggests that Olympic female competitors are continually advocating to be taken seriously as athletes at the Olympics level, as well as in other sport and physical activity spaces. The IOC is consistently viewed as the quintessential "good old boys network" and is continually scrutinized for its lack of advocacy, support, and inclusion of female Olympic athletes.

See Also: Coaches, Female; Figure Skating; Kim, Yu-Na; Olympics, Summer; Sports, Women in.

Further Readings

Hargreaves, J. "Olympic Women: A Struggle for Recognition." In Jean O'Reilly and Susan K. Cahn, eds., *Women and Sports in the United States: A*

Documentary Reader. Lebanon, NH: Northeastern University Press, 2007.

Kidd, B. "The Pioneering Role of Madame Alice Milliat and the FSFI in Establishing International Track and Field for Women." *Journal of Sport History*, v.4/1 (1977).

Laurendeau, J. and C. Adams. "'Jumping Like a Girl': Discursive Silences, Exclusionary Practices and the Controversy over Women's Ski Jumping." *Sport in Society*, v.13/3 (2010).

Nelson, M. B. "Who We Might Become." In Nike is a Goddess. New York: Atlantic Monthly Press, 1998.

Remley, M. L. "Women in the Olympics." *Journal of Physical Education, Recreation and Dance*, v.65/7 (1996).

Rintala, J. "Women in the Olympics—Making a Difference." *Journal of Physical Education, Recreation and Dance*, v.59/3 (1988).

Story, R. "A Guide to the Olympic Gold Rush." *Women's Sports & Fitness*, v.16/1 (1994).

Donna Duffy
University of North Carolina, Greensboro

Oman

Oman is a country in the Middle East with a long seacoast on the Arabian Sea and the Gulf of Oman; it shares land borders with Yemen, Saudi Arabia, and the United Arab Emirates. Oman is a Sultanage with a freely elected parliament and, in an official decree in 1970, was declared to be Arab and Islamic. The population of 3.4 million includes Arabs, south Asians, and Africans; most are Muslims, with Ibadahi Muslims predominant (75 percent).

Omanis enjoy a high standard of living with a per capita gross domestic product (GDP) of $20,300 in 2009 and life expectancies of 71.87 years for men and 76.55 years for women. Oman prohibits discrimination on the basis of gender, but the laws are frequently not enforced, and Islamic law and tradition, as well as social customs, may act to put women at a disadvantage. The World Economic Forum ranks Oman low on gender equality of the 134 countries it studied. On a scale where 0 is inequality and 1 is perfect equality, in 2009, Oman received an overall score

A mannequin wearing a hijab *(headscarf) in a storefront in Oman, with cosmetics in the background. Women wear* hijabs, *and while some women cover their faces and hands, not all do.*

of 0.5928 (123rd of 134 countries). Oman received a score of 0.960 on health and survival (95th), 0.974 on educational attainment (93rd), 0.406 on economic participation and opportunity (128th), and 0.025 on political empowerment (128th).

Omani women have made great gains in education. Although female literacy is only 86 percent, that figure includes many older women who grew up before universal education became the norm. Girls today are as likely as boys to attend primary and secondary school and constitute a majority in tertiary education. In 2009, women held 10 percent of ministerial positions in the Omani government and none of the seats in parliament, although women have served in parliament in the past as well as in the cabinet and on the council of Oman.

Women make up just 34 percent of the labor force in Oman, and despite constituting a majority of students in tertiary education, they hold less than one-third of the tertiary teaching posts. Omani women earn 70 percent of what men earn for comparable work.

One reason for the low rates of employment among Omani women is that Oman has one of the highest fertility rates in the world, at 5.53 children per woman. Abortion is permitted only to save the mother's life, but birth control is available, and about one-quarter of Omani women report using contraception. Almost all births are attended by trained personnel, but results are less than the country's prosperity would suggest: the maternal mortality ratio is 64 per 100,000 live births and the infant mortality rate is 10 per 1,000 live births. Save the Children ranks Oman 67th of 75 less developed countries on its Mother's Index, 66th on its Women's Index, and 61st on its Children's Index.

See Also: Abortion, Access to; Contraception Methods; Equal Pay; Islam.

Further Readings

Hausman, Ricardo, Laura D. Tyson, and Saadia Zahidi. The Global Gender Gap Report 2009. Geneva: World Economic Forum, 2009. http://www.weforum.org/en /Communities/Women%20Leaders%20and%20 Gender%20Parity/GenderGapNetwork/index.htm (accessed June 2010).

Save the Children. "State of the World's Mothers 2009: Investing in the Early Years." http://www.savethe children.org/publications/?WT.mc_id=1109_hp_hd _pub (accessed June 2009).

U.S. Department of State. "2005 Country Reports on Human Rights Practices: Oman." http://www.state.gov /g/drl/rls/hrrpt/2005/61696.htm (accessed June 2009).

Sarah Boslaugh
Washington University School of Medicine

Operation Rescue

Operation Rescue is a controversial Christian organization that opposes abortion. Its nationwide actions against abortion have ranged from civil disobedience to members being involved in clinic violence. Supporters believe it is answering a spiritual calling to save "unborn children." Opponents believe Operation Rescue has violently and criminally limited the reproductive rights of women by intimidating them and the doctors who provide their care.

Founded by Randall Terry in 1986, Operation Rescue garnered attention for drawing thousands of anti-abortion protestors to its "rescues" (protests in which participants attempted to unlawfully block entrance to abortion clinics). Two notable actions included a mass protest at the 1988 Democratic National Convention in Atlanta and the "Spring of Life" protests in Buffalo, New York, in 1992. Autonomous chapters of the organization arose, and Operation Rescue West of California gained prominence. Terry's original organization, under the leadership of Flip Benham, split from the other branches and became known as Operation Save America in 1994. The former Operation Rescue West maintained the organization's original name.

Pro-choice opponents of Operation Rescue blamed the organization and others like it for espousing radical rhetoric to its members. Throughout the 1980s and 1990s, there were incidents of arson and bombings at abortion clinics in several states. In 1993, Dr. David Gunn of Pensacola, Florida, was murdered during a protest outside of a clinic where he practiced. Terry was blamed by some for circulating a "wanted" flyer with Dr. Gunn's home information on it during an earlier protest. George Tiller, a doctor in Wichita, Kansas, was also shot by antiabortion extremist Rachelle "Shelly" Shannon later that same year. Shannon frequently attended protests organized by Operation Rescue, and outsiders believed that she may have had a role within the organization. In 1994, then-President Bill Clinton signed the Freedom of Access to Clinic Entrances Act (FACE), making it a federal crime to prohibit individuals from obtaining or providing reproductive rights by the use of physical obstruction, force, or the threat of force. Opponents also filed a number of lawsuits against the organization, including a federal lawsuit alleging criminal conspiracy. However, the violence continued. In 1998, Dr. Barnett Slepian, an abortion provider in Buffalo, was shot and killed by James Kopp, a long-time Operation Rescue member.

Under the leadership of Troy Newman, the group relocated to Wichita in 2002 with the intent of closing Tiller's clinic. In 2006, Operation Rescue bought the building where Tiller's practice was housed. That year, Operation Rescue also petitioned Kansas to convene a grand jury to investigate the death of one of Tiller's patients who died of complications. Tiller was cleared of all wrongdoing. On May 29, 2009, Tiller was shot and killed by antiabortion extremist, Scott Roeder. Despite its public condemnation of the slaying, Tiller's murder caused renewed media attention on the group as the name and phone number of their senior policy adviser was found in Roeder's car when he was arrested. The adviser, Cheryl Sullinger, had once served two years in jail for her role in conspiring to bomb an abortion clinic. She says she had no involvement in Tiller's death.

Operation Rescue lost its nonprofit standing in 2006 and, after Tiller's murder, issued a release stating that it was suffering financial difficulties and would likely close if it did not receive funding from its supporters.

See also: Abortion, Access to; Abortion, Late; Abortion Laws, United States; Pro-Life Movement; Reproductive and Sexual Health Rights.

Further Readings

Operation Rescue. http://www.operationrescue.org (accessed June 2010).

Robb, Amanda. "The Last Clinic Standing." *Marie Claire* http://www.marieclaire.com/world-reports/news /latest/last-clinic (accessed July 2010).

Solinger, Rickie, ed. *Abortion Wars: A Half-Century of Struggle, 1950–2000.* Berkeley: University of California Press, 1998.

Jeanette Koncikowski
*Buffalo State College,
State University of New York, Buffalo*

Organization of Women's Freedom in Iraq

The Organization of Women's Freedom in Iraq (OWFI) was established by Yanar Mohammad, a prominent Iraqi feminist and advocate for women's rights, and a few of her associates in 2003. The organization was established after the United States–led invasion of Iraq and was created in response to serious concerns about women's wartime safety and security, as well as concerns about the political future of Iraq.

Today, OFWI has established itself in Iraq as a national women's organization dedicated to advocacy for women. Since its inception, OWFI has conducted several antiviolence campaigns, political empowerment campaigns, and other advocacy campaigns to assert women's rights to be free from violence and persecution and to demand basic human rights for all Iraqis. OWFI's work has had particular significance amid evidence of escalating trends in both violence against women and religious fundamentalism in Iraq.

One of the organization's primary activities is the operation of five women's shelters across Iraq to provide Iraqi women with comprehensive services related to the prevention and aftercare of domestic violence and "honor" killings. The organization estimates that its shelter home services have prevented at least 50 honor killings and numerous other incidents of violence against women and girls.

OWFI aggressively lobbies for tougher laws on violence against women and works to protect women and girls from sex trafficking and other forms of sexual victimization. Unfortunately, the rise in war widows and the poor economic conditions of many Iraqi families have resulted in a growing number of women being forced into prostitution and sexual slavery. OWFI is working to raise awareness about this growing problem and to provide alternatives for women in desperate situations.

To spread its message across Iraq, OWFI provides training to interested parties on methods to fight intolerance and misogyny. OWFI also conducts regular advocacy campaigns in the news media via newsletters, radio, and television. In fact, Mohammed serves as the editor of the *Al-Mousawat* (*Equality*) newsletter, which regularly reports on incidents of violence against women. In 2009, OWFI launched the "Al Mousawat Radio" broadcast to reach out to even more people to further spread a progressive message to counter the fundamentalist mindset of the mainstream media and inform the public about available support services.

Although OWFI is dedicated to serving the immediate needs of Iraqi women, it is more broadly committed to rebuilding Iraq according to secular principles that guarantee freedom and human rights for all. To establish a more democratic government, OWFI has vigorously campaigned to increase women's participation in local and national politics and government civil service positions. OWFI has also called for the full participation of women in the establishment of any new Iraqi government. In 2008, Mohammed was awarded the prestigious Gruber Foundation Women's Rights Prize for her work.

See Also: Arab Feminism; Iranian Feminism; Religion, Women in.

Further Readings
Arato, Andrew. *Constitution Making Under Occupation: The Politics of Imposed Revolution in Iraq*. New York: Columbia University Press, 2009.
The Organization of Women's Freedom in Iraq. http://www.equalityiniraq.com/home (accessed April 2010).

Julie Ahmad Siddique
City University of New York Graduate Center

Orthodox Churches

Orthodox Christianity is the second largest Christian communion in the world (250–300 million people), encompassing various national and regional churches that are united by their shared theological vision and sacramental practices while retaining their organizational independence.

Most of the original Orthodox Churches that trace their history back to the first centuries of the Christian era (e.g., the Patriarchates of Jerusalem and Constantinople; the Armenian Apostolic Church; and the national Church of Greece) are associated with the ethnic groups in the Middle East and Eastern Europe. However, the last three decades has witnessed a considerable increase in the Orthodox presence in North America, Western Europe, and Australia—often referred to as the "Orthodox diaspora"—through immigration and, increasingly, through conversion. These changes in the ethnic-cultural situation of the church, along with the ongoing global political, social, and cultural transformations, present some serious challenges as well as new, exciting possibilities to the Orthodox tradition in general and to Orthodox women in particular.

Growing communication between women representing different Orthodox churches worldwide, as well as their participation in the ecumenical dialogue with their Western Christian sisters, has led to an increased awareness of both the important role that women can play in the life of the Church and of the existing barriers for their fuller participation. Some of the important changes in the experiences and status of women that are currently underway in the Orthodox Church are related to the renewal and expansion of female ministries, increased access to theological education, and liturgical reform aimed at the elimination of gender-restrictive ritual practices and customs.

Historic and Contemporary Roles of Women in the Church
Historically, the ministry of women in the Orthodox Church has included a wide variety of vocations and roles, ranging from philanthropic work and social outreach to religious education and liturgical functions. Women serve on the parish boards and take an active part in diocesan, national, and international charity programs. They are involved in missionary and outreach activities, including such inter-Orthodox projects as the Orthodox Christian Mission Center, the Orthodox Peace Fellowship, and Orthodox Women in the Healing Professions. The position of the priest's

wife (*Presbytera; Matushka*), with its combination of social and spiritual obligations, is regarded as an important ministry in the Orthodox Church; traditional female responsibilities such as care of home and family and organization of household devotional life are likewise seen as crucial areas of religious service. In some Orthodox churches nowadays women also take active part in public ritual practices, as choir directors, scriptural readers, and acolytes.

Religious education involves women on multiple levels and in a variety of roles: women direct educational programs in the parishes, participate in conferences and workshops, and engage in producing academic and communal journals that inform their readers about the Orthodox tradition and provide a forum for the exploration of women's issues and roles (e.g., *St. Nina Quarterly; MaryMartha; The Handmaiden*). The number of female students enrolled at Orthodox seminaries has been steadily increasing in the past three decades; women scholars and theologians such as Susan Ashbrook Harvey, Verna Harrison, Kyriaki FitzGerald, and the late Elisabeth Behr-Sigel have pursued successful writing and teaching careers, both at Orthodox seminaries and colleges and other educational institutions.

Finally, female monasticism that had traditionally been an essential part of Orthodox spirituality and praxis is currently on the rise in the Orthodox churches worldwide; in North America alone eight new female monasteries have been established since 1970. In addition to leading contemplative life of prayer and meditation and offering spiritual counseling to the visitors, the members of these communities are often engaged in demanding professional activities, such as publication of liturgical and spiritual literature and creation of liturgical objects and icons.

Seeking Fuller Participation

Although women's involvement in these traditional ministries in many national Orthodox churches and especially in the Western diaspora is steadily growing, Orthodox women today are increasingly voicing a concern regarding what they perceive as unfortunate restrictions on their full participation in the ecclesiastical and liturgical life of the church. A series of inter-Orthodox consultations organized by the World Council of Churches from 1976 to 1997 that brought together participants from different countries have been especially instrumental in raising Orthodox women's awareness of the existing problems and possible ways of addressing them. Their recommendations challenged a number of ritual practices and customs that continue to be perpetuated in some of the Orthodox communities, such as gender segregation in the churches, sacramental restrictions associated with menstruation and childbirth, etc. These were characterized as manifestations of historically limited and culture-specific perspectives that do not properly reflect Orthodox theology; the recommendations asked for their revision.

They also advocated serious consideration of the uses of gender-inclusive language; sustained theological exploration of gender, sexuality; and "the sin of sexism"; and women's active engagement in theological and spiritual education. Finally, they called for a fuller participation of women in the life of the church through existing lay ministries and through revival of the ordained ministry of deaconesses.

As a number of recent historical studies (including the works by Orthodox women scholars) have demonstrated, the order of the deaconess flourished in the Christian East from the apostolic times well into the Byzantine period. Its members belonged to the ranks of ordained clergy and exercised various liturgical functions, such as assisting bishops in female baptism; they also had important catechetical, missionary, and philanthropic responsibilities. The restoration of the female diaconate is currently under consideration in several Orthodox churches whose members see it as an effective way of responding to the needs of the present age and of making the female presence more central in the church.

The Open Question of Ordination

A more controversial issue is presented by an ordination of women to the sacramental priesthood. Until recently, this possibility was categorically rejected by the majority of Orthodox hierarchs and theologians on the grounds of its incompatibility with the church tradition (no female apostles or presbyters attested in scriptural and patristic writings), liturgical symbolism (the priest is an "icon" of Christ and thus must be a man), and theological anthropology (sexual differentiation entails different spiritual "gifts" and roles). Many Orthodox women themselves likewise tended to dismiss the issue of women's ordination as an "outside" question informed by secular ideas or Western feminist theology and foreign to their own convictions and concerns. However, in the past two decades a number of leading Orthodox theologians, both male and female (Bishop Kallistos Ware, Metropolitan Anthony Bloom, Elisabeth Behr-Sigel, Verna Harrison, and others) have argued for the necessity of acknowledging the validity of this question and of addressing it in a way that would be both open-minded and faithful to the authentic Tradition of the church.

As Behr-Sigel and Harrison demonstrate in their works, traditional Orthodox teaching about human nature and salvation does not provide grounds for the exclusion of women from sacramental priesthood and in fact may be used to support their participation in this ministry. Behr-Sigel's analysis also challenges an overly literalist interpretation of the priest's "iconicity," arguing for a more inclusive and polyvalent reading of liturgical symbolism.

As many Orthodox theologians point out, faithfulness to tradition does not imply dead fundamentalism: the tradition must be received and lived anew by each generation, with a willingness to respond to "the signs of the times." Although ordination of women to the priesthood does not appear to be an immediate possibility in today's church, it remains a critical "open question" that stimulates both a creative reappropriation of Orthodoxy's rich spiritual and theological inheritance and a productive dialogue with other traditions and perspectives.

See Also: Christianity; Gender Roles, Cross-Cultural; Ministry, Protestant; Priesthood, Episcopalian/Anglican; Priesthood, Roman Catholic; Religion, Women in.

Further Readings

Behr-Sigel, Elisabeth and Kallistos Ware. *The Ordination of Women in the Orthodox Church.* Geneva: World Council of Churches Publications, 2000.

FitzGerald, Kyriaki, ed. *Orthodox Women Speak: Discerning the "Signs of Time."* Geneva: World Council of Churches Publications, 1999.

Hopko, Thomas, ed. *Women and the Priesthood.* Crestwood, NY: St. Vladimir's Seminary Press, 1999.

Olga Solovieva
Union College

Orthodox Judaism

Contemporary Orthodox Jewish women practice traditions that have existed for thousands of years. Yet a small but vocal minority calling themselves Orthodox feminists are confronting issues of inequality within Judaism of the 21st century. Several prominent Jewish women such as Blu Greenberg, Rachel Adler, and Judith Plaskow are promoting dialogues that they hope will lead to transformations for women.

The Jewish bible consists of the Torah, which is the first five books of the Old Testament, sometimes known as the five books of Moses or the Pentateuch, and Prophets and Writings. The Talmud is a record of rabbinic discussion that pertains to Jewish law, ethics, custom, and history. The Talmud includes the Mishnah, written around 200 C.E., and is considered to be the first written compilation of Jewish oral law and legal opinions and debates. Also part of the Talmud is the Gemara, written around 500 C.E., which includes a discussion of the Mishnah and the wisdom of rabbis and also expounds upon the Torah. Throughout these works, women are encouraged to be modest, submissive, and maintain forbearance in a world in which they must know their place.

The Halakah is a body of religious law that includes 613 *Mitzvot*, or commandments, as well as laws revealed in the Talmud and written by rabbis. Customs and traditions are included in Halakah that are considered to be divinely inspired. The Mitzvot, which are given in the Torah, include 365 prohibitions and 248 positive obligations.

In these religious commandments, a woman is exempted from any time-bound obligations because she must always be available to take care of her family's needs and responsibilities. Women are also excused from many Mitzvot because they do not face all the temptations that men face in their professional and personal lives. Women, by their nature, represent sensuality and seductiveness for men. Therefore, because of these distractions, men must be controlled by more rules than women are. Thus, it is believed that women complement their husbands but basically have fundamentally different roles. Consequently, women have traditionally been discouraged from study beyond the pragmatic aspects of the Torah that relate to how a woman should run her home.

Issues

With the belief that the Torah as well as the oral law was revealed to Moses at Mt. Sinai, Orthodox Jews feel that their practices are divinely inspired. Thus, any discussions about changes or revisions are extremely difficult to initiate. Issues that are prominent among feminists include women's exemption from the *minyan,* or the quorum of 10 or more adult males (including 13-year-old boys who have had a bar mitzvah) for daily prayer. The ramifications of not accepting women are great because, for example, in order to say the mourner's prayer for a deceased mother or father, a minyan must be present. Therefore, a woman has to request that a man says the prayer for her deceased parent.

Other issues are the exemption from time-bound commandments, the inability to initiate divorce, and the limited leadership positions in the synagogue. Women cannot be rabbis because that would contradict Jewish law. Women are allowed to read the Torah but are not permitted to do so in front of a congregation during a religious service.

Agunah and Other Concerns

One of the most controversial issues is the *agunah,* women who have not received an official divorce from their husbands because either the husband's whereabouts are not known or he refuses to grant her a "get," an official bill of divorce that releases her from the marriage. The agunah are women who cannot remarry or find if they do without a "get," that their subsequent marriage will not be recognized and children of the new marriage will be referred to as bastards. In order to get around these requirements, feminists and others are proposing several solutions. They try to prove that the woman didn't consent to the original marriage, or groups try to force the recalcitrant husband to issue the "get" either by revoking any professional licenses he has or sometimes even putting him in jail. Advocates for change are also trying to promote specific life-cycle rituals for girls as well as legal rights for women in religious courts, where often a woman's testimony is not accepted even on such personal matters as divorce.

Jewish Orthodox Feminists

Blu Greenberg, an Orthodox rabbi's wife, founded the Jewish Orthodox Feminist Alliance in 1997. Since she is a believer in the divinity of Jewish law, she seeks changes that will be acceptable within the confines of Orthodox Judaism. She wants to stay within the bounds of Halakah. Her view is that some Halakah are based on customs and thus there is a possibility for reinterpretation. And if a hierarchy serves no religious function, perhaps change is possible. She particularly resents the laws surrounding menstrual purity and impurity and the labeling of the woman a *niddah,* a menstruating woman, which is often a metaphor for moral impurity and debasement.

Judith Plaskow is fighting for women's ordination and new Jewish rituals such as Rosh Chodesh, a celebration of the beginning of each month in the Jewish calendar. She also disagrees with the maleness of God, so often labeled Father of Mercy, Father in Heaven, and King of all Kings. She proposes a degendering of God as well as a recovery of women's history and a resurrection of women's celebrations and symbols that are embedded in the goddess tradition. Rachel Adler would also like to transform the prayers and enrich the words with feminine imagery.

Opposition to these changes abounds. Traditionalists claim that Greenberg, Plaskow, and Adler are undermining the family, destroying the beauty of female modesty, and mixing the sexual roles. But mainly these women are promoting a political agenda for Orthodox Judaism whose very value is the maintenance of roles, rules, and laws for thousands of years. Change, however slowly, seems inevitable.

See Also: Feminist Theology; Israel; Judaism; Religion, Women in.

Further Readings

Adler, Rachel. *Engendering Judaism.* Boston: Beacon Press, 1998.

Davidman, Lynn. *Tradition in a Rootless World: Women Turn to Orthodox Judaism.* Berkeley: University of California Press, 1993.

Greenberg, Blu. *On Women and Judaism, A View From Tradition.* Philadelphia: The Jewish Publication Society of America, 1998.

Plaskow, Judith. *Standing Again at Sinai, Judaism From a Feminist Perspective.* San Francisco: Harper San Francisco, 1990.

Myrna A. Hant
University of California, Los Angeles

Our Bodies, Ourselves

First published in 1970, *Our Bodies, Ourselves* was one of the first books to provide women with comprehensive information about women's health, sexuality, and reproduction. It challenged the medical model by presenting information about women's health in the context of women's life experiences. Currently in its seventh edition, *Our Bodies, Ourselves* continues to provide state-of-the-art information about women's bodies from a feminist perspective.

Our Bodies, Ourselves was written by a Boston-based feminist nonprofit organization named after the book. The founders of Our Bodies Ourselves (OBOS) met while attending a panel on women and their bodies at a women's liberation conference in 1969. The women participating in the discussion quickly realized they had little solid information about women's bodies or women's health; at the same time, they shared similar dissatisfactions with the medical system. Given these realizations, some of the participants decided to keep meeting as a group and began researching women's health, sexuality, and reproduction. In order to conduct their research, they sneaked into medical libraries or borrowed library cards from medical students. They wrote up what they learned in a series of papers and met weekly to discuss what they had written.

Medical Data and Personal Testimonies

The process of learning about their bodies, health, and sexuality was a powerful experience for the women involved, eventually leading them to share what they had learned in book form. Published by the New England Free Press under the title *Women and their Bodies*, the book integrated medical knowledge with women's personal testimonies. The book's focus was sexual and reproductive health; however, the authors also included chapters that spoke to their political concerns, including "Some Myths about Women" and "Women, Medicine, and Capitalism." In 1971, the collective changed the title of the book to *Our Bodies, Ourselves*.

The book was strikingly popular, and demand quickly outpaced the Free Press's ability to produce it. In 1973, the collective began working with Simon & Schuster. The book quickly became a best seller, receiving numerous awards and widespread acclaim.

Simultaneously, the book generated controversy. Numerous high-profile conservatives offered harsh critiques of the book's explicit sexual content and discussions of abortion, leading some high schools and public libraries to remove the book from their shelves.

Expanded and Updated

To date, the English version of *Our Bodies, Ourselves* has sold more than 4 million copies. The subject matter of the book has expanded greatly. Among other things, topics covered in the 2005 edition include entries on alcohol, tobacco, and mood-altering drugs; bodies in motion; complementary health practices; environmental and occupational health; gender identity and sexual orientation; and infertility and assisted reproduction. With the 2005 edition, OBOS launched a companion Website offering up-to-date health information, a blog, historical material about the collective, and links to relevant sites. In spite of these changes, the collective's focus on and validation of experiential knowledge remains consistent. As they have in past editions, the authors intersperse scientific information with women's testimonies while also encouraging readers to consider the information in terms of their personal experiences. The collective has published several books related to *Our Bodies, Ourselves* including *Ourselves and Our Children; Our Bodies Growing Older; Our Bodies, Ourselves: Pregnancy and Birth; Our Bodies, Ourselves: Menopause;* and *Changing Bodies, Changing Lives*, a book directed at teens.

From early in its history, OBOS sought to make the book available to non-English speakers. In 1977, OBOS published a Spanish-language version, *Nuestros Cuerpos, Nuestras Vida*, and by 2007 the collective had published 20 foreign-language editions and made the book available in countries around the globe. Recognizing that women's experiences of health and well-being are grounded in the cultures in which women live, non-English-language versions are translated and revised by health advocates from within the targeted communities with an aim to address readers' unique needs. For example, in Asia, Buddhist nuns are provided information about easing muscle cramps caused by hours of sitting in mediation, and in pronatalist Armenia, the book emphasizes childbirth but downplays the discussion of contraception.

Transforming Doctor-Patient Relationship

Our Bodies, Ourselves was instrumental in the development of a worldwide women's health movement, and it participated in the transformation of the doctor-patient relationship from one in which the doctor is the authority and sole source of information to one in which the doctor and patient work together and in which the patient has ultimate control. More than a simple self-help book, the authors of *Our Bodies, Ourselves* strive to provide the best evidence-based information presented in the context of women's lived experiences. Simultaneously, they present health as an issue of social justice and patients' rights.

See Also: Feminism, America; Health, Mental and Physical; Women's Health Clinics.

Further Readings

Ginty, Molly M. "Our Bodies, Ourselves: Going, Going, Gone Global." *WeNews* (September 14, 2004). http://www.womensenews.org (accessed November 2009).
Hayden, Sara. "Re-Claiming Bodies of Knowledge: An Exploration of the Relationship between Feminist Theorizing and Feminine Style in the Rhetoric of the Boston Women's Health Book Collective." *Western Journal of Communication*, v.6/2 (1997).
Our Bodies Ourselves. http://www.ourbodiesourselves.org (accessed November 2009).
Ruzek, Sheryl. "Transforming Doctor-Patient Relationships." *Journal of Health Services Research & Policy*, v.12 (2007).

Sara Hayden
University of Montana

Overpopulation

In the biological sciences, overpopulation is defined as a state in which the population size of a species has surpassed the carrying capacity of the environment. In this condition, natural resources like food and water will be consumed at a rate at which they cannot be replenished quickly enough. Such a state usually results in the morbidity and mortality of members of the species through famine and disease, such that their numbers are reduced to a population size more compatible with available resources. The application of overpopulation to humans began with the publication of Thomas Malthus's *Essay on the Principle of Population* at the beginning of the 19th century. Malthus proclaimed that because human populations increase geometrically and food production grows arithmetically, in the future the majority of humans would struggle to meet their most basic needs. He warned of an impending crisis and recommended drastic corrective measures. However, with the industrialization of Europe, the birth rate fell and offset the falling mortality rate. In the case of Europe, increased prosperity and the switch from an agricultural to an industrial way of life seemed to result in a desire for fewer children.

This European model of demographic transition proved to be deficient in describing demographic trajectories in all areas of the world. In less developed countries (LDCs) in Asia, Africa, and South America, birth rates remained high despite decreases in mortality rates. Thus in the mid- to late 20th century, the majority of world population growth took place in less developed countries. The observation of dramatic population growth at midcentury in LDCs caused alarm among academic demographers and policy makers in the industrialized world. Out of this alarm grew a neo-Malthusian international population control movement.

The phrase *international population control movement* belies its fractured nature and creates a false sense of a centralized, unified movement. Nonetheless, many major and minor agencies, from multinational aid agencies to small-scale nongovernmental organizations, were driven by similar concerns with overpopulation. And they responded by promoting the use of contraception in LDCs. Some LDC governments embraced the population-control discourse, developing and enforcing coercive population-control projects on their own. The most well-known examples are the one-child policy in China and Indira Gandhi's compulsory sterilization campaign in India. While effective in terms of lowering fertility, such policies have led to human rights abuses. Some feminists agree that the provision of contraceptives is a basic reproductive right, but they have criticized policies that give the decision-making power to someone other than the individual in question. In addition, the safety and acceptability of the

Overpopulation is defined as a state in which the population size of a species has surpassed the carrying capacity of the environment. In this condition, natural resources will be consumed at a rate at which they cannot be replenished quickly enough.

use of certain contraceptives in developing countries, such as intrauterine devices and Norplant, have been challenged because of the lack of sufficient health-care services to handle complications or removal of the devices.

According to neo-Malthusians, rapidly growing populations are a major cause of poverty, and lowering fertility rates through the use of contraception would lead LDCs out of poverty to prosperity. A variety of objections to this position were formed in response. Marxists argued that if systems of production and distribution were made more efficient and equitable, the amount of resources could be sufficient for the world's population. At the 1974 United Nations World Population Conference in Bucharest, delegates from LDCs declared that development was the best contraceptive. Countries with a tradition of

pronatalism also were skeptical of the neo-Malthusian movement. Leaders of LDCs with low population densities thought that population growth would help the economic development of their countries. Some environmentalists argued that more environmental degradation was caused by overconsumption in industrialized nations than by overpopulation in LDCs. And demographers debated the causes of fertility decline and its relationship to economic development at the national level as well as prosperity at the household level.

The 1990s brought the most significant shift in discourse on overpopulation, which was consummated at the 1994 United Nations Conference on Population and Development in Cairo, Egypt. Prior to this point, international health and development agencies espoused "population control"—a phrase that highlighted the role of the state and international agencies in providing contraception to populations and encouraging or enforcing its use. At Cairo, a feminist population agenda was successfully lobbied for that replaced this phrase and its implied goals with a less coercive approach of promoting "reproductive health" and women's empowerment. The program of action adopted in Cairo stated that addressing gender inequities is essential to decreasing fertility rates in LDCs and that women have the right to control their reproduction. Participating countries endorsed the idea that ending discrimination against women was essential to balancing fertility rates with available resources. It should be noted that some feminists worried that this achievement was a change in language more than in actual motivations and actions of the population establishment.

At the beginning of the 21st century, as fertility rates in LDCs continue to fall, demographers and policy makers in the global north are less concerned with overpopulation. New demographic concerns are emerging: aging populations, below-replacement-level fertility in several European countries, and migration patterns and their effects on ethnic compositions of wealthy countries. Governments in the north may become increasingly pronatalist as a result, and one potentially positive outcome is that policies in the workplace may become more supportive of procreation and raising children. In both a pronatalist scenario and the formerly described scenario of overpopulation, the challenge is the same: ensuring that women have adequate reproductive choices yet remain free of coercion that impinges upon their reproductive rights.

See Also: Contraception Methods; Fertility; Reproductive and Sexual Health Rights; Sterilization, Involuntary.

Further Readings

Connelly, Matthew. *Fatal Misconception: The Struggle to Control World Population*. Cambridge, MA: Belknap Press of Harvard University, 2008.

Greenhalgh, Susan, ed. *Situating Fertility*. Cambridge, MA: Cambridge University Press, 1995.

Hodgson, Dennis. "Contemporary Population Thought." In Paul Demeny and Geoffrey McNicoll, eds., *Encyclopedia of Population*. New York: Macmillan Reference, 2003.

Hodgson, Dennis and Susan Cotts Watkins. "Feminists and Neo-Malthusians: Past and Present Alliances." *Population and Development Review*, v.23/3 (1997).

Lane, Sandra. "From Population Control to Reproductive Health: An Emerging Policy Agenda." *Social Science and Medicine*, v.39/9 (1994).

Malthus, Thomas. *Essay on the Principle of Population*. New York: Modern Library, [1798] 1960.

Jan Brunson
Bowdoin College

P

Pacifism, Female

Pacifism is the rejection of war or violence as means to solve disagreement. The relationship between pacifism and women, as well as pacifism and feminism, is complex. Many women are pacifist or have participated in pacifist movements. There are also specific women's movements devoted to pacifism. Further, there are also feminist pacifist movements. Some of the most renowned proponents for female pacifism are Carol Gilligan, Betty Reardon, Birgit Brock-Utne, and Sara Ruddick.

The linking of women to peace has a long historical tradition in Western societies, with female goddesses representing both birth and peace in Greek and Roman cultures. Essentialist feminists, often placed within "difference theory," link the specific characteristics of the female body to peace, thus attributing female pacifism to biological attributes. In this view, woman's capability to give birth and thus her connection to life makes her unqualified to conduct war. This emphasizes and glorifies women's stereotypical roles as mothers, nurturers, and peacemakers, which are considered opposite to men as violent, aggressive, and warmongering.

Standpoint feminists take a wider stance on the relationship between feminism and pacifism, as they link patriarchy, domination, and war. According to this perspective, feminism and pacifism equally aim to eliminate violence in both public and private.

Feminism and pacifism also are based on a premise of equality, focus on the concept of rights, and aim toward a unified sisterhood. Another approach, which combines difference theory and standpoint theory, is provided by the theories of maternal peace or the "ethics of care." This perspective emphasizes maternal instincts of love, nurturing, and relations. It is argued that both men and women, whether they are parents or not, can conduct maternal politics; it is thus not limited to actual mothers' behavior.

These more or less essentialist feminist strands of pacifism have been criticized by other feminist scholars, mainly poststructuralists. It is claimed that by focusing on women as nurturing and mothering, these theories simply uphold the Cartesian dichotomies of women and men as opposites, following from binaries such as passive/active, caring/violent, nurturing/killing. Further, it is alleged that focusing on women as mothers upholds the binarical war system, thus perpetuating war. Further, other feminists question the perceived male monopoly of violence and claim that women should participate in military forces and revolutions, as well as arm themselves through, for example, self-defense training and participation in armed conflict.

Historically, women have taken part in various pacifist movements, and there have also been women's movements working for peace. Berta von Suttner was the first woman to be awarded the Nobel Peace Prize. Jane Addams and Emily Green Balch founded the Women's International Committee for Permanent Peace, which was later renamed the Women's International League for Peace and Freedom (WILPF). In addition to international movements such as WILPF and Women in Black, national and regional organizations have excelled in working for peace. In Latin America, Madres de Plaza de Mayo has used maternalistic rhetoric when protesting against the disappeared persons after the Argentinean military coup in 1976. In similar fashion, the Russian Mothers Against the War in Chechnya has also emphasised their roles as mothers. In southern Asia, organizations such as Women's Initiative for Peace in South Asia (WISPA) and Women's Action Forum (WAF) are vocal opponents to the conflict between India and Pakistan. Aung San Suu Kyi has opposed the military regime in Myanmar since the early 1990s, a cause for which she has both spent most of the last 20 years imprisoned and received the Nobel Peace Prize.

See Also: Global Feminism; Military, Women in the; Peace Movement; Women in Black; Women's International League for Peace and Freedom.

Further Readings

Pierson, Ruth Roach, ed. *Women and Peace: Theoretical, Historical and Practical Perspectives*. New York: Croom Helm, 1987.

Ruddick, Sara. *Maternal Thinking: Towards a Politics of Peace*. London: The Women's Press, 1990.

Snyder, Anna C. *Setting the Agenda for Global Peace*. Aldershot, UK: Ashgate, 2003.

Emma Brännlund
National University of Ireland, Galway

Pagels, Elaine

Elaine Hiesey Pagels (1943–) is a foremost religious scholar, with a specialty in probing and interpreting the Gnostic traditions of Christianity. After growing up on a farm in Palo Alto, California, Elaine Hiesey attended Stanford University, where she received both a B.A. (1964) and an M.A. (1965). She then traveled east to attend Harvard, obtaining her Ph.D. in religious studies (1970). In 1969, she married Heinz R. Pagels, a noted theoretical physicist, and subsequently gave birth to two children. Professionally, Pagels successfully climbed the academic ladder. In 1982, she left a position as a fully tenured professor at Barnard College, Columbia University, to become the Harrington Spear Paine Foundation Professor of Religion at Princeton University.

In 1987, Pagels's 5-year-old son succumbed to chronic lung disease. Fifteen months later, her husband was killed in a hiking accident. These events caused Pagels, an Episcopalian, to question her religious beliefs. Afterward, her ongoing journey to understand the truth of the origins and development of Christianity led her to become one of the most respected religious scholars in the world. Her contributions were recognized through the awarding of a Rockefeller Fellowship (1978–79), a Guggenheim Fellowship (1979–80), and the MacArthur Fellowship (1980–85).

When Elaine Pagels was only 2 years old, two Egyptian brothers stumbled onto a ceramic jar filled with books while digging for natural fertilizer in Jabal-al-Tarif. The discovery of this 4th-century treasure trove, which came to be known as the Nag Hammadi Library, proved to be a watershed in the study of the historical aspects of Christianity and provided Pagels with a wealth of material. Pagels's studies ultimately led her to study Greek, Latin, Coptic, Hebrew, French, Italian, and German, and she participated in translating two of the documents in the 48-volume collection.

Her doctoral dissertation was published as *The Johannine Gospel in Gnostic Exegesis* (1973), an exposition of Heracleon's Commentary on John's Gospel. In *The Gnostic Paul* (1975), she presents 2nd-century Valentinian Gnostic interpretations of Paul that are based on secret oral traditions traced back to the apostle through his pupil Theudas, demonstrating that sin and redemption in Paul's letters were read by Paul's interpreters in both a Gnostic and an anti-Gnostic fashion. Two different pictures of Paul emerge, neither of which are exclusively correct.

Advanced Scholarship and Women in Gnosticism

Pagels' analysis of the Nag Hammadi documents provided the basis for *The Gnostic Gospels*, which sold 400,000 copies, Pagels argued that differences between Gnostic and Orthodox Christians are better explained by politics and organization than by theology. Gnostic texts are based on intuitive insight (gnosis) and apprehension of the divine origins of humanity. Valentinian Christian Gnostic texts convey visions of Jesus. Reviewing the book for the *New York Sun* in 2008, Professor Bruce Chilton notes, "No single contribution has shaped the popular impression of the significance of the find and the meaning of Gnosticism more than her book."

In the chapter titled "God the Father/God the Mother," Pagels became the first religious scholar to correlate female divine imagery with the positive roles of women in Gnostic groups. Many women scholars and writers have subsequently explored this connection with greater methodological sophistication, arguing, for example, that there may be no connection between female imagery and women's social roles or that they may be something altogether more nuanced. All such discussions have been forced to consider the devaluation of "femaleness" in several texts and the variety of texts considered Gnostic. Categories of "male" and "female" in myths of origins are distinct from statements about male and female relations on the one hand and more abstract descriptions of the human condition on the other. Recent discussions have questioned the value of the Gnosticism classification.

Pagels also initiated debate on her analysis of Catholicism's interpretations of the resurrection, authority, martyrdom, knowledge, and the identity of the true church. While recognizing Pagels's contributions to her field, Chilton finds fault with her for neglecting to adequately address the role of the Roman Empire in the development of both Christianity and Gnosticism.

In *The Origin of Satan* (1996), Pagels explores Christian and Jewish concepts of evil, arguing that to give meaning to suffering is an essential human need. In *Adam, Eve and the Serpent* (1988), she examines the creation stories and the development of sexual attitudes in the Christian West. In 2003, Pagels published *Beyond Belief: The Secret Gospel of Thomas*, arguing that John's Gospel knew and disagreed with teachings presented in the Gospel of Thomas. Pagels's most controversial work may be *Reading Judas: The Gospel of Judas and the Shaping of Christianity* (2007), coauthored with Karen King of Harvard. The book evolved from a National Geographic Society project in which Pagels served on a team of religious

scholars translating documents discovered in Egypt in the 1970s. It presented Judas not as a traitor but as a close friend of Jesus who was only carrying out Christ's intentions when he betrayed his presence to Roman soldiers for 30 pieces of silver.

Pagels is currently preparing an analysis of Revelation, the last book of the New Testament. She has remarried and, along with her husband and two children, regularly attends an Episcopal church.

See Also: Christianity; Orthodox Churches; Religion, Women in; Roman Catholic Church.

Further Readings:

Bartlett, Thomas. "The Betrayal of Judas." *Chronicle of Higher Education*, v.54/8 (May 2008).

Chilton, Bruce. "The Gospel According to Pagels: Reconsiderations." *New York Sun* (April 2, 2008). http://www.nysun.com/arts/gospel-according-to-pagels/74033 (accessed July 2010).

Pagels, Elaine. *The Gnostic Gospels* (c.1979). New York: Vintage Books, 1989.

Rogers, Diane. "The Gospel Truth." *Stanford Magazine* (January/February 2004).

Dierdre Good
The General Theological Seminary

Paglia, Camille

Camille Paglia is well-known both for her controversial ideas and for the signature incendiary style in which she delivers them. Born on April 2, 1947, in Endicott, New York, Paglia earned a Ph.D. in English from Yale University in 1974, where Harold Bloom supervised her dissertation. She is currently a professor of humanities at the University of the Arts in Philadelphia. Paglia became famous as both a popular and scholarly figure with the publication of her contentious first book, *Sexual Personae: Art and Decadence From Nefertiti to Emily Dickinson* (1990). Here, Paglia reinterprets works from the early Greeks through the English, French, and American literary canons. *Sexual Personae* was rejected by seven major New York publishers before being accepted by Yale University Press.

The sweeping 700-page text argues that paganism was never defeated by Judeo-Christianity, in contrast to the arguments of conventional histories. Instead, Paglia argues, paganism was merely driven underground and has returned during three important historical moments: the Renaissance, Romanticism, and modern pop culture. Paglia sees world history as an ongoing struggle between two principles: the Apollonian, which is associated with the male, civilization, art, order, and reason; and the Dionysian, which is associated with the female, nature, sex, chaos, and emotion.

Paglia stresses the importance of biological differences between men and women. Women, in her view, are more powerful than men because women control the sexual realm and have since antiquity. She writes, "I see the mother as an overwhelming force who condemns men to lifelong sexual anxiety, from which they escape through rationalism and physical achievement." This effort to separate from nature (the feminine) and conquer it comes directly out of male biology and is responsible for all the great achievements of Western civilization, such as architecture and science: "The male projection of erection and ejaculation is the paradigm for all cultural projection and conceptualization. . . . Women have conceptualized less in history not because men have kept them from doing so but because women do not need to conceptualize in order to exist. . . . Concentration and projection are remarkably demonstrated by [male] urination [which] really is . . . an arc of transcendence. . . . Women, like female dogs, are earthbound squatters. . . . If civilization had been left in female hands, we would still be living in grass huts."

Since the success of *Sexual Personae,* Paglia has commented on a wide range of charged issues in her essays and op-ed pieces; these have been collected in *Sex, Art, and American Culture: Essays* (1992) and *Vamps and Tramps: New Essays* (1994). Of date rape, for example, Paglia insists that sex always carries with it the threat of violence, and women should take responsibility for their own safety by learning how to avoid or fend off unwanted sexual advances. Paglia has also authored *The Birds* (1998) and *Break, Blow, Burn: Camille Paglia Reads Forty-Three of the World's Best Poems* (2005).

See Also: Christianity; Gender, Defined; Judaism; Rape, Cross-Culturally Defined; Witchcraft: Worldwide; Womanist Theology; Women's Studies.

Further Readings

Ivins, M. "I am the Cosmos." *Mother Jones*, v.16/5 (1991).

Paglia, C. "A Pornographic Nun: An Interview with Camille Paglia." Thomas J. Ferraro, ed. *Catholic Lives, Contemporary America.* Durham, NC: Duke University Press, 1997.

Stanfill, F. "Woman Warrior," *New York*, v.26/16 (1991).

Christina Shouse Tourino
College of Saint Benedict/Saint John's University

Pakistan

The Islamic Republic of Pakistan has a population of 147 million, of which 51.4 percent are male and 48.6 percent are female. The majority lives in rural areas; about 48.3 percent of females reside in rural areas, as compared to 57.7 percent males.

Since inception in 1947, Pakistan has had a tumultuous history. It was created as a homeland for Muslims in south Asian when the British Indian Empire crumbled and consisted of two large areas, East Pakistan and West Pakistan, divided by Indian land. In 1971, after a civil war between East and West Pakistan, East Pakistan broke loose and Bangladesh was created. Women were among the greatest victims in both this War of Partition and the Bangladesh War, wherein women of all religions and nationalities were abducted, raped, and killed.

Islam has had a focal position in the history of Pakistan; it has often been used by governments and civil society agents as a tool to control women's lives and bodies. *Purdah*, seclusion of women in the private domain, and *izzat*, honor, are central notions in Pakistani culture. These are, however, constantly negotiated and contested; Pakistan is not a homogenous society, thus social class, region, and tribal customs affect the status of women.

Position of Women Today

Women's labor force participation is to a large extent invisible, at officially 19 percent of work, while simultaneously, 9 percent are recorded as unemployed. In rural areas, the labor force participation figure is 23 percent and in urban areas 11 percent. However, this does not consider the role of women working on family-owned farms or in informal sectors. It is estimated that women's participation in crop and livestock production is 79 percent. Women take part to a large extent in livestock management and production, as well as crop production. Urban women work in the government and industrial sectors, and male migration to jobs in the Persian Gulf has given educated women the opportunity to enter the labor force.

In Pakistan, there are three kinds of educational institutions: public, private, and *madrasas* (religious schools). Despite attempts by various governments to reform the education system, literacy and enrollment rates remain low. Male literacy rates are 64 percent and female 42 percent. The urban literacy rate is 63 percent, while the rural rate is 34 percent. Poverty and unemployment are the main causes for low enrollment rates, as child labor, within or outside the home, is an opportunity for income. Lack of public schools for girls, in particular, has the effect that parents are reluctant to send their girls to school. Religious groups have also attempted to prevent girls from attending school, either through propaganda, threats, closing of schools, or other means.

Health, Sexual Issues, and Political Activism

Women's health is often ignored, and despite policies to improve the situation, there has been little advancement. Maternal mortality rates are high, due to marriages at young age, lack of adequately skilled health services during delivery, and reduced distribu-

Despite government attempts to reform the education system, literacy and enrollment rates for girls in Pakistan remain low.

tion of Tetanus Toxoid vaccination. Malnutrition is prevalent among adult Pakistani women, which poses a serious threat for pregnant women during delivery. Abortion is illegal in Pakistan, except within the first four months of pregnancy if the woman's life is at risk. Social stigma, underreporting of illnesses, and lack of funding are some of the reason why women are less likely to seek medical care. Besides biomedicine, many people trust traditional medicine, healing, and prophetic medicine.

The most prominent law regarding women was the *Hudood* Ordinances implemented in 1979, which introduced Islamic Shari`a law into the Pakistani penal code. It criminalized, among other acts, *Zina* (extramarital sex), and thus made rape victims prosecutable. This law was amended in 2006, in order to protect women who had been raped. Honor killings, dowry murders, sexual and domestic violence, and bride burning are among the gender-specific violence directed toward women. These are criminalized by the law, but women's weak social status inhibits their legal access.

Women's political activism has taken different shapes. Prominent public figures were Benazir Bhutto, the country's first prime minister, and Fatima Jinnah, sister of the founder of Pakistan, Muhammad Ali Jinnah. Despite Bhutto's elaborate rhetoric on women's rights, her two periods in office achieved very little. Jinnah, on the other hand, founded the Women's Relief Committee, which developed into the All Pakistan Women's Association (APWA). This organization campaigns for the economic and social welfare of Pakistani women. Another organization, Women's Action Forum (WAF), is working for equality, democracy, and peace. A majority of the political parties have women's wings; there are also strong women's sections in the religious parties that campaign for women's enhancement within an Islamic structure.

See Also: Abortion, Access to; Abortion Laws, International; Bangladesh; Bhutto, Benazir; Government, Women in; Islam; Rural Women.

Further Readings

Bhasin, Kamla, Ritu Menon, and Nighat Said Khan, eds. *Against All Odds: Essays on Women, Religion and Development from India and Pakistan.* New Delhi: Kali for Women, 1994.

Rizvi, Narjis and Sania Nishtar. "Pakistan's Health Policy: Appropriateness and Relevance to Women's Health Needs." *Health Policy*, v.88/2–3 (2008).

Shaheed, Farida. *Imagined Citizenship: Women, State & Politics in Pakistan.* Lahore, Pakistan: Shirkat Gah Women's Resource Centre, 2002.

Emma Brännlund
National University of Ireland, Galway

Palau

The Republic of Palau, which is made up of a group of islands located in the North Pacific Ocean, was once part of the Caroline Islands. In 1978, the people of the islands chose to become independent rather than join the Federated States of Micronesia. Palau ultimately attained independence in 1994. Tradition continues to govern many aspects of life in Palau, and women play an important role because the basic family is defined as a mother and her children. Groups of families make up clans. Ranking female members work with the other leaders to elect a meal leader for each clan. A separate council with equal status is composed of ranking female members. A council composed of clan chiefs from 16 states serves as advisers to the democratically elected president of Palau. Suffrage is universal.

By 2008, 81 percent of islanders were living in urban areas. The per capita income is $8,100. Income is derived chiefly from government jobs, tourism, and U.S. aid. Ethnically, Palauans make up almost 70 percent of the island's population. A number of religions are represented in Palau, including Roman Catholic (41.6 percent), Protestant (23.3 percent), and Modekngei (8.8 percent), an indigenous religion.

The median age for Palauan females is 32.7 years. With an infant mortality rate of 11.36 deaths per 1,000 live births, female infants have an advantage over male infants (14.83). This higher survival rate continues throughout life, and females have a life expectancy of 74.54 years, compared to 68.08 years for males. In 1973, Palauan women produced an average of 7.7 children. Today, the fertility rate has declined to 1.82 children per woman. Although males (93 percent) have a higher literacy rate than females (90 percent),

females (15 years) generally stay in school longer than males (14 years).

According to law, no barriers exist to prevent women from entering politics. In 2006, there were no women in Palau's parliament. Within two years, two women had been elected to Palau's senate, and women held 16 percent of state legislative seats. Three governors were female, and five of nine supreme court judges were female. Domestic violence is a problem that is often associated with the use of alcohol and drugs. Evidence suggests that many incidences go unreported. Rape is rare on the islands. Although prostitution is illegal, it continues to flourish. There are no official reports of problems with sexual harassment or sex discrimination, but there are reports of human trafficking into Palau. Women's rights groups are active on the islands, and they have made health, education, drug abuse, prostitution, and traditional customs and values priorities on their agendas.

See Also: Domestic Violence; Infant Mortality; Property Rights; Trafficking, Women and Children.

Further Readings
Central Intelligence Agency. "The World Factbook: Palau." https://www.cia.gov/library/publications/the-world -factbook/geos/ps.html (accessed February 2010).

"Pacific Women Run for Politics." *We!* (February 28, 2006).

United Nations. "Core Document Forming Part of the Reports of State Parties: Palau." http://www.unhchr.ch /tbs/doc.nsf/0/ff1daab2d350d3ab802568a5005d4fad ?Opendocument (accessed February 2010).

U.S. Department of State. "2008 Human Rights Project: Palau." http://www.state.gov/g/drl/rls/hrrpt/2008/ eap/119052.htm (accessed February 2010).

Elizabeth Rholetter Purdy
Independent Scholar

Palestine

Today, descendants of the ancient people of Palestine generally reside in the West Bank, the Gaza Strip, or East Jerusalem. After the British pulled out of the area in 1948, the United Nations was asked to broker a settlement between the competing claims of Arabs and

Jews. This resulted in the land being divided among the newly created Jewish state of Israel and the Arab states of Jordan and Egypt. Through the Arab-Israeli War of 1967, Israel won control of both the West Bank and the Gaza Strip. The following decades were filled with occupation and strife, but by the 1990s, Israel had agreed to allow self-government in Palestinian-populated sections of the West Bank and the Gaza Strip. However, conflicts continued between Hamas, the Islamic Resistance Movement, and the Palestinian Authority. In 2007, Hamas conducted a takeover of the Gaza Strip, leaving Palestine to maintain a fragile existence on the West Bank. As a result of decades of fighting for lands and a national identity, Palestinian women have been subjected to major instability. As Muslim women, they have also had to fight for the right to be respected as individuals.

Within the West Bank, 72 percent of the population live in urban areas. Ethnically, 83 percent of the people are Palestinian. From a legal perspective, women have equal standing with males. However, according to religious laws, the rights of males predominate. Palestinians have a per capita income of only $2,900 and an unemployment rate of 16.3 percent. Poverty is widespread on the West Bank, and 46 percent of the people, mostly women and children, live below the poverty line.

The infant mortality rate is 15.76 deaths per 1,000 live births. Female infants (13.93) have an advantage over male infants (17.87), and that advantage continues throughout life. Women have a life expectancy of 76.65 years, compared to 72.54 years for males. That advantage does not apply to literacy, however, and only 88 percent of females are literate, compared to 96.7 percent of males. Despite that handicap, women are more likely to pursue higher education. Palestinian women have a fertility rate of 3.22 children per female, and a median age of 20.8 years.

By the 1990s, Palestinian women's organizations began banding together to create the Action for Legal Reforms, designed to reform family codes and grant women equal rights in inheritance, marriage, divorce, and maintenance and custody of children. The plan also called for the abolition of child marriages, "honor killings," genital mutilation, and being treated as property. According to a 2004 United Nations report, almost a fourth of Palestinian girls between the ages of 15 and 19 are married, divorced, or widowed.

Another report revealed that 40 percent of all marriages are the result of parental decisions. Polygamy continues to be accepted by Islamic dictates, and some Palestinian males have up to four wives. In the case of divorce, mothers retain custody of sons until the age of 10 and of daughters until the age of 12. If women remarry, they forfeit custody.

Women who leave their husband's home without permission can be forced to return. Citizenship is conferred only by fathers. No laws exist to check violence against women. One 2006 report indicated that 60 percent of Palestinian women have been psychologically abused. Additionally, 23 percent have been physically abused, and 11 percent have been sexually abused.

See Also: Domestic Violence; Israel; Marriages, Arranged.

Further Readings

CIA World Factbook. "West Bank." https://www.cia.gov /library/publications/the-world-factbook/geos/we.html (accessed February 2010).

"Palestine: Despite Democracy, Women Still Fear for Their Freedoms." We! (2005/2006).

SIGI. "Gender Equality and Social Institutions in West Bank and Gaza." http://genderindex.org/country/west -bank-and-gaza (accessed February 2010).

"Women and Violence: Palestine Has Largest Number of 'Honor Killings' of Women." WIN News, v.25/3 (1999).

Women Watch. "Palestine." http://www.un.org/women watch/daw/Review/responses/PALESTINE-English.pdf (accessed February 2010).

Elizabeth Rholetter Purdy
Independent Scholar

Palin, Sarah

Sarah Louise Heath Palin is a social conservative, and a Republican politician. In 2006, she became the first female governor of Alaska and the youngest individual (age 42) ever elected to that position. In August 2008, Republican presidential candidate John McCain announced Palin as his running mate. Palin was the first female ever nominated by the Republican Party on a presidential ticket.

Sarah Palin is the first female ever nominated by the Republican Party on a presidential ticket.

Palin was born February 11, 1964, in Sandpoint, Idaho, the third of four children in the Heath family. The family moved from Idaho to Alaska when Palin was only a few months old. Her father taught school in a variety of communities in Alaska, finally settling in Skagway, a suburb of Anchorage. Palin studied journalism at the University of Idaho; she graduated with an undergraduate degree in 1987. Shortly after graduation, in 1988, she eloped with her high school sweetheart, Todd Palin. The Palins have five children.

Palin's political career began in 1992 when she was elected to the Wasilla, Alaska City Council. In 1996 she was elected mayor of Wasilla; she served two, three-year terms as mayor (1996–2002). In 2002, Palin entered the Republican primary as a candidate for lieutenant governor, but was defeated. She was appointed to the Alaska Oil and Gas Conservation Commission by the newly-elected governor, Frank Murkowski. After a brief period on the Commission, Palin resigned and raised ethics concerns about another appointee on the Commission. Her concerns prompted a federal investigation.

In November 2009, Palin's book, *Going Rogue*, was released, and she commenced a national book tour. White House press secretary Robert Gibbs described Palin as "the most formidable force in the Republican Party." She became a contributor to Fox News, and has become a popular and sought-after speaker and leader at Tea Party rallies, the 2010 Southern Republican Leadership Conference, universities, foundations, and other political and current issues forums.

See Also: Attainment, College Degree; Government, Women in; United States; Working Mothers.

Further Readings

Barnes, Fred. "The Most Popular Governor Alaska's Sarah Palin is the GOP's Newest Star." *The Weekly Standard*, v.12/41 (2007).

Palin, Sarah. *Going Rogue: An American Life*. New York: HarperCollins, 2009.

Anita M. Pankake
University of Texas–Pan American

Panama

The Central American Republic of Panama forms a land bridge connecting Central and South America. The majority of the population are mestizo, Creole, or indigenous; Hispanic is the dominant culture; and Roman Catholic is the dominant religion. Women have entered the workforce and political arena, but the traditional view of male dominance remains largely unchallenged. Women enjoy good educational access, high literacy rates, and good medical care and overall living standards. Panama ranked 43rd of 134 countries in the World Economic Forum's 2009 Global Gender Gap Report.

The traditional Hispanic concepts of machismo and marianismo provide a sexual double standard, as male sexual promiscuity is viewed as a sign of virility while there is an equally strong emphasis on female virginity and purity. Both common law and church marriages are common.

The 2009 fertility rate was 2.6 births per woman. Skilled healthcare practitioners attended 91 percent of births. The 2009 infant mortality rate was 18 per 1,000 live births, and the maternal mortality rate was 130 per 100,000 live births. The state social security fund provides women with 14 weeks of paid maternity leave at 100 percent of their wages, with employers covering any funding differences. The civil legal system provides for liberal divorces.

Living Standards and Access to Education Show Increasing Improvement

The Panamanian population is becoming increasingly urban, although there is a substantial rural population. Most Panamanians live in nuclear families, although extended families are also common. There is an effective public school system. Female school attendance rates stand at 98 percent at the primary level, 67 percent at the secondary level, and 56 percent at the tertiary level. The literacy rates for women and men are almost equal, at 93 percent and 94 percent respectively. There is a good state system of social security and public healthcare, and most have access to safe drinking water. Healthcare is becoming increasingly privatized. Life expectancy is age 68 for women and age 64 for men.

Many women work outside the home in a variety of professions. About 52 percent of women participate in the labor force. Women constitute 43 percent of the paid nonagricultural workforce and 52 percent of professional and technical workers. Government and education are primary employers of professional women, although women can be found in top-level positions in most professions. Many women also work in agriculture and service. Subsistence agriculture is dominant among rural families. A gender gap still exists in terms of average estimated earned income in U.S. dollars, which stands at $7,728 for women and $12,481 for men, and unemployment rates, which stand at 9.3 percent for women and 5.3 percent for men. Women enjoy public equality with men, and public social interactions are not segregated by gender. Women have the right to vote. Women hold 9 percent of parliamentary seats and 23 percent of ministerial positions. There has been a female head of state for five of the last 50 years. Many nongovernmental organizations (NGOs) and other international organizations operate in Panama.

See Also: Gender Roles, Cross-Cultural; Machismo/Marianismo; Marriage; Roman Catholic Church.

Further Readings

Dore, Elizabeth and Maxine Molyneux. *Hidden Histories of Gender and the State in Latin America*. Durham, NC: Duke University Press, 2000.

Hausman, Ricardo, Laura D. Tyson, and Saadia Zahidi. *The Global Gender Gap Report 2009*. Geneva: World Economic Forum, 2009. http://www.weforum.org /en/Communities/Women%20Leaders%20and%20 Gender%20Parity/GenderGapNetwork/index.htm (accessed February 2010).

Hepburn, Stephanie and Rita J. Simon. *Women's Roles and Statuses the World Over*. Lanham, MD: Lexington Books, 2006.

Marcella Bush Trevino
Independent Scholar

Panchita's House: Domestic Workers Rights in Lima, Peru

Panchita's House (*La Casa de Panchita*) opened in 1998 as a place for domestic workers in Lima, Peru, to meet and support one another. It offers visitors a wide array of resources and activities, some of which are free of charge. Services include tutoring, English and computer classes, employment and placement in domestic services, legal advice in labor problems, consultation about sexual and reproductive health, self-esteem workshops, and recreational outings. In addition to these resources, Panchita's House advocates for domestic workers to maintain contact with their family and friends.

Panchita's House was founded by *Asociación Grupo de Trabajo Redes* (AGTR), a nongovernmental organization. The aim of AGTR is to defend the rights of and empower those who experience discrimination as a result of poverty, age, gender, or culture. Specific objectives of AGTR involve defending the rights of domestic workers in Peru, where the overwhelming majority of workers (about 90 percent) are indigenous and rural young women who moved to the cities to find work and escape from poverty.

Work conditions are often poor, as many workers work up to 16 hours a day with no rest days and little or no payment. Many workers are also underage, illiterate, barred from attending school, and/or fall victim to physical and sexual abuse. Since its inception, AGTR has been instrumental in introducing and changing laws that protect the rights of domestic workers of all ages. One such law is Law 27986, the Domestic Workers' Act 2003, which requires—among other rights—an eight-hour work day, 15 paid vacation days a year, and either a verbal or written work contract between the domestic worker and her or his employer.

In 1998, AGTR published a booklet featuring the fictional story of Panchita, a young girl from the country working as a domestic worker who overcomes many difficulties in her life. (The booklet also included information on AGTR and the services it provided.) Domestic workers who read her story declared that Panchita needed a home—this declaration eventually evolved into what is now Panchita's House.

Since 2007, Panchita's House has also acted as an employment agency for domestic workers and employers. Anyone interested in being placed through Panchita's House must attend job-training sessions either in full-service home care or nursing. Panchita's House volunteers also help potential employers search, select, and contract with workers.

See Also: Child Labor; Domestic Workers; Educational Opportunities/Access; Global Feminism; Indigenous Women's Issues; Mentoring; Peru; Poverty; Social Justice Activism; Women's Resource Centers.

Further Readings

Anti-Slavery International. "Child Domestic Workers: Finding a Voice." http://www.antislavery.org/includes /documents/cm_docs/2009/a/advocacyhandbookeng .pdf (accessed March 2010).

Asociación Grupo de Trabajo Redes. http://www.grupo redes.org (accessed March 2010).

La Casa de Panchita. http://www.lacasadepanchita.com (accessed March 2010).

Mick, Carola. "Las Empleadas Domesticas como Promotoras del Cambio Social en Peru?" http:// interpol.uasnet.mx/migracionesglobales/ponencias/ Mick_Carola.pdf (accessed March 2010).

Ojeda Parra, Teresa. "Domestic Worker Victims of Sexual Violence in Lima, Peru." http://www.dvcn.org /Documents/DomesticworkersVol1No3.pdf (accessed March 2010).

Florence Maätita
Southern Illinois University Edwardsville

Papua New Guinea

Although one of the fastest-growing developing countries in the southwest Pacific, with a total population of 6.25 million and an annual growth rate of 2.7 percent, Papua New Guinea (PNG) has one of the highest infant mortality rates, at 64 percent, due to the poor health of women and an inadequate healthcare system. Approximately 70 percent of the population are children. The vast majority of PNG's population live in rural areas, and 87 percent of the land remains in "customary" land tenure. However, an increasing number of people are migrating to urban areas due to the deterioration of essential services. Migration is causing an expansion of unplanned settlements with inadequate services and a dependency on cash income to meet basic household needs; many young women are driven into informal survivor sex work to obtain cash to survive.

Due to the influx of transnational corporations engaged in resource extraction, and the consequent uneven distribution of the benefits of "development" surrounding mine sites, land disputes often arise in which women are embroiled. Customary exchange patterns are disrupted by the influx of large compensation payments to landowner groups of men. As women are frequently not allowed to speak in public or to be involved in decision making, and men increasingly represent their own interests with little or no reference to women in their communities, women endure hardships including starvation.

Women have strong social roles within church women's groups and there is a growing nongovernment organization movement that is working toward the empowerment of women, but the pace of reform in slow. Violence against women and children is often sanctioned by culture, custom, and religion. Because it is often considered to be the most effective way to correct the behavior of women and children, violent practices are difficult to challenge and change; they have been successful tools of men's power for many centuries.

The role of adoption increases female children's vulnerability to violence. Traditional adoptions and the practice of bride price brought families and communities together, and the well-being of the child was of paramount importance. Unregulated adoptions now extend into casual arrangements outside the natal family and may not be agreed to by one of the birth parents. Such practices demonstrate the friction that is arising between aspects of modern law, the globalizing economy, and traditional ways of being.

While an independent media exists, it is devoid of critical analysis, particularly of government and public-sector activities. Despite these challenges, women are becoming educated, and in the villages, the rise of "grass-skirt activism" is enabling women to raise their voices to obtain opportunities emerging from the global economy.

See Also: Adoption; Domestic Violence; Reproductive and Sexual Health Rights.

Further Readings

Amnesty International. "Violence Against Women in Papua New Guinea." http://asiapacific.amnesty.org/library/pdf/ASA340022006ENGLISH/$File/ASA3400206.pdf (accessed September 2009).

Macintyre, Martha. "Petztorme Women: Responding to Change in Lihir, Papua New Guinea." *Oceania*, v.74/1–2 (2003).

Tickner, Jo Ann. *Gender in International Relations: Feminist Perspectives on Achieving Global Security.* New York: Columbia University Press, 1992.

Zimmer-Tamakoshi, Laura. "The Last Big Man: Development and Men's Discontents in the Papua New Guinea Highlands." *Oceania*, v.68/2 (1997).

Helen Johnson
University of Queensland

Paraguay

Paraguay is a landlocked country in South America, sharing borders with Bolivia, Brazil, and Argentina. The population of about 7 million is primarily Roman Catholic (89.6 percent), with 6.2 percent Protestant. The 2009 per capita gross domestic product (GDP) of $4,100 is among the lowest in South America, while income distribution is highly unequal (Gini index of 56.8 in 2008, ninth highest in the world) and 32 percent of the population lives below the poverty line.

The World Economic Forum ranks Paraguay near the median in terms of gender equality. On the Gender Gap Index, where 0 signifies inequality and 1 perfect equality, overall Paraguay's score in 2009 was 0.687, ranking 66th out of 134 countries. On health and survival, Paraguay scored 0.980 (highest in the world), while in subcategories Paraguay scored 0.997 (40th) on educational attainment, 0.669 (58th) on economic participation, and 0.102 (85th) on political empowerment.

Good Literacy Rates, but Gender Gap Exists

Literacy is approximately equal for men and women in Paraguay, at 94 percent and 93 percent respectively. Females outnumber males at every stage of enrollment, with about 13 percent more women than men enrolled in tertiary education. About 74 percent of women are in the labor force, as compared with 86 percent of men, but on average women earn about 60 percent of what men do. Women hold about half the technical and professional positions in Paraguay and about a third of positions as legislators, senior officials, and managers. Working mothers in Paraguay are entitled to 12 weeks of maternity leave at 50 percent of their salary.

Women in Paraguay received the right to vote in 1961, making them the last in Latin America to do so. In 1992, the constitution was revised to incorporate gender equality. Women's participation in politics has been aided since 1996 by a quota requiring that candidate lists must include 20 percent women. In 2009, women held 19 percent of the seats in regional legislatures (up from 5 percent in 1993), and in 2006 women held 21 percent of city council positions versus 14 percent in 1996. At the national level, in 2009 women held 14 percent of parliamentary seats and 23 percent of ministerial positions.

The international organization Save the Children ranks Paraguay in the middle of 75 Tier II or less developed countries on issues of importance to women and children. The country is ranked highest on the Women's Index (28th), lower on the Mothers' Index (38th), and much lower on the Children's Index (50th). Paraguay has a high fertility rate (3.8 women per children) and a young population structure (36.7 percent age 14 or younger). Infant mortality is 24.68 per 1,000 live births, among the highest in Latin America.

See Also: Gender Quotas in Government; Gender Roles, Cross-Cultural; Poverty; Roman Catholic Church.

Further Readings

Hausman, Ricardo, Laura D. Tyson, and Saadia Zahidi. *The Global Gender Gap Report 2009.* Geneva: World Economic Forum, 2009. http://www.weforum.org/en/Communities/Women%20Leaders%20and%20Gender%20Parity/GenderGapNetwork/index.htm (accessed February 2010).

Save the Children. "State of the World's Mothers 2009: Investing in the Early Years." http://www.savethechildren.org/publications/?WT.mc_id=1109_hp_hd_pub (accessed February 2009).

United Nations Statistics Divisions. "UNdata: A World of Information: Gender Info." http://data.un.org/Explorer.aspx?d=GenderStat (accessed February 2010).

Sarah Boslaugh
Washington University School of Medicine

Parental Leave

Parental leave is defined by the International Labour Organization (ILO) as "leave granted to fathers and mothers during a period after the termination of maternity leave to enable parents in employment to look after their newborn child for a certain time, whilst giving them some degree of security in respect of employment, social security and remuneration. Parental leave is also granted to adoptive parents."

This definition states the co-responsibility of parents, both natural and adoptive. Parental leave differs from maternity leave because it is focused on the care and upbringing of young children, making both parents eligible for the benefit. The mother's and baby's health is the prime consideration of maternity leave, including extended or optional maternity leave. Paternity leave is distinguishable from parental leave in that it is immediately post birth and of short duration.

Family leave is sometimes granted, although it need not be for childcare and is of short duration. Parental leave need have nothing to do with issues of force majure (or emergency leave for family reasons), although many countries have included this concept in their parental leave legislation. The conceptual distinctions between the above are prone to overlap. The ILO definition envisages parental leave as different from maternity leave because it can be taken by the father and/or the mother and is an employment right.

The ILO on Parental Leave

The Employment of Women with Family Responsibilities Recommendation 1965 (No. 123) was adopted to protect the rights of women workers. It sought to institute measures such as childcare services and facilities, and appropriate counseling, placement, and training, to enable parents to enter or reenter employment after comparatively long absences due to family responsibilities. The International Labor Conference (1975) recommended that gender equality of opportunity and treatment could only be achieved by extending rights to all workers with family responsibilities, both women and men. This was in recognition that any change in the traditional role of women needs to include change in the traditional role of men. Such a development would be a move toward an enhanced status for the exercise of parental duties. The availability of parental leave would be a contributory factor in this development.

The ILO Convention 1981 No. 156 and Recommendation 1981 (No. 165) set out the rationale for Equal Opportunities and Equal Treatment for Men and Women Workers with Family Responsibilities. This convention was adopted to extend the concept of a gender balance in parental responsibility. The convention applies to all workers with children and other immediate family members who need support. Article 3 states that national policies should ensure that workers with family responsibilities should not be subject to discrimination or conflict between their employment and family roles. Article 8 states that family responsibilities should not constitute a valid reason for termination of employment. Other articles invoke measures that enable workers to exercise free choice within the context of the prevailing national policies of each country. Articles reference the requirement that public authorities in each country should make available information and education designed to create a climate of opinion that is conducive to assisting workers with family responsibilities.

Council of Europe

Principle 4 of the Committee of Ministers Recommendation No. R (94) 14 on Coherent and Integrated Family Policies states that: "The Family must be a place where equality, including legal equality, between women and men is especially promoted by sharing responsibility for running the home and looking after the children, and, more specifically, by ensuring that mother and father take turns and complement each other in carrying out their respective roles."

The European Social Charter (revised) was agreed in Strasbourg on May 3, 1996. In addition to protection of employed women, in relation to maternity (Article 8), Article 27 relates to "the right of workers with family responsibilities to equal opportunities and equal treatment."

The charter refers to measures for workers with family responsibilities to enable them to enter, remain in, and reenter employment. Vocational guidance and training should be made available to facilitate this. Measures should take account of the prevailing conditions of employment and social security and should develop or promote childcare services and arrangements.

In addition, Article 27 sought to ensure that family responsibilities should not constitute a valid reason for termination of employment. A prime goal is "to provide a possibility for either parent to obtain, during a period after maternity leave, parental leave to take care of a child, the duration and conditions of which should be determined by national legislation, collective agreements or practice."

The COE adopted a Recommendation No. R (96) 5 of the Committee of Ministers to Member States on Reconciling Work and Family Life, which acknowledges the need for a number of innovative measures that would reconcile working life and family life. The recommendation sought paternity leave for fathers of newly born children and in addition that: "both the father and the mother should have the right to take parental leave during a period to be determined by the national authorities without losing either their employment or any related rights provided for in social protection or employment regulations. The possibility should exist for such parental leave to be taken part-time and to be shared between parents."

U.S. National Legislative Provisions

All developed U.S. state governments have provisions for the support of parents with newborn children. Parental leave laws can support new parents in complementary ways:

- By offering job-protected leave, which protects at least one parent's job for a period of weeks, months, or years at and after the birth of a child.
- By offering financial support during that leave.
- By providing the important right to take parental leave on a part-time basis, which enables a worker to combine leave with part-time employment.

European Union

The first commission proposal for a directive on parental leave dates back to 1983. However, it was not until 1995 that an agreement could be reached, which led to the formal adoption of the Council Directive 96/34/EC of 3 June 1996 on the framework agreement on parental leave concluded by the European Trade Council, the Union of Industrial and Employers' Confederations of Europe, and the European Centre of Employers and Enterprises Providing Public Services.

The directive required member states to grant parental leave as an individual worker's right—for both women and men. The purpose of the parental leave is to facilitate the care of the child for at least three months, or until a certain age defined by member states, which could be up to the age of 8 years. By definition, parental leave granted to each parent may be shared, but it is not transferable between parents for the purposes of increasing the parental leave entitlement of an individual parent. The directive leaves member states the option to regulate whether parental leave is granted on a full-time or part-time basis, in a piecemeal manner, or in the form of a time-credit system. The directive obliges member states to take measures that protect workers from dismissal for having applied for, or for having taken, parental leave. It furthermore guarantees the worker's right to return to the same job, or a similar job, when the leave is over, and that the worker will keep any accrued rights.

The directive anticipated that parental leave would be a right of wage earners, in full- or part-time employment within both the public and private sectors. It did not include self-employed or family workers, nor does it cover care responsibilities for other members of the family, such as elderly or sick relatives. The directive makes no specific reference to single parents or children with disabilities.

The experience of countries that are compliant with "best practice" suggests that a generous, universal, gender-egalitarian, and flexible parental leave policy—financed through social insurance—would go a long way toward spreading the costs of caring for children more equitably between mothers and fathers, parents and nonparents, and employers and employees.

See Also: Equal Pay; Household Division of Labor; Parental Leave Act; Part-Time Work; Working Mothers; Work/Life Balance.

Further Readings

Haas, L. "Parental Leave and Gender Equality: Lessons from the European Union." *Review of Policy Research* v.20/1 (2003).

International Labour Organization. *Maternity Protection Database.* Geneva: ILO Conditions of Work and Employment Programme. http://www.ilo.org/travail database/servlet/maternityprotection (accessed March 2010).

Plantenga, J. and C. Remery. "Reconciliation of Work and Private Life: A Comparative Review of 30 European Countries." Luxembourg: European Commission Directorate-General for Employment, Social Affairs and Equal Opportunities, 2005. http:// www.cecot.es /harmonitzacio/documentacio/estudi%20CE.pdf (accessed March 2010).

Kadriye Bakirci
Istanbul Tecnical University

Parental Leave Act

All developed world governments have provisions for the support of parents with newborn children. Parental leave laws support new parents by offering job-protected leave and financial support during that leave. The right to take parental leave on a part-time basis can be another important aspect of family leave policy. New parents in the United States may access leave through the Family Medical Leave Act (FMLA) of 1993.

The FMLA entitles eligible employees to take up to 12 weeks of unpaid, job-protected leave in a 12-month period for specified family and medical reasons. Amendments to the FMLA by the National Defense Authorization Act NDAA for fiscal year 2008, Public Law 110-181, expanded the FMLA to allow eligible employees to take up to 12 weeks of job-protected leave in the applicable 12-month period for any "qualifying exigency" arising out of the fact that a covered military member is on active duty, or has been notified of an impending call or order to active duty, in support of a contingency operation. The NDAA also amended the FMLA to allow eligible employees to take up to 26 weeks of job-protected leave in a "single 12-month period" to care for a covered service member with a serious injury or illness.

FMLA applies to all public agencies, including state, local, and federal employers; local education agencies (schools); and private-sector employers who employed 50 or more employees in 20 or more work weeks in the current or preceding calendar year, including joint employers and successors of covered employers. To be eligible for FMLA benefits, an employee must work for a covered employer, have worked for the employer for a total of 12 months, have worked at least 1,250 hours over the previous 12 months, and work at a location in the United States or in any territory or possession of the United States where at least 50 employees are employed by the employer within 75 miles.

While the 12 months of employment need not be consecutive, employment periods prior to a break in service of seven years or more need not be counted unless the break is occasioned by the employee's fulfillment of his or her National Guard or Reserve military obligation, as protected under the Uniformed Services Employment and Reemployment Rights Act, or a written agreement, including a collective bargaining agreement, exists concerning the employer's intention to rehire the employee after the break in service.

A covered employer must grant an eligible employee up to a total of 12 work weeks of unpaid leave during any 12-month period for one or more of the following reasons:

- For the birth and care of a newborn child of the employee
- For placement with the employee of a son or daughter for adoption or foster care
- To care for a spouse, son, daughter, or parent with a serious health condition
- To take medical leave when the employee is unable to work because of a serious health condition

- For qualifying exigencies arising out of the fact that the employee's spouse, son, daughter, or parent is on active duty or called to active duty status as a member of the National Guard or Reserves in support of a contingency operation

A covered employer must also grant an eligible employee who is a spouse, son, daughter, parent, or next of kin of a current member of the armed forces, including a member of the National Guard or Reserves, with a serious injury or illness up to a total of 26 work weeks of unpaid leave during a "single 12-month period" to care for the service member.

Spouses employed by the same employer are limited in the amount of family leave they may take for the birth and care of a newborn child, placement of a child for adoption or foster care, or the care of a parent who has a serious health condition to a combined total of 12 weeks (or 26 weeks if leave to care for a covered service member with a serious injury or illness is also used). Leave for birth and care, or placement for adoption or foster care, must conclude within 12 months of the birth or placement.

Upon return from FMLA leave, an employee must be restored to the employee's original job, or to an equivalent job with equivalent pay, benefits, and other terms and conditions of employment. An employee's use of FMLA leave cannot result in the loss of any employment benefit that the employee earned or was entitled to before using FMLA leave, nor be counted against the employee under a "no fault" attendance policy.

If a bonus or other payment, however, is based on the achievement of a specified goal, such as hours worked, products sold, or perfect attendance, and the employee has not met the goal due to FMLA leave, payment may be denied unless it is paid to an employee on equivalent leave status for a reason that does not qualify as FMLA leave. An employee has no greater right to restoration or to other benefits and conditions of employment than if the employee had been continuously employed.

Current U.S. policy includes a key feature of gender-egalitarian parental leave policy—the non-transferability of leave between fathers and mothers. FMLA includes strict nontransferability between parents.

With the exception of a handful of U.S. states, U.S. law provides no right to paid parental leave.

Employer-size and long-job-tenure restrictions also mean that a large proportion of working parents are either not covered or are not eligible for leave under FMLA.

Current U.S. labor law and social policy places almost the entire responsibility for caring for young children—and for combining that care with employment responsibilities—on individual parents.

See Also: Gender Roles, Cross-Cultural; Household Division of Labor; Parental Leave; Working Mothers; Work/Life Balance.

Further Readings

Ray, R. "A Detailed Look at Parental Leave Policies in 21 OECD Countries." Washington, DC: Center for Economic and Policy Research Briefing Paper, 2008. http://www.lisproject.org/publications/parentwork /parentleavedetails.pdf (accessed June 2010).

Turk, J. "The United States' Lack of Parental Leave Benefits: An Analysis of the Negative Impacts on Working Mothers and Recommendations." *Brandeis University Graduate Journal* (2006). http://www .brandeis.edu/gsa/gradjournal/2006/pdf/jematurk.pdf (accessed June 2010).

U.S. Department of Labor. "Federal vs. State Family and Medical Leave Laws." Washington, DC: DOL, 2009. http://www.dol.gov/esa/programs/whd/state/fmla /index.htm (accessed June 2010).

Washington State Department of Labor and Industries. "Family Care and Family Leave Laws." Olympia: WSDLI, 2007. http://www.lni.wa.gov/Work placeRights/files/FamilyLeaveLawsTable.pdf (accessed June 2010).

Kadriye Bakirci
Istanbul Technical University

Parents, Families and Friends of Lesbians and Gays

Parents, Families and Friends of Lesbians and Gays (PFLAG) formed amid national social movements whose leaders challenge oppression rooted in missionary ideology that considers humans to be drawn to the same value bases. The journey to organization

A Parents, Families and Friends of Lesbians and Gays contingent marches at San Francisco Pride 2004. PFLAG has 200,000 members and supporters in 500 chapters in the United States, providing support and advocacy for gay loved ones.

for PFLAG began when Jeanne Manford, a retired mother and school teacher in New York City, attended the 1972 annual gay pride parade in support of her son. Manford and parents like her wanted to form a community of interest, not only to support the children they loved but to serve as a catalyst for activism, designed to codify the dignity and integrity of their children in the laws of the United States.

PFLAG's support, education, and advocacy began in parents' homes. From 1972 to 1979, support groups for families of lesbians and gays formed throughout the United States, but it was not until the 1979 National March for Gay and Lesbian Rights when these parents formed the predecessor organization to PFLAG, known as Parents FLAG and incorporated in California in 1982 as the Federation of Parents, Families and Friends of Lesbians and Gays, Inc. PFLAG

has always represented family members of bisexual orientation, and since 1998 has included transgender individuals in its mission statements and mandates. As of 2009, PFLAG in the United States has 200,000 members and supporters in 500 chapters.

PFLAG's goal has always been to restore and renew bonds of love and friendship among families and friends faced with a loved one's disclosure of sexual orientation; its members and staff educate governments and school boards on all matters concerning sexuality; and it has advocated on behalf of LGBT individuals in discussions on family and caregiver, education, healthcare, employment, and housing policies. PFLAG began when Americans noticed the efforts of one mother who criticized hateful behavior of some police officers in New York City, and the more than 65,000 households in the United States that belong to PFLAG tie their criticisms of the repression of the American federal government and substantial numbers of Christians back to their one desire: to love and support their families.

See Also: Coming Out; Gay and Lesbian Advocacy; Heterosexism; Homophobia; Sex Education, Comprehensive; Sexual Orientation–Based Social Discrimination: United States; Social Justice Activism.

Further Readings

Bernstein, R. A. *Straight Parents, Gay Children: Inspiring Families to Live Honestly and with Greater Understanding.* New York: Thunder's Mouth Press, 1995.

Broad, K. L. "Social Movement Selves." *Sociological Perspectives*, v.45.3 (2002).

Parents, Families, & Friends of Lesbians and Gays. "Vision, Mission and Strategic Goals." http://community.pflag.org/Page.aspx?pid=237 (accessed September 2009).

Jonathan Anuik
Lakehead University Orillia Campus

Partner Rights

Partners are typically defined as unmarried adult cohabitants who are emotionally and financially interdependent, have reached the age of consent, do not have a different domestic partner or spouse, and are in a long-term committed relationship. Despite the financial and legal disincentives, over the past 30 years, there has been an upward trend worldwide in industrialized countries in the number of unmarried partners cohabitating. Underlying this shift in living arrangements is the broad social and cultural shift from a society in which religious ideology encouraged social conformity regarding marriage to a more secular society in which individual choice, autonomy, and freedom are encouraged. The extension of legal rights around the world to opposite-sex and same-sex cohabitants has evolved unevenly and varies both among and within nations.

This broad cultural shift is reflected in the 2000 U.S. census: the number of households headed by cohabitating partners doubled from 1990 to 2000. Cohabitating households make up slightly over 5 percent of all U.S. households and include 5.5 million people; there are minor children in 41 percent of these households. Currently, over half of all marriages are preceded by cohabitation in the United States.

The growth in the rate of cohabiting couples reflects changes in the institution of marriage and concerns about its stability over the life course. Marriage, once strongly fortified by law, religion, and economics, is being replaced by cohabitation. There is a growing movement in the United States to further the separation of church and state by privatizing marriage so that the word *marriage* no longer appears in any laws. This would eliminate any confusion created by the fact that the word *marriage* currently refers to both a legal status and a religious status.

The concern about cohabitation, particularly for the person with fewer resources, is that, unlike marriage, there is no obligation for the person with more resources to support their partner outside marriage by the contractual obligations of divorce should the relationship dissolve. Public policy has not kept pace with this shift in living arrangements and continues to support, preserve, and encourage marriage by reserving many rights and privileges to married persons. Cohabitants in most countries around the world are unclear about their legal rights in areas such as child custody, property ownership, healthcare access, responsibility for debt, and survivorship.

Only 50 years ago, it was illegal in the United States for adults to live together as loving partners. Today, many nations in Europe, North America, and South America extend rights through civil unions and registered partnerships to unwed couples. India's Supreme Court recently ruled that unmarried couples have the right to live together and, as part of its ruling, pointed out that "even the Hindu gods, Lord Krishna and Radha, were cohabitating lovers rather than man and wife."

In the majority of northern European countries, cohabitation is an accepted new social institution. In several Scandinavian nations, cohabitating partners share nearly the same legal rights as their married counterparts. Denmark and Sweden are currently the world's "cohabitation leaders," where cohabitants have the same rights and obligations in childcare, taxation, inheritance, and welfare benefits as married couples.

Cohabitation Around the World

Currently, the vast majority of nations around the world do not offer the same social and legal protections to unmarried partners that they offer to married partners. In China, for example, contraception needs for unmarried women are not being met. There are approximately 13 million abortions performed every year in China for young single women (and 10 million abortion pills sold annually to them), often because young single women know little about contraception; the state widely promotes and subsidizes contraception for married women but tends to ignore the needs of unwed women. There are no rights for unmarried same-sex partners in most Muslim-majority countries; homosexual activity in many Muslim-majority countries is considered a crime and can be punished by death, imprisonment, fines, or corporal punishment. Since the Islamic revolution in Iran in 1979, at least 4,000 individuals charged with homosexual acts have been executed by the government. In Saudi Arabia, gays and lesbians can be publicly executed if found participating in lesbian/gay/bisexual/transgender (LGBT) movements. On the other hand, there are some relatively secular Muslim-majority countries where same-sex partnerships are tolerated, such as Turkey, Indonesia, and Jordan.

Opposite-sex couples in many Muslim-majority countries also receive few rights. Although little can be said in general about all women in Islam, sexual abstinence before marriage is often expected. This severely limits the number of unwed couples that exist. Among particular Muslims sects, in some communities, contact of any kind between an unmarried man and an unmarried woman can be interpreted as adultery and result in a vendetta or an "honor killing," whereby a woman's father or other male relative will kill her to protect the family's honor before the facts of "adultery" are investigated. More than 300 women per year are victims of "honor killings" in Pakistan. If her family waits for justice (four witnesses are required to provide proof of adultery), the penalty of death by stoning has come to be accepted.

What Are Partner Rights?

What does the term *partner rights* mean? Classical liberal theorists, such as John Locke, envisioned human rights as the way to protect individuals from the power of the state (the private realm was considered apoliti-

cal and devoid of power relations). This public/private divide has raised many rights concerns. The term *partner rights* in the United States comes from both a structural concept of the Constitution and a substantive concept of it. By structural concept of the Constitution, one refers to the "zone of privacy" that defines privacy as "beyond the reach of government," where citizens have "the right to be let alone." Unfortunately, for the person who is the weaker party in the partnership and needs more state protection, the language of rights does not extend into the zone of privacy. By substantive rights, one refers to rights that may be unwritten and vaguely defined but that are protected (e.g., all rights claims for same-sex marriage are substantive due process claims and have been asserted based on the constitutional right to marry, right to privacy, and right to intimate association). Laws have evolved (beginning with common-law marriage protections) in response to legal dilemmas, such as for women abandoned by men after providing them years of carework or who were left destitute upon the death of their long-term opposite-sex partners.

An important goal of family law is to protect adults in long-term relationships of emotional and economic dependence and interdependence as well as their children. This goal is not being achieved for growing numbers of cohabitants and their children around the world, especially in the areas of taxation, immigration, property ownership, survivors' benefits, hospital visitation, and inheritance. In the United States, for example, in the case of Social Security, only "spouses" (as defined by state law) may receive survivors' benefits; cohabitants are not allowed to file joint federal income tax returns, claim a spousal exclusion from federal gift and estate taxation, or claim one another as dependents. Domestic partners have no rights at all in Illinois, Georgia, and Louisiana yet receive nearly the legal equivalent of marriage rights in Oregon, Washington, Maine, Nevada, Maryland, and California. Unlike opposite-sex married couples, who receive more than 1,000 different federally based benefits, many or most of such benefits are not available to cohabitants because federal law does not apply to them. Married same-sex couples do not receive the same federal benefits in most states as married opposite-sex couples. Signed into law by President Bill Clinton in 1996, the Defense of Marriage Act (DOMA) allows states the right not to recognize marriages between same-sex couples performed in other states; it defines the term *marriage* to be between one man and one woman; and it defines the term *spouse* as an opposite-sex wife or husband for federal purposes.

Today, in many nations around the globe, cohabitating couples are creating formal "living together contracts" in which partners state clearly what their rights are should the relationship break down. In short, the more an unwed cohabiting relationship resembles a business contract, the more likely it will be recognized legally, and individual partners will have their rights secured.

There are significant legal consequences for cohabitants with children. This is particularly important in parts of the world where the rate of births to unwed mothers is rising quickly, such as in many parts of Britain where 70 percent of all births are now to unwed mothers. In some countries, cohabitation can mean losing custody of a child after the relationship ends. Custody and visitation rights often focus on biology, which may not be a problem for heterosexual domestic partners, but because the children of same-sex parents are not biologically related to both parents, legally these same-sex parents are generally not treated the same as opposite-sex parents. In most countries, the nonbiological parent in a same-sex couple will be treated as a legal stranger to that child and can be denied visitation and custody rights. Co-parent adoption for same-sex couples is now a legal option in some countries; this can provide some remedy to the problems associated with custody and visitation rights by protecting the rights of both adoptive parents.

See Also: Divorce; Fatherlessness; Marriage; Same-Sex Marriage; Sexual Orientation–Based Legal Discrimination: Outside United States; Sexual Orientation–Based Legal Discrimination: United States; Single Mothers.

Further Readings

Batalova, J. and P. Cohen. "Premarital Cohabitation and Housework: Couples in Cross-National Perspective." *Journal of Marriage and Family*, v.64/3 (2002).

Booth, A. and A. Crouter, eds. *Just Living Together: Implications of Cohabitation on Families, Children and Social Policy.* Mahwah, NJ: Lawrence Erlbaum, 2002.

Bumpass, L. and H. Lu. "Trends in Cohabitation and Implications for Children's Family Contexts in the United States." *Population Studies*, v.54/1 (2000).

McLanahan, Sara. "Family, State, and Child Well-Being." *Annual Review of Sociology*, v.26 (2000).

Shanley, Mary. "Unwed Fathers' Rights, Adoption, and Sex Equality: Gender-Neutrality and the Perpetuation of Patriarchy." *Columbia Law Review*, v.95/1 (1995).

Thaler, Richard and Cass Sunstein. *Nudge: Improving Decisions About Health, Wealth, and Happiness.* New Haven, CT: Yale University Press, 2008.

Wu, Zheng. *Cohabitation: An Alternative Form of Family Living.* Oxford, UK: Oxford University Press, 2000.

Lynn Comerford
California State University, East Bay

Parton, Dolly

Dolly Parton is an American singer-songwriter, musician, actress, author, businesswoman, and philanthropist. She has enjoyed success in each of these areas but remains most closely identified with her country-and-western musical roots. Parton is described as an icon variously for her music, fashion, feminism, and sexuality.

Parton was born on January 19, 1946, the fourth of 12 children. Her family lived in a rustic, one-room cabin in Locust Ridge, Tennessee. As a child, Parton taught herself how to play guitar, began performing on local radio and television shows when she was only 8 years old, and debuted on the *Grand Old Opry* at age 13. The first in her family to graduate high school, Parton immediately left for Nashville to pursue a musical career. There she met her famously reclusive husband, Carl Dean, to whom she has been married since May 30, 1966.

Between 1967 and 1976, Parton appeared on the weekly, syndicated, country-music television program, *The Porter Wagoner Show*. Ultimately, the song she wrote about her professional break with Wagoner, *I Will Always Love You*, became one of her most influential songs. Whitney Houston's 1992 cover of this song for the movie *The Bodyguard* became one of the best-selling singles of all time. Parton's other most recognizable songs include *Joshua*, *Just Because I'm a Woman*, *Coat of Many Colors*, *Jolene*, *Two Doors Down*, and *9 to 5*. Parton has penned more than 3,000 songs, and in 2001 she

Dolly Parton, an American singer–songwriter, musician, actress, author, businesswoman, and philanthropist.

Her "dumb blonde" image emphasizes her physical endowments, glittery costumes, and big blonde wigs. She is never seen publicly without being fully "made up;" often uses her physical appearance in her self-deprecating stage humor; and is known famously for quipping, "It takes a lot of money to look this cheap." Yet, Parton's public persona also conveys a genuineness that relates back to her background as being "dirt poor" and from the Great Smokey Mountains. Her sexuality, ambition, talent, spirituality, generosity, and humor have made her a complex and compelling icon for men and women, heterosexuals and homosexuals, feminists and traditionalists alike.

See Also: Country and Western Music, Women in; Entrepreneurs; Poverty.

Further Readings

Havranek, Carrie, *Women Icons of Popular Music: The Rebels, Rockers, and Renegades.* Westport, CT: Greenwood Press, 2009.

O'Dair, Barbara, ed. *Trouble Girls: The Rolling Stone Book of Women in Rock.* New York: Random House, 1997.

Parton, Dolly. *Dolly: My Life and Other Unfinished Business.* New York: HarperCollins, 1994.

Shannon Stettner
York University

was inducted into the Songwriters Hall of Fame. Her chart success has spanned over four decades, during which she has sold more than 100 million records worldwide. Parton has had 25 number one singles and 41 top 10 country albums.

Parton also has enjoyed considerable success outside of music. She has acted in several films, most notably *9 to 5*, *The Best Little Whorehouse in Texas*, and *Steel Magnolias*. In 1986, she opened the entertainment theme park Dollywood in the Smokey Mountains of Tennessee, which both preserves and honors her heritage. It also employs more than 2,000 residents and sees more than 2 million yearly visitors, earning Parton the title successful businesswoman as well. Parton has many philanthropic ventures, raising money for the American Red Cross, HIV/AIDS charities, and medical centers. Her Dollywood Foundation supports literacy efforts in the United States, Canada, and the United Kingdom.

Parton is often called the "iron butterfly" in a nod to the seemingly contradictory interplay of her ultrafeminine appearance and her business acumen.

Part-Time Work

The International Labour Organization's Part-Time Work Convention of 1994 (No. 175) and the European Union Directive 97/81 of 1997 concerning the Framework Agreement on Part-Time Work concluded by the Union of Industrial and Employers' Confederations of Europe; the Center for Economic and Environmental Partnership, Inc.; and the European Trade Union Confederation have similar contents and define a part-time worker as an employee whose normal hours of work—calculated on a weekly basis or on average over a given period of employment—are less than the normal hours of work of a comparable full-time worker.

The term *comparable full-time worker* means a full-time worker in the same establishment having the same type of employment contract or relationship who is engaged in the same or a similar work or occupation, with due regard being given to other considerations, which may include seniority and qualifications or skills.

The definition of part-time work varies considerably in national laws. Essentially, three main approaches can be distinguished: a classification based on the worker's perception of his or her employment situation; a cutoff (generally 30 or 35 hours per week) based on usual working hours, with persons usually working fewer hours being considered to be part-timers; and a comparable cutoff based on actual hours worked during the reference week.

Part-time work can take special forms, such as job sharing (one full-time job is split into two part-time jobs), work on call (a worker on an "accessibility shift" who is not required to be present at the workplace), progressive retirement (reduced working time for older workers close to retirement age), and parental leave that can be taken on a part-time basis (reduced working hours for parents).

Part-Time Workers

In most industrialized countries, the share of part-time workers as a proportion of total employment has increased by one-quarter to one-half over the last 20 years, although the United States is a notable exception to this trend. However, the incidence of part-time work remains low in most developing countries, as well as in countries in transition. In industrialized countries, the proportion of part-time workers is especially high among women. In many countries, the share of part-time workers is also particularly high in the service sector and among low-skilled employees.

Advantages and Disadvantages of Part-Time Work

Some common advantages that can result from part-time working, for employees, are that part-time work can be an entry point into the labor market for women and it can provide a better balance between work and family life. Recommendation number R(96)5 of the Council of Europe on Reconciling Work and Family Life of 1996 provides that employers be encouraged to develop flexible employment practices enabling their workers, both women and men, to meet the demands of their family responsibilities in the most satisfac-

tory manner possible. Insofar as is possible, account should be taken of the individual circumstances of each worker in relation to their family responsibilities and the needs of the persons dependent on them (e.g., the size of their family; whether they are a single parent; or whether their dependent relatives are ill, elderly, or have a disability).

A flexible and voluntary employment practice widely agreed between employers and workers should include as many as possible of the following options:

- easier access to part-time work for those workers who so wish;
- easier access, where possible, to options for "distance employment" such as telework or homework for those workers who so wish;
- the possibility for workers to vary their working hours and the organization of their working time, while retaining the possibility of reverting to their original hours;
- leave arrangements to care for family members who are ill or who have a disability;
- acting as an entry point into the labor market for young people;
- acting as an entry point into the labor market for disabled people; and
- providing the potential for job creation.

However, part-time work can entail several disadvantages for employees. First, there is the potential for gender discrimination. Part-time work can reinforce traditional family roles and offer poorer terms and conditions of work to women. Part-time work also has adverse effects on career development for women. Second, part-time work offers lower incomes because of its shorter hours and lower hourly wages than earned by comparable full-time workers. Third, lower social security benefits and limited career progression and training opportunities are available to part-time workers. Fourth, there is the potential for work intensification (i.e., working part-time hours with a full-time workload). Finally, there is the potential for irregular working hours.

International and European Instruments on Part-Time Work

The International Labour Organization Part-Time Work Convention grants to part-time workers the "same protection as that accorded to comparable full-time workers" in relation to a number of rights. It also states that measures shall be taken to ensure the equal treatment of part-time and comparable full-time workers, particularly regarding discrimination in employment and occupation; hourly basic wage rates; maternity leave, termination of employment, paid annual leave and paid public holidays, and sick leave; participation at the workplace; occupational safety and health; statutory social security schemes; and the right to organize, the right to bargain collectively, and the right to act as workers' representatives.

The convention provides that measures shall be taken to facilitate access to productive and freely chosen part-time work that meets the needs of both employers and workers. These measures shall include, inter alia, special attention in employment policies to the needs and preferences of specific groups, such as the unemployed, workers with family responsibilities, older workers, workers with disabilities, and workers undergoing education or training.

The purpose of the European Union Part-Time Directive is to provide for the removal of discrimination against part-time workers, to improve the quality of part-time work, to facilitate the development of part-time work on a voluntary basis, and to contribute to the flexible organization of working time in a manner that takes into account the needs of both employers and workers.

According to the directive, employers should give consideration to workers' requests to shift from full-time to part-time work and vice versa.

In the European Union, it has also been established that discrimination against part-time workers may constitute indirect discrimination against women because nationally, and in most organizations, the majority of part-time workers are women. Indirect sex discrimination can occur when a requirement or condition is applied equally to men and women, but the proportion of one sex that can satisfy the condition is much smaller than the proportion of the other sex. Unless it can be shown that the condition is essential for the job, indirect discrimination may have taken place.

The directive also stipulates that there can be no discrimination "solely because they [the workers] work part time, unless different treatment is justified on objective grounds." To determine whether there is discrimination against part-time workers, a comparator, or standard, against which such an evaluation can be made is required.

The main principles of the directive have been integrated into national laws across Europe.

See Also: Childcare; Discrimination; Parental Leave; Working Mothers; Work/Life Balance.

Further Readings

Booth, A. L. and J. C. van Ours. "Part-Time Jobs: What Women Want?" Discussion Paper 2010–05. Tilburg University, Center for Economic Research, 2010. http://arno.uvt.nl/show.cgi?fid=97350 (accessed March 2010).

International Labour Organization. "Part-Time Work, Conditions of Work and Employment Programme." http://www.ilo.org/public/english/protection/condtrav/pdf/infosheets/wt-4.pdf (accessed March 2010).

Maxwell, P. "Discrimination Against Part-Time Workers." *Web Journal of Current Legal Issues,* 1995. http://web jcli.ncl.ac.uk/articles1/maxwell1.rtf (accessed March 2010).

Murray, J. "Social Justice for Women? The ILO's Convention on Part-Time Work CELRL Working Paper No. 15." http://celrl.law.unimelb.edu.au/assets/Working%20Papers/celrl-wp15.pdf (accessed July 2010).

Sciarra, S., et al., eds. *Employment Policy and the Regulation of Part-Time Work in the European Union: A Comparative Analysis.* Cambridge, UK: Cambridge University Press, 2004.

Kadriye Bakirci
Istanbul Technical University

Patrick, Danica

Danica Patrick is a famed auto racing driver who has gained tremendous notoriety for both her driving prowess and media presence. Her racing exploits include being a top star in the IndyCar Series and, more recently, her emergence in the world of stock car racing. Beyond auto racing, Patrick has amassed a great deal of attention for her diversified talents, including modeling, product endorsement, and media appearances.

Patrick has evolved into a national celebrity in recent years, with her fame extending beyond the United States. She has participated in IndyCar racing since 2005, and her racing credentials include being selected as the Rookie of the Year for both the 2005 IndyCar Series season and 2005 Indianapolis 500, placing third in the 2009 Indianapolis 500, being the first woman to win an IndyCar race (the 2008 Indy Japan 300), and being a multiple-time selection as IndyCar's most popular driver.

Patrick currently drives in both the IndyCar Series and the National Association for Stock Car Auto Racing (NASCAR) Nationwide Series, the latter of which she began in 2010. Entering the world of stock car racing marked a new phase of the Danica Patrick brand. She embarked in a joint venture as driver of the #7 GoDaddy.com Chevrolet Impala, a part-time juncture with JR Motorsports, which is owned in part by Dale Earnhardt Jr. Her entrance into NASCAR and the Nationwide Series, including the association with NASCAR poster boy Dale Jr., will increase her visibility.

Patrick is not the first or only woman to participate in the high-stakes world of auto racing. Women drivers have preceded Patrick in both IndyCar and NASCAR racing, and there are others waiting in the wings to see whether they can amass widespread success. Though the precedent has been set, the widespread crossover attention that Patrick has received is unparalleled for a woman race car driver.

Patrick has a multifaceted image. Based on speed, beauty, fashion, and style, the Patrick brand thrives in multiple media venues. Whether it is through the stylistic presentation of her personal Website, appearing on GoDaddy.com commercials at halftime during the Super Bowl, serving as a model in the *Sports Illustrated Swimsuit Issue*, winning a Nickelodeon Kid's Choice Award, or guest starring on *CSI: Miami*, Patrick has proven to be a highly visible crossover star. Being associated with famed management group IMG, Patrick is positioned to continue as a dominant force in the world of product endorsement and other media ventures. With sponsors such as Tissot watches, PEAK Antifreeze, Hot Wheels, and GoDaddy.com, Patrick has proven to be one of the premiere product endorsers today.

Although Patrick is a highly successful crossover star, she is not without her share of critics. Critics have said that Patrick is more style than substance and guilty of using her looks to get ahead, and doubts have been expressed regarding her ability to compete in a "man's world," to name but a few critiques. Though she is not without her critics and naysayers, Patrick is a remarkable sport personality who has been positioned among the most visible and popular sport stars internationally. She has brought great attention to the IndyCar Series and has more recently provided a shot of added exposure to NASCAR. It will be interesting to see how Patrick uses her celebrity power and what the ramifications of such actions will produce.

See Also: Auto Racing, Formula One; Auto Racing, NASCAR; Celebrity Women; Sports, Women in.

Further Readings

Danicaracing.com. "Danica." http://www.danicaracing .com/main.html (accessed July 2010).

Newton, D. "Patrick Signs With JR Motorsports." http:// sports.espn.go.com/rpm/nascar/nationwide/news/ story?id=4725025 (accessed July 2010).

Smith, M. "Danica + Junior = Opportunities." *Street & Smith's SportsBusiness Journal.* http://www.sports bus inessjournal.com/article/64342 (accessed July 2010).

Smith, M. "Danica Patrick Signs With IMG." *Street & Smith's SportsBusiness Journal.* http://www.sports businessjournal.com/article/61403 (accessed July 2010).

Smith, M. "Patrick Makes the Most out of Making History." *Street & Smith's SportsBusiness Journal.* http:// www.sportsbusinessjournal.com/article/58836 (accessed July 2010).

Jason W. Lee
University of North Florida
Elizabeth A. Gregg
Jacksonville University

Peace Movement

Peace movement is a general term commonly used to describe any social movement that seeks to end warfare and promote world peace, both on a domestic and on a global scale. Peace movement activists work to raise awareness about social injustices as well as advocate against practices such as war, racial discrimination, and violence. These movements often stand out from specific "antiwar movements" because their objectives often tend to be global and longer term rather than targeted at a specific armed conflict. Peace movement activists often articulate their purpose in terms of social transformations, such as those found in the civil rights and women's movements, rather than in terms of personal development common to self-help transformational movements. In the academic world, peace study scholars focus on a number of central issues, including how individuals act collectively to end war and how private citizens affect government peace policies.

Women and Peace Activism

Women are specifically affected by warfare due to their particular experiences of rape and forced impregnation for the purposes of ethnic cleansing, sex trafficking, and systematic violence against children and families. Given their potential roles as both victims and active agents, women occupy a unique position in peace movements and peacekeeping initiatives. On the one hand, they are perceived as victims and thus too vulnerable to directly participate in formal peacekeeping efforts. On the other hand, given their idiosyncratic experiences of war, women can be seen as powerful members of peace-building movements and energetic advocates for women's rights during conflict and subsequent postconflict rebuilding efforts.

In a process known as movement spillover, peace movement leaders often share tactics and ideologies with feminist activists, including acts such as staging peace camps at military bases, raising awareness about the connection between militarism and patriarchy, and acting as key contributors to international policy.

In the last decade, women's involvement in peace activism has risen sharply, both formally with the United Nations (UN) and in grassroots organizations. These contributions have greatly increased awareness of gendered violence in conflict-afflicted societies. Although many groups have similar goals, peace movement activism can take different forms. Today, women's activism combines both new and traditional forms, from grassroots groups in Nepal and Somalia, participation in political institutions in Kabul and Kigali, and in more traditional forms of activism such as providing services to the sick and elderly, and ensuring the survival of the family unit.

United Nations Initiatives

In 1995, the UN sponsored the Fourth World Conference on Women in Beijing, China. The conference was the catalyst for a more globally conscious discussion of women's experience in war and women's activism for peace. Conference delegates drafted Chapter E (Women and Armed Conflict) of the Platform for Action, which called for an increased presence of women in peace-building projects. Delegates who worked on this project brought together women from Israel and Palestine, survivors of the Rwandan genocide and the Bosnian war, and South African peace activists.

In 2000, a groundbreaking study was launched to investigate women's roles and gender bias in global peacekeeping efforts. UN Special Advisor to the Secretary -General on Gender Issues and the Advancement of Women Angela King spearheaded an investigative report titled "Mainstreaming a Gender Perspective in Multi-Dimensional Peace Support Operations." Concentrating on previous missions in Namibia and South Africa, the project's purpose was to define and locate areas where women were specifically discriminated against in peacekeeping efforts and to recommend improvements to the procedures of the UN's Peace Operation units. Suggestions centered on the practice of gender mainstreaming, which refers to a specific initiative emphasizing women's roles in peacekeeping missions, as well as support for the equal participation of women in the expansion of peacekeeping actions around the world. Study results were finalized in the Windhoek Declaration and the Namibia Plan of Action, which were presented at the fifth anniversary review conference called the "Beijing +5 Council." The Beijing +5 Council was held in 2000 and aimed to formally recognize women's participation in peacekeeping efforts and enhance their protection in war zones.

As a result of the Windhoek Declaration, the UN Security Council recognized Resolution 1325 in 2000. This groundbreaking resolution declared the inextricable link between women's rights, gender equality, and the desire for an increased presence of women in all peacekeeping operations. Council members acknowledged that women were to be involved equally in all efforts to maintain peace and to end conflicts globally. Resolution 1325 is the result of years of work that began with Eleanor Roosevelt and her tireless efforts to include gender equality in the

Charter of Rights and Freedoms. When the first UN Assembly was held in 1946, Roosevelt participated on the Security Council and worked to declare freedom of equality for every human being regardless of sex, race, or creed. Although the protection of women specifically from sexual violence was already part of the UN Security Council's mandate, Resolution 1325 legally bound participating countries to enact these goals, support women's nongovernmental organizations (NGOs), and increase the number of women in leadership peacekeeping roles around the world.

In 2000, the UN declared an "International Year for the Culture of Peace." The plan was initiated by the UN Educational, Scientific and Cultural Organization (UNESCO) and all of the Nobel Peace laureates. The declaration was a bold initiative to create cultures of peace and nonviolence and to promote a viable alternative to violence against women, discrimination and exploitation of all individuals, and war education programs. The grander objectives of this declaration included creating a vision of the future where all individuals would collectively establish a peaceful global culture. During the 2005 annual UN Commission on the Status of Women, 1,000 women peacekeepers were honored as part of the Nobel Peace Prize Initiative and the 1,000 Women Peace Activists campaign.

Notable Peace Activists

Cora Weiss currently presides at the Hague Appeal for Peace. She is an ardent peace supporter, notably active in the anti–Vietnam War movement and a cofounder of Women Strike for Peace (WSP) in the early 1960s, which fought to end the testing of nuclear weapons. From 2000 to 2006, she served as president of the International Peace Bureau, an organization that was awarded the Nobel Peace Prize in 1910. She also serves as joint-principal of the Peace Boat's Global University and sits on the advisory board of the Peace Child International's Millennium Action Fund.

Aung San Suu Kyi is a loyal advocate of Burma's National League for Democracy (NLD), and her efforts to promote peace, democracy, and human rights are recognized globally despite violent retaliation from Burma's (Myanmar's) State Peace and Development Council (SPDC). She was awarded the Sakharov Prize from the European Parliament in 1990, the Nobel Peace Prize in 1991, the United States Presidential Medal of Freedom in 2000, and the Con-

gressional Gold Medal in 2008. Since 1990, she has repeatedly been held under house arrest in Myanmar for her involvement with the NLD. In 2009, Aung San Suu Kyi's continued detention and intrusive monitoring by the SPDC were declared unlawful according to the international legal standards set by the UN Working Group on Arbitrary Detention.

Jody Williams, jointly with the International Campaign to Ban Landmines (ICBL), was awarded the Nobel Peace Prize in 1997 for her efforts. Williams founded the ICBL in 1992 with the goal of implementing a global ban on the creation, stockpiling, and use of landmines. Along with Wangari Maathai and other Nobel laureates, Williams created the Nobel Women's Initiative as a means of using their activist experiences and public visibility to recognize and promote the particular contributions of women peacemakers and to raise global awareness of gendered experiences of violence. Specifically, the Nobel Women's Initiative hopes to determine the root causes of women's experiences of violence during war, to advance women's rights, and to promote peace on the global stage. Williams also remains an ambassador of the ICBL.

Wangari Muta Maathai was awarded the Nobel Peace Prize in 2004 for her efforts with the Green Belt Movement (GBM), a nonprofit NGO based in Kenya. Maathai and GBM work with Kenyans to develop environmentally sound farming by promoting awareness of sustainable practices, self-sufficiency, and community solidarity. Maathai and GBM members supervise numerous projects, including tree planting and sustainable farming education programs and promote indigenous food planting.

See Also: Conflict Zones; Maathai, Wangari; Pacifism, Female; Social Justice Activism; United Nations Conferences on Women; Women's International League for Peace and Freedom.

Further Readings

Anderlini, Sanam Naraghi. *Women Building Peace: What They Do, Why It Matters.* Boulder, CO: Lynne Rienner Publishers, 2007.

Association of 1,000 Women for the Nobel Peace Prize 2005. *1,000 Peace Women Across the Globe.* Zurich: Scalo, 2005.

The Laureates. http://www.nobelwomensinitiative.org /about-us/laureates (accessed June 2010).

Meyer, David S. and Sidney Tarrow, eds. *The Social Movement Society: Contentious Politics for a New Century.* Lanham, MD: Rowman and Littlefield, 1998.

Olsson, Louise and Torunn L. Tryggestad, eds. *Women and International Peacekeeping.* Portland, OR: Frank Cass Publishers, 2001.

Adriane Bilous
Fordham University

Pedophilia Online

Pedophilia online is a misnomer, because pedophilia is often a thought not an action. The American Psychiatric Association defines pedophilia as recurrent, sexually arousing thoughts or fantasies, urges, or behavior that last at least six months and involve sexual activity with a child under the age of 13. It is crucial to understand that all individuals who prey on children online are not pedophiles, just as all pedophiles do not commit sexual crimes against children.

The Internet can still be a dangerous place that provides an opportunity for adults to exploit or victimize children. Three types of danger exist: children are solicited online to meet in person for sexual encounters, minors obtain access to pornographic Websites, and children are exploited for their depiction in child pornography. Although child sexual abuse and pornography have existed throughout history, the advent of the Internet added the extra danger from anonymity.

Legislation to Protect Minors

This is apparent in the extent of recent legislation aimed at protecting children from online predators and pornography. As early as 1988, the U.S. Congress made it illegal to possess, sell, or distribute child pornography over the Internet, and in 1996 the Telecommunications Act prohibited the use of pornographic images sent over the Internet to engage children in sexually explicit conversation or behavior. Despite legislation, the sexual exploitation of children over the Internet is still a problem today. It has become increasingly difficult to police child pornography Websites, primary due to multijurisdictional issues. Many of these sites or hosts are located outside the jurisdiction of the United States, where different laws apply to child pornography. As such, there are millions of images of children uploaded to the Internet, with an estimated 200 million new images being uploaded daily. It has become a big business endeavor with instant availability, anonymous and private access, and the ability to access different formats (including live Webcam videos) for different interests.

Users of child pornography are not usually involved in hands-on child sexual abuse or solicitation of minors for sexual encounters. Still, the Internet is often used as a facilitator for other forms of illegal activities directed at young children. These acts may include cyber-stalking, using the Internet to seek out victims or to solicit a child for sexual purposes, encouraging sex trafficking, and promoting child sex tourism. The most well known would be solicitation of a child for sexual purposes, and many prominent figures have been arrested and charged for this type of behavior. Often, the sex sting operations and subsequent arrests are televised via the MSNBC series *To Catch a Predator.* Typically, the sting operation involves a police officer entering an Internet chat room, pretending to be an underage child. Eventually, the "child" and an adult begin communicating and may continue to do so for varied periods of time. When the two agree to meet in person, the adult is arrested for soliciting a minor.

Legislation and law enforcement tactics to reduce and prevent these crimes are well intended and are applauded by many; however, they are often based on misinformation and distorted truths about online solicitation. For instance, research suggests that the majority of online solicitations do not involve adults and that despite popular belief adult solicitation of minors is a relatively rare occurrence. That said, when it does occur, most adult-child conversations online involve nothing more than what children hear or discuss with their peers. In addition, when minors were aggressively solicited, more often than not the offender was also a minor. Nevertheless, adult solicitation of minors for sexual behavior causes harm to the child. Although Internet sex stings are well intended, the best prevention measure is to educate parents about the potential dangers of the Internet.

See Also: Adolescence; Crime Victims, Female; Megan's Law; Pornography/Erotica; Rape, Incidence of; Sex Offenders, Male.

Further Readings

Finkelhor, D., K. J. Mitchell, and J. Wolak. "Online Victimization: A Report on the Nation's Youth." Crimes Against Children Research Center. Washington, DC: National Center for Missing and Exploited Children, 2000. http://www.missingkids.com/en_US/pub lications/NC62.pdf (accessed October 2010).

Terry, K. *Sexual Offenses and Offenders: Theory, Policy, and Practice.* Belmont, CA: Wadsworth, 2006.

Wright, R. "Internet Sex Stings." *Sex Offender Laws: Failed Policies, New Directions.* Richard Wright, ed. New York: Springer, 2009

Alissa R. Ackerman
University of California

Pelosi, Nancy

Nancy Patricia D'Alesandro Pelosi (Democrat, California) was the first woman in U.S. history to be elected to top party leadership positions in the U.S. Congress. A member of the House of Representatives since 1987 from the 8th District in San Francisco, she was elected House minority whip in 2002, House minority leader in 2003, and Speaker of the House in 2007. As of this writing, no woman has ascended to any other top-tier leadership positions in either party in the U.S. House of Representatives or the U.S. Senate.

Pelosi was born on March 26, 1940, in Baltimore, Maryland, to a political family. Her father served in the U.S. House of Representatives and as Mayor of Baltimore; her brother also served in the latter position. In 1969, Pelosi and her husband Paul settled in San Francisco. As the mother of five children, Pelosi focused primarily on raising her family and volunteering in Democratic politics. After many years of service, she was elected chair of the California Democratic Party in 1981. In 1987, Pelosi's friend and congressional representative, Sala Burton, died shortly after winning reelection to her House seat. Before her passing, Burton persuaded Pelosi to run for the seat. Pelosi agreed, won a special election, and assumed office in June 1987. She has been reelected handily ever since. During her years in the House, Pelosi has served on several committees including the Intelligence Committee and the powerful Appropriations Committee.

Nancy Pelosi was the first woman in U.S. history to be elected Speaker of the House of Representatives, in 2007.

Pelosi's voting record in the House is considered generally to be liberal. She has supported the Fair Minimum Wage Act of 2007, human rights in China, energy conservation and renewable energy, women's rights, gay/lesbian/bisexual/transgender (GLBT) rights, and abortion rights. Her opposition votes have included authorization for the Iraq War, the Secure Fence Act of 2006, the Defense of Marriage Act, and welfare reform in both the Clinton and Bush administrations. However, Pelosi also supported the USA Patriot Act of 2001, the No Child Left Behind Act, and the bank and auto industry bailouts of 2009.

In 2007, Pelosi ascended to the Speakership on the strength of her record as a leading fund-raiser and party strategist. This position made her second in the line of presidential succession and the most powerful elected woman in U.S. political history. In her first speech as Speaker, Pelosi acknowledged the significance of her ascension: as quoted in her book, cited below, she noted: "This is a historic moment— for the Congress, and for the women of this country. It is a moment for which we have waited more than 200 years." Pelosi considered her rise as having shattered the "marble ceiling" after which anything would be possible.

See Also: Government, Women in; Political Ideologies; United States; Working Mothers.

Further Readings

Bzdek, Vincent. *Women of the House: The Rise of Nancy Pelosi.* New York: Palgrave MacMillan. 2008.

Pelosi, Nancy with Amy Hill Hearth. *Know Your Power: A Message to America's Daughters.* New York: Doubleday. 2008.

Sue Thomas
Pacific Institute for Research and Evaluation

Perpetrators, Female

Historically, the reasons why females commit crimes and what female offenders need have been overlooked in the criminal justice and criminological literatures. In fact, female offenders are often referred to in the academic literature as "invisible women" or the "forgotten offenders" because academia has been focused on understanding male offending patterns. The feminist movement in the 1970s brought a renewed interest in issues impacting females in society, including female offenders. Over the past several decades, female offenders have received increased attention from researchers in the criminal justice and criminological literatures. This article devotes discussion to a description of female perpetrators in the United States and internationally, the types of crimes female perpetrators commit, risk factors for female criminality, and policy implications for female perpetrators of crime.

Description of Female Perpetrators Cross-Culturally

In the United States, according to the Uniform Crime Reports (2008), adult females accounted for approximately 1.9 million arrests for index crimes (e.g., murder, rape, robbery, burglary, sexual assault, larceny-theft, arson, and motor vehicle theft). Compared to males, the arrest rate is substantially lower, as adult males experienced approximately 6 million arrests for index crimes. Specifically, females were arrested for approximately 25 percent of index crimes, and males were arrested for approximately 75 percent of index crimes. The Uniform Crime Reports (2008) state that arrest trends for adult females has increased (i.e., 11.6 percent) since 1999; however, the arrest trends for juvenile females has decreased (i.e., 7.8 percent) since 1999. In terms of race, the Uniform Crime Reports (2008) indicate that 69.2 percent of those arrested were white, 28.3 percent were black, and the remaining 2.4 percent were other races (i.e., American Indian/Alaskan Native or Asian/Pacific Islander).

It is important to note that while Caucasian offenders were arrested more, a disproportionate numbers of African Americans were arrested given their population numbers in the United States. According to the U.S. Census Bureau (2007), African Americans represent approximately 13 percent of the total U.S. population. Thus, with 28.3 percent of all arrests attributed to African Americans in 2008, their arrest rate is not proportionate with their population numbers. However, findings from self-report criminal surveys do not support the official statistics. Results of self-report criminal surveys reveal that Caucasians and African Americans report similar levels of involvement in criminality regardless of gender.

In regard to age, the majority of those arrested in 2008 were overage. However, researchers have long identified an age-crime curve, wherein those who commit crimes are more likely to be between the ages of 16 and 24. The relationship between age and crime is consistent for both genders.

Female perpetrators of crime are more likely to commit property crimes as opposed to violent crimess. Females are more likely to be involved in robbery, burglary, and larceny-theft crimes. When females do commit a violent crime, it is usually directed at a relative or an intimate. Females are also likely to engage in drug offenses. More often than not, females are not the sellers of drugs but rather the "mules" or carrier of drugs for a boyfriend or spouse. Additionally, a female's use of illegal drugs often contributes to her arrest.

Similar to the United States, the Ministry of Justice (2010) reports that in the United Kingdom (UK), females were less likely to be arrested for committing crimes than males. However, between the ages of 10 and 17, juvenile females were more likely to be arrested (25.7 percent vs. 20.5 percent, respectively). Moreover, those arrested in the UK are more likely to be members of a minority group. Results from the Offending, Crime, and Justice self-report survey (2008) conducted in the UK reveal that females are less likely to self-report involvement in crime than are males. When females did commit crimes, they self-reported far fewer serious offenses than males. Additionally, results from the survey revealed that the average peak age of offending for females was 14 through 17 and that minorities did not self-report more criminal involvement than their Caucasian counterparts.

The Australian Institute of Criminology (2009) reports that males were responsible for most criminal activity, and females comprised approximately 23 percent of all offenders in 2007–08. For those females committing crimes, they were more likely to commit theft crimes as opposed to violent crimes such as homicide. Additionally, females had the most involvement in crime in the age range of 15 through 19. Thus, female offenders in Australia are similar in nature to their U.S. counterparts.

It is difficult to determine if the characteristics of female offenders are similar for all female offenders around the world. One reason for this difficulty is the inconsistent crime statistic data collection, particularly in Third World countries; this has resulted in researchers' providing estimates of female offenders. For example, while the Ministry of Home Affairs (2007) publishes data on crime statistics in India, it does not report these offenses by gender or race for all crime categories. In Russia, females are less likely to commit violent crimes such as homicide.

Risk Factors for Female Criminality

Historically, early criminologists from the late 19th through the mid-20th centuries attributed female criminality to their biology—that is, these criminals were born this way. Cesare Lombroso (1920) posited that females who committed crimes were masculine and exhibited an excess of male characteristics (e.g., excess body hair, moles, broad shoulders). Pollak (1950) claimed that female offenders were deceitful and were able to hide their crimes so well due to their biological makeup. In the United States, it was not until the 1970s that there was a renewed interest in understanding female criminality. The feminist

movement spurred budding female criminologists to examine female offenders around the world. The renewed interest in understanding female criminality has led to a departure from biological explanations for female criminality; instead, other risk factors have been identified as contributing to this behavior.

Since the departure from examining biology as the sole contributor to female criminality, researchers have been able to identify multiple risk factors for female offending patterns. In the Unites States, both physical abuse and sexual abuse have been linked to onset of female criminality. Overwhelmingly, female offenders report two to three times higher rates of sexual abuse than in the general population. Researchers have consistently identified prior sexual abuse as a risk factor for female criminality. Oftentimes, the offenders are sexually victimized by a male family member (e.g., father, stepfather, uncle, or brother) and, thus, the females run away from home and turn to the streets for survival. In order to survive, females will turn to prostitution to gain income.

Given their involvement in prostitution, females will often use drugs and/or alcohol as a way to numb previous abuse and to numb their feelings about being involved in prostitution. If females are not involved in prostitution, they may become involved in the drug trade as a method to gain income. Their entry into the drug trade often leads to drug addiction or further addiction if they were not involved in the drug trade previously.

For instance, Covington and Kohen (1984), in an examination of addicted and nonaddicted women, found that 74 percent of addicted women reported prior sexual abuse, compared to 50 percent of non-addicted women. Risk factors for female offenders in Australia and the UK include experiencing violence in the home as a child and drug addiction. Besides prior sexual abuse and addiction, other risk factors for entry into female criminality include association with delinquent peers. Edwin Sutherland (1947) asserts that those who associate with other delinquents will be more likely to engage in delinquent acts. Research has found empirical support for this assertion for female offenders in the United States. The association with antisocial others has been found to be a risk factor for female offenders in other countries such as the UK. Other risk factors for female offending in the United States include poor socialization by parents, biology, gender inequality, poverty, and low self-control. For females in other countries, risk factors for entry into offending include poverty, inequality, and marginalization.

Policy Implications

With the increased attention given to female perpetrators of crime by criminologists, it is important that researchers provide gender-specific policy recommendations to those in the criminal justice system to assist female offenders. While some researchers have claimed that rehabilitation does not work, a wealth of empirical research has indicated that rehabilitation can indeed be useful in reducing recidivism rates. Additionally, female offenders have needs (i.e., mental, physical) that are different from male offenders and correctional programming should reflect that.

Clearly, prior sexual abuse is a risk factor for onset and persistence in criminality for females in several countries. Thus, programming in jails and prisons should adopt specialized programs to assist female offenders in coping with their trauma. By healing wounds, female offenders may more successfully reintegrate into their communities upon release. Additionally, many female perpetrators of crime have drug and/or alcohol addictions. Thus, correctional programming should continue to offer female offenders drug and/or alcohol treatment programs. Finally, for some female perpetrators of crime around the world, marginalization and inequality are the root causes of their involvement in crime. Thus, any macro-level policy that reduces the inequality and marginalization of these women may reduce their involvement in crime.

See Also: Prisoners, Female; Sex Offenders, Female; United Kingdom; United States.

Further Readings

Chesney-Lind, M. *The Female Offender: Girls, Women, and Crime.* Thousand Oaks, CA: Sage, 1997.

Gibson, M. *Born to Crime: Cesare Lombroso and the Origins of Biological Criminology.* Westport, CT: Praeger, 2002.

Pollak, O. *The Criminality of Women.* Philadelphia: University of Pennsylvania Press, 1950.

Elaine Gunnison
Independent Scholar

Peru

Women make up approximately half of Peru's 29 million inhabitants. Although they hold a variety of roles within contemporary society, their rates of literacy, economic activity, formal schooling, and government positions continue to be lower than those of men.

Life expectancy is 72 years for women compared with 67 years for men. Over half of Peruvians are poor, and nearly a quarter are extremely poor. Peruvian women experience varying access to resources depending on region of residence, urban versus rural location, language, and race. Although just over one-third of the country's population lives in rural settings, the population in rural settings makes up almost 60 percent of those living in poverty. Women in rural areas have higher fertility and maternal mortality rates. Leading causes of maternal mortality include hemorrhage, toxemia, and complications related to abortion. Differences in maternal mortality rates are partly the result of the concentration of resources in urban areas and to the marginalization of rural areas, where the population is made up mostly of indigenous people.

The contraceptive prevalence rate among married women aged 15–49 years is 48 percent for modern methods and 71 percent for all methods. In 2008, women had an average of 2.4 children. The dominant religion in the country is Catholicism, and abortion is illegal except in cases in which it is necessary to preserve the life or health of the woman.

Over the last two decades, the government designed policies to address maternal and infant healthcare, as well as reproductive health. The National Program of Reproductive Health and Family Planning 1996–2000 made sterilization and reproductive health education free to all Peruvians. However, within two years of the program's implementation, over 200 cases of forced or coerced sterilization of mainly poor indigenous women had been documented. In 2001, the National Family Planning Program underwent reorganization, and family planning and reproductive health lost priority and funding.

Primary education is mandated for all Peruvians, and public schools are free, yet in practice, not all Peruvians have equal access to education. Women continue to receive less formal schooling than men, and women in rural areas have less access to schooling than women in urban areas. Peru's two official languages are Spanish and Quechua—the most widely spoken indigenous language in the Andes—yet in practice, access to bilingual education is not guaranteed, and Spanish continues to be the dominant language within the education system. In addition to Quechua, there are several dozen other indigenous languages spoken across Peru, especially in the Amazon.

Peru ratified the Convention on the Elimination of All Forms of Discrimination Against Women (CEDAW) in 1982 and the regional Convention of Belém do Pará in 1996, thereby formally recognizing violence against women as a form of discrimination and as a human rights issue. In 1993, Peru became the first Latin American country to pass laws specifically on domestic violence. As a result of modifications in 1997, 1998, 2000, and 2003, the Family Violence Law includes physical, psychological, and sexual violence as forms of domestic violence, regardless of an individual's class, race, or gender. Women can file complaints in the family violence sections of regular police stations, specialized women's police stations, Women's Emergency Centers, and the public prosecutor's office.

In 1988, Peru established women's police stations to focus on women's complaints of violence. Women police officers constitute 15 percent of the entire police force, but women's police stations are staffed exclusively by women officers. In 2009, the police announced that Lima's notoriously hectic and dangerous traffic would be directed exclusively by women police officers. It was widely publicized that the rationale behind the decision was the belief that women officers are less corruptible and more disciplined than men.

See Also: Convention on the Elimination of All Forms of Discrimination Against Women; Law Enforcement, Women in; Poverty.

Further Readings

Amnesty International. "Peru: Denial of the Right to Maternal and Child Health." Washington, DC: Amnesty International, 2007.

Physicians for Human Rights. "Deadly Delays: Maternal Mortality in Peru." http://physiciansforhumanrights .org/library/documents/reports/maternal-mortality -in-peru.pdf (accessed June 2010).

M. Cristina Alcalde
University of Kentucky

Philanthropists, Female

Philanthropy is giving for a purpose, an outcome, a change, or a social cause. Philanthropy occurs through contributions of time, volunteer efforts, or wealth. Women philanthropists give their personal earnings, inheritances, marital wealth, or family assets. Philanthropy is part of the third sector. The third sector includes nonprofit organizations and volunteer organizations. The other sectors are the public sector and the private sector.

Examples of prominent U.S. women philanthropists include Oprah Winfrey, Joan Kroc, Teresa Heinz, Marian Wright Edelman, and Catherine S. Muther. Winfrey is cited by *Forbes* magazine as one of the seven most influential individuals in the world based on her influence on people through her prominence on television and through her initiatives, her extensive financial resources, and her powerful presence in many spheres.

The Angel Network is one example of her philanthropic efforts. Winfrey's focus is on women, children, and families with an emphasis on empowerment. According to *Forbes*, she is the first African American woman billionaire.

Kroc, widow of Ray Kroc, founder of McDonald's, used her philanthropic contributions in the promotion of peace initiatives. Peace institutes at the University of Notre Dame and the University of San Diego were established with these funds. She also contributed to National Public Radio, the Salvation Army, animal welfare, the homeless, and children's charities. Kroc's contributions were given "quietly."

Heinz is the head of the Heinz Family Philanthropies and chair of the Heinz Family Foundation's Women's Institute for Secure Retirement. Edelman established the Children's Defense Fund in 1973. This children's advocacy organization is a private nonprofit funded by foundations, corporate grants, and individual donations.

Muther, former Cisco System senior marketing officer, founded the Three Guineas Fund in 1994. The fund combines philanthropy and entrepreneurship with a focus on social change, girls, and equity. The fund makes grants focused on innovative ideas, social change, teamwork, and results.

The first women's fund, the Ms. Foundation, was created in 1973 to support the empowerment of women and girls in the United States. According to its history, the foundation was established to deliver funding and other strategic resources to organizations that were elevating women's voices and solutions across race and class in communities nationwide.

The Center on Philanthropy at Indiana University includes academic and research initiatives as well as a fund raising school and the Women's Philanthropy Institute. The Center's Website notes the focus on increasing understanding of philanthropy and improving its practice.

Philanthropic Groups Worldwide

Women's philanthropy and philanthropic groups are accompanied by terms such as collaboration, teamwork, and sharing in their descriptions. The emphasis on outcomes, goals, social change, and social causes is evident in the descriptions as well.

Women may give anonymously to avoid publicity. When gifts are given quietly or secretly, accurate public information about the contributions is unavailable.

Women's giving may be stimulated by personal involvement with a social cause or organization. The personal involvement may then result in the contribution of wealth to the cause or organization. The giving may be directed at a specific desired outcome.

The number of philanthropic groups, institutes, and organizations reveals the extent of women's philanthropy and wealth. Based on its Website, the Women's Funding Network is described as more than 155 organizations that fund women's solutions across the globe.

See Also: Social Justice Activism; Winfrey, Oprah; Women's Funding Network.

Further Readings

Center for the Study of Philanthropy, The Graduate Center, City University of New York. http://www .philanthropy.org (accessed July 2010).

Kroc Institute for International Peace Studies. http://kroc .nd.edu (accessed July 2010).

Ms. Foundation for Women. http://ms.foundation.org (accessed July 2010).

Shaw-Hardy, Sondra C., Martha A. Taylor, and Buffy Beaudoin-Schwartz. *Women and Philanthropy: Boldly Shaping a Better World.* Hoboken, NJ: Jossey-Bass, September 2010.

Women's Donor Network. http://www.womendonors.org (accessed July 2010).

Marilyn L. Grady
University of Nebraska–Lincoln

Philippines

The 1987 Philippine Constitution provides that "[the State] shall ensure the fundamental equality before the law of women and men." This supported the passing of a number of laws to ensure gender equality and the elimination of discrimination against women, as well as the ratification of international human rights treaties, including the Convention on the Elimination of All Forms of Discrimination Against Women (CEDAW) and other covenants.

The nation's population is estimated at 92.23 million people, with women comprising 49.72 percent. The fertility rate is 3.5 children per woman, and although declining, this rate is relatively high compared with other Southeast Asian countries. There are 172 maternal deaths to live births, with 56.5 percent of babies delivered at home. More than half of all pregnancies in the Philippines are unintended due to low use of contraception methods. Just over half, 50.6 percent, of childbearing women are using a family-planning method, and only 35.9 percent are using modern methods. The Catholic hierarchy exerts great power over the political debate concerning reproductive rights. Abortion is forbidden and punished by law. Abortion complications are common or increasing, including deaths from unsafe abortions due to the legal restrictions. Some municipalities, like Manila, have issued executive orders banning city health centers and hospitals from providing contraception.

There is no marked difference in the educational status of Filipino women and men. The illiteracy rate for men is higher than it is for females, at 11 in 100 people versus eight of 100. Women account for 56 percent of the total school graduates. Almost half, 48 percent, of women participate to the labor force, with men accounting for 78 percent of all workers. Females are predominantly employed as low-wage workers but comprise the majority of the bureaucracy, accounting for 57.6 percent of government personnel.

Without affirmative action, many women can be found in the political sphere. Women account for 21 percent of the total 240 representatives, and a women's rights organization, Gabriela, has secured party-list representation in Congress since 2004.

But women often earn political seats by belonging to a clan and are often used as "seat warmers" when their relative cannot run for the election. In Mindanao and Sulu archipelago—because of the state's low-intensity conflict strategy in the civil war—women are broadly victimized, especially as displaced persons. Manila and Clark—a former American military base—as well as some other tourist places, are known as sexual tourism spots. These areas tend to be frequented by Japanese, American, and Australian males. Thousands of Philippine women travel abroad as sex workers or "entertainers" (mostly in Japan) and as "mail-order brides" (mostly in United States, Australia, and Japan). Of the 2 million Filipino migrants in 2008, female, were estimated to account for almost half, or 968,000. They are mainly employed as domestic workers in the Persian Gulf states and in other Asian countries, where they face much discrimination.

See Also: Abortion, Access to; Conflict Zones; Domestic Workers; Mail Order Brides; Migrant Workers; Sex Workers.

Further Readings

Darroch, Jacqueline E., et al. "Meeting Women's Contraceptive Needs in the Philippines." *Brief,* v.1 (2009). http://www.guttmacher.org/pubs/2009/04/15/IB_MWCNP.pdf (accessed November 2009).

National Commission on the Role of Filipino Women, "Factsheets on Filipino Women." www.ncrfw.gov.ph/index.php/statistics-on-filipino-women/14-factsheets-on-filipino-women (accessed November 2009).

G. Ricordeau
University of Lille 1, France

Photography, Women in

In a world full of images, it is easy to become desensitized to the power of the still photograph. It is also easy to forget that women have played an important role in the development of photography as it rose from a curious new discovery that began as a documentary medium and evolved to become a respected profession, an admired art form, and a popular pastime. Women have been active in photography since its inception in the 1840s. From the start, the medium was accessible to women as users of the camera and producers of photographs, not merely subjects of male-held lenses. As a new occupation, photography did not have the same social barriers to women participants as the traditional art forms did, and the profession of photographer was not off limits to women. Nevertheless, even today, women photographers are often ignored and slighted, underrecognized in historical records for their contributions to the development of photography and underrepresented in nongendered photography exhibitions and collections.

In the beginning, photography consisted of heavy equipment and smelly chemicals that left dark stains on hands and clothes. Taking a picture was a labor-intensive process that included arranging the shot, making the exposure, and preparing the print (which had to be done immediately or it was lost). In the 19th century, it seemed unlikely that women would be interested in such a procedure. But they were.

An expensive activity, photography was only accessible to those with resources. But the rise of the middle class in the 19th century meant that more women had both resources and leisure time. Largely barred from the public sphere and serious art forms such as painting and sculpture, women found photography open to them. Whether as a hobby, a serious artistic endeavor, or a business venture, women participated fully in its development. In business situations, women often worked with their husbands as helpers or as collaborators and innovators, their contributions often going unnoted if the results appeared publicly. For instance, English photographer Harriet Taylor's name was not included on official records of the photographs both she and her husband took of the Indian Mutiny of 1858.

Despite their open participation in the new discipline, women were still on the receiving end of criticism merely because of their gender; critics accused them of being out of place, of being competent but not creative and of being mere button pushers. Also, employment compensation was subject to gender inequity: as labor, women were cheaper than men.

Nevertheless, by 1900, more middle-class women realized they could pursue self-fulfillment outside the domestic realm through photography. In 1880, there were 271 professional women photographers in the United States. By 1910, there were 4,900, and the number was rising. Women with some artistic sensibility and a reasonable feel for business saw opportunities for themselves in an otherwise restrictive world.

Photography required a relatively small financial investment; it was fairly easy to get started by studying the manuals and apprenticing in a studio. Moreover, photography was adaptable to individual schedules. Women could use their cameras in their own environments if they didn't want to venture out into locations unconventional for their gender. Unlike other professions, where men had the advantage of access to higher education and wider opportunities, in photography, men and women started out somewhat even.

In this era, women photographers tended to favor portraiture and often idealized their subjects, especially their children, posing them in carefully constructed settings. Nevertheless, many women photographers grew adept at creating individualized portraits. From 1900 to the beginning of World War I, women were seen to provide a much-needed softer touch to society in general and to photography in particular. Believing that men were not naturally nurturing as parents, the portrait-seeking public turned to women photographers to produce images that portrayed middle-class assumptions about family and motherhood.

Women were not limited to portrait photography. Many also became good landscape photographers. In Canada, women such as Geraldine Moodie and Hannah Maynard were pioneering forces. In the United States, Eliza Withington made photographic expeditions to the West and also wrote extensively about her photography experiences.

In the early 20th century, the rise of illustrated magazines meant a growing need for good photography. A strong demand grew for idyllic images of rural life, prominent people, attractive women and children, architecture, and products for advertising. This

Women have been active in photography since its inception in the 1840s. From the start, the medium was accessible to women as users of the camera and producers of photographs, not merely subjects of male-held lenses.

created new opportunities for women because many magazines targeted female audiences and required domestic images such as child-care products and domestic scenes.

Nevertheless, women did not limit themselves to female-oriented work. They photographed news events, racial living conditions, ethnic situations, and workplaces outside the domestic sphere, such as mines and factories. Some publications took care to assure their audiences that, while pursuing photographic assignments, female photographers were not neglecting their domestic responsibilities.

However, no matter their beliefs, their philosophies of life, or their social situations, women photographers recognized the value of photography not only as a source of income but also as a documentary force, an educational tool, a life-expanding endeavor, and an art form. Women brought as much talent and dedicated work ethic to photography as did their male counterparts, but, as with so many facets of their lives, they made less money doing it and have been under-recognized for their contributions to the discipline.

As photography grew during the 20th century, so did the number of photographic societies and organizations. Many did not admit women and photography as a discipline finally succumbed to prevalent social and cultural attitudes about gender. When the discipline of photography gained status as an art form, women did find recognition, but not without tension. Some claimed exclusion when male photographers did not like the competition.

After World War I, most women were relegated back to the domestic arena to make room in the workforce for returning servicemen, resulting in fewer opportunities for women photographers. During the 1920s, photographic trends changed: maternal images were no longer desirable. New directions toward precision and clarity in photography reflected rising modernist values. But women photographers became adept at new techniques and made notable contributions to the various modernist movements such as Bauhaus and Dada; however, these contributions have not received the same rigorous retrospective investigation as those of their male colleagues.

The rise of the 35mm camera, along with the growing news magazine industry, created more photographic employment opportunities in both advertising and photojournalism. It was tough for women to break into either field as photographers, both domains largely reserved for men. Nevertheless, women such as Gertrude Krull, Margaret Bourke-White, and Dorothea Lange made much progress. Later, photographers as different as Diane Arbus and Linda McCartney had much positive impact on public perceptions of the quality of women photographers' work. However, even as second-wave feminism made gains for women's equality in the 1970s, women photographers still had to work hard to be taken seriously.

In the late 1990s, digital photography revolutionized the medium once again by releasing it from the need for chemical processing. As seen in work produced by photographers such as Nancy Clendaniel, Joyce Tenneson, and Annie Leibovitz (just to name a few), women photographers adapted well to their discipline's ongoing changes. Today, women continue to be creative contributors in all areas of photography, from portraits to landscapes, from people and events to art, nature, and news.

Over the years, women photographers have learned to draw on each other's expertise and knowledge. As an example, in 1981, a small grassroots organization began in the United States with nine founding members. Almost three decades later, Women In Photography International (WIPI) is a global organization that works to promote the visibility of women photographers and their work. With thousands of members, WIPI holds exhibitions and workshops, offers networking and support, and promotes collaboration among professional and amateur women photographers around the world.

See Also: Arts, Women in the (21st Century Overview); Leibovitz, Annie.

Further Readings

Chapman, H. C. *Memory in Perspective: Women Photographers' Encounters with History.* Nexus Series: Theory and Practice in Women's Photography, Marsha Meskimmon, Series Editor. London: Scarlet Press, 1997.

Rosenblum, N. *A History of Women Photographers.* New York: Abbeville Publishing, 1994.

Women in Photography International. http://www.women inphotography.org (accessed June 2010).

Myrl Coulter
Independent Scholar

Physician Assistants, Female

Physician assistants (PAs) are healthcare professionals who are educated according to the medical model and licensed to practice medicine under the supervision of a physician. The profession developed in response to a growing population and an increased demand for medical care. The first PAs were graduates of Duke University's pioneering program. By design, these first graduates were male, with a single exception, and many were former military medics with experience in the Vietnam War. Conflicts between the American Medical Association and the American Nursing Association (ANA) helped to limit the number of women becoming PAs in the early years, but by the end of the first decade of the 21st century, women made up nearly 60 percent of practicing PAs.

As early as 1961, Dr. Charles Hudson, writing in the *Journal of the American Medical Association*, proposed the creation of a new class of healthcare providers who would work with a physician to perform routine medical care. At the end of the decade, Dr. Ernest B. Howard, executive vice president of the American Medical Association, in an address at Boston University's School of Medicine, proposed the recruitment of 100,000 nurses to be trained as PAs. Turf wars began almost immediately when Dorothy Cornelius, president of ANA, objected to Howard's speaking for the nursing profession. Nurses had fought a long battle to be viewed as professionals in their own right, rather than as "doctors' handmaidens," and Cornelius and others in ANA were fierce in protecting their gains. It is worth noting that nurse practitioners are licensed as independent healthcare providers, without mandated physician supervision, although some states require them to have a supervising or collaborating physician to whom they can turn for advice. The first nurse practitioner program was begun at the University of Colorado the same year that the first program for PAs was introduced at Duke University.

In 1965, Dr. Eugene Stead of Duke University's School of Medicine began the first program for PAs. Bitter about the failure of an advanced nursing program he had championed, Stead reluctantly agreed to leave the program open to women, but he made it clear that he expected his first students to be men. He actively recruited former military medics, believing that their experience made them ideal candidates for his program. Three years after Stead began instructing his first class, Joyce Nichols, an African American licensed practical nurse, became the first woman to enter the program at Duke. In 2008, 142 education programs for PAs were accredited or provisionally accredited by the Accreditation Review Commission on Education for the Physician Assistant. A decade after Nichols's graduation in 1970, women made up 36 percent of the country's nearly 30,000 PAs. By 2007, the total number of PAs approached 100,000, and the percentage of women in the profession had risen to 66 percent.

Growing Numbers of Women PAs

The number of women PAs has provoked concern about the "feminization" of the profession, but with the proportion of female to male students gaining admittance to PA programs still increasing, it appears unlikely that the picture will change. Although some of the gains can be attributable to the effects of Title IX, women PAs have cited numerous reasons for choosing the profession. Many say that it allows them to provide diagnostic, therapeutic, and preventive healthcare services without the heavy investment of time and money medical school would demand. A PA can perform about 75 percent of a doctor's tasks, but typically a PA's education costs about one-fifth that of a physician. Although most PA programs now offer a master's degree, PAs may begin work with only a bachelor's degree.

Upon graduation, PAs take a national certification examination developed by the National Commission on Certification of PAs in conjunction with the National Board of Medical Examiners. The return on the PA's investment is good. Income varies by specialty, practice setting, geographical location, and years of experience, but the median income for PAs in full-time clinical practice was $85,710 in 2008. Women also report that the less-demanding schedule of a PA is compatible with family life. Female PAs most frequently choose to concentrate in practice areas of women and children's health, but studies suggest that more are choosing nontraditional female specialties such as internal medicine and surgery.

The future of PAs is promising as well. Employment of PAs is predicted to grow by 39 percent from 2008 to 2018—much faster than the average for all occupations. Some countries have already incorporated the U.S. model as a means of increasing healthcare access while controlling its costs. Canada, the United Kingdom, the Netherlands, South Africa, and Taiwan already have programs in place. The battles for PA acceptance within the medical communities in these countries appear to replicate those that were fought in the 1960s and 1970s in the United States. Doctors, jealous of their position, challenge the competency of PAs and express fears for patient safety. Nurses protest that expanding the role of the nursing profession would be a better and fairer alternative. However, the admission of women into these programs no longer seems to be an issue.

See Also: Health, Mental and Physical; Nurses; Physicians, Female.

Further Readings

Holt, Natalie. "'Confusion's Masterpiece': The Development of the Physician Assistant Profession." *Bulletin of the History of Medicine*, v.72/2 (1998).

Lindsay, Sally. "The Feminization of the Physician Assistant Profession." *Women & Health*, v.41/4 (2005).

U.S. Department of Labor. "Physician Assistants." http://www.bls.gov/oco/ocos081.htm (accessed April 2010).

Wylene Rholetter
Auburn University

Physician Specialties

Occupational sex segregation is a persistent feature of the organization of work and contributes to gender inequalities in pay, status, and power. For physicians, intraoccupational sex segregation by medical specialty remains entrenched despite the rapid influx of women into medicine. Women physicians tend to be overrepresented in primary care specialties and underrepresented in surgery and surgical subspecialties. Explanations range from those focused on women's gendered choices to those emphasizing structural and external barriers. Equalizing women's status in medicine necessitates parity within medical specialties and more equity across specialties in terms of pay and prestige.

Medical specialization emerged in most Western countries in the 19th century as the separate fields of medicine and surgery began to merge. With the rise of other medical specialties in the middle and latter parts of the 19th century, surgery and internal medicine were relegated to specialty status. While some argue that the advent of an information age and new technologies forced rapid specialization in medicine, others contend that the transformation of intellectual perspective—especially an emphasis on organs and specific areas of the body—was behind the shift. During the 19th century, a more complex division of labor emerged in society generally—setting the stage for highly specialized occupations. Furthermore, as bureaucratization and administrative rationality became dominant forms of organization in the professions, people were increasingly classified and categorized. Medical associations devoted to individual specializations emerged, and specialty training and licensure soon followed.

In 1875, the International Medical Congress listed eight medical sections. In the United States, a 1933 meeting of physicians led to discussion on the education and certification of medical specialists. This discussion sparked the formation of the American Board of Medical Specialists (ABMS), whose mission is to oversee certification of physician specialists in the United States. In short, a national qualifying board determines who is competent to practice in any given specialty. Currently, there are 24 approved ABMS Member Boards that certify in 145 specialty and subspecialty areas. Accordingly, the number of doctors who specialize has risen dramatically, and recent research indicates that fewer than 20 percent of all U.S. medical students are choosing a primary care specialty such as family medicine, general internal medicine, and pediatrics.

In 2009, the Council of Graduate Medical Education advocated for health reform that would provide financial and educational incentives to produce more primary care physicians. The letter outlines five changes recommended by the Council on Graduate Medical Education, including training in nonhospital primary care settings, reducing the income gap between primary care and subspecialty physicians, and providing support for an infrastructure to coordinate patient care and reduce administrative burden. In addition, since growth in specialty areas is largely driven by the workforce needs of teaching hospitals, realignment requires monitoring and regulation by the federal government.

Women's Entrance Into the Medical Profession

Across the globe, one of the most dramatic changes in the profession of medicine has been the rapid influx of women. In the United States, affirmative action policies of the 1970s and 1980s opened up educational opportunities for women. In 1960, approximately 5 percent of medical students were female compared to about 48 percent in 2008. However, relative parity in medical school has not given way to parity in the active physician workforce given the skewed gender cohorts of prior decades. Approximately 27.5 percent of all active physicians are currently women—a number that will increase slowly as younger, more gender-balanced cohorts replace older, male-dominated cohorts.

Despite increasing parity in the numbers of women attending medical school, gender disparities persist in medical specialization. Women continue to be underrepresented in the most prestigious and highly remunerated medical specialties, particularly surgery and surgical subspecialties. Currently, 45 percent of practicing female physicians practice in specialties beyond general primary care or primary care subspecialties, compared with 64 percent of male physicians. A glance at the number of females per specialty for resident physicians reveals internal medicine, pediatrics, and family medicine as the top choices for women. In terms of percentages, obstetrics and gynecology and pediatrics are most likely to have women residents, with 77 percent and 73 percent female, respectively. Finally, residents in radiology are 27 percent female, compared with 31 percent in surgery and 35 percent in anesthesiology.

Gender segregation in medical specialization holds across different types of healthcare systems, from the market-driven systems like the United States to welfare states like Scandinavia with gender-equality policies. Furthermore, gender segregation persists even in post-Soviet societies such as Lithuania and Russia where women physicians have dominated for more than five decades.

Women comprise over 45 percent of medical students in Finland, about 31 percent in Spain, and 12 percent in Switzerland. Healthcare delivery systems and types of remuneration vary by country and influence specialty patterns, as do national variations in gendered employment patterns, state support for childcare, gendered educational systems, and variation in domestic labor.

For example, women are generally not well represented in most prestigious specialties in Britain, France and Norway—and are more likely to be located in specialties with controllable hours. However, historic and relatively high levels of state support for working mothers in France, combined with recent changes in the French educational process, have resulted in incoming cohorts that are predominantly female (about 70 percent). Since women tend to score higher on exams, they are more likely than men to have access to the most prestigious specialties.

Much of the available research on physician specialties hails from research conducted in Western medical settings. Only about 30 percent of medical students in Japan are female, although the rate is on the rise. Research on the changing medical profession in the developing world is scarce. Survey research indicates that between 30 and 50 percent of physicians in Chile, Costa Rica, and Uruguay are women. Recent evidence from Mexico shows a very rapid influx of women into medical schools; currently, about 50 percent of medical students are women. This is a result, in part, of the rapid influx of women into the labor force generally in Latin America. However, women physicians face higher rates of unemployment than do men upon completion of their training.

Why is intraoccupational sex segregation so persistent, even across varied national contexts? Explanations range from those focused on individual level gender socialization (early life and throughout medical training) and the experience and persistence of discrimination. In addition is the recognition that the medical specialty hierarchy is gendered. The most prestigious specialties are characterized as masculine and appropriate for those who embody toughness, while the less prestigious specialties, such as primary care specialties, are characterized as more feminine and appropriate for those who embody a caring nature and possess good communication skills. The barriers, then, are not only overt discrimination and bias but are also cultural and symbolic—those, too, vary cross-culturally. In sum, gender equity in physician specialties will come about when structural, cultural, and symbolic barriers are reduced. The challenge is to understand how national and local contexts influence gendered barriers.

See Also: Japan; Mexico; Physicians, Female; Russia; United States.

Further Readings

Accreditation Council for Graduate Medical Education. http://www.acgme.org/acWebsite/home/home.asp (accessed January 2010).

Association of American Medical Colleges. http://www.aamc.org (accessed January 2010).

Boulis, A. K. and J. A. Jacobs. *The Changing Face of Medicine: Women Doctors and the Evolution of Healthcare in America.* Ithaca, NY: Cornell University Press, 2008.

Hinze, S. W. "Gender and the Body of Medicine or at Least Some Body Parts: (Re)constructing the Prestige Hierarchy of Medical Specialties." *The Sociological Quarterly*, v.40/2 (1999).

Knaul, F., J. Frenk, and A. Mylena Aguilar. "The Gender Composition of the Medical Profession in Mexico: Implications for Employment Patterns and Physician Labor Supply." *Journal of the American Medical Women's Association*, v.55/1 (2000).

Riska, E. *Medical Careers and Feminist Agendas. American, Scandinavian and Russian Women Physicians.* New York: Walter de Gruyter, Inc., 2001.

Weisz, G. *Divide and Conquer. A Comparative History of Medical Specialization.* Oxford, UK: Oxford University Press, 2006.

Susan W. Hinze
Case Western Reserve University

Physicians, Female

Female physicians are increasingly common in many countries in the world, and this trend of more female physicians is now also true in the United States, although this has occurred more slowly in the United States than in many European countries. Over the past 30 years, both in the United States and in Europe, women have been entering medical schools in much greater numbers. This is a positive trend for many women, in terms of greater equity in professional attainments and in terms of income, since physicians are among the best paid professionals in the United States. This is even truer for women, and among high-earning American women, about one in 10 is a physician.

Numbers of Women in the Field and Issues by Subfield

The number of women physicians has been increasing in the United States, especially from 1970 on. Prior to that date, only a small percentage of the entering medical school classes each year were women. In 1970, women were 11 percent of medical students, but by 2005 they were 48.9 percent of medical students, according to the Association of American Medical Colleges (AAMC). Because the 1970s were an era of expansion in numbers of medical school seats, the number of new male physicians continued to grow. Beginning in the 1980s, the number of new male physicians began to decline, as the numbers of new physicians produced stabilized, at about 15,000 per year, and women continued to make up increasing proportions of medical school classes. Because many practicing physicians have been practicing since before 1985, there are still many more practicing male physicians (about 650,000) as compared to about 235,000 female physicians.

While in 1970 women were only 7.6 percent of all physicians, by 2004 they were almost 27 percent. Female physicians are more diverse in terms of race and ethnicity than are men, and the representation of women is also increasing among foreign-born physicians now working in the United States.

In contrast, in many European countries, and especially in Nordic countries, by 1998 women physicians were already over one-third of the medical profession, and as high as 50 percent in Finland. Within 20 years, it is expected in those countries that the medical profession will be gender balanced, according to E. Riska. By 1998, for physicians under 30, almost 60 percent or more of the physicians were women in Finland, Norway, and Denmark.

Do women specialize in the same fields within medicine and have similar practices? While women can increasingly be found in all the subfields of medicine and the representation of women increased in all medical specialties between 1975 and 2005, there is

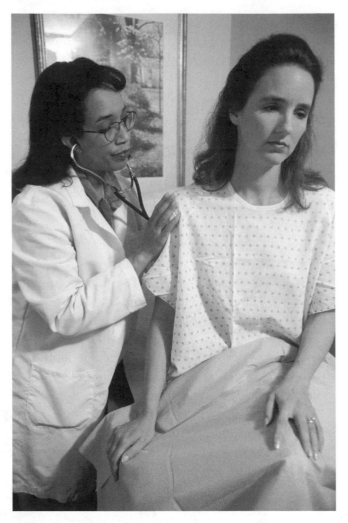

The representation of women is increasing among physicians now working in the United States.

gender stratification within the practice of medicine in terms of specialty, and this is also true in European countries. One specialty (pediatrics) had a majority of female practitioners (53 percent in 2005). Four specialties (neurologic, orthopedic, thoracic, and urological surgery) all had less than 6 percent female representation. Other specialties with more than 35 percent female representation include child psychiatry, obstetrics and gynecology, dermatology, general preventive medicine and physical medicine.

Women are underrepresented among physician administrators and physician researchers and are more likely to work as employees rather than as physician practice owners in the United States. Some of this latter difference is probably due to more recent graduation into the profession, and the number of male physician employees is also increasing, as part of a general trend in the practice of medicine.

Another aspect of practice in which women differ from men is in earnings. Based on the 2000 census, the gender gap in pay in medicine is larger than for most other professions, with women physicians earning an average 63 percent of the earnings of male physicians. Some past research has emphasized that these differences relate to individual choices in specialties and work patterns linked to marriage and childbearing, but some more recent research has found that even after an allowance is made for work and specialty, practice types, and a variety of other factors, earnings gaps remain. The gender gap is declining, however, but at a fairly slow rate.

Linkages With Family and Marriage

One debate in recent years relates to labor force participation rates of educated women. The idea that women would not fully utilize their medical training by remaining as active physicians was one reason for discrimination against admitting women to medical schools prior to 1970. The argument was that once women married, they would not continue in practice or practice at the same rates once they had children. Recent data show clearly that, at least for female physicians, this is a false argument. All physicians have high labor-force-participation rates, both men and women, and this is true for married women also. In 2000, 99 percent of male married physicians aged 30 to 50 were working, as were 96 percent of women. Figures are almost as high for mothers of preschool children.

While married women physicians with children at home under 18 years of age do work fewer hours than male physicians, both groups work more than 40 hours a week. In 2000, female physicians from 30 to 50 worked 47 hours a week, versus 55 hours a week for male physicians in the same age group. As fewer male physicians are married to nonworking spouses, long work hours may become an issue for both male and female physicians.

Practice Differences and the Future

Do women have a different practice style from men, and are they better for women patients? Physicians do generally set the tone for physician-patient interaction. Some sources argue that women exhibit more empathy to others in general and that this should also be true for women physicians. Other sources see increasing similarities in how male and female physicians interact with patients, although there are some stylistic differences in communication patterns of women. In general women physicians talk to their patients more and allow the patients more time to talk to them and ask them questions. Their nonverbal communication style seems to encourage greater participation by patients.

Use of preventive services also is encouraged more by women physicians, according to some research. Some studies argue that this is party because of practice patterns; that women are more likely to be primary care providers and to practice in managed care environments; and that it is these practice characteristics, rather than gender, that explain the difference in encouragement of use of preventive measures.

Despite growing numbers of women physicians, women have not been moving rapidly into leadership roles in medicine, although this has started to increase in the last decade. This issue of lower representation of women in leadership positions and in medical school positions is true in most European countries as well as in American medicine, although there has been more change in Europe. If women move into top leadership positions, they may bring some changes to medicine, such as perhaps greater attention to the psychosocial needs of patients. However, it is not yet clear whether the growing numbers of women in medicine will alter the impact of medical training and the standard biomedical outlook of the profession or not, especially in the United States.

See Also: Equal Pay; Health, Mental and Physical; Health Insurance Issues.

Further Readings

Baker, Lawrence C. "Differences in Earnings Between Male and Female Physicians." *New England Journal of Medicine*, v.334/15 (1996).

Boulis, Ann K. and Jerry A. Jacobs. *The Changing Face of Medicine: Women Doctors and the Evolution of Care in America.* Ithaca, NY: Cornell University Press, 2008.

Hoff, T.J. "Doing the Same and Earning Less: Male and Female Physicians in a New Medical Specialty." *Inquiry*, v.41/3 (2004).

Lorber, Judith and Lisa Jean Moore. *Gender and the Social Construction of Illness,* 2nd ed. Lanham, MD: AltaMira Press, 2002.

Riska, Elianna. "Toward Gender Balance: But Will Women Physicians Have an Impact on Medicine?" *Social Science and Medicine*, v.52/2 (2001).

Sasser, Alicia. "Gender Differences in Physician Pay: Tradeoffs Between Career and Family." *Journal of Human Resources*, v.40/2 (2005).

Weinberg, Daniel. "Evidence From Census 2000 About Earnings by Detailed Occupation for Men and Women." *Census 2000 Special Reports* (2004). http://www.census.gov/prod/2004pubs/censr-15.pdf (accessed July 2010).

Jennie Jacobs Kronenfeld
Arizona State University

Physics, Women in

Physics is a discipline of natural sciences defined as "the scientific study of matter and their interactions using the electromagnetic, gravitational and nuclear forces of nature." Historically, the percentage of women contributing to new discoveries in physics and academic teaching of physics has been considerably less than the percentage of men. Despite the modern feminist movement, the number of women in physics continues to be less than the number of men, particularly in leadership positions. As there is no rational reason for women to trail men in achieving new scientific discoveries or excel in academic teaching, the cause of this trend is attributed to existing gender biases in the perception and practice of science. Thus, increasing the number of women in physics as well as emphasising their relevance in physics have emerged as women's issues.

Women in History of Physics

Hypatia (370–415) lived in Alexandria in Egypt and taught philosophy and astronomy. She is one of the earliest women scientists in recorded history. Contributions of women astronomers have been recognized for centuries. In 1786, J. K. Lalande published his "Astronomy for Ladies," which has a history of the women astronomers. Physicist Laura Bassi (1711–78) became the first woman to be awarded a university professorship in Europe and is known for her work in fluid mechanics and devising experiments in electricity. Emilie Marquise du Chatelet (1706–49) translated Newton's *Principia* in French. Emmy Noether (1882–1935) is perhaps the most famous woman scientist, whose mathematical theorems gave birth to modern algebra. "Noether theorem" is used in physics to obtain conserved charges in systems with continuous symmetries. Marie Curie (1867–1934) was the first woman to receive two Nobel Prizes in physics and chemistry for her work in radioactivity. Maria Goeppert-Mayer is the only other women to have received a Nobel Prize in physics, awarded in 1963 for her work in nuclear physics.

Statistics of Women in Physics in Today's World

The percentage of women in physics at undergraduate and graduate levels is high (30–50 percent) in most developed countries (e.g., in the United Kingdom and the United States). The number reduces considerably for midcareer women (10–20 percent) to very low (less than 5 percent) for senior and leadership positions. This gives rise to a scissors diagram in the plot of male-female ratios in physics career graphs. The details differ in some countries. A set of illustrative examples taken from the proceedings of the 3rd International Conference on Women in Physics are listed below. In Australia, approximately 24 percent of undergraduate students are female, and 28.3 percent of postgraduate students are women.

Selected universities in Australia have 22 percent women as academic staff, whereas women in government research labs are about 9 percent of the total. Across Canada, the percentage of women at undergraduate level in physical and life sciences and technology is 55.7 percent and 46.5 percent at graduate level. The percentage of women in full-time teaching positions in Canadian universities in mathematical and physical sciences is 14.6 percent (in 2004). In France, 25 percent of undergraduate and graduate students are women; 21 percent of faculty at French universities are female. The percentage of female graduates from the Physical Society of Japan (JPS) is 9 percent, and the percentage of women members of the JPS is 5 percent.

At the undergraduate and graduate levels in Kenya, the percentage of women is below 10 percent. In Kenya, the percentage of women teaching staff is less than 1 percent. In Lebanon, 45 percent of the undergraduates

in the physics department at St. Joseph's University are female, and 15 percent of the professors are women. In Peru, the percentage of women at NMU University is 53 percent at the undergraduate level and 14.6 percent at the graduate level. In South Africa, 33.3 percent of the students are female, whereas at the researcher level 16 percent of the members of the South African Institute of Physics are women. Some prestigious universities like Harvard University in the United States have tenured their first female faculty, Melissa Franklin and Lisa Randall, in recent years.

Feminism and Physics

The issue of women in physics is deeply rooted in the rise of the feminist movement in the world. The feminist movement aims for equal rights and opportunities for women in all spheres of human endeavour. In the first wave of the feminist movement, women obtained the right to vote. Scientific institutions and universities started admitting women students and hired women teachers and researchers in the natural sciences. The second wave of feminism rose as an effort to end gender biases and discrimination and is based on the idea of difference feminism.

This movement is reflected in the sciences and as an effort to find sociological and cultural reasons that discourage women from pursuing a career in physics. The number of women in biological sciences has risen to be significant, as it is considered a "soft science," whereas the number of women in physics remains low, as it is perceived as a "masculine science" requiring mathematical and logical skills, which are traditionally deemed as masculine. Similarly, women remain underrepresented in academics in countries where physics is considered prestigious, as in the United States and in Germany. On the other hand, in countries like Turkey, the percentage of women in academics is comparatively higher (30 percent) because a teaching job is not well paid and men prefer disciplines such as law, which is considered prestigious in Turkish culture.

Gender Bias in Physics

Conclusive physiological evidence for innate differences in the practice of science by men and women has not been found. However, there is evidence of differences induced due to social conditioning of men and women, and this is known as "gender bias." Societal gender biases in science teaching and practice start at a very young age. Girls are encouraged to take up feminine roles advocated by school books and toy manufacturers. The Barbie doll's vocabulary had the words *math class is tough* before the manufacturers removed it due to protests by women. Physics is an exact science; the laws of physics are based on experimental data. Devising experiments is sometimes deemed as masculine in textbooks. At the undergraduate level this discouragement persists when a female chooses a career. Graduate, postdoctoral, and tenure-track positions require intense focus for career building; however, these stages coincide with a woman's childbearing age. Provisions of good maternity benefits and day care facilities are limited in universities and research institutes in most countries. It has been found that work environments in physics departments are not female-friendly. Women researchers are isolated in the male-majority departments and are ignored in promotions or in assigning of duties, preventing their progress to senior and leadership positions.

Establishing a Gender-Sensitive Practice of Physics

Several organized efforts have started to counter existing discrimination in the practice of science and encourage women to take up a career in physics. Scientists in School is a Canadian effort formed by women who interact with elementary school children to inspire them to develop an interest in science. The Indian government has announced the introduction of flexible working hours of mothers of children under age 3. The Hertha Sponer Prize, named in honour of a German female physicist, is awarded by the German Physical Society to a young female researcher. The International Union of Pure and Applied Physics has a working group focused on women that organizes an international conference for women in physics. This is a very concerted effort to bring women of all countries together to brainstorm on encouraging women in physics. The European Commission's aim to have gender equity in science and achieve 25 percent representation of women in permanent academic positions is a very positive action.

The American Institute of Physics (AIP), the Canadian Association of Physics (CAP), and the Institute of Physics (IOP) in the United Kingdom have specific working groups devoted to gender issues. These seek to build networks of women, to increase their visibility, and to increase awareness about existing gender-based biases. The use of site visits to assess the environment of a physics department or institute was initiated by the AIP and the IOP. This has served to increase gender sensitivity in the work environment. Affirmative action has been implemented in various Universities and research institutes in the world to encourage women in physics. Key goals of women in physics are to work toward minimizing biases, to engage in activities designed to educate the broader community about the impact of physics in daily life, and to take every opportunity to highlight positive female role models in physics. Furthermore, the images of physics and physicists that are presented in textbooks and the media must ensure that women are well represented.

See Also: Affirmative Action/Equal Opportunity; American Association of University Women; Astronomy, Women in; Education, Women in; Science, Women in Science Education for Girls; STEM Coalition.

Further Readings

Baki, P., et al. "Kenya Women in Physics: Societal, Cultural and Professional Challenges." Proceedings of 3rd IUPAP International Conference in Physics, AIP Proceedings, v.1119 (2008).

Beyers, N. "Contributions of 20th Century Women to Physics." http://cwp.library.ucla.edu (accessed June 2010).

Foley, C. P. "Status of Women in Physics in Australia." Proceedings of 3rd IUPAP International Conference in Physics, AIP Proceedings, v.1119 (2008).

Predoi-Cross, A., et al. "Women Physicists in Canada." *Proceedings of 3rd IUPAP International Conference in Physics, AIP Proceedings*, v.1119 (2008).

Schiebinger, Londa. *Has Feminism Changed Science?"* Cambridge, MA: Harvard University Press, 2001.

Tajima, S. and M. Nishitani-Gamo. "`Recent Progress in Promoting Gender Equality for Japanese Scientists." Proceedings of 3rd IUPAP International Conference in Physics, AIP Proceedings, v.1119 (2008).

Thibault, C., et al. "French Women in Physics: Status and Actions." *Proceedings of 3rd IUPAP International Conference in Physics, AIP Proceedings*, v.1119 (2008).

Arundhati Dasgupta
Adriana Predoi-Cross
University of Lethbridge

Pilates

Pilates is a method of exercise that can be performed on a mat with specialized equipment. The exercises condition the body, strengthening and lengthening the body's muscles. Pilates improves posture and has antiaging qualities, as it strengths the abdominal muscles, inner thighs, and upper arms without affecting the joints. The exercises place emphasis on reducing the incidence of back pain and injury.

The Developer of Pilates

Pilates was developed by German-born Joseph H. Pilates, who was a skier, boxer, dancer, and gymnast. Pilates developed an obsession with physical fitness, and during World War I, he designed exercise equipment to rehabilitate injured war victims. He opened his first studio in New York City, with his wife Clara, in 1926. Many of their clients were prominent dancers, including Martha Graham.

His method of exercise was called Contology until after his death, when it became known as the Pilates method. Clara Pilates was a trained nurse and is credited for incorporating his concepts to benefit more ill or injured clients. Romana Kryzanowska and Eve Gentry are two famous elders who popularized the benefits of this method for ordinary people.

The Pilates method emphasizes breathing with movement, body mechanics, balance, coordination, body positioning, spatial awareness, strength, and flexibility. Yoga shares similar goals with Pilates, placing emphasis on stretching and strengthening the muscles in a noncompetitive arena; however, unlike Yoga, Pilates works the body as a whole, coordinating upper and lower musculature with the body's core. It is this holistic approach that sets Pilates apart from many other forms of exercise.

Pilates views the muscles at the center of the body, including the abdomen, lower back, hips, and buttocks, as the "powerhouse." Pilates exercises begin from this core and flow outward to the limbs. The original Pilates method included 34 exercises done on the floor on a padded mat. Pilates also invented several apparatuses, each of which has their own set of exercises. The most common apparatus is the "reformer, which has pulleys and cables that one can push or pull. The reformer enables the practitioner to stretch further and into positions unreachable on the mat alone.

Popular perceptions hold that Pilates is "just for women," and Pilates during pregnancy has been claimed to be highly valuable and a beneficial form of exercise. However, practitioners argue that Pilates can be beneficial for almost anyone, regardless of age, gender, or fitness level.

Men have played an important role in the evolution of the Pilates method. Many women who were dancers choose teaching Pilates as a second career, making the exercise even more appealing to women. Practitioners argue that this may be why Pilates is increasingly associated with feminine characteristics.

Famous women who practice Pilates include Jennifer Aniston, Madonna, Vanessa Williams, Martha Stewart, Sigourney Weaver, and Martina Navratilova.

See Also: Dance, Women in; Diet and Weight Control; Exercise Science; Fitness; Yoga.

Further Readings

Pilates, Joseph. *Pilates' Return to Life Through Contrology.* New York: Presentation Dynamics, 1928.

Winsor, M. and M. Laska. *The Pilates Pregnancy: A Low Impact Exercise Programme for Maintaining Strength and Flexibility.* London: Vermilion, 2002.

Danai S. Mupotsa
Monash University

Pink, Advertising and

The color pink has been used in advertising and popular culture since the 1940s. Drawing upon and reinforcing gender stereotypes, the subtlety and consistency of pink symbolism has adapted to different generations and contexts to shape popular understandings of what it means to be a woman in America.

From the 1940s to the 1970s, advertising created a feminine ideal packaged in pink. The color became an iconic symbol to convey a set of duplicitous traits, in which the feminine could be a source of assurance or alarm.

Pink girlhood was represented as soft, pure, impressionable, and pretty, but it was accompanied with trickery, mysteriousness, and volatility. In turn, pink womanhood was characterized in terms of morality, emotionality, and nurturance, as well as seduction, manipulation, and secrecy. Physical attractiveness and beauty habits were crucial for both girls and women, and it was never too early to surround girls in pink accouterments (ribbons, ruffles, dresses, and jewelry). Pink also became popular from its connection with the iconic Barbie doll. Clothing and accessories for Barbie from the 1970s on were predominately pink, and a bright pink color came to be associated with the doll.

The color pink gained new momentum in the form of the pink breast cancer ribbon, established in 1992 as the symbol for breast cancer awareness. The pink ribbon easily conjured feminine imagery and discourse that was already prevalent in popular culture. Focusing on goodness, morality, and woman's domain in the private sphere, pink was used to evoke innocence, thereby rendering breast cancer a virtuous illness and a good cause.

Although women's health advocates successfully used the ribbon to promote awareness, October's National Breast Cancer Awareness Month became so closely identified with a *feminized* version of the cause that it is now commonly referred to as "Pinktober." Pinktober is an array of awareness and advertising campaigns that encourage people to buy pink products, while it uses the color pink to reinforce idealized versions of survivorship that are steeped in feminine stereotypes.

The *pinking* of breast cancer has turned the illness into one of the most popular, and most advertised, causes in contemporary culture. As with other common advertising techniques, pink marketing capitlizes on the sexualization, objectification, and infantalization of women. From "Boobie-Thons" to T-shirts with statements such as, "Stop the War in My Rack", these representations reduce women to their usefulness as sexual objects.

Pink ribbon ads for teddy bears, rubber duckies, M&Ms, and Barbie dolls suggest that femininity and adulthood are incompatible. And, many pink ribbon ads depict women in their proper domestic roles— cooking, cleaning, and satisfying the needs of others with pink kitchen aids, pink vacuum cleaners, pink cosmetics, and other feminine accessories. Pink advertising is part of an ongoing cultural project that draws upon and strengthens gender stereotypes for the purpose of selling products and ideas.

See Also: Advertising, Aimed at Women; Advertising, Portrayal of Women; Breast Cancer; Femininity, Social Construction of.

Further Readings

King, S. *Pink Ribbons, Inc.: Breast Cancer and the Politics of Philanthropy.* Minneapolis: University of Minnesota Press, 2006.

Peril, L. *Pink Think: Becoming a Woman in Many Uneasy Lessons.* New York: W. W. Norton & Company, 2002.

Sulik, G. *Pink Ribbon Blues: How Breast Cancer Culture Undermines Women's Health.* New York: Oxford University Press, 2010.

Gayle Sulik
Independent Scholar

Plan B

Unintended pregnancy is a public health problem with major significance worldwide. Plan B, a progestin-only type of emergency contraception, is an effective yet underutilized method of pregnancy prevention. Plan B is 75 to 89 percent effective in preventing pregnancies when taken within 120 hours (five days) after sexual intercourse; however, the medication is more effective the earlier it is used. Although Plan B has been controversial and wrapped up in the abortion debate, it is not effective if a woman is already pregnant and therefore does not disrupt an established pregnancy. It has been estimated that wider access and acceptability of Plan B could reduce the number of unintended pregnancies and could prevent 1 million abortions annually. This form of contraception is important in that, unlike most forms of contraception, it is effective after sexual intercourse but before pregnancy.

Plan B is orally administered and consists of two white pills—one pill is taken within 120 hours of unprotected intercourse and the second pill is taken 12 hours later. In 2009, Plan B-One Step was developed, which consists of one pill that is taken within 72 hours of unprotected intercourse. Overall, Plan B is a safe form of contraception with very few side effects and contraindications. The mechanism of action of Plan B is the same as oral contraceptives. Plan B can work to inhibit:

- *Ovulation*: can suppress hormone needed for ovulation
- *Fertilization*: can inhibit movement of egg/sperm
- *Transport*: can inhibit path of the fertilized egg to uterus
- *Implantation*: can change the endometrium so the blastocyst cannot implant

Although emergency contraception has become more available in both developed and developing countries, three main barriers to access to Plan B seem to perpetuate a lack of awareness and utilization of this birth-control method. First, the public, including providers and women themselves, either do not know about it or have certain misunderstandings about Plan B. Second, some healthcare providers and professionals do not prescribe or dispense it. For example, there have been numerous accounts of doctors refusing to write prescriptions and pharmacists refusing to dispense it. Third, inadequate education is provided to women about it.

In an effort to remove barriers to accessing Plan B, there has been a push for over-the-counter (OTC) access; however, in some countries this proposal has been met with great trepidation. In the United States, over-the-counter approval is for women 18 years and older, with prescriptions required for those 17 years and younger. Plan B advocates globally continue to work toward the removal of barriers to access of this important form of contraception.

See Also: Contraception Methods; Planned Parenthood; Reproductive and Sexual Health Rights.

Further Readings

Ellertson, C., et al. "Modifying the Yuzpe Regimen of Emergency Contraception: A Multicenter Randomized Controlled Trial." *Obstetrics & Gynecology*, v.101/6 (2003).

Piaggio, G., et al. "Timing of Emergency Contraception with Levonorgestrel or the Yuzpe Regimen." *Lancet*, v.353 (1999).

Richman, A. R. "Emergency Contraception: Do We Have the Political Will to Increase Access?" *Women's Health Issues*, v.14/5 (2004).

Trussell, J., C. Ellertson, and L. Dorflinger. "Effectiveness of the Yuzpe Regimen of Emergency Contraception by Cycle Day of Intercourse: Implications for Mechanism of Action." *Contraception*, v.67/3 (2003).

Alice R. Richman
University of North Carolina at Chapel Hill

Planned Parenthood

Planned Parenthood is an organization committed to providing access to sexual and reproductive health education and services throughout the world. The Planned Parenthood Federation of America (PPFA), often referred to simply as Planned Parenthood, began with the work of American birth-control advocate Margaret Sanger, who opened the first birth-control clinic in New York in 1916 and founded the American Birth Control League in 1921. Sanger was committed to making contraceptive information and devices available to women and also helped secure funding for new research that led to the development of oral contraceptives (or "the Pill") in the early 1960s. Although Planned Parenthood thus traces its own history back to the early 20th century, Sanger's activist and research organizations merged to officially operate under the name Planned Parenthood Federation of America in 1942. Sanger served as president of PPFA until 1962.

The International Planned Parenthood Federation (IPPF) was founded in 1952 out of the Third International Conference on Planned Parenthood in Bombay, India. IPPF is now based in the United Kingdom, with regional offices in Kenya, Tunisia, Belgium, India, Malaysia, and New York City. Representatives from each of these regions form the decision-making board, or Governing Council, of IPPF. In addition to the IPPF's Western Hemisphere program offices in the United States, Latin America, and the Caribbean, the PPFA operates as the U.S. affiliate of the IPPF. The IPPF is a nongovernmental organization that receives both government and private funding to operate sexual education and family-planning clinics in close to 200 countries. The IPPF has also had a voice in international commissions, such as those organized by the United Nations and the World Health Organization, to address issues related to population control, development, children's issues, public health, and women's rights. Challenged by conservative politicians and the Catholic Church throughout the 1990s and early 2000s, the IPPF lost as much as 20 percent of its funding under former U.S. President George Bush's 2001 policy that prevented U.S. funds to any international nongovernmental organization providing abortion services; this policy was reversed by President Barack Obama in 2009, and funding was restored.

Both IPPF and PPFA have been at the center of controversies and court cases involving primarily abortion rights and services. In its more than 800 clinics in the United States alone, Planned Parenthood offers a range of sexual and reproductive health services for both men and women, including pregnancy testing; birth control information and prescriptions; surgical sterilization; prevention, testing, and treatment of sexually transmitted diseases; HIV tests; Pap tests; breast exams; and other cancer screenings. Planned Parenthood has also become a clearinghouse for information and education about sexuality, about sexual orientation and gender identity, and about body image and other social and psychological issues.

Still, for many people, Planned Parenthood remains synonymous with abortion services, and PPFA has been at the forefront of pro-choice campaigns to influence or challenge legislation that limits abortion rights and access. Since the 1980s, Planned Parenthood has been a critic (and often target) of antiabortion activists, including staged protests outside of clinics and even violence directed at clinics and abortion providers. Planned Parenthood has also been involved in several court cases regarding abortion, arguing against attempted legislative restrictions such parental or spousal consent, mandatory waiting periods, restrictions on doctors providing abortion information to patients, or violating the privacy and free-speech rights of both patients and doctors who perform abortions by publicizing medical and personal information.

In 1992, Planned Parenthood challenged the legality of a series of Pennsylvania restrictions on abortion. In *Planned Parenthood (of Southeastern Pennsylvania) v. Casey*, the U.S. Supreme Court upheld the basic tenets of *Roe v. Wade* (the 1973 case that established the trimester framework for determining a woman's access to abortion) and declared it unconstitutional for states to require married women to obtain spousal consent for abortion services. The case

Planned Parenthood is committed to providing access to sexual and reproductive health education and services worldwide.

was only a partial victory for Planned Parenthood and pro-choice advocates, however, for the court allowed the state to impose a 24-hour waiting period for a woman requesting an abortion, to require "informed consent" in the form of doctor-provided information about the health risks of abortion, and to require parental notification and consent before a minor could receive an abortion. Planned Parenthood continues to challenge limitations on abortion access at the local and state levels.

PPFA and its political affiliates have raised funds and lobbied the U.S. Congress on a range of other issues related to reproductive rights and women's health. It has launched a major campaign to make accessible FDA-approved emergency contraception (also known as the "morning after pill") and has advocated for healthcare reform that makes health insurance more affordable to low-income families and prevents gender discrimination by insurance companies (such as not covering pregnancy, birth control, or breast cancer screenings). Finally, Planned Parenthood has been critical of abstinence-only sex education programs in public schools, promoting instead a comprehensive sex education program that includes support for abstinence alongside information about birth control, pregnancy, sexually transmitted diseases, and human immunodeficiency virus and acquired immune deficiency syndrome (HIV/AIDS).

After Margaret Sanger, Dr. Alan Guttmacher served as president of PPFA (1962–73). Both Sanger and Guttmacher were associated with eugenics movements of their day, which has attracted more controversy and criticism over Planned Parenthood's beginnings. Faye Wattleton became the first African American president of PPFA in 1978 and served until 1992. Other presidents to date are Pamela Maraldo (1993–95), Gloria Feldt (1996–2005), and Texas Democratic activist Cecile Richards, who has been president of PPFA since 2006.

See Also: Abortion, Access to; Contraception, Religious Approaches to; Contraception Methods; Pregnancy.

Further Readings

Davis, Tom. *Sacred Work: Planned Parenthood and Its Clergy Alliances.* New Brunswick, NJ: Rutgers University Press, 2006.

International Planned Parenthood Federation. http://www.ippf.org/en (accessed June 2010).

Sanger, Margaret, et al. *The Selected Papers of Margaret Sanger, vol. 3: The Politics of Planned Parenthood, 1939–1966.* Chicago: University of Illinois Press, 2010.

Tiffany K. Wayne
Independent Scholar

Plumwood, Val

Val Plumwood is an Australian ecofeminist philosopher and activist who participated in movements to preserve biodiversity and to stop deforestation from the 1960s until her death in 2008. Prominent in the development of radical ecosophy (a contraction of the phrase *ecological philosophy,* frequently used to refer to different and often conflictual concepts espoused by Norwegian philosopher Arne Naess and French post-Marxist philosopher and psychoanalyst Félix Guattari), she helped establish the interdisciplinary field of eco-logical humanities, which aims to bridge gaps between the sciences and the humanities, as well as Western, Eastern, and indigenous ways of knowing nature.

Plumwood was born in 1939 and was married for a time to Richard Routley, also a philosopher and a proponent of deep ecology (a branch of ecological philosophy that conceptualizes humankind as an integral part of its environment and that calls for major changes in our attitudes toward nature and the adoption of voluntary simplicity as a lifestyle). Formerly Val Routley, she changed her last name to Plumwood after their separation in the early 1980s. During her lifetime, she held positions at North Carolina State University, the University of Montana, and the University of Sydney. At the time of her death, she was an Australian Research Council Fellow at the Australian National University.

The author of four books and over 100 papers, Plumwood draws upon feminist theory to critique what she calls the "standpoint of mastery," a phrase that refers to a set of views about the Self and its relationships to the Other with respect to sexism, racism, capitalism, and the domination of nature. Her two major theoretical works are *Feminism and the Mastery of Nature* (1993) and *Environmental Culture: The Ecological Crisis of Reason* (2002). In *Feminism and the Mastery of Nature*, she argues, following the ecofeminist line of reasoning, that the current environmental crisis originates in the West's dualistic ways of conceptualizing things. What she calls the "hyperseparation" of humans from nature is also part of the colonizing dynamic we see in the West's relationship with the rest of the world. She counsels us to abandon these dualisms in favor of an ecological ethic founded on empathy for the Other. Although she is not opposed to spirituality, she thinks that the predominant forms of Western spirituality have located the sacred above and beyond a fallen Earth, a notion she considers misguided.

In her last major theoretical work, *Environmental Culture: The Ecological Crisis of Reason*, Plumwood argues that contemporary forms of ecological denial are dangerous and can be traced back to historical warpings of reason and culture. After documenting the profound effects of such distortions upon the fields of economics, politics, science, ethics, spirituality, and the current hegemonic form of globalization, she presents a radically different vision of how our culture must change in order to develop a society that is ecologically rational.

See Also: Ecofeminism; Environmental Activism, Grassroots; Social Justice Activism; Social Justice Theory.

Further Readings

Griffin, Nicholas. "Val Plumwood." In Joy A. Palmer et al., eds., *Fifty Key Thinkers on the Environment*. London: Routledge, 2001.

Plumwood, Val. "The Crisis of Reason, the Rationalist Market and Global Ecology." *Milennium Journal of International Studies*, v.27 (1998).

Plumwood, Val. "Deep Ecology, Deep Pockets and Deep Problems: A Feminist Eco-Socialist Analysis." In E. Katz, A. Light, and D. Rothenberg, eds., *Beneath the Surface: Critical Essays on Deep Ecology*. Cambridge, MA: MIT Press, 1999.

Plumwood, Val. "Ecological Ethics from Rights to Recognition: Multiple Spheres of Justice for Humans, Animals and Nature." In Nicholas Low, ed., *Global Ethics and Environment*. London: Routledge, 1999.

Plumwood, Val. *Environmental Culture: The Ecological Crisis of Reason*. London: Routledge, 2002.

Plumwood, Val. *Feminism and the Mastery of Nature*. London: Routledge, 1993.

Plumwood, Val. "Paths Beyond Human-Centeredness: Lessons From Liberation Struggles." In Anthony Weston, ed., *An Invitation to Environmental Philosophy* New York: Oxford University Press, 1999.

Danielle Roth-Johnson
University of Nevada, Las Vegas

Poets, Female

Sappho, a Greek poet whose work remains only in fragments, is one of the foremothers of poetry in the Western tradition. Although women have been central to the history of poetry, at various times female poets have been dismissed and minimized, sometimes with the gendered label "poetess." In spite of this, women poets have created an impressive body of work. At the beginning of the second millennium, there is new recognition of contemporary female poets, new publishing opportunities for women poets exist, and critical appraisal of the work of female poets from the past continues.

There are no themes or styles that define poetry by women. Female poets, like male poets, write poetry that is diverse, idiosyncratic, and defies categorization. The work of an individual woman poet is loyal only to her own vision and sensibility. For every major poetic movement, there are women engaged in its aesthetic practices. During the 20th century, women poets were major innovators, for example, in modernism, confessionalism, and L=A=N=G=U=A=G=E poetry. During the Women's Liberation Movement in the 1970s and 1980s, poetry was both an artistic and a political practice, shaping and promoting the goals of feminism. Today, women poets write narrative poetry, lyric poetry, epic poetry, formal poetry, and free verse, among many other types of poetry. Women poets engage with tradition and innovation, supporting a vibrant contemporary poetics.

Equal representation in journals, book publishing, and anthologies is important for female poets. Women poets are represented in all major journals, though their numbers as contributors and editors vary widely. In 2007, Juliana Spahr and Stephanie Young surveyed anthologies of experimental poetry for their inclusion of women; they found that while the number of women had increased during the 1990s as a result of feminist interventions, in most anthologies, the number of women included was still below 50 percent. In the Spahr and Young survey, the place in the world of poetry where women have the most equity is in book publishing at university presses.

Even though there is not gender parity in book publishing, women poets are published by all major publishing houses and by small, independent poetry publishers. Established poets like Adrienne Rich, Rachel Blau DuPlessis, Marilyn Hacker, Rita Dove, Alicia Ostriker, Marie Ponsot, Carolyn Forche, and Sharon Olds have committed commercial publishers. Emerging poets like Meg Kearney, Lyrae Van Clief-Stefanon, Christina Davis, Elizabeth Bradfield, and Sandra Beasley have published exciting first books of poetry, primarily at small, independent presses. Some of them have published acclaimed second books or have anticipated second books in press. In spite of the prominence of women poets in publishing, there remains a need for publishing dedicated to the work of women poets. New, small presses dedicated to publishing women poets have launched recently, including Perugia Press, Kore Press, and Arktoi Press.

While women have made strides in publishing and received concomitant recognition for their work, sexist exclusion continues. Recently, however, women poets broke new barriers. In 2009, the poet laureates of the United States and the United Kingdom were both women. (Poet laureates are appointed by the government and charged with representing poetry nationally.) In May 2009, Queen Elizabeth II appointed Carol Ann Duffy as poet laureate of the United Kingdom. Duffy is the first woman to occupy the position in the three centuries. The Library of Congress appointed Kay Ryan poet laureate in the United States in July 2008. Of the 49 poet laureates (or consultants in poetry, as the position was titled between 1937 and 1986), 12 have been women (25 percent). While the history of national poet laureates is one of exclusion, more women are being appointed to these positions, providing a partial remedy.

Critical Acclaim

Just as poet laureateships are not an exclusive measure for the engagement of women in poetry, neither are prizes an exclusive measurement of achievement in poetry. They do provide, however, an indication of the current reception of female poets. The Pulitzer Prize for poetry has been awarded since 1918, when the inaugural prize was awarded to Sara Teasdale. Two women, Natasha Trethewey (*Native Guard*, 2007) and Claudia Emerson (*Late Wife*, 2006), have won the Pulitzer Prize in poetry during the past 10 years. Of the 19 finalists named for the Pulitzer Prize in poetry since 2000, seven were women (36 percent).

Since 1950, the National Book Foundation has given the National Book Award for poetry; each year, a panel of poets selects a winner and four finalists from nominated books. Between 2000 and 2009, three women—Jean Valentine (*Door in the Mountain: New and Collected Poems*, 2004), Ruth Stone (*In the Next Galaxy*, 2002), and Lucille Clifton (*Blessing the Boats: New and Selected Poems 1988–2000*, 2000)—won the National Book Award for poetry. A survey of finalists reveals that of the 40 finalists, 14 were women (35 percent). The National Book Critics Circle (NBCC), an organization of book critics and reviewers, awards prizes annually. Of the nine awards for poetry given by the NBCC since 2000, four have been awarded

to women, or 44 percent; women were 11 of the 32 finalists, or 34 percent. Thus, although women are recognized by award-giving institutions, there is not gender parity among prize recipients.

Two prestigious fellowships in poetry demonstrate gender parity. The Witter Bynner Fellowship is awarded by the Library of Congress to two or more poets a year. Of the 20 Witter Bynner Fellowships awarded since 2000, 11 awards were given to women, for a rate of 55 percent. The Ruth Lilly Poetry Prize, given by the Chicago-based Poetry Foundation and accompanied by a fellowship of $100,000, was given to five women, or 50 percent of the recipients, since 2000. The five women who received the prize are Lisel Mueller, Linda Pastan, Kay Ryan, Lucille Clifton, and Fanny Howe. Thus, some strides have been made for women poets in recent years in terms of professional recognition, particularly in the realm of fellowships, but in literary prizes, women continue to be underrepresented as winners and finalists.

In addition to the contemporary reception of women poets through book circulation, awards, and fellowships, literary appraisal by critics is essential to position women poets more broadly in the canon, to place them in relationship to other poetic movements, and to understand the history and significance of women's poetry. Feminist literary criticism has been responsible for the reclamation of a number of women poets, including Anne Bradstreet, Michael Field, Angelina Weld Grimké, and Charlotte Mew, and for repositioning poets whose reputation had been influenced by sexist ideas, like Emily Dickinson. The loss of work by women poets through books falling out of print, lack of critical attention, and lack of inclusion in anthologies contributes to a cultural amnesia that erases women's poetry. Critical work on behalf of women poets is an evolving area of inquiry, and vital work remains for the next decades. Most assuredly, the women poets writing now will be recognized in part through the labor of thoughtful and informed literary criticism.

See Also: Arts, Women in the (21st Century Overview); Duffy, Carol Ann; United States.

Further Readings

Budy, Andrea Hollander. *When She Named Fire: An Anthology of Contemporary Poetry by American Women*. Pittsburgh, PA: Autumn House Press, 2008.

Moore, Honor. *Poems from the Women's Movement.* New York: Library of America, 2009.

Sparh, Juliana and Stephanie Young. "Numbers Trouble." *Chicago Review*, v.54 (Autumn 2007).

Julie R. Enszer
University of Maryland

Poland

Christianity was established in Poland by Mieszko in 966; in 1569, Poland became a kingdom in the Union of Lublin, the Polish-Lithuanian Commonwealth, which collapsed in 1795. Then, for more than 120 years, Poland was not on the map; Russia, Austria, and Prussia governed the territory. The Second Polish Republic was established following World War I, but then Nazi Germany and the Soviet Union occupation followed in World War II. Years later the socialist People's Republic of Poland emerged within the Eastern Bloc. Polish language, education, and culture were often quashed under occupation, thus women's significance in the family was critical to maintain the Polish cultural heritage. The Third Polish Republic was established in 1989 when communism was overthrown. Poland is a member of the European Union, North Atlanta Treaty Organization, United Nations, World Trade Organization, and Organisation for Economic Co-operation and Development.

Fifty-one percent of Poland's population of nearly 39 million people is female. Poland's population grew at a rate of 1 percent per year from 1970 to 1984, and then declined due to a lower fertility rate. In the mid-2000s, Poland's economic crisis mimicked that of others within the Council for Mutual Economic Assistance, yet Poland is one of the more robust transformed economic states. Younger generations compete for education and economic opportunity. Women's life expectancy is approximately 76 years, compared to 68 years for men, primarily due to lifestyle behaviors associated with tobacco use and alcohol consumption.

The economic and social transformation of Poland from communism to a democratic, privatized market economy has had mixed results. Gender differences continue to be accentuated, and some benefits for women, including access to subsidized childcare and paid maternity leave, have diminished. In the late 1970s, more than 70 percent of Polish women were gainfully employed while maintaining household duties, putting a strain on their ability to balance "women's two jobs" because of role competition and unsatisfactory state assistance. Class issues remain predominant; lower-class women can more easily hold a coprovider status along with a domestic role, whereas this challenges the social status of upper class women.

Partner relationships have been typically egalitarian, with the head of household described as that person who disposes of the income of both providers. Divorce is less common than in other former communist countries, likely because of the country's Catholic roots. Single mothers tend to retain custody of children. Birth control was typically limited to abortion due to lack of other options; abortion was more restricted in 1993, however. Increasing grassroots democracy efforts included challenges to church doctrine on birth control in the 1990s.

Women in the Workforce and Politics

Education has remained the biggest predictor of women's roles outside the home. Women tend to go on to post-secondary education more often then men. However, fewer women are educated than in other Eastern European countries. Recently, only 10 percent of women aged 30 to 39 had a college degree. Women's workforce participation is high, yet women comprise the majority of the unemployed in the country. Women tend to make less money than men, largely due to their gender-segregated occupations and less access to private sector and state employment. They account for less than 20 percent of faculty in higher-education institutions. Growth in the number of women-owned businesses has occurred, although they compose less than 10 percent of the workforce.

Women's involvement in politics dropped from a guaranteed approximate 20 percent proportion of women in the Sejm (the Polish legislature) under communism and increased slightly in 1993 around the time of the new abortion legislation. The post-Communist women's movement is evident in groups like the Enthusiasts and the Union for Equal Rights for Polish Women; identifiable activists, including Narcyza Zmichowska, Kazimiera Bujwidowa, and Romualda

Baudoin; and the Polish Socialist and National Democratic Parties. The roots of this involvement can be derived from the Stalinist era, when women's leagues were encouraged to raise membership through their "talkativeness."

Poland is a source, transit, and destination country for women trafficked for commercial sexual exploitation. The government's limited response includes victim-assistance programs and prevention efforts. Despite such issues, Polish women tend to disagree with American feminism; if anything has spoken to their experience, it is bell hooks' black feminist perspective that designated a feeling of otherness amid gender discrimination. Polish women identify that socialism had discriminated against women and men. Like Western women, east-central European women identify conceptually as postfeminist "superwomen" who balance work and domestic realms.

See Also: Gender Roles, Cross-Cultural; Germany; Lithuania; Ukraine.

Further Readings

Hoff, Joan, and Christie Farnham. Editor's Note and Acknowledgements: "The More Things Change the Worse They Become for Women." *Journal of Women's History*, v.5/3 (Winter 1994).

Lobodzinska, B. "Married Women's Gainful Employment and Housework in Contemporary Poland." *Journal of Marriage and the Family*, (May 1977).

Nowak, Basia A. "Constant Conversations: Agitators in the League of Women in Poland during the Stalinist Period." *Feminist Studies*, v.31/3 (Fall 2005).

Oleksy, Elzbieta H. "American Feminism and Pedagogy: The Case of Poland." *American Studies International*, v.38/3 (October 2000).

Siemienska, R. "Winners and Losers: Gender Contracts in the New Political and Economic Situation." *International Journal of Sociology*, v.35/1 (Spring 2005).

Sokolowska, M. "The Role and Status of Women in Poland." *Studies in Comparative Development*, (Fall 1975).

Velkoff, Victoria A. U.S. Department of Commerce, Economics and Statistics Division. Bureau of the Census. "Women in Poland." July 1995. http://www .census.gov/ipc/prod/women_po.pdf (accessed December 31, 2009).

United States Department of State. *Trafficking in Persons Report 2008—Poland.* June 2008. http://www.unhcr .org/refworld/docid/484f9a3632.html (accessed December 31, 2009).

Elesha L. Ruminski
Frostburg State University

Political Ideologies

The meaning of the term *political ideology* can be ambiguous, due in large part to differing understandings of the word *ideology*. In everyday usage, ideology has a pejorative connotation: the ideology of another person or group is seen to distort or distract from social and political realities. This usage contrasts "ideology" with "truth" and understands the former to be biased and the latter to be value neutral. Everyday usage of "ideology" differs from academic applications. In Marxist thought, ideology is linked to class. The ideology of the ruling class is thought to pervade the lower classes: the latter suffer from "false consciousness," that is, they are tricked into accepting a social and political order that is not in their interest. In feminist thought, ideology is linked to gender. Ideology has been used to theorize how women are conditioned to accept a sexist (or patriarchal) social and political order. Political ideology and ideology are related but distinct concepts. Political ideology can be defined as a comprehensive set of ideas that attempt to make sense of the social and political world and provide a foundation for action. In other words, political ideologies have two dimensions: first, how society should be organized and function; and second, the best way to achieve these goals.

Following from the second dimension, political ideologies are concerned with the justification of authority (that is, demonstrating that a particular form of authority will benefit society). To examine political ideologies is to examine the content of these ideologies and how they concretely impact people as well as assess the nature of ideology in a more abstract manner. As such, political ideologies are important to women today less because of the way ideology has been theorized in academic feminism (or elsewhere) and more because of how different political ideologies have played a significant role in women's lives.

All contemporary political ideologies are gendered, including liberalism, socialism, conservatism, nationalism, and fascism. In setting out how society ought to be organized and function, political ideologies involve an understanding of gender-appropriate behavior. For example, conservatism understands women's inequality as both natural and functional. Men "by nature" are assertive, rational and logical, and women "by nature" are passive, emotional, and nurturing. Women's inequality is functional in that the traditional division of labor—in which women are stay-at-home mothers and helpmates to their male partners—is seen to benefit society as a whole. Political ideologies also are gendered in that women are used as symbols representing ideological goals.

For example, nationalism often involves an idealized figure of a woman, often a mother, representing the nation. Such images here would be the Statue of Liberty, Mother India, Mother Ireland, and Mother Russia. Finally, political ideologies are gendered in their understandings of authority. For example, liberalism understands power as existing primarily within institutions of the state, namely, the legislature and courts. As such, many abuses of power affecting women, such as domestic violence, have not always been treated seriously. In this entry, the basic ideas of each of the political ideologies of liberalism, socialism, conservatism, nationalism, and fascism will be considered along with further concrete implications for women today.

Liberalism, Socialism, and Conservatism

Liberalism, socialism, and conservatism have dominated political life for two centuries. Although adherents to these schools of thought accuse each other of being ideological, all can be defined as political ideologies. They all arose in Europe and North America in conjunction with several forces, including the Enlightenment, the industrial revolution, and the political revolutions of the 17th and 18th centuries. They became increasingly global with 20th-century struggles against colonial rule and recent expansions of globalized capitalism. Although all remain influential, liberalism is the predominant political ideology today.

The starting point of liberalism is the individual. The state grants the individual rights and liberties. Liberals understand power and politics as being conducted in the state (for example, through elected representatives). The state has two primary functions: to secure a citizen's rights and liberties within the state and to protect its members from dangers outside the state.

Outside of these functions, the state should intervene in individual's lives as little as possible. Individual liberty is maximizing self-interest and acting according to one's desires. Liberals understand differences such as gender and race as irrelevant to citizenship; equality means individuals are equal before the law. Liberal political ideology has had various and contradictory implications for women. On the one hand, it has been mobilized by feminists for women's education, basic political rights—such as the right to vote—and the wider inclusion of women in public life. On the other hand, in the last three decades the liberal idea of minimal state intervention has translated into the "market" being understood as the main regulator of public life. This has resulted in the dismantling of health and social services upon which women tend to rely.

Although quite different political ideologies, the starting point of both socialism and conservatism is not the individual but society as a whole. Both emphasize the community and collective good and critique the liberal emphasis on self-interest and individualism. Both understand society to be hierarchical; however, while socialists critique hierarchies, conservatives wish to "conserve" them. The socialist critique of hierarchy is a critique of how the capitalist mode of production exploits the working class. Socialism contends that anything contributing significantly to the production, distribution, and delivery of socially necessary goods must be controlled for the benefit of everyone. Socialism can take many forms, only one of which is Marxism. Conservatives wish to maintain hierarchy. They believe the social fabric that has carried on for generations is delicate, and as such, each person should be born, live, and die according to their station.

While socialism is not hostile to women's equality in the manner of conservatism, both socialism and conservatism have been problematic for women. Socialism tends to privilege class over other forms of oppression including gender. This is evident in the marginalization of many women within unions. On the other hand, socialists, along with left-leaning liberals, have pushed for the expansion of social services benefiting women, including affordable childcare and maternity leave. Conservative ideology understands many women's issues as threatening the social fabric, including access to contraceptives and other reproductive rights, lesbian parenting, and affirmative action.

Nationalism and fascism are different political ideologies with one shared belief: that people naturally fall into separate groups. Nationalism understands that all people within the group, or nation, have similar needs and desires, and as such, require a nation-state of their own. Fascism combines nationalism with militarism and totalitarian forms of authority; it is the only political ideology to reject democracy. Fascists understand people to be fundamentally irrational, defined by difference like race, gender, religion, language, and nationality, and perpetually locked in conflict. Although most closely identified with Italy and Germany up to World War II, neo-Nazism in North America and Europe is on the rise. In both nationalism and fascism, women play an important role distinguishing "us" from "them."

Most political ideologies, with the sometimes exception of liberalism and socialism, are hostile to feminism or women's equality. At the same time, in conservatism, nationalism, and even fascism, women's roles as mothers and "reproducers of the nation" are recognized and respected, at least rhetorically. Liberalism, socialism, conservatism, nationalism, and fascism are not the only political ideologies affecting women today. There are several other "isms" that also might be considered political ideologies, such as religious fundamentalism and environmentalism. However, the Encyclopedia contains other entries on these topics.

See Also: Affirmative Action/Equal Opportunity; Childcare; Domestic Violence; Ecofeminism; Environmental Activism, Grassroots; Feminism, American; Household Division of Labor; Lesbian Adoption; Religious Fundamentalisms, Cross-Cultural Context of; Reproductive and Sexual Health Rights; Stay-at-Home Mothers; Voting Rights.

Further Readings

Charles, Nickie and Helen Hintjens, eds. *Gender, Ethnicity and Political Ideologies.* New York: Routledge, 1998.

Mathews, Donald G. and Jane S. De Hart. *Sex, Gender, and the Politics of ERA: A State and the Nation.* New York: Oxford University Press,, 1992.

Yuval-Davies, Nira. *Gender and Nation.* Thousand Oaks, CA: Sage, 1997.

Julie E. Dowsett
York University

Polygamy, Cross-Culturally Considered

Polygamy refers to simultaneity of marital bonds with two or more partners and is thus (if only legally) distinguished from serial (sequential or successive) monogamy and nonmatrimonial, polyamorous relationships. Polygyny (a man marries two or more co-wives) is much more prevalent than polyandry or group marriage, and would be a preferential system in 75 percent of ethnographic communities drawn from the mid-20th-century World Ethnographic Sample. In the contemporary West, sensitivity over polygamy is politically oscillating with that over immigrant, denominational, and ethnic minority status of the polygamist (or bigamist, in legal terms focusing on the ceremonial act of marriage rather than the polygamous state it inaugurates), inviting confrontations between de facto practice, legal climate, and collateral political sensibilities, for instance, over same-sex marriage. It brings together a range of discourses about women, often in terms of custom, rights, and identity.

International Law

The United Nations Human Rights Committee has occasionally reaffirmed their General Comment No. 28 (2000), according to which polygamy violates the dignity of women and should be definitely abolished wherever it continues to exist. Polygamy is not prohibited or protected under international human rights law, and legal status varies markedly across national jurisdictions. Polygamy may be illegal (as in most Western countries); recognized under civil or customary law; partially recognized for purposes of welfare benefits if legally obtained abroad (in the United Kingdom and Australia); permitted only to certain denominations and delimited by sex and number of partners (e.g. four wives permitted to Egyptian Muslim men); otherwise rendered conditional (requiring written consent from a first wife and a man's ability to provide for co-wives); and/or regionally exempted from national bans by Shari`a (Islamic) Law (e.g., Eritrea). In the West, prosecution is rare. In Canada, for instance, polygamy is practiced by a breakaway Mormon sect in Bountiful, British Columbia, but prosecution for polygamy has not occurred for more than 60 years, and statistics are not kept. Today polygamous unions are recognized civilly in approaching 50 (mostly Arab) countries. It is widely practised in Africa; in Burkina Faso and Togo, according to 2002 data, more than half of women would be in polygynous marriages.

Cross-Cultural Practice

Legal globalization has tended to abolitionism, and but also to a rise in de facto forms that hide from the legal gaze under various guises (e.g., "concubinage" in China). De facto polygyny may be interwoven with commuting across borders, thus evading, or pertaining to, multiple jurisdictions—many married Hong Kong men who cross the border regularly on business have taken second wives or mistresses in China. In de facto cases, plural marriage is not legally or ritually codified but depends on informal or customary arrangements related to domestic tasks, sexual access, kinship-based obligations, or other aspects. Many semiformalized social arrangements resist reduction to legal codification. Examples include wife sharing, "sugar daddy–

gold digger" liaisons in sub-Saharan Africa, and *enjo kosai* ("compensated dating") in Japan. Ultimately, the definition of polygamy depends on that of the family as a demarcated socioeconomic unit and of marriage as codified type of sociality both in terms of spousal union and as alliance between families or kin groups. However, it often remains delivered to an administrative, legalistic, and Western gaze. In contemporary urban African settings, especially, people move in and out of a range of conjugal relationships, with varying degrees of formality, and in which marriage is encountered more as fluid and processual than contractual.

In a 2005 comparative policy assessment, Angela Campbell reviews social status, economic, and health implications of polygamy, finding such implications to vary considerably across research settings and studies and to invite careful legal maneuvering. The female experience of plural-wife (co-wife) systems differs with respect to: rivalry, hierarchy, and favoritism; economic support, companionship, task sharing, and conflict resolution; and resources for containing abuse. These differences are often compounded by

An early 1900s photograph from the Utah Quarterly Journal, *of Joseph F. Smith, his wives and children. Smith was the nephew of Joseph Smith, Jr., founding prophet of the Church of Jesus Christ of Latter-day Saints.*

prohibitive legislation introducing constraints on who can act as "real wife" in the public eye, with implications for mobility and social insulation—important factors with regard to consent and potential for abuse. Legal status is a political objective for women in some countries; in nonstatutory marriages, widows may be unable to inherit property, receive insurance benefits, or gain child custody. If divorced, they may not be able to sue for support.

Studies suggest that viability in plural marriages depends on a range of factors, including acceptance of polygamy as divine wish or destiny, household separation, equality in allocation of resources among non-resident families and cross-household communication patterns (if non-co-resident), and patterns of dealing with "minor" conflicts or disagreements. Some Africanists differentiate between *affluent polygamy* and *interventive polygamy*; the former motivated by the urge for social prestige and economic ambitions, and the latter as a response to family stress, particularly as a therapeutic for childlessness or sonlessness. Introduction of a second wife into a childless marriage when the problem is proved to be that of the first wife is understood to serve as relief of, rather than stress to, the first wife. However, preferential polygyny is often overdetermined given traditional valuation of female fertility, female hypergamy and male hypogamy (marrying upward or downward with respect to a partner's socioeconomic status), male display of wealth through co-wife number, and the insurance of male progeny.

It is questionable, then, that the cultural and ethical assumptions of the *affluence-intervention* distinction are exhaustive whether in terms of a final arbitration between use and abuse or as a continentwide teleological typology. Nevertheless, the basic administrative question remains whether the conditions for polygamous practice can be optimized or whether the institution needs to be abandoned entirely. Research suggests that higher regional prevalence of polygyny correlates with marginalization in social, economic, and reproductive decision making for married women both in monogamous and polygynous unions.

In higher-polygyny environments, women's household position and roles are seen as easily replaceable, which undermines their bargaining position relative to that of their husband's in major household decisions. The choice to enter or leave polygamous marriages is intrinsic to cultural value systems, given that evaluations of economic, reproductive, and matrimonial status determine the conceptualization of free choice as a situated possibility. Current legal debates, as a consequence, inform a perennial standoff between valuations of community, tradition, and strategic alliance on the one hand and [inter]nationalist proclamations of equality and [reproductive] autonomy on the other, a standoff characterizing feminist internationalism in general. Important here, for instance, is whether one can see polygamy as symptomatizing or even epitomizing patriarchy or whether its situational merits should be considered in relation to the question of whether it may happen to, or usually does, coincide with a wider patriarchal context. Local evaluations of such a coincidence may alternatively stress the possibilities for viable pluralism or a totalizing verdict of incompatibility with female "autonomy."

A number of demographic and biomedical factors may determine much of the course of the politicization of polygynous traditions in sub-Saharan Africa, given their association with markedly low female marriage age, large spousal age gap, high household fertility, and bride price. Polygynous countries are also on average poorer than monogamous countries.

Contemporary and future politics over polygamy in minority polygamous communities revolve around excesses considered either inherent or associated with isolation, secrecy, and anxiety over expulsion, such as underage and incestuous liaisons and domestic violence. A specific problem is purging of surplus young males in communities where seniority is a marked factor in obtaining wives and where the number of young bachelors becomes a problem to community stability.

Health

Controlling for a set of social and biodemographic factors, it is reported that substantial risks of mortality are associated with polygyny. Polygyny's impact, however, may differ from country to country. Polygyny has been associated with an accelerated transmission of sexually transmitted diseases (STDs), specifically human immunodeficiency virus (HIV), because it both allows multiplication of sexual partners and correlates with low rates of condom use, poor communication between spouses, and age and power imbalances. Recent research, however, suggests to the contrary that HIV prevalence is lower in countries where the practice of polygyny is common, and within countries, it is lower in areas with higher levels of polygyny. Female fertility may be variably affected by the interplay of marital rank, household status, and cultural norms. Men from polygynous families are more likely than their monogamous counterparts to be unemployed and to suffer from myriad psychological problems, including anxiety, depression, and somatization. According to other research they may be more likely to perceive the functioning of their families as problematic, their marriage as less satisfying, and their relationship with their children as more troublesome.

See Also: Africa; Fundamentalist Church of Jesus Christ of Latter-Day Saints; HIV/AIDS: Africa; Marriage.

Further Readings

Campbell, Angela. "How Have Policy Approaches to Polygamy Responded to Women's Experiences and Rights? An International, Comparative Analysis." *Polygamy in Canada*. Ottawa: Status of Women Canada, 2005.

Cook, Cynthia. "Polygyny: Did the Africans Get it Right?" *Journal of Black Studies*, v.38 (2007).

Nwoye, Augustine. "The Practice of Interventive Polygamy in Two Regions of Africa: Background, Theory and Techniques." *Dialectical Anthropology*, v.31 (2007).

Tertilt, Michèle. "Polygyny, Women's Rights, and Development." *Journal of the European Economic Association*, v.4 (2006).

Zeitzen, Miriam Koktvedgaard. *Polygamy: A Cross-Cultural Analysis*. Oxford, UK: Berg, 2008.

Diederik F. Janssen
Independent Scholar

Pornography, Portrayal of Women in

Pornography in the United States is a multibillion-dollar industry that transcends media boundaries, from magazines to films to books to the Internet. Its popularity, however, has not come without criticisms, drawing a unique group of opponents that includes left-wing feminists and conservative right-wing fundamentalists working in concert to challenge pornography's portrayal of women. From a historical standpoint that stems from the Puritanical roots of the United States, adult entertainment has a longstanding tradition of being considered taboo. Those participating in pornographic media, sometimes referred to as adult entertainment, have often been deemed as deviant, with adult entertainment actresses commonly stereotyped as sluts and whores while its actors are similarly characterized and viewed as perpetuating a misogynistic culture.

From a critical perspective, contemporary pornography objectifies women by reducing them from complete human beings to a collection of body parts designed to satisfy and gratify men. Women are seen as playthings that must be subservient to their male counterparts, either physically or emotionally. They may be dressed in childlike outfits (school or cheerleading uniforms) and wear pigtails or ribbons in their hair. This infantilizing process delegitimizes any power or voice the women may have and establishes the other half of the whore/virgin dichotomy that exists in pornography.

In turn, the subservience may be followed or accompanied by force which affords detractors the opportunity to link pornography with violence against women that extends beyond a mediated reality (or fantasy) and into actual reality. Furthermore, as the pornographic portrayal of women bleeds into more mainstream media, opponents contend that young women and girls are given a false sense of what it means to be popular, loved, and happy.

From a legal standpoint, First Amendment scholars make certain it is known that pornography is a protected form of speech and not synonymous with obscenity, which is considered unprotected speech and defined by *Miller v. California*. Women, provided they are of a legal age and capable of consenting, have every right to engage in such activities if they so desire. Some third-wave feminists consider pornography to be empowering to women, affording them control of their sexuality and allowing them to be sexual for their own benefit and not assuming it is for a man. This perspective further complicates the pornography debate by pitting feminist against feminist and adding an additional critical component.

Historical Look

Even before technological advancements in the mid-19th century made it easier to reproduce photographic images, pornography as an industry had been a part of U.S. culture, albeit not without periods of marginalization. Politicians and morality watchdogs like Anthony Comstock, who was the impetus for the Comstock Act of 1873, have long fought against pornography, often calling the material obscene and a detriment to the American public. Hugh Hefner's introduction of *Playboy* magazine in 1953 can be considered pornography's introduction into mainstream culture. Hefner offered a higher-quality medium than had been shown previously in pornography. His female models were portrayed as the average girl and not the destitute women who had been featured in print.

Similar to *Playboy*, the 1972 release of the movie *Deep Throat* was also said to elevate the portrayal of women in pornographic films. Linda Boreman, better known as Linda Lovelace, was the lead actress in the film and played the role of the girl next door. The role of prostitutes and drug addicts common to earlier stag films was abandoned in favor of something more relatable to audiences. However, Boreman's actual life, which included abuse and prostitution, was indicative of the stag film industry. She eventually said she was forced to perform in *Deep Throat* by her then-husband, Chuck Traynor, and described the film as depicting her rape. Boreman detailed her life in her autobiography, *Ordeal.* She died on April 22, 2002, at the age of 53.

Larry Flynt's launch of *Hustler* magazine in 1974 gave readers a much more explicit look at naked women, compared to Hefner's *Playboy.* Flynt's raw and detailed photographs of female genitalia were criticized as obscene and his pushing-the-envelope photo spreads condemned as objectifying women and promoting a culture of violence and misogyny, or a hatred of women. Flynt continues to publish *Hustler* as of 2009, along with other magazines, and has film, retail stores, and strip club holdings. *Hustler* magazine continues to depict women in a more hardcore fashion than Hefner's *Playboy.* Flynt is reportedly worth more than three-quarters of a billion dollars.

Boreman's success in the 1970s was unprecedented at the time. Her accomplishments, however, are incomparable to the industry's postmillennium porn queen: Jenna Jameson. Born April 9, 1974, Jameson has successfully infiltrated mainstream media, including book publishing, television, and film, to become a popular culture icon. Her 2004 book, *How to Make Love Like a Porn Star: A Cautionary Tale,* details her life in and out of the pornography industry and spent multiple weeks on the *New York Times* Bestseller List.

Misogyny Versus Empowerment

As pornography has become more mainstream in recent decades, its prevalence has likewise come under more scrutiny. While one side of the pornography debate sees the destigmatization of pornography to be a liberating factor and another step away from viewing sex as a taboo subject, or the female body as innately dirty, challengers question if the increasing presence of pornography has created a desensitization toward violence, particularly sexual violence against women. This desensitization process creates a trickle-down effect that extends to nonadult entertainment, including network and basic cable television programming, children's video games and music videos. Nelly's 2003 "Tip Drill" video is an example of this bleeding; the term *tip drill* refers to a woman with an attractive body, but an unattractive face—good only for sex.

In the music video for "Tip Drill," which has been labeled by some as soft-core pornography, men and women are shown drinking and dancing, scantily clad, at a palatial home. The women, often shown topless and wearing little more than thongs, are shown in hypersexual positions with same- and opposite-sex partners, while rap artist Nelly sings, "It must be ya ass, cuz it ain't yo face, I need a tip drill." To further show the objectification of the women, a male actor is shown swiping a credit card down the buttocks of a woman, while at another point, dollar bills are strewn onto a woman's crotch area as she lays on a table.

Jameson maintains she held complete control over her sex activities during her career as a pornographic actress, explicitly stating what she would and would not do. In 2006, Jameson retired from performing and moved behind the camera, directing her first film, *The Provocateur.* She argues that her films do not mirror pornography that blatantly degrades women or portrays them in subservient or victimized roles. Instead, Jameson focuses on empowering women and allows women to be sexual for their own—and not a man's—pleasure. This type of feminist pornography challenges patriarchal ideologies and focuses on empowering not only the actresses involved in the film production but those viewing the finished product. This exemplifies one aspect of third-wave feminist ideology.

Not one to buy into the argument of feminist pornography or the ability to empower women through adult entertainment was the late radical feminist, Andrea Dworkin. As the author of *Intercourse* and *Pornography: Men Possessing Women*, Dworkin was a vigilant crusader against pornography and claimed obscenity laws were ineffective and innately anti-women in construction. Pornography, according to Dworkin, maintains male supremacy through the portrayal and promotion of female inferiority. She disputed the argument that pornography is a form of fantasy entertainment, pointing again toward acts of sadism against, and the objectification of, women. Dworkin died on April 9, 2005, at the age of 58.

Obscenity Versus Free Speech

Degradation, hyperfeminization, and hypersexualization, as well as sadism and masochism involving women, may be unattractive to pornography's opponents, but provided they are not obscene, they are legal, according to the U.S. judicial system. The term *obscene* is often incorrectly utilized, with some individuals using it synonymously with pornography. This is not accurate, however. The 1973 decision of *Miller v. California* provides a three-prong test for determining what is obscene. The statute's requirements include that the work: appeals to a prurient interest in sex when taken as a whole and judged by contemporary community standards by an average person; is patently offensive as defined by state law; and lacks serious literary, artistic, political, or scientific value. Thus, while those in the adult entertainment industry may create work that some may find offensive and exploitative of women, mainstream pornographers are businessmen and businesswomen who adhere to state and federal statutes to avoid costly court battles. And when arguments occur, they are often based on what is ethically—not legally—correct.

Nadine Strossen, a professor of law at the New York Law School, has been a vocal advocate for the First Amendment protection of pornography and served as the president of the American Civil Liberties Union from 1991 to 2008. Her publications include *Speaking of Race, Speaking of Sex: Hate Speech, Civil Rights and Civil Liberties* and *Defending Pornography: Free Speech, Sex and the Fight for Women's Rights*. Advocates of censoring pornography under the guise of protecting women have drastically decreased as the world entered a new millennium, yet the topic remains in the issue loop for politicians. Politicos argue that the negative portrayals and exploitation of women in pornography provide false ideals, harmful messages, and unrealistic expectations for young women who may view porn stars as icons, particularly since some, like Jameson, Nina Hartley and Stormy Daniels, have crossed into nonadult entertainment, thereby increasing their visibility to the under-18 demographic.

Impact on Young Women

Mainstream pornography may be legally protected by the U.S. Constitution, and its detractors may be quieter now than in the previous millennium, but there remain groups that continue to criticize pornography as detrimental not only to women but to young girls. The Massachusetts-based Media Education Foundation has produced a series of videos that challenge what it believes to be misogynistic, violent, hypersexual, and demeaning messages conveyed through the portrayal of women in not only pornography but nonadult entertainment, including video games, music videos, and popular culture in general. Documentaries like *Generation M: Misogyny in Media & Culture*; *Hip-Hop: Beyond Beats & Rhymes*; and *Price of Pleasure: Pornography, Sexuality & Relationships* target high school and college-age viewers and challenge them to critically analyze media.

As pornographic images become more mainstream and less shocking to the general public, the perceived objectification and hypersexualization of women in everyday media become more apparent. Furthermore, as pornography actresses move in and out of "the business" and nonindustry women experiment with the fame of pornography, how women are portrayed is becoming less the issue. Jameson has appeared in Abercrombie & Fitch advertisements, and Olympic gold-medalist Amanda Beard is just one of multiple Olympians who have posed for *Playboy*; she appeared in July 2007. Other Olympians include, but are not limited to Haley Cope and Amy Acuff, both of whom appeared in the September 2004 edition.

See Also: Feminism; Pornography/Erotica; Pornography Produced by Women; Third Wave.

Further Readings
Calvert, C. and R. D. Richards. "Porn in Their Words: Female Leaders in the Adult Entertainment Industry Address Free Speech, Censorship, Feminism, Culture and the Mainstreaming of Adult Content." *Vanderbilt Journal of Entertainment and Technology Law*, v.9/2 (2006).
Paul, P. *Pornified: How Pornography Is Transforming Our Lives, Our Relationships, and Our Families.* New York: Times Books, 2005.
Sarracino, C. and K. M. Scott. *The Porning of America: The Rise of Porn Culture, What It Means, and Where We Go from Here.* Boston: Beacon Press, 2008.
Stark, C. and R. Whisnant, eds. *Not for Sale: Feminists Resisting Prostitution and Pornography.* North Melbourne, Australia: Spinifex Press, 2004.

Kalen M. A. Churcher
Niagara University

Pornography Produced by Women

In recent decades, women have been actively diversifying sexual expression in the male-dominated pornography industry by moving from in front of the camera to behind the scenes. By contributing as directors and producers of pornography, in addition to acting, women participating in the pornography industry are now able to professionally construct their visual conceptions of sexuality. Until recently, these female-generated conceptions have been strategically overlooked within the modern pornography industry. Due to the fact that this industry derives profit from the continued success of otherwise "masculine-centric" cultural scripts and representations including power, domination, and aggression, the omission of female fantasy within mainstream pornography had become an industry standard. However, as women began developing an interest in the production side of por-

nography, these unchallenged scripts began to shift. Keeping in mind the notion that not all women conceptualize sexuality in the same way, female pornographers project elements of female sexuality that initially draw from common experiences and interpretations, including the absence of violence, women enjoying the sexual encounter, women initiating the sexual encounter, egalitarian lovemaking, and the construction of a narrative. However, as an anti-essentialist form of expression, pornography produced by women does not follow a grand narrative; instead, each film offers a unique interpretation of sexuality, depending on various factors including the director, the production company, and funding. Historically, audiences of pornography have been exposed to a sexual construction made for and by men, but with the inclusion of women as producers of pornography, this historical construction is now being challenged and modified.

While most mainstream or traditional pornography constructs an otherwise patriarchal and sexist representation of women, female pornographers claim that they construct a female sexuality that transcends oppression. It is important to note, however, that sexuality is subjective. In other words, one woman's interpretation of female desire might not match another woman's. Pornography produced by women, therefore, is not able to represent the sexuality of all women. Rather, it represents a progressive movement toward the inclusion of women's voices in the pornography industry. As the number of female pornography producers continues to increase, so will the various depictions of female sexuality and desire.

Some of the most notable female producers of pornography include Candida Royalle (Femme Productions), Tristan Taormino (Smart Ass Productions), Joanna Angel (Burning Angel), Madison Young (Madison Bound Productions), Shine Louise Houston (Pink & White Productions), Erika Lust (Lust Films), Veronica Hart (works for VCA Pictures), and Dana Dane (Erockatavision). Most of these women have emerged as producers as a result of their experiences as actors within the mainstream industry.

For example, Royalle, who claims to be the first woman filmmaker to try to appeal to women viewers, was a successful pornography actor in the 1970s. She later established Femme Productions in 1985 as a way to address the overlooked sexual needs of women by introducing a more loving attitude toward sex and women. While Royalle's work falls under the category of pornography, she prefers to refer to her work as "erotica" or "adult entertainment," due to the otherwise oppositional stance that women take toward traditional pornography. Two of her films include *Eyes of Desire* (2000) and *The Bridal Shower* (2003).

While female producers of pornography continue to put female desire and sexual empowerment at the forefront of their work, their participation in the pornography industry has been challenged as part of a historical debate between feminism and pornography. While attitudes toward pornography have existed for hundreds of years, it wasn't until the 1980s that radical feminists began publicly challenging the pornography industry's incorporation of violence, victimization, and objectification of women. At the same time, however, liberal feminists voiced their support for sexual expression and found radical feminism's opposition to pornography to place limitations on the construction of women's sexual liberation. This conflict was part of the Feminist Sex Wars, a larger feminist debate that centered on women, sexuality, and representation.

This conflict was never resolved, and there still exists a split within feminism regarding female participation and promotion of pornography. It is important to note, however, that while the feminist movement is not solely responsible for legitimizing female desire, it does offer a helpful theoretical framework for understanding sexuality, marginalization, oppression, and violence.

The Feminist Sex Wars illustrate the fact that not all women approach sexuality, desire, or fantasy the same way. Therefore, while female participation in pornography is problematic for many, it is also liberating, helpful, and enjoyable for others. Pornography produced by women has created an opportunity for the construction of female desire in the pornography industry as well as the development of a female audience that feels represented in a more respectful and accurate manner.

However, while some female pornographers feel that particular sexual acts, toys (including bondage), or settings may be particularly liberating, other women will continue to find these representations of women destructive and oppressive. As stated earlier, sexuality is subjective and therefore so is pornography, whether or not women produce it.

See Also: Feminism, American; Pornography, Portrayal of Women in; Pornography/Erotica; Representation of Women; Sex Workers.

Further Readings

Baumgardner, J. and A. Richards. *Manifesta: Young Women, Feminism, and the Future.* New York: Farrar, Straus & Giroux, 2000.

Cornell, D., ed. *Feminism and Pornography.* Oxford, UK: Oxford University Press, 2000.

Dworkin, A. *Pornography: Men Possessing Women.* New York: Plume, 1991.

Kipnis, L. *Bound and Gagged: Pornography and the Politics of Fantasy in America.* New York: Grove Press, 1996.

Milne, C. *Naked Ambition.* New York: Carroll & Graf, 2005.

Nagle, J. *Whores and Other Feminists.* London: Routledge, 1997.

Royalle, C. *How to Tell a Naked Man What to Do: Sex Advice from a Woman Who Knows.* New York: Fireside, 2004.

Rachael Liberman
University of Colorado at Boulder

Pornography/Erotica

The term *pornography* is a compound of two Greek words: *porno*, meaning prostitute, and *graphos*, meaning writing or depiction; erotica is rooted in the Greek word *eros*, meaning passionate love. The inception of modern pornography is closely tied to technological development. At the forefront of each emerging medium is the application of the technology for producing or distributing pornography, such as printing capabilities in the 18th century and then photography in the 19th century, especially the production and trade of erotic postcards in the 1890s. In the early 20th century, short "stag films" or "loops" were produced on 8mm film. The porn industry took off in the 1970s, when feature-length pornographic films such as *Boys in the Sand, Deep Throat, Behind the Green Door, Devil in Miss Jones, Score,* and *Debbie Does Dallas* were given X ratings and shown in regular movie theaters. As VHS cassette tape technology was created in the late 1970s and toward the start of the 1980s, this technology became mainstream, bringing pornography into private homes in America. Likewise, when DVDs were created and began to replace VHS tapes in the late 1990s, porn producers embraced this new medium.

The explosion of the Internet has had a profound effect on the porn industry. Today there is so much pirated pornography available that mainstream studios have given up trying to shut them down and instead provide video-on-demand options on their Websites so viewers can select and download millions of videos from a multitude of Websites onto their personal computers. In 2005, video sales and rentals were $4.28 billion and Internet sales were $2.5 billion. One year later, video sales had dropped to $3.62 and Internet sales increased to $2.84 billion a year. While China, Japan, and South Korea exceed the United States in video sales, the United States is home to about 90 percent of pornographic Websites. Currently, about 80 percent of pornography made in the United States is produced near Los Angeles, California. The major producers in the industry participate in the Adult Video News (AVN) Awards, an awards show held in Las Vegas that celebrates the achievements of producers, directors, and performers.

Legal Issues

Pornography has been subjected to censorship from three forces: second-wave feminists such as Catherine MacKinnon, Andrea Dworkin, and Gloria Steinem who argue that porn is in itself degrading to women; government agencies supported by conservative politicians; and fundamentalist religious groups such as the Family Research Council. In 1970, President Richard Nixon instigated the "Report of the Commission on Obscenity and Pornography," emphasizing First Amendment rights to the consumption of pornography by adults and recommendations for education and restriction of access to porn by children. In 1986, President Ronald Reagan commissioned the Meese Report, a 1,960-page document describing the history of pornography, linking the industry to organized crime, and postulating about the negative social effects of pornography on society.

Many objections to pornography by these groups attempt to make a causal link between pornography production and consumption and violent behavior such as rape or compulsive sexual behavior, but no empirical research has supported these claims. These groups also object that pornography is easily acces-

sible to minors on the Internet. Some attempts have been made to disambiguate "pornography" from "erotica" in an attempt to codify which materials have artistic merit and are thus acceptable to community standards and which do not. Many legal and academic theorists describe erotic media on a continuum, starting from a "love scene" in a movie that depicts sex between characters, to erotica or softcore porn that features sex as a major theme but does not show explicit penetration, to pornography that is built around a story, to hard-core pornography with little or no plot, to extreme "horror" porn produced mainly for shock value. Many proclaim that sexual stories or narratives of fantasies are erotica, since the written word contains no visually explicit element. One must question whether or not sexual expression and pleasure are as defensible a motivation as artistic or scientific exploration of human sexuality.

In the United States, porn performers must be 18 years or older and sign consent forms before working. Currently, pornography producers and directors of mainstream studios follow a set of guidelines developed by attorney Paul Cambria, who represented *Hustler* magazine for several years. The "Cambria List," as it is known in the industry, is a list of behaviors that are considered too extreme to show on film and may leave the producers open to obscenity charges. The list is based on prior obscenity convictions during the Bush administration, such as that of Max Hardcore (a.k.a. Paul Little) in 2008; Little was sentenced to four years in prison for charges of obscenity.

Safety Concerns

In the early 1980s, the human immunodeficiency virus and acquired immune deficiency syndrome (HIV/AIDS) epidemic began to come to the forefront of national consciousness, prompting new health and safety regulations and safer sex outreach. However, this trend did not reach the adult industry until more than a decade later. The Adult Industry Medical (AIM) Healthcare Foundation is a nonprofit organization founded in 1997 by Sharon Mitchell, former adult performer. AIM has become the industry safety standard, regularly testing adult performers for HIV, chlamydia, gonorrhea, and hepatitis. All performers must now produce a negative test from AIM that is less than 30 days old before working. In 2004, four performers were found to have HIV, and the industry briefly came to a halt. The outbreak was traced to a performer's sexual contact with someone outside the adult industry. Several companies stated that they would be implementing a condoms-only standard, but by two years later these measures were abandoned.

Most straight porn is currently shot without condoms or other safer-sex measures. In April 2010, the AIDS Healthcare Foundation, an AIDS advocacy group, filed a lawsuit against nine adult talent agencies, citing unsafe labor practices for exposing employees to HIV and other sexually transmitted infections. Steven Hirsch, the head of major production company Vivid Entertainment, has stated that if state laws mandate condom use, the porn industry will leave California. The Occupational Safety and Health Administration (OSHA) is currently attempting to enact stricter guidelines about "cross-contamination" on porn sets, instructing companies to use red bins labeled "biohazard" for all trash and laundry that has come into contact with bodily fluids.

Feminism and Pornography

Pornography has fractured modern feminism into two camps: anti-porn feminists who see pornography as entirely exploitative to women (some may favor legal intervention/regulation, others may not be in favor of legislation of pornography but still see it as a social ill) and others who see the potential for pornography to empower women. In 1978, Andrea Dworkin, Adrienne Rich, and others founded Women Against Pornography (WAP), testifying before the Meese Commission about the degradation of women resulting from pornography and demanding laws restricting the production and distribution of porn.

In the early 1980s, a countermovement of sex-positive feminists emerged, and in 1982, the Feminist Anti-Censorship Taskforce (FACT) was formulated. These scholars see pornography as a complicated issue of sexual labor, which may exploit women in certain ways just as other labor industries exploit women. These feminists are likely to see pornography as a red herring: a distraction from the creation of opportunities for women such as equal access to healthcare, opportunities in education and career advancement, and representation in top levels of corporations and government.

This debate has continued to rage for the past several decades. However, the sex-positive movement grew throughout the 1990s and 2000s, resulting in the rise in popularity of feminist pornography led by authors Betty Dodson, Susie Bright, Gayle Rubin, Annie Sprinkle, Carol Queen, Violet Blue, Tristan Taormino, and others. Taormino produces the *Chemistry* series that mimics popular reality television shows in which several performers spend two days living together and engaging in whatever unscripted sexual behavior they wish while a crew follows them with cameras. Taormino also conducts interviews with the performers, asking them about their sexual preferences, experiences, and desires. This links the production of pornography to feminist ideals in an entirely new way, foregrounding the sexuality of the performers themselves instead of the perceived desires of the audience and allowing them more participation in the production of the films.

Good For Her, a feminist sex-toy store in Canada, sponsored the first annual Feminist Porn Awards June 5, 2006, in Toronto, Ontario. To be eligible for consideration of a Feminist Porn Award, a film or other project must meet at least one of the following criteria: (1) a woman is substantially involved with the making of the film, (2) the film depicts genuine female pleasure, (3) the project expands the range of sexual expression for women by showing something new about female sexuality.

Race and Sexual Identity

In the history of pornography in the United States, racial themes have echoed historical patterns of racial hegemony and have been reproduced through the eroticization of racial transgression. Porn scholars such as Mireille Miller-Young and Celine Parreñas Shimizu are complicating the experience of women in porn by studying the intersections of race and ethnicity in porn. These researchers work within the sex-positive movement to challenge the idea that "women" is a monolithic category, arguing that porn that features only white women is not empowering for all women and describing the widespread erasure of women of color in pornography. Films like *Afrodite Superstar*, produced by Candida Royalle, and *Dangerous Curves* by Carlos Batts attempt to disrupt this paradigm and celebrate the sexuality of people of color without exotification. Several directors have produced projects including queer women of color, such as Shine Louise Houston of Pink & White Productions, Manuela Sabrosa of Femme Productions, and Courtney Trouble of Nofauxxx Productions.

In the first part of the 20th century, "sexploitation" films depicted lesbianism in porn as a transitional time of experimentation in a young girl's life before she settled down into a heterosexual relationship. The 1968 film *The King* (director Looney Bear) was the first to address itself to a lesbian audience instead of portraying lesbian sex as deviant, temporary, or inferior to heterosexual activity. In 1970s mainstream theatrical releases such as *Behind the Green Door*, sex between women was shown as foreplay to heterosexual intercourse.

In 1984, the lesbian erotica magazine *on our backs* was created by Nan Kinney and Debbie Sundahl, who later went on to create Fatale Video, a production company still in the business of making authentic lesbian porn. The 1990s saw an emergence of self-labeled "dyke porn" in San Francisco, portraying female-identified people with bodies of all shapes and sizes having safer sex with each other. Queer or dyke porn is abundant online as well; the *Crash Pad Series* created by Houston is similar in vision to Taormino's *Chemistry* series but depicts transgender, queer, and female-bodied people engaged in various forms of sexual expression.

Instructional/Educational

A popular trend in feminist pornography has been instructional videos. Nina Hartley has been a prolific source of educational porn videos over the last two decades. Hartley entered the industry in 1984 as a performer and now produces the *Nina Hartley's Guide to...* series, including over 30 instructional videos. Carol Queen, sexologist and author of several sex education books, produced one of the most popular instructional videos to date, *Bend Over Boyfriend* (1998), a guide for male anal penetration for straight couples. Jaiya and Jon Hanauer produce a series for New World Sex Education about sensual massage and Tantric eroticism called *Red Hot Touch*, as well as a guide for erotic massage during pregnancy. Tristan Taormino, feminist sex educator and author, started a line of educational videos through VividEd (a division of mainstream company Vivid Entertainment) and has produced over 10 award-winning titles.

See Also: Feminism, American; Pornography, Portrayal of Women in; Pornography Produced by Women; Representation of Women; Sex Workers.

Further Readings

Cornell, D., ed. *Feminism and Pornography*. Oxford, UK: Oxford University Press, 2000.

Easton, S. M. *The Problem of Pornography: Regulation and the Right to Free Speech*. London: Routledge, 1994.

Kipnis, L. *Bound and Gagged: Pornography and the Politics of Fantasy in America*. New York: Grove Press, 1996.

Steinem, G. "Erotica and Pornography: A Clear and Present Difference." *Pornography: Private Right or Public Menace?* New York: Prometheus Books, 1991.

Williams, L., ed. *Porn Studies*. Durham, NC: Duke University Press, 2004.

Emily E. Crutcher
University of California, Santa Barbara

Portugal

The democratic revolution of 1974 brought Portuguese women a different status and new spheres of social participation. However, the conservative residue in Portuguese society is still affecting women's lives in terms of health, employment, and access to full citizenship. Several aspects characterize the reproductive health situation of Portuguese women. Although women's average maternity age has been increasing, mainly as a result of their strong presence in the job market, Portugal is still one of the countries in the European Union with the highest rate of teenage pregnancy. This may be due to a dearth of information on reproductive issues as well as by the cultural importance of the Catholic Church in the country. Nevertheless, there has been a steady increase in the use of contraceptives by Portuguese women, 85 percent of whom used some contraceptive method in 2007.

Another aspect affecting women's health is availability of abortion. Until 2007, abortion in the first 10 weeks of pregnancy was illegal except for certain specific circumstances. This made women revert to clandestine abortions, the main cause of maternal death until then. The liberalization of abortion laws had been greatly debated by political parties, nongovernmental organizations and the general population over the previous 10 years and involved the active struggle of many women. The official antiabortion position of the Catholic Church and the media coverage of the trials of women involved in illegal abortions in 2001 and 2004 contributed substantially to both sides of the argument.

Portuguese law explicitly recognizes the right to equal opportunities at work and considers sexual discrimination a serious offence. Such a progressive law could explain why Portuguese women have a higher rate of employment within the European Union. However, their wide participation in the job market should be further justified by the rapid growth of the service sector, women's access to higher education, and the average standard of living of the Portuguese family, which is one of the lowest in the Union.

Despite the law, Portuguese women experience gender discrimination in the job market. Not only are women the majority of nonqualified workers, but women who are highly qualified are more likely to follow careers in intellectual fields. Thus they tend to be underrepresented in the higher ranks of the public sector or private companies. In addition, women suffer with unemployment more than men because they are often subject to precarious working contracts. Consequently, they are less protected by social welfare and more exposed to poverty. There also is pay discrimination: in 2004 women earned 80 percent of what men earned.

Although most Portuguese women share job responsibilities with their male partners, the same does not happen in the domestic sphere, where there is still a gender asymmetry. As a result, women often balance a paying job with domestic responsibilities and family care. This situation has restricted women's civic and political participation.

Despite these drawbacks, Portuguese society is gradually changing. Important steps have been taken toward women's emancipation and empowerment in several spheres of the public life (e.g., the 2006 parity law, concerning mixed gender representation in political party lists) and education, namely in terms of access to further education, where women are largely more represented than men.

See Also: Abortion, Access to; Equal Pay; Household Division of Labor; Reproductive and Sexual Health Rights.

Further Readings

Anderson, James Maxwell. *The History of Portugal: (The Greenwood Histories of the Modern Nations)*. Westport, CT: Greenwood Press, 2000.

Disney, A. R. *A History of Portugal and the Portuguese Empire: From Beginnings to 1807*. Oxford, UK: Cambridge University Press, 2009.

Maria Luisa Coelho
University of Minho, Portugal

Post-Abortion Trauma Syndrome

Post-abortion trauma syndrome or post-abortion syndrome (PAS) is a term primarily used by antiabortion advocates who posit there is a relationship between abortion and adverse mental health effects in women. It is derived from the term *post-traumatic stress disorder* and, for women who have had abortions, is said to occur frequently and include long-term consequences such as depression, substance abuse, sexual dysfunction, and/or suicidal tendencies. As outlined below, PAS is important in the current abortion dialog because it is used to argue for more restrictive abortion access. It is important to note that the American Medical Association, the American Psychiatric Association, and American Psychological Association have found no empirical support for this concept

The term *PAS* originated in 1981 when psychologist Vincent Rue, testifying before a subcommittee of the U.S. Senate Judiciary Committee, used it to describe what he perceived as women's severe reactions to abortion. In 1984, under the Reagan administration, the antiabortion president requested then Surgeon General C. Everett Koop, a known abortion foe, to report on the effects of abortion on women. Despite his personal beliefs, Koop was unable to conclude that abortion had either significant positive or negative effects on women's health. This finding remains true almost three decades later.

Neither the American Psychological Association nor the American Psychiatric Association recognizes PAS as a legitimate condition. Moreover, in 2008 the American Psychological Association released a taskforce report indicating that while women may experience grief, sadness, or a sense of loss after undergoing one abortion, there is no evidence that these feelings are specifically caused by having had an abortion. Rather, such feelings are generally attributed to preexisting emotions or the woman's life circumstances influencing the abortion decision.

Further evaluations suggest that the studies that are done to demonstrate the existence of PAS are methodologically unsound. A recent survey by Johns Hopkins University scholars Charles, Polis, Sridhara, and Blum found flaws with most investigations conducted between 1989 and 2007 regarding the mental health effects of abortion. They identified two key weaknesses with such studies: the failure to identify what the women's pregnancy intentions were (i.e., whether the pregnancies were unplanned or unwanted) and the erroneous attribution of cause to certain variables. Specifically, they were critical of studies that found a relationship between having an abortion and adverse mental health effects since such studies failed to explore alternate explanations for women's emotional health following an abortion. They concluded that the higher-quality studies deduced that there is little or no difference between the mental health of women who had undergone abortions and the comparative group of women who did not terminate their pregnancies.

PAS is important to the abortion debate because it is used to argue for antiabortion legislation. In 2007, the U.S. Supreme Court referenced negative mental health effects as justification for limiting late-term abortions. Such research also is used to implement "informed consent" laws that require women to be given certain information, including disputed medical facts, before having an elective abortion. Such misinformation, like the possibility of experiencing adverse mental health effects, could, as Weitz, Moore, Gordon, and Adler argue, adversely affect the mental health of women who seek elective abortions.

See Also: Abortion, Access to; Abortion, Ethical Issues of; Pro-Life Movement.

Further Readings

American Psychological Association, Task Force on Mental Health and Abortion. "Report of the Task Force on Mental Health and Abortion 2008." http://www.apa.org/pi/wpo/mental-health-abortion-report.pdf (accessed October 2009).

Charles, Vignetta E., Chelsea B. Polis, Srinivas K. Sridhara, and Robert W. Blum. "Abortion and Long-Term Mental Health Outcomes: A Systematic Review of the Evidence." *Contraception*, v. 78/6 (2008).

Cohen, Susan A. "Abortion and Mental Health: Myths and Realities." Guttmacher Policy Review, August 2006. http://www.guttmacher.org/pubs/gpr/09/3/gpr090308.html (accessed October 2009).

Stotland, Nadia L. "The Myth of the Abortion Trauma Syndrome." *Journal of the American Medical Association*, v.268/15 (1992).

Weitz, Tracy A., Kirsten Moore, Rivka Gordon, and Nancy Adler. "You say 'Regret' and I say 'Relief': A Need to Break the Polemic About Abortion." *Contraception*, v.78/2 (2008).

Shannon Stettner
York University

Postpartum Depression

Postpartum depression, also known as postnatal depression, is a form of depression that occurs in the days, weeks or months after childbirth. It can have profound effects on parents, infants and wider family. The prevalence of postpartum depression has been estimated in recently delivered women at between 10 and 15 percent internationally, though far fewer women than this receive treatment. Identifying postpartum depression is a key concern for maternal healthcare professionals.

Symptoms

Postpartum depression can affect women in different ways. The symptoms can begin soon after the birth and last for several months. Approximately half of all cases of postpartum depression start within the first three-and-three-quarters months within the first six months after childbirth. There is some evidence to suggest that its initial onset may occur beyond six months postpartum and extend well past one year. Symptoms fall into three groups: physical, psychological, and behavioral. Physiological symptoms include difficulty sleeping, low mood for prolonged periods of time (i.e., a week or more); tearfulness; and physical signs of tension, such as panic attacks, headaches, stomach pains, or blurred vision. A mother's psychological symptoms can include lack of interest in herself and the new baby; difficulty concentrating; lack of motivation; feeling trapped, lonely, guilty, rejected, or inadequate; and feeling overwhelmed or unable to cope. Finally, behavioral symptoms may include irritability and becoming withdrawn.

Postpartum depression can be distinguished from baby or maternity blues, which have milder symptoms, such as feeling sad, anxious, or overwhelmed, having mood swings, crying spells, loss of appetite, or trouble sleeping. These usually begin a few days after birth and end within a couple of weeks without the need for treatment, though women who suffer them are at higher risk of developing postpartum depression than women who do not. Postpartum psychosis, also known as postnatal or puerperal psychosis,

is a rare but very severe form of postpartum depression. It develops in about 1 or 2 out of 1,000 mothers. Symptoms can include irrational behavior, confusion, hallucinations, and delusions, as well as suicidal or psychotic thoughts. Recently, men have been increasingly identified as suffering from postpartum depression though opinion is divided as to whether their symptoms should be described as such.

Risk Factors

The causes of postpartum depression are usually multifaceted. Stressful events during pregnancy and birth are associated with depression after birth, and include worry and anxiety about the responsibility of having a new baby, a difficult delivery, money problems, lack of support at home, relationship worries, and not having close family or friends around to help her transition into her new role. Certain groups of women are at higher risk than others, including

Symptoms of postpartum depression can include lack of interest in the new baby; difficulty concentrating; lack of motivation; feeling trapped, lonely, guilty, rejected, or inadequate; and feeling overwhelmed or unable to cope.

women who have had mental health problems in the past like depression or previous postpartum depression; mothers who have had physical health problems following the birth; younger mothers; women whose pregnancy was unplanned; low-income individuals; those with more children; moms who are not breastfeeding; and women whose child has health problems or has died. As depression tends to run in families, genetics are thought to play a part in postpartum depression, but the exact nature of the link between the condition and genetics is not fully understood. Opinion is divided as to whether the changes in hormone levels that occur during and after pregnancy may directly cause some cases of postpartum depression or whether they cause a set of symptoms similar to postpartum depression.

Diagnosis

To identify possible cases of postpartum depression women may undergo a full clinical interview, but shorter screening instruments are commonly used in both clinical and epidemiological settings. These include the Edinburgh Postnatal Depression Scale (EPDS), a dedicated 10-item postpartum depression screening. The EPDS is composed of 10 questions that ask mothers about their feelings over the past seven days, which are scored, summed, and compared to thresholds for caseness. Other dedicated tools such as the Postpartum Depression Screening Scale (PDSS) and its shorter form, PDSS-SF, also have been developed. More general screening tools commonly used include the General Health Questionnaire screening for nonpsychiatric morbidity, a 60-item questionnaire commonly found in shortened versions of 30 and 12 questions, respectively, and the Beck Depression Inventory. Healthcare professionals often ask a smaller selection (possibly just two or three) of such questions or discuss the general topics of feelings rather than directly asking all the questions from any tool.

Treatment

Many women do not seek or receive treatment for postpartum depression. Treatment will depend on the severity of the depression and the mother's situation. Treatments include support and self-help, counseling for milder depression, psychological therapy for moderate depression, and antidepressants for moderate

and severe depression. Treatment to raise low levels of thyroid hormone also may be given where indicated. Women with postpartum psychosis generally require specialist psychiatric treatment and medication.

Self-help and support groups may include support online and by telephone as well as face to face, providing encouragement and advice on how to cope. Some women also benefit from sessions with a trained counselor. Support from family and friends might include both talking about feelings as well as practical support and childcare. Physical exercise may help, too. Some of the symptoms of postpartum depression, such as low mood, poor sleep, difficulty concentrating, and irritability, are often reduced with antidepressants, though they do not work immediately and not all types of antidepressants are suitable for breastfeeding mothers. Many mothers are keen to continue breastfeeding because they feel that it helps them to bond with their child and boosts their self-esteem and confidence in their maternal abilities.

Psychological treatment, including cognitive behavioral therapy and interpersonal therapy may be considered. For moderate depression, the proportion of people who improve with cognitive behavioral therapy is similar to those given antidepressants. Psychological treatments may not be as useful for some people with severe depression because motivation is required for these treatments and people with severe depression often find motivation difficult. Psychological treatments may not be practical for women with postpartum depression because of the time commitments required. Computer-based cognitive behavioral therapy may be available or via telephone using interactive voice response systems or the Internet. Some research suggests that a combination of an antidepressant plus a psychological treatment may be better than either treatment alone.

See Also: Depression; Health, Mental and Physical; Mental Health Treatment, Access to; Mental Health Treatment, Bias in; Mental Illness, Incidence Rates of; Postpartum Psychosis.

Further Readings

Kleiman, Karen R. *Therapy and the Postpartum Woman: Notes on Healing Postpartum Depression for Clinicians and the Women Who Seek Their Help.* London: Routledge, 2008.

U.S. Department of Health and Human Services, "Postpartum Depression." http://www.womenshealth .gov/mh/conditions/postpartum.cfm (accessed June 2010).

U.S. National Institute for Health and Clinical Excellence "Antenatal and Postnatal Mental Health: Clinical Management and Service Guidance." http://www.nice .org.uk/CG45 (accessed June 2010).

Nicola Shelton
University College London

Postpartum Psychosis

Only experienced by one or two women out of 1,000, postpartum psychosis (PPP) is a rare and extreme form of postpartum mood disorders and is seen in women who lose touch with reality shortly after birth. Usually occurring during the first three months after childbirth, women with PPP are often misdiagnosed with postpartum depression (PPD), a less severe form of PPP. The defense attorneys for Andrea Yates—in her highly publicized 2001 case about the drowning of her five young children in a bathtub—built a case around PPP. Yates was later found not guilty by reason of insanity and committed to a Texas state mental hospital.

The number of women with PPP has not changed since it was first recognized as a disorder in 1850. PPP is thought to be caused by a number of possible events, such as hormone changes after birth, low self-esteem due to postpartum appearance, lack of social and emotional support, financial strain, and a host of other factors. PPP has a 5 percent suicide rate and a 4 percent infanticide rate. Women who have a personal and/or family history of psychosis, bipolar disorder, or schizophrenia are at an increased risk of developing PPP. Those who have had past experience with PPP are between 20 and 50 percent more likely to develop the condition again.

There are a number of symptoms and signs that a woman is experiencing PPP, but the best course of action is to seek urgent help from a healthcare professional, since PPP can often be treated with immediate medical attention. Symptoms often develop during the first two to three weeks after birth, and can include guilt, delusions, hallucinations, illogical thoughts, refusal to eat or drink, insomnia, suicidal or homicidal thoughts, periods of mania, extreme feelings of anxiety and agitation, and the inability to distinguish reality from imagination.

Women with PPP are often misdiagnosed as having PPD and suffer from a lack of adequate treatment. Some women are unaware that anything is seriously wrong, misinterpreting their feelings as the "baby blues," and thus find it difficult to consult a physician. PPP is typically treated with antipsychotic medications, which may be combined with antidepressants or antianxiety drugs, and also may benefit from individual psychotherapy or group therapy. With proper treatment, women with PPP usually recover. Without proper treatment, a woman can be hospitalized for failure to adequately care for herself and her child.

See Also: Anxiety Disorders; Depression; Health, Mental and Physical; Infanticide; Mental Illness, Incidence Rates of; Postpartum Depression; Psychological Disorders by Gender, Rates of; Suicide Rates; Yates, Andrea.

Further Readings
McNamara, Melissa. "Andrea Yates Found Not Guilty by Reason of Insanity; Will Be Committed to State Mental Hospital." http://www.cbsnews.com /stories/2006/07/26/national/main1837248.shtml (accessed November 2009).

Pregnancy Info.net. "Post-Partum Psychosis." http://www .pregnancy-info.net/postpartum_psychosis.html (accessed November 2009).

Valerie R. Stackman
Howard University

Post-Traumatic Stress Disorder in Female Military

Since the early 2000s, post-traumatic stress disorder (PTSD) has increasingly become part of people's consciousness around the world, particularly in the United States and the United Kingdom. This can be partially attributed to the impact of the wars in Afghanistan and Iraq. A new openness about the experiences of people involved in these conflicts has brought attention to the complexities of PTSD. Individuals develop PTSD after experiencing a single or series of traumatic events that often involve death, threat of death, or serious physical or psychological injury, including threat to the physical integrity of oneself or others. For men in the military, the most common cause of PTSD is experience in combat, and while this can happen for women as well, the majority of women develop PTSD from experiences related to military sexual trauma (MST).

Underreporting and Uneven Participation

The number of veterans and people still serving in the military with PTSD is unknown. Estimates range from 5 to 10 percent of all men and 10 to 30 percent of all women veterans in the United States have PTSD, compared to 4 percent of the British military. These approximations are limited, as many are based on self-reporting to medical personnel within the government or at government supported facilities versus people seeking care via private healthcare providers as well as people who do not seek treatment.

Information on women serving in the military is limited in comparison to men, partly due to the fact that women's participation in the armed services varies around the world. For example, one report noted that Nepal claims a 30 percent participation rate, while nations such as Argentina or France record less than 10 percent of the military as being female.

Traditionally, women serve in service-support positions rather than in occupations that are directly combat related. Only 10 countries—Canada, Denmark, Finland, France, Germany, Israel, New Zealand, Norway, Sweden, and Switzerland— allow women to serve in active combat roles, while the United Kingdom and the United States permit women to serve in combat arms (but not direct combat) positions. Additionally, scarce information is available regarding women involved in organizations or movements that are categorized as rebellions or resistance movements, yet these often mirror traditional military structures. Substantial research does exist on women developing PTSD due to their experience as civilians in a war zone. Similar to people who get PTSD as civilians, it is believed that most people with PTSD go undiagnosed and therefore untreated.

PTSD itself has existed for centuries but was labeled and described differently than it is today. During the Civil War it was called "soldier's heart;" in World War I it was "shell shock," and in World War II it became known as "battle fatigue" or "combat fatigue." While many studies have focused on PTSD related to the impact of trauma due to accidents, various forms of violence, and natural disasters and the impact of war on civilians, the vast amount of research on the connections of PTSD related to the military focus on males in combat zones. Studies related to women's experiences particularly connected to MST (as well as men experiencing MST) are quite recent and limited in scope.

Diagnosing PTSD

There are six main criteria in diagnosing an individual with PTSD. The person's response to the trauma must involve helplessness, intense fear or horror, and a persistent reexperiencing of the event, which can occur as dreams, images, thoughts, or perceptions. Some individuals may feel or act as if the event was recurring, and this can take the form of flashbacks, illusions, or hallucinations. Additionally, individuals avoid conversations, feelings, and thoughts associated with the trauma and tend to avoid activities, places, and people that may make them recall the event; many are unable to remember important aspects of the trauma. Avoidance behavior also includes an inability or lack of interest in maintaining intimate relationships, diminished interest or participation in significant activities, and feelings of disassociation or detachment from others. Hyperarousal is another symptom: this includes outbursts of anger, an exaggerated startle response, and difficulty concentrating, sleeping, or staying awake.

Many of these symptoms—intrusive recollection, avoidance or numbing and hyper-arousal—must occur for longer than one month for an individual to be diagnosed with PTSD. Lastly, these symptoms must cause clinically significant distress or impairment in social, occupational, or other important areas of functioning. If these symptoms last less than three months, a person is diagnosed with acute PTSD; if it is longer than three months, then the PTSD is considered to be chronic.

Women have been involved in the military both as civilians and military personnel since military organizations have existed. Often, women serve in auxiliary units and their integration is limited to select, largely noncombat positions. In some countries, such as Israel, women are subjected to the draft just as men are but often are excluded due to religious regions, marital status, or if they are pregnant or have children. As of the mid-2000s women served in over 80 percent of available positions. Since the rise of feminism and shifts in culture in many industrialized nations, women have become more integrated into military structures. Due to changes in warfare, particularly in the Iraq and Afghanistan wars, despite official policy many women are serving in combat zones, often as guards, construction workers, or drivers throughout Afghanistan and Iraq.

MST and Low Reporting Rates

While all women face potential discrimination, many who experience discrimination or MST are in positions where there are few women and are of a lower rank. MST is an umbrella term representing a range of behaviors, such as rape, attempted rape, and various forms of force and sexual harassment, including intimidation and abuse of authority. Similar to PTSD, women experience fear related to their personal and psychological safety as well as their career. Due to military structures, MST represents a deep betrayal of trust, as often the perpetrator is someone they are reliant on for their job and perhaps their safety.

Research and anecdotes have shown that men often discount reports of rape or harassment, and the military structure is not designed to recognize or end sexual misconduct or gender-related violence within the ranks. Some research has suggested that approximately 90 percent of all women serving in the United States have experienced discrimination or harassment based on gender. Additionally, many women also are subjected to inappropriate behaviors or discrimination based on race or ethnicity or speculation that they may be lesbian or bisexual; this can add an additional level of fear and hostility in militaries that ban homosexuality or bisexuality.

Military structures around the world have recognized PTSD; the sophistication and level of the response is largely cultural. For many countries that have strong gender integration in the military, the need for services for PTSD is recognized but reportedly low. As of 2010, the United States has the widest array of information and research available regarding PTSD for military personnel and veterans; countries such as Canada, Australia, and Britain reference U.S. sources for information. This is possibly due to greater need in the United States due to involvement in Iraq and Afghanistan.

Widespread reluctance to report assault and other forms of misconduct continues, as the burden of proving these behaviors remains placed on the victim, and the stigmas associated with this can cause someone to be outcast from their fellow soldiers and can negatively impact a woman's career.

Many countries report offering education and training programs as well as counseling, but the impact of these programs is difficult to determine. For some countries, PTSD is not widely recognized, which could be an indicator of limited cases but also a lack of acknowledgment of the extent of people suffering from it.

Research has shown that the main cause of PTSD in women, even if they have experienced combat on some level, is military sexual trauma. Many women have experienced MST and developed PTSD from serving in noncombat related positions throughout the entire time women have been in the military. However, research examining veterans who served before the Iraq and Afghanistan wars is sparse. Studies have found that while women are more likely to seek services for MST and PTSD, many have found military services to be a barrier to care. One example is the trend in the U.S. military in which men and women are being diagnosed as having pre-existing conditions that are attributed to causing their PTSD, thus limiting or eliminating their access to benefits or services.

Many women who enter the military have experienced various forms of assault, abuse, and discrimination before joining. Knowing that they will likely have to fight for a proper diagnosis, many women simply seek help outside of the military or government-sponsored healthcare services, even though they've earned the benefits. Many women also face lack of full recognition of their contributions to the military, largely because most societies recognize men as veterans and tend to honor men with combat experience over others who have served. This creates yet another barrier to care and resistance to recognizing the need for treatment.

See Also: Gender Roles, Cross-Cultural; Military, Women in the; Rape in Conflict Zones; Sexual Harassment.

Further Readings

Benedict, H. *The Lonely Soldier: The Private War of Women Serving in Iraq.* Boston: Beacon Press, 2009.

Herman, J. *Trauma and Recovery: The Aftermath of Violence from Domestic Abuse to Political Terror.* New York: Basic Books, 1997.

Himmelfarb, N., D. Yeager, and J. Mintz. "Posttraumatic Stress Disorder in Female Veterans with Military and Civilian Sexual Trauma." *Journal of Traumatic Stress,* v.19/6 (2006).

Hotopf, M., et al. "The Health of UK Military Personnel who Deployed to the 2003 Iraq War: A Cohort Study." *The Lancet,* v.367 (2006).

Kelly, M. M., D. S. Vogt, E. M. Scheiderer, P. Ouimette, J. Daley, and J. Wolfe. "Effects of Military Trauma Exposure on Women Veterans' Use and Perceptions of Veterans Health Administration Care." *Journal of General Internal Medicine,* v.23/6 (2008).

Yeager, D., N. Himmelfarb, A. Cammack, and J. Mintz. "DSM-IV Diagnosed Post-Traumatic Stress Disorder in Women Veterans With and Without Military Sexual Trauma." *Journal of General Internal Medicine,* v.21/65,69. (2006).

Kristina Wolff
University of Maine, Farmington

Poverty

Globally as well as in America, women are more likely to be poor than men. In fact, America has the largest gap in the Western world between men and women in poverty across all racial groups. This disparity exists in spite of substantial gains made by women over the last 40 years. Almost 63 percent of American women are the primary or co-primary source of income for their family; yet an American woman is 35 percent more likely to be poor than an American man.

The economic downturn that began in 2007 strained many good-paying jobs for both men and women. Women in particular were caught in a bind; the availability of lower-paying pink-collar jobs (e.g., secretarial and customer-service oriented jobs) remained strong. However, women in these positions continued to face discrimination and inadequate social policies, ensuring that they remained trapped in a cycle of poverty.

Goals Face Demographic Obstacles

Women fare worse when examining their standing in the world writ large. Over half of the food in the world is produced by women, even though they own less than 1 percent of the land. Educational opportunities, including reproductive health education, escape young women, resulting in high rates of pregnancy-related deaths. The general lack of social standing and extremist discrimination behaviors (e.g., genital mutilation, honor killings) force women into a life of poverty that is difficult, if not impossible, to overcome.

To date the most comprehensive and universally agreed-upon strategic initiative to eliminate poverty is the United Nations (UN) Millennium Development Goals (MDGs), a set of eight goals to reduce global poverty by 2015. Adopted in 2000, the MDGs' aim to reduce global poverty by 50 percent. Gender equity in primary and secondary education is one of the eight goals; subgoals include an increase in female workforce participation and increases in elected positions held by women globally.

The MDGs' initiative is important, not only because of its international acceptance and implementation but because it provides a largely comprehensive approach to eradicating poverty.

The one area lacking in the MDGs is the growing aging population. Globally by 2045, people over age 60 will outnumber children. This population shift will produce profound changes in international policy and healthcare. Fifty-five percent of the aging population are women, and almost 65 percent of the 80-plus year-olds are women. Elderly women often find themselves in double jeopardy, suffering discrimination because of their age and their gender.

Overcoming the high poverty rates for women around the world is difficult when women face immediate discrimination at birth. For example, only 26 percent of older women in China can read and write, compared to 66 percent of older men. Such lack of formative training has resulted in a higher percentage of elderly women working into their retirement years than men across the globe. International pressure prompted Japan to enact gender equity in the workplace in the mid-1980s, but it has proved largely symbolic, as a substantial pay gap remains. The Euro-

A homeless woman in Porto City, Portugal. As they tend to be the primary caregivers for children and the elderly, women are particularly vulnerable to poverty and homelessness, especially women of color.

pean Union, particularly in Portugal and Italy, has a better track record on the pay gap, but much remains to be done.

Women across the world are unable to accumulate wealth because in every advanced industrialized nation, women still earn less than men for equal work. The passage of time has done little to close the discrimination gap; in fact, the UN recently reported that global discrimination is worsening rather than abating.

Gender Disparity and Ethnic Disadvantages

In the United States, the poverty rate has fluctuated since the late 1950s. Although the poverty level is updated yearly to account for inflation, the method to calculate poverty levels has largely remained unchanged since 1964 when the yearly cost of food, along with family size and a few additional variables, determined poverty status. While food was the major area of expense up through the 1960s, that is no longer the case; accordingly, many scholars believe a new poverty formula should be created.

The poverty trap is particularly harmful to women; as primary caregivers for children and aging parents, women are overrepresented in single parent households, and women and people of color are over-represented in poverty figures. From 2000 to 2008, the most current data available, the poverty rate rose to 13.2 percent, or 39.8 million Americans—the highest since 1997.

Women, in particular women of color, are most likely to live in poverty; in fact, women in general are more likely to be poor than men in any racial or ethnic group. In 2008, 59 percent of adults (18 years and older) living in poverty were women. Especially hard hit are single-women (including those divorced or widowed) households where over 28 percent reside in poverty, compared to 5.5 percent of married women. Compared with men and married women, single women are disproportionately more likely to live at or below the poverty level.

Numerous factors account for this disparity. Overall in 2008, women earned around 77 percent of their male counterparts—down 1 percentage point from the prior year. Single women of color, 30 percent of African Americans, and almost 30 percent of Hispanic women, live in poverty—compared to 18 percent of Caucasian single women. Women of color make less than 70 cents per dollar made by men in general. These income disparities are largely unchanged since the 1960s.

Further hampering financial security, women are less likely to receive unemployment benefits than men. Women are also more likely to suffer hiring discrimination and when hired for lower-paying jobs. In addition, pregnancy affects work-cohesion and the return to work. Being female and having children doubly increases the likelihood of living in poverty, termed the "pauperization of motherhood." Childcare and caring for elderly parents disproportionately falls to women; termed the "sandwich generation," many women hold full-time employment outside the home and complete a second shift of unpaid caregiving at home. And, variable child support from fathers further hampers the likelihood single women will stay out of poverty. Further, domestic violence has been shown a primary cause of female homelessness.

The income disparity between men and women continues throughout the lifespan, where the risk for poverty for women more than doubles after age 65. In part, the wage gap over the collective years of working produces lower savings and pension benefits. On average, women over 65 live on 57 percent of the annual income of their male counterparts. Male-headed households on average exist on 62 percent more income than female-headed households. African American–headed households live on 26 percent less than white–headed households in general. The marriage-income disparity continues throughout the golden years as well, where married households live on twice the income of single households. Education positively influences yearly income in all households with one major exception: full-time working women have closed and exceeded the education gap with men yet still earn less for the same work.

What the Future Holds

Looking toward the future highlights a mixed bag of possibilities. Recently, white and Latina women have made strides in reducing the wage gap with men. The opportunities for voice, discussed earlier, are likely to coalesce in future gains for women. It is uncertain whether pink-collar jobs will provide higher pay even though women have gained greater access to education and the labor market over the last 30 to 40 years.

Some calculations suggest that simply eliminating the pay gap would cut poverty rates in half. However, increases in nontraditional work hours place additional economic demands on women who utilize daycare and other caregiving services. A lack of access to reproductive health services presents another obstacle to some women. Although the birth control pill celebrated its 50-year anniversary in 2010, many parts of Africa have yet to receive the pill or find the $1-per-month price tag too costly.

Further, the overworked woman has less time for what has traditionally been female-oriented services, such as volunteering and at-home healthcare. This growing lack of unpaid work by women trickles down through nonprofits and community-based organizations, those most likely to depend on female volunteers, negatively affecting productivity within local communities. Further, home care remains the responsibility of women even when they are engaged in paid work outside the home.

Reducing the gender disparity in poverty will likely necessitate policy changes, educational opportunities, and stringent domestic violence legislation, along with increased social support services such as child care and parental leave. The opportunity for these types of policy changes has increased substantially since the 1970s, as the number of women holding elected office at state, national, and international levels has increased. Some examples in the United States include the passage of the Violence Against Women Act in the early 1990s, the Family Medical Leave Act (FMLA) in 1993, and the Lilly Ledbetter Act in 2009. Globally, the adoption of the UN-originated Convention on the Elimination of All Forms of Discrimination Against Women act has unfortunately done little to end discrimination or violence against women.

See Also: Aging, Attitudes Toward; Antifeminism; Attainment, College Degree; Convention on the Elimination of All Forms of Discrimination Against Women; Equal Rights Amendment; Financial Independence of Women; Government, Women in; Household Division of Labor; Lilly Ledbetter Act; Poverty, "Feminization" of; Single Mothers; Unpaid Labor; Working Mothers.

Further Readings

Arrichi, Barbara and David Maume, eds. *Families and Children: Child Poverty in America Today*. Westport, CT: Praeger, 2007.

Chen, Martha, Joann Vanek, Francie Lund, and James Heintz. *Progress of the World's Women 2005: Women, Work, & Poverty*. New York: United Nations Development Fund for Women, 2005.

Pierson, Christopher. *Beyond the Welfare State: The New Political Economy of Welfare*. Malden, MA: Policy Press, 2006.

Royce, Edward. *Power and Poverty: The Problem of Structural Inequality*. Plymouth, UK: Rowman and Littlefield Publishers, 2009.

U.S. Census Bureau. "Poverty." http://www.census.gov /hhes/www/poverty/poverty.html (accessed July 2010).

Dana K. Bagwell
Memory Health and Fitness Institute

Poverty, "Feminization" of

The feminization of poverty is a concept developed and popularized by Diana Pearce and other gender scholars to capture the alarming increase in the proportion of U.S. women with minor children living in poverty in the post–World War II years. In 1960, female heads of household with no husband present were about one-fourth of poor families; by the 1980s, women with minor children were a majority of America's poor, with three-fifths of poor families headed by women and nearly half of single-mother families classified as poor.

Feminist scholars have emphasized the relationships among the family, the state, and the labor market in the feminization of poverty. They argue that the gendered division of labor—reproductive and productive work, both paid and unpaid—is deeply embedded in welfare state policies. Thus, trends in the feminization of poverty must be understood in relationship to the welfare state, which can reinforce traditional gender ideologies or offer resources that can potentially empower women. Global comparisons in welfare state policies, work inequality, and family demographics reveal that the feminization of poverty is not a universal phenomenon. Countries with family-friendly social and economic policies have lower rates of poverty and do not display the same trends in female poverty.

Women's Poverty in the United States

Heidi Hartman's *Women, Work, and Poverty* (2005), written for the Institute for Women's Policy Research (IWPR), documents the changing impact of family, marriage, motherhood, work, and welfare reform on trends in women's poverty. Marital dissolution and the burdens of single parenting have played a key role in the feminization of poverty since the 1960s.

This trend has historically intersected with labor-market dynamics, particularly limited work opportunities for low-skilled women, and with increasingly restrictive welfare policies that make it difficult for poor women to escape poverty. Although the overall levels of women's poverty have not changed substantially in the United States since the 1960s, women's lives have changed dramatically. This suggests that the causes of women's poverty may also be changing. Central among these changes is the employment revolution, reflected in a turn from marriage for economic security to the labor market. While most women have adjusted to the changing location of their support, a female under class remains trapped in poverty. The IWPR report concluded that improving conditions in the wage economy holds greater promise for female economic independence than a return to marriage as a primary means of support. This change, however, would need to be accompanied by increased opportunities and support for education and training of working women.

In 1996, the United States passed the most sweeping welfare reform policy in its history. The *Personal Responsibility and Work Opportunity Reconciliation Act* (PRWORA) restricted social support services and welfare income for low-income women with children. Federal guidelines limited lifetime support from Temporary Aid to Needy Families (TANF), formerly known as Aid to Families with Dependent Children, to a total of five years. States were, at the same time, granted the freedom to restrict benefits further in order to conform to mandated budget cuts and reductions to welfare rolls. Ellen Reese, in *Backlash Against Welfare Mothers* (2005), documented that many states in the south and southwest—particularly those with high levels of agricultural, low-wage industries and large minority populations—restricted continuous benefits to two years and denied benefits for additional children born to a recipient under "child exclusion" or "family cap" policies.

Reese attributed these strict and punitive regional practices to a politics of race, class, and gender. She wrote that low-wage employers with business interests built powerful lobbies and alliances with the white middle and working classes by mobilizing racist, classist, and sexist attitudes prevalent in these regions. The welfare reforms were exacerbated by the disproportionate number of single mothers and the demographics of women on welfare, which showed they were below the general population in education and job skills. Increasing sanctions under stricter guidelines resulted in removing women from welfare rolls and/or denying benefits outright, particularly to legal immigrants and minority women. Under PRWORA "work first" policies were implemented that require women to secure employment and/or enroll in vocational training or educational programs prior to receiving benefits.

The goal is to encourage women to quickly make the transition from welfare to work. However, the low earnings from the types of jobs women are forced to take and their inability to complete education or training within restrictive time limits have clearly undermined the self-sufficiency goals of the new policies. Problems for low-income women are magnified further when TANF benefits are stopped, as women typically lose other social and economic supports such as subsidized childcare, housing, and medical services. The benefits of gaining full employment are thus offset by the losses of these other supports.

Although the welfare rolls have radically declined since the passage of PRWORA, the depth and extent of the feminization of poverty have not. Between 1996 and 2002, welfare cases declined from 4.5 million families to 2.1 million families. However, most recipients who left welfare for work remained poor and were earning poverty wages. Many were forced to seek housing and support from families or homeless shelters. With declines in the economy and the increasing scarcity of both jobs and welfare, families with children comprised a growing proportion, about 40 percent, of the nation's homeless and 59 percent of those seeking emergency food. Approximately one-third of former welfare recipients continued to cycle between welfare and work. In the same period, the depth of poverty increased sharply, by 23 per-

cent, even after adjusting for inflation. While welfare caseloads declined in this period, the poverty rates of single, working mothers and child poverty rates did not. The child poverty rates in the United States remain the highest among the industrialized countries. Clearly, while the "work first" philosophy was intended to create more self-sufficiency, it presumes wrongly that any job is better than no job. A stratum of women with children remains trapped in poverty; there are limited resources available to these women to rise above poverty levels from low-wage employment in dead-end jobs. By severely restricting benefits, PRWORA created many obstacles for welfare mothers who want to pursue the American dream through sustained education and training.

Global Comparisons

Between the 1960s and 1980s, Goldberg and Kremen found among seven advanced industrialized countries that economic inequality by gender was present across nations and the feminization of poverty was not. The major factors explaining this included changing demographics, labor markets, equalization policies, and social welfare. In each of the countries studied, except for Japan, there were increases in the levels of single motherhood due to changing family demographics. The occupational concentration of women in low-wage jobs and female-male earnings differentials were associated with greater increases in poverty rates among female-headed households. Insufficient governmental commitment to equalization policies, publicly supported childcare, and the underrepresentation of women in policymaking bodies were similarly related to higher levels of growth in female poverty.

Unlike other countries, the United States has both high rates of female-headed households and labor market earnings inequality along with weak social support programs designed to offset the absence of economic earnings, such as paid family leave, universal family allowances, public childcare, or rent subsidies. In global comparisons, both Japan and Sweden revealed different trends in the feminization of poverty than the United States., but for very different reasons. The gender earnings gap is highest in Japan, and Japan has very minimal social assistance and income transfer programs to benefit women. However, Japan has low rates of single motherhood—about one-fourth of those in the United States and Sweden. Very few women in Japan can risk divorce, given the limited prospects for economic independence through labor market employment. Single women in Japan are at the highest risk of poverty of any of the countries studied. Should separation and divorce rates increase in Japan, as they have in other industrialized countries, Japan is ill equipped to offset the economic consequence for women and children.

Sweden is perhaps the country that has shown the greatest success in severing the tie between single motherhood and poverty. American single parents, for instance, are six times as likely to be poor as their Swedish counterparts. This is due to a combination of labor market and social welfare policies in support of gender equity and families. Canada shows lower trends in female poverty than the United States, but the rates are increasing with the growth of single motherhood. Today, single-mother families comprise about 40 percent of all poor families in Canada. Like the United States, Canada has high rates of occupational sex segregation, female unemployment, and earnings differentials between men and women.

While Canada has more liberal social support programs than the United States, in recent years Canada has moved toward more restrictive social welfare policies. Finally, although conclusive data is absent, in France and the socialist countries of Poland and the former Soviet Union, female poverty has not been as prevalent as it is in the United States. France has more generous social support programs than Canada, the United States, or Japan and relatively low rates of single-parent households. However, women in France have experienced consistently high unemployment rates since the 1960s. In the socialist countries of Poland and the former Soviet Union, women tend to work full time and have paid maternity leaves, yet they still work in low-paying occupations. The wage gap is wider than in Canada and France and about the same (or slightly better) than in the United States. Even though overall economic resources are lower in these countries, social programs are much more extensive than in the United States, which provide a safety net against grinding poverty, hunger, and homelessness.

Future Prospects

Clearly, trends in the feminization of poverty are greatest in countries that have higher disparities in labor market earnings between women and men and fewer social support programs that transfer earnings and benefits to single-parent families. Although the growth of single-parent households is typical in most industrialized countries, it is unlikely that a return to marriage and the traditional family will solve problems related to the growing numbers of women and children living in poverty.

Only the most advanced welfare states have been successful in eliminating female poverty through family-friendly and generous government transfer programs. However, even in countries like Sweden, women experience social and economic inequality. Thus, any successful antipoverty program must be centered in policies that address the inequality of women both in the workplace and in the family. Such a perspective targets both the work and familial roles and contributions that women make to society as single heads of households.

Subsidized and widely available quality childcare, paid maternity and parental leave, and part-time work with benefits and family allowances can reduce some of the burdens of parenthood. Similarly, a parent could be compensated for providing childcare as paid employment, thereby eliminating the artificial distinction between reproductive and productive work. Programs that target single parents, such as government-assured child support, also are used successfully in many countries, both to enforce child-support payments and to subsidize inadequate child support. In the workplace, policies that enlarge women's employment opportunities, including affirmative action and equal pay policies, are necessary to address systematic earnings inequality embedded in segregated job markets. Ultimately, the prevention of the feminization of poverty will require a combination of reformed workplace and social welfare policies. How such strategies, programs and policies are combined will vary in different countries based on their unique histories and cultures.

See Also: Childcare; Children's Rights; Divorce; Educational Opportunities/Access; Effect of Unpaid Labor on Educational Attainment; Equal Pay; Equal Rights Amendment; Gender Quotas in Government; Global Feminism; Household Division of Labor; Marriage; Parental Leave; Parental Leave Act; Part-Time Work; Poverty; Representation of Women in Government, International; Working Mothers.

Further Readings

Edin, Kathryn and Laura Lein. *Making Ends Meet: How Single Mothers Survive Welfare and Low-Wage Work.* New York: Russell Sage Foundation, 1997.

Edin, Kathryn and Maria Kefalas. *Promises I Can Keep: Why Poor Women Put Motherhood Before Marriage.* Berkeley, CA: University of California Press, 2005.

Goldberg, Gertrude Schaffner and Eleanor Kremen. *The Feminization of Poverty: Only in America?* Westport, CT: Praeger, 1990.

Hartman, Heidi. *Women, Work, and Poverty: Women Centered Research for Policy Change.* New York: Haworth Political Press, 2005.

Hays, Sharon. *Flat Broke With Children: Women in the Age of Welfare Reform.* New York: Oxford University Press, 2003.

Pearce, Diana. "The Feminization of Ghetto Poverty," *Society*, v.1 (1983).

Pearce, Diana. "The Feminization of Poverty: Women, Work, and Welfare." *Urban and Social Change Review*, v.11 (1978).

Pearce, Diana. "Welfare Is Not for Women: Why the War on Poverty Cannot Conquer the Feminization of Poverty," Linda Gordon, ed. *Women, the State, and Welfare.* Madison: University of Wisconsin Press, 1990.

Piven, Frances Fox. "Ideology and the State: Women, Power, and the Welfare State. In Linda Gordon, ed., *Women, the State, and Welfare.* Madison: University of Wisconsin Press, 1990.

Reese, Ellen. *Backlash Against Welfare Mothers: Past and Present.* Berkeley: University of California Press, 2005.

Vicky M. MacLean
Middle Tennessee State University

Pregnancy

Examining pregnancy from a global viewpoint reveals marked differences in this universal event. Major differences include access to vital healthcare including contraception, prenatal care, safe abortion, and skilled birth attendants. Another stark difference is that while women are at risk of dying from complications of pregnancy and birth all around the world, lifetime risk varies drastically by country and within countries based on socioeconomic factors. To gain a snapshot of the different experiences of pregnancy around the world, this article begins by examining global statistics on pregnancy and recent demographic trends including fertility rates, maternal age, nonmarital childbearing rates, and maternal mortality. A woman's culture plays an integral role in her pregnancy, and thus cultural variations in advice and birthing are discussed, followed by discussion of the physical and psychological experience of pregnancy.

Becoming Pregnant

In 2008, there were 208 million pregnancies worldwide—40 percent were unintended. One in five pregnancies ends in induced abortion, with 48 percent of these occurring under unsafe conditions. The number of abortions has declined worldwide between 1995 and 2003, with the greatest decrease occurring in developed countries. Abortion rates are similar whether residing in developed (26 per 1,000) or developing (29 per 1,000) countries and whether abortion is legal or illegal. In developing countries where abortion is generally legal, 92 percent are safe, while 60 percent of abortions in Asia and 95 percent in Africa and Latin America are considered unsafe. There are many consequences of unsafe abortion, including 13 percent of maternal deaths worldwide (70,000 maternal deaths per year, which results in 220,000 children losing their mothers each year), and an estimated 5 million women are hospitalized each year due to unsafe abortion-related consequences such as hemorrhage and sepsis.

A major factor in the high percentage of unintended preganancies is a woman's ability to control her fertility. In 2009, an estimated 215 million women worldwide did not have access to modern contraceptives, which is critical in the ability to plan family size. In developing countries, the majority of women who have unintended pregnancies (82 percent) had an unmet need for contraceptives. Other factors associated with unintended pregnancy are maternal/paternal education, poverty status, inaccurate sex education, improper use of contraceptives, and race/ethnicity. For example, in the United States, women of color have much higher rates of unintended pregnancy.

While some women are unable to prevent the number of pregnancies they have, other women are struggling with infertility. For women with financial resources or health insurance coverage, infertility treatment is an option. Advances in assisted reproductive technology (ART) have led to an increased success rate of approximately 36 percent live births in 2006, meaning that for the majority of women who undergo ART, it will not be successful. In vitro fertilization (IVF) occurs around the world, but restrictions on the number of embryos that are allowed to be implanted differ by country, as do costs. ART success rates differ based on number of embryos, age, hormones needed, underlying cause of infertility, and ethnicity. Pregnancy that results from ART is associated with a higher rate of multiple pregnancies and consequent health issues for mothers and infants.

Fertility Rates

The average fertility rate worldwide is 2.6 live offspring, with ranges from a low of 1.3 in Europe and Japan to an average over 7 in some African countries. Fertility rates are highest in Africa, Asia, and Latin America. In developing countries, there has been increased recognition of the socioeconomic burden of high fertility rates, and population growth is decreasing in some areas. Delayed childbirth and lower fertility rates are associated with increased schooling for girls, access to safe and reliable contraception, increased work opportunities for women, marrying at older ages, and less economic incentives for multiple children (including lower infant mortality rates). Fertility is lower in developed countries because women tend to marry later, contraception is widespread and consists of several reliable choices, abortion is legal and safe, and many educated women delay having a family to establish their careers first.

In addition to lower fertility rates, maternal age at first birth has risen in many developed countries; in the United States it rose to 25, and in Switzerland it is now 29. Birth rates in older age groups have also been increasing as a result of both delaying motherhood and second marriages. In the United States, pregnancy rates in age groups technically considered of advanced maternal age (over 35) have increased sharply since 1990. The birth rates increased 57 percent for women aged 35–39, over 70 percent for women aged 40–44, and tripled for women aged 45–49. Since women's fertility begins to decline in their 30s and fertility problems increase after age 35, in some cases these pregnancies are the result of ART. Increased maternal age is associated with a higher risk of medical problems including hypertension and diabetes, increased rates of miscarriages, prematurity and low birth weight of the infants, and higher rates of birth defects and chromosomal abnormalities such as Down syndrome and autism. However, older mothers tend to have higher income and better education, which are associated with improved outcomes.

Teen Pregnancy

Around the world, teen pregnancy rates have declined and currently account for 1 in 10 births. Approximately one-third of these pregnancies are not planned or wanted. Rates of teen pregnancy (out of 1,000 teenage girls) range from 2.9 in South Korea to 143 in sub-Saharan Africa, and in most of Latin America one-third of girls are teenage mothers. Economically impoverished countries like Niger have higher teen pregnancy rates (233 per 1,000), while wealthy countries like Japan have very low rates (4 per 1,000). Poverty is also linked to higher rates within developed countries. For instance, in Italy the poorest area has a rate of 10 per 1,000, while the richest has 3.3 per 1,000; in the United Kingdom, over half of all teen pregnancies occur among the 30 percent most impoverished individuals.

Interpretations of teen pregnancy differ by country and are dependent on cultural norms. In developing countries, there may be no social stigma associated with teen pregnancy, and it often occurs within marriage. For example, in Niger, 87 percent of girls are married by age 18 and 53 percent of them have given birth by 18. Factors associated with teenage pregnancy in developing countries include early marriage, traditional gender roles, poverty, lack of sex education, and lack of access to safe and reliable contraception and abortion.

In many developed countries, teen pregnancy is seen as a social problem, and research has associated it with poorer life outcomes including higher risk of lifetime poverty. The highest rate of teen pregnancy in developed countries occurs in the United States, which has a rate twice as high as any other developed country. Japan and South Korea have the lowest rates. There has been a recent uptick in the U.S. rate beginning in 2006, reversing a pattern of decline that occurred from 1991 to 2005. Currently, one of seven American girls between the ages of 15 and 19 becomes pregnant; 80 percent were unintended, and in over half, no contraception was used. In developed countries, many factors are associated with teen pregnancy including inadequate sex education and access to contraception, family poverty, peer pressure, perception of few opportunities for success, exposure to sexualized media, increased rate of adverse childhood events, and lack of close contact with adult role models. Research also indicates that 11–20 percent of teenage pregnancy is the result of rape, and in 67 percent of teen pregnancies, the male was over the age of 20. Dating violence and histories of sexual abuse are also associated with teen pregnancy; a United Kingdom (UK) study found that 70 percent of teens who had given birth had experienced violence within their relationship.

Worldwide, teen pregnancies are associated with higher rates of premature birth and low birth weight. Approximately one-third of teens do not receive prenatal care, and this lack of quality maternal care is linked to negative outcomes. Further, teenagers in developed countries often have nutritional deficiencies from poor eating habits, fast food, and dieting and, in developing countries, may be suffering from chronic malnutrition and stunted growth. There are particularly high risks for girls under 14 who may have an undeveloped pelvis, which increases the risk of obstructed labor, eclampsia, obstetric fistula, infant mortality, and maternal mortality (MM, the number of maternal deaths per 1,000 live births). Compared to 20–24 year olds, MM is five times higher for girls aged 10–14 and twice as high for teens aged 15–19. In developing countries, complications from birth/pregnancy are the leading cause of mortality among girls aged 15–19, and an estimated 70,000 teen girls die each year. Socioeconomic factors rather than age account for the increased risk for girls over 15. It is also important to note that pregnant teenage girls are at a seven times higher risk for suicide.

Nonmarital Childbearing

Another trend is in nonmarital childbearing in developed countries, with rates doubling and tripling in recent years. Unwed births now account for 50 percent or more of all births in Iceland (66 percent), Sweden (55 percent), Norway (54 percent), and France (50 percent). In the United States, the rate increased 21 percent between 2002 and 2007, when it reached an all-time high of 39.7 percent of births. The UK and the Netherlands have a similar rate, while in other devel-

oped countries, including Ireland, Germany, Spain, and Canada, the rate is around 30 percent. In contrast, the rate is 2 percent in Japan; this low rate is linked to the fact that belief in the traditional marriage system is very strong and birth outside marriage is socially unacceptable. The increase has occurred among all ethnicities and ages and is due to a variety of reasons, including changing beliefs about marriage, lesbian relationships, and single women intentionally becoming pregnant through ART. Although an increase has occurred among well-educated and professional women, it more often occurs among women with lower income and educational level. In the United States, percentages vary by race, with approximately 72 percent of black women, 51 percent of Latinas, and 28 percent of white women having children out of wedlock; 77 percent are over age 20.

Rates of nonmarital childbearing differ significantly in developing countries. Several Central American countries have high rates of unwed births, including Guatemala (67 percent), El Salvador (67 percent), and Honduras (53 percent). In these countries, factors that explain these high rates include pronatalist attitudes and policies, high rates of male mortality, machismo, and male migration. In other countries including India, Indonesia, and Malaysia, early marriage and pregnancy occur at relatively high rates, and thus unwed birth rates are significantly lower.

Maternal Mortality

All pregnancies carry a risk, and 15 percent of pregnancies everywhere are life threatening. Although the global MM rate has declined 35 percent in the last 30 years, approximately every minute a women dies from complications during pregnancy and childbirth, resulting in more than half a million deaths each year. The leading causes of death include hemorrhage, sepsis/infections, hypertensive disorders, anemia, obstructed labor, and complications of unsafe abortion. For every woman who dies, there are another 20 who suffer morbidity. The majority of maternal deaths occur in developing countries, with 84 percent occurring in sub-Saharan Africa and south Asia. In 2008, six countries (India, Nigeria, Pakistan, Afghanistan, Ethiopia, and the Democratic Republic of Congo) accounted for 50 percent of the deaths.

There are significant disparities in MM by country; sub-Saharan Africa has an MM of 920, whereas an MM of 8 is reported in industrialized countries. Recently, the MM has risen in some developed countries, such as the United States, Canada, and Norway. In the United States, the rate recently doubled, and the amount of "near misses" of maternal deaths has increased 25 percent since 1998. One-third of pregnant American women have pregnancy-related complications; the majority are women of color and women in poverty.

Maternal mortality is affected by numerous factors, including poverty, maternal education, maternal health, nutritional status, prenatal care, history of female genital mutilation, medical resources, and maternal age. Access to skilled prenatal and childbirth care is critical wherever one lives, including in developed countries. Lack of quality care for poor and uninsured women of color is one of the factors associated with the consistent finding that in the United States, black women have MM rates almost four times as high as white women (32.7 versus 9.5).

MM can be combined with fertility rates within countries to assess lifetime risk for women. In countries with high fertility rates and high MM rates, a woman repeatedly risks maternal death with each pregnancy. The lifetime risk of maternal death is 1 in 76 in the developing world versus 1 in 8,000 in the developed world. The stark reality of maternal death over one's life is even more glaring when specific country comparisons are made: in Niger, 1 out of 7 pregnant women will die, compared to 1 out of 47,600 in Ireland.

Cultural Differences

Pregnant women are often given advice on what to do while pregnant. Some of the advice tends to be universal, such as sleeping on the left side and drinking more water; however, there are large cultural differences, and sometimes these differences are contradictory. For example, U.S. women are told to abstain from alcohol, while women in Europe are advised to have only one glass a day. Nutritional recommendations often include avoiding certain foods and eating more of others, but the specifics vary by culture. In Sri Lanka, women are told to avoid mango, pineapple, and vinegar, while in Australia, women are told to eat 100 grams of beef every day. Advice may also include what to think about, for example, Korean women are told to focus and look only on that which is beautiful and good and avoid eating things that are broken or have blemishes because it is believed these behaviors

will influence the shape and features of the baby. The consequences of not following some recommendations may be significant. Maternal factors associated with pregnancy/birth complications and poorer infant outcomes include behaviors such as smoking, prenatal visits, and alcohol/drug consumption. In addition, in recent years, pregnant women in the United States have been prosecuted for engaging in conduct such as consuming alcohol that would be legal otherwise.

Another commonality is that all pregnant women will prepare for the impending birth in some manner;,but her culture will play a significant role in how this occurs. For example, in the United States, birth is seen as a medical event that requires frequent medical procedures and needs to occur with an obstetrician in a hospital with an epidural, while in the Netherlands, birth is seen as a natural and healthy process that does not require high-tech medical intervention, and most births take place in the home with a skilled midwife without any pain medication. The contrast can be extreme. In some European countries, women not only have frequent medical visits but may have monthly ultrasounds, while in developing countries, more than a third of pregnant women will not have any contact with health professionals before the birth, and over half of the births will take place without a skilled birth attendant. For example, in Afghanistan, where 1 in 9 women die during or shortly after pregnancy, only 14 percent of women have a skilled attendant. The presence of a skilled attendant and access to medical supplies and timely transportation to hospitals with surgical capability is critical in reducing maternal mortality.

At the other end of the continuum, many pregnant women are experiencing unnecessary medical interventions. Public health organizations have raised alarm about the current epidemic of caesarian section (C-sections) occurring in developing and developed countries. The World Health Organization indicates that the optimal C-section rate is between 5 and 10 percent and rates above 15 percent are too high. Concern about high rates of C-sections are due to the numerous risks associated with this surgery, including sepsis, blood clots, surgical injury, longer recovery, maternal morbidity, maternal mortality, and long-term risks such as ectopic pregnancy, placenta previa, uterine rupture, ongoing pelvic pain, and future infertility. C-section rates vary by country, accounting for 46 percent of births in China, 35 percent in Latin America, 32 percent in the United States, 24 percent in the UK, 18 percent in India and France, 15 percent in Cambodia, 12 percent in the Netherlands, and 9 percent in Africa. Increased patient financial resources and improved medical facilities are some of the reasons for the rising rate of C-sections globally in developing countries. Reasons given for elective C-sections include fear of painful vaginal births, the mistaken belief that a C-section is safer, fear of vaginal stretching, and desire to schedule the date of birth.

Cultural norms also play a role in social support at the birth. In the United States, Canada, and many European countries, the husband plays an instrumental role in the birth, while in many other cultures, birth is seen as a female event and husbands do not participate. In Russia, 70 percent of expectant mothers prefer to be alone during labor, and in Arabic, Korean, Chinese, and Indonesian cultures, female relatives are at the birth instead of the husband.

Subjective Experience

Although women around the world and throughout time have experienced pregnancy, from an individual perspective, pregnancy is a unique experience. Numerous factors influence the experience of pregnancy: was it intended or unintended; was intercourse desired or coerced/forced; is abortion or adoption chosen; experience with infertility treatment; history of miscarriages (20–40 percent of all pregnancies end in miscarriage); previous pregnancies; risk of infant mortality and maternal mortality; whether a live birth results; and demographics of the mother including age, marital status, and socioeconomic status.

However, there are some commonalities among all pregnant women, the primary one being that their bodies are undergoing remarkable and uncontrollable changes. The symptoms of pregnancy vary based on the trimester and manifest differently among women and between pregnancies. Common symptoms include swollen/tender breasts, fatigue/exhaustion, nausea/vomiting, backaches, headaches, frequent urination, food cravings, sensitivity to odors, enlarged breasts, itching from stretching skin, constipation, heartburn, unpredictable allergies, changes in balance, dizziness, sudden weight gain, swollen extremities, stretch marks, darkening pigmentation, varicose veins, insomnia, and hemorrhoids.

Weight gain during pregnancy is of particular import—women who gain too little have a higher risk of having a baby that is too small, while women who gain too much increase the risk of early delivery, large babies, C-sections, diabetes, high blood pressure, and varicose veins. Malnutrition and low maternal weight gain is a serious concern in both developing countries, where chronic malnutrition can lead to anemia and stunted growth, and in developed countries that have high rates of eating disorders. Recommendations about ideal weight gain vary, although the most frequently used guidelines are from the Institute of Medicine (IOM).

The 2009 guidelines provide ranges of healthy weight gain based on prepregnancy body mass index (BMI) categories established by the World Health Organization. The recommendations are as follows: underweight, 28–40 pounds; normal weight, 25–35 pounds; overweight, 15–25 pounds; obese, 11–20 pounds. In Italy, women are advised to gain much less weight than in other countries (2.2 lbs per month), and other countries, including Brazil, Chile, Argentina, and Ecuador, have adopted more conservative ranges than the IOM.

Pregnancy also has challenges and demands that require psychological changes including restructuring, adopting new skills, goal modification, and major role alterations. Although these tasks will differ significantly based upon one's culture, they often include (1) the physical aspect of growing a child (nutrition, physical symptoms, changes in behavior to protect the developing fetus and accommodate changing body); (2) anticipatory and preparatory work for the baby (prenatal care, diapers/clothing/baby items, preparing space and pragmatics for the child); (3) changes in personal relationships and roles with significant other, family of origin, existing children, and family; (4) changes in self-identity as the mothering role is added (both positive and negative aspects including developing relationship with unborn child, loss of autonomy, loss of time); and (5) changes in work life (ability to match needs of work tasks, assessment of goals and priorities). Women who engage in paid employment outside the home may face discrimination when pregnant including being fired, not being hired, or receiving a reduction in pay.

In addition, fears may arise concerning the health of the baby, bodily changes, the birth process, financial issues, infant mortality, and/or maternal mortality. Concerns about the pregnancy ending in a healthy baby and mother will vary, depending on a variety of factors, including maternal health, history of genetic disorders, and experiences with infant mortality (IM; the number of deaths of infants under 1 year old per 1,000 live births in given year). IM rates differ greatly among countries, with the highest in Angola (178.3) and the lowest in Monaco (1.78).

See Also: Abortion, Access to; Adoption; Childbirth, Home Versus Hospital; Infertility, Incidence of; Working Mothers.

Further Readings

Bongaarts, John. "Demographic Trends." http://www .packard.org/assets/files/population/program percent20review/pop_rev_bongaarts.pdf (accessed May 2010).

Guttmacher Institute. "Facts on Induced Abortion Worldwide." http://www.guttmacher.org/pubs/fb_IAW. html (accessed May 2010).

Heron, Melonie, Paul Sutton, Jiaquan Zu, Stephanie Ventura, Donna Strobino, and Bernard Guyer. "Annual Summary of Vital Statistics: 2007." *Pediatrics*, v.125 (2010).

Hilfinger Messias, DeAnne and Jeanne DeJoseph. "The Personal Work of a First Pregnancy: Transforming Identities, Relationships, and Women's Work." *Women & Health*, v.45/4 (2007).

Hogan, Margaret, Kyle Foreman, M. Naghavi, Stephanie Ahn, Mengru Wang, Susanna Makela, Alan Lopez, Rafael Lozano, and Christopher Murray. "Maternal Mortality for 181 Countries, 1980–2008." http://www .thelancet.com/journals/lancet/article/PIIS0140 -6736(10)60518-1/fulltext (accessed May 2010).

Institute of Medicine. "Weight Gain During Pregnancy." http://www.iom.edu/Reports/2009/Weight-Gain -During-Pregnancy-Reexamining-the-Guidelines.aspx (accessed May 2010).

Joslin, Courtney. "Legal Regulation of Pregnancy and Childbirth." http://ssrn.com/abstract=1558517 (accessed April 2010)

Ventura, Stephanie. "Changing Patterns of Nonmarital Childbearing in the United States." http://www.cdc.gov/ nchs/data/databriefs/db18.pdf (accessed May 2010).

Susan Logsdon-Conradsen
Berry College

Premenstrual Dysphoric Disorder

Premenstrual dysphoric disorder, or PMDD, is a severe form of premenstrual syndrome (PMS) that affects 3 to 8 percent of women and involves debilitating emotional, mental, and physical symptoms that interfere with a woman's ability to enjoy a normal life.

Emotional and mental symptoms can include intense sadness, severe anxiety, panic attacks, mood swings, irritability, and anger that seem out of proportion to events in the woman's life. Sufferers also deal with apathy or disinterest in daily activities, insomnia or hypersomnia, feelings of being out of control, decreased desire for sex, increased need for emotional closeness, and difficulty concentrating. Physical symptoms can include bloating, heart palpitations, breast tenderness, headaches, joint and muscle pain, swollen face, food cravings, binge eating, yeast infections, and diarrhea. While many women experience premenstrual symptoms, women with PMDD are thought to have abnormally sensitive reactions to their own hormonal changes.

Originally named late luteal phase dysphoric disorder (LLPDD), the American Psychiatric Association renamed it PMDD in its May 1993 revision of the *Diagnostic and Statistical Manual of Mental Disorders.* It is currently considered a "disorder requiring further study" rather than a diagnosable mental illness. The Food and Drug Administration considers PMDD an illness, but it has not yet been listed as a separate disorder in the World Health Organization's International Classification of Diseases.

Controversies over the development of PMDD as a diagnosable disorder or illness have persisted for nearly two decades. Feminist critics point out that diagnosing women with PMDD represents a trend toward medicalizing women's normal bodily processes, a phenomenon that has been occurring for centuries (e.g., hysteria as a "wandering womb"). Critics of PMDD argue that Western culture values men's bodies and experiences at the expense of women's bodies and experiences. Defenders of PMDD argue that the classification represents a real disorder of women's natural physiological processes and warrants medical intervention. Treatments for PMDD also carry implications of controversy, as drug companies compete with more intuitive or psychotherapy-based treatments. Drug treatments include selective serotonin reuptake inhibitors (SSRIs) like Zoloft, Paxil, Lexapro, and Prozac and have been widely criticized as a way to earn profits for the pharmaceutical industry.

Critics worry that PMDD is marketed to women to convince them they are "sick" when their bodies behave normally. Defenders of drug treatments for PMDD argue that, medically, women with PMDD differently process serotonin and thus require drug interventions. Aside from drug treatments, lifestyle changes such as regular exercise and a well-balanced diet have improved PMDD symptoms, and psychotherapy also has produced effective results.

Research has shown that women typically believe that other women's symptoms are worse than theirs, calling into question the universality of premenstrual symptoms.

Western countries that value women's bodies and advocate for more equal gender roles less often diagnose women with PMDD. This may be viewed through the lens of social and political implications of PMDD as a diagnosable disorder in some camps and as an indicator of gendered relationships, medicalization, and corporate power in others.

See Also: Depression; *Diagnostic and Statistical Manual of Mental Disorders*; *Diagnostic and Statistical Manual of Mental Disorders*, Critiques of; Health, Mental and Physical; Menstruation; Mental Health Treatment, Bias in; Premenstrual Syndrome.

Further Readings

Gurevich, M. "Rethinking the Label: Who Benefits From the PMS Construct?" *Women & Health*, v.23/2 (1995).

Huston, James E. and Lani C. Fujitsubo. *PMDD: A Guide to Coping with Premenstrual Dysphoric Disorder.* Oakland, CA: New Harbinger Publications, 2002.

Kissling, E. A. *Capitalizing on the Curse: The Business of Menstruation.* Boulder, CO: Lynne Rienner, 2006.

Offman, Alia and Peggy J. Kleinplatz. "Does PMDD Belong in the DSM? Challenging the Medicalization of Women's Bodies." *The Canadian Journal of Human Sexuality*, v.13/1 (2004).

Breanne Fahs
Arizona State University

Premenstrual Syndrome

Premenstrual syndrome (PMS) refers to the cyclic recurrence of certain physical, psychological, and behavioral symptoms that begin about a week before the menstrual period and disappear within a few days after menstruation starts.

Although American women commonly say that they have PMS or are "PMSing" anytime they notice a cyclic change, the term *PMS* should only be used to describe the experience of symptoms that are severe enough to interfere with a woman's daily life. According to the National Institutes of Health, symptom intensity must increase at least 30 percent in the six days before menstruation, and this pattern must occur for at least two consecutive menstrual cycles for the symptoms to be called PMS.

PMS symptoms vary from woman to woman, and even from one menstrual cycle to another in some women. Self-help books for women with PMS sometimes list as many as 200 different possible symptoms, but most of these have not been clearly linked to menstrual cycle–related processes.

Among the more commonly reported physical symptoms are backache; bloating; edema (swelling, particularly in the hands, ankles, and feet); breast tenderness; fatigue; insomnia; constipation or diarrhea; appetite changes (e.g., cravings or overeating, loss of appetite); weight gain; acne; and changes in libido (e.g., feeling more or less sexy, increased or decreased sex drive). The more commonly reported psychological and behavioral symptoms include sadness, anxiety, irritability, mood swings, difficulty concentrating, increased sensitivity to rejection, decreased interest in work and social activities, and feeling overwhelmed.

PMS was originally known as premenstrual tension, and it was first described in 1931. However, it did not become well known until the 1980s, when PMS was used as a criminal defense in England. It is interesting to consider that before 1980 few women had even heard of PMS, yet, today, the term is so commonly used in the United States and other Western countries that most women think they have it. Researchers estimate that up to 85 percent of women will report premenstrual symptoms at some point during their childbearing years, but only a small percentage (3–5 percent) of women will experience symptoms that are severe enough to interefere with daily functioning.

Some healthcare professionals and researchers have suggested that PMS is a culture-bound or socially constructed syndrome because it is not experienced in the same way around the world. For example, in China women are much more likely to complain of temperature changes than of emotional changes. PMS seems to be more common in cultures with negative and stigmatizing attitudes toward menstruation. Such a negative view leads women to consider normal physical and behavioral fluctuations to be symptoms of an illness and any stress, strain, nervousness, or unhappiness to be related to the menstrual cycle. In actuality, when most women chart their fluctuations, they find that there is not a cyclical pattern and that the symptoms are not actually severe enough to interfere with daily living. In addition, when men chart their moods and behaviors, they too find changes in energy, libido, and emotions throughout the month, but their changes are obviously not caused by a menstrual cycle or considered to be a medical problem.

Causes, Symptoms, and Treatments

The exact causes of PMS are unknown. A hereditary link has been found; twin studies reveal that the occurrence of PMS is twice as high in monozygotic (identical) twins as in dizygotic (fraternal) twins. Other studies have suggested that: PMS may be caused by nutritional or sleep deficits or by biochemical malfunctions in neurotransmitters (seratonin, dopamine); prostaglandins (hormone-like substances that act on smooth muscle); melatonin (the substance that regulates the biological clock); the renin-angiotensin-aldosterone system (regulates water and electrolyte balance); or ovarian hormone ratios (estrogen, progesterone).

PMS also may be more common in women who are under a lot of stress or who have experienced depression and/or trauma. The ovarian hormone hypothesis is the best known, but the fact is that none of these hypotheses has been reliably substantiated (i.e., results of studies vary considerably, and some findings could not be replicated).

Because of the wide range of possible symptoms and vast differences in women's experiences during the premenstrual phase of their cycles, it is possible that no one "cause" of PMS will ever be determined. More than 80 treatments have been suggested for PMS, but no single treatment works for everyone. Treatments range from medical interventions (e.g., hormonal treatments, painkillers, antianxiety medications, antidepressants) to lifestyle interventions (e.g., exercise, dietary supplements) and psychotherapy (e.g., cognitive-behavioral therapy, relaxation training).

During the 1980s, the favored treatments were progesterone therapy and evening primrose oil, but these have faded away with time, as they did not prove useful in the long run. Most women whose symptoms are not severe would probably benefit from stress management and other self-care activities. Those whose symptoms are severe should consult their doctors about treatments targeted toward the particular symptoms they experience most often. For example, they may need to take diuretics for water retention and edema.

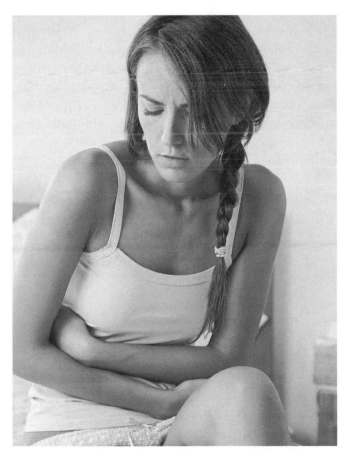

A small percentage of women experience premenstrual syndrome symptoms that affect their daily functioning.

Treatments of PMS also are challenging because premenstrual symptoms can sometimes be caused by other conditions. For example, women with chronic illnesses (e.g., multiple sclerosis, migraine headaches, epilepsy, major depression) sometimes report that their symptoms get worse just before menstruation. This is referred to as PMM or premenstrual magnification of existing symptoms. According the National Institutes of Health, 50 to 60 percent of women with severe PMS have an underlying psychiatric disorder, such as premenstrual dysphoric disorder (PMDD) or major depression (MDD).

See Also: Health, Mental and Physical; Menstruation; Premenstrual Dysphoric Disorder.

Further Readings

Chrisler, Joan C. "PMS as a Culture-Bound Syndrome." In Joan C. Chrisler, Carla Golden, and Patricia D. Rozee, eds. *Lectures on the Psychology of Women*, 4th Ed. New York: McGraw-Hill, 2008.

Golub, Sharon. *Periods: From Menarche to Menopause.* Newbury Park, CA: Sage, 1992.

Taylor, Diana and Stacey Colino. *Taking Back the Month: A Personalized Solution for Managing PMS and Enhancing Your Health.* New York: Penguin, 2002.

Joan C. Chrisler
Jennifer Gorman Rose
Connecticut College

Prenatal Care

Prenatal care, also called antenatal care, refers to medical treatment of pregnant women. Though pregnancy is a normal female physiological process, rather than an illness or disease, it still introduces physical risks to the mother and the fetus; therefore, prenatal care's primary emphasis is on reducing and/or eliminating known threats to maternal and infant health.

Early documented accounts of formal medical attention to pregnant women date back to the 1st century, when the Greek physician Soranus of Ephesus recommended gentle care of pregnant women and abstinence from sexual intercourse during pregnancy. In medieval Europe, physicians reportedly offered herbal remedies for physical discomfort in pregnancy.

Early Formal Prenatal Care Programs

In early-20th-century Western Europe, systematic medical programs to reduce maternal mortality began emerging and involved caring for childbearing women throughout pregnancy and childbirth. Treating primarily poor, urban-dwelling mothers, formally educated nurses with obstetric training—in today's terms, nurse-midwives—conducted repeated home visits to check on expectant mothers' weight and blood pressure and to measure the mothers' abdomens for fetal growth and position.

In countries such as Denmark and Great Britain, prenatal nurse visitation also incorporated educating mothers on safe hygiene in childbirth. In programs such as these, prenatal care was typically coupled with childbirth assistance provided by a trained nurse or midwife. In 1930, a larger-scale, international effort to reduce maternal mortality began officially when the League of Nations' Health Section identified maternal mortality as a global concern. Though not a league member at that time, the United States supported a number of domestic prenatal and childbirth assistance programs for low-income mothers. For example, data from programs treating poor, rural-dwelling women in Kentucky showed that maternal mortality rates dropped to about one-tenth of typical maternal death rates in the early-20th-century United States.

By the 1950s, researchers had learned that the chief causes of maternal mortality—bacterial infection, uncontrolled bleeding, and obstructed labor—were most effectively addressed with the intervention of a skilled attendant in childbirth. Thus, prenatal medicine began shifting away from focusing on maternal survival and more toward fetal development and health. The discovery of ultrasound imaging in the 1940s and 1950s and its growing use in obstetric medicine by the 1960s marked another critical point in the progressive and ongoing decoupling of maternal and fetal health.

Scientific Studies and Prenatal Care Today

The separation of maternal and fetal health has led to research on two major issues in prenatal care: first, how the number of prenatal visits relates to maternal and infant health, and second, what the benefits of specific prenatal procedures may be. On the first matter—the relationship between prenatal visits and maternal/infant health—having from 12 to 14 prenatal visits was an accepted tradition until the 1970s, when U.S. researchers reported that mothers who attended more prenatal visits had fewer premature and low-birth-weight babies than mothers who had fewer visits. Those studies were flawed because they failed to take into account that women attending more prenatal visits were also more often white and socially advantaged compared with women who attended fewer visits.

Controlling for sociodemographic factors, a British medical team published a landmark study in 1985 indicating that reducing the number of prenatal visits from the traditional 13 to eight for first-time mothers, and fewer for multiparous mothers, did not adversely affect mothers or infants. This work triggered an accumulation of research in the United States and abroad supporting reduced visit schedules as safe and effective. In 1998, the U.S. National Institutes of Health recommended 8 to 11 "focused" visits for first-time mothers (seven for women with prior children), rather than the traditional 13 to 14 visits. Global health organizations also have reinforced a reduced visit schedule; for example, the World Health Organization recommended in 2006 four medical checks as a necessary minimum. In the United States today, the American College of Obstetricians and Gynecologists' most recent published guidelines maintain the 13–14-visit schedule, but another widely used treatment guideline in the United States recommends up to 11 but no fewer than eight visits.

In addition to research on the number of necessary prenatal care visits, research on the benefits of specific procedures has also been accumulating. There is a time lag between the time a procedure may be discovered and the time at which long-term data on its safety and efficacy become available. If short-term studies suggest that a procedure may prove more beneficial than harmful, experts may recommend or begin using the procedure. This has proved problematic in the case of, for example, pelvic X-rays, which were conducted routinely on U.S. pregnant women in the 1930s and 1940s, which were later determined to have caused higher rates of cancer in offspring. The U.S. Food and Drug Administration issued a statement on limiting the practice in 1981.

Promoting and supporting adequate caloric intake for pregnant women has long demonstrated cognitive benefits for offspring.

This work is particularly valuable for nations with severely limited healthcare resources. In general, only a handful of prenatal procedures have solid scientific evidence showing they prevent the most severe consequences of childbearing: maternal or infant death or disability. For example, testing mothers' blood for Rh factor, a blood antigen, is unequivocally critical in preventing potentially disastrous consequences to the fetus. Knowing mothers' blood type before birth can allow professionals to prepare for safe blood transfusion in the case of hemorrhage. Assessing fetal position before birth can help make labor and delivery safer. Promoting and supporting adequate caloric intake for chronically malnourished pregnant women has a long history of demonstrated cognitive benefits for offspring.

Other prenatal care procedures may have less solid scientific support, such as advising women in poor relationships to seek treatment or counseling others to reduce stress, but they are nevertheless included in treatment protocols because experts have agreed that the practice is beneficial. Some practices, such as prescribing iron supplements, are recommended as a matter of tradition despite the absence of firm evidence confirming any benefit. Other routine practices showing no clear medical benefit in healthy pregnancies, such as ultrasound, appear to continue as a matter of presumed psychological benefit or consumer demand.

Prenatal Care and Global Maternal Health

Though research tends to treat prenatal care and skilled assistance in childbirth as two separate entities, in practice, maximum benefit of prenatal care can be achieved only when it is accessible to childbearing women and paired with safe childbirth procedures, similar to the structure of prenatal care programs over a century ago. Unfortunately, comprehensive prenatal care and childbirth assistance programs are both scarce and costly to women living in low-income economies, particularly for those residing in remote areas. For these reasons, maternal mortality is perhaps the most profound indicator of differences between poor and rich nations. Of the total maternal deaths occurring in 2005, 99 percent occurred in developing countries, with nearly 87 percent occurring in sub-Saharan Africa and South Asia. Translated into individual risk, 1,600 mothers die for every 100,000 live births in economically poor and war-torn Afghanistan, whereas only a single death occurs for every 100,000 live births in Ireland. Even within wealthy nations such as the United States, economically disadvantaged women face up to a three to four times higher maternal mortality risk.

To address dramatic differences in maternal survival by national income, in February 1987, the World Health Organization and partners launched the Safe Motherhood Initiative (SMI), in which prenatal care and skilled childbirth assistance are promoted as human rights. SMI has drawn opposition stemming from deeply held traditional and cultural beliefs surrounding women's roles and the value of maternal relative to fetal life, making the SMI mission of maternal healthcare for all childbearing women challenging to achieve. In response, for example, SMI proponents have had to adjust their approach to addressing maternal mortality caused by illegal and/or unsafe abortion, which accounts for up to 13 percent of global maternal death. Alongside such adjustments, in 1999 the World Health Organization produced a cost analysis outlining the minimal investment needed to dramatically reduce maternal mortality and the overall economic benefit of long-term maternal survival to communities.

To ensure the availability and acceptability of prenatal care and skilled birth assistance to women across the globe, cooperation among political forces, medical systems, and the women and families receiving intervention appears necessary and effective. Using a multitarget and collaborative approach, remarkable progress has been made in nations such as Sri Lanka. Despite an overall poverty rate of more than 30 percent, national and medical officials have worked together to guarantee safe, free, and culturally acceptable maternity care to women even in the remotest areas. The results of such efforts show that the 2006 maternal mortality rate of 60/100,000 births is a 100-fold reduction from the 600/100,000 rate of just 50 years ago. The dramatic improvements produced by Sri Lanka's efforts underscore the importance of pairing prenatal care with safe and hygienic practices in childbirth and in making maternal medical services accessible.

See Also: Infant Mortality; Maternal Mortality; Pregnancy; World Health Organization.

Further Readings

AbouZahr, Carla. "Safe Motherhood: A Brief History of the Global Movement 1947–2002." *British Medical Bulletin*, v.67/1 (2003).

Center for Global Development. "Millions Saved: Proven Successes in Global Health Case 6: Saving Mothers Lives in Sri Lanka." http://www.cgdev.org/section /initiatives/_active/millionssaved/studies/case_6 (accessed October 2009).

Drife, J. "The Start to Life: A History of Obstetrics." *Postgraduate Medical Journal*, v.78/919 (2002).

Dunn, Peter. "Soranus of Ephesus (circa AD 98–138) and Perinatal Care in Roman Times." *Archives of Disease in Childhood*, v.73/1 (1995).

Institute for Clinical Systems Improvement. "Routine Prenatal Care." http://www.icsi.org/guidelines_and _more/gl_os_prot/womens_health/prenatal_care_4 /prenatal_care__routine__3.html (accessed April 2008).

Kirkham, Colleen, et al. "Evidence Based Prenatal Care: Part I. General Prenatal Care and Counseling Issues." *American Family Physician*, v.71/7 (2005).

Marsh, G. N. "New Programme of Antenatal Care in General Practice." *British Medical Journal (Clinical Research Ed.)*, v.291/6496 (1985).

McDuffie, Robert, et al. "Effect of Frequency of Prenatal Care Visits on Perinatal Outcome Among Low-Risk Women: A Randomized Control Trial." *Journal of the American Medical Association*, v.275/11 (1996).

Posmontier, B. "Antepartum Care in the 21st Century." *Nursing Clinics of North America*, v.37/4 (2002).

Strong, Thomas. *Expecting Trouble: The Myth of Prenatal Care in America.* New York: New York University Press, 2000.

U.S. Department of Health and Human Services, National Institutes of Health. "Caring for Our Future: The Content of Prenatal Care, Report of the Expert Panel on the Content of Prenatal Care" (report NIH-Pub-90-3182). Bethesda, MD: National Institutes of Health, 1989.

U.S. Food and Drug Administration. "Statement on Use of Pelvimetry X-Ray Examination." *FDA Drug Bulletin*, v.11/3 (1981).

Walker, Deborah. "Evidence-Based Prenatal Care Visits: When Less is More." *Journal of Midwifery & Women's Health*, v.46/3 (2001).

Woo, Joseph. "A Short History on the Development of Ultrasound in Obstetrics and Gynecology." http://www.ob-ultrasound.net/history1.html (accessed July 2010).

World Health Organization. *Maternal Mortality in 2005.* Geneva: World Health Organization, 2007.

Elizabeth Soliday
Washington State University Vancouver

Priesthood, Episcopalian/Anglican

Anglican churches are split on the question of women's ordination. Since the 1970s, thousands of women have been ordained as priests in the Anglican Communion, and more than 20 have been ordained as bishops. The issue remains controversial, however, especially as it has led a few conservative congregations to break away from their provinces. Nonetheless, in most areas of the communion, the prohibitions against women's ordination are continuing to be removed.

Women Priests

The Worldwide Anglican Communion is made up of 38 individual, autonomous provinces, including the Church of England and the Episcopal Church, USA (EC-USA). In 1968, the Lambeth Conference—the meeting of Anglican bishops and primates held every 10 years—decided that arguments both for and against women's ordination were "inconclusive" and that women's ordination would be a vivid representation of the universality of redemption. However, this position threatened the church's relationship with the Roman Catholic Church, which strongly opposes women's ordination. Hong Kong was the first province to allow women priests, ordaining Joyce Bennett and Jane Hwang in 1971. Following the "irregular" ordination of 11 women in Philadelphia in 1974, the Anglican Church of Canada authorized women's ordination in 1975, as did the EC-USA in 1976 and the Church of England in 1992. By 1998, the majority of provinces were in favor of women's ordination. Women made up about one-quarter of clergy in the EC-USA by 2004 and in the Church of England by 2008. Approximately half of students now training for ordination are women. However, as of 2008, 10 Anglican provinces allow women to be only deacons or do not allow women's ordination at all.

Bishops

The first female bishop in the Anglican Communion was the Right Reverend Barbara Harris, who was consecrated as Suffragan (assistant) bishop of Massachusetts in 1989; Penelope Jamieson was elected to be the first female diocesan bishop by the Anglican Church of New Zealand later that year. Subsequent bishops included Victoria Matthews (Canada, 1995), Nerva Cot Aguilera (Cuba, 2007), and Kay Goldsworthy (Australia, 2008). As of 2008, 24 women were bishops in the Anglican Communion. Ten other provinces allow for women bishops but have not yet consecrated any. In the Church of England, legislation in support of women bishops is currently moving forward. In 2009, Los Angeles elected the Reverend Canon Mary Douglas Glasspool, an openly lesbian woman, as bishop of that city.

In 2006, the Most Reverend Katharine Jefferts Schori was elected as the presiding bishop of the Episcopal Church, USA—the first woman to lead a national church in the Anglican Communion.

Church Divisions

This issue is particularly difficult to resolve because many who oppose women's ordination claim that the church cannot legitimately ordain women and thus that women priests and bishops are not truly ordained and administer invalid sacraments. Therefore, acceptance of women's ordinations has not, for the most part, been mandatory; instead, concessions of "conscience," including England's "flying bishops," have been made for dioceses and parishes that see women's ordination as unscriptural. Because of this, many women seeking ordination have faced unusual obstacles, and their ordinations are not necessarily recognized by other bishops or dioceses. The ordination of Presiding Bishop Jefferts Schori and the 2003 ordination of Gene Robinson, the first openly gay man to be consecrated as an Episcopal bishop, deepened the split between the EC-USA and some more conservative parishes. About 700 theologically conservative churches have seceded from the Episcopal Church to form the Anglican Church in North America—a "province" not recognized by the Anglican Communion.

The EC-USA dioceses that most vocally opposed women's ordination were Fort Worth, Texas; Quincy, Illinois; and San Joaquin, California. During 2007 and 2008, delegates in the dioceses of San Joaquin, Quincy, Forth Worth, and Pittsburgh, Pennsylvania, voted to leave the Episcopal Church and join the Argentina-based Anglican Province of the Southern Cone. The EC-USA then reorganized the Episcopalian parishioners remaining in those dioceses, and the reorganized Episcopal dioceses of San Joaquin and Fort Worth ordained their first woman priests in 2009. Meanwhile, many provinces are working against the discrimination of ordained women by removing their "conscience clauses" (Canada) and making acceptance of women's ordination mandatory (United States).

See Also: Anglican Communion; Lesbian/Gay Clergy; Priesthood, Roman Catholic; Schori, Katharine Jefferts; Winkett, Canon Lucy.

Further Readings

Darling, Pamela W. *New Wine: The Story of Women Transforming Leadership and Power in the Episcopal Church*. Cambridge, MA: Cowley, 1994.

The Episcopal Church Welcomes You. http://www .episcopalchurch.org/index.htm (accessed July 2010).

Harris, Harriet and Jane Shaw, eds. *The Call for Women Bishops*. London: SPCK, 2004.

Vanessa Baker
Bowling Green State University

Priesthood, Roman Catholic

According to the *Catechism of the Catholic Church*, the priesthood still interconnects Christ and men. In 1965, Vatican II emphasized that the church was to be led by the lay people and there would be an increase in social justice advocacy. Since then, Catholic women have taken on various leadership roles within the church, such as religious education, social ministry, music ministry, and scripture lectors. More recently, girls and women have been altar servers and Eucharistic ministers. However, movements toward allowing women to be priests have not been successful.

Biblical Arguments

The church argues that there were no women ordained in the New Testament and that Jesus chose only men to be his apostles, who in turn then chose only men to follow them. This, according to church authorities, established the perception that only men could sacramentally represent Christ. Feminist and philosophical arguments regarding social structures of biblical times, the roots of Jewish tradition, and Greco-Roman influences have had no impact on today's church leaders who continue to espouse the idea that only men can consecrate the Eucharist.

Historical Arguments

In the *Didascalia Apostolorum*, a 3rd-century Christian text, both widows and deaconesses are mentioned as being church officials. However, later arguments, especially those of the 13th century, dismissed these functions as not being tied to the sacrament of Holy Orders.

The two best-known opponents of women in the priesthood were St. Thomas Aquinas (1225–74 C.E.) and St. Bonaventure (1217–74 C.E.). Aquinas's main argument consisted of the theological position that the female sex cannot signify eminence of degree. This is based on the multiple levels of female inferiority: women are biologically inferior to men, women are socially inferior to men, and women were created to be dependent upon men. These inherent defects will not allow women to represent Christ. Bonaventure agreed that women are inherently inferior to men and endorsed the idea that Christ's maleness required his representatives on earth, priests, to also be male. Bonaventure also argued that women were expressly forbidden to handle sacred objects, they cannot hold power, and they do not bear the image of God. These detrimental arguments continue to hold sway in today's church, and women are still considered unfit for Holy Orders.

Sacrament of Holy Orders

Holy Orders is one of the seven sacraments of the church. Originally, there was a division between major Holy Orders and minor Holy Orders; however, from the late Middle Ages on, the minor ones were considered mostly ceremonial. The sacramental rite of Holy Orders is generally reserved for men who are entering the priesthood, although deacons undergo a similar ritual. Through this sacrament, priests share in the universal mission of the church that Christ assigned to the apostles—to preach the Gospel to the congregation and perform the sacrament of Eucharist.

Only baptized men are qualified to receive this sacrament. The official stance of today's church is that Christ chose 12 men for his apostles and the apostles did the same when they chose who succeeded them in the ministry. The church considers itself bound to Christ's choice; hence women's ordination is not possible. However, women are allowed study to become priests, although they cannot take the final vows.

Recent Papal Responses

In 1976, the report of the Pontifical Biblical Commission found that there were no Scriptural grounds for

In May 1994, Pope John Paul II wrote an apostolic letter that stated that women's ordination is not allowed, that all conversation for pro-women's ordination should be silenced, and that the church does not have the authority to grant priestly ordination to women.

denying priestly ordination to women. However, in May 1994, Pope John Paul II wrote an apostolic letter titled *Ordinatio Sacerdotalis* ("On Ordination to the Priesthood"). It addresses the traditional prohibition of women's ordination. It maintains that women's ordination is still not allowed and directs that all conversation for pro-women's ordination be silenced. The Jesuit Order came under censure because of failure to comply with this second regulation. The letter also states that the church does not have the canonical authority to grant priestly ordination to women and that the church's entire congregation holds this same judgment. The letter rests on the fact that the prohibition of women's ordination is a part of the written work of God and an integral part of God's plan.

In particular, Pope John Paul II stressed that the role and presence of women in the church is necessary and irreplaceable. He relaxed his stance against female altar servers and Eucharisitic ministers and encouraged women to pursue roles better suited to them, such as religious education leaders and music ministry. This letter was followed by the papally endorsed *Responsum ad Dubium* issued by the Congregation for the Doctrine of the Faith (1995). Together, these documents have officially closed discussion of Roman Catholic women's ordination, and women continue to play no part in the decision making of the church.

Several organizations, including Women's Ordination Worldwide (WOW), have fought continually against the discussion ban, which has never officially been reversed. However, since the matter is considered doctrinal and not dogmatic, dissenters are not classified as heretics.

Women's Ordination Worldwide (WOW)

Women's Ordination Worldwide was founded in 1996 at the First European Women's Synod in Gmunden, Austria. Its primary mission is "to promote worldwide the ordination of Roman Catholic women to a renewed priestly ministry in a democratic church, and to stand in solidarity with women who are ordained in the ongoing renewal of the church." Although WOW is specifically directed toward the Roman Catholic tradition, other denominations are not excluded from participation.

Originally organized as a loose network of similarly minded individuals, the movement solidified its international presence with its first conference held in Dublin, in 2001. Despite pressure from the Vatican, the conference was deemed a success, and the organization has subsequently become a viable force across the world, with branches in numerous countries. WOW also serves as an umbrella for other organizations. In the United States, the main organization working for women's ordination is the Women's Ordination Conference (WOC). This group was founded in 1975 and has worked solely for the rights of Roman Catholic women to be ordained. This goal reflects the prevailing beliefs of U.S. Catholics, 63 percent of whom support women's ordination.

See Also: Lesbian/Gay Clergy; Priesthood, Episcopalian/Anglican; Roman Catholic Church; Women's Ordination Conference.

Further Readings

Bonavoglia, Angela. *Good Catholic Girls: How Women Are Leading the Fight to Change the Church.* New York: HarperOne, 2006.

John Paul II. *Ordinatio Sacerdotalis.* May 22, 1994. http://www.vatican.va/holy_father/john_paul_ii/apost _letters/documents/hf_jp-ii_apl_22051994_ordinatio -sacerdotalis_en.html (accessed June 2010).

Macy, Gary. *The Hidden History of Women's Ordination: Female Clergy in the Medieval West.* New York: Oxford University Press, 2007.

Torjesen, Karen Jo. *When Women Were Priests: Women's Leadership in the Early Church and the Scandal of their Subordination in the Rise of Christianity.* San Francisco, CA: Harper San Franscisco, 1993.

U.S. Catholic Church. *Catechism of the Catholic Church.* Liguori, MO: Liguori Publications, 1994.

Michelle M. Sauer
Emily D. Hill
University of North Dakota

Prison Administration

Before the passage of the Civil Rights Act of 1964, which banned discrimination on the basis of sex in employment, women were generally excluded from the field of prison administration. Those who did work in the prison system were generally confined to clerical jobs, teaching, support positions, or working with adult and juvenile female offenders. In 1969, when women made up 40 percent of the total workforce, only 12 percent of those working in the corrections field were female. A year later, barriers that banned women from working with male prisoners were removed, and females were provided with greater opportunities for employment. Between 1985 and 2002, the number of women correctional officers rose from 13 percent to 22.7 percent.

In the late 19th century, female reformers had bullied their way onto corrections boards in order to improve the lot of prisoners generally and female offenders particularly. In 1870, reformers founded the American Correctional Association (ACA). Initially, female members focused on the rights of female offenders, but as the number of women working in corrections expanded, ACA broadened its scope to address the issues of women working in the field of prison administration. By 1912, the Association of Women Members (AWM) of the American Prison Association was founded under the guidance of Maud Ballington Booth, a well-known prison reformer who had cofounded the Salvation Army in 1887.

Dedicated to promoting the Public Correctional Policy on Employment of Women in Corrections, by the 1970s, the Women's Task Force, which later became the Women Working in Corrections Committee, had evolved as a working arm of the AWM. In the 21st century, much of the work of AWA is accomplished through national conferences that bring women together to address issues of interest to women working in prison administration and furnish them with training and support.

Individuals working in prison administration may be employed as correctional or detention officers or they may work in various administrative or support positions. In most cases, they work five-day workweeks and may be either on an eight-hour schedule or on rotating shifts. They are often required to work on holidays and weekends as well. Applicants for correctional officers must have at least a high school diploma or its equivalency. Many individuals employed in the field also have military experience. Those who work in federal prisons are required to have at least a bachelor's degree and at least three years of field experience. At the administrative level, a college degree is generally required. Training is conducted according to guidelines established by the ACA. Additional training is required at the federal level. New applicants must be between the ages of 18 and 37 and have no felony convictions. Career advancement may occur as a result of job experience, educational advancement, testing, or bidding on higher-level positions. In 2008, the median annual wage of those working in corrections was $38,380, and salaries ranged from $25,300 to $64,110. For supervisors, the median annual salary was $57,380, and salaries ranged from a low of $32,300 to a high of $86,970.

Even though legal barriers to female employment have been removed and females have demonstrated over time that they are capable of handling the rigors of life in prison administration, women continue to face subtle and informal on-the-job discrimination. This is due in large part to an ingrained belief that women are physically incapable of dealing with crisis situations because of both physical characteristics and female socialization. Research into this subject has borne out the fact that women do indeed approach their jobs in prison administration with different skills than those of males. They tend to be more service oriented on the job, and they are less confrontational and more positive when interacting with male offenders. However, this difference in approach has proven quite successful for women in prison administration, and women are generally ranked high in job performance.

Job Satisfaction

While women in prison administration express job satisfaction equal to that of males, there is considerable on-the-job stress, and turnover is high. Much of the stress is related to hostilities exhibited toward them by male colleagues. Sexual harassment, which consists of behaviors such as swearing, unsolicited touching, intimidation, and expressions of inappropriate humor, also causes a good deal of stress.

Research on women in the field of prison administration has documented the existence of a glass ceiling evoked through both intentional and unintentional male behaviors. As in many male-dominated fields, women are shut out of informal social networks that tend to advance the rise of males in any business. There is also a lack of mentoring of females in the field. In some cases, there is a tendency of males to exhibit paternalistic behaviors toward females rather than treating them as equals. Many women in prison administration insist that they are held to different standards of behavior than those set forth for males, making it more difficult for them to advance up the career ladder.

See Also: Gender Roles, Cross-Cultural; Law Enforcement, Women in; Prison Guards, Female (U.S.).

Further Readings

Carlson, Peter M. and Judith Simon Garrett. *Prison and Jail Administration: Practice and Theory.* Sudbury, MA: Jones and Bartlett, 2007.

Collins, Pamela A. and Kathryn E. Collins. *Women in Public and Private Law Enforcement.* Boston: Butterworth Heinemann, 2002.

Josi, Don A. and Dale K. Sechrest. *The Changing Career of the Correctional Officer: Policy Implications for the 21st Century.* Maryland Heights: MO: Elsevier Science and Technology Books, 1998.

Morton, Joann Brown. "ACA and Women Working in Corrections." *Corrections Today* (October 1, 2005). http://www.allbusiness.com/human-resources /employee-development-leadership/991754-1.html (accessed April 2010).

U.S. Department of Labor. *Occupational Outlook Handbook 2010–11 Edition.* http://www.bls.gov/oco /ocos156.htm (accessed April 2010).

Elizabeth Rholetter Purdy
Independent Scholar

Prison Guards, Female (U.S.)

Women were first hired as prison guards in the 1830s, but it was not until the mid-20th century that female correctional officers began pushing for equal opportunities in the field. At first, female officers were primarily assigned to women's institutions, but today woman are employed at all levels of the correctional system. The fundamental basis for equality in prison work stems from Title VII, a 1972 amendment to the 1964 Civil Rights Act, declaring it is illegal to base any terms of employment on race, sex, religion, or national origin. However, there was a stipulation that stated that employment could be restricted for one's gender, if the individual did not meet certain job requirements. In *Dothard v. Rawlison* (1977), the Supreme Court ruled that minimum requirements were not job related. Thus, Title VII is hailed as pivotal for equality in hiring women in male-dominated professions.

In the 1990s, the rate of women working in corrections began to increase. In the mid 1990s, it was estimated that 19 percent of correctional officers in both state and federal prisons were women. By 2005, this number had increased to 27.4 percent. Regarding jails, women account for 34 percent and 40.8 percent of guards in government and private facilities, respectively. It is difficult to distinguish employment by rank or institution, but it has been estimated that 65 percent of correctional officers in women's facilities are female, but less than 15 percent of guards in male facilities are women. There appears to be a correlation between level of security and percentage of female staff.

There are three objections to women working in male facilities. Though the issue of privacy was never an issue until women started staffing male facilities, some have argued that female officers invade the privacy rights of male inmates. In some instances women have been prohibited from working posts that have increased contact with male inmates, but the courts have favored the rights of employees over privacy concerns. Concern has been voiced, too, regarding the security of institutions where some feel women are weaker than men, but there is no evidence to support this notion. Further, it has been argued that female officers are likely to be attacked by an inmate, but research finds that females are no more likely to be assaulted than male officers. In fact, a 1996 study found that men were four times more likely to be attacked by an inmate than women and that female officers tend to relax tension and conflict, sometimes improving dress code, behavior, and language among inmates. The presence of female officers reportedly has normalized the prison environment.

There are two general models used to explain why gender differences exist in job performance. The "gender model" suggests that individuals bring certain characteristics to the job, while the "job model" implies that the organizational structure influences how each individual operates. Regardless of theoretical models of behavior, studies find that both male and female correctional officers report gender differences in job performance. Male officers report that women are "soft" or "nice" and act in a maternal fashion. Some might see this as invective, but female officers stated that they were more "human-service oriented" and likely to use appropriate interpersonal skills when interacting with offenders.

Courts and legislative findings often support equality for women. Consequently, women have slowly gained access to occupations within corrections institutions. Still, recent research suggests that full equity has not yet been garnered. Sexism still exists in this field, but in time female prison guards will achieve full equity.

See Also: Equal Rights Amendment; Glass Ceiling; Judges, Female; Law Enforcement, Women in; Prisoners, Female (U.S.); Stereotypes of Women.

Further Readings

Belknap, Joanne. *The Invisible Woman: Gender, Crime, and Justice,* 3rd ed. Belmont, CA: Thomson Wadsworth, 2007.

Bureau of Justice Statistics (Law Enforcement Statistics). http://www.ojp.usdoj.gov/bjs/lawenf.htm (accessed July 2010).

Jenne, D. and R. Kersting. "Aggression and Women Correctional Officers in Male Prisons." *Prison Journal,* v.76 (1996).

Alissa R. Ackerman
University of California, Merced

Prisoners, Female (U.S.)

Historically, female prisoners have played a somewhat invisible role in the criminal justice system. During the 19th century in the United States, it was highly unlikely for a judge to sentence a woman to prison, unless she was a habitual offender. Prison was considered the end of the road. Until the 1870s, women were housed in the same facilities as men and were often imprisoned for public order offenses. Reform slowly occurred, and by 1873, the first female prison was established in Indiana. As new women's reformatories were built around the country, domestic values flourished. Women could decorate their rooms and learned feminine vocations. After World War II, values did not change, and female offenders were provided with traditionally feminine occupational and vocational trade skills. Though no new correctional model for women has been introduced since that time, in recent years more attention has been given to women in prison, primarily because the number of women being incarcerated continues to rise. In 1970, there were 5,600 female inmates in the United States, whereas in 2007, 105,500 women remained behind bars. From 1980 to 1994, the number of women in prison increased 386 percent, but when assessing the increase over three decades—from 1977 to 2007—the female prison population grew 832 percent. Still, female prisoners constitute a small portion of those behind bars.

Demographic Makeup

Female prisoners comprise between 5 and 7 percent of the prison and jail population in the United States and typically are incarcerated for less serious offenses. In fact, as incarceration for violent offenses decreased, the number of women incarcerated increased dramatically. Prior to the 1980s, women were more likely to be sent to prison for property crimes; since that time, women have been incarcerated primarily for drug-related offenses. Women are at least twice as likely to be sent to prison for drug offenses as men and are more likely to suffer from alcohol and drug dependencies. Despite the dramatic increase in the number of women incarcerated in the United States, today two-thirds of them are imprisoned for nonviolent offenses. Research suggests that only 35 percent of incarcerated women were convicted of a violent offense, whereas 28 percent and 25 percent were convicted of drug and property offenses, respectively. In the 1990s, it was reported that women convicted of drug offenses made up half of the growth in the prison population.

As with incarcerated men, minority women are disproportionately represented in U.S. prisons. Though roughly 45 percent of incarcerated women are white, the proportion of black and Hispanic women relative to white women is higher. For instance 349, 147, and 93 out of every 100,000 black, Hispanic, and white women, respectively, are incarcerated.

Challenges Facing Incarcerated Women

Between 60 and 80 percent of incarcerated women have children under the age of 18, and most report having at least two. In 2007, 65,000 incarcerated women reported being the mothers of almost 150,000 minor children. It is also estimated that about 8 percent of women are pregnant during their incarceration. These statistics are critical because separation from one's child is reported as one of the worst situations faced by the female offender. Once incarcerated, the woman faces the breakdown of her family while learning to cope with her new life behind bars. This is exacerbated by the Adoption and Safe Families Act of 1997, whereby states may seek to terminate parental rights when a child has been in foster care for 15 of the previous 22 months. The average prison sentence for a woman is 19 months, and almost 50 percent of incarcerated mothers reported being a single parent prior to going to prison. The formal loss of a child to the system is a very real possibility.

Women who come into contact with the criminal justice system exhibit severe societal deficits. In a recent study, almost two-thirds of incarcerated women reported not having a high school diploma, and 50 percent were unemployed in the month prior to their incarceration; prior to arrest, 15 percent of women reported being homeless at least once in that year. Almost half of incarcerated women reported that an immediate family member has been incarcerated, and six out of 10 women reported growing up with one parent being absent from the home.

In other studies, 24 percent of female inmates and probationers reported mental health issues and 74 percent reported regular drug use. In a recent study of female jail inmates in the northeastern and mid-Atlantic United States, 75 percent of women reported a history of drug or alcohol abuse, 60 percent reported committing an offense to obtain money for drugs, and 52 percent reported that they were under the influence at the time of their arrest. The women were less likely to report receiving drug treatment while in jail (35 percent) and even fewer (10 percent) received mental health counseling.

Drug and alcohol issues are not the only problems faced by incarcerated women. A high-risk population, incarcerated women are more likely to be infected with human immunodeficiency virus (HIV) than incarcerated men and are more likely to be sexually abused. These two issues are not mutually exclusive, as research suggests that women who are sexually abused are more likely to engage in risky sexual behavior and to inject drugs intravenously. Incarcerated women are also more likely to report use of the more dangerous drugs crack-cocaine and heroin than incarcerated men. Statistics such as these suggest that many of the women imprisoned in the United States face serious challenges prior to their incarceration. It is important to understand the relationship between these types of issues and criminal behavior.

Despite the challenges facing incarcerated women, often they do not receive the necessary services or treatments that are crucial to their successful reintegration into society, post-release. In a study by the U.S. Department of Justice, the number of women in acute need of services and the number for whom services were actually provided were illustrated. Over 65 percent of those in need of mental health services received treatment. With regard to substance abuse, employment, and educational needs, only half of those in acute need for treatment or services received it. While substance abuse and mental health treatment are crucial, they are often all that is provided, despite the need for various forms of rehabilitation, including family reunification and counseling, therapy aimed at dealing with prior victimization, and proper aftercare. Unfortunately, the small number of incarcerated women makes it difficult to justify the use of diverse programs for educational and vocational training and to provide specialized treatment. Not providing services may make it more difficult for women to effectively deal with the obstacles that previously landed them in prison.

In addition, many women report sexual abuse while incarcerated. In a national study of sexual misconduct in prisons in 2004, women were overrepresented as victims. Though women comprise less than 10 percent of the overall prison population, 46 percent of victims of abusive sexual acts were women. It is impossible to understand the full extent of the problem because sexual abuse is severely underreported. However, states are taking action to prevent sexual misconduct by staff. By the turn of the century, 41 states had enacted legislation criminalizing sexual misconduct against inmates.

The Prison Subculture

The first account of the female prison subculture was by Giallambardo, who, in the 1960s found that women interacted in a different fashion than men. Whereas men reported "doing their own time," women were more likely to confide in staff about their everyday problems and were more likely to take an interest in each other's lives and to take care of one another. Incarcerated women often create pseudofamilies upon whom they rely for hope and support to cope with the harsh realities and challenges of prison life. One will often hear women referring to other members of their pseudofamilies by titles including dad, mom, grandma, sister, and even cousin. Members take on caring, nurturing roles in lieu of their roles beyond prison walls.

Research and Policy

Unprecedented growth since the 1980s in the number of women's prisons and prisoners has provided the impetus to study this seemingly unknown population. In fact, it was not until the 1960s that studies of female prisoners were conducted, and women were not mentioned in the President's Commission on Law Enforcement and the Administration of Justice of 1967. Very little was known about women and women's prisons until the 1970s. As noted, this was primarily because of the small number of incarcerated women and the nonviolent nature of their crimes in comparison to men. The implications of crime prevention policies have adversely affected women for whom prison would have never been an option prior to their enactment. The war on drugs, determinate sentencing, and mandatory minimum sentencing have all increased time spent under criminal justice sanction, and because of these phenomena, over the last decade, researchers and advocacy organizations have begun giving more attention to women in the criminal justice and corrections system.

Research and policy publications from organizations like the Women's Prison Association (WPA), first established in the 1840s, highlight the special needs of incarcerated women and provide recommendations for prevention, treatment, and reintegration strategies, including access to employment, public assistance, healthcare, child care, community involvement, and policies to promote healthy family life. The WPA is an advocacy organization focused on assisting women with criminal justice histories with the reintegration process. The organization adheres to a strict research and policy agenda aimed at shedding new light on issues related to women and incarceration. Recent research has focused on the use of prison nurseries, the growth of the imprisonment rate, the use of state commissions and task forces, and the demographic makeup of women's prisons. In 2009, the WPA authored a national study on prison nurseries and community-based alternatives for incarcerated mothers. Research shows that the bond between a mother and child, early in development, provides positive outcomes to the mother and the baby. Despite this research, many babies born to incarcerated mothers are immediately placed with other family members or in foster care. The WPA recommended the use of prison nurseries to foster the relationship between mother and child and highlighted prison nurseries around the United States that utilized such a method.

Prison itself will not correct unwanted behavior and may even increase criminality. Effective use of treatment and services both behind bars and in the community may be effective in decreasing and preventing future crime.

See Also: Crime Victims, Female; Girl Gangs; HIV/AIDS: North America; Mental Health Treatment, Access to; Perpetrators, Female; Poverty, "Feminization" of; Sexual Harassment.

Further Readings

Beck, Allen J. and Timothy A. Hughes. *Sexual Violence Reported by Correctional Authorities, 2004.* Washington, DC: Bureau of Justice Statistics: July 2005.

Belknap, Joanne. *The Invisible Woman.* Belmont, CA: Wadsworth, 1996.

Clear, Todd R., George F. Cole, and Michael D. Resig. *American Corrections*, 8th ed. Belmont, CA: Wadsworth, 2009.

Frost, Natasha, A., J. Greene, and K. Pranis. *The Punitiveness Report-HARD HIT: The Growth in Imprisonment of Women, 1977–2004.* New York: Women's Prison Association, 2004.

National Institute of Corrections (NIC). *Sexual Misconduct in Prisons: Laws, Remedies, and Incidence.* Washington, DC: NIC, 2000.

Snell, Tracy and Danielle Morton. *Survey of State Prison Inmates, 1991: Women in Prison.* Washington, DC: Bureau of Justice Statistics: March 1994.

U.S. General Accounting Office (GAO). *Women in Prison: Sexual Misconduct By Correctional Staff.* Washington, DC: GAO, 1999.

West, Heather C. and William J. Sabol. *Prison Inmates at Midyear 2008.* Washington, DC: Bureau of Justice Statistics: March 2009.

West, Heather C. and William J. Sabol. *Prisoners in 2007.* Washington, DC: Bureau of Justice Statistics: December 2008.

Women's Prison Association. "Addressing Women's Incarceration: A National Survey of State Commissions and Task Forces on Women in the Criminal Justice System" (2008). http://www.wpa online.org/pdf/Mothers%20Infants%20and%20 Imprisonment%202009.pdf (accessed August 2009).

Women's Prison Association. "Mothers, Infants and Imprisonment" (2009). http://www.wpaonline.org/pdf /Mothers %20Infants %20and %20Imprisonment %20 2009.pdf (accessed August 2009).

Alissa R. Ackerman
University of California, Merced

Prisoners of War, Female

Since its first documented usage in 1660, the term *prisoner of war (POW)* has commonly referred to men, and now women as well, who have been imprisoned by an enemy power during or immediately after an armed conflict. Chapter Two of the 1907 Hague Convention was one of many attempts made during the 20th century to fully outline the parameters of POW categories. The 1949 and 1950 Geneva Convention (III and IV) Relative to the Treatment of Prisoners of War mentions very little about women prisoners. However, several articles in the treaty (13, 14, 25, and 29) call for separate housing, acknowledgment of specific hygiene and health needs, and the right to receive the same favorable treatment as men.

Joan of Arc

Despite being denied the right to serve in their respective militaries, women worldwide have historically found ways to aid the nation's war efforts, often risking capture, imprisonment, even death. One of the most poignant examples in history is Joan of Arc, an illiterate French peasant teenager who successfully led French male troops in battles against England to win some decisive victories for France in the 100 Year War. At 19, she was captured by the Burgundians in 1431, imprisoned, sold to the British, and ultimately burned at the stake on May 30, 1431, for being a religious heretic.

Confederacy and Union Spies

During the American Civil War of 1860–65, espionage became women's preferred weapon of service choice. Spying for the Confederacy as well as the Union forces did not come without risks. Dr. Mary Walker, the only female Congressional Medal of Honor recipient, was imprisoned in 1864 for four months by the Confederacy. Another female Union spy, Pauline Cushman, barely risked being hanged by the Confederacy after being found guilty of espionage. She was rescued by Union troops. For the Confederates, 20-year-old Confederate spy Nancy Hart was briefly imprisoned and managed to escape from her jailers. Twice imprisoned by Union forces, Washington, D.C., socialite Rose O'Neal Greenhow proved so formidable a Confederate that she earned personal praise from Confederate President Jefferson Davis.

World War II

World War II was the first conflict in which American military women were captured and imprisoned by enemy forces. On December 9, 1941, two days after the infamous Pearl Harbor attack, the Japanese captured five American Navy nurses on Guam and imprisoned them in Japan. In 1942, 83 U.S. Army and Navy nurses were captured in the Philippines and held prisoner for three years in the infamous Japanese Los Banos Internment Camp. The German forces imprisoned Lt. Reba Whittle, a member of the Army's Nursing Corp., who was wounded during a thwarted aeromedical evacuation mission. While in the camp, she continued her nurse's duties, taking care of other POWS. She received the Purple Heart and the Air Medal, but it took years for the United States to formally grant her POW status. Although there are no precise numbers, French and other European women who were a part of the famed Resistance Movement also were imprisoned by the Germans. Some were executed.

Desert Storm

Approximately 40,000 American servicewomen deployed in support of Operation Desert Shield/ Storm fought in the Persian Gulf. Thirteen were killed and two became POWs. Army Transportation Specialist Melissa Rathbun-Nealy was captured January 30, 1991, after she and Specialist David Lockett got lost while driving a heavy equipment transport vehicle near the border of Kuwait and Saudi Arabia. The military did not declare her a POW until February 12, 1991. She was the first American servicewoman captured in war since World War II. She was taken to a prison in Basra, Iraq, and held in solitary confinement until she was released three weeks later, on March 4. Rhonda Cornum, an Army flight surgeon, was on a aerorescue mission and captured when Iraqi combatants shot down the Black Hawk helicopter carrying her and seven aircrew members. Cornum was severely injured with a bullet lodged in her shoulder, two broken arms, and significant damage to the ligaments in her knees. She was held in a prison in Basra, Iraq, for eight days and released March 5, 1991, one week after the war officially ended. During her imprisonment, she was interrogated and had been sexually assaulted by one Iraqi captor.

In early 1993, Congress eliminated the combat exclusion policy for women, an action that allowed women to fly combat aircraft and serve on all surface ships. Additionally, Secretary of Defense Les Aspin revoked the "risk rule," a 1988 Bush administration mandate that had previously kept women from serving in military jobs that could put them in the direct or even indirect line of combat.

Operation Iraqi Freedom

On March 23, 2003, another wrong turn in the Iraqi desert caused three U.S Army women in the 507th Maintenance Company (a Fort Bliss, Texas, unit, near El Paso) to become POW during Operation Iraqi Freedom. Iraqi forces attacked the 33-person unit that got separated from other convoying coalition forces. The action ended with 11 U.S. soldiers killed and six taken prisoner by Iraqi irregular forces. Sixteen of the element's members evaded capture and were later rescued by U.S. Marines.

Specialist Shoshana Johnson, the first African American female POW, was wounded and taken by Iraqi forces, imprisoned, and kept in solitary confinement. Private Jessica Lynch, a supply clerk, was severely wounded, captured, and taken to an Iraqi hospital. Private First Class Lori Ann Piestewa also was severely injured when the Humvee she was driv-

Garrison Commander Col. Edward Manning and Shoshana Johnson, the first female African American prisoner of war.

ing was hit by explosives and crashed into another Humvee. (Lynch was in Piestewa's Humvee.) Piestewa was taken to the same Iraqi hospital as Lynch but did not survive her injuries. She was initially classified as Missing in Action (MIA), but her body was found later, buried in an unmarked grave with the bodies of the other male soldiers who had died in the ambush. U.S. forces later recovered their remains. Piestewa became the first Native American woman killed in combat and the first U.S. servicewoman to die in Operation Iraqi Freedom.

Private Lynch was rescued by U.S. Army Rangers from their Iraqi hospital on April 1, 2003, although controversy surrounds the validity of the rescue. Johnson was released from captivity along with five other males from the 507th on April 13, 2003. In 2004, Iraqi POW women claimed they had been beaten and raped by American soldiers in Abu Ghraib prison.

Forced Conscription and Sexual Slavery

Historically, women frequently have been the primary targets of extreme inhumane physical abuse and sexual violence during military conflicts. In 1937–38, 50,000 Japanese soldiers marched into

Nanking China and over a six week period captured, raped, and tortured 20,000–80,000 Chinese girls and women. Thousands of other young Chinese women throughout the country were forced to serve as "Comfort Women" in a notorious sex slave/prostitute system and labor pool designed to service Japanese soldiers.

From May 1998 to June 2000, thousands of Eritrean women were involuntarily conscripted as soldiers and forced to serve on the front lines for Eritrea during the end of the Eritrean–Ethiopian War when it became evident that the Eritrean Army was losing the conflict. Its predominantly male force, composed of both career soldiers and conscripts, had been decimated and then plagued with mass desertions. After receiving a minimal amount of military training, many of these women voluntarily surrendered to Ethiopian forces to avoid being killed.

Forced conscription and sexual slavery continues. In Darfur, rebel militia and Sudanese government forces have captured and sexually abused thousands of Dinka women, forcing them into a life of forced military conscription, labor, and sexual slavery. Women in the Congo also have been captured by rebel forces, raped, and used as sex slaves.

Globally, there have been many women, military and civilian, whose imprisonment by enemy forces have not been fully documented or recognized in the annals of history. Today, combat battle lines continue to blur and disappear, and women are volunteering for military service in record numbers as more countries allow women to serve in more military combat jobs previously reserved for males. As a result, the numbers of women POWs will likely increase.

See Also: Military, Women in the; Military Leadership, Women in; Prisoners of War, Female.

Further Readings

Bragg, Rick with Jessica Lynch. *I Am a Solider Too. The Jessica Lynch Story.* New York: Knopf Publishing, 2003.

Cornum, Rhonda. *She Went to War: The Rhonda Cornum Story* (with Peter Copeland). San Francisco, CA: Presidio Press, 1992.

The History Place. "Genocide in the 20th Century, The Rape of Nanking 1937-1938 300,000 Deaths." http://www.historyplace.com/worldhistory/genocide/nanking.htm (accessed July 2010).

The Liz Library—Military History. http://www.theliz library.org/undelete/military/prisoners.html (accessed July 2010).

Ramasastry, Anita. "What Happens When GI Jane Is Captured? Women Prisoners and the Geneva Convention." http://writ.news.findlaw.com/ramasastry/20030402.html (accessed July 2010).

U.S. Department of State. "Diplomacy in Action: Sudan. Bureau of Democracy, Human Rights and Labor 2005," (March 8, 2008). http://www.state.gov/g/drl/rls/hrrpt/2005/61594.htm (accessed July 2010).

Elizabeth Frances Desnoyers-Colas
Armstrong Atlantic State University

Professional Education

Professional, or trade and vocational, education has traditionally been one of the most gender-segregated educational sectors. Professional education remains an important avenue for workforce training and economic development even as it has changed to reflect changing trends in labor needs. Professional education has been increasingly emphasized on an international level as a means for aiding development and assisting marginalized girls and women in developing countries. Although gender inequities have been reduced in the late 20th and 21st centuries, gender gaps in female enrollment in nontraditional careers remain. Gender inequities in professional education reflect and contribute to gender inequities in the labor market.

Trends in Professional Education

Professional education is also known as vocational, career, or technical education. Internationally, professional education is usually referred to by the phrase *trade and vocational education and training (TVET)*. Professional education encompasses family and consumer sciences as well as training for the labor market or a specific career or trade. Professional education is centered on skills application, often through hands-on training or work experience. In countries such as Germany, professional education is coupled with an apprenticeship system, and in other countries, many professional education students simultaneously hold full- or part-time jobs.

Professional education programs vary internationally based on individual country educational systems and requirements. Women have access to professional education courses and programs at a variety of levels, including high schools, postsecondary trade schools, community colleges, four-year colleges and universities, and collaborative tech prep programs between secondary and postsecondary schools. Most women enroll in professional education at the high school or postsecondary trade school level. Professional training is also available through other avenues, such as the military, employers, and government or community-based workforce programs.

Common professional education fields of study include beauty, service and hospitality, bookkeeping and clerical, computer technology, nursing and health sciences, construction and related fields, art and design, media, mechanical and automotive, education, paralegal, criminal justice, real estate, travel, and interior design. According to the U.S. Department of Education's 2004 National Assessment of Vocational Education, approximately half of the nation's high school students and one-third of college students were enrolled in vocational courses or programs.

Most vocational students enroll in order to obtain the skills necessary to become employed or advance in their chosen professions. Traditionally, professional education students were not expected to obtain bachelor's or higher degrees, a trend that still hold true for many students. While many vocational students are enrolled in degree programs, most do not attend four-year institutions, instead earning either associate's degrees or vocational certificates. The number of women in professional education courses or programs has been affected by overall trends in vocational education in the late 20th and early 21st centuries.

The rising demand for new information- or service-based occupational skills and global economic recession has increased the number of adult workers who return to school to enhance or broaden their skills or change careers, many attending evening and weekend classes in programs designed specifically for adult students. Single parents and displaced homemakers comprise another large segment of adult professional education students.

Overall, professional education enrollment has declined in some industrialized countries, such as the United States, most notably in the 1990s, due to the shift toward an information-based society requiring workers with more academic skills, such as critical thinking. In the United States, this emphasis could be seen in rising high school graduation requirements, reductions in vocational course offerings, and increased integration between academic and vocational education. Professional education enrollments rebounded in the 21st century.

The rise of information-based skills and service-based occupations and a decline in manufacturing in some industrialized countries, such as the United States, has affected vocational education. One outcome has been lowered enrollments in trade and industry-related courses and rising enrollments in in-demand fields such as healthcare, computers and technology, service-based industries, and childcare. Other industrialized countries, however, such as Germany, Italy, and France, maintained high percentages of professional education students and workforce participants in industry and manufacturing. Internationally, almost all countries experienced rising percentages of the workforce employed in service occupations and a concomitant rise in professional education enrollments in those areas. Other determinants of professional education offerings include funding mechanisms and levels, employment availability options and competition levels, demographic differences, and unionization levels.

International Partnering

Internationally, many governments and nongovernmental organizations (NGOs) have partnered with local and community-based organizations to promote technical and vocational education and training (TVET), in part driven by the ongoing success of universal primary education movements. Collaborative efforts such as the United Nations Educational, Scientific and Cultural Organization and International Centre for Technical and Vocational Education and Training (UNESCO-UNEVOC) have studied TVET trends and benefits and implemented programs and conferences designed to increase TVET access and educational quality worldwide. Other groups involved in the promotion of TVET include the Organisation for Economic Co-operation and Development (OECD) and the Women's Entrepreneurship Development and Gender Equality (WEDGE).

These organizations and programs have promoted TVET as an important component in the achievement of gender equity and labor market inclusion, development and sustainability goals, the reduction of poverty, and the integration of socially marginalized groups. In developing countries, the need to increase professional education enrollments overall and for women in particular is a key component to the elimination of poverty and the achievement of development goals. Technical and vocational training provide girls and women with the skills necessary to enter the workforce or become entrepreneurs, thereby increasing their family income, food security, healthcare, and savings. Studies have also shown that women who increase their earnings are more likely to reinvest those earnings into their families and communities.

Gender in Professional Education and Its Impact

Gender segregation was traditionally commonplace in professional education in most countries, and gender equity issues are still present. Government legislation such as the U.S. Vocational Education Act of 1976 and Carl D. Perkins Vocational and Technical Education Act and its updates, commonly known as the Perkins Act, addressed gender segregation and stereotyping, expanding women's access to all fields of professional education. Although many of the legal barriers to gender equity in professional education have been removed, women and men still limit themselves to certain courses or programs due to social pressures against challenging accepted gender roles and stereotypes or the belief that women are physically unable to perform required job tasks in male-dominated fields such as construction or firefighting. Women and girls in developing countries often face additional barriers to professional education, including poverty, rural residency, or physical disability.

Many women and men are discouraged from pursuing professional education in careers or trades that have traditionally been associated with the opposite gender, which can be viewed as threatening to traditional social gender roles. Historically, women professional education students were concentrated in such fields as family and consumer sciences or home economics, clerical and general office work, and beauty careers such as cosmetology and hairdressing. Women's enrollments remain low in traditionally male-dominated fields such as industrial, mechanical, and construction careers. While overall female enrollments in professional education and in nontraditional female fields of study have increased, the latter still remain low.

Excpectations and Experiences

A large body of research has documented the differences in male and female educational experiences in education at large, which is also applicable to professional education. Both men and women who enroll in professional education programs in nontraditional careers often encounter isolation or ridicule and feelings of nonacceptance by their fellow students. They may also be more likely to encounter sexual harassment. The low percentage of female teachers and administrators in nontraditional career programs means fewer mentors for female students and can increase their feelings of isolation. Vocational students may also suffer from lowered expectations of achievements such as obtaining a bachelor's or advanced degree or the educational practice of tracking low-performing students into professional education and the accompanying stereotypes.

The effects of gender segregation and stereotyping in professional education carry over to impact issues such as unequal pay, sexual harassment, and the glass ceiling in the workplace. In the United States, Department of Labor statistics show that more than 75 percent of the female workforce is employed in occupations traditionally dominated by women, a statistic that mirrors professional education enrollment gender statistics. Many of the careers or trades traditionally dominated by male workers also have better wages and advancement possibilities than those careers or trades traditionally dominated by female workers. Women who do enter nontraditional fields may leave due to male-dominated workplaces and feelings of not being accepted or experiences of sexual harassment. Other women considering professional education in these fields may reconsider when learning of these experiences.

While gender stereotyping continues to impact women in professional education, the continued reduction of gender inequities has allowed increased numbers of women to share in the benefits of such education. High school students enrolled in vocational programs or courses were less likely to drop out and increased their academic achievement levels. Those who earn a degree or certificate demonstrate to potential employers that they possess the skills necessary for their chosen career or trade, which often translates into easier job placements and salary benefits. The U.S. Department of Education's 2004 National Assessment of Vocational Education study showed that professional education training correlated to higher short- and long-term earnings for both high school and postsecondary school students after they entered the workforce. Many schools also offer their students valuable assistance in meeting licensing requirements and job placements in their chosen fields.

Many professional and general education programs in developing countries are addressing and reducing the gender and other inequities found in both professional education and the labor market, as well as to adapt local programs to local social and labor market needs. Professional education programs also help address the traditional gender biases in labor markets found in many developing countries, where women are disproportionately represented among the unemployed, underemployed, low wage earners, and those employed in the informal economy. Many women work as street vendors, laundresses, agricultural laborers, or in other unskilled jobs. Access to professional education and skills increases the numbers of women who are able to find better-paying skilled trades or careers or to open their own businesses.

See Also: Education, Women in; Educational Opportunities/Access; Nontraditional Careers, U.S.; Professions by Gender; Vocational and Trade School Faculty.

Further Readings
Adamuti-Trache, Maria and Robert Sweet. "Vocational Training Choices of Women: Public and Private Colleges." *Gender and Education*, v.20/2 (2008).
Biklen, S. K. and D. Pollard. *Gender and Education*. Chicago: NSSE, University of Chicago Press, 1993.
Freeland, Brett. *International Comparisons of Vocational Education and Training*. Adelaide, Australia: National Centre for Vocational Education Research, 2000.
"Gender Issues in Vocational Education and Training and Workplace Achievement of 14–19 Year Olds: An EOC Perspective." *Curriculum Journal*, v.10/2 (1999).
International Rescue Committee (IRC). "Assessment Report on Female Enrollment in Technical and Vocational Training, Particularly in Non-Traditional Occupations for Women." New York: IRC, 2009. http://legacyinitiative.net/pubs/TVET_final.pdf (accessed July 2010).
Jejeebhoy, Shireen J. *Women's Education, Autonomy, and Reproductive Behavior: Experience from Developing Countries*. New York: Oxford University Press, 1995.
King, Elizabeth M. and M. Anne Hill. *Women's Education in Developing Countries: Barriers, Benefits, and Policies*. Baltimore, MD: Johns Hopkins University Press (for World Bank), 1993.
McWhirter, Ellen. "Perceived Barriers to Education and Career: Ethnic and Gender Differences." *Journal of Vocational Behavior*, v.50/1 (1997).
Solomon, Barbara Miller. *In the Company of Educated Women: A History of Women and Higher Education in America*. New Haven, CT: Yale University Press, 1985.
Tembon, Mercy and Lucia Fort. *Girls' Education in the 21st Century: Equality, Empowerment, and Growth*. Washington, DC: World Bank, 2008.
Van der Meulen Rodgers, Yana and Teresa Boyer. "Gender and Racial Differences in Vocational Education: An International Perspective." *Human Resources Abstracts*, v.42/4 (2007).

Marcella Bush Trevino
Barry University

Professions by Gender

Women's experiences in the labor force have changed significantly since the 1950s. Women are no longer relegated to the domestic sphere or "pink-collar" jobs. Expanding opportunities in high-status and male-dominated occupations, changing attitudes toward women's roles in the family and workplace, increasing educational attainment, and the passage of protective and affirmative legislation have created a new structure of occupational opportunity for women. At the same time, women continue to face unique challenges at work and in their family lives. Despite improvements, women still experience discrimination and harassment on the basis of their gender. Women continue to receive unequal pay for equal work and are underrepresented among the most prestigious and highly paid professions. Race, ethnicity, and class compound professional gender differences, producing diversity in the experiences different women face at work and at home.

Domestic Work, the Alienated Housewife, and the Shift to Paid Work

Prior to modern industrialization, when the domestic sphere included a farm or small business, men and women both labored to meet their needs as a productive family unit. In addition to child rearing, cooking, and cleaning, women produced household necessities such as soap, candles, and clothes and farmed alongside their husbands and children. Industrialization and urbanization separated the workplace from the home. Many middle-class women were relegated to the private, domestic sphere to preserve morality in an increasingly capitalist society in which men went out into the public work world to singlehandedly support their families. Meanwhile, working-class, African American, and immigrant women in the United States were often compelled to work in other people's homes as domestic servants or in factories, in sweatshops, in saloons, in brothels, or on plantations. Since morality was equated with domestic housewifery, working women's morality and social status suffered as a result of employment.

In the 20th century, middle-class and affluent women began to openly acknowledge a sense of alienation that resulted from their isolation at home and their economic and social dependence on men. In the classic feminist manifesto *The Feminine Mystique*, Betty Friedan argued that women's self-fulfillment depends on the pursuit of a career in lieu of an unpaid and devalued domestic role. By entering semiprofessions such as social work, teaching, librarianship, and nursing and lucrative high-status professions such as law, medicine, science, and business, women would transform widespread attitudes concerning their status, abilities, and appropriate social roles.

Women across the class spectrum heeded Friedan's call to paid work. Women enrolled in college in increasing numbers, joined the paid labor force, and pushed their way into occupations formerly monopolized by men. Today, women constitute the majority of college students and at least half of the students enrolled in medical, dental, and law schools in the United States, and women's postsecondary educational attainment rates are rising globally. Educational parity has enabled women to increasingly participate in the paid labor force. As of 2008, women constitute nearly half of the American paid labor force. Whereas less than 30 percent of American women were employed in 1950, today approximately 72 percent of women between 25 and 64 years old work for pay, and the labor force participation rate increases to 80 percent for women with college or higher degrees. By contrast, 86 percent of men in the same age group are in the paid labor force, and 92 percent of those with at least a college degree work for pay.

Today, more women work full time, and women with children are one-and-a-half times as likely to work for pay as women in the 1970s. In addition, the dual-earner couple has become the norm in marriage: in nearly 60 percent of married couples, both husband and wife contribute earnings to the household, as compared to 44 percent in the 1960s. Nevertheless, men continue to work for pay more than women, on average.

While many of these trends characterize women's workforce participation in nations around the world, women's labor force participation rates vary considerably. Among developed nations, Canadian, U.S., Swedish, and Australian women have the highest labor force participation rates. In Europe, women's labor force participation varies by region. For example, Norway, Sweden, and other northern European countries have high workforce participation by women; in contrast, women in Spain, Portugal, and Italy have low labor force participation and especially low full-time employment rates. Women's labor force participation throughout Latin America varies by country.

For example, in Argentina, Brazil, Ecuador, Peru, and Uruguay, 40–46 percent of women participate in the labor force, whereas women in Brazil, Colombia, and Paraguay have lower rates. Except in China and Thailand, where approximately 75 percent of adult women work, women in most Asian countries have substantially lower labor force participation rates, with less than 40 percent working in the formal economy. Notably, less than a third of Indian and Korean women are in the formal labor force. In Muslim countries in the Middle East, north Africa, and south Asia, less than 40 percent of women participate in the formal labor force.

Occupational Gender Segregation and Integration

The majority of men and women work in occupations with 70 percent or more of the same sex. Men are more likely than women to work in gender-integrated occupations. Women are one-and-a-half times as likely as men to work in an occupation dominated by the opposite sex. In addition to the gender segregation of occupations, men and women often specialize in distinct subfields or positions within the same occupation.

Pink-collar or female-dominated semiprofessions such as teaching, nursing, social work, and secretarial work have grown with the influx of women into the workforce. The few men in these fields enjoy a professional advantage. For example, while the majority of teachers are women, the higher the level of teaching and age of students, the higher the proportion of male teachers becomes. Nearly all prekindergarten teachers are female, while the majority of college and university faculty are male. The gender composition of the professoriate varies by discipline, with relatively high proportions of women in the humanities and education and men in science, engineering, business, and law. In addition, colleges and universities that place greater emphasis on teaching than on research tend to be less gender segregated. Male educators also enjoy an advantage in promotion to leadership positions; men in all levels from elementary to post-secondary education advance into administrative positions faster and more frequently than female educators do. Men in nursing, social work, and librarianship also experience the global phenomenon of the "glass escalator," or rapid advancement to supervisory and managerial roles.

International Perspective

Whereas the majority of women in the United States, Europe, and Brazil work in the service sector, the overwhelming majority of employed women in most Asian and African countries work in agriculture. While agriculture remains gender integrated, most skilled nonagricultural work in nearly all of Asia and Africa is male dominated. The percentage of women employed in nonagricultural work in these countries tends to reflect the level of national economic development. For example, in 1990, in highly industrialized Japan, women held more than a third of the nonagricultural jobs in the country, whereas in India less than one in nine nonagricultural jobs were performed by women.

The rise of industrial manufacture in developing nations in Asia, Latin America, the Caribbean and of information technology centers in the Middle East to service globalized production has generated new nonagricultural employment opportunities for more women and men; however, most of these jobs are low-wage, low-skilled assembly, production, and customer service positions. In addition, primarily middle-class and urban women in Asia, Africa, the Pacific, and Latin America tend to be employed in nonindustrial, nonagricultural work such as teaching, nursing, banking, and clerical positions.

In the United States, men have dominated certain lower-status professions, such as law enforcement and firefighting, as well as the majority of blue-collar and manual labor occupations, such as factory work, construction, skilled trades, transportation, and sanitation. Women have made little headway into these occupations, with the exception of women's temporary entrance into industrial manufacturing during World War II. Today, American women in factory jobs are largely limited to the textile and apparel industry, which tends to offer low pay and lack union representation.

While most people are employed in occupations dominated by the same sex, the gender segregation of occupations has steadily declined since the 1950s, and women have worked their way into high-status, male-dominated professions including law, medicine, and finance. Around the globe, eastern European women occupied the highest proportion of professional jobs, while east Asian and Middle Eastern women occupied less than 30 percent of professional positions. In Latin America, women's representation in professional occupations varies greatly, with women holding more than 60 percent of professional jobs in Uruguay and Paraguay and less than 40 percent in Colombia. While women have made headway in both political and business leadership positions, they often remain underrepresented in both occupations.

For example, while women's labor force participation rates are similar in Australia, South Africa, Canada, and the United States, women's representation in managerial, professional business, and executive positions in these countries varies considerably. South African women are two-and-half times as likely as Australian women, twice as likely as U.S. women, and almost twice as likely as Canadian women to be corporate executives. Canada has 30 percent more female CEOs than the United States, while the United States has 30 percent more women in managerial and professional business specialties. In Latin America, women hold anywhere from nearly half of the managerial, senior official, and legislative positions in Colombia to less than 6 percent of the same positions in Peru, a nation where women hold the majority of professional jobs.

Several high-status profession, such as finance and engineering, remain male dominated; yet, other high-status, high-paying occupations, including medicine, law, and accounting, have become gender integrated in economically advanced nations such as the United States. Nevertheless, women in these professions are more likely to specialize in female-dominated subfields such as pediatrics, obstetrics, family or real estate law, and bookkeeping. These subfields are typically less prestigious and/or lucrative than male-dominated subfields such as neurosurgery, litigation and corporate transactional law, and certified public accounting. Women are also more likely to assist doctors and lawyers as nurses and paralegals than to work as their peers. In addition, women who enter high-status professions that remain male dominated such as finance are disproportionately relegated to lower-paying positions within their field.

The gender composition of professions is not universal; for example, the majority of doctors in the former Soviet states are women. Likewise, the majority of judges in Hungary, Romania, the Czech Republic, Estonia, Croatia, and Lithuania are women, and the majority of judges on the International Criminal Court are women.

Women have also altered the gender balance in certain professions including real estate sales, bill collection, and bank telling, where women went from gross underrepresentation in 1950 to the majority by 2000.

Race and ethnicity also impact occupational gender segregation. Compared to blacks, Latinos, and Asians, white workers experience the most gender segregation of occupations in the United States. White and Asian women have made the greatest strides in entering high-status male-dominated professions, while black and Latina women are more likely to work in service and office support occupations. In addition, Latina and Asian women are more likely to work in manufacturing than white or black women. In Europe, occupational gender segregation reflects patterns of transnational migration. Women migrating into Europe are largely relegated to low-skilled, low-status occupations such as retail sales, personal service, and clerical work. Women who migrate between European nations fare better than their non-EU counterparts; however, in nearly every EU nation, native-born women enjoy a distinct advantage in terms of employment rates and securing full-time employment that matches their skills and education level. Men hold the overwhelming majority of the highly skilled, highly paid jobs available to migrants into the EU.

Like women migrating to Europe, migrant women around the globe predominantly work in the service sector. Skilled migrant women frequently find work in healthcare as nurses and home health aides; highly skilled and highly educated migrant women from former Soviet states with advanced medical training find work as doctors and dentists. Unskilled migrant women with limited education typically find domestic work in childcare and cleaning. Some migrant women, particularly from eastern Europe, the former Soviet states, the Philippines, and southeast Asia, work in prostitution as part of the global sex trade. Women's mass entry into the labor force has engendered some unintended consequences, including differences in compensation, career trajectories, workplace discrimination, and work-life balance challenges.

Gendered Wage Gap

Whereas women in the United States, the United Kingdom, and Canada earn approximately 80 cents for every dollar men earn, women in Europe earn 84 cents for every dollar men earn. European women in France, Belgium, and the Nordic and Mediterranean countries enjoy the narrowest wage gap, earning 90 cents for every dollar their male counterparts earn; however, Mediterranean women tend to have low labor force participation rates, and the gendered segregation of occupations in Nordic countries is high compared to the United States. Since World War II, the gender pay gap has decreased significantly. For example, American women earned only 50 cents for every dollar men earned in 1950 compared to 80 cents today. Nevertheless, women continue to earn less than men, even when men and women are equally qualified and employed in the same occupation. For example, 32 percent of doctors in the United States are female, but full-time female doctors earn only 61 percent of full-time male doctors' earnings. Female-dominated occupations typically pay less than male-dominated occupations regardless of the worker's sex. Moreover, men typically earn more than women in the same field, regardless of gender composition. Among all racial and ethnic groups, the gendered wage gap is greatest for white women in the United States.

Gendered Professional Trajectories

Women have made great advances in traditionally male-dominated professions such as law, medicine, business, academia, and politics, but they have not reached parity with men. For example, half of U.S. law school students are women, yet they constitute less than 20 percent of partners at major law firms and only two of the nine justices on the U.S. Supreme Court. While some notable women have made it to top positions in the corporate world (e.g., Carly Fiorina, former CEO of Hewlett Packard), most professional women confront a "sticky floor," or slower and fewer promotions, and a "glass ceiling," or an informal, invisible barrier that keeps them from occupying the highest ranks in male-dominated fields, even when women have educations and experience comparable to their male counterparts.

The informal male-dominated management circles often pivotal in advancement in corporations and expectations of gender-appropriate personality, degree of competitiveness, and family roles can limit women's professional advancement. Women in male-dominated, high-status professions also experience greater isolation and harassment at work; are more likely to have their authority challenged by coworkers, subordinates, and clients; and receive fewer referrals than their male counterparts. Together, these explanations suggest that informal discrimination, stereotypes, and social expectations promote persistent gender inequality in the workplace.

Despite increasing opportunities in high-status, high-paying occupations, a significant number of well-educated women in elite occupations are exiting their careers to become full-time, stay-at-home mothers. The gendered division of domestic labor, work conditions, and organizational intractability contribute to the recent trend of "opting out." Women are still expected to perform a greater share of domestic duties, even in two-earner couples; unpaid domestic labor compounds women's work obligations, creating a "double shift." Extremely long hours, productivity demands, and extensive travel also explain why successful women feel compelled to opt out of their careers to have children. While more employers are offering flexible and part-time work schedules even for professional staff, women who take advantage of "family-friendly" work arrangements often find themselves stuck on the "mommy track," with curtailed opportunities for professional advancement. Few men take advantage of alternative work arrangements, especially in the United States, further stigmatizing family-friendly options and limiting their appeal to women accustomed to academic and professional success. Countries with policies that encourage women to take extended maternity leaves and/or work part time while they raise young children, such as Denmark, Sweden, and Norway, often have fewer stigmas attached to family-friendly work arrangements and are able to keep highly skilled, highly educated women in the workforce more effectively.

Anti-Discrimination Legislation and Affirmative Action

In addition to informal mechanisms that promote gender inequality in the workplace, overt and formal systems of gender inequality have limited women in occupations. Acknowledging such inequity, lawmakers have enacted legislation designed to counteract and prevent sexism and gender discrimination. Title VII of the U.S. Civil Rights Act of 1964 banned employment discrimination on the basis of sex, and the Lilly Ledbetter Fair Pay Act of 2009 strengthened women's legal claims to equal pay for equal work. For example, the height, weight, and strength requirements of certain jobs in fire and police departments have been challenged as forms of gender bias. In addition, affirmative action programs have been developed in various fields to compensate for past gender discrimination. For example, fellowships are offered to encourage women to enter science and engineering. Like affirmative action programs that target racial and ethnic inequality, sex-based affirmative action programs are still controversial, despite their apparent effectiveness in ameliorating women's underrepresentation in professions.

See Also: Administrative Assistants/Office Managers; Affirmative Action/Equal Opportunity; Attorneys, Female; Business, Women in; Education, Women in; Glass Ceiling; Lilly Ledbetter Act; Midlife Career Change; Parental Leave; Part-Time Work; Physicians, Female; Work/Life Balance.

Further Readings

Blau, Francine D., et al, eds. *The Declining Significance of Gender?* New York: Russell Sage Foundation, 2006.

Solis, Hilda L. and Keith Hall. *Women in the Labor Force: A Databook (2009 Edition).* Report 1018. Washington, DC: U.S. Department of Labor and U.S. Bureau of Labor Statistics, 2009. http://www.bls.gov/cps/wlf -databook2009.htm (Accessed April 2010).

Williams, Christine. *Gender Differences at Work: Women and Men in Nontraditional Occupations.* Berkeley: University of California Press, 1989.

Judith R. Halasz
State University of New York, New Paltz

Progressive Muslims (U.S.)

American Muslims are a vibrant, diverse, and highly visible religious community in the United States. They are composed of both immigrant and native-born populations, express different sectarian perspectives, and represent an array of cultural and ideological positions. American Muslim woman are active members of their religious community, and American society in general, and play a vital role as representatives of their faith. A central focus of Muslim women's activism has been to improve women's status and participation in Muslim religious life through the recognition of their equal status as human beings before God.

The majority of American Muslim women are college educated and employed, but they do not necessarily share a strong commonality of experience, given the highly diverse character of Muslims in America. Over the past quarter century, Muslim women's involvement and leadership has grown significantly in intellectual production, community structures, and activism. An important moment for Muslim women in America was the 2006 election of

Ingrid Mattson as the president of the Islamic Society of North America, the largest Muslim organization in North America.

A central organizing principle for American Muslim women has been the promotion of women's equality in Islam. In response, some Muslim women engaged in this effort challenge women's inequality in Islamic practice and Islamic thought by identifying the theological and social structures in the Muslim community that perpetuate injustices against women. In their recognition of God as the final authority of truth, these American Muslim women have developed progressive feminist positions through the study and interpretation of Islamic sacred texts, which they claim reveal a fundamental egalitarian principle for humanity. Independent interpretation, or *ijtihad*, is deemed necessary because of the limitations placed on the sacred texts by traditional Islamic interpretations premised on women's inferiority.

Progressive feminist reformulations of Islamic thought on the basis of God's justice and equality for humanity are manifested in social action dedicated to Muslim women's emancipation and empowerment in both the United States and the global Muslim community. Central social concerns include women's access to spiritual education and literature and leadership roles, respect in the domestic sphere, and equality in the mosque. More moderate and conservative voices in the American Muslim community have disagreed with elements of progressive interpretations of the sacred texts and ritual practice on gender, such as the permissibility of female-led ritual prayer.

American Muslim feminist activity can be roughly divided into three categories: scholarship and literature; social services for women's education, health, and civil rights; and organizations that promote Muslim women's voices and participation in the Muslim community and the American public. American Muslim men are also active in these projects in recognition of their own liberation through the establishment of human equality and cooperation.

Key Muslim feminist scholars include Khalid Abu El Fadl, Leila Ahmed, Kecia Ali, Asma Barlas, Aminah Beverly McCloud, Riffat Hassan, Mohja Kahf, and Amina Wadud. Representative of more popular literature is the magazine *Azizah*, founded by Tayyibah Taylor, which promotes a positive self-image of

American Muslim women and brings their voices into popular media.

Karamah: Muslim Women Lawyers for Human Rights is a well-known Muslim organization that promotes progressive Islamic values of human dignity and gender equality. Karamah's central activities include Muslim women's religious and legal education, legal consultation, and community outreach. It absorbed the flagship North American Council for Muslim Women in 2004. The Muslim Women's League, based in California, is also a model organization.

Larger Muslim bodies in the American Muslim community have robust women-focused divisions or initiatives, such as the American Society for Muslim Advancement and Women's Islamic Initiative in Spirituality and Equality, led by activist Daisy Khan.

See Also: African American Muslims; Feminist Theology; Islam in America; Wadud, Amina.

Further Readings

Abdul-Ghafur, S., ed. *Living Islam Out Loud: American Muslim Women Speak*. Boston: Beacon Press, 2005.

Barlas, A. "Believing Women." *Islam: Unreading Patriarchal Interpretations of the Qur'an*. Austin: University of Texas Press, 2002.

Haddad, Y. Y., et al. *Muslim Women in America: The Challenge of Islamic Identity Today*. Oxford, UK: Oxford University Press, 2006.

Karim, J. *American Muslim Women: Negotiating Race, Class, and Gender Within the Ummah*. New York: New York University Press, 2009.

Wadud, A. *Inside the Gender Jihad: Women's Reform in Islam*. Oxford, UK: Oneworld, 2006.

Webb, G., ed. *Windows of Faith: Muslim Women Scholar-Activists in North America*. Syracuse, NY: Syracuse University Press, 2000.

Katherine Rose Merriman
Harvard University

Pro-Life Movement

The pro-life movement, also referred to as the right to life movement or antiabortion movement, is copmosed of several distinct forms of activism: political lobbying, direct action, crisis pregnancy centers, awareness-raising campaigns, "postabortion" advocacy groups, and secular/nonpartisan efforts. Some factions within the movement are increasingly likely to address women in unplanned pregnancies as opposed to an exclusive focus on the rights of the fetus and subsequently have adopted a public health framework that downplays the religious motivations of many activists. Others groups take a deliberately secular approach. Recent developments such as the movement's successful efforts to block public funding of abortion in federal healthcare reform legislation indicates the movement is a significant social force in the United States. Abortion rights advocates respond to these efforts with a number of criticisms that reveal the struggles over women's rights and role in the contemporary United States.

The majority of pro-life activists are white and middle or working class. Most are women, although certain types of activism are more likely to be led by men. Originally a Catholic movement focused primarily on state and federal legislation, evangelical Christians predominate in the pro-life movement today, alongside a sizable Catholic minority and some secular activists.

Prior to *Roe v. Wade*, the 1973 Supreme Court ruling legalizing abortion in the United States, pro-life efforts were sporadic and focused on individual states that already permitted abortions. After *Roe*, Catholics began mobilizing in larger numbers to reverse the legalization of abortion or at least to restrict access to abortion through state and federal legislation. The largest political lobbying group in the United States today is the National Right to Life Committee (NRLC). Originally a Catholic organization, NRLC leaders made a strategic decision in the 1970s to downplay the organization's religious roots due to widespread anti-Catholic sentiment and to recruit Protestant and secular activists into the movement.

As of 2010, there are more than 3,000 NRLC chapters in all 50 states and the District of Columbia. Most members, including leaders, are women, but men remain a sizable minority. At the national level, NRLC and similar organizations consistently support political candidates who oppose abortion and played instrumental roles in both instating the so-called "partial birth" abortion ban in 2003 and the passage of a conscience clause in 2005 giving medical personnel the legal right to refuse to participate in abortion procedures. Most recently, these groups successfully lobbied Congress to maintain various restrictions on public funding and access to abortion in the federal healthcare reform bill passed in 2010.

Critics of these efforts argue that political-lobbying pro-life groups seek to impose their own moral norms on women, regardless of women's circumstances or own sense of morality. They also argue that legally restricting abortion does nothing to prevent unintended pregnancies or to help women faced with pregnancies made problematic by financial need or a lack of support from male partners and family members. Abortion rights advocates object to the apparent dismissal of women's ability to make key decisions for themselves. Activists in political pro-life groups respond with arguments claiming that science offers irrefutable proof that human life begins at the moment of conception, that the difficulties faced by pregnant women are not solved by abortion nor do these problems justify ending another life, and that restrictions on abortion are necessary because women do not always understand the magnitude of abortion decisions and must be protected through mandatory delays and "informed consent" stipulations prior to having abortions.

Direct Action

Direct action activism consists of protests, picketing, demonstrations, vigils, and acts of civil disobedience at freestanding abortion clinics. Activists, who are often religiously motivated, emphasize "fetal rescue tactics" that focus on stopping abortion and saving the fetus through the use of persuasion or force. Activists, who are predominantly women, try to forcefully interact with women clients entering abortion clinics to convince them to continue their pregnancies. Strategies include the public display of posters and placards graphically depicting aborted fetuses; public sharing of narratives by women who regret their abortions; and the distribution of brochures and flyers on fetal development, the alleged medical and psychological complications of abortion, and the purported link between abortion and breast cancer.

Direct action, often associated with the religious antiabortion group Operation Rescue, founded by Randall Terry, originally involved mass blockades of abortion clinics. Direct-action tactics gained notoriety in the 1980s as this part of the movement became

increasingly violent. Direct-action activists vandalized and even bombed abortion clinics and harassed clinic workers and clients at their homes. The violence came to a head when four clinic workers were murdered and another eight were subjected to murder attempts in 1994. In Kansas, Scott Roeder was convicted of murdering Dr. George Tiller, who worked at a clinic where late-term abortions were performed. In April 2010, Roeder was sentenced to life in prison without being eligible for parole for 50 years.

With the passage of the Freedom of Access to Clinic Entrances (FACE) law in 1994 and the increasing use of the Racketeer Influenced and Corrupt Organizations Act (RICO) to prosecute abortion protesters, direct action today is less confrontational but no less controversial. Critics claim direct action interferes with women's reproductive decision making, privileges the fetus, casts women as selfish and immoral, trivializes contextual factors of women's lives, and distorts the safety of the procedure. In response, direct-action activists argue that abortion workers deceive women about the facts of abortion, abortion kills a preborn person entitled to full rights of personhood, and direct action represents an opportunity to directly impact the number of abortions.

Crisis Pregnancy Centers

Crisis pregnancy centers (CPCs) constitute the largest wing of the pro-life movement. There are approximately 2,500 to 4,000 local, community-supported CPCs in the United States seeking to dissuade women in problematic pregnancies from aborting. Both lay activists and leaders are overwhelmingly likely to be women. Centers offer free pregnancy tests; peer counseling by lay activists (not professional social workers or counselors); and some free goods; including maternity and baby clothing, formula, diapers, housing, and social service referrals.

Approximately half of CPCs offer limited ultrasound services to pregnant clients and use sonogram images to persuade clients to continue their pregnancies. Most CPCs are evangelical organizations and consider proselytizing to clients to be part of the core mission of the center. CPCs have attracted widespread criticism from pro-choice activists and politicians who accuse centers of giving women clients inaccurate information about the medical risks of abortion, of falsely advertising themselves as full-service medical clinics offering abortion, and of using emotionally coercive tactics with clients considering abortion. In response, CPC activists argue that centers provide women with social support and material resources they are unable to obtain elsewhere and that without these resources, women would feel compelled to have abortions they do not want.

Changing Public Perception

Yet another contemporary approach to pro-life efforts involves mass-media efforts designed to change public perceptions of abortion. Representative efforts involve posting signs on public transportation, billboards, Websites, and television commercials aimed at reframing the abortion debate in pro-life terms. In 2010, 2,000 posters hung in New York City subways featured young women and men in pensive poses with captions explaining that abortion has a profound, long-term negative effect on those who choose to terminate pregnancies, including depression, regret, and grief. That same year, University of Florida football star Tim Tebow and his mother appeared in a Super Bowl commercial describing how his mother did not have an abortion when pregnant with Tebow, against medical advice. Two years prior, during the 2008 presidential campaign, a similar commercial aired, but the focus this time was President Barack Obama's mother's decision to continue her pregnancy (Obama did not participate in the ad; his mother is deceased). These efforts attempt to recast abortion as a devastating choice and continuing pregnancies despite difficult circumstances as the path to a bright future for both women and their potential children.

Positioning Abortion as a Race Issue

Other mass-media efforts attempt to recast abortion as a race issue. In Atlanta, the Georgia chapter of Right to Life sponsored dozens of billboards likening the disproportionate rates of abortion among African American women to genocide. The billboards refer to African Americans as an endangered species and is part of a larger campaign to cast abortion clinic workers and pro-choice activists as racists bent on reducing or eliminating the African American population. Simultaneously, many pro-life organizations are creating diversity positions and campaigns to attract African Americans to what is, by pro-life activists' own admissions, historically seen as a white,

conservative movement. Opponents to these mass-media campaigns argue that framing abortion as always damaging is little more than an effort to restigmatize abortion and the women who choose to end pregnancies. Efforts such as the Tebow commercial are dismissed as misleading about the life chances of marginalized women by these critics. Race-based campaigns garner the most protest, as abortion rights groups decry the characterization of African Americans as a separate species from whites and claim pro-life shifts toward multiculturalism are more strategic than a sign of actual change. Pro-life activists involved in these efforts respond by arguing that they are trying to correct the movement's historical blind spots with regard to minorities and that such efforts should be seen as sincere. Moreover, these activists may also see pro-choice objections to their efforts as further proof of the pro-choice complicity in obscuring the harmful effects of abortion.

Post-Abortion Syndrome

Post-abortion syndrome (PAS) counseling and advocacy groups engage in public outreach to address the purported psychological and behavioral consequences attributed to abortion. Pro-life claims that abortion causes negative emotional responses including regret, depression, and anger first appeared in public abortion discourses in the late 1980s. Although the major medical associations refuse to recognize the legitimacy of PAS and scientific evidence supports the safety of legal abortion in the first trimester of pregnancy, public support for PAS continues to gain momentum. Support for PAS and the availability of postabortion counseling groups coincided with growing internal conflict among pro-life supporters, particularly women, in the early 1990s. Pro-life women argued that fetal rescue strategies ignored the needs of pregnant women and should be expanded to include more woman-focused strategies. Advocates argued the inclusion would decrease negative media attention, broaden the movement's appeal, and counter increasing apathy among the public over the issue of abortion. Using the feminist language of womancare, the movement was able to downplay religious motivations and emphasize more secular and public health–oriented strategies into their opposition to abortion.

PAS supporters argue that abortion is a public health concern because it hurts women. A key example, Women Exploited by Abortion (WEBA), uses narratives of women who regret their abortions to dissuade women from having abortions. Claiming that abortion clinic workers deliberately lie about the health consequences of abortion in order to hide their profit-driven motivations, WEBA and similar groups seek to change women's understandings of abortion. These groups define abortion as the intentional rejection of motherhood (and for men, the rejection of the responsibilities of fatherhood). This rejection causes hurt and pain that can only be resolved through the reclaiming of traditional gender roles. Critics argue that PAS overgeneralizes the consequences of abortion, rests on empirical data that is methodologically flawed, fails to recognize that women experience a range of emotions including relief after an abortion, and presumes that motherhood and traditional gender roles are appropriate for all women.

Secular Focus

Finally, a number of pro-life efforts focus on secular and/or nonpartisan practical efforts, often identifying the aspects of the pro-choice platform that can be incorporated into pro-life activism. These groups are officially secular (although individual activists may be religiously motivated) and do not endorse political candidates based on political party. The Nurturing Network and Feminists for Life are advocacy groups arguing that women are driven to abortion by socially unjust conditions targeting women, such as having to choose between continuing education and continuing an unintended pregnancy. Both emphasize the need to establish resources for pregnant and parenting students on college campuses and in communities, so students may finish their educations without aborting unintended pregnancies. Other pro-life groups take a single-issue approach to politics, supporting only those candidates who promise to implement policies that are logically linked to decreased abortion rates, regardless of whether the candidate identifies as pro-life or pro-choice. For example, the group ProLife, Pro Obama, founded during the 2008 presidential campaign, argues that Obama's favorable attitudes toward social welfare policies such as subsidized healthcare and child care would translate into programs alleviating the need for abortion despite his pro-choice stance. Secular/nonpartisan organizations sometimes explicitly disavow any connection to political efforts to restrict or ban abortion or deliberately do not discuss or act on the issue.

Critics argue that secular/nonpartisan efforts are little more than thinly veiled ploys to advance an anti-abortion agenda by pointing out that these efforts did not emerge until political and legislative strategies failed to reverse *Roe* or to restrict abortion access to the extent pro-life activists desired. Reproductive rights advocates also express concern that these efforts will be used to restrict women's right to abortion in the future, as some of these pro-life activists argue that practical assistance to pregnant women negates the need for legalized abortion. Pro-life activists respond that practical assistance efforts have a long history in the pro-life movement without such groups making any overt efforts toward banning abortion. Moreover, activists claim that these also are policies that should logically be supported by pro-choice groups.

See Also: Abortion, Access to; Abortion Laws, United States; Crisis Pregnancy Centers; Feminists for Life; Mothers Against Choice; Operation Rescue; Post-Abortion Trauma Syndrome.

Further Readings

Jordon, Beth and Elisa S. Wells. "A 21st-Century Trojan Horse: The 'Abortion Harms Women' Anti-Choice Argument Disguises a Harmful Movement." *Contraception*, v.79/1 (2009).

Lee, Ellie. "Reinventing Abortion as a Social Problem: 'Post-Abortion Syndrome' in the United States and Britain." In *Spreading Social Problems: Studies in the Cross National Diffusion of Social Problems*, Joel Best, ed. Hawthorne, NY: Aldine de Gruyter, 2001.

Luker, Kristin. *Abortion and the Politics of Motherhood.* Berkeley: University of California Press, 1984.

Munson, Ziad W. *The Making of Pro-Life Activists: How Social Mobilization Works.* Chicago: University of Chicago Press, 2009.

Williams, Rhys H. and Jeffrey Blackburn. "Many Are Called but Few Obey: Ideological Commitment and Activism in Operation Rescue." In *Disruptive Religion: The Force of Faith in Social Movement Activism*, Christian Smith, ed. New York: Routledge, 1996.

Kimberly Kelly
Jonelle Husain
Independent Scholars

Prom

The prom (short for promenade) is a formal dance event that celebrates student graduation from high school and commemorates the transition from adolescence to adulthood. Within contemporary U.S. and popular culture, the prom is an iconic event and a multibillion-dollar industry that plays a significant role in the lives of American teenage girls. Prom is conventionally understood as an important rite of passage for adolescent girls and maintains significant investments in notions of romance, beauty, and femininity. The prom is also a site of student resistance, cultural tension, controversy, and change; however, students (and their parents) have resisted racial segregation and/or separation in the prom setting.

The prom ritual emerges from the historical tradition of a debutante ball and, as such, is signified as a particularly feminine domain despite the involvement of both adolescent boys and girls. Each year, high schools organize and sponsor the prom for its senior and sometimes junior students, with typical attendees ranging from 16 to 18 years of age. Students and teachers work together to organize the event, and preparation often begins as early as September; the event itself is held at the end of the school year in May or June to coincide with student graduation. As a school-based event, the prom is highly regulated and monitored by adults and authorities. Regulations include attendance, dress code, student conduct, and pre- or post-prom activities.

American popular culture plays a large role in defining the significance of the prom to adolescent girls' lives. Popular teen magazines and films focus on a narrative of product consumption, investment in traditional beauty standards, and normative femininity as central to the prom ritual. Adolescent girls and their families spend hundreds to thousands of dollars in preparation for prom—typical expenses include formal dress, shoes, hair, nails and makeup; body work such as tanning, teeth whitening, diet and exercise; transportation; photos; and boutonnieres, jewelry, and various other accessories.

Prom is also strongly associated with notions of heterosexual romance, virginity, and rebellion. Prom night remains symbolically tied to girls' sexuality and virginity, while the culture of prom is further associated with alcohol, drugs, and adolescent experimentation.

The articulation and inclusion of social differences including sexuality, gender, and socioeconomic status continues to challenge the normative construction and regulation of prom culture. Increasingly, the institutionalization of prom and its associated rituals have come under scrutiny, particularly as high school students actively challenge the conventional boundaries of prom itself.

Students resist, negotiate, and redefine prom in a variety of ways. To protest the exclusion of LGBTQ students and couples, students have collectively boycotted the prom and/or staged alternative proms. To challenge the romance narrative and assumed coupling at prom, students attend the event as singles, friends, or groups. Adolescent girls wear tuxedos, refuse makeup, or choose inexpensive or pre-owned dresses to confront beauty standards and traditional gender norms. Students also organize "anti-proms" or limited-budget proms to ensure the participation

The prom is an important rite of passage for girls, and plays a part in future perceptions of romance, beauty, and femininity.

of all students, regardless of socioeconomic status, as well as to reject prom's assumed culture of consumerism and financial excess.

See Also: Adolescence; Cosmetic Industry; Educational Administrators, Elementary and High School; "Femininity," Social Construction of; Sexual Orientation–Based Social Discrimination: United States.

Further Readings

Best, Amy L. *Prom Night: Youth, Schools, and Popular Culture*. New York: Routledge, 2000.

Zlatunich, Nichole. "Prom Dreams and Prom Reality: Girls Negotiating 'Perfection' at the High School Prom." *Sociological Inquiry*, v.79/3 (2009).

Emily Bent
National University of Ireland, Galway

Property Rights

The importance of women's property and inheritance rights is recognized in international legal instruments and in a growing number of national laws, such as the Convention on the Elimination of All Forms of Discrimination Against Women (CEDAW, 1979) and the Beijing Platform of Action (1995). Property rights usually include the legal rights to acquire, sell, own, and transfer property; to keep and collect rents; to keep one's salary; to make contracts; and to bring lawsuits. In the land market, property rights laws for instance, determine who can possess land and who can buy and sell property.

Thus, a fundamental step to achieve gender equality is to establish equal basic rights, especially in family law, property rights, and political rights. Yet, women often face legal, cultural, and/or religious discrimination that restricts their ability to own or inherit property in both developing and developed countries. Gender inequality regarding property rights has strong and perverse ties to traditions within the family, the state, and the marketplace.

Divergent Challenges and Progress Globally

Property rights are not completely equal for women vis-à-vis men in any country of the world, despite the fact that women can individually acquire, sell, own, and transfer property; keep and collect rents; and keep control over their own wages in many world areas.

In fact, several countries of the developing world adopted significant reforms in these matters during the second half of the 20th century. One example is the Chinese government-sponsored Marriage Law (1950) that established standards of equal rights for women and men with respect to marriage, divorce, and custody of children. In the 1980s, Colombia and Costa Rica introduced land reform that explicitly addressed gender inequalities in inheritance and expanded considerably women's land ownership. In 1997, Mozambique revised the Land Law, giving women a chance to become individual owners when 10 years of usufruct over land was proved. A loose coalition composed of the highest Egyptian government leaders and groups from civil society broadened women's rights under Family Law there in early 2000.

Law reforms are not enough, however, since legal and political rights alone do not guarantee equality in Europe, Asia, America, Africa, or Oceania due to cultural, political, and economic interferences. There is often a gap, at times huge, between formal and real equality in property rights for women.

More often than not, property rights refer to land or family-related property and thus are linked to marriage and family laws. This is because, historically, a woman's property has usually, though fortunately not always, been under the control of her father (or her brother, if orphaned), and when married, her husband. In many countries, the law has generally followed that of the mother countries, being England, France, or Spain, among other former colonial powers. The United States, for instance, used to follow British law, and thus women's property was under the control of their husbands until the beginning of the 20th century, when several states introduced important reforms in women's access to property.

Dowry and Bride Price

Property rights for women have often been and continue to be dependent upon marriage due to dowry and bride price arrangements. These payments mean a transfer of property (land or other goods) between families, as well as of the custody of offspring. Sometimes, such payments are returnable when or if the marriage ends.

Dowry usually refers to a payment by a bride's family to the bride, who in turn brings it to the marriage, theoretically retaining some power over it, while in fact her husband demands control over that payment. Dowry systems are common in Europe and Asia, in contexts of intensive agriculture, where men are usually the ones to inherit the family's property. Dowry is found in ancient Roman and Greek traditions and is known today in China, in northeastern Spain, and particularly in south Asia, where "dowry deaths" are a terrible problem, whereby a husband sometimes abuses or tortures his bride as a threat to increase a dowry obligation.

Brice price, or bride wealth, refers to a payment usually valued in cattle, goat, or other animals or the equivalent in money to the bride's father and/or other male kin. Such transactions are more typical of sub-Saharan Africa, in contexts of extensive agriculture and divergent family inheritance. Bride wealth in this region relates to the central role of women in agriculture, as well as the high value given to productive and reproductive rights, especially in rural areas.

In Latin America, women's movements have strongly fought to have family and civil codes revised in the 1980s and thus gain property rights. That was Guatemala's case in 1986. However, while article 78 of the Civil Code established equal rights for men and women, article 109 kept the male as the one and only domestic authority. In such instances, as in several other areas of the word, consuetudinary or traditional law based on family and communitarian traditions and the dynamics of the labor market collide with the state legal machinery to the detriment of the women's predicament.

Collision of Family, State, and Market

Women's property rights, thus limited by customs, social norms, and even legislation, hamper their economic status and chances to overcome poverty. Ownership of land and property empowers women and provides income and security, but when that ownership is mostly based on her marital status rather than on individual rights ensured by law, women have limited say in household decision making and no recourse to the assets during crises. This is often related to other vulnerabilities, such as domestic violence and human immunodeficiency virus and acquired immune deficiency syndrome (HIV/AIDS) infection.

In regions of conflict or war, the impact of unequal land rights has particularly serious consequences for women. Without their husbands, brothers, or fathers—in whose name land and property titles have been traditionally held—they find themselves denied access to their homes and fields by male family members, former in-laws, or neighbors. Without the security of a home or and income, women and their families fall into poverty traps and struggle for livelihoods, education, sanitation, healthcare, and other basic rights.

The family, the state, and the market often collide regarding property rights. A strong system of property rights is the most fundamental requirements of a capitalist economic system and one of the most misunderstood concepts. Social critics in the United States and other areas of the Western world have complained for decades that property rights might take precedence over human rights, resulting in unequal treatment and opportunities for people. Pioneering studies over several regions of the world argue that the single most important economic factor affecting women's position is the gender gap in command over property. More studies and continued action are needed regarding gender, women, and property rights.

See Also: Children's Rights; Marriage; Convention on the Elimination of All Forms of Discrimination Against Women; Economics, Women in; United Nations Conferences on Women; United Nations Development Fund for Women.

Further Readings

Agarwal, Bina. *A Field of One's Own. Gender and Land Rights in South East Asia.* Cambridge MA: Cambridge University Press, 1995.

Alchain, A. A. "Property Rights." *The Concise Encyclopedia of Economics* (2008). http://www.econlib.org/library /Enc/PropertyRights.html (accessed July 2010).

De Soto, H. and F. Chenewal. *Realizing Property Rights.* Zurich, Switzerland: Rüffer & Rub, 2006.

Lastarria-Cornhiel, Susana. "Impact of Privatization on Gender and Property Rights in Africa." *World Development*, v.25/8 (1997).

Meinzen-Dick, Ruth S., et al. "Gender and Property Rights: Overview." *World Development*, v.25/8 (1997).

Ruqadya, Margaret A., Hema Swaminathan, and Cherryl Walker, eds., *Women's Property Rights, HIV and AIDS & Domestic Violence: Research Findings from Two Districts in South Africa and Uganda.* Cape Town, South Africa: Human Science Research Council, 2009.

Sandefur, Timothy. *Cornerstone of Liberty: Property Rights in 21st Century America.* Washington, DC: Cato Institute, 2006.

World Bank. *Engendering Development Through Gender Equality in Rights, Resources, and Voice.* Washington, DC: World Bank and Oxford University Press, 2001.

Soledad Vieitez-Cerdeño
University of Granada

Prostitution, Legal

Legal prostitution broadly refers to the ability of consenting adults to buy and sell sexual intercourse or other sexual services without incurring legal penalty. International legislative approaches to prostitution vary enormously and can be grouped into three broad categories: legalization, with associated state involvement in regulating prostitution; decriminalization, which makes prostitution neither illegal nor legal; and criminalization, in which prostitution is entirely illegal.

Heated debates surrounding legal prostitution can be divided into two primary camps: those opposing prostitution as a public nuisance and/or a form of violence against women and others who recognize that prostitution is an enduring reality and a form of work with associated risks that can be minimized by state regulation of its practice. Given that the vast majority of prostitutes throughout the world are women, it has been suggested that unique socioeconomic issues associated with women's status, vis-à-vis men, must be considered in any discussion of the subject.

International Approaches to Prostitution Legislation

Legal prostitution takes many forms throughout the world, and some countries vary even in their national approaches to legislation. One approach to legal prostitution advocates direct state regulation, which usually involves the construction of areas specifically designated for prostitution, or tolerance zones. These regulated areas feature a police presence to maintain order and mandate regular health checks such

An openly HIV-positive prostitute, and a member of the Brazilian sex worker project Davida, models its fashion line.

as screening of prostitutes for sexually transmitted diseases. This approach is believed to improve prostitutes' health and safety while providing valuable tax revenue for the local and national governments. A number of countries follow this legislative pattern, including the Netherlands, Ecuador, Germany, and Greece. In those nations, both brothels and pimping are legal, provided that neither involves coercion. In Brazil, sex workers are active partners in designing national healthcare policy, particularly in regard to human immunodeficiency virus and acquired immune deficiency syndrome (HIV/AIDS).

With decriminalization, there are varying degrees of permissiveness and enforcement. Numerous countries throughout Western Europe and the Americas have experimented with decriminalization for prostitutes but not for their clients. Often considered to be a deterrent to prostitution without punishing the prostitutes, decriminalization recognizes that prostitutes sometimes (but not always) choose this line of work as a last resort. For instance, it is not illegal for adults to sell sex in Canada, but soliciting, brothel ownership, and pimping are all illegal. This focus on demand from clients rather than the supply of prostitutes simultaneously deters potential clients without further marginalizing those who sell sex. Clients may be deterred by the difficulty in separating illegal from legal activities in decriminalized systems, as clients rarely know the full reality of the prostitute's circumstances. In Iceland and Sweden, it not illegal to sell sex but it is illegal to pay for it. Such seemingly contradictory legislation is part of a broader philosophy that holds that prostitutes are often desperate and would not engage in such behaviors if a demand for them did not exist.

All countries in the world have prostitution, but the degree to which laws are enforced even in areas where it is completely criminalized and socially stigmatized varies enormously. One of the possible penalties for prostitution in Iran includes death by stoning, yet in most other countries characterized by criminalization, prostitution is tolerated in certain areas that the police ignore as a consequence of several factors: low levels of concern with the problem; a lack of regard for the safety and well-being of prostitutes; the need for law enforcement to urgently respond to crime scenes; and the tacit understanding of police officers that the arrest, release, and rearrest of prostitutes is a wasteful, cyclical process. Experienced police officers in such situations sometimes believe that prostitution is a relatively victimless crime.

Their feeling is that women who sell sex are at least, theoretically, making a choice to do so and thus must accept the consequences of their actions. In many countries, the stance that prostitution is morally and legally offensive results in the sex trade being concentrated in low-income neighborhoods that have been abandoned by businesses, middle-class families, and other indicators of social and civic well-being.

India and the United States are particularly strong examples of nation's that apply varying levels in criminal penalties to prostitution. In India, prostitution is illegal, but it also is highly visible and tolerated by the police in certain urban neighborhoods that are well known for such activity. The same is true in the United States, where prostitution is illegal everywhere except for 11 rural counties in Nevada—and only restricted to brothels. Yet it is very easy in almost any American city to find areas frequented by prostitutes and their clients, although these areas are periodically subject to crackdowns by police.

Debates on Legal Prostitution

There are two schools of thought on legal prostitution: one opposes it as a sexist and/or socially dangerous practice and the other recognizes it as a form of work in need of state regulation and harm reduction. Many national governments, including the United States, maintain laws against prostitution because it is believed to be harmful to the fabric of society, including families and communities. Most faith-based organizations also oppose prostitution on similar grounds.

A significant number of feminist activists contend that prostitution itself is a violent act both in its intention of placing intimacy in the marketplace and in its consequence of making women's bodies into marketable commodities. More radical proponents of this belief argue that legal prostitution is oriented toward protecting the health and anonymity of male clients by screening prostitutes for sexually transmitted diseases and designating certain geographic areas for the trade. They argue that legalization is tantamount to state complicity in what they believe is an essentially sexist and violent act.

Governments, organizations, and individuals who believe prostitution should be legal often argue that criminalizing prostitution simply pushes it further underground, making it a more dangerous practice by raising the risk of violence, abuse and the involvement of organized crime. Some feminist activists believe that prostitution should be legal because individual women, rather than society at large, should have the right to determine what to do with their bodies. Activists for prostitutes' rights organizations contend that the prostitutes are simply filling a service demand and should be treated like any other worker. Such rights groups find the beliefs and policies of people opposed to the legislation of prostitution offensive and patronizing because they assume that individual women are incapable of making responsible decisions about what to do with their bodies.

Debates on prostitution have spurred equally vibrant exchanges between the two opposing groups on appropriate language to describe prostitution and its practice. Some feminist activists and prostitutes' rights organizations argue that the word *prostitute* is a morally loaded term that should be replaced with what they believe is the more neutral description: "sex worker." This latter phrase is thought to more sensitively describe the labor of a highly stigmatized community. However, some sex workers' rights advocates outright reject the use of this term and instead embrace their outsider status by challenging prevailing social norms regarding sexuality.

Health and Safety Issues

One of the central arguments for the legalization of prostitution is that it minimizes risks to the health and safety of prostitutes and their clients through state regulation. Prostitutes and their clients incur a number of risks to their health and safety by choosing to engage in a paid sexual encounter with a nonmonogamous partner. Foremost among these risks is HIV/AIDS as well as other sexually transmitted diseases that cannot be prevented through the use of condoms. While many prostitutes throughout the world now insist their clients use condoms, their ability to do so can be severely constrained by poverty, the need for drugs to feed their addiction, or control by a pimp or other third party. Prostitutes who have less control over the circumstances under which their sexual labor is carried out—including the right to use condoms—are much more likely to contract sexually transmitted diseases from their clients, which are in turn spread to other clients and the general population.

Mental health is another issue for many prostitutes. Intense emotional processes of separation and rationalization are necessary for women who engage in sex work because of the stigmatized nature of prostitution in almost every society in the world. Individuals who are pushed to the margins of society in this way are more likely to suffer low self-esteem and, as a result, may be less able to engage in loving relationships of equality because of the numbing and socially stigmatized behavior they engage in on a regular basis. Some prostitutes turn to self-medication through drugs and alcohol to deal with these emotional issues, thus creating a vicious spiral in which intoxication and/or addiction can make them even more vulnerable to risks to their health and safety.

Legal prostitution is believed to address and reduce the frequency of abuse prostitutes endure by clients, pimps, or other authority figures. Sex trafficking, in which girls or women are forced to engage in prostitution for a third party's economic gain, is a particularly insidious aspect of prostitution now receiving increased attention by governments because of its high potential for illicit income. Prostitutes can be vulnerable to abuse by pimps, who support themselves economically from the earnings of the prostitute. These relationships are often described by those involved in them as romantic bonds, despite the exploitation they entail. Such complex dynamics can make it difficult for individuals to leave prostitution because their networks of emotional support are completely dependent upon those who are involved in the business.

People who advocate for the criminalization of prostitution often believe that prostitution has a deleterious impact on communities, schools, and property values. For many people, prostitution is associated with drug use, violence, marital infidelity, and other undesirable social behaviors thought to damage the social fabric of society. Those in favor of legal prostitution tend to argue that criminalizing prostitution only serves to push the sex industry further underground and thus less visible to policymakers and the voting public. This invisibility in turn puts prostitutes at a greater risk of violence and abuse by both clients and the police because of their status as criminals and members of a socially stigmatized group. Overall, it is clear that there are serious consequences to public health and safety incurred by both approaches.

Legal Prostitution and Gender Relations

It has been argued that prostitution is a manifestation of unequal gender relations, that it is an easy metaphor for male economic power and female submission. The worldwide feminization of poverty through lower pay and higher expectations for unpaid labor such as childcare and eldercare among women have a direct correlation to the number of women who sell sex to survive. Such economic crises at the individual level often combine with regional conflicts to push poor women in many countries into sex work, at least in part because of the demand for prostitutes created by military bases and economies dominated by tourism.

Many feminist scholars have argued that the universality of prostitution stems at least in part from pervasive beliefs that men must demonstrate sexual virility to be considered masculine. This is problematic, such scholars argue, because so many societies associate femininity with passive behavior and a lack of sexual desire. As a consequence of this enduring paradox, it has been argued that prostitution is a result of a system that forces women to deny desire while forcing men to embrace it so that both sexes fulfill their culturally appropriate roles.

See Also: "Femininity," Social Construction of; "Masculinity," Social Construction of; Pornography/ Erotica; Prostitution in Combat Zones; Sex Workers; Trafficking, Women and Children.

Further Readings

Bernstein, Elizabeth. *Temporarily Yours: Intimacy, Authenticity and the Commerce of Sex.* Chicago: University of Chicago Press, 2007.

Day, Sophie. *On the Game: Women and Sex Work.* London: Pluto Press, 2007.

Kuo, Lenore. *Prostitution Policy: Revolutionizing Practice Through a Gendered Perspective.* New York: New York University Press, 2002.

Weitzer, Ron, ed. *Sex for Sale: Prostitution, Pornography, and the Sex Industry,* 2nd. ed. New York and London: Routledge, 2010.

Susan Dewey
Indiana University Bloomington

Prostitution in Combat Zones

Prostitution in combat zones is defined as the exchange of sexual intercourse or sexualized attention for money or something of value in an area experiencing war or active conflict. Strong evidence from many combat zones suggests a direct correlation between the presence of military troops and a dramatic rise in prostitution.

This has been particularly marked in the 20th and 21st centuries, which have featured historically unprecedented levels of violence against civilian noncombatants. The nature of contemporary military engagement in combat zones directly impacts neighboring countries, which may or may not be embroiled in the conflict, and sometimes functions to increase the number of women forced or compelled to engage in prostitution for economic or other constraining circumstances. The presence of large numbers of unaccompanied male soldiers and associated stereotypes about male sexuality are thought to encourage

this practice. Countries that have experienced particularly significant problems with prostitution due to their proximity to combat zones include Bosnia-Herzegovina, the Democratic Republic of Congo, the Philippines, Thailand, South Korea, and Vietnam. The worldwide prevalence of this phenomenon has led to increased expressions of concern on behalf of the international community.

It is difficult in combat zones to distinguish between prostitution and survival sex, which involves the exchange of sexual favors for basic items necessary for human existence, such as food or shelter. The majority of contemporary refugees are girls and women, all of whom are vulnerable to gender-based violence due to the feminization of poverty and conflict-associated chaos. It has been argued that sexual relations between soldiers and war-affected women and girls cannot be considered consensual because of inherent inequalities of status, power, and authority. Serious accusations have emerged in recent decades regarding the alleged involvement of United Nations peacekeepers and other armed forces in patronizing prostitutes who may have been held against their will. This is especially true in Bosnia-Herzegovina and the Democratic Republic of Congo. Many governments have adopted "zero tolerance" policies toward this behavior as a result, but reports have suggested that conflict may create a permissive environment in which soldiers sometimes operate with impunity. Part of this stems from widely held assumptions linking masculinity to aggressive sexuality, a social construct that may pressure soldiers to patronize prostitutes to demonstrate their "masculinity."

Prostitution in combat zones has had an enduring impact on many countries. An estimated 200,000 eastern Asian females, known as "comfort women," were held against their will by Japanese forces in World War II. Victims and their advocates continue to pressure the Japanese government for official acknowledgement of military wrongdoing, without success. Approximately 50,000 children, known as AmerAsians, were fathered by American soldiers stationed in southeastern Asia. Although not all of their mothers were prostitutes, such children faced stigma in their home countries due to the political significance of U.S. soldiers' involvement with local women. It has been suggested that the legacy of prostitution in former southeastern Asian combat zones can be seen in the region's popularity as a destination for sex tourists, who plan their visits with the sole intention of visiting prostitutes.

Given the conflicted debates surrounding prostitution in combat zones, the international community has begun to efforts to reduce its prevalence, particularly among destitute women and underage girls. Many proponents of restitution contend that any sexual relationships between females in positions of conflict-related vulnerability and soldiers constitute a violation of human rights. Most suggestions center upon soldiers' demand for prostitutes' services and include raising gender sensitivity among peacekeepers and the general public, adopting stricter policies regarding the interpretation of military misconduct, and stationing increased numbers of female soldiers and peacekeepers in combat zones to promote greater gender equality.

See Also: Combat, Women in; Conflict Zones; "Masculinity," Social Construction of; Prostitution, Legal; Rape in Conflict Zones.

Further Readings

Enloe, Cynthia. *Maneuvers: The International Politics of Militarizing Women's Lives.* Berkeley: University of California Press, 2000.

Hicks, George. *The Comfort Women: Japan's Brutal Regime of Enforced Prostitution in the Second World War.* New York: W. W. Norton & Company, 1997.

Lowry, T. P. *The Story the Soldiers Wouldn't Tell: Sex in the Civil War.* Mechanicsburg, PA: Stackpole Books, 1994.

Susan Dewey
Indiana University Bloomington

Psychological Disorders by Gender, Rates of

Psychological disorders are understood as patterns of experience and behavior that deviate from the population norm and are associated with subjective distress. Various disorders also have been distinguished, such as mood disorders or substance-related disorders.

It has been shown that men and women have differing vulnerabilities with various psychological disorders. Such differences are documented in the diagnostic compendium *Diagnostic and Statistical Manual of Mental Disorders, 4th Edition.* The most typical differences are that women have about twice the risk of men of being affected by mood, anxiety, or eating disorders. Men, in contrast, have a somewhat higher risk with respect to antisocial personality and substance-related disorders.

Age-Related Changes

Psychological disorders can be divided into two groups: externalizing (i.e., aggressive and delinquent behavior) and internalizing (i.e., anxious and depressive behavior, physical complaints and social withdrawal) disorders. Longitudinal studies have shown that in infancy there are no significant gender differences in psychological disorders.

From infancy to early adolescence, boys show higher rates of psychological disorders than girls do, and school-age boys are affected by depressive disorders more frequently than girls. In late adolescence and early adulthood, however, the pattern is reversed, and depression becomes twice as frequent among women than among men. This is in line with the general age trend of decreases in internalizing disorders with boys and increases in these disorders with girls. Furthermore, boys in elementary school and young men exhibit externalizing disorders more frequently than others. Among young men, substance-related disorders and antisocial personality disorders are especially frequent.

Cultural Aspects and Risk Factors

Cross-national and epidemiologic surveys have shown that gender differences in psychological disorders are relatively independent of cultural setting. Across countries in America, Africa, Asia, Europe, the Middle East, and the Pacific, the risk for most mood disorders (except bipolar disorder) and anxiety disorders is 1.3 to 2.6 times higher in women than men. Men have 0.3 to 0.8 times higher risks of most externalizing disorders (e.g., attention-deficit/hyperactivity, conduct disorder, or intermittent explosive disorder) and most substance-related disorders.

Rates of major depressive disorders and substance-related disorders vary between countries that differ in their emphasis of traditional gender roles. In countries with less traditional role orientations, the prevalence of major depressive disorders among women is lower than in more traditional countries. In less traditional countries, female and male drinking behaviors converge, and substance-related disorders among women become more frequent.

There are indications that certain sociodemographic risk factors (e.g., being single, separated, divorced, widowed, or unemployed) increase the risk of psychological disorders in both genders, with a stronger effect seen on men. Other risk factors are relatively specific to one of the two genders: entering retirement is associated with increased risk for any depressive disorders in women, but not in men. In contrast, male, but not female, single parents have higher rates of substance-related disorders and mood disorders.

Possible Explanations

Various explanations have been proposed to explain the gender ratios. Biological explanations suggest that gender differences in the rates of psychological disorders are based on differences in brain structure and endocrine functioning. For instance, a gender-specific hormone system is considered a starting point for the development of psychological disorders. Psychosocial explanations focus on gender-role-associated prescriptions of hiding or showing distress (internalizing vs. externalizing); risk factors such as women's lower socioeconomic status, specific experiences of stress, negative life events, or traumatic events during childhood (e.g., sexual abuse); and protective factors such as women's larger resources of social support and social networks. Artifact explanations suggest that differences in internalizing disorders can at least in part be accounted for by differences in reporting symptoms. With externalizing disorders, the case may be different, for they are often more obvious. At this time, however, none of the approaches mentioned seems sufficient to account for the full variation that has been observed.

See Also: Anxiety Disorders; Depression; *Diagnostic and Statistical Manual of Mental Disorders;* Eating Disorders; Gender Roles, Cross-Cultural.

Further Readings

Klose, M. and F. Jacobi. "Can Gender Differences in the Prevalence of Mental Disorders Be Explained by Sociodemographic Factors?" *Archives of Women's Mental Health*, v.7 (2004).

Seedat, S., et al. "Cross-National Associations Between Gender and Mental Disorders in the World Health Organization World Mental Health Surveys." *Archives of General Psychiatry*, v.66 (2009).

J. Röhner
A. Schütz
Chemnitz University of Technology

Psychology/Psychiatry, Women in

Women participate in the fields of psychology and psychiatry as providers, researchers, subjects, teachers, students, critics, and consumers. Increasing numbers of women are entering the fields and taking leadership positions in professional organizations; more than half of those training as psychologists and psychiatrists today are women. Their presence has affected the mental health treatment of women and minorities. Men's voices continue to dominate, however, especially in certain subfields of psychology and psychiatry, and critiques of the fields' impact on disadvantaged groups (e.g., women, people of color, sexual minorities) remain strong.

Early Women in Psychology and Psychiatry

Throughout history and across cultures, women have been providers of emotional caretaking, empathy, and mental health services. Rather than being concentrated (and compensated) in a separate professional mental health role, this work has often come about in the course of women's other roles, such as friend, relative, teacher, childcare provider, midwife, and healer. As the fields of psychiatry and psychology grew with and branched from their roots in philosophy and medicine, they became professionalized through academic training and credentialing. This process was generally dominated by white, educated men, leaving women marginalized in early professional psychiatry and psychology.

Modern psychiatry is a medical specialty. Psychiatrists are medical doctors who study, diagnose, and treat mental disorders. With their medical degree and licensure as physicians, psychiatrists can order and interpret laboratory tests, prescribe medication, and conduct physical evaluations, in addition to counseling patients. As in other medical fields, women were historically excluded from many training programs and from membership in professional societies. For example, the American Psychiatric Association (APA) did not admit women as members until the 20th century. This is not to say that women had no participation in the field prior to this time, however. Many women, especially those with connections to men in the field (e.g., husbands, fathers), provided important insights and critiques that helped shape the early development psychiatry.

Modern psychology is a social and behavioral science. Psychologists study the behavior and mental processes of humans and animals. Trained psychologists hold a doctoral degree (Ph.D., Psy.D., or Ed.D.) and can conduct psychological tests and engage in psychotherapy processes such as counseling and behavior modification. Again, as in other specialized fields requiring advanced degrees, women were historically excluded from training and advancement in psychology. When the American Psychological Association formed in the late 1800s, all members were white men. In the 1890s, Mary Whiton Calkins attended Harvard psychology lectures as a "guest" and even presented a thesis in 1895, but she was denied a degree. She became an Instructor of Psychology at Wellesley College, however, and went on to later become the first woman president of the American Psychological Association.

Training and Advancement of Women Today

Before the 1970s, fewer than 20 percent of advanced psychology degrees were granted to women. Today, women outnumber men in both undergraduate and graduate psychology programs, and 67 percent of doctoral degrees in psychology are earned by women. The American Psychological Association Task Force on the Changing Gender Composition of Psychology noted that this shift is likely a result of women's increased access to education, as well as a decline in men's enrollment. As in other fields, the feminization of psychology coincided with a decline in the profession's prestige and earning power.

The distribution of men and women in psychology varies by subfield. For example, women are more likely to identify their specialization as developmental psychology than experimental psychology.

Psychiatry has also seen a great increase in women's participation since the 1970s. In the United States, 42 percent of new certifications in psychiatry and neurology went to women in the year 2000, up from 8 percent in 1970. This trend has been influenced, in part, by an increase in women patients requesting women physicians.

Women are less likely than men to enter and remain in academic positions in psychology and psychiatry. One possible reason for this is that traditional academic timetables do not accommodate the childbearing and parenting expectations many women face. Private practice and other work settings may provide more flexibility. Worldwide, men continue to hold more advanced positions in the fields.

Women's Presence in Professional Organizations

Although women now outnumber men entering the field of psychology and its professional organizations, men frequently comprise a disproportionate percentage of the leadership of these organizations. In the APA, more men than women hold elected "fellow" status, reserved for those with "unusual or outstanding contribution or performance in the field of psychology." As of 2009, only 11 of the APA's 110 elected presidents have been women.

Similar trends have been noted in other professional organizations, including the Canadian Psychological Association and the British Psychological Society. In 1984, Carol Nadelson was the first woman elected to serve as president of the American Psychiatric Association, which consists primarily of medical doctors. She also holds the distinction of being the first woman editor-in-chief of the *American Psychiatric Association Press*.

Some women have responded to concerns about women's participation and leadership in the fields of psychiatry and psychology by forming professional organizations or subgroups dedicated to women's advancement in the fields. These include the Association for Women in Psychology (AWP), Canadian Psychology Association/Societe Canadienne de Psychologie Section on Women and Psychology (SWAP), the British Psychological Society's Psychology of Women Section (POWS), the Association for Women Psychiatrists (AWP), the Australian Psychological Society's Women and Psychology Interest

Group, and the American Psychological Association's Women's Program Office.

Prominent Contemporary Women in the Fields

Despite their increased numbers in the fields, women's contributions receive little recognition in psychology and psychiatry academic courses and textbooks. While some claim this is due to women's lack of significant contributions, others point out that systematic bias often determines whose accomplishments are noticed and what research is recognized as influential. Many important theories and practices in modern psychiatry and psychology were developed by women.

Elizabeth Loftus is an award-winning psychology professor at the University of Washington. She is frequently called upon as an expert witness on false memories and the reliability of eyewitness testimony, due to her research findings that have challenged popular psychological theories about repressed and recovered memories. Her expertise has changed the way courts view recollections as evidence in trials.

Nancy Coover Andreasen holds the Andrew H. Woods Chair of Psychiatry at the University of Iowa Roy J. and Lucille A. Carver College of Medicine. She is a leading expert on schizophrenia and is frequently cited for her scales measuring both positive symptoms (the presence of an atypical behavior or experience such as hallucinations) and negative symptoms (the absence of a typical behavior or experience—for example, emotional numbness). Prior to her work, negative symptoms had received much less attention, despite their significant effect on the lives of those with schizophrenia.

Patricia S. Cowings is a research psychologist at the National Aeronautics and Space Administration's (NASA's) Ames Research Center. As a young, black woman, she struggled to be taken seriously as a scientist but was eventually selected to be the first American woman astronaut. Though she never ended up in space, her research on how astronauts adapt to new environments has provided important insights and tools for the voluntary control of body processes such as heart rate and blood pressure. These can be used by doctors and therapists to address a wide variety of medical and psychological conditions, including hypertension, motion sickness, and attention deficit disorder.

Other prominent women in contemporary psychology and psychiatry include former American Psychological Association presidents Norine Johnson and Diane Halpern. Johnson was an early advocate of integrating children with disabilities into community schools. She has developed measures, written books, and launched businesses dedicated to the practice of feminist psychology. Halpern's research, writing, and speaking has centered on critical thinking and sex differences in cognitive ability. She has called for improved fairness in the practice of using standardized tests for college admissions and other selection processes.

Bringing Attention to Marginalized Voices

Many women in psychology and psychiatry have focused their work on underrepresented populations. The annual Association for Women in Psychology's Women of Color Psychologies Award recognizes the importance of work by and for women of color. Past recipients have included Beverly Greene, who has written prolifically on ethnic and gender identity in psychotherapy; Oliva Espin, an expert on the psychology of immigrant and refugee women; Aida Hurtado, author of books on Chicana/o identity; NiCole Buchanan, whose research has led to increased understanding of racialized sexual harassment; and Lillian Comas-Diaz, an expert in ethnocultural psychotherapy.

Other women in psychology and psychiatry have focused on the experiences of people with disabilities, sexual minorities, and people of low socioeconomic status. Esther Rothblum's clinical work and research has brought attention to the experiences of people of size, challenging the pathologizing of size diversity. Her work in this area has spanned decades, most recently including the development of *The Fat Studies Reader*, an interdisciplinary compilation of scholarly writings about fatness.

Women as Critics of Psychiatric Practices

Even before they were permitted formal participation in psychology and psychiatry, women were vocal critics of certain trends in the fields. Sigmund Freud's theories of women's psychosexual development, for instance, led to several critical responses from women. In the late 1960s and early 1970s, Phyllis Chesler cofounded the Association for Women in

Psychology and also published a book, *Women and Madness,* asserting that labels of mental health and illness are often biased along classifications such as gender and race. Paula Caplan and other feminist psychologists have written extensively on modern controversies such as whether or not "premenstrual syndrome" and "premenstrual dysphoric disorder" should be considered mental disorders.

Today, the AWP continues to have an active committee on Bias in Psychiatric Diagnosis. In the development of the fifth edition of the *Diagnostic and Statistical Manual of Mental Disorders,* used by psychologists and psychiatrists to categorize mental conditions, the committee has raised concerns about eating disorder and obesity classifications, the label of gender identity disorder, and the influence of classism and racism in psychiatric diagnosis.

Women's Impact on Services for Women

One goal of many women entering the fields of psychology and psychiatry is to improve services for women. Feminist psychology developed, in part, as a result of this desire. Psychologists such as Rhoda K. Unger have developed courses, produced textbooks, and written articles and chapters on the psychology of women and feminist psychology to correct what they perceived as a lack of representation of women's voices in the field and a resulting harm to women seeking services. Women's presence in the field has led to increased understanding of women's experiences. For example, psychologist Lenore Walker's work has produced valuable information about the cycle of abuse experienced by many in domestic violence situations. Through feminist critiques, original research, and their own practices, women in psychology and psychiatry continue to change the way women—from patients to practitioners—are treated in the fields.

See Also: Attainment, Graduate Degree; *Diagnostic and Statistical Manual of Mental Disorders,* Critiques of; Mental Health Treatment, Access to; Mental Health Treatment, Bias in; Mental Illness, Incidence Rates of; Physician Specialties; Physicians, Female; Professional Education; Professions by Gender.

Further Readings

Bender, Eve. "Prominent Minority Psychiatrists Say 'The Sky's the Limit.'" *Psychiatric News,* v.41/22 (2006).

Caplan, Paula J. *They Say You're Crazy: How the World's Most Powerful Psychiatrists Decide Who's Normal.* Reading, MA: Perseus Books, 1996.

Chin, Eliza Lo, ed. *This Side of Doctoring: Reflections from Women in Medicine.* Thousand Oaks, CA: Sage, 2002.

Hirshbein, Laura D., Kate Fitzgerald, and Michelle Riba. "Women and Teaching in Academic Psychiatry." *Academic Psychiatry,* v.28 (2004).

O'Connell, Agnes N. *Models of Achievement: Reflections of Eminent Women in Psychology (Vol. 3).* Mahwah, NJ: Erlbaum, 2001.

Rutherford, Alexandra and Wade Pickren. "Women and Minorities in Psychology." Davis, Stephen F. and William Buskist, eds. *21st Century Psychology: A Reference Handbook.* Thousand Oaks, CA: Sage, 2008.

Warren, Wini. *Black Women Scientists in the United States.* Bloomington, IN: Indiana University Press, 1999.

Virginia Dicken
Southern Illinois University, Carbondale

Psychotropic Medications

In general, the term *psychotropic medication* is interchangeable with the terms *psychoactive* and/or *psychotherapeutic medications,* since all three terms are used to describe chemical elements that work principally on the central nervous system. In all cases, these medications change one's perception of time, awareness of external reality, and behavior. While the drugs were created for specific purposes, they are used frequently as a means of recreation.

Since psychotropics cause an individual to experience changes in perception and frame of mind, which are often seen as enjoyable, many psychotropics are misused, as people can tend to take more than they should, regardless of the potential dangers. With continued abuse, the individual could develop a physical dependency on the drug, making it harder to stop. Drug rehabilitation often necessitates a mixture of counseling, support groups, and other psychotropics, such as methadone, to sever the person's dependency.

Specific types of psychotropic medications include antidepressants: a type of medication used primarily for the treatment of depressive disorders such as major depression, dysthymic disorder, nervousness, eating disorders such as anorexia and bulimia, as well as borderline personality disorder; Stimulants: medicine prescribed principally to take care of disorders such as attention deficit hyperactivity disorder or ADHD; Antipsychotics: used to help deal with psychotic disorders like schizophrenia; Mood stabilizers: frequently prescribed to treat either bipolar disorder and/or schizoaffective disorder, which is a combination of schizophrenia and bipolar disorder; anxiolytics: usually prescribed to treat problems with nervousness and/or phobias; and depressants: primarily prescribed as a sedative or hypnotic.

Psychotropic Medications and Health

Psychotropics work by momentarily changing an individual's brain chemistry, causing an obvious alteration in his/her frame of mind, cognition, discernment of external phenomena, and behavior. Psychiatrists often prescribe psychotropics to control the symptoms rather than to cure them, as the medical field is still unsure why psychotropic medication works. In addition, psychotropics often affect men differently than women and are not recommended for pregnant women. Psychotropics could adversely affect both mother and child.

Various researchers have stated unequivocally that using psychotropics should be limited. In 2004, the U.S. Food and Drug Administration issued a warning indicating that using certain antidepressants by pregnant women in their third trimester might affect the baby. In addition, another antidepressant medicine, selective serotonin reuptake inhibitors, or SSRIs, could cause a miscarriage or possibly lead to a child born with birth defects. Using antianxiety medications like benzodiazepines may lead to birth defects and a bevy of other probable adverse problems for the child if ingested during the first trimester.

After the baby is born, if the mother decides to breast-feed, she should know that a possibility exists that a minute amount of the substance could pass into the breast milk. Whether pregnant women should take psychotropics to treat mental illness can be a difficult decision and should be based on each woman's unique needs and circumstances. Pregnant women and/or breast-feeding mothers need to discuss any potential risks and benefits with their doctors, and physicians should closely observe their pregnant patients, both before and after delivery of the child.

Studies conducted in Europe and North America indicate that physicians are more likely to prescribe psychotropic medication to women than men. In fact, survey results indicate that physicians prescribed tranquilizers to only 8.5 percent of men, while prescribing them to 16.5 percent of women, largely to overcome anxiety and insomnia. In addition, male physicians are more likely to diagnose women with psychiatric problems and to treat the illness with psychotropics.

One possible reason for this is that male doctors tend to view women as the "weaker sex" and more emotional and vulnerable. Culture plays a role in these viewpoints, too, with sexist attitudes regarding the vulnerable state of women leading doctors to prescribe more medication for them than men. Another likely cause is the belief that women need medication to handle their emotional needs. Some also feel that women are more apt to need psychiatric treatment. Until society as a whole soundly rejects these notions, women will continue to receive greater amounts of psychotropic medication than do men.

See Also: Health, Mental and Physical; Mental Health Treatment, Access to; Mental Health Treatment, Bias in; Mental Illness, Incidence Rates of; Pregnancy.

Further Readings

Gitlin, M. and V. Hendtick. *Psychotropic Drugs and Women: Fast Facts*. New York: W. W. Norton, 2004.

Kohen, D. "Psychotropic Medication in Pregnancy." *Advances in Psychiatric Treatment*, v.10/1 (2004).

Muirhead, Greg. "Psychotropic Drugs May be Needed in Pregnancy: Maternal Psychiatric Illness, if Inadequately Treated or Untreated, May Result in Poor Compliance With Care." *Ob.Gyn. News*, v.43/9 (2008).

Rubin, Peter C. and Margaret Ramsey. *Prescribing in Pregnancy*. London: BMJ Books, 2008.

U.S. National Institutes of Health. "Mental Health Medications." http://www.nimh.nih.gov/health/publications/mental-health-medications/complete-index.shtml (accessed November 2009).

Li-Ching Hung
Overseas Chinese University
Cary Stacy Smith
Mississippi State University

Puberty

Puberty is defined as the period of human development during which physical growth and sexual maturation occur and a child's body becomes an adult's body, capable of reproduction. Strictly speaking, the term *puberty* (derived from the Latin word *puberatum*, meaning "age of maturity") refers to the bodily changes of sexual maturation, whereas adolescence, by contrast, is the term that refers to the psychosocial transition between childhood and adulthood. That said, the boundaries of puberty and adolescence overlap, thus, this entry will discuss both the physical and psychosocial characteristics of this particular stage of female development.

Puberty is an experience that unites women worldwide, from all cultures and social status. Puberty in a girl tends to begin two years earlier than it does in a boy and can start as early as 8 years old or even as late as 15, although the more common age is around 10 or 11. This means that a girl can find herself going through puberty when her best friend of the same age is not, and this can be an isolating and turbulent experience. Puberty is not something that happens overnight but rather is a process that occurs in different stages. Puberty is initiated by hormonal changes triggered by a part of the brain called the hypothalamus, which stimulates the pituitary gland, which in turn activates other glands from which comes a flood of reproductive hormones. These changes begin about a year before any of their results are visible. Both the male reproductive hormone testosterone and female hormone estrogen are present in children of both sexes. However, their balance changes at puberty, with girls producing relatively more estrogen and boys producing more testosterone.

The experience of puberty unites women worldwide, as the shame, uneasiness, embarrassment, and displeasure that a young girl feels at some point during the physical changes of puberty are almost universal.

Five Phases of Puberty

The Tanner Scale, established by British pediatrician James Tanner, identifies five distinct physical stages in female sexual development. During the first stage, the prepubertal stage, which occurs generally between the ages of 8 and 11, there are no major outward signs of sexual development. However, a girl's ovaries are enlarging, and hormone production is beginning.

The second stage of female sexual development is said to occur around the age of 11 or 12, although the full age range for this stage is 8 to 14, and involves accelerated height increase, weight gain, breast growth (palpable breast buds and areolae enlargement), and the emergence of minimal coarse, pigmented hair, mainly on the labia. Stage three usually takes place at the age of 12 or 13 (full age range: 9 to 15) and brings about peak height increase, elevation of the breast contours, further enlargement of the areolae, further growth of pubic hair (coarser and darker), production of vaginal discharge, and perhaps the onset of menstruation toward the end of this stage. Other changes that can occur during stage three concern the skin, with the possible outbreak of acne vulgaris due to increased secretion of sebum and perspiration body odor, as a result of hormonal changes.

During stage four, generally at 13 or 14 years old (full age range: 10 to 15), a secondary mound appears on the breast, pubic hair takes on the triangular shape of adulthood but still does not cover the entire area, underarm hair appears, and ovulation begins in some girls but does not really establish itself into a monthly routine until stage five. Once stage five sets in, typically at the age of 15 but possible anywhere between 12 and 19, physically, the girl is considered an adult. Breast and pubic hair growth are complete, and full height has, generally, been attained by this point. Menstrual periods are well established, and ovulation occurs monthly.

Alongside these five stages of female sexual development are five terms that can also be said to indicate the milestones of puberty in a girl: adrenarche; gonadarche; thelarche; pubarche, and menrache. Adrenarche is an early stage of sexual development referring to the start of the secretion of androgens by the adrenal glands, occurring at around 6 to 8 years of age in girls. Gonadarche indicates that true central puberty has begun and is associated with growth in the size of the ovaries in a girl, in response to changes in the pituitary gland. Thelarche, which occurs in conjunction with gonadarche, refers to the beginning of breast development in a girl. Pubarche signifies the emergence and spread of pubic hair, and, finally, menarche marks the onset of menstruation. It is important to note that several other factors can play a role in the process of female sexual maturation, such as nutrition (undernourished girls often suffer from delayed menarche, whereas obesity can bring about early menarche), level of exercise (a high level can slow down puberty), stress, social factors, and ill health (all of which can hinder sexual development).

The Psychosocial Consequences

Given the extent of the physical changes that take place in a girl's body during puberty, it is not surprising, therefore, that the psychosocial consequences of sexual maturation are equally substantial. In *The Second Sex* (1949), a groundbreaking text with regard to its detailed analysis of the female body in society, Simone de Beauvoir discusses the emotional trauma that can occur in a girl during puberty due to the dramatic transformation of her physiology, which is beyond her control. De Beauvoir describes puberty as a "crisis" that the young girl meets with uneasiness and displeasure. The young girl feels that her body is getting away from her, becoming foreign to her. She often develops a sense of shame and extreme modesty with regard to her new physical form, embarrassed to show herself naked from this point on and both astonished and horrified at what is happening to her. Furthermore, the changes that occur are painful, particularly in the case of menstruation (cramps, nausea, etc). The latter, according to de Beauvoir, is not helped by the fact that while the penis is seen to symbolize the glory of manhood, menstruation is considered a "monthly curse" and is rendered taboo in society, to the extent that, even among themselves, women are reluctant to discuss it.

Due to the abhorrence that puberty has the potential to inspire, many young girls will go to great lengths to deny it, for example, refusing to eat so as to slow down the sexual maturation of the body. For a long time, it was believed that such disgust at the weight gain brought on by puberty was essentially a Western problem, but studies such as Susan Bordo's *Unbearable Weight* (1993) reveal that the issue now extends to girls from cultures worldwide, even those where weight is traditionally valued (such as black

African cultures). An additional factor contributing to young girls' repulsion at and rejection of puberty is its connotations with sexual reproduction and the fear of penetration or perforation by the male.

During puberty, de Beauvoir states, the young girl feels condemned to a physical existence that is beyond her control; her sense of inferiority is increased and she goes on toward adulthood, wounded and shamed. Although written 60 years ago, this element of taboo and humiliation surrounding the sexual development of the female body described in *The Second Sex*, especially where menstruation is concerned (for example, in Muslim countries menstruating women are considered "unclean"), remains very much intact in the 21st century and must be addressed if young girls are to feel at ease with their changing female bodies. Until television advertisements for sanitary products (tampons and pads) change the test liquid from blue to red, we cannot say that, even in the supposedly liberal Western world, that we are at ease with menstruation.

See Also: Adolescence; Body Image; Diet and Weight Control; Health, Mental and Physical; "Femininity," Social Construction of; Menstruation.

Further Readings

Beauvoir, Simone de, H. M. Parshley, trans. *The Second Sex,* London: Penguin, 1972.

Bordo, Susan. *Unbearable Weight.* Berkeley: University of California Press, 2003 (1993).

Simmons, R. and D. Blyth. *Moving into Asolescence.* New York: A. de Gruyter, 1987.

Tanner, J. *Growth and Adolescence.* Oxford, UK: Blackwell Scientific, 1962.

Julie Anne Rodgers
National University of Ireland, Maynooth

Puerto Rico

Puerto Rico is a commonwealth politically allied with the United States since 1898, and Puerto Ricans have been U.S. citizens since 1917 but do not vote for the U.S. president and have only a nonvoting representative in the U.S. Congress. Puerto Rico has been governed by popularly elected officials (including a governor and bicameral legislature) since 1948. The commonwealth consists of one large island and several small islands in the Caribbean Sea, with an area of 13,790 square kilometers and a population of just under 4 million (as of July 2009).

Puerto Rico was claimed for Spain by Christopher Columbus in the 15th century and was a Spanish colony for several centuries before being ceded to the United States at the conclusion of the Spanish American War. This history is seen in the population, which is primarily Roman Catholic (85 percent), and the major ethnic groups are Caucasian (76.2 percent, mostly of Spanish origin) and black (6.9 percent), with small numbers of Asians, Amerindians, and people of mixed race. Spanish and English are the official languages.

Aid for Women and Children Living Below Poverty Line

The Puerto Rican economy has benefited from substantial U.S. investment; in 2009, the per capita Gross Domestic Product (GDP) was $17,100. Women constituted 41.5 percent of the nonagricultural labor force in 2007, including 40.5 percent of managers and legislators. In 2005, 10.2 percent of women age 15 and older were unemployed, and women and children are disproportionately represented among people living below the poverty line. The total fertility rate in 2009 was 1.6 children per woman, and the birth rate is 11.7 per 1,000 population, with a migration rate of minus 0.96 per 1,000 (Puerto Ricans are free to live and work in the mainland United States, and many leave during their working years then return for retirement), resulting in a population growth rate of 0.3 percent.

Women in Puerto Rico are far more likely than men to be divorced, separated, or widowed than men. In 2000, 38.4 percent of women age 60 or older were widowed versus 12 percent of men; 20 percent of women age 30 to 39, 22.5 percent of women age 40 to 59, and 13.3 percent of women age 60 or older were divorced or separated, whereas the comparable numbers for men are 13.2 percent for age 30 to 39, 15.3 percent for age 40 to 59, and 11 percent for age 60 and over.

Improvements in Healthcare and Education

Puerto Rico has made major efforts to improve health services over the past decade. Today, the most common causes of death are similar to those in other industrialized countries, primarily chronic diseases such as heart disease, cancer, and stroke. Life expectancy is comparable to the entire United States at 74.9 years for men and 82.4 years for women, although infant mortality is higher at 8.28 per 1,000 live births. Almost all births are attended by skilled healthcare personnel. The maternal mortality rate has fluctuated between about 5 to 20 per 100,000 live births; in 2005, it was 17.6 per 100,000. Birth rates among adolescent mothers (age 10 to 19 years) have decreased from 42.9 per 1,000 in 1997 to 31.4 per 1,000 in 2004. From 2002 to 2004, 29 percent of induced abortions were performed on women age 15 to 19.

Education is theoretically universal in Puerto Rico, but in practice more boys than girls attend primary school while more women attend secondary school and university. Literacy is about equal, at 94.4 percent for women and 93.9 percent for men.

Women in Politics and Sports

One woman has served as governor of Puerto Rico: Sila Maria Calderón of the Popular Democratic Party, who served from 2001 to 2005. She previously held several other government offices, including mayor of San Juan (capital of Puerto Rico) as well as secretary of state in the federal government. San Juan had one previous female mayor, Felisa Rincón de Gautier, who served from 1947 to 1969 and was the first woman to serve as governor of a capital city in the Americas. Several women currently serve in the legislature for Puerto Rico, including President Pro Tempore Margarita Nolasco Santiago; Melinda K. Romero Donnelly and Norma E. Burgo Andújar in the Senate; and Albita I. Rivera Ramirez, Liza Fernandez Rodriguez, and Jennifer Gonzalez Colon in the House of Representatives.

Many Puerto Rican women have achieved success in sports and sports administration. In 2008, Natasha Sagardia became the first Puerto Rican to win a gold medal at the International Surfing Association world championship. Maria Elena Batista competed in the 1988 Olympics as a swimmer. She is currently working as a sports administrator responsible for building or upgrading many athletic venues in Puerto Rico and founding several sports schools for low-income children. Rebekah Colberg competed internationally in several sports, including softball and track and field, and is often called the "mother of women's sports" in Puerto Rico for her pioneering efforts to promote female participation in sports. Ivelisse Echevarría, currently director of sports and recreation for the city of Guaynabo, carried the Puerto Rican flag in the 1996 Olympics and competed as a pitcher for the softball team. She was inducted into the International Softball Hall of Fame in 2003.

See Also: Abortion, Access to; Government, Women in; Poverty; Roman Catholic Church.

Further Readings

Lewis, Linden. *The Culture of Gender and Sexuality in the Caribbean*. Gainesville: University Press of Florida, 2003.

United Nations Statistics Divisions. "UNdata: A World of Information: Gender Info." http://data.un.org/Explorer .aspx?d=GenderStat (accessed April 2010).

World Health Organization. "Puerto Rico: Health in the Americas." http://www.paho.org/hia/archivosvol2 /paisesing/Puerto%20Rico%20English.pdf (accessed April 2010).

Sarah Boslaugh
Washington University School of Medicine

Purity Balls

A purity ball (also called a "purity wedding" or a "father-daughter purity ball") is a formal event that encourages the virginity of preteen and teenage girls until marriage and is attended by fathers and their daughters. Girls are encouraged to dress up in a formal white gown (resembling a wedding gown) for the event, which usually includes a "ceremony" in which the girl pledges to remain abstinent until marriage and her father pledges to protect his daughter's purity. Often the father will present his daughter with a "purity ring" or another piece of jewelry symbolizing his pledge to her. The event usually includes a dinner and dance, in addition to the ceremony. Purity balls are an American phenomenon and often associated with U.S. Evangelical Christian churches. The phenomenon is spreading in popularity though to other nations like Australia and to some European nations. Purity balls have been criticized as maintaining sexual double standards and traditional gender roles by feminist organizations.

The purity ball is a derivative of the larger abstinence movement, which has been promoted by conservative or religious right organizations in the United States since the 1980s. Pastor Randy Wilson and his wife, Lisa, organized the first purity ball in Colorado Springs, Colorado, in 1998. The couple runs Generations of Light, a popular Christian Ministry in town, and their Colorado Springs' Annual Father-Daughter Purity Ball has since become a well-known national event, placing the congregation as a leader in the abstinence movement. Since then, other churches and conservative organizations from around the country have held their own purity balls based upon the Wilson's model.

Feminists have criticized purity balls for maintaining a sexual double standard, in that young woman are prevented from controlling their own sexuality, instead placing the control in the hands of their fathers. They also point out that young women within these conservative movements are also not given access to information about their sexuality, including sexual health options, and are thus placed at risk for unplanned pregnancy and sexually transmitted diseases when they do become sexually active. Furthermore, purity balls have received criticism for promoting traditional gender roles, where girls are groomed for their roles as wives and mothers rather than as independent young women with a world of life options to choose from.

Purity balls have received a lot of attention from the press in recent years, with the *New York Times*, *Time* magazine, and *Glamour* magazine all covering the phenomenon. Abstinence Clearinghouse, a South Dakota–based organization involved in the purity movement, sends out over 700 "Purity Ball Planner" booklets a year to churches and abstinence organizations, encouraging them to hold their own purity balls. However, despite the media coverage and promotion by conservative organizations, it is difficult to know exactly how many purity balls are held annually in the United States, since most are grassroots organized and can range in size.

See Also: Chastity Pledges; Focus on the Family; Fundamentalist Christianity; Pro-Life Movement; Sex Education, Abstinence-Only.

Further Readings

Banerjee, N. "Dancing the Night Away, With a Higher Purpose." *New York Times* (May 19, 2007). http://www.nytimes.com/2008/05/19/us/19purity.html (accessed July 2010).

Baumgardner, J. "Would you Pledge Your Virginity to Your Father?" *Glamour* (January 2007). http://www.glamour.com/sex-love-life/2007/01/purity-balls (accessed July 2010).

Gibbs, N. "The Pursuit of Teen Girl Purity." *Time* (July 17, 2008). http://www.time.com/time/magazine/article/0,9171,1823930-1,00.html (accessed July 2010).

Valenti, J. *The Purity Myth: How America's Obsession with Virginity is Hurting Young Women.* Berkeley, CA: Seal Press, 2009.

Jessalynn Keller
University of Texas at Austin

Qatar

Located on the coast of the Arabian peninsula and surrounded by the Persian Gulf, Qatar is an oil-rich country with one of the fastest growing economies in the world. A monarchy controlled by the Al Thani family, Qatar's government rules by religious law, with councils of leading citizens. While the constitution bans discrimination against women, law and social customs restrict women's rights and freedoms. Shari`a, or Islamic law, gives men some controls over women.

In education and the workforce, Qatar women experience some equality. Women have equal access to education, although it can be harder for them to travel abroad for college, as their movement can be limited without male escorts. Women comprise 26 percent of the national workforce, primarily in teaching, health, and government sectors. Women also receive equal pay for equal work.

Migrant women face significant hardships in Qatar, which has a national problem with forced domestic service and the mistreatment of domestic servants. Women are forced into labor in homes, are given no access to assistance, and are often abused and beaten. Foreign embassies have gone so far as to establish shelters for runaway maids.

While Islamic law prohibits physical abuse of women, it does protect men for "crimes of honor," or assaults on women who displayed defiant behavior or were immodest. Husbands can restrict the activities of their wives and make it difficult for a woman to travel unaccompanied. In court, a woman usually has to be represented by a male relative, and it takes the testimony of two women to equal that of one man.

Shari`a law compromises the freedom of women. Yet, Qatar women do have certain guarantees to an equal education and fair wages.

See Also: Honor Killings; Islam; Shari`a Law.

Further Readings

Abdala, Ikhlas A. "Attitudes Towards Women in the Arabian Gulf Region," *Women in Management Review,* v.11/1 (1996).

Alsharekh, Alanoud. *Popular Culture and Political Identity in the Arab Gulf States.* London: Saqi Books, 2008.

Bahry, L. "Elections in Qatar: A Window of Democracy Opens In The Gulf." *Middle East Policy,* v.6 (1999).

Crystal, Jill. *Oil and Politics in the Gulf: Rulers and Merchants in Kuwait and Qatar.* Cambridge, UK: Cambridge University Press, 1995.

Peterson, J. E. "The Political Status of Women in the Arab Gulf States," *Middle East Policy,* v. 33(1989).

Zahlan, Rosemarie Said. *The Making of the Modern Gulf States: Kuwait, Bahrain, Quatar, the United Arab Emirates and Oman.* Ithaca, NY: Ithaca Press, 1999.

Monica D. Fitzgerald
Saint Mary's College of California

Queen Latifah

Born Dana Elaine Owens on March 18, 1970, the premier female rap star is better known by her stage name Queen Latifah. Latifah began her career in the 1980s, and is considered a pioneer. Her career has also encompassed acting and writing. She continues to be a force in today's world as a spokeswoman for companies such as Cover Girl and Curvations. Her 1999 memoir, *Ladies First: Revelations of a Strong Woman*, was a bestseller, hailed as a self-esteem manual for young women.

Young Dana Owens grew up in Newark, New Jersey. At age 8, she was dubbed Latifah, which means "gentle" in Arabic, by a cousin; she adopted "Queen" later. In 1987, she began beatboxing for the rap group Ladies Fresh. At the age of 19, she produced a solo album, *All Hail the Queen* (1989), which incorporated techniques beyond rap, such as soul, hip-hop, and reggae, and is often hailed as a feminist expression. Since then, she has gone on to produce an impressive discography: *Nature of a Sista* (1991), *Black Reign* (1993), *Order in the Court* (1998), *The Dana Owens Album* (2004), *Trav'lin' Light* (2007), *Persona* (2009). *Black Reign* was the first album by a female MC to go gold, and the single *U.N.I.T.Y.* earned the Grammy for Best Rap Solo Performance. Latifah has earned an additional four Grammy nominations as well.

Other Talents

Besides singing, Latifah also directed her talents toward acting. Early movie ventures included *Jungle Fever* (1991), *House Party 2* (1991), *Juice* (1992), *My Life* (1993), *Set It Off* (1996), and *Hoodlum* (1997). After guest appearances on *The Fresh Prince of Bel-Air*, Latifah starred in her own TV series, *Living Single*, which ran on Fox from 1993 to 1998. She also hosted *The Queen Latifah Show*, which ran in syndication from 1999 to 2001, and continues to make occasional guest appearances on other TV series.

After *Living Single* ended, Latifah turned her attention more fully to movies. Parts in *Sphere* (1998), *Living Out Loud* (1998), *The Bone Collector* (1999), and *Brown Sugar* (2002) led to her notable part in the movie musical, *Chicago* (2002), for which she earned nominations from the Screen Actors Guild and the Golden Globes for Best Supporting Actress.

Other movies followed, including *Bringing Down the House* (2003), *Scary Movie 3* (2003), *Taxi* (2004), *Barbershop 2: Back in Business* (2004), *Beauty Shop* (2005), *Stranger Than Fiction* (2006), *Last Holiday* (2006), *The Perfect Holiday* (2007), *Hairspray* (2007), *The Secret Life of Bees* (2008), *What Happens in Vegas* (2008), and *Mad Money* (2008). Latifah also starred in an HBO movie, *Life Support* (2007), for which she earned a Golden Globe Award, a Screen Actors Guild Award, and an Emmy nomination.

Recently, Latifah has also made forays into the realm of voice-overs. She has worked on several TV shows, such as *The Fairly Oddparents*, but she is perhaps best known for portraying Ellie the Mammoth in *Ice Age: The Meltdown* (2006) and *Ice Age: Dawn of the Dinosaurs* (2009). She has also penned a children's book, *Queen of the Scene* (HarperCollins, 2006), which sends a message of female empowerment to the younger generation.

Besides singing, acting, and writing, Latifah also discovers and manages other acts. Her management company, Flavor Unit Entertainment, was responsible for discovering Naughty by Nature and Outkast, among other acts.

Latifah's own career is still going strong. She has several movies premiering in 2010, and has appeared as a guest judge on *American Idol*. She also signed a deal with Grand Central Publishing to release a book in 2010, and her new fragrance, Queen, was launched in November 2009. She will continue in her role as spokeswoman for Cover Girl and Curvations, sending the message that all women are beautiful, no matter their race, size, or background.

See also: *American Idol*; Arts, Women in the (21st Century Overview); Celebrity Women; Film Actors, Female; Hip Hop; Stereotypes of Women.

Further Readings

Mizejewski, Linda. "Queen Latifah, Unruly Women, and the Bodies of Romantic Comedy." *Genders*, v.46 (2007).

Queen Latifah. http://www.queenlatifah.com/pages/home (accessed November 2009).

Queen Latifah. *Ladies First: Revelations of a Strong Woman*. New York: William Morrow, 1998.

Michelle M. Sauer
University of North Dakota

Queen Noor of Jordan

Prior to her marriage to King Hussein of Jordan in 1978, the woman who would become Noor al-Hussein, Queen of Jordan, was Lisa Halaby, an American urban planner working in Tehran. Born to a Swedish American mother, Doris Carlquist, and an Arab American father, Najeeb Halaby, in Washington, D.C., on August 23, 1951, Halaby's interest in politics was sparked by her father's work as a government official and by the prominence of the U.S. civil rights and peace movements. She was aware of the contrast between her privileged upbringing and the poverty of others. This contrast grew to define her work, even as her personal and professional life transformed completely.

After working in Tehran, Halaby intended to return to the United States to attend graduate school. Instead, after visiting Jordan, she accepted a job with her father's Jordanian aviation company. While in Jordan she met King Hussein, and on June 15, 1978, she exchanged her American identity to become Her Majesty Queen Noor.

Noor's immediate domestic responsibilities included raising King Hussein's children from previous marriages as well as their own four children. As Jordan's queen, Noor chaired a national task force for children and the National Committee for the International Year of the Child, established the first Arab Children's Congress, and initiated children's services and programs.

Noor's appreciation for the region's arts and culture culminated in her 1980 inauguration of the Jerash Festival for Culture and Arts and her support for the National Handicrafts Development Project. As a state leader, she broke with convention by wearing traditional dresses to official events, drawing national and international attention to Jordan's rich heritage while promoting the importance of sustainable economies for women in the region. Noor also challenged some of the gendered norms of her office. For example, she held *iftars*—evening meals when Muslims break their fast during the month of Ramadan—which are traditionally prepared by women for their husbands. Instead, Noor held these events for female friends, diplomats, associates, students, and representatives of organizations.

In addition to her efforts on behalf of women and children, Noor strived for a revised Western perception of the Arab world. Guiding reporters through the Jordanian camps for refugees from Kuwait and Iraq, campaigning to ban and remove landmines, and conducting speaking tours in the United States, Noor offered a perspective on life in the Middle East that was different from images commonly portrayed in Western news and entertainment.

In 1999, when King Hussein died from cancer, Noor assumed the responsibility of chairing the newly established King Hussein Foundation. Since then, Noor has served as an advisor to the United Nations, Seeds of Peace, and the International Campaign to Ban Landmines, and as an advisor, board member, or trustee for a number of other women's, refugee, environmental, and peace organizations. She also is currently president of United World Colleges, a global educational organization that brings students together from all over the world to foster peace and international understanding. Queen Noor has received numerous commendations and awards for her work, including honorary doctorates in law, international relations, and humanities. Her autobiography, *Leap of Faith: Memoirs of an Unexpected Life*, was a *New York Times* best seller and has been published in many languages.

See Also: Arab Feminism; Children's Rights; Council of Women World Leaders; Islam; Jordan; Peace Movement; Representation of Women in Government, International.

Further Readings

Fenton, Matthew McCann. "A Revealing Talk With the American Who Became Queen of Jordan." *Biography* (September 2003).

Noor, Queen. *Leap of Faith: Memoirs of an Unexpected Life*. New York: Miramax, 2003.

Noor Al Hussein Foundation. "Her Majesty Queen Noor." www.nooralhusseinfoundation.org/index.php?page r=end&task=view&type=content&pageid=80 (accessed December 2009).

Rompalske, Dorothy. "The All-American Girl Who Became Queen." *Biography* (September 1997).

Wright, J. W., Laura Drake, eds. Foreword by Queen Noor. *Economic and Political Impediments To Middle East Peace: Critical Questions and Alternative Scenarios*. New York: Palgrave Macmillan, 2000.

Emily Plec
Molly Mayhead
Western Oregon University

Queer Theory

Queer theory in North America grew in prominence in the early 1990s, having developed from gay and lesbian studies, which was an outgrowth of feminist studies and feminist theory in the mid-1980s. Feminist theory challenged the humanist notion of an essential, unique, and coherent self. It promoted the idea that identity is culturally constructed and inspired the shift in understanding from self to subject. The subject, as produced and constructed, is local, partial, provisional, and fluid.

Queer theory insists that all sexual behaviors—that is, all concepts linking sexual behaviors to sexual identities—and all categories of normative and deviant behaviors are socially constructed. It also rejects the idea that sexuality is biologically determined. Queer theory contends that sexuality is a constructed aggregate of social codes and influences, individual tastes and activities, and institutional power. These social constructions are dialectically informed by what is considered normative or deviant in particular cultural milieus. Prominent queer theorist Judith Butler suggests that sexuality is not just a construct but a performance, something that we do as in "doing gender" rather than thinking of sexuality and gender as innate aspects of a person. Cultural practices shape beliefs that sexualities are natural, essential, and biological; however, queer theory posits that sexualities are culturally bound and historically constructed.

The term *queer* is imbued with myriad meanings and cultural interpretations. Queer could be considered a "zone of possibilities" that defy clear articulation, as a definitive claim that queerness is antithetical to what it means to be "queer." Queer is paradoxically inclusive and exclusive. There are no definitive limits to what it means to be queer. Queer is both a noun and a verb: one is queer; one queers a text. Queer describes the spaces between; the liminal; and the mismatches between sex, gender, and desire. Queer theory contests heteronormative metanarratives and positions against compulsory heteronormativity.

"It Is Unqueer to Define Queer"

The theory seeks to destabilize heterosexuality by locating and questioning the inconsistencies in this category that have been taken for granted in their stability, unity, and coherence. Queer theory works against the trope of heterosexuality by making transparent the fragility and slippage in language. Because of this language slippage and the instability of categories, it is unqueer to define queer. Queer theory seeks to illustrate that sexuality is liminal, partial, and subjective. Queer theory contends that language is not a mirror of experience but produces experience in cultural and historical contexts.

Humanist traditions suggest that one becomes or develops into a self with a unique and coherent identity; queer theory contests unity and proposes that subjects are culturally produced and thus are unstable, nonunified, and in a constant state of unbecoming. Subjectivity, according to queer theory, could best be described as a culturally informed journey not an ahistorical or predetermined destination. Subjects are located in relation to others and within specific systems of power and knowledge that privilege specific ways of being, while delineating alternative ways of being as deviant and unintelligible. Intelligibility describes the operations of rendering subjects visible or invisible. Queer theory illuminates the intelligibility of heterosexuality as reflective of power relations and knowledge constructions that privilege heteronormative sexuality and opposite sex/gender relationships.

Queer theory proposes that identity and sexuality are not essential aspects of humanity and seeks to make transparent the ways that heterosexuality is propped up by homosexuality, since homosexuality is all that heterosexuality is not. Queer theory seeks not to determine sexuality but to show the ways that sexuality is determined by discursive operations of culture that privilege heterosexuality. Queer theory contests grand narratives and binaries that position man/woman, heterosexual/homosexual as exclusive categories. It argues against the stability of these categories as essential or fixed. Queer is thus antiheteronormative without fundamental logic or a consistent set of characteristics. Queer is whatever is at odds with the normal, the legitimate, the dominant. Queer is an identity without essence; queer contests what is normalized or naturalized within culture.

Queer theory promotes reflexivity rather than proposing stable ideals, fixed identity or subject position. The theory invites critical analysis of subjects in cultural and historical contexts. It contests homogenized identities and politicizes subjectivity as relational, contextual, and historical, arguing for the problematization of stable categories. Queer theory questions systems of oppression that naturalize particular regimes of truth and argues for investigations of sexuality and gender norms that are presumed to be intrinsic.

Queer theory can be used as a strategy to denaturalize heteronormative understandings of sex, gender, sexuality, social life, and all the relations between systems of power/knowledge. It politicizes sex, gender, and sexuality in ways that disrupt or make apparent the fractures in the notions of stable or fixed identities. Because gender, sexuality, and compulsory heterosexuality are so pervasive, queer theory promotes the need for constant deconstruction as a political imperative. Like poststructural feminism that promotes the politicization and contestation of language as reflective of meaning, queer theory invites challenges to the idea that language is a mirror of experience, identity, or sexuality. Queer theory allows for and invites contradictory understanding of sexuality and gender, disrupts definitive meaning making, and promotes the interrogation of identity as prefigured or categorical.

See Also: Coming Out; "Femininity," Social Construction of; Lesbians; LGBTQ; "Masculinity," Social Construction of, Sexual Orientation.

Further Readings

Jagose, Annamarie. *Queer Theory: An Introduction.* New York: New York University Press, 1996.

Klages, Mary. *Literary Theory: A Guide for the Perplexed.* New York: Continuum, 2006.

Sullivan, Nikki. *A Critical Introduction to Queer Theory.* New York: New York University Press, 2003.

Wilchins, Riki. *Queer Theory, Gender Theory: A Primer.* New York: Alyson Books, 2004.

Joani Mortenson
University of British Columbia, Okanagan

Quinceañeras

A quinceañera is the celebration of a Latina girl's 15th birthday. From the Spanish word *quince*, meaning "15," a quinceañera marks the end of a girl's childhood and entrance into adulthood and womanhood. The term *quinceañera* means both the celebration itself and the 15-year-old girl. For some families, the celebration of their daughter's 15th birthday is symbolic of a girl's freedom to date and her growing responsibilities as a young woman. Today, quinceañeras are celebrated throughout Latin America and the United States in cities with large numbers of Latino people.

Some scholars believe that a girl's 15th birthday was considered highly significant to the Aztec people who ruled present-day Mexico and parts of the western United States before the arrival of the Spanish in the early half of the 16th century, indicating that contemporary celebrations owe their origins to both indigenous and Spanish–Catholic influence. Scholars have indicated that at the age of 15, a young Aztec girl was old enough to marry; however, as scholars argue, a wedding celebration and quinceañera are not one and the same and hold different meanings to Latino people. It must also be noted that many nationalities make up the label *Latino*, and thus there is no single way a quinceañera is celebrated. The celebrations themselves reflect each family's way of interpreting this special day.

Although some contemporary quinceañeras may be more secularized than others, certain Roman Catholic elements, such as a Mass and blessing of the quinceañera, continue to be a part of many celebrations. Some Latino families have chosen to omit a religious ceremony from the celebration, instead organizing a reception with food, dancing, and music—not unlike many wedding festivities. Yet, although a Catholic wedding is symbolic of a couple's freedom to engage in sexual intimacy, a quinceañera for many Latinos represents the girl's commitment to sexual purity until marriage.

To symbolize each of her 15 years, the quinceañera will often have 15 other young girls, known as *damas*, accompany her, in addition to 15 male escorts, called *chambelanes*. However, some quinceañeras may choose to not have *damas* accompany the birthday girl, which attests to the variation and diversity of contemporary celebrations. In some celebrations, the Mass begins with the entrance of the 15 *damas* and *chambelanes*, followed by the quinceañera, who is walked down the church aisle by her father or a male relative. Because the ceremony is often marked by religious symbolism, the quinceañera may choose

A girl in a pastel gown celebrates her quinceañera, or 15th birthday, surrounded by some of her male escorts, called chambelanes. *For many, the celebration is symbolic of a girl's entrance into adulthood and womanhood.*

to wear a white gown to mark her purity, although it is becoming more common, and even fashionable, to wear pastel colors like pink or purple.

Although quinceañeras are celebrated in some fashion among Latino families, factors such as economics may influence a family's decision not to celebrate. An elaborate ceremony and party, for example, may cost a family up to $20,000. A large number of Latino families do not celebrate quinceañeras, which indicates that the meaning behind the celebration is not universal or monolithic but is fluid. In addition, some Latino families may choose to mark the 15th birthday in other ways, such as buying a special gift or having a more intimate family party rather than in the form of a ceremony or reception.

See Also: "Femininity," Social Construction of; Mexico; Purity Balls; Roman Catholic Church.

Further Readings

Alvarez, J. *Once Upon a Quinceanera: Coming of Age in the USA.* New York: Viking, 2007.

Cantu, N. E., et al. *Chicana Traditions: Continuity and Change.* Chicago: University of Illinois Press, 2002.

Castro, R. G. *Chicano Folklore: A Guide to the Folktales, Traditions, Rituals and Religious Practices of Mexican-Americans.* New York: Oxford University Press, 2001.

Cristina Herrera
California State University, Fresno

R

Rabbis, Female

In the last three decades, hundreds of women have chosen to become rabbis. This growth parallels and follows the demand for change in women's roles in public ritual life and family laws and is due to the profound impact of feminism, especially in North America. In English-speaking countries, women call themselves rabbis, but in countries such as Germany, the woman rabbi is referred to as *rabbina* and in Israel often as *rabba*. The Orthodox ABR (all but rabbis in name) refer to themselves as *maharat*, a newly coined term. Women rabbis' contribution has broadened the concept of Judaism and the image of women in general by providing female models of leadership.

In 1890, Ray Frank, the "Girl Rabbi of the Golden West," who was born in San Francisco in 1861, arranged services for the community in Spokane, Washington, on Yom Kippur of 1890. Since there was no rabbi, Frank was invited to preach. She studied at the Hebrew Union College, receiving a Bachelor of Hebrew Letters. In the 1920s, there were several women who entered seminaries with the intention of becoming rabbis, but all were refused ordination, including Helen Levinthal (1910–89), who became the first woman to complete the rabbinical course at Rabbi Isaac Meyer Wise's Jewish Institute of Religion in 1939.

The first known woman rabbi ordained privately in 1935 was Regina Jonas of Germany, who died in Aus-chwitz. In 1972, the first woman to be ordained by a theological seminary in the United States was Sally Preisand of the Reform Movement. In 1968, women were accepted into the Reconstructionist Rabbinical College, and Sandy Eisenberg Sasso was its first woman rabbi to be ordained in 1974. Amy Eilberg was already studying at Jewish Theological Seminary of America (JTSA) when women's ordination was approved and in 1985 became the first woman ordained as a rabbi by the Conservative Movement. The Orthodox movement in the United States does not ordain women, but in 2009, Sara Hurwitz received the title maharat (leader in *halachic*, spiritual and pastoral counseling, and in teaching Torah) after completing a rabbi's full curriculum of study.

Rabbinical Seminaries Ordain Women

In Israel, the rabbinical seminaries began ordaining women after much debate. Some felt that Israeli society was too traditional to stomach female leadership. The first conservative woman to be ordained by the Shechter Institute in 1993 was Valerie Stessin. At least four women served in pulpits in the *masorti* (Conservative) movement (in Beersheba, Omer, and two in Jerusalem). Yalta is a forum that works as a support group for Conservative female rabbis and students and advocates for greater recognition. There are more Reform rabbis in Israel since they began admitting women in 1986, and Naamah Kelman made history as the first woman in Israel to be ordained as a rabbi in 1992. Mimi Feigelson, Eveline Goodman-Thau, and Haviva Ner-David were privately ordained with Orthodox *semicha* (rabbinic ordination). Ner-David documented her journey in *Life on the Fringes: A Feminist Journey Toward Traditional Rabbinic Ordination* and identifies herself as a "post-denominational rabbi." In 2008, the modern Orthodox Shalom Hartman Institute of Jerusalem started a nondenominational program to prepare women and men for rabbinic ordination in order to train them as Jewish educators, not for pulpit positions.

Jacqueline Tabick was the first woman rabbi in Britain. She enrolled at the Progressive (Reform) Leo Baeck College, where she completed her rabbinical training in 1975. The Leo Baeck College has ordained more than 25 female students in 24 years. It trains rabbis to serve in Europe.

In the Reform movement, the discussion for decades revolved around whether or not it was seemly for a woman to preach from the pulpit. In the Conservative movement, the issues of a woman serving as prayer leader, or conducting weddings where she might serve as a witness, were taken into account. One of the biggest arguments against women serving as rabbis in non-Orthodox settings was that of *kevod ha-tzibbur* (the "honor of the community"). This argument suggests that women's participation casts shame on the males in the congregation by demonstrating superiority in knowledge over the ignorant males. Others interpret the term *kevod ha-zibbur* as an allusion to the sexual distraction posed by women to men. This sociological argument has been swept over by the new reality. Women are now actively participating in and leading religious activities such as daily prayer, the weekly public readings of the Torah, and teaching and studying the Torah. Women's roles are no longer peripheral in communal life. Even in the modern Orthodox world, women are separate but equal. There are still some halakhic objections to women rabbis, such as women serving as witnesses, but the major obstacles are social convention and "the weight of tradition."

The relationship between the rabbi and the congregant has changed with the coming of women to a relationship of greater closeness and greater informality. Women tend to stay in smaller communities, they are less interested in climbing the ladder from small to bigger congregations, and they form close relationships with the congregants they have. Many women rabbis prefer not to take pulpit positions and serve as educators, chaplains in hospitals, rabbis of day schools, and college campus rabbis. Some of them have senior positions in nonprofit organizations. The fact that women are redefining the pulpit impacts positively on their male colleagues, who often choose less competitive ways of life as well.

See also: Lesbian/Gay Clergy; Orthodox Judaism; Religion, Women in; Women's Ordination Conference.

Further Readings

Greenberg, S., ed. *The Ordination of Women as Rabbis.* New York: JTS, 1988.

Nadell, P. *Women Who Would Be Rabbis: A History of Women's Ordination 1889–1985.* Boston: Beacon Press, 1998.

Ner-David, H. *Life on the Fringes: A Feminist Journey Toward Traditional Rabbinic Ordination.* Needham, MA: JFL Books, 2000.

Wenger, B. "The Politics of Women's Ordination: Jewish Law." *Tradition Renewed: A History of the Jewish Theological Seminary (JTSA).* New York: JTSA, 1997.

Naomi Graetz
Ben Gurion University

Rachel's Network

Rachel's Network (RN) was established in 1999 by Winsome McIntosh with a grant from the McIntosh Foundation. McIntosh gathered a group of fellow women philanthropists who had committed at least $25,000 annually to environmental causes to form the "Founder's Circle" of the organization. The founders chose "Rachel's Network" as the name of their group to honor Rachel Carson (1907–64), whose book *Silent Spring* is credited with beginning the environmental movement in the early 1960s. Believing that collaboratively the group could be more effective than as individual voices, the founders determined to strengthen the representation of women on the boards of nonprofits, corporations, and government commissions and to use their power to protect the earth and the health of its citizens.

Seventeen women made up the original group. McIntosh served as president for the first 10 years. McIntosh brought to the job decades of experience on the board of the McIntosh Foundation, a family philanthropy established in 1949 by Josephine H. McIntosh, whose grandfather George Hamilton Hartford founded the Great Atlantic & Pacific Tea Company (later renamed A&P). In 2009, Lisa Renstrom, a former Sierra Club president and a trustee of her family's foundation, Bonwood Social Investments, succeeded McIntosh, who became board chair. By the time McIntosh stepped down as president, RN had more than 90 members. Among them were foundation presidents, board directors, businesswomen, and community leaders from across the United States and representing a range of political ideologies connected by their commitment to environmental causes and to the empowerment of women in shaping the policies that addressed those causes.

The diversity within the membership of RN allows the organization to use innovative ways of fostering collaboration even among unlikely partners. The Congressional Women's Networking Initiative provides resources and events that encourage women in Congress to work together in a nonpartisan, informal setting to solve environmental problems. RN has served, since 2005, in an unofficial capacity to connect leaders in the National Association of Evangelicals, for whom "Creation Care" has become an increasingly important issue, and in the environmental community. RN also founded as a separate organization Rachel's Action Network, a nonpartisan 501(c)(4) organization that promotes the engagement of women in the political process and campaigns for female candidates committed to environmental issues.

RN has also worked closely with the Environmental Working Group (EWG), funding studies for that research and advocacy organization. Eighteen members of RN and their families went beyond funding and volunteered to participate in a 2005 Body Burden test conducted by EWG. Researchers sampled the volunteers' blood and urine and analyzed them for toxic chemicals. Although RN member volunteers lived in various parts of the country, the study showed their toxic chemical load to be similar, with all of them testing positive for 60 percent of the 75 chemicals evaluated, including fire retardants, Teflon chemicals, fragrances, bisphenol A (found in plastics), and perchlorate—a rocket fuel ingredient. In 2007, RN funded a second EWG study that tested the umbilical cord blood of U.S. newborns. For the first time, synthetic fragrance chemicals were detected in cord blood, providing evidence that infants in the womb are contaminated with toxic chemicals used in cosmetics and other consumer products. Such studies help to build a case for improved regulation of controversial chemicals.

See Also: Ecofeminism; Environmental Activism, Grassroots; Environmental Issues, Women and; Philanthropists, Female.

Further Readings

Doheny, Kathleen. "Household Chemicals May Show Up in Blood." http://www.medicinenet.com/script/main/art.asp?articlekey=99927 (accessed March 2010).

MacGillivray, Alex. *Rachel Carson's Silent Spring (The Manifesto Series)*. Hauppauge, NY: 2004.

Rachel's Network. "What We Do." https://www.rachels network.org/whatwedo.php (accessed March 2010).

Wylene Rholetter
Auburn University

Rape, Cross-Culturally Defined

Defining rape is a complicated exercise as different definitions abound in legal, media, academic, and political discourses. Feminists are not in agreement on whether rape should be considered a sex crime or a crime of violence. A rigid definition has normative significance, so the definition of rape requires a degree of flexibility and contestation. That said, rape can be defined as the assault by a person involving sexual contact with another person without that person's consent. This definition is not explicit about the range of sexual contact or abuse involved, nor is it explicit about the gender of the survivor/victim and perpetrator. This ambiguity lends itself to a number of factors. For instance, this definition of rape is cautious not to explicitly identify perpetrators of rape as "men" as a result of the debates concerning the multiple forms of rape, including male-to-male rape. Additionally, the explicit identification of "men" as perpetrators bears the potential to individualize rape, rescinding responsibility for these acts of violence from the state or patriarchal cultural practices. On the other hand, some argue that gender neutrality regarding definitions of rape assumes that rape can be desexualized and that the social norms of heterosexist and patriarchal societies can automatically change. These assumptions are deeply flawed and potentially injurious to women.

Feminists have long labored for a legal definition of rape, and ongoing country-specific debates concerning the juridical definition of rape shed some insight into the complexity of a universally applicable definition of the term. The legal restrictions that regulate what does and does not constitute rape often depend on what does or does not appear to be an effect of violence. The term *rape* is implicitly linked with numerous and often-contested meanings and contestations about power, desire, morality, and justice and the legal laboring for a definition reflects the larger family, community, and generational debates concerning social norms and expectations. The multiplicity of definitions of rape reveal the differences between men's and women's understandings of what constitutes rape, and these understandings are influenced by other social factors, such as age, socioeconomic status, education, and the perceptions of a community's general vulnerability to crime. Legal definitions often differ across and within nations, particularly when nations have two or more legal frameworks. Legal definitions of rape are also often considered too narrow. Feminist interventions aim to highlight the socioeconomic, historic, political, and cultural contexts in which definitions of rape are produced.

Rape is a widespread international problem. Globally, acquaintance, date, and marital rape appear to be more common than stranger rape. Women and girls are at greater risk of being raped than boys and men. Rape statistics are heavily contested, due to underreporting and the crisis of defining rape in the first place. Rape is also a common feature of war violence, and evidence suggests that the rate of rape is higher in zones of armed conflict. Mass rape during wartime has been documented in Liberia, Uganda, Nicaragua, Japan, Peru, Cambodia, Somalia, Rwanda, Bosnia, Yugoslavia, Mozambique, and many other countries, and some would argue that rape is a feature of all armed conflict. The social context in which rape is perpetrated impacts upon the forms that it takes and the manner by which it is perceived. Due to the public and concentrated violence of mass rape in war, greater moral outrage is expressed, as compared to rape during peacetime. This violence is relegated to the private domain, discursively constructed as a symptom of dysfunctional relationships between individual men and women, and this privatization ultimately masks the social relations of power that create the conditions for violence against women.

There are several types of rape, including date rape, gang rape, marital or spousal rape, child sexual abuse, prison rape, male rape, war rape, and statutory rape. Victims/survivors of rape experience a range of consequences, including depression, guilt, anxiety, fear, sexual difficulties, and anger. Physical injuries may include sexually transmitted disease and human immunodeficiency virus and acquired immune deficiency syndrome (HIV/AIDS) and pregnancy, and depend on the context and range of physical violence of the assault. Social stigmas regarding rape are a common feature in many cultures and can result in suicide. Stigma and victim blaming are also reasons why victims/survivors of rape may not pursue criminal or other recourse.

Discourse on Rape

Feminist discourse has challenged the notion that rape is an act of nature, positing that it is in fact a mode through which male cultural power and domination are exercised, offering the notion of a "rape culture" or "rape cultures" as cultures in which systematic dominance and control of and over women are aspects of the practice and performance of masculinity, and that, ultimately, rape is implicitly condoned. If rape emerges out of specific structural, social, and cultural conditions, this raises questions concerning the universal applicability of theories of a "rape culture" in cross-cultural analysis. Northern, northern-biased, and southern feminists have argued that rape is a weapon of intimidation and one that functions to keep all women in a state of fear, with some degree of agreement. Some researchers argue that there are some cultures in which there is no rape or in which masculinities are "anti-rape," urging further investigations into these "non-rape cultures." Others reveal a concern with the proposition of a "rape culture," as it fails to capture the full myriad of hierarchical gendered relationships within and between different cultural contexts. Some argue that identifying perpetrators as "men" solely by their gender fails to account for the manner by which women are differently vulnerable to rape and also fails to fully account for the experiences of sexual violence in various social and cultural contexts. The complexity of a universal definition of rape can be ethically, theoretically, and practically paralyzing; however, for activists internationally organizing against rape, broad perspectives may be necessary.

Critical Race theorists and feminists in the United States query the degree to which black women have benefited from prevailing feminist interventions. For instance, media sensationalism of white women being raped by nonwhite men not only purports racist myths of "black peril" but also does little to reflect the reality that most women are raped by men of their own race and class. The rape of women of color, receiving much less attention and often being ignored outright, leaves the impression that women of color are not victims of rape. Identity politics in the case of feminist interventions concerning violence against women appears to depend upon a problematic elision of difference.

Racism and sexism function together to coproduce dominant discourses and definitions concerning rape. Examining the early common-law practice in which women alleging rape were asked to show how they resisted male advances and were in fact put on trial themselves, legal frameworks legitimized the good woman/bad woman dichotomy. Rape law reform measures did not appear to challenge or engage with historically produced and maintained narratives that are read onto black women's bodies, associating black femininity with hypersexuality and ultimately leading up to the oppression of black women in rape trials. Critical race feminists note that both feminist and antiracist agendas on the issue of rape are ineffective in politicizing the treatment of black women, offering intersectionality as a tool through which rape can be examined as a product of both racism and patriarchy.

International Debates and Definitions

There is no clear international law or agreement that defines rape or comprehensively deals with gender-based violence and violations, although rape is considered a crime against humanity in the Statute of the International Criminal Court and the Geneva Convention of 1949. Generally, international conventions take the view that cultural and traditional practices are often the cause of gender-based violence. The tenor of the United Nations conference on Women continued in this grain, with a series of recommendations for governments to reconcile the conflicts that arise between women and the harmful effects of traditional practices. This tenor created a rift between northern- and southern-based feminists, as those cultural practices presented as harmful and patriarchal were often cultural practices occurring in the global south. This led to accusations of a Western, objectifying, and homogenizing gaze from southern feminists, as these discourses seemed to suggest that women's rights and gender equality are characteristics of the Western world and Western culture. Furthermore, southern feminists argue that these conclusions failed to acknowledge the role of the combination of traditional patriarchies with the imposed colonial and postcolonial forms of patriarchy in and through which contemporary gendered cultural practices emerge in the world.

Analyzing national debates, one can observe the close relationship between discourses on cultural practice and legal definitions of and punishment for rape. Many countries have both a civil and customary framework. The result can be and is often a contradiction in regard to the meaning of women's rights. Many national constitutions claim to be committed to equality between men and women but also require that traditions be preserved. Oftentimes, it is when issues related to gendered cultural practices arise that calls for cultural preservation emerge. The "curative" rape of lesbians, for instance, is considered a practice intended to preserve "traditional" and normative sexualities in some countries.

The term *violence against women* aims to describe a spectrum of gender-based violence, paying particular attention to gender-based violence that disproportionately victimizes women and girls, such as sexual assault or rape. The term wishes to draw attention to the manner by which certain violence or violations are due to gendered or sexual stereotypes or expectations of masculinity and femininity, considering the intersections of race, class, ethnicity, religion, nationality, age, and inequality in shaping women's experience of violence and violations such as rape. Some theorists argue that violence against women is an insidious and invisible global war against women. National and international legal instruments declare that rape is illegal, yet most incidences of rape are ignored and unofficially condoned. This global war on women often becomes visible during wartime, as incidences of mass rape and "ethnic cleansing" come to the fore. International structures and laws prohibit rape in domestic and armed conflict; however, these provisions are infrequently enforced, reflecting national and international complicity with violence against women.

The term *gender-based violence* aims to locate rape within a continuum of sexed and gendered violence in the world by illuminating the conditions under which people become vulnerable to rape and how in these situations, being gendered "woman" or "man" holds particular significance in regard to who is injured, with what, and the manner by which rape is rationalized, legitimized, and normalized within different social contexts. The use of the terms *gender-based violence* and *violence against women* aims to place rape within an analytical and theoretical framework that emphasizes the complexity and plurality of violence. This violence and violations include the sexual abuse of children, sex trafficking, forced prostitution, forced pregnancy, female infanticide, female genital surgery, dowry burnings, and pornography. These forms of violence are mutually reinforcing, and these terms allow us to examine both the intersections and disjunctures of gendered violence.

See Also: Child Abuse, Perpetrators of; Child Abuse, Victims of; Children's Rights; Crime Victims, Female; Critical Race Feminism; Dating Violence; Domestic Violence; Gender Roles, Cross-Cultural; Global Feminism; Honor Suicides; Morrison, Toni; Pornography, Portrayal of Women in; Rape, Legal Definitions of; Rape and HIV; Rape in Conflict Zones; Sexual Orientation–Based Violence: Outside United States; Trafficking, Women and Children.

Further Readings

Allen, B. *Rape Warfare: The Hidden Genocide in Bosnia-Herzegovina and Croatia.* Minneapolis: University of Minnesota Press, 1996.

Brownmiller, S. *Against Our Will: Men, Women and Rape.* New York: Simon and Schuster, 1975.

Crenshaw, K. "Mapping the Margins: Intersectionalist, Identity Politics, and Violence Against Women of Color." *Stanford Law Review,* v.43/6 (1991).

Hill Collins, P. *Black Feminist Thought: Knowledge, Consciousness, and the Politics of Empowerment.* London: Routledge, 2000.

Jayawardena, K. and M. de Alwis. *Embodied Violence: Communalizing Women's Sexuality in South Asia.* London: Zed Books, 1996.

Mama, Amina. "Heroes and Villains: Conceptualizing Colonial and Contemporary Violence Against Women in Africa." In M. Alexander and C. Mohanty, eds., *Feminist Genealogies, Colonial Legacies, Democratic Futures.* London: Routledge, 1997.

McKinnon, Catherine A. *Towards a Feminist Theory of the State.* Cambridge, MA: Harvard University Press, 1989.

Moffett, Helen. "'These Women, They Force Us to Rape Them': Rape as Narrative of Social Control in Post-Apartheid South Africa." *Journal of Southern African Studies,* v.32/1 (2006).

Mohanty, C. "Under Western Eyes: Feminist Politics and Colonial Discourses." *Feminist Review* (1988).

Muholi, Z. "Thinking Through Lesbian Rape." *Agenda* (2004).

Peacock, D. and B. Khumalo. "'Bring Me My Machine Gun': Contesting Patriarchy and Rape Culture in the Wake of the Jacob Zuma Rape Trial." In Pumla Gqola, et al., eds., *Sexual Politics and Gender Relations: The Jacob Zuma ersus Khwezi Rape Trial in South Africa,* Tshwane: HSRC Press. http://www.genderjustice.org.za/resources/organisational-documents/sonke-gender-justice-network-capacity-statement/download-3.html (accessed November 2009).

Stiglmayer, A., ed. *Mass Rape: The War against Women in Bosnia-Herzegovina.* Lincoln: University of Nebraska Press, 1994.

Danai S. Mupotsa
Monash University

Rape, Incidence of

Rape is a violent crime that victimizes women worldwide. A 2001 World Bank report estimates that one in three women throughout the world has been raped or sexually assaulted. Rape incidents lead to trauma and involve physical violence and mental anguish associated with injury, pain, fear, and humiliation. Although public awareness and research on rape have increased in the past 30 years, measuring the extent and mag-

Underreporting of rapes by victims to law enforcement authorities is a troubling issue, and factors such as fear of the attacker, self-blame for being attacked, and embarrassment discourage victims from reporting rape.

nitude of rape incidents and their toll on victims remains difficult. Variations in research methodologies and definitions of rape complicate understanding rape's global impact.

In the United States, the FBI's Uniform Crime Reporting (UCR) Program distinguishes between forcible rape (rape by force) and statutory rape (rape without force). According to the UCR, forcible rape is "carnal knowledge of a female forcibly and against her will," which refers to sexual intercourse forced on a female of any age. Assaults and attempts to commit forcible rape are included in this category. Statutory rape refers to nonforcible rape involving females under the age of consent, who are not considered mature enough to understand and engage in consensual sex. Age of consent laws are meant to protect young people from being manipulated and sexually exploited by adults. While ages of victims are crucial in determining legality of consensual sex involv-

ing young women, ages of consent vary according to national laws.

In some societies, gender-biased legal systems make it almost impossible for women who report rape to authorities to validate their claims. For example, Islamic law requires rape victims to provide credible male witnesses. Muslim women who do not provide such witnesses are often charged with adultery. In some Latin American countries, such as Costa Rica, Peru, and Uruguay, penal codes permit rapists to be exonerated if they propose marriage to their victims and receive their consent.

Underreporting of rapes by victims to law enforcement authorities is another troubling issue. UCR estimates that about 89,000 women in the United States were forcible rape victims in 2008. However, these figures do not reflect actual numbers of rape victims. Factors such as fear of the attacker, self-blame for being attacked, and embarrassment discourage victims from reporting rape to police or taking legal action. Assumptions that rape is often committed by strangers who randomly seek out victims are also problematic. About 80 percent of all rapes in the United States are identified as incidents of date rape or forcible rape, committed by people the victims know as friends or as current or former intimate partners such as spouses and dates. Date rape occurs frequently in settings familiar to attackers and their victims, such as homes and college campuses. Given the nature of most relationships between victims and attackers, date rapes are less likely to be reported to police, compared with rapes by strangers.

Date rapes are also common in cultures outside the United States where traditional attitudes toward date rape tend to justify male actions. In Cambodia, nearly one-third of respondents in a demographic survey stated that refusing sex to husbands is not justified for reasons such as recent childbirth and knowing that husbands have human immunodeficiency virus and acquired immune deficiency syndrome (HIV/AIDS). In Papua New Guinea, almost half of the 95 women interviewed for a study said their husbands forced them to have sex.

International Scope of Rape

Armed conflicts in international or noninternational war zones are another arena where women are at risk for violence in the forms of rape, sexual abuse, abduction, and forced pregnancy. Rape is often used as a military weapon against women to undermine national, political, and cultural solidarity. In 1994, as many as one-half million Rwandan women were raped by Hutu soldiers during the period of genocide. Many of these Rwandan women were killed or took their own lives after being raped. Rwandan women who survived often suffered from HIV or from fear of HIV-infection, since many Hutu rapists were HIV-positive. Military rape is also associated with forced impregnation. In the early 1990s, Serbian soldiers carried out mass rapes of Muslim and Croatian women during ethnic conflicts in Bosnia-Herzegovina. To carry out ethnic cleansing, their attackers raped these women repeatedly until they became pregnant. In many cases, pregnant rape victims were detained until abortion was no longer an option.

Insufficient attention to rape's prevalence throughout the world makes understanding the long-term impact of rape on survivors difficult. Rape survivors suffer mental and physical trauma personally, but in patriarchal societies such trauma is blamed for undermining family cohesion. During the 1991 war between East Pakistan (now Bangladesh) and West Pakistan (now Pakistan), hundreds of thousands of Bangladesh girls and women were raped by Pakistani soldiers. After the war, many Bengali men rejected their wives and daughters who had been raped and sometimes impregnated by Pakistani soldiers. Bangladesh is an example of a society where sexual violence is regarded as shameful not just for its victims but also for their families. Instead of blaming male attackers, communities and families stigmatize female victims for loss of honor. Rape survivors endure hostility within and ostracization from their own societies. There are also concerns about HIV infection among rape survivors, since their attackers may have transmitted the virus. Transmission of HIV from HIV-infected mothers to succeeding generations is another problem, especially in countries with inadequate or minimal healthcare and medical treatments for HIV and AIDS patients.

See Also: Crime Victims, Female; Rape, Cross-Culturally Defined; Rape, Legal Definitions of; Rape and HIV; Rape Crisis Centers; Rape Trauma Syndrome; Sex Offenders, Female; Sex Offenders, Male.

Further Readings

Card, Claudia. "Rape as a Weapon of War." *Hypatia*, v.11/4 (Fall 1996).

George Mason University Sexual Assault Services. "Worldwide Sexual Assault Statistics." http://www.gmu .edu/depts/unilife/sexual/brochures/WorldStats2005 .pdf (accessed May 2010).

Kilpatrick, Dean G. "Rape and Sexual Assault." National Violence Against Women Prevention Research Center. http://www.musc.edu/vawprevention/research /sa.shtml (accessed December 2009).

Sharlach, Lisa. "Rape as Genocide: Bangladesh, the Former Yugoslavia, and Rwanda." *New Political Science*, v.22/1 (2000).

Tjaden, Patricia and Nancy Thoenners. "Extent, Nature, and Consequences of Rape Victimization: Findings From the National Violence Against Women Survey." U.S. Department of Justice. Office of Justice Programs, National Institute of Justice, January 2006. http://www .ncjrs.gov/pdffiles1/nij/210346.pdf (accessed May 2010).

U.S. Department of Justice. Federal Bureau of Investigation. "Crime in the United States, 2005." http://www.fbi.gov/ucr/05cius/offenses/violent_crime/forcible_rape.html (accessed December 2009).

U.S. Department of Justice. Federal Bureau of Investigation. "Crime in the United States, 2008." http://www.fbi.gov/ucr/cius2008/index.html (accessed December 2009).

U.S. Department of Justice. Federal Bureau of Investigation. "Uniform Crime Reporting Handbook, 2004 (revised date)." http://www.fbi.gov/ucr/handbook/ucrhandbook04.pdf#page=26 (accessed December 2009).

Ayako Mizumura
University of Kansas

Rape, Legal Definitions of

A recent United Nations report suggests that, on average, over 250,000 cases of rape or attempted rape are reported each year worldwide, while the U.S. Department of Justice estimates that nearly 200,000 incidents of rape or sexual assault occurred in 2005 in the United States alone. Because most rape victims are women, these data suggest that approximately one in six women in the United States become the victims of actual or attempted rape each year, excluding the countless rapes that go unreported. Although rape is a serious offense punishable by law, there exists no consensus regarding the precise definition of this crime. Legal definitions of rape vary from state to state and are subject to continual debate. Conflicting understandings of exactly what constitutes "rape" highlight the inevitable difficulties that arise in any attempt to legislate the sexual encounter. English common law defined rape as the carnal knowledge of a woman forcibly and against her will. In contemporary legal usage, rape generally refers to unwanted sexual intercourse that involves the use of force and the lack of consent. Yet there is widespread disagreement regarding the meanings of "penetration," "force," and "consent"—the primary elements of this legal definition.

Defining Rape

Disagreement also prevails with respect to the manner in which a rape victim is expected to behave or respond to the perpetrator. Women who dress a certain way or behave aggressively are often either blamed for or perceived to enjoy rape. In addition, a range of special conditions and circumstances necessarily modify the legal definition of rape. For example, sexual intercourse with a child under the age of 18 is considered statutory rape, as the child is legally regarded as unable to consent. Rape may also be found when a person has sex with someone deemed legally incapable of consenting due to mental illness, impairment, or intoxication. Other types of rape include acquaintance rape, spousal rape, prison rape, gang rape, incest, and rape during wartime. Despite the formal legal classification of rape as a criminal offense, many cases that seem to adhere to this legal definition are either not perceived as such or not prosecuted by their victims. Rape victims often fear that they will experience additional humiliation, exposure, and violation within the legal system. This leads to the phenomenon of underreporting, which thwarts official attempts to collect accurate data regarding the incidence of sexual assault. The growing use of date-rape drugs also impedes rape victims' ability to resist or recall unwanted sex. Collectively, these issues complicate the prosecution of rape charges within the U.S. legal system and compound the emotional, legal, and psychological implications of rape for survivors.

Etymologically, the word *rape* derives from the Latin verb *rapere*, to seize or take by force. The legal history of rape yields a complex and shifting patchwork of meanings rather than a linear progression of definitions. Under Roman law, rape was classified as a crime of assault. By late antiquity, rape was regarded instead as a crime against male property. Through this gradual transformation of meaning, rape came to be understood as an attack against the victim's husband or father and as a crime that devalued women through their presumed loss of virginity.

Since the 1970s, feminist scholars have sought to expose the masculinist biases of these historical as well as contemporary definitions of rape. Noteworthy are the efforts of Susan Brownmiller, Andrea Dworkin, Catherine MacKinnon, Sharon Marcus, and Susan Estrich to demystify rape as a crime of power and control rather than one motivated solely by sexual desire or passion. Through their scholarship and legal activism, these and other scholars have consistently exposed the masculinist underpinnings of traditional notions of penetration, force, and consent.

They have also critiqued the popular characterization of rape victims as "damaged goods" as well as the primacy of penetration to legal definitions of rape. The women's liberation movement of the 1970s also led to the establishment of the first rape crisis centers in the United States.

Rape Versus Sexual Assualt

Although rape is closely related to sexual assault, state laws often distinguish between the two with respect to the details of penetration. While some jurisdictions explicitly define "rape" as an act that involves penile penetration of the vagina, other jurisdictions define all nonconsensual sex as rape. Similarly, some legal definitions of rape encompass oral sex, masturbation, and penetration with any foreign object, including, but not limited to, the penis. Other definitions of rape are gender specific. In Scotland, for example, male rape was not officially recognized as a form of "rape" until 2009. Similarly, Brazil narrowly defines rape as nonconsensual vaginal sex. As a result, nonconsensual male, oral, and anal sex are not recognized as "rape," contrary to prevalent European and American definitions. These definitional distinctions have important implications for whether or not certain forms of rape, such as gay and lesbian rape, will "count" as rape and be recognized as such under the law. Penetration-based definitions of rape are especially consequential in specific national and cultural contexts. Until 2006, for example, Pakistan's Hudood Ordinance required four male witnesses to attest to a woman's penetration in order to establish the occurrence of rape.

Debates about the precise nature and degree of force involved in rape also contribute to ongoing ambiguities of definition. Yet perhaps the most controversial aspect of contemporary legal definitions of rape is the notion of consent. What exactly does it mean to "consent" to sexual intercourse, and what happens when initial consent is subsequently withdrawn? In an effort to resolve these questions following a surge of acquaintance rape on campus, Antioch College drafted a Sexual Offense Prevention Policy in 1993. The objective of Antioch's policy was to highlight the imperative to obtain and recognize consent in every step of the sexual encounter. Although this effort attracted nationwide ridicule, it nonetheless highlighted the importance of subjecting familiar concepts to ongoing efforts of critical inquiry.

Rape in War

Legal definitions of rape have proven no less controversial in the international sphere. Rape myths continue to inform understandings of rape worldwide, as in South Africa, Zambia, and Nigeria, where common belief holds that sexual intercourse with a virgin will cure a man of human immunodeficiency virus and acquired immune deficiency syndrome (HIV/AIDS). For centuries, rape has been used as an instrument of war. Japanese soldiers raped approximately 80,000 women during the Nanking Massacre. Rape was a common practice in Japanese "comfort stations" during World War II, where thousands of women, most of whom were Korean, were coerced into various forms of sexual servitude.

The International Criminal Tribunal for the former Yugoslavia similarly confirmed rape as a crime against humanity in 2001 and thereby challenged mainstream understandings of rape as an inevitable by-product of war. Hopefully, these significant efforts to redefine and bring new visibility to the crime of rape in the international sphere will gradually arrest ongoing campaigns of mass rape in places like Darfur and the Democratic Republic of Congo.

In the context of armed conflict including war, rape has been defined within the international community as a crime against humanity and an integral component of genocide if it is part of a widespread or systematic practice. Serbian soldiers raped at least 20,000 Bosnian Muslim women in mass rape camps during the Bosnian civil war in conjunction with a military campaign of ethnic cleansing. Rape was first recognized as a crime against humanity in 1992, when the International Criminal Tribunal for the former Yugoslavia issued arrest warrants on the basis of the systematic and widespread gang rape of Muslim women by Bosnian Serb soldiers. A major breakthrough in international women's human rights law came in 1998 in response to atrocities in Rwanda, where the International Criminal Tribunal for Rwanda found that systematic rape had been used as a means of forced pregnancy and a tool of genocide during the protracted civil war. The International Criminal Tribunal for Rwanda found that the systematic rape of Tutsi women was a deliberate strategy within the Rwandan genocide. An estimated half million women were raped during the 1994 Rwandan genocide. A few years later, in 2001, the International Criminal Tribunal for the former Yugoslavia similarly defined rape as a crime against humanity.

In the Democratic Republic of Congo, where the prevalence of rape is described as the worst in the world, analysts also define rape as a weapon of war. Despite increased public awareness of the widespread use of rape in the Congo, rape has continued at a staggering rate. In 2006, Congo's parliament passed a law on sexual violence that broadened the legal definition of rape and increased the penalties against it. Yet enforcement of the new law has been weak and has led to the convictions of no senior military officers or commanders.

Today, mass rape—often instigated by military officers—is endemic in the Darfur region of Sudan. Yet rape victims lack legal recourse, as the government is more likely to prosecute those who report and document the crime of rape than those who commit it. Sudanese laws, regulations, and customs offer inadequate measures with which to address rape in the region. In particular, Sudan's legal definitions of rape often expose victims to further abuse. Rape is defined as the offense of *zina*, or intercourse between a man and a woman who are not married to one another.

Blurred Boundaries

This legal definition effectively blurs the boundaries between sex and rape. If a woman voices a rape accusation in the Sudan, she herself may be charged with *zina* because she has confessed to an act of extramarital sex. Unmarried women convicted of *zina* in the Sudan receive 100 lashes; married women are sentenced to death by stoning. In 2001, two women were sentenced to death by stoning for committing adultery. If a woman chooses to prosecute for rape, many judges require the sexual act to have been witnessed by four competent men—evidence that is extremely difficult to obtain. It is virtually impossible to prosecute rape in the Sudan because Sudan grants immunity to individuals with government affiliations, including military officers. Within this climate, few women come forward to report rape or to access vital medical, legal, and psychosocial services.

The precise acts and organs associated with rape vary across jurisdictions as well as national and cultural borders. Some jurisdictions define "rape" exclusively as penile penetration of the vagina. For example, rape in Brazil is defined as nonconsensual vaginal sex. As a result, male rape, anal rape, and oral rape are defined not as rape, but as a violation of modesty (*atentado violento ao pudor*).

Although rape is defined primarily in relation to lack of consent within adversarial legal systems, the International Criminal Tribunal for Rwanda, in its landmark 1998 ruling, used a definition of rape that did not explicitly use the word *consent*. Instead, it described rape as "a physical invasion of a sexual nature committed on a person *under circumstances which are coercive.*"

Rape in Marriage

Historically, marriage has been construed as a form of implicit consent to sexual intercourse. Today, however, nations are increasingly contesting this understanding of marriage as a defense to rape. Most nation-states now formally recognize rape in the context of marriage.

Pakistani law defines rape as sexual intercourse in the absence of a valid marriage and without the consent of the victim. Pakistani law does not recognize marital rape as a criminal offense. Yet sexual intercourse with a girl under the age of 16 is always construed as rape, whether or not she is a consenting partner. Female victims of rape are ostracized in Pakistani society, where rape is traditionally perceived as a source of dishonor to the victim's family.

In France, rape is defined as any act of sexual penetration committed against another person using violence, restraint, threats, or surprise. Although the law mandates up to 20 years in prison for rape, the average punishment for rapists is six years in prison. The General Civil Penal Code of Norway (2000) expansively defines rape to include a broader spectrum of unwanted sex, including sexual activity by means of violence or threat, or sexual activity with a person who is unconscious or otherwise incapable of resisting. Following conviction, rapists in Norway may be imprisoned for a maximum of 10 years. Longer sentences apply in the case of prior convictions, extreme brutality, gang rape, and serious injury or death of the victim.

Whereas countries like the United States with adversarial legal systems define rape in relation to the absence of consent, investigative systems define rape in terms of force. Yet both of these legal definitions have evolved significantly over the past decade or so. States have increasingly defined rape as a gender-neutral offense and have broadened their legal definitions to include male rape. Norway recently convicted a woman of rape (2005) after she performed oral sex on a man who was asleep on a sofa in her apartment. Norwegian government officials explained that amendments to the legal definition of rape in 2000 permitted more expansive interpretations of "unwanted sexual contact." Other states have similarly expanded their legal definitions of rape by opening them up to include multiple forms of penetration.

See Also: Crime Victims, Female; Rape, Cross-Culturally Defined; Rape in Conflict Zones; Violence Against Women Act.

Further Readings

Estrich, Susan. *Real Rape*. Cambridge, MA: Harvard University Press, 1987.

MacKinnon, Catharine. "Rape: On Coercion and Consent." In Katie Conboy, ed., *Writing on the Body: Female Embodiment and Feminist Theory*, New York: Columbia University Press,1997.

Stetz, Margaret. "Wartime Sexual Violence Against Women: A Feminist Response." In Katie Conboy, ed., *Writing on the Body: Female Embodiment and Feminist Theory*. New York: Columbia University Press, 1997.

Karina Eileraas
University of California, Los Angeles

Rape, Prosecution Rates of

Rape Prosecution Rates are often used to judge how well a particular justice system is combating the crime of rape by measuring how many rapists have been prosecuted. It is, however, important to distinguish among unreported claims of rape; reported claims of rape, which sometimes never go to trial; prosecution rates; and actual conviction rates. The vast majority of these rape cases are perpetrated by adult heterosexual males, and most victims or survivors are women.

Rape prosecution and conviction rates are very low worldwide; research from the United Kingdom, United States, Canada, Ghana, and Sweden has shown that the number of women reporting rape to

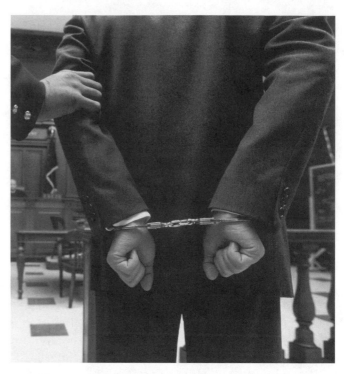

The vast majority of rape cases are perpetrated by adult heterosexual males, and most victims or survivors are women.

the authorities is usually below 10 percent. Sometimes crimes go completely unreported, as in the Ghana National Survey. The number of rapists finally convicted is usually a very small percentage of those who are identified and/or tried in court, and though prosecution and conviction rates vary internationally, worldwide attrition is endemic.

The failure to properly prosecute rape cases and convict rapists tends to be attributed to two factors: the prevalence of "rape myths" in public opinion and the judicial system;,and the intimidating tactics of defense teams in rape cases, which refocus both the judge's and jury's attention on the moral fiber of the rape survivor rather than on the rapist. The situation is slightly different when rape is tried as a war crime, or a crime against humanity, though rates of prosecution and conviction are still low.

Factors like the race, age, and job of the perpetrator and of the victim are significant in rape cases. In the United States, black men are far more likely to be convicted of rape than white men, and, historically, in the West, working-class and black survivors of rape have been far more likely to be disbelieved than their middle-class or white counterparts. Juries can be influenced by the victim's presented character, behavior, and possible drug or alcohol use. In a British poll conducted by Amnesty International in 2006, substantial numbers of respondents blamed the survivor for her own rape if she was drunk (37 percent), if she was wearing sexy or revealing clothing (26 percent), or if she had many sexual partners (22 percent). Juries are more likely to find a rapist guilty in cases where the assailant is a stranger, when a weapon is used, or when the rape survivor is physically injured. All of these responses reveal the power of rape myths surrounding women's consent to sexual acts.

Prosecuting Rape

Prosecution of rape cases often depends on the ability of the rape survivor to testify in a convincing manner. This can be extremely difficult, however, in the face of hostile defense legal strategies like "whacking," where the defense lawyer seeks to intimidate and humiliate the survivor to discredit her (or him). Such strategies reframe the rape as a pornographic scenario in which the survivor becomes a participating and willing agent, or the survivor's character is disparaged via histories of substance or alcohol abuse, sexual trauma, shoplifting, or mental illness. The main aim is to destroy, in the jury's mind, the image of moral purity that the rape survivor needs to be a reliable witness.

While some women feel too ashamed to report rapes, the ability of the authorities to prosecute and convict rapists is questionable. Strategies for combating the failure to convict rapists are being developed; these strategies include employing specialist police teams, improving the quality of medical investigation in rape cases, clarifying the law on consent, and using expert psychological evidence that clarifies the responses of the rape survivor for the jury. Within the Anglo-Saxon model of adversarial justice, rape survivors have been known to win rape cases, even when they do not fit the feminine ideal of the cautious, sensible, middle-class housewife. These winning cases succeed mainly because of strong witness testimony and when rape survivors stand up to cross-examination and probing questions and continue to maintain their nonconsent. The Anglo-Saxon model may, however, be inadequate for rape cases, and some experts have suggested adopting instead a kind of community justice to work alongside the retributive mode.

Beyond the context of the individual rape case, it is extremely significant that rape can now also be prosecuted as a war crime, as decreed by the Geneva Convention. This was in response to the systematic rape and impregnation of mainly Muslim women by Serbian soldiers in Bosnia-Herzegovina during the Serbian-Croatian conflict in the former Yugoslavia. The International Criminal Tribunal for Rwanda first convicted a subject accused of rape as a crime against humanity in 1998, swiftly followed by the International Criminal Tribunal for the former Yugoslavia in 2001. The Yugoslavia Tribunal also expanded the term *slavery* to include sexual slavery. The prosecution rates in these cases, however, are far lower than the number of actual rapes committed in war would warrant.

See also: Rape, Incidence of; Rape, Legal Definitions of; Rape in Conflict Zones; Violence Against Women Act.

Further Readings

Amnesty International. "Sexual Assault Research." http://www.amnesty.org.uk/news_details.asp?NewsID=16618 (accessed February 2010).

Bourke, Joanna. *Rape: Sex, Violence, History*. Berkeley, CA: Shoemaker Hoard, 2007.

Child and Women's Studies Abuse Unit. "Attrition Rates." http://www.cwasu.org/page_display.asp?pageid=STATS&pagekey=35&itemkey=39 (accessed February 2010).

Koss, Mary P. "Blame, Shame and Community: Justice Responses to Violence Against Women." *American Psychologist*, v.55/11 (2000).

Larcombe, Wendy. "The 'Ideal' Victim V Successful Rape Complainants: Not What You Might Expect." *Feminist Legal Studies*, v.10.2 (2002).

Zoë Brigley Thompson
University of Northampton

Rape and HIV

Gender violence and the human immunodeficiency virus (HIV) are two of the major social and health problems affecting women worldwide. HIV is the virus that causes aquired immune deficiency syndrome (AIDS). HIV destroys the white blood cells (CD4 cells, also known as T cells) that the immune system requires to fight disease. AIDS is the final stage of HIV infection, and it is diagnosed when CD4 cell counts fall below 200. HIV infection can initially produce no symptoms, and some people remain asymptomatic for years before developing AIDS. HIV is transmitted through bodily fluids, such as blood, semen, vaginal secretions, or breast milk. The burden of the worldwide HIV pandemic has disproportionately fallen on the developing world. Africa has been hit the hardest; approximately 75 percent of all women living with HIV today reside in sub-Saharan Africa. Women are at a greater risk of HIV transmission through heterosexual intercourse than men. Today, women constitute about half of an estimated 31.3 million adults living with HIV and AIDS, and AIDS is the third-leading cause of death for women, behind cancer and heart disease.

Gender violence is an umbrella term that includes a host of violations that are predominantly committed by men and against women. Gender violence occurs worldwide. Studies have consistently demonstrated a clear link between gender violence and HIV. Rape is a particular kind of gender violence. Legal definitions of rape vary from state to state and from country to country, as well as within international law. Most generally, rape is defined as nonconsensual sexual interaction. Definitions of rape typically involve the concept of penetration. Sexual assault is a broader term that includes various forms of sexual interaction. Within international law, definitions of rape often employ the concept of invasion, which is intended to be gender-neutral. When committed as part of a widespread or systematic attack against civilians, rape and sexual assault can be considered crimes against humanity. When women and girls are targeted because of their inclusion in a particular national, ethnic, racial, or religious group, rape and sexual assault can be used as a tool of ethnic cleansing and genocide. In some cases, genocidal regimes have deployed HIV-positive men as rapists to intentionally infect women and girls from the targeted national, ethic, racial, or religious group.

The risk of contracting HIV through rape is unknown. Although rape and sexual assault increase a woman's vulnerability to HIV infection, the probability of contracting HIV through a single sexual interaction is actually quite low. However, the structural inequalities that underlie gender violence have a profound effect on the relationship between rape and HIV. In addition to contracting HIV through nonconsensual sex with an infected partner, women may be infected through other forms of gender violence. For example, gender inequality may limit a woman's ability to negotiate HIV-preventative behaviors, such as condom use, during sexual interactions. Along these lines, many married women and women in long-term monogamous relationships become infected as a result of unfaithful partners. In addition, risk of physical and sexual violence, as well as other harmful outcomes, increases when women disclose HIV-positive status to their partners.

Taking antiretroviral medication (ARV), also called postexposure prophylaxis (PEP), after rape or sexual assault may reduce the risk of HIV transmission. However, these medications must be administered as soon as possible after the assault, and they are no longer effective if more than 72 hours have passed. The medications must be taken every day for 28 days, and they may cause side effects, including headaches, nausea, and stomach problems.

See Also: HIV/AIDS: Africa; Rape and HIV; Rape, Cross-Culturally Defined; Rape, Legal Definitions of.

Further Readings

Brownmiller, S. *Against Our Will: Men, Women and Rape.* New York: Simon and Schuster, 1975.

Kim, Julia C., Lorna J. Martin, and Lynette Denny. "Rape and HIV Post-Exposure Prophylaxis: Addressing the Dual Epidemics in South Africa." *Reproductive Health Matters*, v.11/22 (November 2003).

Stetz, Margaret. "Wartime Sexual Violence Against Women: A Feminist Response." In Katie Conboy, ed., *Writing on the Body: Female Embodiment and Feminist Theory.* New York: Columbia University Press, 1997.

Jenna Appelbaum
New York University

Rape Crisis Centers

Historically, feminists in various parts of the world establish rape crisis centers to cater to the specific needs of rape victims/survivors, ranging from immediate support services to long-term goals to change the unequal social relations between men and women. Currently, rape crisis centers have also advertised their services to cater to sexually abused males. Nonetheless, females are more at risk for sexual assault, and they remain the main clients.

While initially rape crisis centers rely on the fundraising efforts of its founders, which include securing grants from the government, the advocacy work has resulted in allocations for services to sexual assault victims provided for by law in certain countries. In the United States, the Violence Against Women Act (VAWA) of 2005 includes provisions for rape crisis centers to support direct services to adult and minor sexual assault victims as well as their family and household members. On the other hand, in the Philippines, the law mandates the creation of rape crisis centers in every province and city by a partnership between government agencies and nongovernmental organizations. Budgetary allocations are also channeled under the law to the various government agencies involved, for example, the Social Welfare Department.

Immediate Support Services

Sexual assault is a traumatic event for its victims, even in cases where there are no physical injuries. The victim may suffer from rape trauma syndrome, which impacts him or her emotionally, physically, and even financially. In cases of sexual assault, the cards are also stacked against the victim, as there is a tendency to blame women for "inviting" rape by the way they dress and behave. Similarly, minors who are sexually assaulted may find it difficult to be believed because it is their word against an adult's. Typically, the sexual assault victim may blame herself/himself for being raped. Since sexual assault is a medico-legal case, it becomes more complicated, as the victim will have to deal with the legal system as well.

With a vision to heal and lessen the trauma experienced by sexual assault victims, rape crisis centers offer immediate support services to empower and convey the message that the victim is never at fault for being sexually assaulted. However, the range of immediate support services differs from one rape crisis center to another. In cases where a particular service is not offered, the rape crisis center will provide referrals. These support services provide emotional support and information through telephone hotlines as well as online hotlines in this Internet age, face-to-

face counseling, and support groups. Because understanding and support from family members and friends are necessary for sexual assault victims and because they are also impacted, support programs are in place for them. For sexual assault victims who are alcohol and/or drug dependent, there is a specific program to cater to their needs.

When needed, rape crisis centers have personnel to accompany sexual assault victims through the medico-legal process, which includes treatment and documentation of any injury and collection of forensic evidence. Sexual assault victims are also mentally and emotionally prepared for what to expect in a trial and, when necessary, are accompanied through the court process. In addition, emergency shelters are available for those who need it. In the provision of these immediate support services, rape crisis centers strive to be inclusive, with services available in different languages. The particular needs of the client—whether due to disability, ethnicity, religion, class, sexual orientation, or displacement—are also considered to ensure effective delivery of services.

Education, Advocacy, and Networking for Change

The educational dimension of rape crisis centers has three main components. First, it works toward increasing awareness among the public of the facts of sexual assault cases and debunks the myths. Some of the facts are that men can control their sexual urges if they exercise their choice to do so and that not only women who are sexily dressed are raped; women who are decently dressed, children, and the elderly have been targets for sexual assault perpetrators. These facts question the tendency to blame the victim in crimes of a sexual nature and direct the responsibility back to whom it belongs—the rapist who committed the crime. In other words, there is awareness rising to change public opinion and garner support for sexual assault victims. Sexual assault victims are encouraged to come forward and report the incidence of rape rather than feeling ashamed or guilty and enduring the violation in silence.

Second, the educational dimension focuses on prevention. Among the information provided are precautionary measures for safety, what to do in the event of an attack, self-defense classes, and esteem-building programs. Specifically, for children there are educational programs for differentiating between a "good" and a "bad" touch and where they can get help if sexually abused. There is also a program on Internet safety for parents and older children to guard against pedophiles on the prowl on networking sites such as MySpace and Facebook. Third, the educational dimension focuses on gender-sensitized services and policies to lessen the trauma experienced by sexual assault victims as they go through the medical process and the legal system. Personnel from rape crisis centers are part of the resources to facilitate an understanding of the dynamics of rape and related ethical issues not only for their new staffs and volunteers but also for other service providers in the medical and the legal systems.

Complementing the educational dimension are advocacy and networking. Rape crisis centers are typically part of a network to campaign and lobby government to enact and amend policies and laws so that they are sensitive to the needs of sexual assault victims. Consequently, there are now sexual assault units in place in hospitals and police departments to handle such cases.

Furthermore, in some countries like Bangladesh, Canada, Malaysia, Namibia, South Africa, Thailand, and the United Kingdom, the concept includes establishing the one-stop center (even though it may be named differently) for sexual assault victims. At the one-stop center, typically located at hospitals, sexual assault victims have access to medical services; counseling; and, should they choose to report it, the police. Follow-up services related to pregnancy and sexually transmitted diseases, including human immunodeficiency virus and acquired immune deficiency syndrome (HIV/AIDS), are also provided. Advocacy and networking are also important for rape crisis centers to highlight best practices, pool resources for research to support advocacy work, and respond collectively to practices that work against the interest of sexual assault victims.

Both the immediate support services and long-term nature of educational and advocacy activities aim to lessen the stigma of rape and to increase the incidence of reporting as well as the prosecution and conviction rates of rape casaes. The broader vision of the rape crisis center is to have a violence-free society where both females and males can live in an environment that fosters respect for each other's bodies and spaces.

See Also: Crime Victims, Female; Rape, Incidence of; Rape, Prosecution Rates of; Rape and HIV; Rape Trauma Syndrome.

Further Readings

Pittman, Karen J. *The Internal Dynamics of Rape Crisis Centers.* Baltimore, MD: Urban Institute, 1984.

Scott, Ellen Kaye. "How to Stop the Rapist? A Question of Strategy in Two Rape Crisis Centers." *Social Problems,* v.40/3 (1993). www.jstor.org/stable/3096884 (accessed November 2009).

Zilber, Tammar B. "Institutionalization as an Interplay between Actions, Meanings, and Actors: The Case of a Rape Crisis Center in Israel." *Academy of Management Journal,* v.45/1 (2002).

Suat Yan Lai
University of Malaya

Rape in Conflict Zones

Rape in conflict zones is a weapon of war that is used to degrade, humiliate, and dehumanize civilian populations. History demonstrates that sexual violence during times of war is not a new phenomenon. However, the recent conflicts in Bosnia-Herzegovina, Rwanda, the Democratic Republic of Congo, Darfur, Liberia, and other parts of the world have brought increasing attention to the ways in which rape is used as a weapon of terror and, consequently, represents a barrier to peace.

During times of conflict, some military leaders encourage the use of sexual violence as a military strategy intended to increase the morale of troops, to demoralize the enemy, and to lay claim to the "spoils of war" (in this case, the women of the enemy). Although rape is the most common form of such violence, other forms may include forced prostitution, sexual slavery, forced sterilization, and forced impregnation. Perpetrators are typically armed military personnel; however, it is not uncommon for enemy civilians and even those charged with protecting and providing aid to civilian populations to commit rape during times of war. Women and girls are most often the victims—although men and boys may also be affected, particularly those who are prisoners of war—and targeted not only because they are female but often because of their race, ethnicity, or religious affiliation.

Rape may be committed by an individual or by groups (gang rape). It may involve vaginal or anal intercourse; it may also involve the use of objects such as guns, knives, sticks, bottles, or pipes. It is common for a woman to be raped in front of family members or members of her community as a means of terrorizing both the woman herself and those forced to witness the rape. After raping a woman, and in an effort to inflict as much physical damage as possible, some perpetrators will discharge a gun into the woman's vagina. Perpetrators may also kill victims after raping them. Some rapes are committed with the express intent of impregnating victims (who then may be forced to continue the pregnancy to term) or infecting them with HIV or other sexually transmitted diseases. Rape victims in conflict zones range in age and may include infants, adolescents, adult women, and the elderly. Victims suffer physical and psychological harm, both immediately and long term. They are often stigmatized within their communities and punished for adultery or for having sexual relations outside of marriage. Perpetrators are rarely brought to trial or punished.

International bodies (such as the United Nations) and nongovernmental organizations have attempted to address the issue of rape in conflict zones in a variety of ways. Key strategies include prevention, increasing awareness, providing additional support and services for victims, and strengthening laws in an attempt to bring perpetrators to justice. Such efforts have helped to draw attention to sexual violence as a war crime, a threat to security, a form of torture, and an act of genocide. Still, the cultural stigma and silence that continues to surround rape and other forms of sexual violence has meant that such efforts have had limited effect.

See Also: Conflict Zones; Prostitution in Combat Zones; Rape, Incidence of; Rape, Legal Definitions of; Rape and HIV; Sexually Transmitted Infections; United Nations Development Fund for Women; Violence Against Women Act.

Further Readings

Barstow, Anne Llewellyn, ed. *War's Dirty Secret: Rape, Prostitution, and Other Crimes Against Women.* Cleveland, OH: Pilgrim Press, 2001.

Carpenter, R. Charli. *Born of War: Protecting Children of Sexual Violence Survivors in Conflict Zones.* Bloomfield, CT: Kumarian Press, 2007.

Greer, Gill. *Rape: The Oldest and Newest War Crime.* http://www.ippf.org/NR/exeres/AD977915-0C90-4 BFB-90EE-27D4DEBC704B.htm (accessed June 2010).

Nordland, Rod. "More Vicious than Rape." *Newsweek,* (November 13, 2006). http://www.newsweek.com /id/44653/page/1 (accessed June 2010).

United Nations. "Stop Rape Now: UN Action Against Sexual Violence in Conflict." http://www.stoprapenow .org (accessed June 2010).

Jillian Duquaine-Watson
University of Texas at Dallas

Rape Trauma Syndrome

Rape trauma syndrome (RTS) includes the acute or immediate phase of disorganization following rape; an intermediate and often superficial appearance of adjustment; and a long-term, nonlinear process of reorganization typically including flashbacks and periods of regression. RTS was first identified in two phases by Ann Burgess and Lynda Holmstrom, who found physical and emotional reactions to a life-threatening experience to characterize the acute phase and lifestyle changes, such as moving and job switches, along with sleep disturbances and generalized phobias to characterize the reorganization phase.

Rape Crisis Movement

In the 1970s and 1980s, a rape crisis movement brought RTS to public awareness through education and advocacy aimed at increased reporting and countering public stereotypes and self-recriminations associated with rape. Community centers with trained volunteers helped victims cope with the criminal justice system and work toward reorganization of their lives. Public education placed blame for rape on the perpetrator and on a society that engenders a rape culture. Lectures, magazine articles, films, and public service announcements were aimed at building public support and understanding among family and intimates who often wanted nothing more than for the victim to put the rape behind her and move on with her life.

The media disseminated information and publicity surged as researchers, clinicians, and criminal justice practitioners studied rapists, rape victims, and the social, psychological, and legalistic aspects of rape. As the rape crisis movement achieved a degree of success and feminists took up other causes, both publicity and interest in rape waned by the early 1990s, leading some to conclude prematurely that the problem was solved.

The concept of a rape trauma syndrome has its roots in crisis theory, defining a crisis as: (1) a hazardous, threatening event; (2) an inability to respond with adequate coping mechanisms; and (3) temporary disruption of one's typical pattern of functioning. Implicit in the definition is the notion that the trauma resulting from rape will be time limited because crises are time limited. Individuals recover, reorganize, and are able to resume some semblance of their life prior to the crisis. This explanation of the problem was preferable to the previously popular psychoanalytic theory of women's subconscious "rape wish" but had its drawbacks, most notably that victims were expected to recover from the crisis and get on with their lives.

Feminists embraced the rape-as-crisis explanation while simultaneously engaging in public education that placed responsibility on men as perpetrators and on a society where men were socialized to be aggressive and to exercise control while women were socialized to be "feminine," sometimes to the point of accepting themselves as sex objects and thus accepting the blame for rape.

Revisions in the Rape-as-Crisis Model

Research subsequent to Burgess and Holmstrom's work has led to revisions and reconceptualization of rape trauma syndrome as comprised of at least three stages and as more than a temporary crisis. While most survivors effect a reorganization of their lives, this often entails acceptance of an altered post-rape life. One of the earliest empirical works to document the fact that rape is a "prolonged crisis" was that of Joyce Williams and Karen Holmes, who found that survivors, whether by a few months or years, still manifested symptoms of rape trauma. They suffered from health issues, their functionality (work, school, travel) was impacted, and they experienced feelings of generalized discomfort toward men. Those who achieve some resolution of the rape and the accompanying sense of disempowerment do so by incorporating the experience into their lives and moving ahead as survivors, not as victims.

See Also: Rape, Incidence of; Rape, Legal Definition of; Rape, Prosecution Rates of; Rape Crisis Centers.

Further Readings

Burgess, Ann Wolbert and Lynda Lytle Holmstrom. *Rape: Victims of Crisis.* Bowie, MD: Robert J. Brady, 1974.

Roberts, Albert R. *Crisis Intervention Handbook: Assessment, Treatment, and Research.* New York: Oxford University Press, 2005.

Warshaw, Robin. *I Never Called it Rape.* New York: Harper and Row, 1988.

Williams, Joyce E. and Karen A. Holmes. *The Second Assault.* Westport, CT: Greenwood Press, 1981.

Joyce E. Williams
Texas Woman's University

Reality Television

Reality television, a wide-ranging genre purporting to depict the "real" lives, experiences, and/or circumstances of its subjects, is rooted in shows such as *Candid Camera*, which first appeared in 1948 and lasted through 1992; the British documentary *Up Series* (1964–2005); and 1970s game shows produced by Chuck Barris, including *The Dating Game*, *The Newlywed Game*, and *The Gong Show*.

Current reality television programs appear in varying forms, generally falling into broad categories such as the "docudramas" or "docusoaps" that chronicle the supposedly candid experiences of "ordinary" individuals (such as *The Real Housewives*) or celebrities along with their friends and families (for example, *The Osbournes*). Celebrity reality shows are vehicles meant to elevate the star of the show—and/or his/her family—to a higher level of fame/fortune through book deals, fashion lines, and record contracts marketed through the Internet. Non-celebrity individuals who appear on reality shows often attempt to parlay their appearances on reality television into securing recognition and renown, by appearing on more reality shows and/or starring in their own program. Moreover, individuals who are somewhat "infamous" for their outrageous and/or controversial behavior will often successfully transform their public personae into a reality show, such as "Octomom" Nadya Suleman.

Competition shows are another major category of reality television, in which groups and/or individuals use their talents to compete for entry into as well as recognition in a designated field and/or to win a monetary prize by successfully competing in extreme physical challenges. Another popular group of reality television shows are the "makeover" shows, of which perhaps Bravo's *Queer Eye* (originally titled *Queer Eye for the Straight Guy*) is the most well known. *Queer Eye* paved the way for the genres of makeover, home- and self-improvement and dating reality shows, some of which combine aspects of the makeover, self-improvement, and the competition reality genre. Yet another group of reality television programs focus on personal/family issues and crises, including rehabilitation for drug/alcohol addiction, unplanned teenage pregnancy/motherhood, and dealing with out-of-control children. Still other reality shows combine aspects of lifestyle change/self-improvement with documentary and competition, while many of the competitive shows require that cast members live together in a group setting.

The phenomenon of reality television, whose influence has increased exponentially throughout the world at the onset of the 21st century, arguably since the competition program *Big Brother* first appeared in 1999 in the Netherlands, is a pervasive element of broader global popular culture since the late 20th century. Subsequently, reality television took the world by storm. The current success of reality television is undeniable: 21st-century American reality shows such as *Survivor* and *American Idol*—both based on similar, earlier UK programs—have remained top-rated shows.

Stereotypes of Women in Reality Shows

Reality shows often pander to and capitalize upon stereotypes, particularly of women. Some of the most notorious reality TV personalities who are vilified in the blogosphere and in tabloids include, among others, Omarosa Manigault-Stallworth; Wendy Pepper; Heidi Montag; Tila Tequila; Kim Zolciak; and the late Jade Goody, who in 2003 received the title of "fourth worst Briton" in the British TV station Channel 4's list

of "100 Worst Britons." Women on reality television shows are often represented in an unflattering light as embodying female archetypes such as the "bad" girl (*Bad Girls Club*); leading double and/or hidden lives (*Secret Lives of Women*); and playing into the stereotype of the inability of women to form sustainable and supportive friendships (most of *The Real Housewives*).

Other female tropes and stereotypes embraced and exploited by reality television include "bridezillas"; "cougars"; mistresses; ditzes; desperate housewives trapped in loveless marriages and filling emotional voids through conspicuous consumption and cosmetic surgery; frigid career women incapable of successful romantic relationships and/or marriages; "gold diggers"; stage mothers pushing very young children to compete in beauty pageants; incompetent mothers of problem children. The presence of the wedding industry in reality television, in particular, reinforces stereotypes of the predatory bride demanding an outlandish, fantasy "princess" wedding at all costs. The prevalent use of the term *famewhore*—and the act of "famewhoring"—when referring to those seeking a place on reality television demonstrates how enmeshed reality television is with misogyny and stereotypes of women. Despite capitalizing upon and reinforcing pernicious stereotypes of women, marriage, and motherhood, as well as projecting negative attitudes toward female aging, many of the most successful reality shows air on channels specifically targeting a female demographic (WEtv, Lifetime, Bravo, and Oxygen).

The success of reality television in the 21st century can be understood as a true Warholian moment, in which everyone is entitled to 15 minutes of fame. It also invokes and reflects the Baudrillardian theories of the hyperreal, simulation, and simulacra, as it promotes Jean Baudrillard's claim that reality occurs only on television.

See Also: Banks, Tyra; Beauty Pageants (Babies/Young Children); "Bridezillas"; Celebrity Women; Cho, Margaret; Cosmetic Surgery; "Cougars"; Diet and Weight Control; Diet Industry; Fashion Industry, Theoretical Controversies; Goody, Jade; MTV; Palin, Sarah; Suleman, "Octomom" Nadya; Wedding Industry.

Further Readings

Brandt, Jenn. "Here's to Not Being Fake: Bravo TV's *The Real Housewives* and the Construction of the

Postfeminist Heroine." In Marcelline Block, ed., *Foregrounding Postfeminism and the Future of Feminist Film and Media Studies.* Newcastle, UK: Cambridge Scholars Press, 2010.

Carter, Bill. "Bravo's Chief Reaches Out to the Prosperous Urban Woman." *New York Times (*March 31, 2008).

Glynn, Kevin. *Tabloid Culture: Trash Taste, Popular Power, and the Transformation of American Television.* Durham, NC: Duke University Press, 2000.

Marcelline Block
Princeton University

Religion, Women in

The multiplicity of women's issues in religion depends on a complex relationship of variables, such as the specific religious tradition in question, the variance of locations in which it is practiced, the multiple ethnicities of practitioners, the differences in social class among believers, and individual or communal economic issues. One way to approach this complex and changing relationship is through addressing issues that speak to important cross-cultural themes that affect many women. For example, Hinduism provides an interesting context for looking at sexuality and gender since the Hindu pantheon includes many goddesses and addresses sexuality in many of its texts. Closely related to sexuality and gender is the idea of the human body as a site of signification. A discussion of veiling, practiced by many Muslim women, addresses this idea in a religious context.

Personal and communal identity is a vital component of religious traditions. There is a significant discussion in contemporary media on issues of women's spiritual authority and the continued refusal of the Catholic Church to ordain women priests. An increasing number of women find that the religions they have participated in have not offered them a fulfilling spirituality because of their inherent patriarchal structures. Many of these women have found spiritual solace in the Earth-based traditions of Paganism. Although the examples in this entry are in no way exhaustive of the issues encountered by women in religious traditions, they are representative of the ways scholars approach the general subject of women and religion.

Sexuality and Gender

Most living religious traditions have rules and strictures that speak to how human sexuality is properly expressed, embodied, deployed, and experienced. These strictures commonly focus on women's sexuality in reference to that of men, and imply that a woman's social status is dependent upon her sexual behavior. One common stereotype that emerges from these rules is the female as temptress whose sexuality must be held in check by complying with normative models portrayed in religious imagery and texts. Hinduism presents an interesting example for an examination of images of women's sex roles and how those same rules determine her social role as a woman.

Scholars generally divide Hindu goddesses into one of two categories: goddesses who are consorts of gods and speak to the domestic role of women, and goddesses who are independent and seen as fierce, terrifying, and sexual. One example of the ideal gender embodiment for Hindu women is the goddess Parvati, second wife of Shiva. Parvati is described as virtuous, maternal, and her sexual fidelity to Shiva is never questioned. Parvati's central purpose is to domesticate Shiva so he may enter the householder stage. Householder is one of the stages on the Hindu path to *moksha*, the liberation a person from the cycle of reincarnation. The goddess Parvati teaches that a woman's purpose is to serve her husband, care for their children, and maintain the family home in a way that facilitates the husband's path to enlightenment.

During and after the British occupation of India, many of the social structures particular to Western culture were either adopted by or forced upon Hindus, causing significant transformations in the social landscape. These transformations included a more noticeable division of public and private realms; this division inevitably binds women to the private sphere of the household in light of the gender roles assigned to her sex. In rural areas of India, where a majority of the country's population lives, women are still expected to embody the traditional role displayed by Parvati, while women who live in urban centers are more likely to look toward fierce and independent goddesses like Kali and Durga for spiritual inspiration.

The Body

In the context of religious traditions, proper presentation of the body speaks to outward signs of identification, and those outward signs typically signify the moral codes that govern that body. Perhaps the most pervasive signification of Muslim women in the global media is the veil. It is easy to assume that Islamic women who cover their body in accord with the laws of modesty found in the Qur'an are forced to do so by an oppressive patriarchal system bent on denying women full human status. It is important to note that not all Muslim women, or men for that matter, encourage or approve of veiling. In fact, the Qur'an also has prescriptions for men's modest apparel. Finally, it is significant to note that many Muslim women in the contemporary world see veiling as liberating.

While it is true that in some Islamic countries, women's basic human rights are affected by interpretations of Islam's holy book the Qur'an and its accompanying *hadith*, scholars have pointed out there may be reasons other than strict interpretations of religious law that motivate women in the contemporary world to embrace hijab—the idea of modest dress. For Muslims, the bodies of both women and men have what is called *awrah*, sometimes translated as nakedness or shame. Exposition of these parts of the body in public is considered a sin. Although there is no consensus among Muslims as to what exactly the specific parameters of this concept are, women's bodies are thought to have more *awrah* then men's. Furthermore, the extent of *awrah* of the female body differs among schools of Islamic thought, and thus dress can range from full body and face coverings to just a veil covering the hair, to wearing modest, everyday clothing.

For many women today wearing the hijab is not necessarily connected to the insistence that this patriarchal system insists on the oppression of women through the denial of their feminine bodies. Many women who live in Muslim dominated areas wear the hijab because it allows them to move freely in public without being harassed. Here, the covered body is thought of as liberated, albeit in terms of negotiation, giving them access to education and jobs. Some Islamic women feel that wearing the veil frees them from sexual objectification and the harsh, socially constructed ideals of beauty in much of Western culture.

Identity

Among present-day Native Americans, religious identity is thoroughly intertwined with both cultural traditions and historic interactions with modernity. This reality is even more marked among Native women. Prior to contact with Euro-Americans, American Indian tribal traditions often allocated very important positions of authority and sacred power to the female sphere, and much of the nature of Earth-centered spirituality draws connections between the sacred nature of the universe and the bodies of women. Both menstruation and childbirth are seen as microcosms of the larger cosmos, thus women provide tangible and present connections to the sacred.

This reality is evident in the fact that the Apache puberty rite for girls, the Sunrise Ceremony, remains the largest ritual complex in nearly all Apache communities. The Sunrise Ceremony, also called the *Isanaklesh Gotal*, not only ushers a girl into womanhood, but draws the community into an intimate relationship with perhaps a key holy figure—the goddess *Isanaklesh*. *Isanaklesh* is in fact the creatrix of the Apache people, bringing them into being using her own skin and minerals associated with the four directions. The ceremony consists of four days of rituals designed to instruct the girl in Apache sacred culture, test her dedication through a grueling schedule, and reiterate the Apache sacred system through songs, dances, and performances of the creation narrative. The sing concludes after the initiate, who has danced all night long, runs toward the rising sun, then back again, symbolizing her transformation into a woman. The young woman is said to embody *Isanaklesh* upon her completion of this run, and she in turn blesses the community using the traditional form for such blessings—corn pollen—symbolizing fertility.

Authority

The highest authority on religious matters in the Catholic Church is the Pope, whose power is based on the doctrine of Apostolic succession. This doctrine states that Jesus Christ, understood in Christianity as God incarnate, conferred full sacramental authority upon his apostles, in effect naming them the first bishops of the Church. That same sacramental authority is passed today through ordination into the priesthood, a ritual carried out primarily by bishops and sometimes the Pope. It is sacramental authority that allows a Catholic priest to perform the sacred rites of the Catholic Church through which its followers attain salvation. In light of this, feminist scholars have pointed out that salvation in the Catholic Church can only be attained through men. This puts women into a position of both dependence and subordination that ultimately maintains the patriarchal structure of Catholic Christianity.

It is hardly surprising, then, that one of the most contentious issues in the feminist encounter with Catholicism is the subject is the demand for the recognition of women's ordination. Although the majority of Protestant Christian churches do ordain women today, a few still maintain a strictly male priesthood. In response to the call for women's ordination, the Roman Catholic Church has argued that they do not have the authority to change what they cite as divine revelation as well as historical precedent. In response, many critics argue that the continued discrimination of women is based on an outdated social system that characterized women as incomplete persons, in fact, as deficient men, and that the Catholic Church should align itself with contemporary laws regarding human rights.

Feminist Theology

Feminist theology developed as a mode of critical inquiry in the social activism and scholarly work of women engaged in second wave feminism. There is no one feminist theology, but the discourse can be generally divided into two streams of thought. One mode of feminist theology focuses on reforming and reconstructing living religious traditions by working within them to make women's experience as central to the tradition as men's experience has been. Another equally important approach to feminist theology works from the starting point of women and celebrates their differences from men as meaningful. This latter approach also involves breaking with major world religions and creating, or recreating, more women-focused religious traditions.

Although these ways of thinking about religions through a feminist paradigm differ greatly in terms of how to take action, they do have some common starting points. Feminist theologians recognize that women's religious experience is fundamentally different from that of men. In light of this, scholars have pointed out that there is no way to build a complete theology for humans without including women, since roughly half the human race identify themselves as women. A theology, regardless of tradition, that does not include this basic fact of human existence simply cannot claim to be comprehensive. Furthermore, the absence of women's experience in religions is often pointed out as a form of patriarchy because it subordinates women's religiosity to that of men.

Theology built around men's experience of religion is androcentric—a discourse that situates the male experience as central to one's world view—and results in figuring the male experience as the normative mode of human being. One of the ways feminist theology confronts androcentrism is at the level of language. Feminist theologians, most famously Mary Daly, claim as their own right the naming of reality: this includes the divine and women's experience with it. At a very fundamental level, using gendered language, such as masculine pronouns when referring to the divine, has the effect of presenting a gendered image in the mind regardless of claims of neutrality. Additionally, this use of masculine pronouns reinforces the male model of experience as the generic human experience.

Feminist theologians who work from within a particular religious tradition approach their work on many different levels. For instance, influential feminist scholars such as Judith Plaskow, Elizabeth Schüssler Fiorenza, and Rosemary Radford Reuther have critiqued and reconstructed major world religions. Plaskow has worked in the tradition of Judaism to critique and reconstruct Jewish history in the Torah, in the Five Books of Moses, to include Jewish women's experience. Reuther is a Christian feminist who argues that the Christ of biblical texts can be separated from the patriarchal hierarchy of the church. The method she prescribes is to look at the Jesus of the synoptic Gospels—the books of Matthew, Mark, and Luke in the New Testament—which, she argues, are well-suited to feminist theology. Finally, women who have found the religions they practice unchangeable have looked to history, often to the traditions of Paganism, to create their own spiritual systems.

As feminist theology grew around second wave feminism, whose earliest work was done predominantly by white, middle-class women in the United States, the United Kingdom, and western Europe, many women found they could not identify with the experiences of these scholars and activists because of the distinctiveness of their own situations. This critique has lead to a growing discourse of multiple feminisms and feminist theologies that originated, and are still being developed, by women in many different social, religious, economic, and ethnic contexts.

Paganism

Paganism is an overarching term that encompasses many different practices and beliefs. Although this term was used in a derogatory sense throughout Christian history to denote nonmonotheistic religions, it has taken on a new and more positive meaning today. As it is often referred to, Neo (new) Paganism includes revitalizations of past practices and modern religious movements that incorporate different elements of spirituality to create alternative religious traditions. These traditions tend to favor individual experience over inflexible doctrine and dogma, and most Pagan traditions share a belief in more than one goddess or god as well as a reverence for nature. This reverence takes the form either of pantheism, an understanding that the ultimate divine and nature are identical, or panentheism, the belief that the ultimate divine permeates all of nature, but also extends endlessly beyond the material world to encompass totality.

A significant aspect that attracts women to Pagan traditions is the concept of veneration and respect for the natural world. One of the most salient features of the major of world religious traditions, at least as they are practiced on the ground today, is a dualism that attaches women to the material aspect of the world, and affords men a "higher" distinction by associating them with the immaterial or transcendent realm. With Earth-based traditions, women's bodies are celebrated as creative forces for the divine. The immaterial realm, while still imagined, takes on less prestige than it does in religions that focus considerable amounts of attention on salvation and the afterlife. Most rituals and practices of Neo Paganism are based on the cycles of the natural world and the that people can interact with the power inherent in nature—the immanent divine.

See Also: Buddhism; Chinese Religions; Christianity; Hinduism; Indigenous Religions, Global; Islam; Judaism; Native American Religion; New Age Religion; Priesthood, Episcopalian/Anglican; Priesthood, Roman Catholic; Progressive Muslims (U.S.); Roman Catholic Church; Wicca; Witchcraft: Worldwide; Womanist Theology; Women's Ordination Conference.

Further Readings

Bagley, Kate and Kathleen McIntosh. *Women's Studies in Religion: A Multicultural Reader*. Upper Saddle River, NJ: Prentice Hall, 2006.

Castelli, Elizabeth A. and Rosamond C. Rodman. *Women, Gender, Religion: A Reader*, 1st ed. New York: Palgrave Macmillan, 2001.

Fisher, M.P. *Women in Religion*. New York: Longman, 2006.

Ruether, Rosemary Radford. *Feminist Theologies: Legacy and Prospect*. Minneapolis, MN: Fortress Press, 2007.

Sharma, Arvind and Katherine K. Young. *Feminism and World Religions*. Albany: State University of New York Press, 1998.

Kate S. Kelley
University of Missouri

Religious Fundamentalism, Cross-Cultural Context of

When originally coined in the late 19th century, the term *fundamentalism* referred to a strand of theologically conservative Protestantism in the United States. Today, the term *religious fundamentalism* applies to conservative religious groups across the globe that protest or reject some aspects of modernity and secularization, and, in some cases, Westernization. Fundamentalist religious groups tend to hold traditional views on gender, sexuality, and the family. Since the emancipation of women and the diversification of family forms and sexualities are among the hallmarks of modernity and secularization, religious fundamentalism is often portrayed as an archaic, patriarchal, and oppressive regime.

Defining Fundamentalism

The word *fundamentalism* is often used by the media and in political discussions to refer to politicized forms of religiosity and to groups that take religion seriously. References are typically critical of attempts to enhance the role of religion in public life. However, students of religion vary in their definitions of fundamentalism and in their assessments of whether attempts to enhance the role of religion in public life threatens democratic political culture. There is also disagreement to what extent fundamentalism compromises women's interests. These debates are a product of the history of the term as well as observers' own range of intellectual and political perspectives on the role of religion in the modern world.

Fundamentalism was originally used in reference to a conservative strand of Protestantism that developed in the United States in the late 19th century. The original movement was a theologically conservative and culturally separatist group that opposed attempts to modernize Christianity. The term remained confined to this context through the 1970s.

The late 1970s and 1980s saw an influx of conservative religious movements around the globe in a process that has been termed the resurgence of religion. The 1979 Iranian Revolution, the emergence in the 1980s of a politically active form of conservative Christianity in the United States, and the rise of politically engaged and theologically conservative religious movements on all continents defied the accepted wisdom that modernization and secularization are inseparable processes. Scholars sought to explain the resurgence of religion and to identify the features common to conservative religious groups. Some observers view fundamentalist groups as antimodern, an attempt to return to an authentic and unchanging social order that preceded modernity.

The notion that fundamentalism and modernity clash with one another is a product of this perspective. The dominant view is that fundamentalist groups are modern movements that emerge within and respond to modern conditions. There is also disagreement whether fundamentalist religiosity represents historically accurate and culturally authentic patterns. The dominant view is that despite claims for authenticity, a return to a timeless tradition, and cultural purity, fundamentalist groups engender new forms of religiosity. For example, studies find that veiling had not been a central feature of all Muslim and Arab societies. Moreover, the way women veil (headscarf or a full body covering; in private or public)—and their reasons for doing so—do not necessarily correspond with historical forms of veiling.

The most comprehensive study of fundamentalism, the Fundamentalism Project, brought together historians, sociologists, political scientists, and anthropologists who contributed dozens of case studies on movements from seven religious traditions and numerous geographical locations. The Fundamentalism Project identified nine ideological and organizational features that characterize fundamentalist groups and defined fundamentalism as a modern global phenomenon that is premised on the inerrancy of sacred texts and aims to gain political power while defending religious tradition against the eroding forces of modernization and secularization.

The Fundamentalism Project's findings and definitions are held in high regard, and most subsequent definitions view fundamentalism as an ideology rather than a theology and emphasize scriptural literalism. However, some disagreements persist. First, the application of the term *fundamentalism* outside Western Christianity is still the subject of controversy. Some critics note that the Fundamentalism Project's emphasis on the commonalities between very diverse phenomena, geographical locations, and religious groups disregards key differences. Of particular concern is the difference between Western conservative religious movements and those that emerge in postcolonial contexts, in which the legacy of European colonization and its impact on local culture, society, and religion are related to the emergence of politicized religiosity.

Second, critics note that despite the emphasis on fundamentalism as a global phenomenon, in popular discourse fundamentalism is often associated with Islam as an irrational, morally inferior, and violent religion that oppresses women. These critics prefer terms such as Islamicization or political Islam. A third line of criticism points out that the notion of religious resurgence is based on a faulty reading of the historical record about religion's demise. Far from a universal phenomenon, religious demise was experienced primarily by Western Christianity. Therefore, the lines between the old forms of religion and newer conservative and politicized movements are more blurry outside Western Christianity. These critics prefer to label the current phenomenon a reinvention rather than revival of religious traditions. In this, critics agree with one of the main findings of the Fundamentalism Project: fundamentalist groups are highly selective in their use of religious tradition.

Women and Fundamentalism

Women's emancipation is a hallmark of modernity, as is the diversification of family forms and sexualities. Consequently, a key feature of religious fundamentalist groups' protests and rejections of modernity is apparent in their traditionalist views on gender, family, and sexuality. Despite the controversies about the definition of religious fundamentalism, commentators agree that religious fundamentalism impacts women's lives. However, observers diverge on the extent of these implications, explanations for women's involvement with such movements, and interventions that may improve the lives of women who are members of fundamentalist religious groups.

Some critics, and especially feminist critics, hold that fundamentalism is a patriarchal and oppressive political and cultural system that is detrimental to women's interests, livelihoods, and dignity. In this view, fundamentalist regimes are akin to other patriarchal configurations of economic and political interests that favor men. By identifying women and sexuality with political, cultural, and religious goals, religious fundamentalism legitimizes a patriarchal social order that happens to be based on religion. Under this view women's acquiesce can only be explained as a form of oppression or false consciousness, and interventions from outside groups—or nations—are welcome.

Other commentators point out that while fundamentalism limits women's opportunities and regulates their bodies, these regulations and limitations must be understood within particular historical and cultural contexts. One claim is that given the structural forces that shape their lives, women are simultaneously oppressed and empowered by their religion. For example, veiling allows women access to public spaces that are typically reserved for men. Second, commentators note a gap between religious prescriptions and lived realities. The process of adaptation provides women with opportunities to subvert and resist religious prescriptions through imaginative interpretations and practical realities.

For example, although fundamentalist Christian women in the United States say that they support male headship and traditional gender roles, the realities of their lives are such that they work outside of the home and participate in financial decision making. Finally, research indicates that women strategize and appropriate religion to further a variety of ends, such as economic opportunities, domestic relations, political ideologies, and cultural affiliation. For example, for many women the veil has become a symbol of national belonging and cultural affiliation in the face of colonial legacies. Similarly, women use religious rationales to avoid unattractive employment or potential partners. Under this perspective, women's acquiesce to fundamentalist regimes does not necessarily indicate oppression but a strategic choice within a given set of cultural and political circumstances, and interventions that aim to improve the lives of women who are members of conservative religious groups must be a product of indigenous efforts to improve women's lives.

See Also: Arab Feminism; Evangelical Protestantism; Fundamentalist Christianity; Iranian Feminism; Islamic Feminism; Orthodox Judaism; Religion, Women in; Secularity Law, France; Taliban.

Further Readings

Antoun, R. T. *Understanding Fundamentalism: Christian, Islamic and Jewish Movements*. Walnut Creek, CA: AltaMira, 2001.

Emerson, M. O. and D. Hartman. "The Rise of Religious Fundamentalism." *Annual Review of Sociology*, v.32 (2006).

Marty, M. E. and R. S. Appleby, eds. *Fundamentalism Comprehended*. Chicago: Chicago University Press, 1995.

Moallem, M. *Between Warrior Brother and Veiled Sister: Islamic Fundamentalism and The Politics of Patriarchy in Iran*. Berkeley: University of California Press, 2005.

Orit Avishai
Fordham University

Representation of Women

The first decade of the 21st century offers a complicated set of contradictions for analyzing representations of women in the media. These tensions come from changing ideas in feminist inquiry. Newer ideas accept and even celebrate displays of femininity, sexuality, and beauty through revealing clothes, styled hair, and makeup as forms of empowerment. Older ideas disregard the personal choices behind these displays as just reinforcing oppressions through dominant media. These tensions do not reduce readings of a representation but instead encourage negotiated ones. These multiple readings allow reconsiderations and appropriations of old stereotypes and revisions of them.

Mainstream films of the early part of the 21st century in some ways reify traditional stereotypes and roles, while at the same time adjusting to allow the feminine a degree of power. With the current industry releases dominated by blockbusters, action films, and the science fiction and fantasy genres, women appear to have few heroic places within those narratives.

Women's Film Roles

Women more often serve as love interests or damsels in distress, such as Mary Jane Watson in the *Spider-Man* franchise (2002, 2004, 2007) and Pepper Potts in the *Ironman* franchise (2008, 2010). Other women hold token places in male-dominated science fiction and fantasy worlds, such as in the *Harry Potter* series (2001–09), with Hermione; the *X-Men* series (2005, 2007); the *Fantastic Four* series (2000, 2003, 2006); and *Watchmen* (2009).

Woman-centered action films, however, cast women in strong lead roles. These women wield weapons, engage in hand-to-hand combat, and defy death through series of challenges, all while wearing tight clothing that accentuates both musculature and curves. In *Tomb Raider* (2001, 2003), Angelina Jolie wore a padded bra one cup size smaller than her character's cup size in the original video game. Close-up shots emphasize the tight clothing and the exposed skin on Jolie's body. The prostitutes in Frank Miller's *Sin City* (2005) also show this contradiction: Although they dress for attracting men, these women also use machine guns to stop an attack in their territory. Uma Thurman's Bride character in the *Kill Bill* series (2003, 2004) manages to slay an entire room of martial experts with a sword and other weaponry. Michelle Yeoh also demonstrates martial arts skills in *Crouching Tiger, Hidden Dragon* (2000). Other examples of these characters include Charlize Theron in *Aeon Flux* (2006) and Milla Jovovich in the *Resident Evil* (2002, 2004, 2007) series. In general, these representations show women adopting traditionally male violence and methods to defend and assert themselves.

"Chick flicks" represent a popular genre wherein women also obtain lead roles. In these films, the main character is often an intelligent woman with a career, her own life, and supportive friends, but who desires someone to love and someone to love her. These women often embody and even enjoy traditional ideas of consumer-based femininity, such as through expensive clothing, jewelry, and salon visits, often with their friends. The narrative arcs of these films focus on the female lead finding, losing, and finding love again, usually ending with some kind of marriage or other coupling. Examples of chick flicks include *Bridget Jones's Diary* (2001), *Legally Blonde* (2001), *The Devil Wears Prada* (2006), and *Sex and the City* (2008, 2010). The latter film features four fashion-conscious friends pursuing love and new shoes along with their careers in New York City. All four celebrate different aspects of femininity, from home decorating to shopping, along with their independence, but the men in their lives often play important roles in their careers and other decisions.

This assertive, strong woman also appears in a newer-emerging genre that focuses on white men who embody a man-boy or man-child stereotype. These men exhibit immaturity, irresponsibility, and even ignorance of their actions and lives. The women in these films demonstrate the opposite, showing maturity, confidence, responsibility, and accomplishment. To get the right man, however, she must teach the man-child how to grow up and must be patient with him while he figures out how. This role shifts some of the leadership responsibilities to the woman in the relationship, but ultimately they return to the male after he matures. Examples of this kind of film include *Talladega Nights* (2006), *Knocked Up* (2007), *The 40-Year-Old Virgin* (2005), and *Zack and Miri Make a Porno* (2008).

Precious (2009) provides an example of a new direction for women's roles in film. Based on the novel *Push* by Sapphire, *Precious* focuses on an unlikely lead character: an overweight, pregnant Harlem teenager who is molested by her father and abused by her mother. Claireece "Precious" Jones struggles with living, and she gets enrolled in a special program where she finds some love and support, even as the rest of her life crumbles around her. After her abusive father dies, she finds out she is human immunodeficiency virus (HIV)-positive, although, thankfully, her unborn child is not. This film offers none of the uplifting, happy endings that chick flicks and other films provide, nor does it offer the coupling ending. Its bleakness represents a reality not often seen on screen.

Overall, contemporary films offer opportunities for women to assert more confidence, strength, and choice. In some the feminine remains a choice, but even if not chosen, it still becomes part of a complex association with the masculine.

Women on Television

The last decade of television saw an increase in programming and networks targeted primarily at women. Following the success of Lifetime, other networks such as Oxygen and Women's Entertainment began to offer similar programming appealing to women. Overall, women gained stronger roles in various shows, particularly dramas, while at the same time situation comedies and reality shows often reinforced traditional women's roles.

The amount of dramatic programming that featured women in leading roles or strong women as part of ensembles has increased. Shows such as *Ally McBeal* (1997–2002), *Judging Amy* (1999–2005), and *Strong Medicine* (2000–06) showed women as a lawyer, a judge, and doctors working within high-pressure environments while at the same time juggling issues with children and significant others (or lack thereof). *The West Wing* (1999–2006) featured several strong women in prominent political roles never previously held by a woman in real life, but the show regularly puts limitations on their abilities to succeed, both professionally and personally. The *Law & Order* (1990–) franchise regularly casts women as lawyers, detectives, forensic scientists, and even police chiefs, but these women still work under male supervisors among primarily male casts. Olivia Benson on *Law and Order: SVU* (1999–) regularly pushes the boundaries for investigations of rape cases, only to meet resistance from her male partner and superiors.

Unlike in dramas, situation comedies sometimes reinforce the dominant stereotypes for women's roles. The man-child or man-boy becomes a key masculine stereotype within these shows, and the wives, often of different ethnic backgrounds such as Italian or Hispanic, must maintain their patience and their households. The *King of Queens* (1998–2007) often found husband and Italian wife butting heads over the husband's antics, and Patricia Heaton's character on *Everybody Loves Raymond* (1996–2005) regularly lost her patience and temper with her bumbling husband. These women retain strength for the household and the family, but overstepping certain bounds results in their seeming bitter and opening them up for mockery from their husbands.

Sex and the City (1998–2004) offered representations of four strong, single women trying to find the perfect careers, perfect clothes, and perfect men. Though the main character, Carrie, sustains herself through her writing career, she still seeks men for relationships and goes through a series of boyfriends before finally marrying Mr. Big. Miranda, the lawyer, asserts a greater degree of confidence in her career, but at one point her employers assume she is a lesbian and set her up with another lesbian. This moment demonstrates the lines women characters must remain behind in order not to appear too masculine.

Other shows have taken up themes of polygamy and homosexuality, with mixed results in terms of gender stereotypes. In HBO's *Big Love* (2006–), for example, one man marries and has families with three women. While he retains the role as head of household, the three wives develop a pecking order that still works under their husband. Showtime's *The L-Word* (2004–09) follows a group of lesbian friends who live in Los Angeles. It gains support for showing positive representations of lesbians, but it also draws criticism for its emphasis on glamour, and its overly melodramatic story lines.

Reality programming offers a division between positioning women on equal planes as men and reinforcing stereotypical gender roles. Multiple "game show"– or competition-type reality shows divide their contestants with equal numbers of men and women—including *American Idol* (2002–), *So You Think You Can Dance* (2005–), and *Survivor* (2000–) —superficially suggesting that both sexes are on equal planes. Other shows reinforce women's traditional roles and beauty expectations, such as seeking a man in *The Bachelor* (2002–) and *Joe Millionaire* (2003), becoming more beautiful in *What Not to Wear* (2003–), and maintaining households and raising children, as in *Jon and Kate Plus 8* (2007–2009), *Wife Swap* (2004–), and *Little People Big World* (2006–). Only a few reality shows represent experiences primarily from women's points of view, though again from traditional viewpoints. *The Bachelorette* (2003–) offers another take on the finding a spouse theme, and *The Girls Next Door* (2005–) represents the glamorous and objectified life of being one of Hugh Hefner's girls. Hefner chooses these girls, but they also choose to display themselves according to standards, such as dying their hair blonde.

Although the visibility for women on television has increased and the niche markets for women's programming also has increased, women's overall representations remain divided. On one hand, the representations of women flaunting their sexuality and femininity, such as in *The Girls Next Door*, *Sex and the City*, and even the dating shows, could demonstrate an empowerment through ownership of their own identities. In contrast, these representations in other shows, particularly in their stereotypes of women as homemakers and as in their seeking affirmation through getting a man, reaffirm the traditional representations of women throughout television and other media.

Women's Documentary

Unlike fiction filmmaking and television, documentary productions provide a prominent place for representations of women. The recent decade saw increased documentary production in both mainstream and independent venues, but unlike Hollywood and television, documentary represents real women and their stories. Some recent documentaries balance social issues with those stories, but in general, the women represented remain the primary subjects.

Some male directors bring forward women's stories in their documentaries. Bob Ray's *Hell on Wheels* (2008), about contemporary roller derby revived by a team in Austin, Texas, showcases the women's power and sexuality in the sport. David Schisgall's more serious *Very Young Girls* (2007) focuses on girls as young as 12 and 13 years old who have been forced into prostitution, and the efforts made to help them.

Most of the women's stories, however, are brought forward by other women, who make up about half of all documentary makers. Some of these women work in mainstream venues, such as Barbara Kopple and Liz Garbus for HBO. Two-time Oscar winner and veteran documentary maker Kopple, along with Cecilia Peck, tells the story of the Dixie Chicks in *Shut Up and Sing* (2006). The group's lead singer, Natalie Maines, disparaged then-president George W. Bush during a European performance, and news of her statement caused an uproar among the group's U.S. fans, with demands for apologies, boycotts of concerts, and burning of CDs taking place in response. The directors weave the band's story with interviews and raise questions about working full time in music and trying to raise families at the same time.

Liz Garbus's work focuses on multiple issues, including women and girls within the prison system.

The Execution of Wanda Jean (2002) follows the final days of Wanda Jean Allen, who was charged with murder and sat on Oklahoma's death row hoping for an appeal or a stay of execution. Garbus represents Allen, whose low IQ bordered on retarded, with sensitivity and deep emotion and without highlighting the sensational nature of her case. In *Girlhood* (2003), Garbus follows Shanae and Megan through their years in juvenile detention and through their attempts at reintegrating into society. Her access to these girls again shows emotional depths bordering on melodrama, particularly through the troubled relationship of Megan with her estranged mother.

Other documentary makers balance stories with key social issues and institutions that affect women directly. Similar to *Girlhood*, *Girl Trouble* (2004) follows three girls and their experiences in the juvenile justice system. Lexi Leban and Lidia Szajko address the limitations and failings of the system, at the same time focusing on Lateefah Simon's efforts at the Center for Young Women's Development. Directed by Meg McLagan and Daria Sommers, *Lioness* (2008) represents women who served in ground combat during the Iraq War despite official orders disallowing it. Still other women documentary makers focus on issues of race, such as Yvonne Welbon's *Sisters in Cinema* (2003) and Cyrille Phipps's *Seen But Not Heard: AIDS and the Untold War Against Black Women* (2008).

Other documentary makers address global women's issues unseen in mainstream media, calling attention to the stark realities faced by women around the world. Lisa F. Jackson's *The Greatest Silence* (2007) tells stories about women who suffered rape and mutilation during the war years in the Congo. Directed by Mary Olive Smith and Amy Bucher, *Walk to Beautiful* (2008) follows five Ethiopian women who suffer from obstetric fistulas and their journeys to get help with a health problem largely invisible in Western nations with developed healthcare systems. *God Sleeps in Rwanda* (2005), directed by Kimberlee Acquaro and Stacy Sherman, follows five women rebuilding their lives after the 1994 genocide. *Mrs. Goundo's Daughter* (Barbara Attie and Janet Goldwater, 2008) documents Mrs. Goundo's fight to remain in the United States to prevent her daughter from undergoing a clitorectomy in her home country. Overall, documentary directors bring forward representations of women unseen in other media.

Women and New Media

New digital technologies present possibilities and challenges to women's representations. Until recently, the pornography industry provided the primary representations of women most viewed online, but with social media use recently eclipsing that dominance, more women partake the opportunity to represent themselves. Social media offer multiple outlets for representations, including Facebook, Flickr or PhotoBucket, YouTube or Vimeo, Twitter, MySpace, blogs, and personal Websites, frequently in combination. Some women write their own blogs about various topics and associate with collectives such as BlogHer. Others, such as performers Lady Gaga and Tila Tequila, combine Twitter and home pages to further their images and promote their shows and songs. Sex-positive educators such as Annie Sprinkle use Websites to inform and educate through self-representation and humor. Some even upload their own videos and documentaries, such as Abiola Abrams's *Knives in My Throat.* Although these women gain some opportunity to retain control over the images, words, and ideas that compose their representations, they also face a more immediate response, either support or backlash, from other social media users.

Representations of women across the media show a complex intersection of changes. These representations can demonstrate degrees of greater power and agency, sexuality, and femininity. They also can affirm limits of this empowerment, particularly through labels of homosexuality and through limits in potential development. These representations vary through medium and format, with documentary forms and new media outlets offering greater degrees of freedom of expression than the more traditional television and film outlets. Women makers also find more opportunities in the former set than the latter set. Overall, however, how all these representations get decoded—as empowering, as disempowering, as negotiated—lies primarily with the audience.

See Also: Advertising, Portrayal of Women in; Arts, Women in the (21st Century Overview); Celebrity Women; Feminist Publishing; Film Directors, Female: International; Film Production, Women in; Representation of Women in Government, International; Representation of Women in Government, U.S.

Further Readings

Akass, Kim and Janet McCabe, eds. *Reading Sex and the City.* London: I. B. Taurus, 2004.

Brunsdon, Charlotte and Lynn Spigel, eds. *Feminist Television Criticism: A Reader,* 2nd ed. New York: Open University Press/McGraw-Hill, 2008.

Ferriss, S. and M. Young, eds. *Chick Flicks: Contemporary Women at the Movies.* New York: Routledge, 2008.

Hurd, Mary G. *Women Directors and Their Films.* Westport, CT: Praeger, 2007.

Johnson, Merri Lisa, ed. *Jane Puts It in a Box: Third Wave Feminism and Television.* London: I. B. Taurus, 2007.

Lotz, Amanda D. *Redesigning Women: Television After the Network Era.* Urbana: University of Illinois Press, 2006.

Schubart, Rikke. *Super Bitches and Action Babes: The Female Hero in Popular Cinema, 1970–2006.* Jefferson, NC: McFarland, 2007.

Tadiar, Neferti X. M. and Angela Y. Davis, eds. *Beyond the Frame: Women of Color and Visual Representation.* New York: Palgrave Macmillan, 2005.

Heather McIntosh
Northern Illinois University

Representation of Women in Government, International

As of November 2009, women accounted for only 14 of the world's heads of government and 18.6 percent of all parliaments. Following the September 2008 elections, Rwanda led the world with the largest number of women in government, with 56 percent of its lower-house seats filled by women.

No other country has achieved this percentage of female governmental representatives. The Nordic countries as a region, however, lead the world, with 42.5 percent of the parliamentary seats filled by women. Two factors may contribute to higher numbers of women in parliaments worldwide: the system of government and constitutional and/or party rules, which promote gender equity, including quotas. Rwanda uses a proportional system with quotas to elect its parliament. Nearly one-third of its seats are elected by a "women's only" ballot. The Nordic countries also rely on a proportional system and if quotas are implemented, they are done so voluntarily at the party level.

Proportional Systems

Proportional systems increase women's levels of representation, not only in parliaments but in the highest levels of political leadership. According to Table 1, two of the 14 women identified are from the Nordic region. The majority of the women in Table 1 were elected directly to the top position through a plurality/majority (P/M), usually a two-round system (TRS). With P/M, the person who receives the required threshold of votes wins the election. It's a winner-takes-all scenario. By contrast, with proportional systems (PR), multiple seats are filled, and the percentage of votes won by a party indicates the percentage of seats that party will fill in the legislature. All but two of the women leaders in Table 1 are from

countries that rely on some form of proportionality to fill parliamentary seats. All but three have quotas (required or voluntary) in place at some level. Thus, a correlation exists between proportional systems, which increase women's representation at the parliamentary level, and women elected at the highest levels of government. Often these women have worked their way up the party ranks, secured the party's nomination for president, and collaborated with other parties to develop a winning coalition.

P/M systems institutionalize disadvantages for women's political representation since they ascribe to the winner-take-all arrangement and usually are composed of single-member districts (one elector per district). In some cases, winners only need to win a

Table 1: Recent Women Presidents and Prime Ministers, as of October 2010

Name	Position	Country, Year	Parliamentary Election System (as of 2005)	Quotas	Pres. Election System (as of 2005)
Sheikh Hasina Wajed	Prime Minister	Bangladesh, 1996–2001; 2009–	FPTP (P/M)	Yes, constitutional level	—
Mary McAleese	President	Ireland, 1997–	STV (PR)	Yes, party level	AV (P/M)
Tarja K. Halonen	President	Finland, 2000–	List PR	No	TRS (P/M)
Gloria Macapagal-Arroyo	President	Philippines, 2001–2010	Mixed (FPTP and List PR)	Yes, national and party level	FPTP
Luisa Diogo	Prime Minister	Mozambique, 2004–2010	List PR	Yes, party level	TRS
Angela Merkel	Chancellor	Germany, 2005–	Mixed (FPTP and List PR)	Yes, party level	—
Ellen Johnson Sirleaf	President	Liberia, 2006–	FPTP	Yes, national level	TRS
Michelle Bachelet	President	Chile, 2006–2010	List PR	Yes, party level	TRS
Emily de Jongh-Elhage	Minister President	Nederlandse Antillen, 2006–2010	List PR	No	—
Pratibha Patil	President	India, 2007–	FPTP	Yes, national and party level	—
Cristina Fernández de Kirchner	Executive President	Argentina, 2007–	List PR	Yes, national and party level	TRS
Nino Burjanadze	Acting President	Georgia, 2007–2008	Mixed (FPTP and List PR	No	TRS
Dr. Ivy Matsepe-Casaburri	Acting President	South Africa, 2008	List PR	Yes, national and party level	—
Jóhanna Sigurðardóttir	Prime Minister	Iceland, 2009–	List PR	Yes, party level	FPTP

plurality of the votes cast rather than a majority. P/M systems are the most popular worldwide, functioning in nearly half of the nation-states and territories that have direct elections. P/M systems provide a major barrier for high levels of women's representation in government because there is only one seat to be filled rather than multiple seats; no mechanism exists for including candidate diversity on the ticket.

First Past the Post (FPTP) is the most often used P/M structure, functioning in roughly one-quarter of countries worldwide, including the United States. In this system, the candidate who secures the largest number of votes wins. The Two-Round System (TRS) is found in a large number of countries that elect presidents directly, and it is the second most often used P/M system. Roughly 20 national legislatures use TRS. As the name suggests, two rounds of voting may be used, though specific rules for how this occurs vary from country to country. Generally, the first round functions as a FPTP election. If no candidate receives the specified threshold of votes, a second round is held between the top two candidates.

Proportional representation (PR) systems attempt to assure that if a party wins a certain percentage of the vote, that party fills that percentage of the seats available. Usually this means that parties put forward lists on which citizens vote. More countries and territories use List PRs than any other single electoral system, including nearly two-thirds of new democracies. One advantage for women in PR systems, which list the candidates, is district magnitude; the more seats available, the more likely a party will include a diversity of candidates on the list.

List PR systems operate using one of two types of list systems: closed and open lists. In closed-list systems, the party determines the candidates and the order of candidates on the list. Many closed-list systems require that candidates are ordered so that at least one woman must be listed for every two men. Sometimes lists alternate one woman, one man, according to the voluntary party rules in some Nordic countries.

Depending on the percentage of votes the party secures, legislative seats are filled by going down the list, from top to bottom, based on the percent of the vote won by the party. Open-list systems, used by many European democracies, allow voters to indicate their preference for individuals on the party list. An individual vote also is a vote for a party. While the party still determines the list, candidates are ordered randomly, and the candidates who secure the highest number of preference votes will fill the percentage of seats won by the party.

Proportional representation systems are twice as likely as P/M structures to elect women to office. For example, Germany elects its parliament using a mixed system. In 1994, 13 percent of the winning candidates on the P/M vote were women. On the PR portion of the ballot, 40 percent of the winning candidates were women. Similarly, in New Zealand in 1999, 24 percent of the P/M winners were women; 40 percent of the PR winners were women.

Government Quotas

One of the greatest benefits to women's representation has been the implementation of quotas, most likely to be found in proportional systems. In addition to Rwanda, India designates a group of "women's only" seats, guaranteeing approximately one-third of the seats reserved for women. Requiring a certain percentage of the ballot to be female generally accelerates women's representation, but women must be strategic when lobbying for quotas. Quotas of 20–30 percent seem to provide women with increased political opportunities and, with time, increase the number of viable female candidates. Higher quotas, though, do not return a comparable benefit to women. Quotas do not always translate into political power; some women have argued against their implementation because being elected to a "reserved" seat results in further political marginalization.

The Nordic countries as a region (Sweden, Iceland, Finland, Norway, and Denmark) lead the world in women's political representation, ranging from 38 percent in Denmark to 47 percent in Sweden. Each country uses List PR but does not have a formalized quota system at the national level. The high levels of women's political representation can be attributed to sustained pressure by women's groups, which have urged political parties to voluntarily implement quotas. In doing so, the parties focus on their initial recruitment strategies to get more women involved in the process and into the electoral pipeline. Once involved, these women have the visibility and garner the experience they need to eventually be nominated by their party.

Women are still underrepresented in politics worldwide. The electoral system and party rules, including quotas, impact the level of visibility and viability that women may achieve in politics. The Nordic countries provide an example of a region achieving a high level of women's political representation. Getting women into the pipeline through the party structure and parliamentary elections provides the first step to reaching the goal of parity.

See Also: Council of Women World Leaders; Denmark; Finland; Gender Quotas in Government; Government, Women in; Heads of State, Female; Iceland; Norway; Representation of Women in Government, U.S.; Sweden.

Further Readings

Amy, Douglas J. *Real Choices/New Voices*. New York: Columbia University Press, 2002.

Inter-Parliamentary Union. *Women in National Parliaments*. http://www.ipu.org/wmn-e/world.htm (accessed November 2009).

Jones, Mark P. and Patricio Navia. "Assessing the Effectiveness of Gender Quotas in Open-List Proportional Representation Electoral Systems." *Social Science Quarterly*, v.80/2 (June 1999).

Reynolds, A., B. Reilly, and A. Ellis. *Electoral System Design: The New International IDEA Handbook*. Stockholm, Sweden: International Institute for Democracy and Electoral Assistance, 2005 (Reprinted 2008).

Rule, Wilma. "Parliaments of, by, and for the People: Except for Women? *Electoral Systems in Comparative Perspective: Their Impact on Women and Minorities*. Westport, CT: Greenwood Press, 1994.

Kristina Horn Sheeler
Indiana University, Purdue University Indianapolis

Representation of Women in Government, U.S.

In 2009 in the United States, women comprised 16.8 percent of Congress. At a state level, the percentage is slightly higher, with women holding nearly one-quarter, 22.9 percent, of elected offices. These numbers have risen significantly over the past 20 years, when women held only 5 percent of the elected offices at a national level and 14 percent of elected offices at a state level. However, given that women comprise over half the population, these numbers still raise a number of questions about the representation of women in government. First, does having women in office matter? Second, why are women a significantly smaller number of elected officeholders than men? And third, what obstacles, if any, do women face when running for office? This entry first discusses whether or not it is important to have women in office. Next, it will review the hypotheses that provide explanations for why women are less politically involved and effective than men. Finally, this article will discuss the various hurdles that women sometimes must overcome when running for office.

Descriptive Representation

Descriptive representation occurs when groups are represented by people who share similar physical traits or background experience. The alternative, substantive representation, argues that it is possible for elected officials to adequately represent the interests of their group even though they share very few characteristics. Many scholars debate that descriptive representation leads to increased participation among the group that is descriptively represented. People will be more likely to become actively involved in politics when they view their representative as responsive to their concerns. Additionally, the greater the number of descriptive representatives a group has, the more power they have to focus on issues that are a significant concern for their group. Some research shows that women are more likely than their male counterparts to vote for legislation that pertains to women's issues. Other researchers, however, argue that there is little support that descriptive representation is any more effective than substantive representation.

The Gender Gap

The gender gap states that differences in policy preferences and party preferences exist between men and women. Women are more likely to associate with the Democratic Party and support more liberal social policies than men. Conversely, men are far more likely to be members of the Republican Party and are more concerned with masculine issues such as foreign policy and defense. There are many hypotheses for what causes the gender gap. The attitude hypothesis argues that party positions on specific issues determine which party voters support. Based on this theory, it follows that if women are more focused on social issues than their male counterparts, they would be more likely to side with the party that traditionally is viewed as more capable of handling social issues, or the Democratic Party. Some posit that the gender gap results from issues men and women find more important during any given election. A third explanation states that the main reason for the gender gap since 1980 has been the movement of men from the Democratic Party to the Republican Party. Thus, the gap is not a result of changing attitudes among women but rapidly changing attitudes and values among men.

Political Participation

In many measures of political participation, women and men participate equally. Both groups vote at roughly the same rate, protest at equal rates, and are equally involved in local politics. In other areas of politics, however, women are far less likely to be involved than men. These areas include making campaign contributions, holding positions of leadership and running for office.

Many theories seek to explain why these differences exist. One explanation is based on socialization and encouragement. Women are less likely than men to view themselves as capable of holding office, and require more encouragement from others before deciding to run. Parties, however, are less likely to give women encouragement to run, which limits the number of women running for office. Another explanation is based on resources. Because women have less time and money than men, they are less able to participate in some levels of political activity, such as making contributions or belonging to a political organization. Women also tend to have lower levels of education than men and are less likely to participate in fields that frequently lead to politics, such as law. Therefore, the type of job one holds, in addition to other leadership positions, provide one with the opportunities needed to develop good social skills. Since women have less of these opportunities than men, this may partially explain their lower levels of political participation.

Women as Candidates

How women are treated as candidates may significantly explain the lack of descriptive representation women face in the United States. Of the obstacles that women must overcome during the campaign, two of the most difficult are stereotypes and the type of media coverage. When it comes to stereotypes, women face a distinct disadvantage. Voters typically prefer candidates whom they perceive as competent, strong leaders, and assertive. All of these traits are stereotypically associated with male candidates.

Conversely, female candidates are more likely assigned traits of compassion, kindness, and accessibility. Images of women as weak leaders may decrease their ability to win elections. Along the same lines, women also are associated with liberal issues, such as education, poverty and welfare, whereas men are associated with issues that may have a broader appeal, like defense, the economy, and foreign affairs. Because women are associated with issues that affect a smaller number of people, they may not hold the same broad appeal as their male counterparts. In addition, voters view competence on traditionally male issues as more important in the higher offices. If women are not seen as capable of representing a wide range of interests, it could make it more difficult for them to win votes on Election Day.

Media coverage also may impede the ability of women to be elected to office. On average, women receive far less campaign coverage than do their male adversaries. In addition, when women do receive media coverage of their campaigns, it tends to be more negative than positive, with a greater emphasis on horse-race coverage and viability than issue coverage. When reporters cover stories, they tend to focus on issues that are frequently associated with women, even if that issue is not central to the candidate's campaign. This type of coverage can lead to skewed opinions of a candidate and assign more concern for an issue than is actually the case. It may lead to perceptions of female candidates as concerned with only a narrow range of issues, which could translate to a lack of votes on Election Day. The situation is exacerbated when little information is available on a candidate, forcing voters to rely more on visual cues than substance, such as name or photo in lieu of researching the candidate's positions on important issues.

See Also: EMILY's List; Gender Quotas in Government; Glass Ceiling; Government, Women in; League of Women Voters; National Organization for Women; National

Women's Political Caucus; Representation of Women; Representation of Women in Government, International.

Further Readings

Box-Steffenmeier, Janet M., Suzanne De Boef, and Tse-Min Lin. "The Dynamics of the Partisan Gender Gap." *American Political Science Review*, v.98/3 (2004).

Carroll, Susan J. "Political Elites and Sex Differences in Political Ambition: A Reconsideration." *The Journal of Politics*, v.47/4 (1985).

Huddy, Leona and Nayda Terkildsen. "The Consequences of Gender Stereotypes for Women Candidates at Different Levels and Types of Office." *Political Research Quarterly*, v.46/3 (1993).

Kahn, Kim Fridkin. *The Political Consequences of Being a Women*. New York: Columbia University Press, 1996.

Mansbridge, Jane. "Should Blacks Represent Blacks and Women Represent Women? A Contingent 'Yes.'" *Journal of Politics*, v.61/3 (1999).

McDermott, Monika L. "Voting Cues in Low-Information Elections: Candidate Gender as a Social Information Variable in Contemporary United States Elections." *American Journal of Political Science*, v.41/1 (1997).

Sanbonmatsu, Kira. "Gender Related Political Knowledge and the Descriptive Representation of Women." *Political Behavior*, v.25/4 (2003).

Swers, Michele. 2001. "Understanding the Policy Impact of Electing Women: Evidence From Research on Congress and State Legislatures." *PS: Political Science and Politics*, v.34/2 (2001).

Angela L. Bos
Heather Madonia
College of Wooster

Reproductive and Sexual Health Rights

Since antiquity, cultures have developed and adopted technology and practices to promote or inhibit reproduction in response to their sociophysical environments and needs. Although most cultures have historically been pronatalist, this attitude has been highly dependent on intersections of class, race, ethnicity, age, sexual orientation, and disability, among others. The inherently iniquitous nature of society along these interstices has meant that reproductive rights, despite their fundamental nature, have not been a universal phenomenon. Even in the 20th century, the focus on women's reproductive health issues was more demographic than human rights–oriented. The language of reproductive "rights" is relatively new, owing its birth to the U.S. civil rights movements of the 1960s leading to the "sexual revolution" that gave women more freedom regarding their reproductive and sexual lives.

Recognizing the absence of any explicit reference to reproductive rights in international charters, the 179 participating countries of the International Conference on Population and Development, held in Cairo in 1994, and the subsequent Fourth World Conference on Women, held in Beijing in 1995, sought to address this oversight. Using language from preceding charters such as the 1948 Universal Declaration of Human Rights, the definition and assurance of reproductive rights was specifically spelled out during these conferences. The definition of reproductive rights may be framed within all reproduction-related issues from preconception to pregnancy and postreproductive health. Within this spectrum lie many considerations, including whether, when, and on what terms to engage in reproductive processes, and access to all appropriate information, reproductive technology, and healthcare options without discrimination or coercion, at all relevant lifestages.

Because sex is typically central to reproduction, reproductive rights discourse usually includes sexual health and rights, which encompass the freedom to engage in or deny sexual activity, control its terms, and exercise one's sexual preferences.

In addition, as women are the crucial end links in reproduction, gender equity issues and sexual politics are an important part of the reproductive rights discourse. Finally, international and intranational geographic variations in reproductive and sexual health and rights (RSHRs) are the rule rather than the exception, as women's overall life experiences are embedded in their socioeconomic-political contexts and determine many of their choices, both voluntary and imposed. Thus, RSHRs encapsulate biological processes, political considerations, and sociocultural practices/mores related to procreation, sexuality, and gender, as framed within the twin principles of right to reproductive health and right to self-determination.

Global Scenario Within Sociocultural Contexts

The constitution of the World Health Organization defines health not just as the absence of disease but also as overall mental, physical, and emotional well-being and acknowledges this to be a basic human right. Reproductive health is the most basic and mandatory of women's rights. Reproductive rights within the reproductive health principle seek foremost to address access to basic and reproductive healthcare to ensure safe pregnancy and motherhood, and prevention of diseases of the reproductive system, including human immunodeficiency virus and acquired immune deficiency syndrome (HIV/AIDS) and other sexually transmitted diseases. Rights within the reproductive self-determination principle overlap with the rights within the reproductive health principle to encompass access to contraception and abortion, all relevant information regarding such aspects, and the right to reject the abuse of methods of fertility control.

However, more than half a million women die annually as a result of the lack of these services, either during or after pregnancy or in an effort to terminate it. Less than two-thirds of the poorest women in middle- and low-income countries have access to antenatal care, and less than a third have access to skilled birth attendants at delivery—services that are near-universal in developed countries. Therefore, the lifetime risk of maternal death for women in the developing world is much higher, at 1 in 73, with sub-Saharan Africa presenting the worst odds, at 1 in 22. Comparatively, this risk is 1 in 7,300 in developed regions. Other basic reproductive health services are also inadequate, leading to immensely high maternal morbidity and chronic disability numbers between 10 and 15 million, characterized by sexually transmitted infections including HIV/AIDS, obstetric fistula (vaginal-rectal or vaginal-bladder tissue tear), severe anemia, damage and dysfunction, and chronic infections frequently resulting in infertility. Fully 99 percent of maternal mortality and an overwhelming proportion of morbidity and disability occur in developing countries.

Contraception and Abortion

Today, contraception is available by numerous traditional and modern methods, yet it remains out of reach of many. The global level of contraceptive prevalence by any method is 68 percent, but this figure is only 30 percent in the least developed countries of the world. As a result, the burden of fertility (number of births per women) is higher for women in such areas, where services and relief are most required, yet most inaccessible; for example, in Niger, the average number of children per woman during her lifetime (total fertility rate) is 7.2. Over 200 million women in middle- and low-income countries face an unmet need for contraceptives, resulting in unwanted pregnancies and abortions—the latter causing 13 percent of all maternal deaths worldwide. The flip side of fertility prevention can also be dark: cultural contexts and iniquitous social structures can sometimes lead to abuse, even in the 21st century.

In Slovakia, for example, systemic ethnic bias led to instances of Roma women being subject to forced sterilizations, sometimes without any knowledge that they were undergoing the procedure, until a safeguarding law was passed. Similarly, sex-selective abortions, sometimes forced, still take place in countries like India that display high son preference, despite laws banning them.

The topic of contraception and abortion is highly controversial and is the subject of heated debate in many parts of the world. Religion often plays a central role in these debates. Typically, most religions tend to be pronatalist, with both contraception and termination of pregnancy seen as contrary to religious teachings. Catholicism and Islam are examples of religions with very high levels of pronatalism, reflected in the reproductive rights and policies of many states where they are predominant, as in countries of South America and North Africa/Middle East, respectively.

Industrialized nations are also not immune to such controversy: Decades after the ruling in favor of the plaintiff to the (limited) right to abortion on the basis of the "right to privacy" in the case of *Roe v. Wade* in the early 1970s in the United States, the issue and the decision rendered remain highly contested. Religious conservatism was also responsible for the delayed approval of Emergency Contraception (Plan B or "morning after" pill), which drew resistance in the United States and continues to do so in other parts of the world.

Globally, the levels of reproductive rights accorded to women are characterized by high differentials. Developed countries typically possess both the resources as well as the constitutional setup to accord women a high degree of reproductive rights in terms

On the Brooklyn Bridge during the march for Women's Rights in 2004. As women are the crucial end-links in reproduction, gender equity issues and sexual politics are an important part of the reproductive rights discourse.

of healthcare, as well as self-determination. Scandinavian countries are traditionally leaders in rankings that factor in women's reproductive rights. Among developed countries, the United States is unique in that many indicators of reproductive rights, such as maternal and infant mortality, maternal morbidity, and access to care and contraception, all belie a lack of investment in women's health and rights. However, the consistently worst-performing countries in such indices are mostly located in Africa, followed by South Asia. Causes for such low reproductive health and rights are profoundly linked to economic and sociocultural factors.

Economic barriers arise on both the individual and national scales: Many developing nations do not possess the financial, infrastructural, or skilled human resources to provide adequate and/or universal healthcare. Thus, women have to access them per their own, often-limited, resources. For instance, access to the above-mentioned antenatal and delivery care improves drastically for women in the uppermost

income quintiles, with just over 90 and 80 percent served, respectively. Sociocultural barriers to RSHR include pervasive discrimination against women, often reflected in early marriages; condonement of abuse; and lack of investment in women's health, education, and empowerment. Early marriage is widespread in much of Africa and Asia (except China), constantly placing adolescents and young women at unnecessary risks associated with childbearing (higher mortality and morbidity and particularly obstetric fistula) and earlier exposure to sexually transmitted infections, including HIV/AIDS. This practice, as well as the violence and abuse that are also common in many parts of the developed and developing world, adversely affects women's levels of autonomy regarding sexual encounters and in general.

Sexual Health and Rights

The International Conference on Population and Development guaranteed the right to a safe and healthy sex life, free of coercion, as a major component of reproductive health. However, the patriarchy and heteronormativity present in most cultures often translate into stigma, discrimination, and violence against women and persons not conforming to mainstream sexual lifestyles.

As mentioned earlier, widespread violence and abuse compromise sexual health and rights not simply because of the risk for sexually transmitted diseases and human immunodeficiency virus and acquired immune deficiency syndrome (HIV/AIDS) or unwanted pregnancies but also as an imposition on the integrity of one's body, as enshrined in the Universal Declaration of Human Rights. In addition, rape and sexual violence have become a weapon of choice in areas of war and conflict. Because of women's role as gatekeepers of a culture, sexual coercion over them is seen as a type of conquest, leading to serious breaches of sexual rights.

Another violation of the security of the body is the cultural practice of female genital mutilation/cutting, in which all or part of the external female genitalia may be excised, often with rudimentary tools and without anesthetics. Practiced widely in Africa and West Asia/the Middle East, with prevalence rates between 5 percent (Uganda) and almost 100 percent (Guinea and Mali), female genital mutilation/cutting renders women more prone to infections and reproductive complications, severely disabled or in discomfort, and very often traumatized. With migratory movements, some prevalence is also appearing in other parts of the world, such as Australia and the United Kingdom.

Sexual health and rights overlap considerably with reproductive health rights, including issues such as access to contraception and negotiating safe, noncoercive sex, and protection from harmful practices such as female genital mutilation/cutting. Some scholars note that such intersections between sexual and reproductive rights has lead to sexual rights being subsumed by reproductive rights. They argue that sexual health and rights should extend to cover not just protections from disease and abuse but also promotion of sexual rights encompassing aspects of pleasure and eroticism and the assurance of such rights for nonmainstream expressions of sexuality.

In addition, under the human rights rubric, there are other concerns that must be addressed. In most cultures of the world today, reproduction and motherhood is a social institution in itself. Domi-

nant discourses of motherhood idealize it as central to women's sense of identity and ascribe to it noble attributes of nurturance and selflessness. This is at odds with "discourses of deviancy" that attach to those who do not conform to the mainstream model of the fecund, healthy female who is ready to sacrifice self-interest to the larger interests of child and society. Childless women (by choice or otherwise), lesbians, and HIV-positive women are typical targets of such discourses, and the protection of their rights to choose whether or not to bear children is sometimes overlooked in the more typical concerns of RSHR. Given that the United Nations Millennium Development Goals have been critiqued for not overtly including reproductive rights in their targets and goals, an expanded definition and assurance of RHSR may be necessary. Some ways of addressing these oversights are addressed in the section on policy directions.

Population Control Perspectives

The perspective of population control throws greater complexity into the area of reproductive rights. Fears of a world overrun by an uncontrollably growing population have consumed general populace and development practitioners alike, sometimes resulting in draconian policies. The motivations behind some of these policies can be described as population pressure on limited resources at best, or racism and eugenics at worst. As mentioned, until the International Conference on Population and Development, most population control policies did not consider human or reproductive rights but rather population numbers, often leading to coercive programs in many countries, such as China. Since then, efforts have been made to promote human rights and the "user's perspective" in fertility-control programs.

However, the perspective has shifted yet again, and fertility control, particularly in the world's poorest regions, is deemed essential for sustainable development. International development and aid agencies tend to precede human development agendas with a population-control agenda, but there is adequate evidence to show that the causal relationship is stronger in the reverse. Women's educational levels have been shown to be the most important development indicator in lowering fertility levels, as evidenced by Kerala state in India, raising more policy implications.

Policy Directions

Apart from the obvious policy directions of universal reproductive health and expanding reproductive and sexual self-determination to fulfill the mandates of the Universal Declaration of Human Rights, International Conference on Population and Development, and Millennium Development Goals, other areas still need to be fully addressed by comprehensive policies. The lack of appropriate care often leads to related problems such as infertility, which in turn is stigmatized by most societies, particularly in the developing world. It is also emotionally injurious to many women. Reproductive health rights should thus encompass access to basic healthcare and the provision of technology and medical aid to address infertility.

The increasing feminization of the HIV/AIDS epidemic also means guaranteed provision of antiretroviral therapies for HIV-positive women and for prevention of mother-to-child transmission of the virus. Expansion of RSHR must also extend to marginalized sexualities and women in general, who often suffer from RSHR violations in iniquitous personal or societal settings and institutions such as marriage. Men's frequent control over women's sexuality and reproductive choices has often been the cause of low RSHR outcomes.

Therefore, men's cognizance of their critical role is extremely valuable in the promotion and fulfillment of RSHR needs. Population policies must also seek to address gender equity and empowerment issues first to ensure RSHR, which in turn can lead to better population outcomes.

See Also: Abortion Laws, International; Female Genital Surgery, Geographical Distribution; Female Genital Surgery, Terminology and Critiques of; Female Genital Surgery, Types of; Pregnancy; Prenatal Care; Pro-Life Movement; *Roe v. Wade*; Sterilization, Involuntary.

Further Readings

Arendell, Terry. "Conceiving and Investigating Motherhood: The Decade's Scholarship." *Journal of Marriage and Family*, v.62/4 (2000)

Center for Reproductive Rights. "Gaining Ground: A Tool for Advancing Reproductive Rights Law Reform." http://reproductiverights.org/en/document/gaining -ground-a-tool-for-advancing-reproductive-rights-law -reform (accessed January 2010).

Ehrenreich, Nancy, ed. *The Reproductive Rights Reader: Law, Medicine, and the Construction of Motherhood*. New York: New York University Press, 2008.

Knudsen, Lara M. *Reproductive Rights in a Global Context: South Africa, Uganda, Peru, Denmark, United States, Vietnam, Jordan*. Nashville, TN: Vanderbilt University Press, 2006.

Save the Children. "*State of the World's Mothers 2009*." http://www.savethechildren.org/publications/state -of-the-worlds-mother s-report/state-worlds-mothers -report-2009.pdf (accessed January 2010).

United Nations Population Fund. "State of the World Population 2008, Reaching Common Ground: Culture, Gender and Human Rights." https://www.unfpa.org /webdav/site/global/shared/documents/publications /2008/swp08_eng.pdf (accessed January 2010).

Vandana Wadhwa
Boston University

Reproductive Cancers

Cancer is a group of more than 100 related diseases named after the part of the body from which they originate. Reproductive cancers begin in the reproductive organs in both females and males. Female reproductive cancers, also known as gynecologic cancers, include two types of uterine cancer, ovarian, cervical, vaginal, vulvar, and fallopian tube cancers, and cancerous hydatidiform moles.

Reproductive cancer occurs when a cell's genetic material changes, becomes damaged, and is not controlled by the body's immune response, causing abnormal cell growth to proliferate and invade nearby tissue. If the cancer metastasizes, it then spreads to other parts of the body. Risk factors for reproductive cancers include family history, infection, exposure to ionizing radiation and certain chemicals, and hormones and lifestyle influences, as well as social determinants of health such as lack of access to income, resources, and healthcare. The primary methods of treatment include surgery, radiation and chemical therapies. Success rates for treatments vary by overall health status, type, site, and stage of cancer. It is important to note that mortality rates from cancer are higher in low- and middle-income countries.

Types of Uterine Cancer

There are two types of uterine cancer: endometrial and sarcoma. Endometrial cancer, beginning in the lining of the uterus, is the most common type. It usually occurs after menopause in women whose risk factors include family history, obesity, hypertension, diabetes, and exposure to high levels of estrogen, especially without the balancing effects of progesterone, and exposure to radiation therapy in the pelvic area. The most common symptom is abnormal vaginal bleeding. Diagnosis is made by transvaginal ultrasound and endometrial biopsy. If treated early, and the cancer has not spread beyond the uterus, the survival rate is high. Uterine sarcoma, beginning in the connective or other tissue of the uterus, occurs in only about 5 percent of uterine cancers. Symptoms are similar to that for endometrial cancer, and risk factors include exposure to radiation therapy and the use of tamoxifen to treat breast cancer. Treatment for both is similar and includes hysterectomy, or removal of the uterus—the most common treatment—followed by radiation, chemotherapy, or hormone therapy if the cancer has metastasized.

Cervical cancer begins in the lower part of the uterus that extends into the vagina. It is the fifth most common cancer in women worldwide and the first and second most common in middle-income and developing countries. This slow-growing cancer has few symptoms in earlier stages and is, therefore, usually diagnosed in middle age. Later-stage symptoms include abnormal bleeding and discharge, low back pain, and pain during intercourse and urination. While the predominant risk factor is the very common sexually transmitted human papillomaviruses (HPV), which is highly preventable with the use of condoms, most women with HPV do not get cervical or other reproductive cancers.

The synthetic estrogen diethylstilbestrol (DES), used on pregnant women primarily from the late 1930s to the early 1970s—and "dumped" for profit by pharmaceutical companies into third-world nations for use by pregnant women after it was banned in developed countries—also is known to cause cervical and vaginal cancer. This is particularly true in young girls and younger women. Regular PAP tests and pelvic examination used to detect precancerous changes make cervical cancer highly preventable and, when found early, extremely treatable. Treatment involves removal of the cancerous tissue, which may be accompanied by chemotherapy or radiation. Recently, health agencies have recommended that girls between the ages of 9 and 26 get the HPV vaccine to reduce their risk of cervical, vulvar, and vaginal cancers.

Cancers of the vagina, or the birth canal, and vulva, or external genitals, are both relatively uncommon and most likely to occur in women over the age of 60. The primary symptom for both cancers is abnormal bleeding, and the primary treatment is surgical removal or radiation therapy. The HPV vaccine is now used as a preventative for both, while regular screening increases the probability of early stage abnormality being found in time for effective treatment.

Ovarian Cancer

Ovarian cancer develops from different kinds of ovarian cells. It can be especially virulent because symptoms may not present until the cancer is large or has spread. While ovarian cancer is the second most common reproductive cancer, it is the most fatal. Ovarian cancer is more likely in developed countries because high-fat diets and oral contraceptive use increase risk. Other risk factors include family history, with 5 to 10 percent of cases being related to a specific gene also found in breast cancer. The disease is most common among women of Ashkenazi Jewish descent, older women who had a child late in life, or women who did not have children, as well as females who began menstruating early and those whose menopause began late. Symptoms include discomfort similar to indigestion, enlarged abdomen, bloating and gas, and backache. Diagnosis is by imaging techniques, and treatment is usually surgery, the extent of which is dependent on the stage of the cancer. Ovarian cancer in advanced stages is likely to recur. Having similar risks and treatments to ovarian cancer, fallopian tube cancer, which is unlikely to originate in the fallopian tubes, is rare.

In about 20 percent of cases, a hydatidiform mole, an abnormal fertilized egg, or molar pregnancy becomes cancerous. Symptoms include feeling pregnant and may include nausea, vomiting, and bleeding. If this cancer spreads, women may experience other symptoms. A positive pregnancy test, an unusually large uterus, and no fetal heartbeat make detection easy. The cure rate is virtually 100 percent if the cancer has not spread and 60 to 80 percent if it has spread. Treatment includes removal of the cancerous mole and may be followed by chemotherapy.

Currently, the most controversial issue around reproductive cancers is widespread use of the HPV vaccine. Some argue that the vaccine has not been adequately tested and may have unintended harmful consequences, leaving many questions unanswered. In addition to issues of safety and efficacy, another concern is whether reliance on the vaccine will reduce safe -ex practices and screening procedures.

Important to note is that most research and funding for cancer causes and treatments fall into a biomedical model of medicine with little attention paid to social determinants beyond lifestyle issues or the broader conditions that promote or restrict health. Consequences of globalization, war, environmental disasters and climate change, and allocation of global resources need to be taken into serious account to reduce worldwide cancer rates when considering prevention forms. Reproductive cancers are no exception and have further stigmatizing effects because of relationships drawn to women's sexual practices and disease. Because reproductive cancers often have devastating consequences for fertility and reproduction, the quality of both women's health specifically and the health of nations generally should be matters of serious concern.

See Also: Birth Defects, Environmental Factors and; Breast Cancer; Cancer, Environmental Factors and; Cancer, Women and; Health, Mental and Physical; Infertility, Incidence of; *Our Bodies, Ourselves*; Pregnancy; Prenatal Care; Poverty; World Health Organization.

Further Readings
Hasan, H. *Cervical Cancer: Current and Emerging Trends in Detection and Treatment (Cancer and Modern Science)*. New York: Rosen Publishing Group, 2009.

The International Gynecologic Cancer Society. http://www.igcs.org/ (accessed December 2009).

Muggia, Franco and Esther Oliva. *Uterine Cancer: Screening, Diagnosis, and Treatment (Current Clinical Oncology)*. New York: Humana Press, 2009.

National Women's Health Network. http://www.nnewh.org (accessed December 2009).

Nicolopoulou-Stamati, P. *Cancer as an Environmental Disease*. Boston: Kluwer Academic Publishers, 2004.

Palefsky, Joel and Jody Handley. *What Your Doctor May Not Tell You about HPV and Abnormal Pap Smears*. New York: Grand Central Publishing, 2002.

Salani, Ritu and Robert E. Bristow. *Johns Hopkins Patients' Guide to Ovarian Cancer*. Sudbury, MA: Jones and Bartlett, 2009

Deborah Davidson
York University

Revirginization

Revirginization is the act of regaining one's virginity, after having had sexual intercourse once or many times, through spiritual or surgical means. As conceptions of virginity are highly influenced by religion, motivations for revirginization are often religious in nature. Women may also seek revirginization to comply with familial or cultural expectations. Both spiritual and surgical revirginizations are gaining popularity in the United States and can be seen in many other countries today.

The label *virgin* is traditionally much more important for women than it is for men, and in most societies, including the United States, it is understood primarily, and often exclusively, in terms of women. Definitions of virginity vary according to location and culture, but most include the lack of experience of sexual intercourse and the presence of internal cleanliness and purity. As virginity is seen in both spiritual and physical terms, revirginization can take both spiritual and physical forms.

Spiritual Revirginization
Spiritual revirginization gained popularity in the United States in the early 1990s. The idea that virginity can be regained through spiritual means requires virginity to be thought of as a state of mind or intention, as opposed to a physical, experiential fact. Women working toward becoming a born-again virgin are often religious, most often Christian, and are seeking an innocence that they possessed before being sexually active. Virginity here is defined as the possession of a childlike heart and/or a pure sense of being that is lost when women "give" their virginity away. Women seeking this form of revirginization are often not looking to lose their virginity again.

Spiritual revirginization is achieved through prayer, thought, and meditation.

Physical Revirginization

Physical, or surgical, revirginization is called hymenoplasty or hymenorraphy and involves reconstructing the hymen. As the hymen is often ruptured during a female's first vaginal intercourse, an intact hymen is seen as proof of virginity to many men and women. There are two types of hymenoplasty—one involves sewing together a torn hymen and the other uses an artificial hymen implant. Implants are made to resemble the natural hymen to the extent that some are inserted with a bloodlike solution to be expelled when the implant breaks during intercourse.

Hymenoplasty is more commonly used by women whose lives combine or alternate between two cultures—one that includes premarital sex and another that demands a virgin marriage. Women use the surgery as a means to negotiate between differing societal expectations, although this negotiation does not provide a means to combine cultures into one unifying identity but rather separates ideals and behaviors into stages according to location or life stage, such as the young woman who engages in sex acts in college in the United States but undergoes revirginization surgery before returning to her home country for her marriage, for which she is expected to be a virgin.

Unlike spiritual revirginization, which many women seek for personal reasons, surgical revirginization is often sought as a gift for a woman's husband, as the fulfillment of a requirement of her family, or as a means to avoid the social consequences of sex before marriage. The procedure costs approximately $2,000 to $5,000.

See Also: Female Genital Surgery, Types of; Gender Roles, Cross-Cultural; Marriage.

Further Readings

Alexander, Brian. "Born-Again Virgins Claim to Rewrite the Past." MSNBC.com. http://www.msnbc.msn.com /id/23254178 (accessed June 2010).

Bernau, Anke. *Virgins: A Cultural History*. London: Granta, 2007.

Keller, Wendy. *The Cult of the Born-Again Virgin: The New Sexual Revolution*. Deerfield Beach, FL: Health Communications, 1999.

Katy N. Kreitler
University of San Francisco

Revolutionary Association of the Women of Afghanistan

The Revolutionary Association of the Women of Afghanistan (RAWA) is an independent political and social organization of Afghan women fighting for human rights and social justice for all people in Afghanistan. For over 30 years, it has been actively supporting the most needy women and girls in life-threatening circumstances. RAWA has been doing its extraordinary work by running literacy classes, schools, orphanages, and small business projects while publicly advocating for women's human rights. RAWA's work is courageous, vital, and inspirational. Its main objective is to increase the number of Afghan women in political and social activities and to contribute to the struggle for the establishment of a government based on secular and democratic values in Afghanistan.

Founded in 1977 by a 20-year-old student and activist named Meena, RAWA's goals were to aid and empower Afghan women and to further the peaceful creation of a free and secular Afghan democracy. RAWA's founding leader and her two colleagues were brutally murdered by the Soviet occupying forces in 1978. Since then, RAWA's activists have focused on women's rights and human rights as they have responded to one brutal regime after another: the 1979 Soviet invasion of Afghanistan and the consequent rise of fundamentalist jehadis (1992), the Taliban (1996), the return of jihadi warlords to positions of power in the interim, and now transitional governments in 2001 and 2002. RAWA believes that democracy and freedom cannot be given but rather it is the duty of the country and people to fight for it.

RAWA's work in Afghanistan is aimed primarily at supporting women and girls who are victims of war and atrocities committed by belligerent groups. They provide psychosocial support, trace missing females or their family members, and assist families in evacuation and resettlement and supply them with basic living necessities. However, RAWA's main focus is on girls' education, as they believe that knowledge is a great power that will raise women's awareness about women's human rights, their place in society, and the importance of their engagement in the social and political problems that Afghanistan faces. RAWA also believes that education must go beyond providing basic literacy skills, so they have created diverse educational opportunities available for everyone to achieve enlightenment and raise awareness.

Despite political oppression and grave security risks, RAWA's appeal, courageous work, and influence grew worldwide. In 1981, to spread the news, aims, and objectives of its work, RAWA launched a bilingual magazine *Payam-e-Zan* (woman's message). RAWA's efforts, in Afghanistan and among Afghan refugees in Pakistan, are carried out by some 2,000 core women members and thousands of male supporters, without a paid staff or even an office. The organization has been able to document some of the most shocking images of fundamentalist atrocities, from limb amputations to public executions, and they have been able to spark some of the most profound changes in mindsets in a society in which many have been taught that a woman is worth literally only half of a man.

RAWA has been carrying out its struggle for human rights and social justice for over four decades and has gained much support and sympathy from around the world.

See Also: Afghanistan; Islamic Feminism; Pakistan; Religious Fundamentalism, Cross-Cultural Context of; Taliban.

Further Readings

Brodsky, Anne. *With All Our Strength: The Revolutionary Association of the Women of Afghanistan.* London: Routledge, 2003.

Mehta, Sunita. *Shattering Myths and Claiming the Future: Women for Afghan Women,* New York: Palgrave MacMillian, 2002.

Skaine, Rosemarie. *The Women of Afghanistan Under the Taliban.* Jefferson, NC: McFarland, 2002.

Olivera Simic
University of Melbourne

Revolve

Revolve is a publication of the complete New Testament in the form of a large glamour magazine, targeted at teen girls. Full of quizzes and Q&A advice, the "Biblezine" appeals by making the Bible seem exciting and relevant. Since its initial publication in 2003, *Revolve* has been followed by several similar products—as well as harsh criticism from more conservative Christians who see *Revolve* and its allies as giving bad advice and weakening the Bible's authority.

Revolve: The Complete New Testament is published by Thomas Nelson. Targeted at high school girls who are intimidated by the Bible, *Revolve* uses the New Century Version (NCV), a translation chosen for its "readability," and mimics the format of popular teen magazines. Like typical niche study Bibles, *Revolve* includes informative sections such as "Bible Basics." However, the text is also interspersed with familiar magazine features such as quizzes, "Guy 411" sections, "Blab" columns to answer readers' questions, "Beauty Tips" to help girls achieve "inner beauty," and interviews with popular Christian recording artists and speakers. Nearly a million young readers have been drawn to *Revolve* because it is written in a language they can understand, helps relate the Bible to their daily lives, and is nonthreatening to carry in public.

Since 2003, *Revolve* has been republished in annual new editions, as well as several offshoots, including *Revolve Devos,* a collection of daily devotionals; *Revolve: Psalms & Proverbs and other Wisdom Books*; and *Revolve Study Guides* for the books of Mark and James. There is also a *Revolve Journal*; a Spanish-language edition, *En Órbita*; and *Revolve Spin: An Audio Devotional for Teens*. Besides these magazine-format publications, the *Revolve Devotional Bible* (2006) is a NCV Bible that includes daily devotionals and study sections as well as typical *Revolve* features discussing relationships, culture, and spirituality. The Revolve Tour is a related evangelical outreach event.

After *Revolve*'s successful debut, Thomas Nelson Publishing has launched several other similar "BibleZines." These include *Magnify: Old Testament Stories* for kids and the New Testaments *Blossom* and *Explore* for middle school girls and boys. The male counterpart to *Revolve* is *Refuel*. For women in their 20s, *Becoming* discusses relationships, fitness, and beauty in editions featuring the New Testament and the Wisdom Books; *Align* is the counterpart for young men. The New Testament Biblezine for adults, *Divine Health*, includes features about healing and health.

Some more conservative Christian critics and parents have challenged *Revolve* for compromising

"God's Word" by making the Bible too comforting, too conformed to worldly culture, or without authority and power. Critics also critique the Biblezine for offering weak advice to impressionable girls and embracing cultural relativism, ecology, and feminist values instead of offering God's word as the answer to girls' questions. According to critics, *Revolve* is also dangerous because it advises girls to minister to unsaved friends by showing them God's love and praying for them, not by trying to convert them directly or warning them about Hell. The NCV itself is criticized as being inaccurately translated.

See Also: Adolescence; Christianity; Evangelical Protestantism; Feminist Theology; Women's Magazines.

Further Readings

Friedlin, Jennifer. "New Biblezine for Young Women Markets Beliefs." *We News* (July 11, 2004). http://www .womensenews.org/story/arts/040711/new-biblezine -young-women-markets-beliefs (accessed July 2010).

Revolve 2010: The Complete New Testament. New Century Version. Nashville, TN: Thomas Nelson Inc., 2009.

Tennant, Agnieszka. "Ten Things You Should Know About the New Girls' Biblezine." *Christianity Today* (September 1, 2003). http://www.christianitytoday .com/ct/2003/septemberweb-only/9-15-21.0.html (accessed July 2010).

Vanessa Baker
Bowling Green State University

Rhode, Kim

Four-time Olympian Kim Rhode won her first gold medal in International Double Trap at the 1996 Olympic Games in Atlanta, Georgia. She was the youngest person to ever be on an Olympic shooting team, turning 17 years old just two days before the opening ceremonies. She won two more Olympic medals, a bronze (2000) and a gold (2004), before Double Trap was eliminated from the shooting roster in 2004. Switching to International Skeet, a difficult task for any star athlete, she returned to the 2008 Games in Beijing and won the silver. Other highlights from Rhode's career include eight World Cup gold medals in International

Skeet (2007) and International Double Trap (1996–98, 2000, 2003), two gold medals at the Pan American Games in International Double Trap (1999, 2003), and 11 Ladies National Championships in International Skeet (2007–09) and Double Trap (1995–98, 2000–03). She's also broken numerous records, including the Olympic Double Trap record in 1996 and the World Record in International Skeet at the 2007 World Cup in Santo Domingo. For her outstanding achievements, USA Shooting, the national governing body for the Olympic shooting sports, awarded her Female Athlete of the Year seven times (1997–98, 2002, 2004, 2007–09), and *Time* magazine identified her as one of the 10 "Best Sports Phenoms of 1996."

Rhode was known in the competitive shooting world long before she became an Olympian. Born in Whittier, California, on July 16, 1979, and raised in El Monte, California, the young Rhode accompanied her parents on hunting trips before she could talk and began shooting, with her dad's assistance, before she was tall enough to clear the length of a shotgun. She harvested her first doves when she was 7 years old and began her competitive career in American Skeet at the age of 11 years. At 12 years of age, Rhode was the first girl to break 100 straight, and at age 13 years she was the youngest to win the 1993 Ladies World Championship in American Skeet.

Although she clearly demonstrated Olympic potential, Rhode was too young to live at the Olympic Training Center in Colorado Springs, Colorado. Instead she practiced at her home range, the Oak Tree Gun Club in Newhall, California, and once or twice a week at the Prado Olympic Shooting Park in Chino, California, site of the 1984 Olympic shooting games. After her first gold medal, the owner of the Oak Tree club built her a practice bunker for International Double Trap and gave her a key, allowing her 24-hour access. When Double Trap was cancelled, the bunker was turned into an International Skeet field.

In 2009, Rhode retired her four-time Olympic shotgun, an MX-12 Perazzi, and began shooting with a MX2000 Perazzi. She continues to practice four to six hours a day, six to seven days a week, and shoots 500 to 1,000 rounds per session. To this day, her father, Richard, is her coach, and her mother, Sharon, keeps the schedule. For Rhode, hunting and sports shooting are pleasurable family events, and the shooting range continues to be her second home.

See Also: Olympics, Summer; Shooting Sports, Women in; Sports, Women in.

Further Readings

International Olympic Committee. http://www.olympic .org (accessed July 2010).

Kelly, Caitlin. *Blown Away: American Women and Guns.* New York: Pocket Books, 2004.

Team USA. http://shooting.teamusa.org (accessed July 2010).

Nancy Floyd
Georgia State University

Rice, Condoleezza

Condoleezza Rice is an academic and government official who was the second woman and the first African American woman to hold the post of U.S. Secretary of State (2005–09). Prior to becoming secretary of State under President George Bush, Rice served as a national security adviser (2001–05). She describes herself as a moderate Republican. Currently, Rice is the Thomas and Barbara Stephenson Senior Fellow on Public Policy at the Hoover Institution and professor of political science at Stanford University.

As secretary of state, Rice initiated several innovative policy moves, which included dedicating her department to "Transformational Diplomacy." This focused on building and sustaining democratic, well-governed states around the world (and the Middle East, in particular). Among the strategies implemented were the relocation of American diplomats to such hardship locations as Iraq, Afghanistan, and Angola. Affected diplomats were required to become fluent in two foreign languages. Rice also created a high-level position to "de-fragment" U.S. foreign aid.

Rice was born November 14, 1954, in Birmingham, Alabama. She was an only child to John and Angelena Rice, both of whom were well educated. They provided their daughter with a comfortable middle-class existence. Although she grew up in a segregated Birmingham during the civil rights movement, Rice had a relatively sheltered childhood. She mastered the piano at 3 and was told that she could have had a career as a concert pianist. She skipped first and seventh grades and entered college at age 15. Intelligence, hard work, and determination propelled her through her childhood. After Rice's mother died in 1985, her father moved to California to be closer to her.

Rice holds three degrees: a bachelor's in political science, having graduated cum laude and Phi Beta Kappa from the University of Denver in 1974; a master's from the University of Notre Dame in 1975; and a Ph.D. from the Graduate School of International Studies at the University of Denver in 1981. She was hired as an assistant professor of political science at Stanford University in 1981 and worked there from 1981 to 1999. From 1993 to 1999, Rice also served as Stanford's provost. She was the first woman and the first African American to hold this position.

As an African American woman, Rice held the highest position in a presidential cabinet, yet she has often been criticized for her inattention to "black issues." Though she grew up in the segregated South, she was never really directly involved in the civil rights movement. Rice's parents tried to shield her from racial discrimination, but she was still very much aware of the civil rights struggle and the problems of Jim Crow laws in Birmingham. Rice credited the positive attitude of her parents and friends for their influence when she stated, "They refused to allow the limits and injustices of their time to limit our horizons." Rice also asserted, "My parents had me absolutely convinced that, well, you may not be able to have a hamburger at Woolworth's but you can be president of the United States."

See Also: Government, Women in; United States; Women's History Month.

Further Readings

Biography.com "Condoleezza Rice." http://www.biography .com/articles/Condoleezza-Rice-9456857 (accessed July 2010).

Bumiller, Elisabeth. *Condoleezza Rice: An American Life.* New York: Random House, 2009.

Kessler, Glenn. *The Confidante: Condoleezza Rice and the Creation of the Bush Legacy.* New York: St. Martin's, 2007.

Rice, Condoleezza. *Extraordinary, Ordinary People: A Memoir of Family.* New York: Crown Archetype, 2010.

Anita Pankake
University of Texas, Pan American

Ride, Sally

Sally Ride (1951–), the first U.S. woman in space, is the founder, president, and CEO of Sally Ride Science (SRS). Part of the mission of SRS is to make a difference in girls' lives and in society's perceptions of their roles in technical fields. Ride is concerned about the underrepresentation of women in the sciences. Her efforts focus on middle-level students, since girls often lose interest in the sciences at this time in their lives. Ride wants to bring the excitement and fun of science to young people. A key goal is to encourage women to pursue their interests in science.

Sally Ride was the first U.S. woman in space, and has continued her career winning numerous awards and honors.

The Website for Sally Ride Science details the company's extensive array of activities. Accordingly, SRS hosts programs, events, and workshops, as well as providing curriculum, resources, trainings, and publications, to further the interest in science. Sally Ride Science Festivals include opportunities for girls, their parents, and teachers to attend workshops, hear a featured speaker, meet scientists and engineers, and have fun at a street fair. Hands-on activities, music, and food are part of the festival. Festivals are held throughout the United States on university campuses.

Sally Ride Science sponsors TOYchallenge. This event is designed for fifth- to eighth-grade girls and boys. The challenge is to create a new toy or game. Through the hands-on process of creating the toy, participants learn about science, design, and engineering. Science camps are another aspect of Sally Ride Science. Camps for girls in the middle grades provide opportunities to discover, explore, and experience hands-on science and to make new friends.

Sally Ride Science publications are designed for upper elementary and middle school students, parents, and teachers. Classroom kits of supplemental science materials that include activities and nonfiction science career books are available as well.

Awards and Achievements

Sally Ride received a bachelor of science in physics and a bachelor of arts in English in 1973, a master of science in physics in 1975, and a doctorate in physics in 1978 from Stanford University. She was mission specialist on STS-7, aboard space shuttle *Challenger* that launched on June 18, 1983, and on STS 41-G, aboard space shuttle *Challenger* in 1984. Dr. Ride was training for a third mission, but it was suspended due to the space shuttle *Challenger* accident. Her time in space included 147 hours for the first mission and 197 hours for the second mission.

Dr. Ride created the U.S. National Aeronautics and Space Administration's (NASA's) Office of Exploration for long-range planning and prepared the *Leadership and America's Future in Space* report during her time at NASA. She joined the faculty of the University of California in San Diego in 1989 as a professor of physics and director of the University of California's California Space Institute.

She served as the president of Space.com, a Website focused on all aspects of space. She created NASA's

EarthKam project. This project allows middle school through college students to take pictures of natural phenomena on Earth from cameras aboard the NASA space shuttles. The photos are then downloaded to the Internet, and the images of Earth from space are then available to students.

She is the author or coauthor of the following books: *Mission Planet Earth: Our World and Its Climate—and How Humans Are Changing Them* (2009); *Mission: Save the Planet: Things YOU Can Do to Help Fight Global Warming!* (2009); *Exploring Our Solar System* (2003); *The Mystery of Mars* (1999); *The Third Planet: Exploring the Earth from Space* (1994); *Voyager: An Adventure to the Edge of the Solar System* (1992); and *To Space and Back* (1986).

Her awards include induction into the National Women's Hall of Fame, Astronaut Hall of Fame, California Hall of Fame, and National Aviation Hall of Fame. She received the NCAA's Theodore Roosevelt Award, the highest honor presented to a former student-athlete, the Jefferson Award for Public Service, and the Women's Research and Education Institute's American Woman Award.

See Also: Astronauts, Female; Physics, Women in; Science Education for Girls.

Further Readings

Ride, Sally and T. O'Shaughnessy. *Mission Planet Earth: Our World and Its Climate.* New York: Flash Point, 2009.

Riddolls, Tom. *Sally Ride: The First Woman in Space.* New York: Crabtree Publishing, 2010.

Sally Ride Science. https://www.sallyridescience.com (accessed January 2010).

Marilyn L. Grady
University of Nebraska

Robinson, Mary

Mary Robinson was the United Nations (UN) High Commissioner for Human Rights from 1997 to 2002 and converted the ceremonial office into a bully pulpit for human rights. She also helped make human rights a central focus of the world. From 1990 to 1997, as the first female president of Ireland, Robinson transformed that figurehead post into a forum that brought the excluded Irish—especially women, economic exiles, sexual minorities, the poor, and disabled—to the focus of national policy. She used her high profile as a lightning rod, visiting catastrophically violent sites like Somalia—where she was the first head of state to visit the area after the genocide—Bosnia, and Rwanda, describing with plain words and raw emotion the details to the international press corps.

Born Mary Bourke in County Mayo in 1944, the daughter of two physicians, she was educated at Trinity College, University of Dublin, and Harvard Law School, where she won a fellowship in 1967. In the United States, she was influenced by the antiwar and civil rights movement and came to view the law as a vehicle for social change. As a lawyer, she argued landmark labor and women's cases before both the Irish courts and the European Court. In her roles as senator and then president, Robinson dared to change the antediluvian Irish divorce, contraception, abortion, and equal pay laws and helped facilitate peace with Northern Ireland. Even with her public service career, Robinson balanced a successful marriage and three children while advocating, governing and traveling. Ireland became the "Celtic Tiger," one of the world's wealthiest countries where former immigrants returned, during her tenure as president.

As the commissioner of Human Rights, Robinson created a more effective and professional staff even though her budget was a mere 2 percent of the UN's operating costs. She protested the lack of money to effect necessary changes and raised voluntary funds from states and foundations. She refused to ignore the suffering of millions and the numerous violations caused by violent political oppression, torture, exclusion, racial discrimination, and religious persecution—even more so when the daily denial of rights flowed from poverty, lack of food, clean water, sanitation, shelter, and education.

Robinson shook up the UN and the powerful alliances and nations like the United States and the North Atlantic Treaty Organization for targeting bombs at civilians, and she chastised China for jailing political dissidents and for the erosion of workers rights. Robinson spoke out against growing corporate influence, the erosion of human rights provoked by the war on terror, and the reaction to the September 11, 2001, terrorist attacks in New York. Her outspoken, open criticism of the United States prevented her from serving the remaining three years of her full second term. She is currently the President of Realizing Rights: The Ethical Globalization Initiative, a nongovernmental organization she founded, as well as the honorary president of Oxfam International and one of Nelson Mandela's circle of Elders.

See Also: Ireland; Social Justice Activism; Somalia; United Kingdom; United Nations Conventions.

Further Readings

Boyle, K., ed. *A Voice for Human Rights, Mary Robinson.* Philadelphia: University of Pennsylvania Press, 2006.

Goodman, A. "Interview Democracy Now With Mary Robinson." http://www.democracynow.org/2009/3 /9fmr_irish_president_mary_robinson_joins (accessed March 2009).

Horgan, J. *Mary Robinson, A Woman of Ireland and the World.* Lanham, MD: Roberts Rinehart, 1997.

Siggins, L. *The Woman Who Took Power in the Park, Mary Robinson, President of Ireland, 1990–1997.* Edinburgh, UK: Mainstream Publishing, 1997.

Spillane, M. "Leader Like Robinson Hard to Find." *National Catholic Reporter* (April 13, 2001).

Rosalyn Fraad Baxandall
State University of New York, Old Westbury

Rock Music, Women in

The music industry historically has been, and still is, male dominated, making it a difficult battlefield for women who wish to enter. Prior to the mainstream emergence of rock music in the 1950s, female singers can frequently were found in genres like jazz, however, the numbers of women who played instruments were far fewer. Similar trends can be seen in rock music, a sound that brings to mind the spirit of rebellion. It is often associated with youth or popular culture, through the use of, at least, powerful guitar and vocals but also often features drums and bass, and is most often associated with masculinity.

At the height of her popularity in the early 1960s, Janis Joplin was one of the earliest recognizable women in rock music who was featured as number three on VH1's 100 Greatest Women of Rock and Roll' list compiled in 1999. Joplin broke the conventions associated with her contemporary female singers; she sang in a raspy voice rather than a pretty, sweet-sounding tone, and often performed dressed like her male contemporaries.

It was also in the 1960s, as the second wave of feminism was brewing and gaining momentum, that female singer-songwriters like Joni Mitchell, Grace Slick, Carole King, and Joan Baez started to emerge. These women held spots five, 10, and 27 on the VH1 list respectively. More typically feminine in appearance than Joplin, these four women all used their music to express their politics, whereas overwhelmingly most female singers of their time were singing about love—usually the unrequited type.

Singer-songwriters were liberated from some elements of the largely male-dominated industry, needing only their acoustic guitar and voices to produce music; however, gaining a notable fan base involved negotiation with the larger industry and usually meant acquiring a full band and a manager, all of whom would likely be male. In this scenario, the female singer-songwriter would struggle with not being marked by the public as another band with a female singer that was created more by the industry as a novelty than by the musicians themselves in the name of art. Maintaining authorial control within a patriarchal system of producers and record labels that sought to control public images and music based on what would generate the most revenue was, and still is, a challenge faced by many musicians.

The Late 1960s and Early 1970s

The rock genre as a whole really began to flourish in the late 1960s and early 1970s, with the rising popularity of bands like The Rolling Stones and Led Zeppelin. It is during this period of time and in this culture that the image of "women as groupies" emerges. Groupies are fans who chase rock stars who are often presumed to be sexually available. The 1970s, however, with second wave feminism almost at full force, brought forth singer-songwriter, poet, and now intellectual Patti Smith. Smith sang of her personal experiences and played with both masculine and feminine qualities in her appearance.

The advent of punk music and aesthetics created more room for female musicians. Bands like Crass, which weren't exclusively composed of females, would use the political agenda of punk rock to question gender-role stereotypes and relations. In was in this culture that iconic female rock figures like Joan Jett and Siouxsie Sioux emerged, numbers 32 and 96, respectively, on VH1's list. These women sang songs focused instead on how they saw society at large and their place within it, using music as a tool to express opinions while embodying their artistic and musical talents in the tradition of female singer-songwriters prior. This manifested itself in more aggression than previously seen from female front women and themes of equality that provided inspiration to other female punk rockers. The sentiments in punk lyrics coincided with the upfront, offbeat sexual and shocking punk style of dress that challenged conventional ideas of femininity. Like most genres that gain momentum, however, punk was also picked up by the media and music industry at large and became yet another way to package performers for mainstream consumption.

The 1980s

Starting in the 1980s, women began to be seen in rock bands other than as the lead vocalist. The bassists of popular bands the Pixies, Kim Deal, and Sonic Youth, Kim Gordon, are both female. Both women are featured in the 90s of VH1's list but are two of the few women featured who are not vocalists. Also in the 1980s, a lot of popular rock music contained themes of blatant sexism and, in some more extreme cases, glamorized violence against women. Lyrics from two popular songs that exemplify this are "I used to love her, but I had to kill her," by Guns N' Roses, and "You're All I Need" by Motley Crue, originally written as a straight love song by Nikki Sixx, but upon discovering his girlfriend was unfaithful to him, it was modified into a song about a boy killing his girlfriend.

One of the first manifestations of third wave feminism was in the form of Riot Grrrl music. Riot Grrrl started largely as a reaction to popular misogynist rock music from the 1980s, a good example of this being the song "Suck My Left One" by Bikini Kill, a band that became iconic of the movement. Riot Grrrl seeks to challenge the white- and male-dominated rock canon.

Sexuality and Rock

Two all-female bands present prior to the late 1970s that were popular and highlight the relationship between women in rock music and sexuality, as demonstrated through their band names, were The Shaggs and Fanny. The media attention both these bands received was centered on their sex. Fanny, prior to 1975, produced albums that rarely featured themes of sexuality. However, as their sales dwindled, their focus changed and they began writing material that would capitalize in a market where their sex would sell as fantasies of heterosexual male desire.

Like almost all other facets of culture, throughout all decades, women in rock music have been met with critiques of their sexuality and how it is represented in their public appearances, music videos, day-to-day dress, and lyrics. With female rockers, sexuality and its representation in their work is one of the first things worth noting and thus inherently questioning whether sexuality is a valid vehicle to sell music. Regardless of the feminist debates surrounding this, and what the greater implications are for women more generally, female and feminine sexuality is an important tool for the patriarchal music industry.

Female musicians get trapped in a sexual binary and are either criticized for trying to be too masculine or are seen as being too feminine, and thus it is presumed an impossibility that their image is something that they have produced. Rather, they have fallen prey to the false consciousness and fantasy of the larger male-dominated music industry network of producers and label owners who are looking to capitalize on heterosexual male fantasies. Some of Blondie's early promotional material featured her in a short black dress with a sultry stare and caption reading, "Wouldn't you like to rip her to shreds?" VH1's list of Greatest Women in Rock and Roll is based on popular vote, the implication being that fans elect their favorite female artist based on musical talent; however, many other lists exist on-line and in magazines of "hottest women in rock music." These are just a few of the multitude of examples that demonstrate the emphasis placed on the sexuality of female musicians.

In the contemporary context, there might be a few performers who have mostly escaped this tricky binary, or at least shifted its focus a little. Ani DiFranco, who graced VH1's list at number 90, follows the tradition of the 1960s female singer-songwriter Joni Mitchell. DiFranco's first audiences in the 1990s were mainly queer-identified women, a fan base she has largely retained since her climb to more mainstream popularity. She still sings about menstruation and abortion alongside more conventional topics considered more suitable for the larger music community.

DiFranco proudly sports a queer sexuality like the majority of her fan base, thus making it difficult to oversimplify her image and music in a purely heterosexual economy. DiFranco's sexuality is still subject for discussion alongside her music, there was some outrage from her fans when she became romantically involved with a man. However, her music and image nonetheless challenge the conventional consumption of women in music.

Further, music festivals that feature exclusively female performers like Lilith Fair, founded in 1997 by Grammy singer-songwriter Sarah McLachlan, challenge the idea of female entertainer as exclusively a sexual commodity. These festivals feature a wide array of artists and rock musicians showing multiple dimensions of women in rock music, such as Erykah Badu, Tracy Chapman, the Indigo Girls, Queen Latifah, Sinéad O'Connor, and Liz Phair, all of whom were also featured on VH1's list.

In 1997, Women Make Movies produced a documentary film, *Righteous Babes*, about feminists in rock music. The title of the movie is borrowed from the record label owned by DiFranco and features an in-depth discussion of sexuality and the commercial music market, largely at the expense of the very commercially marketable, and thus very successful, Spice Girls.

See Also: Lady Gaga; Madonna; Nicks, Stevie; Queen Latifah; Stereotypes of Women; Third Wave; Women Make Movies.

Further Readings

Gear, Gillian G. with Yoko Ono. *She's a Rebel: The History of Women in Rock and Roll (Live Girls)*. New York: Seal Press, 1992.

Reddington, Helen. *The Lost Women of Rock Music: Female Musicians of the Punk Era*. Burlington, VT: Ashgate Publishing, 2007.

Whiteley, Sheila. *Women and Popular Music: Sexuality, Identity and Subjectivity*. New York: Routledge, 2000.

Mary Shearman
Simon Fraser University

Rodeo

Women have participated in the rodeo since it originated in the late 19th century. By the 1920s in the United States, women participated in many of the same events as men. However, women's opportunities in the rodeo decreased in the 1930s, and it was not until the rise of all-women's rodeos in the 1940s that the situation began to change. At that time, women formed their own organizations, and since the 1980s have worked to increase their participation and recognition in the rodeo.

Early rodeos included female riders in roughstock events like bronc riding. The Cheyenne Frontier Days, one of the most well-known competitions, did not specifically mention female contestants. Because of this, women were neither officially barred nor admitted. As such, women participated freely in some events yet struggled to gain admittance to others. For instance, one rider was able to take part in bronc riding in 1901 only after she petitioned the board. By the 1910s audiences expected to see cowgirls like Vera McGinnis, Tad Lucas, and Lucille Mulhall compete and perform in many events, including trick riding, relay races, bronc riding, and steer wrestling.

This changed in the 1930s, when the role of women in rodeos was limited dramatically. In 1929, a champion rider was thrown from her horse and killed in the bronc riding competition at the Pendleton Round-Up. Because of this, the rodeo committee eliminated the bronc riding competition for all women. Other rodeos soon followed suit. At the same time, the Great Depression reduced the prize money in women's events, and rodeo also began to professionalize. Female competitors were refused membership to these new organizations, received no voting rights, and lacked the ability to safeguard their purse size and control their involvement in different events.

Seeking a Comeback

By the 1930s, the governing bodies of rodeo largely accomplished their goal of eliminating most events for women by relegating them to a showier, more superficial type of competition. While women were no longer encouraged to participate in many rodeo events, particularly not roughstock events, not all women were willing to accept these limited options. In the 1940s, several all-women's rodeos were held throughout the

By the 1910s, audiences expected to see cowgirls like Vera McGinnis, Tad Lucas, and Lucille Mulhall compete and perform in many events, including trick riding, relay races, bronc riding, and steer wrestling.

West. These rodeos held competitions in bronc riding, calf roping, barrel racing, and team calf tying. In 1948, the Girls Rodeo Association (GRA) was formed, and in 1981 the group's name was changed to the Women's Professional Rodeo Association (WPRA).

Today professional cowgirls are members of the WPRA, but can compete only in barrel racing at Professional Rodeo Cowboys Association (PRCA) rodeos. Other rodeos do permit women to compete in some other events, such as team roping, and the WPRA also holds its own rodeos and includes a division for roughstock competitions. Despite these options, women still face limitations in events and prize money.

The WPRA set an ultimatum in 1980 that required PRCA rodeos to offer equal prizes for all competitors. This has been met, but women still struggle to compete in the all-around competitions and to receive lucrative endorsements, often reserved for male roughstock riders. Women in other countries, including Australia, Canada, and Mexico, face similar restrictions, and many have formed their own rodeo organizations in order to combat this discrimination and provide a place for competition.

See Also: Cowgirls; Gender Roles, Cross-Cultural; Sports, Women in; United States; Xtreme Sports.

Further Readings

Englander, Joe. *They Ride the Rodeo: The Men and Women of the American Amateur Rodeo Circuit.* New York: Collier Books, 1979.

Laegreid, R. *Riding Pretty: Rodeo Royalty in the American West.* Lincoln: University of Nebraska Press, 2006.

LeCompte, Mary Lou. *Cowgirls of the Rodeo: Pioneer Professional Athletes.* Urbana: University of Illinois Press, 1993.

Riske, Milt. *Those Magnificent Cowgirls: A History of the Rodeo Cowgirl.* Cheyenne, WY: Wyoming Publishing, 1983.

Elyssa Ford
Arizona State University

Roe v. Wade

Roe v. Wade (1973) and *Doe v. Bolton* (1973) are two U.S. Supreme Court cases that use the judicially created right to privacy to affirm a woman's right to an abortion under certain circumstances. Although *Doe* focused on the constitutionality of a liberalized Georgia abortion statute that permitted abortion in cases where the mother's health was in jeopardy, the fetus would be born with a birth defect, or the pregnancy was caused by rape, *Roe* arose out of a challenge to a Texas statute passed in 1960 prohibiting all forms of abortion.

Road to the Supreme Court

Norma McCorvey—known in court by the pseudonym Jane Roe—was an itinerant circus worker who was unable to care for her first child. When she became pregnant again, she attempted to seek an abortion at an underground facility in Dallas but found it to be an unsatisfactory option. Unsure of what to do, she consulted with an attorney known for handling adoptions, who referred her to another lawyer, Linda Coffee. In December 1969, McCorvey agreed to work with Coffee and her colleague, Sarah Weddington, to challenge the Texas statute.

Weddington and Coffee filed suit against the state of Texas, represented by Dallas County attorney Henry Wade, in the U.S. District Court for the Northern District of Texas. A three-judge panel heard the case in June 1970; its final decision upheld the enforcement of the statute. The attorneys appealed the case to the U.S. Supreme Court, where *Roe v. Wade*, along with *Doe v. Bolton*, was accepted for review.

The American Civil Liberties Union was deeply invested in litigating *Doe*, and much of their expertise and resources were used in preparing attorney Margie Pitts Hames for oral argument. However, the two young Texas attorneys responsible for *Roe* also were in need of legal guidance. Although they had passion for the abortion issue, neither attorney had prepared a brief for the Supreme Court, let alone argued a case before this body. Recognizing the problem that could result from this inexperience, veteran abortion attorney Roy Lucas attempted to take over oral arguments in the case, even though he had also never appeared before the court.

Although Lucas might have brought more experience to the courtroom than Weddington, interest groups with a stake in the abortion issue, including the National Organization for Women and the National Abortion Rights Action League (now simply NARAL), believed that a woman's voice was necessary in oral arguments. Thus, the American Sociological Association opened its personal library, containing volumes of research on abortion litigation and history, to Weddington. In addition, the association coordinated an *amicus curiae* effort in which groups' briefs complemented each other and presented a variety of facets of the same argument.

The organizational efforts and interest group involvement of the pro-choice lobby strongly contrast with the efforts of the pro-life lobby. This lobby did little to promote the participation of any pro-life interest groups, or even the governments of the 44 other states with laws restricting abortion procedures. The pro-life Nixon administration also chose not to file an *amicus curiae* brief.

By December 1971, when the court heard oral arguments on the cases for the first time, it was uncertain how the seven sitting justices would decide *Roe* and *Doe*. When the court heard the cases for the first time in December 1971, there were only seven justices on the court because justices John Marshall Harlan and Hugo Black had recently retired and the Senate had not yet confirmed their eventual replacements. By the time the court heard the case for the second time, in 1972, justices William H. Rehnquist and Lewis Powell, who participated in the final decision, had filled these seats. Arguments did not go well for either side, and conference was particularly contentious. The justices decided by 4–3 vote that the court had jurisdiction in the case; they were then forced to examine the question of whether women had a right to obtain an abortion. On examining this question, the justices reached a 5–2 decision that the Texas and Georgia abortion laws should be struck down—a woman's right to have an abortion fell within the right to privacy enumerated by the Court in *Griswold v. Connecticut* (1965).

Although Chief Justice Warren Burger was a member of the minority, he defied Supreme Court mores and assigned the writing of the court's opinion to Justice Harry Blackmun. Burger believed that although Blackmun was in the majority, he would write a narrowly drawn decision. Blackmun, however, was previously employed as counsel for the Mayo Clinic— an experience that ingrained in him strong feelings about the right of doctors to make medical decisions. These feelings, and Blackmun's methodical personality, made the task of writing the opinion in *Roe* quite difficult. Although he spent five months laboring over the text, after a late May visit from Chief Justice Burger, Blackmun withdrew his work, telling the other justices that the difficult subject required more research. He requested that *Roe* be reargued during the court's next term, and the other justices assented.

Blackmun spent the summer of 1972 in the library of the Mayo Clinic, researching the medical history of abortion. At the library he discovered doctors' trimester approach to pregnancy. By the time the justices reheard the case in October 1972, Blackmun's new opinion had already begun to take shape.

Blackmun initially concluded that abortion should be legal until the end of the second trimester. However, Burger expressed concern with this conclusion, and as a result Blackmun recast his opinion into a three-trimester approach, which was enumerated in the court's opinion handed down on January 22, 1973.

During the first trimester, Blackmun wrote, a woman had an absolute right to an abortion in consultation with her physician. During the second trimester, the state could regulate abortion procedures only in the interest of the woman's health. During the third trimester, the state's interest in potential life allowed it to prohibit abortion except in the case of the life and health of the mother.

Aftermath of the Decision

Following the court's decision in *Roe*, pro-life groups, largely funded by the Catholic Church, began to organize across the country. Especially in state legislatures, these groups, including Americans United for Life and the National Right to Life Committee, lobbied for legislation that restricted women's access to abortion procedures. These laws, enacted in 32 states, led to a torrent of litigation filed by pro-choice groups. From 1973 to 1989, the court heard more than 10 cases surrounding such restrictions.

One of the most notable of these decisions was *Webster v. Reproductive Health Services* (1989). The court's decision in this case did not overrule *Roe*, but neither did a majority of the court specifically affirm a woman's right to an abortion. *Webster*, instead, gave state governments increased authority to regulate when, where, and how abortion procedures could be

performed. These regulations resulted in more litigation, culminating in the 1992 case of *Planned Parenthood of Southeastern Pennsylvania v. Casey*. In *Casey*, the court's plurality opinion again upheld *Roe* but continued to chip away at its central holding.

Following *Casey*, the court appeared to be uninterested in hearing cases regarding the constitutionality of restrictions on abortion procedures. Thus, pro-life groups turned their efforts to securing the free speech rights of abortion clinic protestors and enacting a ban on partial-birth (late-term) abortions. Although the court declared a state law banning these procedures unconstitutional in 2000, in 2007 it upheld a nearly identical federal partial-birth abortion ban. This decision has raised questions for many commentators about the court's willingness to discard *Roe*, especially if presented with the proper case.

Roe has been the subject of much legal analysis. One of its most vocal critics has been Supreme Court Associate Justice Ruth Bader Ginsburg, who at the time *Roe* was decided was a litigator for the American Civil Liberties Union's Women's Rights Project. Ginsburg has publicly criticized the court for legalizing abortion using the judicially created right to privacy. She and many other legal commentators believe that this makes reproductive freedom much more tenuous than if the decision had been grounded in the equal-protection clause of the Fourteenth Amendment to the U.S. Constitution.

Other legal scholars have criticized *Roe* for being the right decision at the wrong time—a case decided before the public and the government had fully embraced its central holding. Still others have noted that the court's decision may be an example of judicial activism run amok. These observers believe that the court should have used greater legal reasoning to make its decision and should not have made specific policy prescriptions regarding when and where abortion should be legal.

See Also: Abortion, Access to; Abortion Laws, United States; McCorvey, Norma; NARAL; Planned Parenthood; Women's Health Clinics.

Further Readings

Balkin, Jack M. *What Roe Should Have Said: The Nation's Top Legal Experts Rewrite America's Most Controversial Decision.* New York: New York University Press, 2007.

Greenhouse, Linda and Reva Siegel. *Before Roe v. Wade: The Voices That Shaped the Abortion Debate Before the Supreme Court's Ruling.* New York: Kaplan, 2010.

Hull, N. E. H. and Peter Charles Hoffer. *Roe v. Wade: The Abortion Rights Controversy in American History.* Lawrence: University Press of Kansas, 2001.

McCorvey, Norma and Andy Meisler. *I Am Roe: My Life, Roe v. Wade, and Freedom of Choice.* New York: Harper Perennial, 1995.

Alixandra B. Yanus
High Point University

Roller Derby

Roller derby first appeared in 1935 in Chicago, as a marathon skating event invented by Leo Seltzer; it was taken on the road later that year as the "Transcontinental Roller Marathon." By 1937, the skating marathon morphed into a team sport consisting of coed teams and is considered the first sport where women and men played by the same rules.

From the 1950s to the 1970s, roller derby was televised and many participants made a career out of this sport. But by the mid-1970s, roller derby began to lose its popularity and was no longer televised, and many of the professional leagues were dissolved.

Today roller derby is primarily an amateur sport, although there are several professional leagues as well, and currently there are two types of roller derby: banked track and flat track. Banked-track roller derby began in the 1930s; as the sport evolved, so did the newer version, flat-track roller derby, which emerged in 2001.

Structure of the Modern Sport and Leagues

Today there are more than 400 amateur roller derby leagues worldwide. Both types of roller derby, banked track and flat track, are played on an oval track with two teams consisting of blockers, a pivot, and a jammer. Blockers wear solid-color helmet covers, and their role is to assist their jammer through the pack

New Hampshire's Skate Free or Die! women's flat-track roller derby team. Derby players wear expressive and creative outfits and use alter-ego skater names like Raggedy Antics (center), Empress Explosiva, and Dirty Kat Box.

of players while preventing the opposite team's jammer from moving through the pack. The pivot wears a striped helmet cover and sets the pace for the defense, calling out plays for the rest of the team.

The jammer wears a helmet cover with a star on it and is responsible for moving through the pack to score points for the team. Once making it through the pack once, a jammer receives one point for each opponent passed legally in bounds. The jam ends when either the time limit for the jam ends or the lead jammer calls off the jam by placing hands on hips.

Today, roller derby is a sport dominated by women's leagues, especially within flat-track roller derby. These all-female teams and leagues are brought together under the umbrella of the Women's Flat Track Derby Association (WFTDA), which was established in 2004. The goal of this organization is to assist women in developing athletic ability and sportsmanship.

In addition to playing within these leagues, women are primary owners, managers, and/or operators of the leagues and the WFTDA. In order to be considered for membership, a league must demonstrate the following: the league is composed of only female competitors, at least 51 percent of the league is owned by league skaters, the league is managed by at least 67 percent of league skaters, the league utilizes democratic principles, and the league participates in at least four competitions a year. Currently, the WFTDA consists of 78 leagues from across the country, as well as an additional 24 apprentice league members. WFTDA sponsors tournaments and national championships each year.

See also: Business, Women in; Sports, Women in; Team Owners, Female; Xtreme Sports.

Further Readings

Bay City Bombers. *"America's Roller Derby Roots."* http://www.baycitybombers.com/history.html (accessed July 2010).

Mabe, C. *The History and All-Girl Revival of the Greatest Sport on Wheels.* Golden, CO: Speck Press, 2008.

Women's Flat Track Derby Association. *"The Latest."* http://wftda.com (accessed July 2010).

Carrie L. Cokely
Curry College

Roma "Gypsy" Women

Linguistic evidence suggests that the Roma people are of northern Indian origin and migrated between 800 C.E. and 950 C.E. toward Europe, where they settled after 1100 C.E. In the European Union (EU), the umbrella term *Roma* refers to people who describe themselves or are perceived as Roma, Gypsies, Travellers, Manouches, Ashkali, and Sinti, as well as other groups. The term has slowly replaced the other one, "Gypsy," which was perceived as an exonym having a negative connotation.

Roma people are the largest ethnic minority in the European Union (EU) and it is estimated that there are possibly over 10 million Roma in Europe. Many Roma people live also in non-EU countries of the Balkan area (e.g. Serbia, Montenegro, Kosovo, Fyrom, and Albania), in Turkey, and in Russia. Settlements of Roma can be found in the United States and in South America as well.

Allegedly, Roma people have been in the Americas since Columbus transported them in 1498. During the colonial period, some European nations (Spain, France, the Netherlands, and the United Kingdom) shipped "their Gypsies" overseas, especially as slaves to their American colonies (e.g., Spanish Louisiana, Antilles, the Caribbean) and to the southern plantations in Central and South America. New migration streams of Roma people toward the United States were generated by the collapse of communist regimes and by the rising of new anti-Roma waves. Roma women have been impacted by the persecution and discrimination against their ethnic minority and have been the target of various forms of violence motivated by ethnic grounds, for example, forced sterilization. Incidentally, they have been confronted also with restrictions within their minority, by marrying at an early age and by being traditionally confined to the household and childcare. Their situation has been changing along the years, and many Roma women have reached leading positions and advocate for Roma rights.

Roma "Gypsy" Women's Rights

Looking at Roma women's rights, they have been often challenged both within their minority (so called in-group discrimination) and in the society at large (so called out-group discrimination), in which they may suffer from multiple discrimination because of both gender and ethnic origin.

As far as the situation within their minority is concerned, traditionally Roma women are exposed to early marriages, which are in many cases arranged by their families. Consequently, they are also exposed to early and numerous pregnancies as well as, due to the lack of adequate sexual education, to multiple abortions. The Roma minority is still patriarchal and the relation between men and women is quite unbalanced, with the role of women subordinated and restricted to the household, which might prevent them from access to education and job opportunities. Nonetheless, in many Roma groups, Roma women are the *trait d'union,* or liaison, between their communities and the rest of the society, because they typically work outside their community or are in the street begging (*Mangel* in Romani), while at the same time, are the main care providers within their minority.

Coming to the out-group discriminations, Roma women are disadvantaged in almost all fields of society. First of all, as a result of bad housing and living conditions and limited access to healthcare structures, their life expectancy is lower than non-Roma women in many countries. Due to pervasive prejudices and stereotypes, Roma women have difficulty accessing education and job opportunities and are often pushed to informal economy.

In the last decades, the situation of Roma women has been changing a lot, both inside and outside their minority. On the one hand, many programs are promoting education for Roma as a tool for emancipation and empowerment; on the other hand, many Roma women themselves have started networking and joining their efforts to advocate Roma women's rights. For example, the Network Women's Program's "Roma Women's Initiative" (RWI), promoted by the Open Society Institute, served the purpose of engaging a core group of committed Roma women's activists.

The RWI is also involved in the "Decade of Roma 2005–2015," which is a synergy among European governments aimed at improving the social inclusion of Roma people. In this framework, the Regional Campaign "I am a Roma Woman" was launched in April 2010, the International Day of the Roma, under the "Empowerment of Roma Women" three-year regional project. The campaign was implemented by CARE International NWB within the Roma Inclusion Decade, in partnership with several Roma women's nongovernmental organizations. It echoes the campaign "I am a European Roma woman" launched by a group of Roma activists for the 2009 International Women's Day.

Famous Roma "Gypsy" Women

Many Roma women became famous in many fields, ranging from art, science, and education, and more recently European politics. Despite the spread stereotype, which still portraits Roma women just as excellent flamenco dancers and musicians, they reached outstanding positions in many other areas.

Although it is impossible to give a full account of these women, some examples include Micaela Flores Amaya (also credited as "La Chunga" or "The Barefoot Dancer"), who was born in Marseille but grown up in Barcelona, and was both a talented cinema actress and painter. Pablo Picasso admired her work and described it as "shining naïf."

In Sweden, Swedish Roma sisters Rosa and Katarina Taikon became famous artists: the former, a renowned silversmith, has shown her silver jewelry in several exhibitions and museums; the latter was a writer and actress. She wrote the Katitzi book series, which was also filmed, and was an activist for Roma's rights. Philomena Franz became famous for her literary production of Romani tales and for the organization of literary readings at schools and universities in Germany after surviving the Holocaust. In August 1995, she was awarded the "Federal Cross for Merits" by the German government for her "activities endeavouring after understanding and conciliation."

Lívia Járóka was the first Romani woman elected to the European Parliament in 2004, and committed herself to the enhancement of Romani people throughout Europe. In 2006, she was nominated MEP of the Year for Justice and Fundamental Human Rights and elected to the World Young Leaders Forum (associated with the World Economic Forum). In the same period, another Roma woman, Viktória Mohácsi, joined the European Parliament by replacing a party colleague. In 2008 in Rome, she was awarded the "Premio Minerva" for her advocacy of human rights.

See Also: Gender, Defined; Glass Ceiling; Global Feminism; Representation of Women.

Further Readings

Decade of Roma http://www.romadecade.org (accessed April 2010).

Gropper, Rena C. *Gypsies in the City: Culture Patterns and Survival.* Princeton, NJ: Darwin Press, 1975.

Hancock Ian F., *The Pariah Syndrome: An Account of Gypsy Slavery and Persecution* Ann Arbor, Michigan: Karoma, 1987.

Open Society Institute. Network Women's Program. "Roma Women's Initiative" http://www.soros.org /initiatives/women/focus_areas/g_romani_women (accessed April 2010).

Sutherland Anne, *Gypsies: The Hidden Americans.* New York: Free Press, 1975.

Barbara Giovanna Bello
University of Milano

Roman Catholic Church

Forty-five years after the close of the Second Vatican Council (1962–65), ecclesial roles for Roman Catholic women have both evolved and remained the same. Some of the major concerns facing Roman Catholic women today include religious roles within ministry and reproductive rights.

In preparation for the Second Vatican Council, Pope John XXIII issued *Il Tempio Massimo,* or Letter to Women Religious, in which the individual vocations, whether cloistered or not, were affirmed while strongly encouraging religious women who work in the areas of education and social service to obtain higher education degrees that would complement and support their particular vocations. In 1965, the council document *Perfectae Caritatis,* Decree on the Adaptation and Renewal of Religious Life, encouraged religious women to situate themselves and their vocations in the social milieu to which they belonged. Each religious community was to adjust rules and customs to accommodate the needs and demands of particular ministerial vocations.

The pursuit of higher education degrees appropriate to their work was again affirmed. Even the religious habit was updated in order to meet the environmental demands of time and place with the occupational needs specific to each. In 1972, the Leadership Con-

ference of Women Religious, composed of approximately 90 percent of U.S. female Catholic religious communities, endorsed feminism as important in the work of social justice and the structure within their own communities. Emerging from this, the theological discipline of feminist theology began to call into question the lower status of women based on the Genesis account of Creation. Since 1968, the number of women entering into religious vocations has seen a significant decline in numbers worldwide, while a growing number of laywomen participate professionally in new and expanded ministerial roles.

In response to the sharp decrease of vocations to the priesthood, women increasingly fill nonordained roles in the form of parish life directors (PLDs). While sacramental ministry continues to be the reserve of the priest, PLDs, who are mostly women, fulfill the pastoral, administrative, and day-to-day needs of parishes that do not have a resident priest.

Women and Lay Ministry

A renewed theology of the priesthood emerged from the Second Vatican Council, opening new possibilities for the nonordained, or laity. Depending upon one's point of view, the growing participation of laity, particularly women, is attributed to the growing shortage of priests or, as many professional lay ministers argue, the growing participation of laity as foundational to their baptism. Yet the reality of the priest shortage has created a crisis for the institutional church in its inability to provide for the sacramental ministry of parishes. Since then, the council and the number of women (and men) preparing for ministry has increased dramatically, while the number of priests and religious women has witnessed a sharp decline.

Currently, there are more women in graduate programs in theology and ministry in Catholic institution than there are candidates for the priesthood. Out of necessity, bishops are relying on these theologically educated women for parish ministry, which takes multiple forms, including serving as pastoral associates. While sacramental ministry continues to be the domain of the priest, pastoral associates, who statistically comprise more women, fulfill the pastoral, administrative, and day-to-day needs of parishes that do not have a resident priest. To be considered as a pastoral associate, the applicant must hold a Master's degree in divinity, or in pastoral, theological, or religious studies. Given the high percentage of women serving as pastoral associates, there is an emerging schism regarding collaborative ministry between women and the priests they work with. Women find it difficult to be recognized as professionals, reporting high frustration at their exclusion from decision-making processes in their areas of expertise. The National Council of Catholic Bishops has called for further study in the ways that women, as lay ministers, can exercise leadership in parishes, and for the possibility of linking authority to baptism rather than ordination.

The relationship between Roman Catholic women in lay ministry in the United States to women in a global context has not been significantly researched in a systematic manner. Instead, individual experiences from Third World women participating in lay ministry report instances of discrimination and injustice stemming from gender-based myths and stereotypes that exclude them from church leadership. There continue to be collective efforts at reform: for example, the 2002 conference of Ecclesia of Women in Asia, "Gathering the Voices of the Silenced," was held in Bangkok, Thailand. As Asian Catholic women, the forum brought together diverse women in lay ministry, addressing a range of topics from theological method to women in church structures. While it would not be accurate to categorize the experience of all Third World women in Catholic lay ministry as monolithic, there continues to be a double standard with gender discrimination for women in a global context with regard to authority and contributions.

The ordination of women in the priesthood continues to be theologically resisted by the magisterium, in spite of popular belief among the laity and among some practictioners that it is expedient to do so. In 1976, Pope John Paul II rejected women's ordination in "Declaration on the Question of the Admission of Women to the Ministerial Priesthood." Three declarations are given in defense of an all-male priesthood: (1) Jesus did not count women among the 12 apostles; (2) church tradition has always excluded women from the priesthood; and (3) the priest, as a male, is representative of Jesus as a male. In response to the exclusion of women to the priesthood, the Women-Church movement endorses the equitability of all its members in order to forego a hierarchal church structure. Conversely, the Women's Ordination Movement

continues to ordain women using the identical Rite of Ordination to the Priesthood reserved for men. In so doing, they have experienced the backlash of excommunication. The Vatican's latest decision to list women's ordination in the same category as pedophile priest and rapists with regard to both as *delicta graviora,* or seriously grave sin, has created outcry among feminist Catholics and progressive theologians.

Women and Sexual Abuse in the Clergy

New documentation has come forth in what has been described as the church's next wave of scandal: the sexual abuse of young girls, women, and women serving in religious positions by priests. Beginning in 1970, the church changed its position and welcomed girls as altar servers, thus making adolescent girls as venerable as boys to predator priest. Experts in the area of children's sexual abuse argue that disclosure of abuse is typically delayed for about 30 years, which means that women abused as children are just starting to come forward. While a study commissioned by the United States Conference of Catholic Bishops found that boys were overwhelmingly the likeliest targets of predator priests, new information is countering the bishop's claims. According to experts, priests are more likely to abuse females, especially adult women, with four times as many priests becoming involved in a sexual relationship with an adult woman than with children. Typically, underreporting of abuse is more evident in populations of young girls and women. Female victims, it is argued, are scrutinized differently than males.

While the focus of the sex abuse scandal has been on homosexual behavior by priests, and therefore judged as more deviant in nature, abuse by heterosexual priests, on the other hand, casts female victims as the temptress or seductress. Interview techniques differ according to gender as well. For females, questions shift responsibility to them by suggesting their attire or manner gave mixed signals to the priest. Additionally, studies indicate that for female victims, the likelihood of revealing the abuse may impact their current relationships. Opinions differ as to whether women as both ordained and nonordained (laity), as nonsubordinated feminine presences, would have been able to reduce the numbers of sexual abuse cases. The Womenpriests movement favors an end to mandatory celibacy, with canonical recognition of women to the priesthood being a tangible effort that would increase transparency and structural change in the present male-dominated ecclesial hierarchy.

Reproductive Rights

An important and controversial issue that Catholic women face is reproductive rights. In 1968, the papal letter *Humane Vitae* written by Pope Paul IV, affirmed the teachings of the 16th-century Council of Trent, rejecting the use of all artificial contraceptives. Dissent from the laity came mainly in the form of ignoring the decree. Considered by moral theologians as a watershed event, it was the first time in modern history that an official teaching from the pope was by-and-large ignored by many Catholics. Official teaching regarding sexual desire or pleasure, especially for women, was superseded by the intended purpose of sex as procreative.

In 1973, the advocacy group Catholics for Choice was formed for Catholics who believe women, as agents, are able to follow their conscience when it comes to matters of sexuality and reproduction. Due in part to strong lobbying efforts by the Catholic hierarchy, public policy regarding reproductive rights in developing countries continues to affect poor women by denying them access to reproductive healthcare.

Currently, over 40 million people live with the human immunodeficiency virus and acquired immune deficiency syndrome (HIV/AIDS) virus. In the wake of the HIV/AIDS pandemic, withholding condoms through official church teaching has called into question the ethical morality of such a policy.

See Also: Catholics for Choice; Feminist Theology; Machismo/Marianismo; Priesthood, Roman Catholic; Religion, Women in; Reproductive and Sexual Health Rights; Women's Ordination Conference.

Further Readings

Center for Applied Research in the Apostolate. http://cara .georgetown.edu (accessed July 2010).
Fox, Zeni. *The New Ecclesial Ministry: Lay Professionals Serving the Church.* Kansas City, MO: Sheed & Ward, 1997.
Johnson, Elizabeth A. ed. *The Church Women Want: Catholic Women in Dialogue.* New York: The Crossroad Publishing Company, 2002.
Macy, Gary. *The Hidden History of Women's Ordination.* Oxford, UK: Oxford University Press: 2008.
National Association for Lay Ministry. http://www.nalm .org (accessed July 2010).
Rausch, Thomas P. *Catholicism in the Third Millennium.* Collegeville, MN: The Liturgical Press, 2003.
Ruether, Rosemary Radford. *Catholic Does Not Equal the Vatican.* New York: The New Press, 2008.

Cynthia Bond
Claremont Graduate University

Romance Novels

Romance novels are defined as novels that narrate the story of a courtship and have a happy ending. These novels are regarded specifically as a woman's genre. Its readership consists largely of women, and it is written mostly by female authors.

The core of the book is the relationship between the hero and the heroine. The story tells the courtship of these two characters, who overcome all the obstacles that separate them, and in the end they find happiness in each other's arms. The novel's primary focus is on the presentation of the characters' emotions. The story is usually told from the heroine's point of view, either in first or third person.

The narrative is driven forward by the barriers between the two lovers. According to Pamela Reggis (2003), the story unfolds through several main elements: the meeting, the barrier, the attraction, the declaration, the point of ritual death, the recognition, and the betrothal. At the beginning, there is the meeting between the two main characters, which includes setting the social scenery of the novel. Their meeting also discloses the barriers separating them. In novels written in the 18th and 19th centuries, the barrier mainly lies in their different social status. In novels written in the 20th and 21st centuries, the barrier changes from external reasons such as social and economic status to internal reasons. One or both of the characters typically have some emotional reason that makes their union impossible.

There are several scenes in which the hero and heroine's attraction to each other is disclosed to the reader. This attraction is expressed in the declaration by one of the characters. The happy ending seems to be the farthest from realization at the point of ritual death, when hero and heroine's communion becomes impossible. This ritual death, however, leads to the recognition of their inseparableness, which is marked by the betrothal. Romantic novels' plot follows this pattern of elements with different variations. The variations have led to the development of several subgenres. Some of the main subgenres are contemporary romance, historical romance, romantic suspense, science fiction romance, paranormal romance, erotic romance, and fantasy romance.

Development of the Genre

Samuel Richardson's *Pamela, or Virtue Rewarded*, published in 1740, tells the story of the courtship between Pamela, a maid, and Mr. B, the master for whom she works. In the end, Mr. B marries Pamela and turns her into a lady. This novel is considered to be one of the first romance best sellers, since it was an instant success at the time of its publication.

The genre flourished in the 19th century, when novels such as Jane Austen's *Pride and Prejudice* (1813) and Charlotte Brönte's *Jane Eyre* (1847) demonstrated the importance of the genre in the literary field. While *Jane Eyre* introduced the orphaned heroine among the set characters of romance novels, E. M. Hull's *The Sheik* (1919) introduced another one of the iconic images of the romance hero, the alpha male who is tamed by the heroine. The other kind of romantic hero is the sensitive one who has to healed by the heroine.

Inspired by Austen's novels, Georgette Heyer (1902–74) wrote historical romances set in the Regency period (1811–20). The historical period was used by Heyer only as a backdrop to the story. The heroine was out of place in this world, as her behavior and thinking was more characteristic of the 20th century than of that period. Heyer was a very prolific writer, as she wrote one or two historical romance per year. At the beginning of the 20th century, this prolificness became characteristic of the romance writers, who usually produce one novel per year.

Some of the most renowned romantic writers of the 20th century were Mary Stewart (1916–), who wrote romantic suspense; Janet Dayley (1944–), who Americanized the popular romance novel by writing romances set in the West; and Jayne Ann Krentz (1949–), whose novels focus on the taming of the dangerous alpha male. Jennifer Crusie (1949–), a pseudonym for Jennifer Smith, wrote more than 15 novels published in about 20 countries. She won the Romance Writers of America prize twice, in 1995 and 2005. Rosemary Rogers (1932–) and Kathleen E. Woodiwiss (1939–2007) wrote best-selling historical romance novels.

Marketing

From the beginning of the 1980s, the market of the romance novels began to boom. This boom was supported by the marketing strategies of three publishing houses that became the main distribution sources of romance novels. The first to realise the potential of the romance novels' market was Mills and Boon, established in 1908 in Great Britain by Gerald Mills and Charles Boon. By the 1930s, Mills and Boon started publishing hardback romance novels. The Canadian company Harlequin was founded in 1949 as a paperback reprint house. Among others, they republished many Mills and Boon titles. Another brand name is Silhouette, formed in the 1980s, which publishes lucrative paperback romances.

Romances are marketed in two formats: single title and category. The format is defined by the length of the novel and its distribution. The category romance cannot exceed 200 pages; it is distributed in series and has only a single print run. A single title romance can be as long as 350 to 400 pages; when particularly successful, it is reprinted several times. Subgenres exist in romance publishing, often closely related to other literature genres, including historical, science fiction, paranormal, and Christian themes.

Critical Reception

The genre of romance novels has been the source of a long standing critical debate. It is dismissed by some critics on the ground of lack of literary value, and criticized by feminists for its treatment of the subject of women's emancipation. According to some feminists, romance novels ensnare their heroines and women readers into the heteronormative narrative. This narrative suggests that the heroine's quest of happiness has to end in finding the "right" man and consolidating that relationship. Reflecting a heterosexist family ideology, romance novels define monogamy, marriage, and motherhood as the most valuable things in a woman's life. Tania Modelski (1982) considers that Harlequin heroines "can achieve happiness only by undergoing a complex process of self-subversion."

With the development of cultural studies, popular culture has become part of academic analysis. The changes in the academic framework contributed to a shift in the interpretation of romance novels. Since they were so popular, critics became interested in the act of reading romance novels as a social and cultural phenomenon. Janice A. Radway (1984) examined the culture of romance reading, focusing on the habits and motivations of its women readers. In her conclusion, she defines romance reading and writing "as a collectively elaborated female ritual." Through this ritual, women try to explore their social condition as defined by their gender and try to envisage a world in which their needs and dreams would be considered important. Radway recognizes the importance of romance novels in women's lives; her conclusion suggests that these novels are used by women as a source of escapism and/or a way to come to terms with the social requirements imposed on women.

The popularity of romance novels is one of the arguments used by the defenders of this genre, such as Dixon Jay (1999), Pamela Regis (2003), and Deborah Phillips (2006). In their view, the romance genre is all too easily disregarded as not serious enough to study. According to Regis, the importance of romance novels is not only assured by its sale numbers but also by being an old genre that includes masterpieces such as *Pride and Prejudice*, *Jane Eyre*, and *A Room With a View*. Moreover, the happy ending is not a heterosexual entrapment but rather the celebration and the realization of the heroine's freedom. The heroines of the 20th- and 21st-century novels are independent, witty, wilful, and strong heroines who are equals to their heroes. Therefore, these novels do not represent the oppression of women but rather contribute to their emancipation.

See Also: Heterosexuality; Marriage; Novelists, Female; Pornography/Erotica; Stereotypes of Women; Women's Studies.

Further Readings

Dixon, Jay. *The Romantic Fiction of Mills and Boon, 1909–90s*. London: UCL Press, 1999.

Modleski, Tania. *Loving With Vengeance: Mass-Produced Fantasies for Women*. New York: Routledge, 1982.

Phillips, Deborah. *Women's Fiction 1945–2005: Writing Romance*. London: Continuum, 2006.

Radway, Janice A. *Reading the Romance: Women, Patriarchy and Popular Literature*. Chapel Hill: The University of North Carolina Press, 1984.

Regis, Pamela. *A Natural History of the Romance Novel*. Philadelphia: University of Pennsylvania Press, 2003.

Zita Farkas
Independent Scholar

Romania

Romania is an eastern European country and has been a member of the European Union since 2007. The nation has a population of 21.5 million. As of the late 1990s, more women than men were enrolled in universities, and the proportion of women in science, mathematics, and computing exceeded 50 percent.

The participation of women in male-dominated professions is increasing, but gender segregation of work and a 10 percent gender pay gap remains, according to the United Nations Development Fund for Women. The gender employment gap for Romanians aged 25–39 years is 1 percent. The social model for women is that they are expected to fulfill three roles—that of a mother, a wife, and a career woman. Consensual partnership and single motherhood also are relatively accepted roles. Women initiated 36 percent of new businesses in Romania in 2006, being overrepresented both as employers and as employees of small enterprises. Gender-based affirmative actions are uncommon, and there is no governmental commitment to gender mainstreaming. The most acknowledged gender-based discrimination remains sexual harassment, with victims (and not the alleged perpetrators) having the liability of proving the crime.

The political sphere in Romania is predominantly masculine, with severe underrepresentation of women in parliament (9.4 percent) and government (14 percent). The few female leaders have not proposed any systematic advancement of women's agendas. With a small upper class, a growing lower class, and a problematic middle class, Romania struggles with rising poverty in addition to corruption, underemployment, and high living costs. The average annual income in 2008 was $600. Severe disparities are seen between rural and urban areas and between Romanians and

Roma. Almost half of Romania's women live in villages with poor infrastructure, severe demographic declines, and orthodox values.

The public healthcare system is experiencing a severe crisis, with health status indicators below the average for the European Union. Romania has a maternal mortality rate within the second quintile and the highest cervical cancer mortality rate in Europe. The Human papillomavirus (HPV) vaccine was received with hesitation because of the caution expressed in regard to its adverse effects. Abortion is decreasing but still widely accepted (performed at a rate of 26 out of 1,000 women in 2006). In 2005, Romania had the second rate of teenage mothers, after the United Kingdom.

Since 2002, many women (often highly qualified) have migrated for work in the European Union. Their remittances are important contributions to their families and to the state budget. In 2009, Herta Muller won the Nobel Prize in Literature. She is a German, born in Romania, who emigrated to Germany in 1987 as a consequence of political persecution. Her novels recall her experience of repression during Communist rule in Romania.

See Also: Abortion, Access to; Equal Pay; Migrant Workers; Representation of Women in Government, International; Reproductive Cancers; Teen Pregnancy.

Further Readings

Gallagher, T. *Modern Romania: The End of Communism, the Failure of Democratic Reform, and the Theft of a Nation*. New York: New York University Press, 2008.

Klepper, Nicolae. *Romania: An Illustrated History*. New York: Hippocrene Books, 2003.

Surdu, Laura and Mihai Surdu. *Broadening the Agenda: The Status of Romani Women in Romania*. New York: Open Society Institute, 2006.

Maria-Carmen Pantea
Babeş Bolyai University

RU-486

RU-486 is a steroid abortifacient, taken in the first seven weeks after conception to terminate pregnancy. RU-486 causes abortion through pill form rather than through placement of objects into the uterus. RU-486 is known as a medical abortion rather than a surgical abortion because it works without the direct placement of tools into the woman's body. The embryo is expelled, simulating miscarriage, which may occur anywhere—it is not limited to the confines of a medical environment. A lengthy battle took place before RU-486 gained final U.S Food and Drug Administration approval in 2000. RU-486 is also known as mifepristone; this name is gaining popularity in the United States.

RU-486 works by divesting the uterus of progesterone, making the womb inhospitable to the prolongment of pregnancy. The abortion process using RU-486 is lengthier than that of traditional methods, including vacuum aspiration or dilation and curettage, as a result of multiple steps in the abortion process and medical appointments. The process begins with an ultrasound confirming less than 49 days of gestation. Then RU-486, or antiprogestin mifepristone, is taken. Forty-eight to 72 hours later, the woman takes prostaglandin either at home or at a medical facility, orally, by injection, or by suppository. The woman later expels the embryo, usually within a few hours of taking the prostaglandin. A final appointment, generally scheduled within two weeks of the second step,

RU-486 is known as a medical abortion because it works without the direct placement of tools into the woman's body.

is necessary to ascertain the success of the process. There are many possible adverse effects, including uterine contractions, diarrhea, headaches, back pain, heavier bleeding, nausea, abdominal cramps, and fatigue. Rarer complications include excessive bleeding requiring blood transfusion. At this time, the long-term adverse effects of RU-486 are unknown.

Since its introduction to U.S. markets in 2000, use of RU-486 has steadily increased, while the overall abortion rate has decreased. Doctors who may not give surgical abortions may be willing to prescribe the RU-486 regimen rather than making women seek out abortion specialists. A slow adoption of RU-486 as a method of abortion in the United States is similar to the pattern established in European nations allowing RU-486.

First approved for use in France in 1988 by the Ministry of Health, considerable setbacks delayed the use of RU-486 in the United States. Final Food and Drug Administration approval was contingent on knowing manufacturing information, which was impossible because most U.S.-based pharmaceutical companies did not want to upset the pro-life community. Eventually, the Danco Group, a small pharmaceutical company, agreed to back RU-486. Mifepristone is currently produced in China by Shanghai Hualian under the patent Mifeprex. As a result of the increasingly murky situation regarding access to contraceptives and emergency contraceptives at pharmacies across the country, Danco Group distributes Mifeprex to doctors and clinics only. According to the Guttmacher Institute, an estimated 22 percent of all abortions in the first seven weeks are through medical and not surgical abortion.

See Also: Abortion; Abortion Laws, United States; Abortion Methods.

Further Readings
Guttmacher Institute. "Facts on Induced Abortion in the United States." (2008). http://www.guttmacher.org/pubs/fb_induced_abortion.html (accessed July 2010).
Lader, L. *A Private Matter: RU-486 and the Abortion Crisis.* Amherst, NY: Prometheus Books, 1995.
Quindlen, Anna. "On Their Own Terms." *Newsweek*, v.153/7 (February 16, 2009).

Jessica Wall
Indiana University Bloomington

Running/Marathons

Women's long road to securing a place alongside men in running competitions began centuries ago and has been marked by successes, challenges, and controversies. Nevertheless, key 20th-century struggles to gain formal entry into elite races have paved the way for millions of recreational runners to enjoy the benefits of running.

The Long Road to the Start Line
The early history of women's participation in running events is marked by struggles to achieve the right to participate alongside men in the sport. As early as 1919, requests to the International Olympic Committee to include women's track-and-field events in the Olympic Games were denied because of assumptions that physical activity and competition were harmful to women's biological and psychological health. The earliest track-and-field competitions were subsequently held as separate women-only events, such as one sponsored by the Fédération Féminine Sportive de France, in which five countries competed in 1921.

In 1926, succumbing to popular pressure, the International Olympic Committee changed its decision and permitted women's entry into five track-and-field events, including three running events: 100 meter, 800 meter, and 4×100 meter relay. This experiment with women's running had mixed results. When some women suffered heat exhaustion and collapsed after the 800-meter race, concerns about women's physical ability to perform distance running resurfaced as matter of debate. All running events longer than the 200-meter race were subsequently removed from the Olympic program. In 1960, however, the 800-meter event was reinstated.

Going the Distance: Women and Marathons
Formal restrictions on women's entry into the marathon persisted well into the 20th century, notably longer than similar restrictions on shorter events. However, formal barriers to elite running competitions did not deter women from training and participating in long-distance events. In 1966, Roberta Gibb became the first woman to run the Boston Marathon, although she did so unofficially after her formal entry request was denied on the basis that women were not physiologically capable of running longer than 1.5 miles—a

recommendation set by the American Amateur Athletic Union. The next year, Katherine Switzer obtained formal entry into the Boston Marathon by using her first initial and last name. Switzer was discovered partway through the marathon by race coorganizer John Semple, who darted into the race and tried to remove her bib number. Switzer finished the race, and the ensuing controversy garnered widespread public support of women's running. Women were officially permitted to compete in the Boston Marathon in 1972.

Bolstered in part by the second wave feminist movement that opposed sexual discrimination in all areas of life, including sport and fitness, women were actively pursuing equal rights at races throughout the 1970s. Women-only races also reemerged during this period, this time as a source of celebration rather than exclusion, and the first International Women's Marathon was held in Waldniel, West Germany, in 1974. The international lobby for women's long-distance running reached an important milestone when the International Olympic Committee Executive Board ruled that the women's marathon would be included in the 1984 Los Angeles Olympic Games. American Joan Benoit won this race.

Ensuing Controversies in Recreational Running Cultures

Although women from all over the world now compete and excel in running events, the most notable trend is the recent popularity of the sport among recreation enthusiasts. In addition to its cardiovascular benefits, running is thought to promote friendship and self-enhancement at the community level. Women's races have also attained widespread corporate sponsorship, and popular races worldwide are key platforms from which to raise funds for a variety of women's charities. Yet some of these developments have come under criticism in recent years. The commodification of running has resulted in steep entry fees for races and growing apparel, magazine, and sporting goods industries that market expensive products and services, which may pose barriers to participation in the activity for low-income women, and on a global scale, women may be differentially situated with respect to the production and consumption of these commodities. Another lingering issue is the images used to market such products, which often promote unhealthy body types for women.

See Also: Fitness; Health, Mental and Physical; Olympics, Summer.

Further Readings

Davis, P. and C. Weaving, eds. *Philosophical Perspectives on Gender in Sport and Physical Activity.* New York: Routledge, 2010.

Hargreaves, J. *Sporting Females: Critical Issues in the History and Sociology of Women's Sports.* London: Routledge, 1994.

Lenskyj, H. *Out of Bounds: Women, Sport and Sexuality.* Toronto, Canada: Women's, 1986.

Lovett, C. *Olympic Marathon: A Centennial History of the Games' Most Storied Race.* Westport, CT: Greenwood Press, 1997.

Radcliffe, P. *Paula: My Story So Far.* Leicester, UK: Charnwood, 2006.

Tricard, L. Mead. *American Women's Track and Field: A History. 1895 Through 1980.* London: McFarland, 1996.

Sandra Ignagni
York University

Rural Women

Despite global urbanization, more than half of the world's population, including the overwhelming majority of poor women and men, live in rural areas. Around 56 percent of the population in the less-developed countries and 72 percent of the population in the least-developed countries live in rural areas.

Women play a significant role in rural areas. According to International Labour Organization (ILO) data, in 2008, 35.4 percent of the total number of employed women worked in agriculture. ILO Convention 141 of 1977 and Recommendation 149 of 1975 concerning organizations of rural workers and their role in economic and social development define rural workers as any person engaged in agriculture, handicrafts, or a related occupation in a rural area, whether as a wage earner or as a self-employed person such as a tenant, sharecropper, or small owner–occupier.

Gender inequalities are widespread in rural labor markets, in which women and men often work in different combinations of employment; for example, as employers; self-employed farmers; permanent/

full-time, seasonal, temporary/casual, and piece-rate workers; and unpaid family workers. Women often work in the lowest-paid and most precarious forms of employment and experience the effects of the so-called "sticky floor" on the bottom rungs of their occupations. Rural women face occupational health, safety, and environmental hazards. Many of those killed, injured, or made ill are women workers. They are especially at risk because they are often employed on a part-time or casual basis and receive less training and instruction. They also often do repetitive work, which can result in musculoskeletal problems, and face reproductive hazards as a result of exposure to pesticides.

Rural women also generate nonagricultural income through cottage industries. They often work long hours in difficult circumstances, combining agricultural work and domestic work, including caring for children, the elderly, and the sick. The imposition of many care responsibilities onto girls/daughters tends to perpetuate cycles of impoverishment and gender disadvantage. In general, in rural areas women are responsible for fuel and water collection. The lack of infrastructure in many rural areas increases women's work and the demands on their time. The overload of work women undertake is reflected in a sharp rise in the incidence of child labor. Despite the contribution of women in supplying a large proportion of the agricultural labor in many parts of the world—in some cases producing up to 80 percent of food crops—women continue to have less access to financial, physical, and social assets in comparison with men. This result is the frequent denial of women's basic human rights.

Education for women and girls in rural areas remains a problem. The United Nations Educational, Scientific and Cultural Organization reports that 72 million children of primary school age are not enrolled in school, of whom 54 percent are girls. There is a lack of public healthcare services for women, as well as social security protection and other social and economic benefits. Women have less of a voice in public decision making and fewer opportunities to improve their knowledge and skills. Rural women own less than 10 percent of property in the developed world and 2 percent in the developing world. Although they are the heads of family in a fifth of rural homes (and in some regions, of a third of such homes), they only own around 1 percent of the land. A large body of literature has debated the "feminization" of rural labor markets, as war, sick-

ness, death from human immunodeficiency virus and acquired immune deficiency syndrome (HIV/AIDS), and male emigration have increased the proportion of women working in agriculture.

In many countries, the situation of women living in rural areas continues to deteriorate because of the lack of development, migration to towns, aging of the population, and lack of education and training opportunities for women. The inequalities and discrimination faced by rural women are exacerbated by the confluence of crises: the financial and economic crisis, the threat of climate change, and the fuel and food crises. Rural women with disabilities, older rural women, and indigenous women often face multiple discriminations and are among the most vulnerable.

**International Instruments
Related to Rural Women**
In 1921, the ILO adopted Convention 11 concerning the Rights of Association and Combination of Agricultural Workers, extending to agricultural workers the same rights of association as for industrial workers. ILO Convention 141 of 1977 provides independent organizations of rural workers an effective means of ensuring the participation of rural workers without discrimination in economic and social development and in the benefits resulting there from. ILO Convention 169 on Indigenous and Tribal Peoples of 1989 adopts special measures to ensure equal treatment in employment and provides protection against sexual harassment and abuses in the workplace. ILO Safety and Health in Agriculture Convention 184 of 2001 represents an important step forward. Article 20 states that hours of work, night work, and rest periods for workers in agriculture shall be in accordance with national laws and regulations or collective agreements. Article 21 states that workers in agriculture shall be covered by an insurance or social security scheme against fatal and nonfatal occupational injuries and diseases, as well as against invalidity and other work-related health risks, providing coverage at least equivalent to that enjoyed by workers in other sectors.

The United Nations Convention on the Elimination of All Forms of Discrimination Against Women of 1979 is unique among human rights treaties in that it specifically addresses the circumstances of rural women—Article 14 is entirely about this population. It recognizes the particular problems faced by rural women, as well as the significant roles that women play in the economic survival of their families, and calls on states' parties to ensure the application of the entirety of the convention to women in rural areas.

The United Nations Convention on the Rights of Persons with Disabilities of 2006 specifically calls on states' parties to ensure the equal rights and advancement of women and girls with disabilities and makes several references to the rights of people living in rural areas. The United Nations Declaration on the Rights of Indigenous Peoples of 2007 recognizes the human rights of indigenous peoples and calls on member states to ensure that indigenous women and children enjoy full protection and guarantees against all forms of violence and discrimination.

The United Nations General Assembly has addressed the situation of rural women in a number of other resolutions, in which it has emphasized the extreme vulnerability of this group as a result of the global economic downturn and stressed the importance of sound gender-sensitive agricultural policies and strategies. In its resolution on the improvement of the situation of women in rural areas of February 12, 2008, the United Nations General Assembly called on member states and United Nations entities to ensure that the rights of older women in rural areas are taken into account with regard to their equal access to basic social services, appropriate social protection/social security measures, and economic resources, as well as their empowerment through access to financial services and infrastructure. In the same resolution, the United Nations General Assembly established an annual International Day of Rural Women on October 15, which was observed for the first time in 2008. In his message, the secretary-general urged all countries to put the needs of rural women at the top of the global agenda, so as to pave the way for a more secure global future. The United Nations selected October 15 because it is the eve of World Food Day, thus linking this recognition of rural women with their critical role in food production and food security.

See Also: Business, Women in; Indigenous Women's Issues; Microcredit; Migrant Workers; Unpaid Labor.

Further Readings

Fontana, M. and C. Paciello. *Gender Dimensions of Rural and Agricultural Employment: Differentiated Pathways Out of Poverty: A Global Perspective.* Brighton, UK: Institute of Development Studies, 2009.

International Labour Organization. *Every Child Counts: New Global Estimates on Child Labour.* Geneva, Switzerland: ILO, 2002.

International Labour Organization. *Global Employment Trends for Women.* Geneva, Switzerland: ILO, 2009.

United Nations. "Improvement of the Situation of Women in Rural Areas." Report of the Secretary-General (A/64/190), July 29, 2009.

Kadriye Bakirci
Istanbul Technical University

Russia

The lives of women in the Russian Federation in the 21st century are shaped by multiple legacies (demographic, ecological, economic, and social) bequeathed by 70 years of communism in the country's recent past and by Russia as a country, making the difficult and simultaneous transitions from an industrial to a postindustrial society and from a centrally planned economy to market capitalism. Although literacy and employment rates for Russian women are among the highest in the world, the gendered wage gap between men and women and the degree to which women are underrepresented in politics in Russia are also very high. Reproductive and child health, trafficking of women, domestic violence, and questions of family stability also remain important issues for Russian women, as does the work/family balance and lack of affordable childcare.

Demographic trends in Russia significantly affect women, particularly in regard to patterns of marriage and fertility and in the way that the Russian government formulates policy toward its female citizens. Mortality rates have exceeded birth rates in Russia since 1992, and there has been an annual decrease of .5 percent in the Russian population from 2000 to 2006. Although Russian women do outlive Russian men (average female life expectancy is 72 years, and average male life expectancy is 59 years), life expectancy for Russian women is 7 to 12 years lower than rates in other developed European countries, and mortality rates for Russian women are more than twice as high as those for other countries with a similar gross domestic product. The extremely low life expectancy for Russian men means that although the ratio of working-age women (16 to 54 years of age) to working-age men (16 to 59 years of age) in Russia is quite normal (954 women to 1,000 men in 2008), in the postworking-age cohort, women outnumber men by the incredible ratio of 2,600 women to every 1,000 men (in 2008). Similar to other developed European countries, Russia has fertility rates that are below the population replacement levels—in Russia's case, 1.3 births per woman per year, which is 1.65 times lower than replacement level. The average maternal age at time of first birth is also growing in Russia.

Partially as a consequence of the Soviet period of Russian development (1919–91), with its formal legal commitment to education and gender equality, educational and literacy rates for women in Russia are among the highest in the world: 99.2 percent of Russian women older than 18 years are literate, and the combined gross enrollment ratio for women in primary, secondary, and tertiary education in Russia was 93 percent in 2005 (the rate for male students was 85 percent). An impressive 82 percent of women in Russia complete some form of tertiary education, and women outnumber men in tertiary education by a ratio of 1.36 to 1.

The high education achievement of Russian women does not translate into economic success, however. As a result of both the legacy of the Soviet push for full employment for women and the dire economic straits of most families during the transition to capitalism, nearly the same number of women as men are formally employed in the Russian economy, and the number of women participating in the informal economic sector has also continued to grow throughout the 2000s. Despite high rates of employment, the gender wage gap in Russia is quite high and is growing. In 2002, the average woman's wage was 33.5 percent less than the average man's; in 2005, the average woman's wage was 39.2 percent less than the average man's wage.

Although the absolute number of unemployed women and women living in poverty decreased in the 2000s, women remained the majority in both these groups (constituting 66.3 percent of the formally registered unemployed in 2004 and nearly 60 percent of those living below the poverty line in the same year). The main cause of the gender wage gap in Russia is the

sexual segregation of occupations: Women predominate heavily in four of the five least prestigious and most poorly compensated occupations in Russia (the arts and cultural sector, the educational sector, the public catering and trade sector, and the healthcare and social service sector), and nearly twice as many men as women are employed in the more lucrative and prestigious sectors of science and engineering and top management and business, and as heads of public authorities. Research suggests that latent gender discrimination during hiring and firing reinforces this occupational segregation. A survey conducted in 2000 by the Office of the United Nations Resident Coordinator in the Russian Federation found that large majorities of both men and women believed potential employers in all sectors preferred male candidates over women.

Social, Health, and Family Concerns

Low remuneration for paid employment and proportionally higher rates of poverty and unemployment have led to higher rates of social problems for women in Russia. State maternity and child allowances that are far below the European average further complicate the economic and social situation of women in Russia, as does the severe shortage of government-subsidized child care (more than 1 million children are currently on waitlists for government child care in Russia). Thus, working Russian mothers face significant difficulties in trying to meet their work and family obligations—a situation exacerbated by the fact that patriarchal attitudes about the division of childcare and domestic labor in Russia mean that women report spending approximately twice the time per week on these tasks than men do. One troubling indicator of the toll that economic and social insecurity and the burden of the "second shift" of home responsibilities take on Russia's women is the fact that between 1990 and 2002, the rate of female deaths caused by alcoholism tripled. Furthermore, the number of alcohol-related female deaths in Russia, which account for 17 percent of total female mortality, is five times as high as the European average.

Although maternal mortality rates in Russia have decreased from 54 per 100,000 women in 1985 to 23 per 100,000 women in 2003, these rates are still more than twice the European average. Domestic violence is also a significant problem in Russia, where the post-

Soviet government has still not ratified a statute defining and criminalizing domestic violence. As scholar Janet Elise Johnson points out, although credible data are not readily available, even the Russian government estimates that between 12,000 and 15,000 women are killed in domestic violence incidences per year—a staggering number when we consider that in the United States, which has roughly twice the population of Russia, the analogous number is 1,200 women.

Women in Politics

During the Soviet era, quotas ensured elevated levels of female participation in party and state governing organizations. With the collapse of communism, the political landscape in Russia took on a decidedly less gender-egalitarian character. Since the Russian Federation emerged in 1992, only one of Russia's 89 federal subjects has had a female governor, and only three women have led regional parliaments during the same period. Women hold roughly 10 percent of the legislative seats in both the federal and regional bodies, but they make up over 75 percent of the clerical and administrative staff in these bodies.

Women's preoccupation with economic survival and family concerns, an increasing (and increasingly true) perception that politics in Russia is too corrupt and violent for women to participate in, and traditional preferences for strong (read: masculine) leaders help keep down levels of female participation in politics in Russia.

Women in Russia find themselves facing multiple challenges as the country transforms itself economically, politically, and socially. The high rates of female education and female economic participation offer a good base from which Russian women can continue to strive for increased social and political equality.

See Also: Economics, Women in; HIV/AIDS: Europe; Representation of Women in Government, International.

Further Readings

Johnson, Janet Elise. *Gender Violence in Russia: The Politics of Feminist Intervention.* Bloomington: Indiana University Press, 2009.

Kuehnast, Kathleen and Carol Nechemias, eds. *Post-Soviet Women Encountering Transition: Nation Building, Economic Survival, and Civic Activism.* Washington, DC, and Baltimore, MD: Woodrow Wilson Center Press and Johns Hopkins University Press, 2004.

United Nations Interagency Thematic Group on Gender in the Russian Federation and the Institute of Society and Gender Policy. "Monitoring Women's Rights in Russia Federation: Thousand of Women's Stories." http://www.undp.ru/publications/1000_istoriy.pdf (accessed November 2009).

Katherine Graney
Skidmore College

Rwanda

Rwanda is a small, land-locked country just south of the equator in the Great Lakes region of central Africa. It is bordered by Uganda to the north, Tanzania to the east, Burundi to the south, and the Democratic Republic of Congo to the west. Known as the "Land of a Thousand Hills," Rwanda is about the size of Maryland (approximately 10,200 square miles) and has a current population of 10.7 million, growing at an annual rate of 3 percent. Rwanda's population density is among the highest in sub-Saharan Africa. More than 90 percent of Rwandans earn their living through agriculture, and approximately 60 percent live below the poverty line. Average life expectancy for men is 55 years and 58 years for women. The human immunodeficiency virus and acquired immune deficiency syndrome (HIV/AIDS) adult prevalence rate is 3 percent. Rwanda has three official languages: Kinyarwanda, English, and French.

Rwanda became a German colony in 1898. After World War I, Belgium administered Rwanda as a United Nations Trust Territory. In 1935, Belgian colonialists instituted a system of national identification cards: Rwandans with 10 or more cows were registered as Tutsi (approximately 14 percent), and those with less as Hutu (approximately 85 percent). A third group, the Twa, made up about 1 percent of the population. Although these three groups spoke the same Bantu language and frequently intermarried, Tutsi were known as cattle herders, Hutu as cultivators, and Twa as hunter-gatherers and craftsmen. On July 1, 1962, Rwanda was granted formal independence. The first president, Gregoire Kayibanda, was a Hutu. Juvenal Habyarimana, also a Hutu, took control in a bloodless coup on July 5, 1973. In late 1959, *muyaga* ("wind of destruction") swept through Rwanda, and

Women in Rwanda harvest geranium plants, hoping to sell the distilled oil to the international perfume industry. More than 90 percent of Rwandans earn their living through agriculture, with 60 percent living below the poverty line.

tens of thousands of Tutsi were killed. Many Tutsi fled to neighboring countries. On October 1, 1990, the Rwandan Patriotic Front (RPF), predominately Tutsi who had escaped in 1959, invaded from Uganda, igniting a civil war. On 4 August 1993, the Arusha Peace Agreement was signed. On April 6, 1994, the presidential jet was shot down as it approached the Kigali airport. All of the passengers were killed, including President Habyarimana and Burundian President Cyprien Ntaryamira.

Within hours of the crash, roadblocks had been established throughout the streets of the capital city Kigali, policed by soldiers and *interahamwe* (Hutu militias), with instructions to kill anyone who "looked" Tutsi. At the same time, the Presidential Guard and *interahamwe* traveled from house to house, killing Hutu opposition members and individuals whose names appeared on their target lists. The genocide

quickly spread beyond the capital, arriving at various regions at different times, ultimately engulfing the entire country. Over the course of a mere 100 days, an estimated 800,000 Tutsi and politically moderate Hutu were killed. The vast majority of the violence was committed with crude instruments, such as machetes and clubs, by ordinary Rwandan men and women.

Violence committed during the genocide was perpetrated in gender-specific forms. Sexual violence was rampant, used as a tool of a genocidal campaign against Tutsi women and girls. Rape and sexual assault were often committed in public, by many men at a time, and in especially violent ways, using instruments such as sticks, guns, and other sharp objects. Women were also taken by *interahamwe*, members of the Rwandan Armed Forces, and civilians, kept as slaves, and forced to serve as their "wives." Over the course of the three-month-long genocide, at least 250,000

Rwandan women were raped. Many of these women survived the genocide only to discover that they had been infected with HIV/AIDS. A generation of children was also conceived through rapes committed during the genocide. Today, genocidal rape survivors face a host of medical, psychological, and social consequences.

Many remain stigmatized, live in isolation, and experience high levels of trauma. After the genocide, in 1994, the United Nations established the International Criminal Tribunal for Rwanda (ICTR) to try those considered most responsible for the genocide. In a landmark 1998 decision (*Prosecutor v. Akayescu*), the ICTR became the first court to recognize rape as an act of genocide. In 2000, the Rwandan government instituted the *gacaca* ("justice on the grass") court system to try more than 100,000 alleged *genocidaires* who had been languishing in lethally overcrowded prisons.

In the country's 2003 amended Constitution, Rwandan women were granted at least 30 percent of posts in decision-making bodies. In order to meet this mandated quota, separate parliamentary elections were held for women in 2008. In a historically and geographically unprecedented outcome, women gained 56 percent of parliamentary seats. As of 2010, Rwanda is the country with the world's highest percentage of female parliamentarians.

See Also: HIV/AIDS: Africa; Rape and HIV; Rape in Conflict Zones.

Further Readings

Gourevitch, P. *We Wish to Inform You That Tomorrow We Will be Killed With Our Families: Stories From Rwanda*. New York: Picador, 1999.

Larson, C. *As We Forgive: Stories of Reconciliation From Rwanda*. Grand Rapids, MI: Zondervan, 2009.

Zinzer, S. *A Thousand Hills: Rwanda's Rebirth and the Man Who Dreamed It*. Hoboken, NJ: Wiley, 2008.

Jenna Appelbaum
New York University

S

Saint Kitts and Nevis

Saint Kitts and Nevis is a small (162-mile) island nation in the Caribbean Sea. The population of 40,131, as of July 2009, is predominantly black and Christian (Anglican, other Protestant, and Roman Catholic). Although the economy is heavily dependent on tourism and services—the sugar industry, previously a mainstay of the economy, was closed down in 2005—and is somewhat handicapped by the nation's small size, citizens enjoy a standard living similar to many European countries. Per capita gross domestic product (GDP) as of 2009 was $18,800, the 64th highest in the world, and life expectancy is 72 years for women and 69 years for men. The fertility rate is above replacement levels (2.26 children per woman), so although net migration is negative (minus 1.15 migrants per 1,000 population), Saint Kitts has a positive population growth rate of 0.847 percent.

Education and Childcare

Educational expenditures comprise over 9 percent of the national budget, one of the highest percentages in the world. Education is provided through the tertiary level, and the literacy rate is close to 100 percent. Labor-force participation for both women and men is over 80 percent, although men are more than twice as likely to be employers (as opposed to employees). About half of households are headed by single women. Women held no seats in the unicameral National Assembly as of 2007, although in recent years they have held as many as 13 percent of the seats.

Saint Kitts and Nevis has a high standard of maternal care and childcare, as reflected in near-universal prenatal care and births assisted by skilled personnel and high rates of childhood vaccination. The birth rate is 17.67 per 1,000 population, and infant mortality is 13.94 deaths per 1,000 live births. Abortion is legal only to save the women's life or preserve her mental or physical health, or if the pregnancy was a result of rape. Family-planning services are available at health-care centers, and over half of women in Saint Kitts report using contraception. However, teenage pregnancy remains a concern, and in 2001–05, the teenage motherhood rate was 19.1 percent. Human immuno-deficiency virus and acquired immune deficiency syndrome (HIV/AIDS) is also a concern, and women are about 60 percent more likely than men to be infected, with infection rates highest in the 25 to 44 age group.

See Also: Abortion, Access to; HIV/AIDS: North America; Single Mothers.

Further Readings

Pan American Health Organization. "Saint Kitts and Nevis." http://www.paho.org/hia/archivosvol2/paisesing /SaintKittsandNevisEnglish.pdf (accessed May 2010).

Richardson, Bonham C. *Caribbean Migrants: Environment and Human Survival on St. Kitts and Nevis.* Knoxville: University of Tennessee Press, 1983.

United Nations Statistics Divisions. "UNdata: A World of Information: Gender Info." http://data.un.org/Explorer .aspx?d=GenderStat (accessed February 2010).

Sarah Boslaugh
Washington University School of Medicine

Saint Lucia

After almost two centuries of controversy between England and France, the British ultimately established ownership of Saint Lucia in 1814. Slavery was abolished two decades later; however, this Caribbean island remained agricultural, chiefly producing bananas, mangos, and avocados. In 1979, Saint Lucia gained its independence and became more urbanized (28 percent). By the 21st century, the chief industry was tourism. Currently, 80 percent of the workforce is employed in services. The island has a per capita income of $10,900 and is ranked 69th on the United Nations Development Programme's (UNDP) list of countries with Very High Human Development. The island is relatively homogeneous in both ethnicity and religion. More than 82 percent of islanders are black, and more than 67 percent are Roman Catholic. Saint Lucia ranks 66th on the UNDP Gender Empowerment Measure, and the women of Saint Lucia generally enjoy equal rights with males. The government has consistently expressed support for women's rights, and at the national level, the Gender Relations Division has been charged with protecting women's rights.

Domestic violence continues to be of major concern in Saint Lucia. Through the efforts of activists, Saint Lucia passed the Domestic Violence (Summary Proceedings) Act in 1995. In 2004, the act was amended to further reduce violence against women by addressing the issues of marital rape, stalking, and sexual harassment and allowing victims of rape and sexual abuse to receive compensation.

The median age of women on the island is 30.8 years. Women have a life expectancy of 79.3 years as compared with 73.8 for males. The fertility rate is 1.8 children per woman. Saint Lucia ranks 134th in the world in infant mortality (13.43 births per 1,000 live births). At 90.6 percent, female literacy is slightly higher than that of males (89.5). Saint Lucia ranks 29th in the world in spending on education; and overall, female Saint Lucians are better educated than males, attending school for at least 14 years and outnumbering males at the tertiary level.

As might be expected in a country that is predominately Roman Catholic, women on the island have only limited control over their reproductive lives. Abortion is illegal except when a mother's physical or mental health is at risk, or in cases of rape or incest.

Women were granted the right to vote in Saint Lucia in 1951, but it was not until 1979 that a female was elected to Parliament. In 2003, a woman was elected to Saint Lucia's highest elected position. Between 1999 and 2005, 55 percent of legislators, senior officials, and managers were female. During that same period, 53 percent of professionals and technical workers were female. In 2007, 18.2 percent of all Parliamentary seats were held by females, and just over 8 percent of cabinet-level officials were female. Despite their majority in such positions, the ratio of estimated female-to-male earned income was only 0.5.

See Also: Abortion Laws, International; Domestic Violence; Government, Women in; Sexual Harassment; United Kingdom.

Further Readings

Breneman, Anne R. and Rebecca A. Mbuh. *Women in the New Millennium: The Global Revolution.* Lanham, MD: Hamilton Books, 2006.

Central Intelligence Agency. "The World Factbook: Saint Lucia." https://www.cia.gov/library/publications/the -world-factbook/geos/st.html (accessed June 2010).

Ellis, G. *Saint Lucia Helen of the West Indies (Caribbean Guides).* Walpole, MA: Hunter Publishing, 1994.

Elizabeth Rholetter Purdy
Independent Scholar

Saint Vincent and the Grenadines

The early history of Saint Vincent and the Grenadines was marked by battles between France and Britain over control of the island and by internal resistance to colonization. By 1783, Britain had succeeded in colonizing the island. It became a member of the Federation of the West Indies for two years in the 1960s before becoming autonomous in 1969 and declaring independence in 1979. Saint Vincent and the Grenadines, which ranks 91st on the United Nations Development Programme's (UNDP) list of countries with Very High Human Development, has a per capita income of $18,100. By the 21st century, 47 percent of this Caribbean island's population lived in urban areas. The island is heavily dependent on the banana crop and tourism. While 57 percent of the labor force is employed in services, another 28 percent works in agriculture. About 72 percent of all female workers are employed in the service industry. With an unemployment rate of 15 percent, the government is facing major difficulties, and women suffer disproportionately from this phenomenon. Those with a secondary education are twice as likely as males in that group to be unemployed. The majority (66 percent) of Saint Vincentians are black. The island is more diverse from a religious perspective, with the majority declaring themselves either Protestant or Roman Catholic.

The median age for women is 28.9 years, and women have a life expectancy of 75.5 years, as compared with 71.8 years for males. The fertility rate is 1.98 children per woman. With an infant mortality rate of 15.1 deaths per 1,000 live births, Saint Vincent and the Grenadines ranks 126th in the world. At 96 percent, female literacy is equal to that of males, and both females and males attend school for approximately 12 years. Saint Vincent and the Grenadines ranks 14th in the world in educational spending. Women continue to earn considerably less than males on the island. In 2005, for instance, the estimated earned income for females was only $4,449, as compared with $8,722 for males.

Women received the right to vote in 1951, but the first woman was not elected to Parliament until 1979, when the island became independent. By the 21st century, 18.2 percent of the seats in Parliament were filled by females, and women made up one-fifth of the island's ministers.

Problems With Violence Against Women

Teenage pregnancy and violence against women continue to concern female activists. Domestic violence is particularly prevalent in common-law relationships, and the most likely victims are females between the ages of 13 and 34. Incest is also a problem on the island. Many feminists see all of these problems as consequences of low self-esteem among females who are taught to subjugate themselves to males. In 1984, the island passed the Domestic Violence and Matrimonial Proceedings Act and followed it up in 1995 with the Domestic Violence Act. However, anyone convicted under these acts faces civil rather than criminal charges.

See Also: Domestic Violence; Government, Women in; Teen Pregnancy; Marriage; United Kingdom.

Further Readings

Breneman, Anne R. and Rebecca A. Mbuh. *Women in the New Millennium: The Global Revolution.* Lanham, MD: Hamilton Books, 2006

International Women's Rights Action Watch. "Country Report: St. Vincent and the Grenadines." http://www1.umn.edu/humanrts/iwraw/publications/countries/st_vincent_and_grenadines.htm (accessed June 2010).

Elizabeth Rholetter Purdy
Independent Scholar

Same-Sex Marriage

There are an array of international policies that variously legitimize same-sex partnerships, and consequently same-sex family formations, through extending the rights of lesbians and gay men to marry or to live as a legally recognized couple. N. Naples (2007) outlines the different types of relationship policies that can be utilized by same-sex couples, beginning with registered partnerships or civil unions, which include substantively similar—or the same—rights as marriage.

Evolution of the Institution

The first national recognition of same-sex partnerships came in Denmark in 1989, allowing registered partnership, as opposed to "marriage." More recently, sexuality has also been high on the United Kingdom (UK) legislative and policy agenda, with fresh legislation that explicitly addresses sexuality within the context of equality issues, including same-sex partnership (e.g., The Civil Partnership Act, 2004). These moves are mirrored across time and place with countries bringing in policies from full marriage (Belgium, 2003; Canada, 2005; Netherlands, 1998; Portugal, 2010; South Africa; Spain, 2005; Sweden, 2009) to civil unions and registered partnerships (including France's *pacte civil de solidarité* in 1999 and New Zealand's Civil Union in 2004).

The United States now stands apart from Canada and many European countries on same-sex marriage, passing the Defense of Marriage Act (DOMA) in 1996, upholding and "defending" marriage for heterosexuals only. The recent Proposition 8 debates suggest a wider differential "mapping" of same-sex rights in the United States Proposition 8 was a California ballot proposition passed in the November 2008 general election. The measure added a new section (7.5) to Article I of the California Constitution. The new section reads: "Only marriage between a man and a woman is valid or recognized in California." The ProtectMarriage.com organization sponsored the initiative that placed Proposition 8 on the ballot, also attracting the support of a number of political figures and religious organizations.

Arguably, it is paramount that current theoretical considerations of sexuality resonate with new legal and international policy landscapes, in which debates are happening in many parts of the world including, for example, Ireland, Japan, Poland, South Korea, and Uganda.

With increasing international legal recognition of same-sex relationships, commentaries and controversies have been born out of the celebration and condemnation of legally recognized, monogamous coupledom, now extended to same-sex partners. Questions on the propriety of gays and lesbians engaging in such normative practices have created a number of thought-provoking stances. Conflict comes from varied corners and many authors, discussing different international contexts, and have explored the resurgence of Christian right-wing discourses in, for example, the United States and the UK, where the "homosexual" is represented as a threat to "normal" family relations. The conjuring up of "real," "chosen," and "pretend" families endlessly occurs, evident too in political and media discourses. However, who gets constituted as "real," "pretend," or "failing" also rests upon other, intersecting hierarchies, where family-values rhetoric often endangers the rights and inter-

ests of varied disadvantaged groups, including poor single mothers as well as lesbians and gays.

Along with the perhaps anticipated outrage from various evangelical Christian groups, aghast at the appropriation of a sacred traditional convention, there has been opposition from those who believe that gays and lesbians have no place within an institution (even as a facsimile of an institution), that is seen as reinforcing firmly conservative, heteronormative family values. Nevertheless, there has been an international growth of confidence and visibility, inspiring a claiming of rights even as these have been accompanied by a strong assertion of traditional "family values" (specifically in the United States and the UK); often victories remain somewhat problematic, both in terms of their legislative framing and substantive effects. Yet, following such gains, much has been said of the move away from the family and the state as a repressive site, where lesbians and gays seek to escape its injustices, toward an active uptake of state-sanctioned relations, welcoming the blessings and privileges afforded.

Issues of Citizenship

Before interrogating this in a bit more detail, it is important to situate the material and symbolic importance of formal inclusion, in terms of legal rights, as well as in the subjective sense of belonging facilitated in being included as a full citizen with similar (if often not equal) rights to their heterosexual counterparts. Status categories (gender, sexuality, class, race) are used to define and negotiate different levels or degrees of citizenship, where social institutions (family, state, labor market) are implicated in defining the boundaries of citizenship—and in recognizing or rejecting rights. There are practical benefits to be accrued in increasing legal entitlements, offering a material and symbolic validation of partnering and, often relatedly, parenting. In the U.S. context, the protections and benefits extended to married couples under federal law is commonly cited as a reason for same-sex marriage. Such policies themselves materialize families, offering new possibilities for societal recognition, legal recourse, and access to welfare services.

Some commentators have argued that the mainstreaming and extension of marriage to lesbians and gays would "normalize" lesbian and gay relations and will thus solve the all-political concern and that, as such, same-sex marriage is the only reform that truly

The first national recognition of same-sex partnerships came in 1989, when Denmark allowed registered partnerships as opposed to "marriages." More recently, gay rights have also been high on the legislative and policy agenda in the United Kingdom.

matters. Claims are also (re)made on marriage as a bedrock offering material and emotional stability to its members, also judged in the "best interests" of children. Nonetheless, same-sex marriage may offer the most appeal, acceptance, and assets to those already closest to the mainstream. Far from "queering" citizenship, the fight for same-sex marriage and equal rights can in fact uphold rather normative frameworks.

Moving the debate on the meanings of same-sex marriage from the theoretical to the empirical level, Shipman and Smart explore the reasons why same-sex couples in the UK have marriage commitment ceremonies and what meanings such ceremonies might have in legitimating same-sex relationships in the eyes of their (heterosexual) families and in wider society. K. Hull (2006) also notes that in the raging controversies and widespread media coverage in Canada, the United States, and beyond, the voices of ordinary same-sex couples are sometimes difficult

to hear. Much contemporary research now interrogates the ways individuals interact with and utilize the law, in which the pursuit of same-sex inclusion may offer a profound threat to legal institutions and to society more generally and meanings and boundaries are up for grabs. Institutional possibilities—and constraints—are important in everyday negotiations enforcing a (re)consideration of the practicalities and promises in doing and being a family, as sanctioned in changing legal contexts.

Yet, developments in sexual citizenship may only extend to certain citizens and may in fact cement exclusions, renewing and heightening boundaries of (un)acceptability between the "dangerous queer" and the "good homosexual," who preferably resides in a "gay nuclear family," living a homonormative lifestyle. Such distinctions press at whether citizenship struggles inevitably constitute an impossible bid for respectability or a realistic claim on being and becoming "normal."

Writing before the introduction of the UK Civil Partnership, J. Weeks et al. note that none of their respondents wanted to mirror heterosexual coupledom, or establish a new norm of couple commitment that created new divisions within the nonheterosexual world.

Perhaps challenging notions of a sweeping homonormativity, lesbian and gay movements may at once involve both assimilation and transformation, oscillating between a "moment of transgression" and a "moment of citizenship." Many see the dualism between assimilation or transformation as a false one, setting up a weighty expectation of revolutionary potential as against stagnant failure. There are tensions and complexities in establishing ways of belonging within heteronormative frameworks, and such tensions displace the binary of assimilation/transformation stances and the notion of "model" and "paradigm" that they imply. More simply, lesbians and gay men continue to be positioned as threats to the sanctity of the heterosexual order and must complexly situate their citizenship struggles within this positioning. Such a fraught negotiation involves striving to become part of the mainstream and self-positioning as different.

Issues of Identity

Focusing on same-sex marriage specifically and sexual citizenship more generally inevitably leads to a re-visitation of issues of sameness/difference, which have dominated debates on lesbian and gay partnership and parenting, highlighting who gets included, even incorporated, into the good citizen/family and who remains excluded. *Lesbian and Gay Parenting: Securing Social and Educational Capital* explores the uptake, negotiation, and refusal of civil partnerships in the UK, where such legal consolidation may be seen as actively materializing family, making that which was sidelined and undervalued included and recognized. Legislative changes enforce a reconsideration of family, especially for lesbian and gay families who are faced again with the weight of success (anticipated by supporters); and with the burden of failure (endlessly declared by the less enthused). Such negotiations are indeed complex, as lesbian and gay families seek to survive and thrive, and indeed capitalize on such legislative changes. Herein lies a consequential sexual and class difference between those who can afford to conceptualize such changes as beneficial, particularly in relation to finances but also in relation to social status, respectability, and esteem—and those who cannot. To have a new currency is perhaps as much a mobilization and mainstreaming of class privilege as it is of sexual status.

See Also: Fundamentalist Christianity; Gay and Lesbian Advocacy; Gender Roles, Cross-Cultural; Heterosexism; Homosexuality, Religious Attitudes Toward; Marriage.

Further Readings

Duggan, L. "The New Homonormativity: The Sexual Politics of Neoliberalism." In R. Castronova and D. D. Nelson, eds., *Materializing Democracy: Toward a Revitalized Cultural Politics*. Durham, NC: Duke University Press, 2002.

Hull, K. *Same-Sex Marriage. The Cultural Politics of Love and Law*. Cambridge, UK: Cambridge University Press, 2006.

Lewin, E. *Recognising Ourselves: Ceremonies of Lesbian and Gay Commitment*. New York: Columbia University Press, 1998.

Naples, N. "Sexual Citizenship in International Context: Towards a Comparative Intersectional Analysis of Social Regulation." In Nick Rumens and Alejandro Cervantes-Carson, eds., *Sexual Politics of Desire and Belonging*, Amsterdam: Rodopi, 2007.

Richardson, D. "Locating Sexualities: From Here To Normality." *Sexualities*, v.7/4 (2004).

Shipman, B., et al. "'It's Made a Huge Difference': Recognition, Rights and the Personal Significance of Civil Partnership." *Sociological Research Online*, v.12/1 (2007).

Sullivan, A. *Virtually Normal: An Argument About Homosexuality*. New York: Knopf, 1995.

Weeks, J., B. Heaphy, and C. Donovan. *Same Sex Intimacies: Families of Choice and Other Life Experiments*. London: Routledge, 2001.

Yvette Taylor
Newcastle University

Samoa

The Independent State of Samoa is an archipelago of islands, nine of which are inhabited. There is a high population growth rate, offset by a high emigration rate. More than 90 percent of the population is ethnic Samoan and Christian. The culture emphasizes traditional Samoan social values, known as *fa'a*, and Christian beliefs. There are no legal or religious obstacles to equality, and many women enjoy good educational opportunities. Key women's issues include domestic violence and a lack of employment and political opportunities.

Samoan families are generally extended in nature, with membership based on heredity, land, and titles. The fertility rate is high, at 4.16 births per woman, and the infant mortality rate is 24.22 per 1,000 live births. Family members are expected to provide for each other's welfare. Domestic abuse is common and usually handled at the village level without police involvement. All family members are responsible for teaching children traditional values such as deference, politeness, and obedience to elders. Children begin chores at a young age. Education is valued and available through both public schools and missionary schools. Both genders receive an average of 12 years of education. The state supports the National University as well as nursing, teacher training, and trade schools. Many Samoans pursue higher education abroad. The literacy rate is equal at close to 100 percent for both men and women.

The population is mostly rural. There is government healthcare available at a nominal cost, but many residents combine Western-style medicine with traditional medical practices, often distinguishing between Samoan and non-Samoan illnesses. An increasingly Westernized diet has led to growing rates of diabetes. The state provides a social security system with a small old-age pension. Life expectancy for women is 75 years; for men it is 69 years.

The main employers are agriculture and industry, although there is also tourism and its related service industries. Traditional labor is divided by gender. Child labor, underemployment, and the exodus of skilled workers are problems. Women have become increasingly visible in modern Samoan public life. Suffrage is universal, and the constitution provides for equality, but women are still largely excluded from public offices. There is a state Women's Affairs Ministry. Nongovernmental organizations, most religious-based, include the Mothers' Club, Federation of Women's Committees, South-East Asia and Pan-Pacific Women's Association, and Mapusaga O Aiga Samoa.

See Also: Christianity; Domestic Abuse; Gender Roles, Cross-Cultural; Indigenous Women's Issues.

Further Readings

Hepburn, Stephanie and Rita J. Simon. *Women's Roles and Statuses the World Over*. Lanham, MD: Lexington Books, 2006.

Lockwood, Victoria S., ed. *Globalization and Cultural Change in the Pacific Islands*. Upper Saddle River, NJ: Pearson/Prentice Hall, 2004.

Mead, Margaret. *Coming of Age in Samoa: A Psychological Study of Primitive Youth for Western Civilization*. New York: HarperPerennial Modern Classics, 2001.

Marcella Bush Trevino
Barry University

San Marino

San Marino is the third-smallest state in Europe (61 square kilometers) and is a landlocked country completely surrounded by Italy. The population of 30,167 (as of July 2009) is primarily Sammarinese (native of San Marino) and Italian. Roman Catholicism is the dominant religion. Italian is the national language, and San Marino is heavily influenced by political, social, and cultural trends in Italy. Citizens of San Marino enjoy a high standard of living, with a Gross Domestic Product (GDP) of $41,900 (16th highest in the world) and life expectancies of 77.4 years for men (highest in the world) and 84.5 years for women. Literacy is almost universal at 95 percent for women and 97 percent for men.

Women have legal equality in San Marino. Women age 15 or older are employed at a higher rate (91.9 percent) than men in the same age group (86.9 percent), and women outnumber men in tertiary education.

Women received the right to vote in 1960 and the right to serve in political office in 1973. Several women have served as heads of state (Captains Regent: two serve at a time and are elected for six-month terms), including Rosa Zafferani (1999, 2008), Fausta Morganti (2005), Valeria Ciavatta (2003–04), and Maria Domenica Michelotti (2000). Women also serve in the San Marino Cabinet, including currently

Ciavatta (secretary of the Interior and Civil Protection) and Antonella Mularoni (secretary of state for Foreign and Political Affairs and Economic Planning). Women also hold about 11 percent of the seats in the national parliament.

Abortion in San Marino is legal only to save the mother's life. However, neighboring Italy allows abortion on demand, so women who can afford to pay can easily seek an abortion there. The fertility rate is 1.36 children per woman, and a low birth rate of 9.68 per 1,000 population, coupled with San Marino's long life expectancy and high rate of emigration (10.4 per 1,000 population, seventh highest in the world), mean the country has an aging population (median age in 2009 was 41.5 years, with only 16.8 percent age 14). Maternal and child care is of a high standard, with extensive prenatal care services and infant mortality of 5 per 1,000 live births. In recent years, there has not been a single case of maternal mortality.

See Also: Abortion, Access to; Government, Women in; Italy; Roman Catholic Church.

Further Readings

Eccardt, Thomas. *Secrets of the Seven Smallest States of Europe.* New York: Hippocrene Books, 2004.

United Nations Statistics Divisions. "UNdata: A World of Information: Gender Info." http://data.un.org/Explorer .aspx?d=GenderStat (accessed February 2010).

World Health Organization. "Highlights on Health in San Marino 2005." http://www.euro.who.int/document /e88392.pdf (accessed February 2010).

Sarah Boslaugh
Washington University School of Medicine

Santería

Santería is an orally transmitted religion that combines indigenous African traditions with elements of Roman Catholicism. Developed in Cuba, Santería has spread to Latin America and the United States. The religion emphasizes a reciprocal relationship between practitioners and *orishas* ("humanlike spirits"), expressed through religious rituals involving trance, spirit possession, dancing, and animal sac-

rifice. Santería offers spiritual opportunities for initiated female and male practitioners (*santeras* and *santeros*) that are somewhat more egalitarian than many other religions.

Known to practitioners as *la Regla de Ocha* ("The Rule of the Òrìshàs") or *la Religión Lucumí*, Santería developed from the 16th to 19th centuries as African slaves brought the baKongo, Dahomey, and Yorùbá beliefs and rituals of their homelands to sugar plantations in the Caribbean. These beliefs included spirit possession, animal sacrifice, and communication with spirits and ancestors through drumming- and dance-induced trance. Despite their forced conversion to Catholicism, many African slaves maintained their native traditions by nominally converting and combining old and new practices, as demonstrated in the fusion of African deities (*orishas*) and Catholic saints (*santos*) that gives Santería ("Way of the Saints") its name. The *orishas* are male and female spirits who intervene in human affairs to bring messages and healing from the spirit world; in return, *santeros* and *santeras* provide the *orishas* with offerings and prayers.

Santería involves trance and spirit possession. Practitioners may have altars at which to pray, like the one shown here.

These spirits are manifestations of the supreme creator deity, Olódùmarè. Religious practices in Santería are typically not shared with the uninitiated.

Santería recognizes both priests (*babalorishas*) and priestesses (*iyalorishas*), who may become possessed or "ridden" by an *orisha* during some religious rituals (*bembés*). *Santeros* and *santeras* are called by and serve specific *orishas*. The priest or priestess functions as the *padrino* ("godfather") or *madrina* ("godmother") for a new initiate. During initiation, the initiate is "married" to his or her *orisha* in the *asiento* ceremony. Three of the most important *orishas* are female: Oya (ruler of winds, associated with St. Theresa), Oshun (ruler of water, associated with Our Lady of Charity, the patron saint of Cuba), and Yemaya (ruler of seas and lakes, associated with Our Lady of Regla).

The religion's highest spiritual achievement is becoming a priest of *Ifá*, the divinatory aspect of Santería. *Ifá* divination (*idafa*) is performed by a *Babalawo*, an initiated priest. This role is not generally available to women in contemporary Santería, although women may have been initiated into *Ifá* priesthood in the 19th and early 20th centuries, and women continue to be initiated into *Ifá* priesthood in Nigeria and some other parts of the world. Women often lead the *ilé*, the "house" that serves as a ritual center for an extended family of Santería practitioners. Women have been influential in the history and development of Santería, and they continue to experience significant opportunities for spiritual advancement within the religion.

See Also: Candomblé; Cuba; Gender Roles, Cross-Cultural; Indigenous Religions, Global; Religion, Women in; Voodoo.

Further Readings

Baba Eyiogbe, F. "The World of the Orishas and Santería." OrishaNet. http://orishanet.org (accessed March 2010).

Clark, Mary Ann. *Where Men Are Wives and Mothers Rule: Santería Ritual Practices and Their Gender Implications.* Gainesville: University of Florida Press, 2005.

Murphy, Joseph M. *Santeria: African Spirits in America.* Boston: Beacon Press, 1993.

Zohreh Kermani
Harvard University

São Tomé and Principe

The West African islands of São Tomé and Principe were founded by the Portuguese, who exploited the islands for their slave-grown coffee and sugar. The islands became independent in 1975, but the road to democracy has been rocky. The population of 212,679 is made up of mestico descendants of Angolan slaves; Forros descendants of freed slaves; servicais laborers from Angola, Mozambique, and Cape Verde; the children of servicais; and Europeans. Most São Toméans are Roman Catholic (70.3 percent), and Portuguese is still the official language. Despite constitutional and legal guarantees of equality, São Toméan women are discriminated against.

To combat this, the Gender Equality Institute of the Office of Women's Affairs has sponsored a number of seminars and workshops to educate the public about that discrimination. Although two women have served as prime ministers, in 2008, women were vastly underrepresented in positions of leadership. Only two women sat in the 55-member national assembly, only four sat in the 14-member cabinet, and only one sat on the three-member supreme court. Opportunities for women are limited in large part because of family responsibilities. Violence against women continues to be a major social problem in São Tomé and Principe.

The economy of São Tomé and Principe is still heavily agricultural, and most of the workforce is engaged in subsistence farming and fishing. However, more than 60 percent of the people are now urbanized. With a per capita income of only $1,400, 54 percent of the population lives in poverty. The nations' massive foreign debt has been somewhat mitigated by international debt- and poverty-relief programs.

São Toméan social indicators reflect extensive poverty. The islands rank 70th in the world in infant mortality (37.12 deaths per 1,000 live births). Female infants (35.35 deaths per 1,000 live births) have an advantage over male infants (38.84 deaths per 1,000 live births) that continues throughout life, resulting in a life expectancy of 70.04 years for women and 66.65 years for men. Roughly half the population is younger than 15 years. Women have a median age of 17 years compared with 15.9 years for men. São Toméan women have a fertility rate of 5.33 children each and the 11th highest population growth in the world. São Toméans have a high risk of contracting bacterial diarrhea, hepatitis A, typhoid fever, malaria, and rabies. Although 92.2 percent of men are literate, only 77.9 percent of women older than 15 years are able to read and write. Both men and women generally attend school for 10 years.

Domestic violence is a major problem in São Tomé and Principe, and incidences have increased in recent years. Most cases go unreported because of the tendency to treat domestic violence as a family problem. The Office of Women's Affairs has established a hotline and a counseling center, but victims are sometimes unable to contact the hotline because of the nation's unstable telephone system. Rape, including spousal rape, is illegal; in general, however, only cases involving children or violent assault are prosecuted. The government is working with nongovernmental organizations to raise public awareness of violence against women. Prostitution is illegal, but it has become a pervasive problem, particularly in areas that cater to foreigners. No measures have been taken to address the problem of widespread sexual harassment.

See Also: Domestic Violence; Poverty; Rape, Cross-Culturally Defined.

Further Readings

Central Intelligence Agency. "The World Factbook: Sao Tome and Principe." https://www.cia.gov/library /publications/the-world-factbook/geos/tp.html (accessed June 2010).

Skaine, Rosemarie. *Women Political Leaders in Africa.* Jefferson, NC: McFarland, 2008.

Tripp, Ail Mari, et al. *African Women's Movements: Changing Political Landscapes.* New York: Cambridge University Press, 2009.

U.S. Department of State. "2008 Human Rights Report: Sao Tome and Principe." http://www.state.gov/g/drl /rls/hrrpt/2008/af/119020.htm (accessed March 2010).

Elizabeth Rholetter Purdy
Independent Scholar

Sarkozy, Carla Bruni

Carla Bruni Sarkozy is a former model and singer and the wife of French President Nicolas Sarkozy. An Italian heiress whose exploits have been media fodder since she was 19 years old, Bruni Sarkozy has become even more of a celebrity since her 2008 marriage to Sarkozy. She was one of the most successful models of the 1990s, reportedly earning more than $7 million annually. Her debut album, *Quelqu'un m'a dit (Someone Told Me)* sold 2 million copies. However real her accomplishments, her romantic escapades with rock stars, businessmen, and academics made her a focus of media attention—attention that increased when she was first photographed with France's newly divorced president at Disneyland Paris. The international press covered the glamorous couple's courtship, their wedding, and their official travels, commenting on Bruni Sarkozy's style and liberal sexual values. More recently, they have commented as freely on the couple's rumored affairs and troubled marriage.

Carla Bruni Tedeschi was born in Turin, Italy, on December 23, 1968, into a wealthy industrialist family in which arts were as important as business. The man whom she knew as her father, Alberto Bruni Tedeschi, was an accomplished composer; he also ran his family company, CEAT, which manufactured cables and tires. Her mother, Marisa Borini, was a concert pianist. Her biological father was a violinist. When young Carla was 5 years old, the family moved to Paris to escape the threat of kidnapping by a Marxist revolutionary group.

At age 19 years, Bruni Sarkozy signed with a modeling agency and soon became the Guess? Jeans girl, later working with top houses including Christian Dior, Chanel, and Versace. By 1990, she was among the highest-paid models in the world, eventually appearing on 250 covers. Her liaisons with men like Mick Jagger, Donald Trump, and French writer Jean-Paul Enthoven made her the darling of the tabloids. While living with Enthoven, she had an affair with his son—a philosopher 10 years her junior. The affair produced a son, born in 2001.

By 2003, Bruni Sarkozy had begun a second career as a singer. *Someone Told Me*, her first album, was a critical failure but a commercial success, selling over a million copies in France alone. It stayed on the European Billboard charts for 30 weeks and earned Bruni Sarkozy a nod as best female vocalist at the Victoires de la Musique, the French equivalent of the Grammy Awards, in 2004. Her second album, *No Promises*, released in early 2007, included songs inspired by poets W. B. Yeats, Emily Dickinson, Wal-

First Lady Michelle Obama meets with Carla Bruni-Sarkozy, wife of French President Sarkozy at the Palais Rohan (Rohan Palace), April 3, 2009, in Strasbourg, France, in this official White House photo.

ter de la Mare, Christina Rossetti, and others. It was less successful than her first album. By the end of the year, her affair between with Nicolas Sarkozy was attracting far more attention than her music.

The twosome holidayed in the Middle East, with journalists and photographers recording the romance. In January, the French president was dropping hints about a wedding, and on February 2, 2008, French radio announced that Sarkozy and Bruni had wed. The French have strong privacy laws and a sophisticated tolerance for personal scandal, but the growth of American- and British-style celebrity press has meant the new first lady's frankly expressed preference for polygamy received media attention, along with details about her fashion sense.

From Twitter gossip to accusations of a plot to destabilize the president's administration, word about the status of the Sarkozy marriage stirred rumors and speculation in 2010.

See Also: Celebrity Women; Fashion Industry, Theoretical Controversies; France; Italy; Supermodels.

Further Readings

Badiou, Alain. *The Meaning of Sarkozy.* London: Verso Books, 2010.

George, Lianne. "The Love Affair Is Over." *Maclean's,* v.121/29 (2008).

Trebay, Guy. "The French President's Lover." *New York Times* (January 13, 2008). http://www.nytimes.com/2008/01/13/fashion/13bruni.html?ref=europe (accessed April 2010).

Wylene Rholetter
Auburn University

Saudi Arabia

The Kingdom of Saudi Arabia, which is controlled by fundamentalist Muslims, has created one of the most restricted environments in the world for women. When the country held its first-ever local elections in 2005, only men older than 21 years were allowed to vote. At 90 percent, Arabs form a considerable majority in Saudi Arabia, and all Saudis are officially Muslim. The situation for Saudi women has often been compared with that of aborigines living in South Africa under apartheid. Since Saudi women are considered what some women's rights groups have called "perpetual minors," they are answerable to *mahrams*—male guardians—who may be husbands, fathers, brothers, sons, or other male relatives. Saudi women have virtually no freedom of movement. Those younger than 45 years can travel only by permission, and they must be accompanied by male chaperones. Though women older than 45 years technically have the legal right to travel without permission, airport officials usually demand that they show permission to travel outside the country. Saudi women are also forbidden to drive automobiles. They cannot even seek out medical care for themselves or their children without their mahram's permission. After they reach puberty, all females appearing in public are required to wear both *abayas*, black cloaks that cover their bodies, and *niqbas*, which cover their heads.

Mosques are generally reserved for men, and female access to public facilities such as parks, museums, and libraries is limited. Only 5 percent of the Saudi workforce is female, and those few who do work are segregated from male workers. Females must also obtain the permission of male guardians before becoming educated. Schools in Saudi Arabia are segregated by sex after the age of 6 years, and the first school for girls was not established until 1960. Today, the female literacy rate (70.8 percent) is considerably lower than that of men (78.8 percent).

The median age for females is 19.9 years. The infant mortality rate is 11.57 per 1,000 live births, with females (9.91) maintaining an advantage over males (13.15) that continues throughout life, resulting in a female life expectancy of 78.48 years compared with 74.23 years for males. In 1975, a royal decree was issued banning all contraceptives in Saudi Arabia. In 2009, the fertility rate was 3.83 children per woman.

Marriages, Family, and Children

Although forced marriages were officially banned in 2005, the practice continues. In general, marriage contracts are negotiated by potential husbands and the brides' mahrams. According to United Nations reports, 16 percent of Saudi females between the ages of 15 and 19 years have been married, divorced, or widowed. Polygamy is still practiced, although the custom is on the decline. Although men can have up to four wives, women are limited to one husband. Men may obtain divorces by denouncing their wives three times, but women are forced to petition courts for divorce decrees. Women who commit adultery may be subjected to death by stoning. Inheritance laws limit women to only half what male heirs inherit.

According to Islamic law, Saudi fathers have sole guardianship of all children. In practice, mothers may obtain custody of sons until age 7 years and daughters until age 9 years. Guardianship of older children may be assigned to paternal grandparents rather than to mothers. Children born to Saudi mothers and foreign fathers are not considered citizens.

No laws exist in Saudi Arabia to protect women against domestic violence, and honor killings are common. Foreign-born women are particularly vulnerable to violence and suppression. There is some evidence that female genital mutilation continues to occur among Shia Muslims of the Eastern Province and among the Bedouin groups.

Because the daily life of Saudi women is governed by *purdah*, which forbids them from appearing in public without a male escort, outside contact is circumscribed, and contact with nonrelated males is banned entirely. In 2007, a Saudi court sentenced a 19-year-old victim of gang rape to 90 lashes for appearing in public without a male chaperone. When her lawyer objected, his license was suspended and the victim's penalty was raised to 200 lashes. The men who raped her were given prison terms of varying lengths. The victim's husband subsequently reported that she was suicidal and asked the court to revoke her sentence.

See Also: Domestic Violence; Islam; Marriages, Arranged; Rape, Cross-Culturally Defined.

Further Readings

Central Intelligence Agency. "The World Factbook: Saudi Arabia." https://www.cia.gov/library/publications/the-world-factbook/geos/sa.html (accessed June 2010).

DeSantis, Marie. "The Middle East Crisis: Democracy, Kings, and Sexual Apartheid in Saudi Arabia." *Off Our Backs*, v.20/9 (1990).

FreedomHouse.org. "Saudi Arabia: Women's Rights in the Middle East and North Africa." http://www.freedom

house.org/template.cfm?page=384&key=174&parent=16&report=76 (accessed February 2010).

Isis International. "Saudi Arabia: Women's Civil Rights Yet to Materialize." http://www.isisinternational.org/index.php?option=com_content&view=article&id=926:saudi-arabia-womens-civil-rights-yet-to-materialise&catid=22:movements-within&Itemid=229 (accessed July 2010).

Keddie, Nikki R. *Women in the Middle East: Past and Present.* Princeton, NJ: Princeton University Press, 2007.

Seelhoff, Cheryl, et al. "Saudi Arabia: Raped Woman Sentenced for Being With a Man." *Off Our Backs,* v.37/2/3 (2007).

Social Institutions and Gender Index. "Gender Equality and Social Institutions in Saudi Arabia." http://genderindex.org/country/saudi-arabia (accessed February 2010).

Elizabeth Rholetter Purdy
Independent Scholar

School Fee Abolition Initiative (Kenya)

Families' inability to pay school fees is one of the largest barriers to children's educational attainment in countries with high poverty rates, such as Kenya. The United Nations Children's Fund and the World Bank launched the School Fee Abolition Initiative (SFAI) in 2005 as one strategy toward achieving the United Nations Millennium Development Goal of universal primary education by 2015, as well as the United Nations Education for All goals. Millions of primary school-age children cannot afford to attend school. The abolishment of school fees is key to ensuring that no child is denied a quality basic education on the basis of their family's inability to pay. Kenya was one of the first countries to abolish school fees under SFAI, along with Ethiopia, Ghana, Malawi, Mozambique, and Tanzania. Kenya has served as a sustainable model for other countries preparing to initiate similar programs.

A Political Attempt at Solving the Problem

Mwai Kibaki was elected Kenyan President in 2002 with a platform that included the abolition of school fees. Most of the children who were previously denied educational access in Kenya as a result of the inability to pay school fees were from poor rural families. Other disproportionately affected groups included girls, orphans, child laborers, and the disabled, who are generally marginalized and tend to suffer more from poverty's negative effects. Some parents could not afford to send any of their children to school, whereas others could only send some of their children or had to pull them out of school before they completed their primary education. Kibaki abolished school fees before the start of the 2003 school year, resulting in immediate chaos but long-term successes.

The Kenyan government placed management of education resources in the hands of the schools themselves, which used government funds to establish their own bank accounts. Shortly after Kenya abolished school fees, the country's 18,000 public schools saw an enrollment increase of approximately 1.3 million students. Public schools became overwhelmed with large class sizes, unprepared teachers, and a lack of basic supplies and sanitation needs. Private school enrollments also began to surge as many parents transferred their children from public schools. Kenya's results showed that although the abolition of school fees dramatically increased educational access, it did not address all barriers to educational attainment, and more planning is needed for the process to run smoothly. SFAI and its partner nongovernmental organizations (NGOs), constituencies, and research institutions studied Kenya's experience in school fee abolition and its aftermath to create a sustainable model for the development of inclusive and sustainable education systems.

Problems that remained included poor-quality education, overcrowded classrooms, lowered financial resources as fee revenues were lost, continued discrimination, health epidemics such as human immunodeficiency virus and acquired immune deficiency syndrome (HIV/AIDS), and war and violence. The Kenyan government and international NGOs provided schools with millions of dollars in emergency grants to lower class sizes, purchase needed supplies, and train teachers in child- and gender-friendly methods of instruction. Kenya's successes have included a 28 percent increase in school-enrollment rates since 2002, lowered rates of repetition, and higher percentages of students completing their primary educations.

Sharing Information for Furthering Success

As a pioneer in the SFAI, Kenya has shared information on its successes and failures to aid other countries in shaping their own programs to meet the challenges that come with abolishing school fees. Kenya's experience provided invaluable information that the SFAI program used to guide technical and financial assistance provided to other countries. Kenya shared its experiences at a 2006 SFAI workshop in Nairobi titled "School Fee Abolition: Building on What We Know and Defining Sustained Support." In 2009, the United Nations Children's Fund and the World Bank, in cooperation with other NGOs, established a guide for the implementation of school fee abolishment.

See Also: Attainment, Elementary School Completion; Educational Opportunities/Access; Global Campaign for Education; Kenya.

Further Readings

Chinyama, Victor. "Kenya's Abolition of School Fees Offers Lessons for Rest of Africa." http://www.unicef.org /infobycountry/kenya_33391.html (accessed July 2010).

International Bank for Reconstruction and Development. *Abolishing School Fees in Africa: Lessons From Ethiopia, Ghana, Kenya, Malawi, and Mozambique.* Washington, DC: International Bank for Reconstruction and Development/World Bank/United Nations Children's Fund, 2009.

Sobaniam N. W. *Culture and Customs of Kenya.* Westport, CT: Greenwood Press, 2003.

Marcella Bush Trevino
Barry University

Schori, Katharine Jefferts

Katharine Jefferts Schori is the head of the Episcopal Church in the United States (ECUSA). At her 2006 installation as presiding bishop, she became the first woman to lead any branch of the worldwide Anglican Communion and the first woman in the United States to lead a major Protestant denomination. Her short term of service in the church prior to her election, her gender, and her support of the ordination of gay clergy and same-sex marriage increased fears of a rift both within the ECUSA and between that body and the 77 million worldwide Anglican Communion. Schori has not wavered in her progressive allegiances, even in the face of conservative groups such as the diocese of Pittsburg leaving the ECUSA.

Born Katharine Jefferts in Pensacola, Florida, on March 26, 1954, Schori was the first of four children. The Jefferts were Catholic, and Katharine attended parochial school until she was in the fifth grade, when the family moved to New Jersey, where they converted to Episcopalian and enrolled their children in public schools. Schori's father was a Navy pilot and a physicist, her mother a microbiologist and virologist, and Schori decided from an early age that she would be a scientist. She received a B.S. from Stanford University, where she majored in biology, and in 1974, she entered Oregon State University in Corvallis, where she received a master's degree (1977) and a Ph.D. (1983), both in oceanography. By the time she completed graduate work, she was married to Richard Miles Schori, a mathematician, and the mother of one daughter. She worked for the National Marine Fisheries Service, but she began considering the priesthood in the mid-80s. It was not until 1991 that she entered the Church Divinity School of the Pacific, in Berkeley, California. Three years later, at age 40, she completed a Master of Divinity degree and was ordained as both a deacon and a priest in the Episcopal Church.

Schori served as assistant rector at her church, the Episcopal Church of the Good Samaritan in Corvallis, Oregon, where her fluency in Spanish aided her pastoral work with congregants who were native speakers of Spanish. In 2001, she was elected bishop of the diocese of Nevada, the ninth woman to serve as bishop in the ECUSA. She used her skills as a licensed pilot to travel within Nevada, working to establish close ties to minority church members. In 2003, she supported the controversial consecration of the openly gay V. Gene Robinson as bishop of New Hampshire. At the 2006 General Convention of the ECUSA, Schori was the lone female among the seven candidates for the next presiding bishop. On November 4, 2006, she became the 26th person and first woman to head the ECUSA. At the Lambeth Conference in July 2008, a gathering of the worldwide Anglican Communion from which many had demanded Schori be excluded, she compared the battle over women bishops and homosexual clergy to birth pangs and insisted that the changed Episcopal body will prevail over the threat of schism.

See Also: Anglican Communion; Ministry, Protestant; Priesthood, Episcopalian/Anglican; Religion, Women in.

Further Readings

Episcopal Church. "Our Presiding Bishop." http://ecusa .anglican.org/78694_ENG_HTM.htm (accessed March 2010).

Moyers, Bill. "Bishop Katharine Jefferts Schori." http:// www.pbs.org/moyers/journal/06082007/profile3.html (accessed March 2010).

Schori, Katharine Jefferts. *Gospel in the Global Village: Seeking God's Dream of Shalom.* Harrisburg, PA: Morehouse Publishing, 2009.

Wylene Rholetter
Auburn University

Science, Women in

The relationship between women and science is a complex one. For a very long time, women were excluded from scientific institutions. However, historians such as Margaret Rossiter tell us that since antiquity, many women have engaged in scientific enquiry. Well-known examples include Hypatia of Alexandria, an astronomer and mathematician who lived in the fourth century, or Hildegard von Bingen, who contributed to the development of medical sciences and cosmology in the 12th century.

Historical Female Exclusion

The emergence of modern science in the 16th and 17th centuries was based on the exclusion of women. Apart from a minority of upper-class women who were tutored, it was not before the 20th century that women were allowed to access advanced levels of education or to enter scientific institutions. In the 20th century, in the Western world, women started accessing higher education on a wider scale. However, as recalled in the work of Londa Schiebinger, this was not a steady process. In the United States, after women gained access to graduate schools at the beginning of the 20th century, their numbers in postgraduate programs increased quickly before decreasing between the 1930s and 1960s, only regaining their 1920s level in the 1970s. However, although women were allowed into institutions of higher education, social opprobrium continued to restrict their freedom to engage in scientific inquiry and in the production of knowledge. They were, for a very long time, excluded from the science academies where men gathered. For example, although the Royal Academy in London was founded in 1662, it was only in 1945 that a woman first joined the institution. Similarly, although the Académie des Sciences in Paris was founded in 1966, it was only in 1979 that a woman became its first elected member. Even Marie Curie, who won two Nobel Prizes—one in physics, the other in chemistry—had her application to the Paris Academy rejected.

In the 1970s and 1980s, partly under the influence of the women's liberation movement, concerns were raised about the experience of girls in schools. Although in most of the Western world curricula were becoming less gender differentiated and the proportion of women entering higher education and the labor market was increasing, subject choices remained strongly gendered, with girls much less likely than boys to enroll in science courses (except for biology) and, subsequently, to enter science as a field of employment.

This concern remains these days, although in some parts of the world it has been overshadowed by concerns about the lower performance of boys in literacy in schools (sometimes known as the "boys' underachievement debate"). The situation of women in science is on the agenda of many governments and international organizations, including the United Nations Educational, Scientific and Cultural Organization and the European Commission. The rationale for promoting women in science chiefly relates to social justice concerns (i.e., that boys and girls should be given equal opportunities) and to economic matters (i.e., that the waste of women's talents represents a barrier to competitiveness in the global economy). Such concerns have led to various initiatives, including the collection of gendered data on the participation of women in science, the creation of awards for women scientists, the development of mentoring programs and networking opportunities for women scientists, the funding of research about gender and science, and the establishment of committees of experts, such as the Helsinki Group on Women and Science or the United Kingdom Resource Centre for Women in Science, Engineering and Technology.

Women in Science: Current Patterns

The metaphor of a leaky pipeline is often resorted to when describing the situation of women in science today. This illustrates the fact that at all stages of science education, women drop out at a higher rate than men. In most countries, this happens as soon as the study of science ceases being compulsory—the proportion of girls among those studying science decreases dramatically with age, as girls tend to disproportionately drop the subject in post-16-years' education. After they enter higher education, the proportion of women studying science declines further, including at the postgraduate and doctoral levels.

The 2006 report published by the European Commission reveals important variations across countries in terms of the proportion of women among science postgraduates. In 2003, women represented 36 percent of science, mathematics, and computing Ph.D. graduates in the United States and 40 percent in the European Union. However, this proportion was much lower in Japan (20 percent) and much higher in a number of countries where women represented the majority of Ph.D. graduates in the field (e.g., in Bulgaria, Ireland, Italy, Latvia, Portugal, Romania, and Slovakia). There are also important differences across science subjects. Overall, women's levels of participation tend to be lower in computer science and physics and higher in life sciences. For example, in the United States, the proportion of women among Ph.D. graduates is 21 percent in computer science, 28 percent in physical science, and 46 percent in life science. Similarly, in the European Union, women represent, respectively, 19 percent and 33 percent of Ph.D. graduates in computer science and physical science, but 54 percent of Ph.D. graduates in life science. The same patterns can be observed among women employed as scientists.

In most countries, the proportion of women among employed scientists tends to be lower compared with their proportion among science students. In 2003, in the European Union, women represented only 29 percent of employed scientists and engineers, although this figure is slowly improving. As for the proportion of women among science students, there

are important cross-national variations. For example, the proportion of women among researchers is only 12 percent in Japan but 53 percent in Latvia. In general, proportions of women among scientists tend to be higher in eastern Europe compared with western Europe (except for the Czech Republic). However, in these countries, the higher proportion of women scientists is usually associated with fewer opportunities for women to progress up the career ladder (except for Romania) and a crucial lack of resources for research.

As in most professions, the levels of participation of women scientists also tend to decrease as they progress through the ranks. This is sometimes described as a glass ceiling. In the European Union, in 2003, women represented only 9 percent of full professors in science and engineering compared with representing 40 percent of Ph.D. graduates in this field. Similar patterns can be observed in most of the Western world. Women in science also tend to have lower levels of responsibilities. For example, within research funded by the European Commission, women represent only a minority of scientific coordinators of research consortium.

Barriers and Business

Although most studies of women in science concentrate on higher-education institutions, 2003 data show that it is in the private (business enterprise) sector that women's participation is the lowest. For example, in the European Union, women represent 35 percent of scientists working in the higher-education sector but only 18 percent of scientists in industry. Further, women working in industrial research tend to be concentrated in marketing and communication rather than in areas perceived as core, strategic ones, such as research and development.

Some studies have also considered whether women scientists may face particular barriers in securing research funding. A study by Wennerås and Wold, published in 1997, determined that women had to be 2.2 times more productive than men to secure financial support. The study was recently replicated, but this time no gender bias was identified, possibly as a result of the policies implemented in the aftermath of the publication of Wennerås and Wold's findings. Besides, most studies find that success rates for men and women are equivalent once rank is controlled for. However, a number of studies in both the United States and the European Union have determined that men's and women's behavior differs when it comes to applying for funding. They show that women tend to seek and secure funding for smaller research projects and submit fewer applications.

More generally, markers of esteem tend to be disproportionately allocated to male scientists. Since its creation in 1901, only two physics Nobel Prizes, four chemistry Nobel Prizes, and 10 medicine or physiology Nobel Prizes have been awarded to women. Scientists such as Rosalind Franklin and Jocelyn Bell are often referred to when illustrating the lack of acknowledgement of the work of women scientists. Rosalind Franklin's work on the structure of DNA is thought to have been insufficiently credited. After her death, the 1962 Nobel Prize in Medicine or Physiology was awarded to Francis Crick, James Watson, and Maurice Wilkins, who had drawn on her work. Similarly, Jocelyn Bell had discovered the first radio pulsars when she was a postgraduate student. The 1974 Physics Nobel Prize, however, famously went to her supervisor. Women are also less likely to be elected to or co-opted onto management and strategy-making bodies, research committees, and evaluation panels. In particular, available evidence shows that scientific boards are overwhelmingly composed of men. There are, however, considerable cross-national variations in this area, with only 7 percent of women on scientific boards in Cyprus and Poland but 48 percent in Norway and 47 percent in Sweden and Finland.

Theoretical Perspectives

In the past, common explanations for women's low levels of participation in science have drawn on biological essentialist theories. Such explanations go back to Aristotle yet still permeate discourses of women in science; for example, through discourses of brain lateralization. A social essentialist version of these theories tends to explain women's low levels of participation in science by their specific ("feminine") abilities supposedly inherited from gendered role socialization. As with biological essentialism, social essentialism draws on a deficit model, with women lacking the qualities required to become a scientist. In these accounts, women's aptitudes and skills, whether thought of as ingrained in women's biology or in their social experiences, have sometimes been constructed as inadequate for the conduct of scientific investigation, as women are sometimes seen as lacking rationality and objectivity.

In the recent period, there has been a shift toward more complex organizational approaches to women in science. Rather than focusing on women as the "problem," studies have focused on the construction of science as masculine. One strand of this work explores the association between masculinity and doing science in the context of schools and its influence on students' subject choices. Another strand focuses on the association between masculinity and doing science in the context of science organizations and its influence on women scientists.

Studies about the study of science in schools have shown that when asked to draw a scientist, a majority of children from both sexes tend to draw a man (although boys are more likely to do so than girls). As evidenced by the work of Jocelyn Steinke and colleagues, the pattern applies to small children as well as to undergraduates, including science undergraduates. A number of studies have shown that the construction of science as masculine (and of scientists as "mad," "geeky" men) is influenced and reinforced by peers, parents, and stereotypical career advice. In particular, most recent research, such as those conducted by Elizabeth Whitelegg and colleagues, has shown that representations of scientists in popular culture often adhere to a masculine construction of science and scientists, sending the message that science is not an appropriate pursuit for girls and women. As a result of this, girls who study science and women scientists may face tensions between the pursuit of their scientific interest and their gender identity.

Other works have taken a more organizational approach to the study of women in science and focused on the occupations of women in science. Scholars argue that science organizational cultures are biased toward men. Although science work may not be thought of as a vocation, it usually requires long working hours. It also requires spending significant periods of time away from home to attend conferences, conduct observations, or develop collaborations. Writing publications also can be a very lengthy process, yet publishing is a major aspect of science work and a key criterion for career development. Because women are often the main persons responsible for childcare in heterosexual partner-

Jackie Grebmeier, a National Science Foundation–funded researcher at the University of Tennessee, prepares sediment samples taken from arctic waters as part of the Western Shelf-Basin Interactions research project.

ships, they may face particular difficulties in combining the demands of science work with a family. Career breaks in particular may be problematic, as there is a need to keep up to date with science developments, and opportunities for part-time work may be limited and hinder career development, as they clash with the culture of working long hours.

In addition, laboratory work and team work in particular fields of science limit opportunities for working at home and occasionally require coming in the laboratory at weekends. It is also notoriously difficult to gain permanent employment as a scientist. It is not unusual for a scientist to take several postdoctoral positions, often in different countries. As a result, scientists often do not get a permanent position before being well in their 30s—that is, in the usual childbearing years. For women who are in a partnership with

another scientist, finding two jobs in the same institution or region may represent an added complication, with men's careers more often taking priority. Finally, it has been argued that women as a minority in a male-dominated workplace may experience isolation and a lack of career guidance and access to support and network, as well as have difficulties in envisioning a future for themselves.

Women have been excluded from science institutions for a very long time and remain to this day marginalized. They are underrepresented among students of science and even more so among scientists, especially in the higher ranks of the profession. However, this picture also hides important differences across subjects and countries, which suggests that women's marginalization, in science as elsewhere, is not inevitable.

See Also: Astronomy, Women in; Biology, Women in; Chemistry, Women in; Mathematics, Women in; Physics, Women in.

Further Readings

European Commission. "She Figures 2006: Women and Science. Statistics and Indicators." Brussels, Belgium: European Commission, 2006.

National Academy of Sciences. *Beyond Bias and Barriers: Fulfilling the Potential of Women in Academic Science and Engineering.* Washington, DC: National Academies, 2006.

Rossiter, M. *Women Scientists in America: Struggles and Strategies to 1940.* Baltimore, MD: Johns Hopkins University Press, 1982.

Schiebinger, L. "Women in Science: Historical Perspectives." In C. M. Urry, et al., "Women at Work: A Meeting on the Status of Women in Astronomy." Meeting held at the Space Telescope Science Institute, Baltimore, MD, September 8–9, 1992. http://www.stsci.edu/institute/conference/wia (accessed July 2010).

Steinke, J., et al. "Assessing Media Influences on Middle School-Ages Children's Perceptions of Women in Science Using the Draw-A-Scientist Test (DAST)." *Science Communication*, v.29/1 (2007).

Wennerås C. and A. Wold. "Nepotism and Sexism in Peer Review." *Nature*, v.347 (1997).

Whitelegg, E., et al. *(In)visible Witnesses: Investigating Gendered Representations of Scientists, Technologists, Engineers and Mathematicians on UK Children's Television.* Bradford, UK: UK Resource Centre for Women in Science, Engineering and Technology, 2008.

Marie-Pierre Moreau
University of Bedfordshire

Science Education for Girls

For over a century, the nexus of gender issues and educational policy and practice have taken on a cyclical nature—most recently in the early1990s when the American Association of University Women (AAUW) outlined the ways U.S. schools "shortchanged" girls, especially in math and science, and the ways curriculum and teacher-student interactions encouraged the silencing of females. Thereafter, in the late 1990s, the focus switched to boys who, it was argued, were not receiving an equitable education due to the feminization of the teaching profession; the perceived inability of female teachers to understand, reach, and teach boys; and the overemphasis on meeting the needs of female students.

Persistent Achievement Gap

Despite the fact that many people think concerns about girls' development in math and science is a thing of the past, recent research reiterates prior barriers, albeit subtle, that still exist in today's schools. Many researchers admit that blatant barriers women and girls experienced in the 1960s and 1970s have diminished significantly, but girls and women still lag behind men in participation in science, technological, engineering, and mathematical (STEM) fields. Some explain the gender gap by pointing out cognitive differences between men and women. While cause-effect relationships are difficult to ascertain, some contend that girls still face an unintended culture in elementary and secondary classrooms that indicates they do not belong in math, science, or technological fields. Other researchers point to the cumulative effect of numerous long-term societal influences that socialize females to appropriate gender roles that do not include interest, achievement, and future careers in STEM.

Gender Stereotyping Versus Role Models and Mentoring

Stereotyping also continues in secondary schools' occupational training programs. For example, boys enroll in advanced computer science and design coursework while girls are more likely to register in word processing and bookkeeping courses. Also, many girls refrain from taking science coursework, because they are discouraged from doing so by parents and/or school counselors. Moreover, many girls have experienced courses that are taught in a dry, abstract style with a chilly classroom climate. Comparative studies on the effects of the approachability of faculty, peer attitudes, and teacher quality on achievement in science may provide additional insights toward understanding why the science achievement of girls and minorities seems especially sensitive to these variables.

Studies have found that girls in secondary schools who are encouraged by parents, teachers, or friends to learn more about science and computers, face course requirements that oblige them to take computer science and have friends who are taking upper-level STEM coursework are more likely to enroll in science and computer science courses. Guidance counselors play a major role in encouraging or inhibiting girls' participation in advanced science and technology: Providing female students with role models and career information that enables them to envision themselves as professionals in a science discipline is just one technique that shows promise toward increasing girls' participation and achievement in science.

Curriculum and Pedagogy

Feminist researchers have analyzed classical science teaching because it emphasized male-centric concepts such as domination, atomism, hierarchy, order, and detachment. In addition, classic science teaching emphasized the positivist pursuit of ultimate truth through testing and proving hypotheses resulting in decontextualized scientific knowledge. Instead, many feminists forwarded the notion of teaching science in a more gynocentric manner. In other words, it is believed that schools should approach the teaching and learning of science in a more holistic, contextualized way that views the researcher and researched in terms of interaction and mutual respect.

Instead of viewing proper science teaching and learning in either-or terms, Lesley H. Parker (1997) suggests looking at the former dualisms of science as complementary rather than oppositional concepts. The conviction is that merging perspectives that were formerly considered "male" or "female" will open the field to diversity of thought and attract the interest in and achievement of science by a greater variety of the student population.

For example, rather than disputing or proving then choosing between a male-centric science that is atomistic and a gynocentric science that is holistic, one might approach teaching and learning science holistically as well as atomistically. Likewise, instead of viewing male-centric science in terms of "domination" and gynocentric science as "mutual respect and interaction," teachers could lead students to view science according to both perspectives. In addition, the science discipline could be conveyed as consisting of order as well as law; nonhierarchical continuums of difference as well as dichotomies and polarizations; involvement as well as detachment; understanding as

well as predicting; and knowledge contextualized in history and contemporary society as well as nonhistorical and decontextualized scientific knowledge.

Science Achievement Internationally

According to TIMSS 2007 International Science Report, at the fourth grade, Singapore was the top performing country, followed by Chinese Taipei, Hong Kong SAR, Japan, the Russian Federation, Latvia, England, the United States, Hungary, Italy, and Kazakhstan, which also performed very well. Science achievement varies greatly among the U.S. states. For example, Massachusetts, followed by Minnesota, was outperformed only by Singapore. The Canadian provinces of Alberta, British Columbia, and Ontario also performed very well.

In eighth-grade science in 2007, Singapore and Chinese Taipei had the highest average achievement, followed by Japan and Korea. England, Hungary, the Czech Republic, Slovenia, Hong Kong SAR, and the Russian Federation also performed well. Among the U.S. states, Massachusetts' results were similar to that of the four top Asian countries (Singapore, Chinese Taipei, Japan, and Korea) while Minnesota had achievement similar to England, Hungary, the Czech Republic, Slovenia, Hong Kong SAR, and the Russian Federation.

Average science achievement for girls was higher than for boys on average across 37 countries at both the fourth and eighth grades. The difference in achievement between boys and girls at the fourth-grade level averaged a three-point difference. Girls had higher science achievement than boys in six countries, and boys had higher achievement than girls in eight countries, while the difference in average achievement was reported as insignificant in more than half the countries. At the eighth grade, girls had higher average science achievement than boys in 14 countries, and boys had higher achievement than girls in 11 countries, amounting to an average six-point difference between the sexes.

Internationally, research has shown higher science achievement for both boys and girls is associated with several factors, including (1) higher levels of parental education; (2) free access to computers and Internet in the home; (3) positive student attitudes toward science and higher levels of confidence; (4) attending a school where there are robust resources and fewer students who are economically disadvantaged; (5) a majority of teachers report more positive working conditions; and (6) over 90 percent of students speak the language of the test at home.

See Also: Computer Science, Women in; Engineering, Women in; Mathematics, Women in; Science, Women in; Single-Sex Education; STEM Coalition.

Further Readings

Clegg, A., ed. *Girls and Science.* Geneva: United Nations Educational, Scientific and Cultural Organization (UNESCO), Section for Science and Technology Education, Division of Secondary, Technical and Vocational Education, 2006. http://www.unesco.org/en/gender-and-education (accessed June 2010).

Hanson, S. *Swimming Against the Tide: African American Girls and Science Education.* Philadelphia, PA: Temple University Press, 2008.

The Jossey-Bass Reader on Gender in Education. San Francisco, CA: Jossey-Bass, 2002.

Margolis, J. and A. Fisher. *Unlocking the Clubhouse: Women in Computing.* Cambridge, MA: MIT Press, 2001.

Martin, M. O., et al. "TIMSS 2007 International Science Report: Findings From IEA's Trends in International Mathematics and Science Study at the Fourth and Eighth Grades." Chestnut Hill, MA: TIMSS & PIRLS International Study Center, Boston College, 2008.

Parker, L. H. "A Model for Gender-Inclusive School Science: Lessons From Feminist Scholarship." In Catherine Marshall, ed., *Feminist Critical Policy Analysis: A Perspective From Primary and Secondary Schooling.* Washington, DC: Falmer Press, 1997.

Katherine Cumings Mansfield
University of Texas

Secularity Law, France

Popularly dubbed *l'affaire du foulard*, this debate highlights the gray areas that often arise when cultural and religious practices cross national borders. The French headscarf debate tests the limits of national tolerance for "difference" by raising salient questions about how nation-states should manage the transnational flow of cultural and religious practices. In particular, it reg-isters the cultural and political discord—and mainstream resistance—triggered by the "integration" of minority populations within the national body politic. It also highlights the female body as a particularly contested site of national belonging and state regulation.

Separation of Church and State

The headscarf debate has its origins in the French republican ideal of secularity, or *laicite*, which mandates the strict separation of church and state. This ideal was first tested at the national level in 1989, when three Muslim girls were suspended from a public middle school for refusing to remove their headscarves, and culminated in 2004 with the adoption of a law on secularity that bans the wearing of "conspicuous" signs of religious affiliation in public schools. Although the law prohibits Jewish yarmulkes, Sikh turbans, and large crosses in addition to the Muslim headscarf, it

By transforming the headscarf into a symbol of difference, the headscarf ban has enlarged a cultural and political divide.

disproportionately targets girls who wear the *hijab*. The law distinguishes between "conspicuous" and "discreet" religious symbols, including small crosses, stars of David, or small Qur'ans. French Muslim girls have devised several tactics to circumvent the ban, including shaving their heads and wearing bandanas instead of headscarves. Similar bans are under consideration or in effect in Belgium, Canada, Denmark, Kyrgyzstan, Turkey, and the United Kingdom.

By transforming the headscarf into a symbol of radical or inassimilable difference, the headscarf ban has enlarged the cultural and political divide between the mainstream French state and its increasingly visible Islamic immigrant population. The ban reflects an understanding of certain religious practices as incompatible with the ideals of French republicanism and modernity. It also incorporates prevalent Western understandings of the headscarf or, more broadly, the veil as a monolithic symbol of patriarchal oppression, cultural tradition, and Islamic fundamentalism.

The incendiary potential of the French law on secularity with respect to France's "Islamic problem" is evident in a June 2008 legal case. Faiza Silmi, a Muslim immigrant whose husband and children are French citizens, appealed an earlier ruling to obtain French citizenship. France's highest administrative court denied her appeal on the grounds that her "radical" practice of Islam (particularly her wearing of the *niqab*, or full-body veil) was incompatible with the democratic values of the French community. Silmi was denied French citizenship on the basis of "insufficient assimilation."

This case marks the first time that the French judiciary has evaluated an immigrant's capacity for assimilation based on private religious practices such as veiling. It highlights the delicate balance between the civic ideal of republican secularity and the individual right to freedom of religion guaranteed by the French Constitution. The ruling in Silmi's case received almost universal support in France across the political spectrum and within the Muslim community. Yet critics fear that it will set a dangerous precedent, allowing for increasingly arbitrary interpretations of what constitutes "radical Islam." The full political effect of the Silmi ruling remains to be seen. In July 2009, the French Parliament established a committee to determine whether the wearing of headwear such as the *burqa* and *niqab* is compat-

ible with France's republican tradition of equality between the sexes. Soon after, Fadela Amara, French minister of urban affairs, called for a ban on the *burqa* in France to combat the spread of radical Islam.

Assimilation Issues

Opponents of France's headscarf ban suggest that it fails to address the real problems faced by immigrants, including discrimination, harassment, and isolation. Perhaps the best evidence of these claims was the wave of riots among the suburban Muslim population in Paris in 2005. Critics regard the headscarf ban as a human rights violation and as a sign of increased intolerance for ethnic and religious difference since the early 1990s. The headscarf ban coincides with the rise of xenophobic sentiments and conservative immigration policy in Europe. Although many critics perceive the headscarf ban as the result of increasing Islamophobia post 9/11, such sentiment predates the contemporary war on terrorism. It represents part of the legacy of French colonialism and, especially, the Algerian revolution. It also reveals the contentious status of women as symbols of national identity. French law on secularity promises to impact the evolving face of the French republic for years to come, as it welcomes a growing number of members—and critics—into its fold.

See Also: Algeria; Islamic Feminism; France; Religious Fundamentalism, Cross-Cultural Context of; Veil.

Further Readings

Bennhold, Katrin. "A Veil Closes France's Door to Citizenship." *New York Times* (July 19, 2008).

Eshet, Dan. "What Do We Do With a Difference?: France and the Debate over Headscarves in Schools." http://www.facinghistory.com (accessed October 2009).

Islam, Shada. "Headscarf Ban Misses the Point." *Yale Global Online Magazine.* http://yaleglobal.yale.edu/print/1443 (accessed November 2009).

Khosrokhavar, Farhad. "Ce Que la Loi sur le Burqa Nous Voile." *Le Monde.* http://www.lemonde.fr (accessed August 2009).

Meyer, L. and G. Reddy, eds. "The French Headscarf Controversy: Secularism and Transnationalism." *Feminist Studies*, v.32/2 (Summer 2006).

Scott, Joan Wallach. *The Politics of the Veil.* Princeton, NJ: Princeton University Press, 2007.

Winter, Bronwyn. *Hijab & the Republic: Uncovering the French Headscarf Debate.* Syracuse, NY: Syracuse University Press, 2008.

Karina Eileraas
University of California, Los Angeles

"Security Moms"

Security mom is a term used to describe a voter group that was originally thought to be a demographic critical to the reelection of President George W. Bush in November 2004. This term is often traced back to a February 10, 2003, article in *Time* magazine in which journalist Joe Klein highlights an observation made by then-Senator Joe Biden: "When I was out campaigning last fall, this was all women wanted to talk about. Not schools, not prescription drugs. It was 'What are you doing to protect my kids against terrorists?' Soccer moms are security moms now."

Reminiscent of the soccer moms of the early 1990s, security moms could be described as a group of women voters who were concerned about their family's safety in the post–September 11 world. This group was rarely explicitly defined in media coverage, although they were typically described as married, female swing voters who had children and were sometimes characterized as white, suburban, and Republican. The conventional wisdom during the campaign was that these women saw George W. Bush as the best candidate to address their concerns, yet there was significant skepticism raised within the media that questioned the legitimacy of this argument.

Academic scholars have since concluded that this voter bloc did not actually exist. Women with children do not have different issue priorities than women without children. Moreover, women with children were no more likely to vote for Bush in 2004 than they were in 2000. Married women voters were not chiefly concerned with terrorism, as had been suggested during the campaign. In sum, the academic literature examining this voter group does not offer any support to the existence of the security moms voter group.

The discussion of a voter group that does not exist may have significant implications for the voting populace. Susan Carroll posits that the extensive talk of security moms during the 2004 presidential campaign actually deflected attention away from women's issues. More broadly, media coverage of voter groups that do not actually exist may impact the issues on which campaigns choose to focus. This could in turn lead campaigns to address issues that are incongruent with those of most concern to the general public.

See Also: Clinton, Hillary Rodham; Journalists, Broadcast Media; Journalists, Print Media; National Organization for Women (NOW); Palin, Sarah; Representation of Women in Government, United States; Soccer Moms; Stereotypes of Women.

Further Readings

Carroll, Susan J. "Security Moms and Presidential Politics." In Lois Duke Whitaker, ed.,*Voting the Gender Gap.* Chicago: University of Illinois Press, 2008.

Elder, Laurel and Steven Greene. "The Myth of 'Security Moms' and 'NASCAR Dads': Parenthood, Political Stereotypes, and the 2004 Election." *Social Science Quarterly*, v.88/1 (2007).

Klein, Joe. "How Soccer Moms Became Security Moms." *Time.* http://www.time.com/time/columnist/klein/article/0,9565,421149,00.html (accessed January 2010).

Morin, Richard and Dan Balz. "'Security Mom' Bloc Proves Hard to Find." *The Washington Post.* http://www.washingtonpost.com/wp-dyn/articles/A63197-2004Sep30.html (accessed January 2010).

VandeHei, Jim. 2006. "Republicans Losing The "Security Moms."" *The Washington Post.* http://www.washingtonpost.com/wpdyn/content/article/2006/ 08/17/AR2006081701484.html (accessed January 2010).

Angela L. Bos
Abbey Smanik
College of Wooster

Self-Defense, Armed

Self-defense serves as a legal justification in which the action taken was the "right" or "good" thing to do, given the circumstances of the situation. To advance a claim of self-defense, the danger to the individual must be imminent, and the force used must be both necessary and proportional. The individual must reasonably believe that the amount of force used is necessary, without being excessive, to prevent great bodily harm or death. The instrument used in armed self-defense can take a lethal form, such as a gun or knife, or nonlethal form, such as pepper spray or handheld stun gun. However, these two categories are not exclusive. Self-defense can also be unarmed, in which an individual learns an array of techniques, specifically martial arts, to distract his or her attacker long enough to be able to escape. The social, cultural, religious, and political context of a country can influence the use and form of self-defense by women.

Some countries, such as Cameroon and Uganda, have a religious and social context that restricts women's rights and movement. In these types of traditional patriarchal countries, women's inferior status is to some degree accepted, both among women and men. Women in traditional countries may not have the opportunity to engage in self-defense, given the acceptance of violence against women. Furthermore, women in these countries may be killed or exiled by their own families for engaging in self-defense against an abusive partner.

In contrast, women in the United States are afforded greater independence and autonomy, as well as many of the same opportunities and rights as men. Moreover, the United States has a high prevalence of firearm ownership, as well as a culture that approves of firearms. In certain states, citizens can apply to carry a concealed weapon, with some states allowing citizens to carry multiple concealed weapons. The right to carry a concealed firearm is not cross-national.

Thus, women in the United States will have a greater opportunity to engage in self-defense as well as use a lethal instrument than women from a traditional country. It should be noted that firearm ownership is not a phenomenon unique to only developed countries and that women in a number of developed countries do not readily support the use of firearms for self-defense. Clearly, the context of the country a woman lives in, not just the state of the country's development, shapes the availability and use of armed self-defense.

Victims and Imminent Harm

Women are more likely to be victimized by someone they know, such as an intimate partner or acquaintance. Therefore, the majority of females who use self-defense do so against a nonstranger. In spite of these findings, the self-defense justification in the criminal justice system does not resemble the experience of most women. To be acquitted on the basis of self-defense, the jury must find that a reasonable person would have believed there was imminent harm.

However, a woman's perception of "imminent harm" can differ from a man's perception, especially if the woman has been subjected to years of physical and/or psychological abuse. The legal system has allowed for evidence to be presented in cases of women's self-defense that would allow for an explanation of women's behavior when she responds violently in self-defense against an abusive partner—a legal defense better known as the Battered Women's Defense.

There have been numerous critiques of the utility of the Battered Women's Defense. Shana Wallace, as part of her attempt to transform the Battered Women's Defense into something resembling international law on self-defense, advanced the claim that the legal system must move beyond the temporal order of imminent harm in self-defense claims by battered women. In other words, instead of determining whether there was a confrontation before the use of self-defense, the legal system should consider the probability of an attack, the lack of alternatives available, and the magnitude of threatened harm.

It is important to take into consideration that women can also engage in self-defense against strangers. These types of scenarios can include stranger sexual assault as well as the castle doctrine. The castle doctrine, applicable in a certain number of states as well as Israel, Ireland, and Italy, allows an individual to use lethal force against an intruder who enters their home. Depending on where a woman lives, a woman can engage in justifiable armed self-defense against an intruder. Lethal armed self-defense is not the only option—women also can use a number of nonlethal forms of self-defense against an attacker. Even though the instruments are called nonlethal, it is possible for these instruments to cause death or serious injury. For example, a knife wound can lead to death or could be used to make a surface wound to ward off an attacker. This is just one example that highlights the complexity of understanding the form women's armed self-defense takes.

Social and Cultural Contexts

Again, the use of nonlethal forms of self-defense will be influenced by the social and cultural context of the country a woman lives in. In most states in the United States, it is legal for individuals older than 18 years to carry pepper spray. In Hong Kong, pepper spray is classified as "arms," making an individual subject to fines and imprisonment for carrying the spray if he or she does not have a license to carry it.

The law on the use of stun guns also differs cross-nationally. Certain states and cities in the United States do not allow citizens to own personal stun guns. Other developed nations, such as the United Kingdom and Canada, also restrict the ownership of personal stun guns. The country a woman lives in once again influences the available means of nonlethal armed self-defense. Armed self-defense also is not restricted to items created specifically for self-defense. Everyday objects, such as baseball bats and lamps, can be used in self-defense. An exhaustive list of items cannot be created, as most household items can be used by an individual as an improvised weapon.

Women's use of armed self-defense can take a variety of forms that are clearly influenced by where a woman lives, as well as her religious and cultural background. For instance, a Muslim woman may find it entirely unacceptable to carry a concealed firearm in a country that allows citizens to because of her religious and cultural upbringing. To obtain a rich and insightful understanding of the options available to women, one must consider the context as well as the individual's religious and personal beliefs.

Researchers and practitioners must acknowledge women's unique position in society when she advances a self-defense claim within the legal system. Women are uniquely situated in society and influenced by social, cultural, and religious contexts. One must also consider that the majority of women know their attacker before engaging in armed self-defense. These unique interactions present a dynamic view of women's use of force.

See Also: Domestic Violence; Gender Roles, Cross-Cultural; Self-Defense, Unarmed.

Further Readings

Hanna, C. "The Paradox of Progress: Translating Evan Stark's Coercive Control Into Legal Doctrine for Abused Women." *Violence Against Women*, v.15 (2009).

Stark, E. *Coercive Control: The Entrapment of Women in Personal Life.* New York: Oxford University Press, 2007.

Wallace, S. "Beyond Imminence: Evolving International Law and Battered Women's Right to Self-Defense." *University of Chicago Law Review*, v.71 (2004).

Brittany E. Hayes
City University of New York

Self-Defense, Unarmed

Unarmed self-defense involves protecting one's physical and psychological safety against assault, without the use of weapons or external devices. Assault can be verbal or physical (with sexual assault considered a type of physical assault). The same is true for self-defense; verbal self-defense techniques might include the use of clear directive language, de-escalation, lying, and getting others' attention and assistance. Physical self-defense techniques include using one's body to strike, kick, or hit another person, as well as a strong and confident body posture, hand gestures, and facial expressions.

Self-defense is one way that women can protect themselves against violence, and there is a critical need for protection, since violence against women is a global health problem. Increasingly, self defense is seen as a viable strategy for combating violence. Self defense training is offered or encouraged for women in multiple countries, including, but not limited to, Turkey, China, Israel, South Africa, Australia, and the United States. Recent news stories that have highlighted self defense training for specific populations, such as for older women in Kenya and female sex workers in India, underscore that bodily integrity should be a right of all women.

However, women, and women's resistance, are embedded in cultural contexts. Legal battles for women's rights to protect themselves from sexual violence are taking place worldwide, from Iran to the United States. The options women have—or do not have—available to them differ depending on where women are positioned physically, socially, and structurally. Resistance, then, is not just about individual choices, awareness, and motivations, but about the individual, cultural, and legal contexts in which women live.

Historically, strategies for preventing sexual violence have focused on avoidance, requiring women to curtail their own behavior in an attempt to avoid victimization. Women are advised to seek out male protection and to avoid "provocative" or revealing clothing, "unsafe" areas, and walking alone, especially at night. Some organizations (e.g., the U.S. National Rifle Association) suggest women carry firearms as means of self-protection. More typically, women are advised to carry whistles, horns, mace, or pepper spray as methods of thwarting an attacker or gaining outside assistance. These strategies are designed to reduce the risk of stranger assault, yet the data indicate that the greater risk for women is from an acquaintance or intimate partner; clearly, these strategies will do little in reducing that risk. However, feminists, women's health advocates, and others have suggested that these prevention efforts are misguided. Instead, they argue that the best, most effective means of preventing sexual violence is to target those who perpetrate it—namely, men. While women can, and do, perpetrate sexual violence, the data indicate that men are the most likely perpetrators. Focusing prevention efforts on perpetrators places the onus for stopping violence on those committing it, rather than relying on those who might be victimized to try and avoid it.

Regardless, neither avoidance nor primary prevention provides strategies for women when a sexual assault is imminent. The relative dearth of information about what women might do in the face of assault communicates that once an assault is attempted, there is little that women can do to stop it. In fact, women are more likely to be advised what not to do than what to do (e.g., don't fight back because he's bigger/stronger/might get angry/might hurt you).

Yet women do defend themselves in the face of imminent assault, and do so effectively. Reviews of the data on resistance over the last few decades indicate that unarmed self-defense—where women resist verbally and physically without a weapon—is an effective method of thwarting rape and sexual assault. In addition, the more forcefully women resisted, verbally or physically, the less likely the assault is to be completed.

Yet there is little recognition or acceptance that women can defend themselves safely and effectively. There are several reasons for this. First, our cultural constructions of sex and gender position men as larger, stronger, and more physically and sexually aggressive than women, who are positioned as smaller, weaker, and less aggressive; this is consistent with many wom-

Self-defense is one way women can protect themselves against the worldwide problem of violence against women.

en's and men's experience of themselves and their bodies in a gendered world. From this perspective, there is no reason to acknowledge or accept the data on women's effective self-defense, because of the belief that women could not possibly fight off a (presumably) larger, stronger, more aggressive male assailant.

Related to this perspective is the belief that fighting back will "make things worse," that self-defense increases women's risk of injury (beyond the sexual assault itself), in addition to having no chance of success. The data, however, suggest otherwise. Although some earlier studies reported women's risk of injury increased when they fought back, more recent work has concluded that there were no differences in injury rates between women who fought back and women who did not. This is not to say that women never experience additional physical injuries during a sexual assault but rather that the injuries women may sustain are not necessarily due to their resistance.

Others express ambivalence about self-defense—or at least, about promoting self-defense as a strategy for violence prevention. Some suggest that the use of (or training in) self-defense is problematic, in that women are using violence as a way to combat violence. Other feminists and antiviolence advocates voice concerns that promoting self-defense is tantamount to telling victims what they "should" have done differently, thereby blaming them for their own victimization.

In response, U.S. feminist self-defense advocates assert that first, defensive use of aggression is different from the perpetration of violence, and second, self-defense is a choice, not a "should." That self-defense can be an effective means of thwarting assault does not mean it is the best or only choice for anyone in any particular situation; self-defense advocates trust that women make the best choices for themselves in the face of violence. To do that, women should have all choices available to them, including self-defense.

While formal training is not required for effective self-defense—indeed, the number of women in North America with self-defense training is small compared to the number of women who have defended themselves—training offers significant benefits. Women who participate in self-defense training are more likely to believe they would be able to resist an assault than women without such training. In addition, self-defense training is linked to increases in assertiveness and self-esteem. Furthermore, self-defense training has been found to reduce trauma-related symptoms when used as a clinical intervention for trauma survivors. Although there is limited data comparing the efficacy of different self-defense programs, which can vary greatly, some programs are explicitly feminist, and they share some commonalities: head female instructors; accurate data about the effectiveness of women's resistance; education about gender socialization; and an understanding of the physical and emotional challenges that self-defense training poses.

Providing information about the efficacy of women's resistance is critical. When assault is imminent, knowing that self-defense is a viable and safe option makes it a choice worthy of consideration. To deny women that choice—whether by dismissing the data on its effectiveness, promoting myths about injury, suggesting it is a means of participating in rather than resisting violence, or focusing on "protecting" those who were raped or assaulted—is to limit women's options for maintaining their own physical and psychological safety.

See Also: Dating Violence; Rape, Incidence of; Reproductive and Sexual Health Rights; Self-Defense, Armed; Sexual Harassment; Stereotypes of Women.

Further Readings

Brecklin, Leslie R. "Evaluation of Outcomes of Self-Defense Training for Women: A Review." *Aggression and Violent Behavior,* v.13/1 (2008).

de Becker, G. *The Gift of Fear and Other Survival Signals that Protect Us From Violence.* New York: Dell Publishing, 1997.

Hollander, Jocelyn. "'I Can Take Care of Myself': The Impact of Self-Defense Training on Women's Lives." *Violence Against Women,* v.10 (2004).

Jill Cermele
Drew University

Self-Employed Women's Association of India

The Self-Employed Women's Association (SEWA) is a collective organization of women working in the informal urban and rural economy in India. Formed in 1972 in Ahmedabad, a prominent city in the state of Gujarat in western India, SEWA has extended itself across India through the formation of SEWA Bharat. SEWA has emphasized that what women require is not welfare but a strengthening of their position as workers in society. Thus, the exclusion of women who lacked a recognizable employer from the framework of traditional trade unions has been challenged by SEWA. A shift in nomenclature from informal to self-employed also is one of SEWA's contributions to providing visibility to the range of women's work. The fact that SEWA members comprise the poorest and most insecure segment of workers makes such organizing an especially significant imperative.

SEWA is led by Ela Bhatt, a lawyer and social activist, previously associated with the women's wing of the Textile Labor Association (TLA, locally known as Majoor Mahajan) in Ahmedabad. The TLA is a trade union based on Gandhian principles that sought to address capital-labor conflicts through peaceful negotiations. The formation of SEWA was propelled in part by the closure of textile mills in Ahmedabad in 1968 and a realization that the responsibility of providing for the family had now fallen on women. In 1981, TLA and SEWA separated from one another, partly due to the contrast between SEWA's links to international development and the TLA's dependence on local political power. Political differences also came to the fore as SEWA has been outspoken in opposing religious and caste-based violence in

Gujarat, especially since SEWA's members span the spectrum of caste and religious identities.

Expanding Into the Rural Areas

While initially focused on urban women workers, SEWA became involved with rural women in 1976, since it was found that women comprised the majority of landless agricultural laborers. SEWA has organized rural women into cooperatives, which ensures both the creation of job opportunities as well as increases women's bargaining power. In the process, SEWA's strategies became differentiated into the establishment of unions in urban contexts, where work was already available, and the establishment of rural cooperatives, where opportunities for work had to be constructed.

Besides providing visibility and collective strength to women in the informal sector, SEWA also sought to link them to financial services, in the process becoming an important part of demonstrating the creditworthiness of the poor, especially of poor women. Since SEWA's members were not welcome in existing banking institutions, the Mahila SEWA Sahakari Bank was formed in 1974. The rising international stature of microcredit initiatives as a strategy of poverty alleviation can partly be traced to Bhatt's proposal in the First United Nations Conference for Women held in Mexico City in 1975. That proposal called for women's banking to be part of women and development initiatives, which was followed by the establishment of Women's World Banking in 1980. SEWA has thus been successful in augmenting women's economic participation and power within both national and international contexts.

See Also: India; Microcredit; Poverty, "Feminization" of; United Nations Conferences on Women.

Further Readings

Bhatt, E. *We Are Poor But So Many: The Story of Self-Employed Women in India.* New Delhi, India: Oxford University Press, 2006.

Jhabvala, R. "Self-Employed Women's Association." In Sheila Rowbotham and Swasti Mitter, eds., *Dignity and Daily Bread: New Forms of Economic Organizing Among Poor Women in the Third World and First.* London: Routledge, 2004.

Rose, K. *Where Women Are Leaders: The SEWA Movement in India.* New Delhi: Vistaar Publications, 2002.

Self Employed Women's Association. http://www.sewa.org (accessed December 2009).

Pratyusha Basu
University of South Florida

Self-Mutilation

Self-mutilation is the deliberate attempt to inflict damaging pain or harm to one's body. Forms of self-mutilation include cutting, scratching, punching, burning, biting, and pinching. Women practice self-mutilation at higher rates than men and may do it for gender-specific reasons. Self-mutilation has been found throughout diverse groups of women, spanning differences in age, race, ethnicity, and class. While the practice is deliberate, it is often a compulsion that is difficult for women to control.

Adolescent women are the most likely group to practice self-mutilation, especially in the United Kingdom (UK) and the United States. Research suggests that up to four times as many adolescent women have self-mutilated than their male peers. The UK has one of the highest rates of self harm in Europe at about 400 per 100,000 of the population. British south Asian women are more likely to self-harm than their white counterparts, and they account for more than 170,000 hospital visits each year. The specific practice of cutting, often done by damaging the body with sharp objects such as knives, razors, or scissors, is widespread in teenage girls. Cutting is not new to the 21st century, but it is growing in frequency. There is little anthropological literature on self-injury across cultures and statistical analysis is insufficient. Many women hide their activities and may experience shame surrounding their participation in self-harm. This makes it difficult to acquire accurate measurements of the rate of, and reasons behind, women's self-mutilation.

Self-injury is sometimes practiced for religious reasons and is culturally sanctified. Religious mutilation myths in India and Scandinavia have inspired some women to engage in mutilation rituals. In Siberian and Australian Aborigines culture the path to becoming a Shaman entails ritual self-torture. Finger mutilation occurs in Africa. The Dugum Dani tribe in New Guinea has a ritual where young girls cut off their fingers at funerals to prevent sickness. The Hottentot tribe symbolizes marriage or engagement with removal of part of the finger.

Self-mutilation might be used as a coping strategy for women who have not been taught how to deal with overwhelming emotions in a less harmful way. Women may self-mutilate to cope with sudden traumatic life events, such as a death in the family or a parental divorce. They may also use it as a way to cope with past traumatic experiences, like sexual and physical abuse. In Afghanistan, self-mutilation among women has dramatically increased as a response to increased poverty and violence in the region. Women as young as 6 are sold into lives of slavery, and many women commit self-immolation—setting themselves on fire—or severe self-harm as a response to this oppression.

Most women who self-harm do it repeatedly, and evidence suggests that the practice has an addictive quality to it. Women can become accustomed to the "high" they get when they self-mutilate. Theories suggest that women can become addicted to the natural "feel good" chemicals released by the body to counteract pain. Self-mutilation also may be caused by an imbalance of neurotransmitters, such as serotonin, in the brain. Some people may cut because they know others who cut themselves; this is known as the "contagion factor." Self-mutilation may be practiced by women who are suicidal, but there are many women who self-harm without the intent of suicide.

The motivation for self-mutilation may be different for women than for men. The socialization of men and women into appropriate gender roles influences the practice. Women may self-mutilate to relieve emotions they do not know how to handle because they do not feel it is socially acceptable to express anger. Women are often socialized to put the feelings of others ahead of themselves. This can lead some women to believe that injuring oneself is superior to injuring another. Self-mutilation can be a reaction to feeling powerless or silenced in society, which is a common experience of women across cultures. The relationship between low self-esteem and self-mutilation has also been documented. Women may punish themselves, and their bodies, because they feel they deserve it.

Victims of sexual abuse have high rates of self-mutilation and may feel the need to punish themselves for what they perceive to be their responsibility in their abuse. Women with eating disorders are also at risk for self-injurious behavior, and these patients should be screened for signs of this behavior. Women with substance abuse issues also are a high-risk group for self-mutilation. Studies agree that the most common place cutters self-mutilate is their arms and wrists, but women also target parts of their bodies connected to being female such as breasts, genitals, and the face. Many women hide their activities and may experience shame surrounding their participation in self-harm. This makes it difficult to acquire accurate measurements of the rate of, and reasons behind, women's self-mutilation.

Some researchers argue that gender differences are overstated. Some feminists criticize the association between women and self-mutilation, claiming that this association is connected to a history of constructing women as mentally inferior to men in the field of psychology. Gender variance can be partially explained by the difference in the way men and women self-harm. Men may be more likely to self-injure in ways that are less noticeable. Single episodes of self-mutilation are rare and may not be reported in statistics.

See Also: Adolescence; Child Abuse, Victims of; Depression; Health, Mental and Physical.

Further Readings

Fox, C. and K. Hawton. *Deliberate Self-Harm in Adolescence*. London: Jessica Kingsley, 2004.

Levenkron, S. *Cutting: Understanding and Overcoming Self-Mutilation*. New York: W. W. Norton, 1998.

Ross, S. and N. Heath. "A Study of the Frequency of Self-Mutilation in a Community Sample of Adolescents." *Journal of Youth and Adolescence*, v. 31 (2002).

Nicole Richter
Wright State University

Senegal

Senegal is the westernmost country on the African continent. A former French colony, it is a secular republic with a legal system adapted from the French model and is known to be one of the most stable democracies in Africa. The United Nations Human Development Index ranks Senegal 166th of 182 countries with data.

A cooperative in Senegal found that powdering local baobab fruit and jujubes increased their value. A Senegalese woman processes baobab fruit kernels into a powder for sale in the Senegalese capital, Dakar.

The legal code relating to family matters contains an option allowing Muslims, who constitute the majority (more than 90 percent) of the population, to follow a version of Sharia law in relation to marriage, divorce, family authority, child custody, and inheritance. The principle of the equality of men and women before the law is enshrined in the constitution, and in 1981, Senegal ratified, without reservation, the Convention on the Elimination of All Forms of Discrimination Against Women (CEDAW). Women nonetheless experience de facto and de jure discrimination. For example, the provisions of the Islamic law of succession, recognized by the Family Code, favor men by assigning to a daughter half of the inheritance allotted to a son. As men alone are legally considered household heads, and may thus claim tax benefits for dependents, women-headed households face discrimination, as they are taxed at a higher rate and are not entitled to the child allowances paid to men and not women.

The population of almost 14 million people is predominantly rural. Some traditional practices common in rural areas such as early marriage and female genital surgery expose women and girls to reproductive and health problems. Despite the existence of a minimum legal age for marriage (16 years for women and 18 years for men), it is still quite common for girls in rural areas to marry as soon as they have reached puberty. However, urban-educated Senegalese women are increasingly marrying at a later age—a trend encouraged by the government. Civil marriage, as opposed to religious marriage, is more common in urban areas than in the countryside, as it is a condition for the receipt of social welfare benefits, which rural households do not receive. Polygamy is legal (a Muslim man may take up to four wives, and about half of Senegalese women live in polygynous marriages), and before entering into a civil marriage, a husband must declare whether the union will be monogamous or polygamous.

Urban Rural Divide

In Senegal, the urban–rural divide is evident in the domains of education and employment, despite constitutional protections. In the countryside, women perform much of the subsistence farming and child rearing and have limited educational opportunities. In urban areas, women meet with less discrimination and are more active in government, political life, and business. Overall, women lag behind men in educational opportunities, with the disparity in literacy rates (49.1 percent of adult men are literate as opposed to 28.2 percent of women) reflecting this. According to the 2005 Demographic and Health Survey, 28 percent of Senegalese women have undergone some form of female genital surgery. The practice has been outlawed in Senegal since 1999, but the ban is largely unenforced for practical reasons, similar to the parts of the Family Code opposed to by religious leaders. However, Senegal is the site of the massive Tostan grassroots project, which has reportedly led to abandonment of the practice in over 3,700 villages, with continued, rapid spread. The Senegalese government, in partnership with this and other community actors, is currently finalizing a national plan to bring about the complete abandonment of female genital surgery by 2015.

See Also: Convention on the Elimination of All Forms of Discrimination Against Women; Female Genital Surgery, Types of; Shari`a Law.

Further Readings

Balonze, John, ed. *Street Children in Senegal.* Netcong, NJ: Gyan Publishing, 2006.

Creevey, Lucy. "Islam, Women and the Role of the State in Senegal." *Journal of Religion in Africa*, v.26/3 (1996).

Ross, Eric S. *Culture and Customs of Senegal.* Westport, CT: Greenwood Press, 2008.

Máire Ní Mhórdha
University of St. Andrews

Serbia

After the tumult of the 1990s, with the dissolution of Yugoslavia, the Kosovo War, and the reign of Slobodan Milošević, the independent state of Serbia is now trying to regain some stability and develop its economy. Serbia is now a parliamentary democracy, and women have the same legal rights as men. However, Serbia's transition from socialism to capitalism has come at the expense of women, as poverty, new gender ideologies, and economic development compromise women's status. Under the socialist system, the normative gender ideology promoted equality in all aspects of public and private life. However, to appeal to Western investors, Serbia has adopted a more patriarchal ideology. With the slogan "Mothers of the Nation," Serbians campaign for a woman's right to stay at home and be a housewife and mother, instead of fighting for wage equity. In many regards, Serbia is ignoring women's issues for the sake of economic growth.

Women's economic status has suffered in recent years. Although women make up 55 percent of the workforce, they are likely to be the first to lose their jobs, especially high-level positions. Women also are impeded from becoming business owners, with poor access to entrepreneur loans. Women earn 60 percent of university degrees, but 90 percent of those are in education—a traditionally female occupation with lower wages. The socialist welfare system provided women with a safety net, but in the transition to a capitalist economy, Serbia has experienced a feminization of poverty, with more and more women and female heads of household unable to support themselves or their families. Compounding that problem, women make up 58 percent of the refugees that still exist.

There are no laws to protect women from discrimination, and few resources to address women's issues, and as a result, Serbian women have experienced a recent rise in domestic violence and sex trafficking. The Serbian Victimology Society estimates that one-third of women have been physically abused, and half of Serbian women suffered from psychological violence. Statistics are difficult because the majority of women refuse to report the abuse, believing nothing will be done and being fearful of repercussions. High poverty levels have led to an increase in sex trafficking, and Serbia has become a waystation in the sex-trade business, as traffickers import and export women through the country.

Although there are some signs of hope for Serbian women, such as the creation in 2004 of the Council for Gender Equity, the new independent country of Serbia has not made women's status a focal point of their development. The transition to democracy and capitalism altered the gender ideologies and economic welfare of Serbian women.

See Also: Domestic Violence; Educational Opportunities/Access; Poverty; Sex Workers.

Further Readings

Bracewell, Wendy. "Women, Motherhood, and Contemporary Serbian Nationalism." *Women's Studies International Forum*, v.19/1-2 (1996).

Ramset, Sabrina P. *Gender Politics in the Western Balkans: Women and Society in Yugoslavia and the Yugoslav Successor States*. University Park: Pennsylvania State University Press, 1999.

Zarkov, Dubrakva. *The Body of War: Media, Ethnicity, and Gender in the Break-Up of Yugoslavia*. Durham, NC: Duke University Press, 2007.

Monica D. Fitzgerald
Saint Mary's College of California

Sex Education, Abstinence-Only

Abstinence-only sex education promotes sexual activity in the context of marriage. In the United States, this form of sexuality education became commonplace in the mid-1990s, after President Bill Clinton signed the Welfare Reform Law that provided federal funding for states agreeing to promote abstinence-only curricula. State support for this form of sex education has decreased somewhat since 1999.

Abstinence-only sex education is controversial; critics believe that abstinence-only sex education is shortsighted and fails to properly educate schoolchildren. Proponents of abstinence-only sex education assert that students should be discouraged from engaging in sexual intercourse before marriage.

Sex education refers to a disbursal of sexuality related information to a select audience. In the United States, elementary and secondary schools are the most common providers of formal sexual education. The curriculum is typically composed of biological, social, and psychological information related to human development, interpersonal relationships, and sexual knowledge. The specific information provided to students varies widely depending upon the students' age as well as the ideological beliefs of the teacher, the school, and the larger society. There are two predominant ideological forms of sex education in the United States: abstinence-only sex education and comprehensive sex education.

Abstinence-only sex education promotes abstaining from sexual contact during the teenage years and before marriage. This type of sex education includes information regarding conception and emphasizes the failure rates of contraceptive devices. Abstinence-only sex education does not include critically important information on sexual health, in particular regarding pregnancy prevention or sexually transmitted disease (STD) protection.

The federal government does not require public schools to teach sex education; however, many states mandate the practice of sexual education in schools. In the year 2009, sex education was mandatory in 21 states and the District of Columbia. It was not required in other states; however, there was some form of school-sponsored sex education in 48 states. States' individual school districts further elucidate and deploy sex education policies.

In 1981, President Ronald Reagan's administration implemented the Adolescent Family Life Demonstration and Research Program; this program encouraged adolescents to abstain from engaging in sexual activity. In 1996, the U.S. government passed additional legislation encouraging schools to promote abstinence-only sex education. This law, referred to as Title V of the 1996 Welfare Reform Law, granted $50 million a year for five years to establish programs that solely promoted abstinence-only education. In its first year, 49 states participated in the program. California was the only state that did not choose to partake in the Title V program. By 2009, participation had dropped to 25 of 50 states. Title V–sponsored sex education taught the following:

- The social, psychological, and health gains that can be achieved by abstaining from sex
- To remain abstinent until they are married, and to encourage sexually-active teens to become abstinent
- That the only way to avoid pregnancy and STDs is to remain abstinent
- That the appropriate avenue for sexual activity is monogamous marital relationships
- That nonmarital sexual activities can produce harmful physical and psychological effects

- That having babies outside of marriage will negatively affect the child, parents, and society
- How to reject sexual advances and to avoid drugs and alcohol
- That they should become self-sufficient before becoming sexually active

Critics of abstinence-only sex education point to research demonstrating that this form of sex education is ineffective in reducing rates of teens' sexual activity. A 2007 meta-study published in the *British Medical Journal* found that abstinence-only programs are ineffective in changing teens' sexual behaviors. Critics also argue that teens who undergo abstinence-only education are more likely to have unprotected sex, are more likely to become pregnant, and are more likely to contract sexually transmitted diseases than students exposed to comprehensive sex education.

A 2007 study by Mathematica Policy Research showed that students in abstinence-only programs were not more likely to abstain from sex, delay having sex, or have fewer sexual partners than students who received no sex education. Comprehensive sex education proponents argue that by withholding information on human sexuality, abstinence-only education does not give youth the information they need to properly protect their health and well-being.

President Barack Obama's 2010 budget did not renew the Title V grant program, and as of 2010, a five-year, $375 million grant was designated for 28 programs that were proven to lower pregnancy rates among participating youth.

See Also: Adolescence; Puberty; Sex Education in the Home; Sex Education, Comprehensive; Sex Education, Cross-Culturally Compared.

Further Readings

Irvine, Janice. *Talk About Sex: The Battles Over Sex Education in the United States.* Berkeley: University of California Press, 2002.

McClelland, S. and M. Fine. "Embedded Science: Critical Analysis of Abstinence-Only Evaluation Research." *Cultural Studies, Critical Methodologies,* v.8/1 (2008).

Santelli, John. "Abstinence Only Education: Politics, Science, and Ethics." *Social Research,* v.73/3 (2006).

Underhill, Kristin, Paul Montgomery, and Don Operario. "Sexual Abstinence Only Programmes to Prevent HIV Infection in High Income Countries: Systematic Review." *British Medical Journal,* v.335 (2007).

Patricia Drew
California State University, East Bay

Sex Education, Comprehensive

Comprehensive sex education is a common form of sexuality education curricula taught in U.S. elementary and secondary school systems. These programs teach youth about social, physiological, and psychological aspects of sexuality. Comprehensive sex education also incorporates information about contraception and sexually transmitted disease prevention. Additionally, sex education frequently includes information about sexual orientation, sexual desire, and abortion. Public opinion about comprehensive sex education is divided. Proponents assert that students need a wide array of sexuality-related information to make informed choices and protect themselves from potential consequences. Critics argue that comprehensive sex education is overly permissive and fails to discourage teenagers from engaging in sexual intercourse.

There are many sex education curricula characterized as comprehensive. While individual lesson plans differ, curricular goals are often shared. Comprehensive sex education typically includes multiple components. Many aspects of the curricula are not controversial, including discussions of factual information about psychological, social, and biological human development from puberty through adulthood. Students are taught about body changes associated with adolescence, including menstruation. The curriculum also highlights information about conception, pregnancy, and sexual-refusal skills. This factual information is similar to the lessons included in abstinence-only programs.

Comprehensive sex education also incorporates information that is not featured in abstinence-only curricula. The curriculum acknowledges that some students are sexually active or will become sexually active during their teenage years. Lessons include information about ways to lessen risks of sexual activity, including use of contraceptive devices and condoms.

A Broader Perspective

Comprehensive sex education also incorporates discussions of abortion, sexually transmitted infections, and human immunodeficiency virus (HIV)/Acquired immune deficiency syndrome (AIDS), and often mentions sexual orientation as well as acknowledging the existence of homosexuality and heterosexuality.

Comprehensive sex education is occasionally referred to as abstinence-plus sex education. In this variation, the curriculum encourages students to abstain from sexual intercourse during their teenage years and before marriage. However, the curriculum continues to include information regarding birth control and sexually transmitted disease protection.

Sex education is commonly taught in elementary and secondary schools. In 2002, 58 percent of high school principals characterized their schools' sex education programs as comprehensive; 34 percent characterized their programs as abstinence-only. Most principals indicated that their schools' comprehensive sex education programs primarily advocated abstinence among teenagers.

There are no federal regulations mandating the presence or content of sex education in schools. Individual states and school districts create sex education policies. In 2009, 21 states and the District of Columbia mandated that sex education be taught in the public schools. These states further outline the types of information that are included in school curricula. Many other states that do not require sex education courses in their schools have outlined the coursework if sex education becomes part of a school district's curriculum. Fifteen states require that contraception information be included as part of a sex education curriculum. Additionally, 35 states require that schools provide sexually transmitted infection/HIV education. While there is currently federal funding for abstinence-only education, there is no similar federal funding for comprehensive sex education.

Accomplishing Change

Research has demonstrated that youth exposed to comprehensive sex education act differently than other teens. Teens taught comprehensive sex curricula are more likely to delay their sexual initiation and are likely to have fewer sexual partners than other youth. Research additionally indicates that comprehensive sex education leads to higher rates of condom and contraception usage. Girls who have undergone comprehensive sex education are less likely than their peers to become pregnant. Finally, teens with comprehensive sex education training are less likely to contract sexually transmitted infections than their peers.

There are many supporters of comprehensive sex education, including the Sexuality Information and Education Council of the United States, the American Psychological Association, the American Medical Association, and the American Public Health Association. Proponents of comprehensive sex education argue that the curriculum has several benefits. They believe that it is productive to encourage youth to refrain from sexual activity, while still providing all students with sexuality-related information that will be useful to them throughout their lives. Advocates argue that teenagers need a wide array of information to protect their personal health and their well-being. Advocates believe that students who have access to comprehensive sex education are better able to advocate for themselves and make knowledgeable decisions. Supporters also argue that it is important to note that more than half of high school seniors have had sexual intercourse, and that these teens need factual information regarding contraception and sexually transmitted infection protection.

Critics of comprehensive sex education include the Heritage Foundation, the Abstinence and Marriage Education Partnership, and some religious groups. Opponents believe that a comprehensive sex education curriculum is damaging to youth on many fronts and that it provides students with mixed messages about the meaning of sexuality and the proper context for sexual activity. Critics believe that students should be discouraged from having sexual relations as teens and outside of the context of marriage. They assert that discussions of successful contraceptive and sexually transmitted infection protection devices encourage students to engage in youthful and premarital sexual activity. Critics also state that sexually active teens often regret their early sexual experiences and report higher levels of depression than abstinent peers; schools should not discuss contraception or provide neutral messages about sexual activity, as sexually active teens may become pregnant or contract sexually transmitted infections; and comprehensive sex education does not sufficiently promote abstinence as a preferred behavior for teens.

Gender Expectations

Feminist academic researchers in the disciplines of sociology, gender studies, psychology, and education have brought attention to commonplace gender expectations in sex education curriculum. These researchers have noted that comprehensive sex education curriculum often provides different messages about sexual activity, desire, and responsibility for females and males. Teenage boys are often expected to be sexually active and desirous but are not responsible for negative sexuality outcomes, such as pregnancy.

In contrast, teenage girls are not depicted as desirous. Girls are often shown to be sexual gatekeepers and responsible for pregnancy and sexually transmitted infection protection. Feminists contend that gender-based sexuality expectations legitimize men's sexuality and delegitimize women's sexuality. Feminist researchers are actively revealing and contesting gendered messages in sex education curriculum to challenge gendered double standards for teenage sexuality.

See Also: Adolescence; Puberty; Sex Education, Abstinence-Only; Sex Education, Cross-Culturally Compared; Sex Education in the Home.

Further Readings

Alan Guttmacher Institute, "Facts on Sex Education in the United States." http://www.guttmacher.org/pubs/fb_sexEd2006.html (accessed November 2009).

Fields, J. *Risky Lessons: Sex Education and Social Inequality.* New Brunswick, NJ: Rutgers University Press, 2008.

Fine, M. "Sexuality, Schooling, and Adolescent Females: The Missing Discourse of Desire." *Harvard Educational Review,* v.58/1(1988).

Kaiser Family Foundation, "Sex Education in the U.S.: Policy and Politics." http://www.kff.org/youthhivstds/upload/Sex-Education-in-the-U-S-Policy-and-Politics.pdf (accessed November 2009).

Martin, K. A. *Puberty, Sexuality, and the Self: Boys and Girls at Adolescence.* New York: Routledge, 1996.

Rose, S. "Going Too Far? Sex, Sin and Social Policy." *Social Forces,* v.84/2 (2005).

Tolman, D., ed. "Through a Lens of Embodiment: New Research From the Center for Research on Gender and Sexuality." *Sexuality Research and Social Policy,* v.3/4 (2006).

Patricia Drew
California State University, East Bay

Sex Education, Cross-Culturally Compared

Appraising sex education across cultures is increasingly challenging given often-dissonant, overarching structures of sponsorship. Below is an overview of the global needs and frameworks, cultural challenges to these, and contemporary politics of definition that continue to make sex education for girls and young women a hot topic.

Urgency and Health Needs

An estimated 4.4 million abortions are sought annually worldwide by women 15 to 19 years old. At the same time, some 10 percent of births worldwide are to teenage mothers, who experience higher rates of maternal mortality than older women. In Asia, 32 percent of unsafe abortions occur among females 15 to 24. Realities such as transactional and cross-generational sex in sub-Saharan Africa and Latin America heavily impact female decision making about family planning, health-risk containment, and abuse prevention.

Contemporary data shows that more than 60 million marriages, mostly arranged, involve girls under the age of 18 years: approximately 31 million in South Asia, 14 million in sub-Saharan Africa, and 6.6 million in Latin America and the Caribbean. One girl in seven in developing countries (excluding China) marries before age 15, according to 2007 estimates, and 38 percent marry before age 18. Early marriages, especially those before puberty, increase the risk of sexually transmitted diseases (STDs) and cervical cancer, problems related to pregnancy, labor and delivery, and infant mortality. Researchers suggest that school-based sex education may be essential in changing awareness, attitudes, and practices leading to risky sexual behavior in marriage.

The Impact of Human Immunodeficiency Virus

Human immunodeficiency virus and acquired immune deficiency syndrome (HIV/AIDS) has been a major drive for gender-minded attention to sex education worldwide given the evident feminization of the pandemic. In 2004, the World Health Organization (WHO) estimated that more than 2 million people aged 10 to 24 were newly infected with HIV annually, two-thirds of them female. Globally, women constitute half the total number of people living with HIV, but in sub-Saharan Africa, the proportion rises to 61 percent. Three-quarters of infected 15- to 24-year-olds in Africa, or almost 5 million people, are female. Sub-Saharan young women are an estimated two to seven times more likely to be HIV positive than their male peers. Apart from higher biological risks, women have less access to education and economic opportunities, making them dependent in relationships and within their families. This may result in a woman having limited power to refuse sex or negotiate condom use or a woman resorting to bartering or selling sex.

According to review research, the impact of education on HIV vulnerability may not differ remarkably between men and women. Sexual decision making in general may be more dramatically dependent on general degrees of educational and socioeconomic opportunity and empowerment than by thematically dedicated projects. A range of sexual-health-related issues, such as prostitution and trafficking, virgin rape in southern Africa, and war-related sexual violence against girls and women, require education of boys and young men, appropriate legal measures, medical infrastructures, community awareness, and international policy.

Global Frameworks

Sex education worldwide is conceptualized in accordance to the vista of reproductive health (RH). This was defined by the International Conference on Population and Development (ICPD), convened under the auspices of the United Nations (UN) in Cairo, Egypt, 1994. One of the primary goals of the program of action was to make family planning universally available by 2015 as part of a broadened approach to reproductive health and rights, involving expanded access to education. RH was the deal-maker or breaker at the UN Millennium Declaration, signed in September 2000 to achieve approval of the Declaration at the General Assembly. The rubric of RH had to be, and was, omitted under pressure by what was critically called an "unholy religious pact" by the U.S.-backed Holy See. RH is largely considered code language for abortion, and conservative Islamic states oppose family-planning services for adolescents and the very ideas of sexual health and sexual rights.

However, the 2005 UN World Summit in New York reinstated RH in its outcome document against all expectations, although it was ensured that the terms *sexual, sexuality,* and *rights* were not used. Several current Millennium Development Goals (MDGs) include targets either directly requiring or indirectly contributing to improvements in sex education for girls and women. They are monitored (www.mdgmonitor.org) by indicators including primary education attendance, gender disparity in primary and secondary education, condom use, proportion of population aged 15–24 years with comprehensive correct knowledge of HIV/AIDS, contraceptive prevalence rate, and adolescent birth rate. A comprehensive review of ICPD at the midpoint to 2015 (ICPD+10 in 2004) confirmed earlier observations that many countries lagged behind in RH indicators or are not anywhere near the projected goals.

At the 2006 High Level Meeting on AIDS, all UN member states pledged to increase the capacity of women and adolescent girls to protect themselves from the risk of HIV infection, including the provision of full access to comprehensive information and education. UNAIDS, the joint UN Program on HIV/AIDS, aims to expand access to sexual and reproductive (SRH) healthcare programs and integrate HIV into these, as well as promote campaigns and community dialog to change harmful gender norms.

In its platform of action, the last (Fourth) World Conference on Women (Beijing, China, 1995) specifically stressed the need to remove barriers to education for women, particularly pregnant adolescents and young mothers, and recognized that adolescents in many developing countries have limited access to comprehensive SRH information and services. The WHO maintains it is critical that sex education be started early, particularly in developing countries, because girls in the first classes of secondary school face the greatest consequences of sexual activity. Beginning sex education in primary school also reaches students who are unable to attend secondary school. The International Sexual and Reproductive Rights Coalition (ISRRC) urges its member states to ensure that all girls have access to gender-sensitive and comprehensive sex education, in and out of school, based on scientific evidence and within a human rights framework. Organizations such as International Women's Health Coalition (IWHC) join in urging governments, specifically the United States, to implement comprehensive sex education.

Resistance to these objectives, however, can be readily seen in the mixed reception of a draft of proposed UN Educational, Scientific and Cultural Organization (UNESCO) *International Guidelines on Sexuality Education* in 2009. Worldwide sex education, particularly in Africa, continues to be heavily influenced both by the Vatican's position, as summarized in the 1995 Pontifical Council for the Family pamphlet *The Truth and Meaning of Human Sexuality: Guidelines for Education Within the Family*. Reaffirming 1983 guidelines from the Congregation for Catholic Education (*Educational Guidance in Human Love*), it naturalized the domestic setting as educational, maternity, and same-gender educators. Further global influence is evidenced by what is known as the Mexico City Policy or "global gag rule," a ban on U.S. funding for international health groups to engage in a range of educational activities involving the provision of advice, counseling, or information regarding abortion. The ban, originally instituted by President Ronald Reagan in 1984, oscillates with Republican administrations adopting and Democratic administrations rescinding it. The ban was last revoked by President Barack Obama in January 2009.

Local/Cultural Challenges

Since 2002, the UN Population Fund (UNFPA) has systematically aimed to explore needs for culture-sensitive approaches to SHR, as indicated in publications such as *Culture Matters* (2004), *Cultural Programming* (2005), and *Reaching Common Ground: Culture, Gender and Human Rights* (2008). Case studies find that strong religious and traditional norms restrict the open discussion of sex across large parts of the world, norms that usually show highly gendered conceptions of body, decorum, and life course. Western-styled curricula may not cover such gendered issues as polygyny, transactional sex, AIDS orphans, genital cutting, and avoidance

rules ("taboos"). They also may not be effective in the everyday juggling of cultural models, including generational relationships, kinship, and gender, that characterize contemporary developing countries. Teachers may cite religious doctrine and absence of curriculum, as well as fears of promoting promiscuity, of parental prosecution, and of being ostracized by community factions. These factors are now prioritized in international initiatives, many of which analyzed in research journals such as *Culture & Sexuality*, *Culture, Health & Sexuality*, and *Sex Education* (published as of 1997, 1999, and 2000, respectively).

Notwithstanding the international push to professionalize and institutionalize sex education, the ethnographic record is testimony to a variety of semi-formalized and nonformalized contexts that prove important spheres of socialization that are considered exploitable for curricular ends. In various African contexts, themes pertinent to sex are traditionally recited in stories, legends, riddles, and proverbs. A major pan-African factor is the replacement by formal-institutional education of "traditional," usually gender-segregated socialization contexts known as puberty or initiation rituals. While the latter commonly included detailed, comprehensive, and realistic coverage of married life and often formed one of the few intergenerational transmission points, institutional curricula and teachers have been slow to "take over." In some areas, designated gender- and kinship-based lines of communication have eroded, leading to a dependency on schools.

In other areas, contemporary research finds that 90 percent of adult respondents report undergoing formalized initiations, often at puberty. Information about sex and marriage has traditionally been passed on to young girls by aunts such as the *senga*, or father's sister, in rural Uganda. This role has equivalents throughout eastern and southern Africa, and research has suggested such institutional roles are associated with beneficial health outcomes. The information can be disseminated as a model, and where eroded it may respond to affirmative stimuli, enhanced by formal training, and regularly monitored with regard to good practices.

This move toward the professionalization of rituals will enhance existing cultural controversy over these events. Women's rights activists suggest rituals may reiterate male-centred values and practices.

Traditionalists may insist on their continuity as part of a more general reclaiming of precolonial cultural identity—an often paradoxical "invention of tradition"—while church-based sponsors, in continuity with missionary work, judge events in terms of promotion of promiscuity and immorality. The result may be total governmental rejection. In 2009, for example, an Indian parliamentary Committee on Petitions resolutely rejected Western-oriented school programs, arguing that "our country's social and cultural ethos are such that sex education has absolutely no place in it."

Part of the information gap is arguably being closed in some regions by public events known as "virginity testing." Considered a human rights violation by Amnesty International and criminalized in many countries, virginity testing survives in a range of countries, particularly Turkey, India, and KwaZulu-Natal province in South Africa, under fiat of local authorities. In South Africa, reemergence of virginity testing is legitimized by periodic examinations that have a pedagogical effect, is part of a centuries-old custom, and is affixed to public events with a broad pedagogical scope. These tests may, conversely, serve to ensure daughters fetch a higher *lobola*, or traditional payment made by the groom's family to the bride's family. A 2005 Children's Bill outlawed virginity testing under the age of 16, paving the way for national laws.

Participation in sex education for many girls worldwide is limited as a result of early school dropout. Effective delivery of sex, relationship, and HIV education may be specifically hampered in some settings by sexual harassment or abuse of schoolgirls by teachers and nonteaching staff, reported in a number of sub-Saharan African countries and undermining the credibility of institutional education. It has been reported that female students may be marginalized and bullied by male pupils in projects involving peer education. Governmental action may be drastic given suspicions against school-based programs. In 2005, Swaziland's King Mswati III ended a five-year sex ban he imposed on the kingdom's teenage girls a year earlier; since 2001, the girls were ordered to wear large woollen tassels signaling their chastity.

Defining Sex, Gender, and Education

Sexuality and procreation are possibly the most questionable of anthropological universalisms and the most embattled of administrative globalisms. This may be particularly true if the discussion centers on of the subject of needs, rights, and human fulfillment. Feminist presence in the house of anthropology has addressed the vista of sexuality quite variably and with increasing complexity over the past four decades, but the issue, if anything, continues to epitomize the gulf between programmatic and formulaic internationalisms on one end and qualitative anthropology's cultural relativism on the other.

Sex education today is marked by the globalization of an administrative biomedical paradigm that precariously interfaces with often-contradictory local and global infrastructures of sponsorship. While major debates in the United States are narrowly occupied with outcome differences between abstinence-based and comprehensive education programs, studies have found that significant variation exists in youths' definitions of "having sex," abstinence, and virginity, with major implications for research organized around the rubrics of sexual debut, harassment, abuse, and sexualization of girls. For instance, a 2007 *Report of the APA Task Force on the Sexualization of Girls* signaled a vital role for formal education, specifically media, literary, athletic programs (with a focus on body competence and away from body appearance), and comprehensive sex education, to tackle a proliferation of sexualized images of girls and young women in advertising and merchandising in the United States. The report's concept of sexualization, however, was largely based on predefined notions of "exposure" rather than on girls' perspectives and audience response. It also assumed, but did not examine, that both the phenomenon and concern for it are "exported" worldwide and internationalizing its "scope" would be advisable.

Another example entails a movement to ritualize abstinence, often in tandem with abstinence-focused education. Started in 1993 by the Southern Baptist Convention, "virginity/abstinence pledging" now claims more than 2.5 million pledgers worldwide in dozens of countries. In 1996, chastity rings were introduced to signal premarital abstinence; the pioneering "Silver Ring Thing," an evangelical-Christian program based in Pennsylvania, currently sponsors events in eight countries. Approximately 16 percent of teenage girls in America, and 10 percent of teenage boys, would have taken a virginity pledge. However, some studies found that half of adolescents who took virginity pledges denied having taken them the following year. Regardless, most recent studies and meta-reviews suggest that abstinence-only curricula, virginity pledging, chastity rings, and purity balls have either no or counterproductive effects.

Given that the idea of sexuality pertains to strategic interplay of moral, administrative, and empirical idioms, it is generally accepted that what should qualify as adequate, comprehensive, age-appropriate, or gender-appropriate content for curricula seems largely indexical to the variously competing or strategically allied internationalisms that have a stake in defining sexuality's ethical contours and horizons. Some might argue with the French-thinker Michel Foucault that sex education does not inform youth of an entitled sexuality but instills it as a regulatory grammar of selfhood, with the implication that it is a vital instrument in the defining of female nature, womanhood, reproductive roles, and normative heterosexuality—whether as human, transcultural, international, or local projection. Thus, the idea of a bounded sexuality is continuously reaffirmed through education as a way of delimiting the mobility of bodies, identities, and pleasures, and it is evident that any disclosure or informational exchange, from virginity tests to textbooks, further entrenches gendered concerns for moral "health" and ethical "integrity." Observing current globalization of legal and sexological discourse, understanding sexuality in this light is of manifest importance in envisioning which revelatory acts, including which sex acts, will in future decades be elevated to the realm of "proper education" and which will be categorized as "normal experience" and/or "abuse."

Continuously Adapting

The stakes of sex education are continuously recalibrated around developing technologies. In the Anglo-American world, Internet-based peer socialization has reintensified old vigilance regarding sexual predators, exposure, and self-exposure. European girls are warned about immigrant "loverboys." Clearly, minors require continuous updating about shifting legal thresholds with such innovations as Webcamming and "sexting"—a contraction of sex and texting via mobile phones—increasingly since 2005. Girls seem to be overrepresented in the number, or at least coverage, of minors being charged for producing and circulating sexually explicit material of themselves. A 2008 survey of 1,280 respondents co-commissioned by www.Cosmogirl.com reported that 11 percent of girls aged 13–16, 22 percent of girls aged 13–19 and 33 percent of women 20–26 had sent/posted nude or seminude photographs of themselves electronically. This was only slightly more than for their male peers. Efforts to decriminalize consensual sexting between teenagers are to emerge.

See Also: Abortion Laws, International; Sex Education, Abstinence-Only; Sex Education, Comprehensive.

Further Readings

American Psychological Association (APA), Task Force on the Sexualization of Girls. *Report of the APA Task Force on the Sexualization of Girls.* Washington, DC: APA, 2007.

Francoeur, R., et al., eds. *Continuum Complete International Encyclopedia of Sexuality.* New York: Continuum, 2004.

Janssen, D. *Growing Up Sexually,* 3 Volumes. Berlin: Magnus Hirschfeld Archive for Sexology, 2004.

Obermeyer, C. M. *Cultural Perspectives on Reproductive Health.* New York: Oxford University Press, 2001.

United Nations Educational, Scientific and Cultural Organization. "International Guidelines on Sexuality Education: An Evidence Informed Approach to Effective Sex, Relationships and HIV/STI Education." Draft, June 2009.

United Nations Population Fund (UNFPA). "Culture Matters: Working With Communities and Faith-Based Organizations: Case Studies From Country Programmes." New York: UNFPA, 2004.

Diederik F. Janssen
Independent Scholar

Sex Education in the Home

Sex education in the home is often talked about as a new concept, being portrayed by both conservative and liberal organizations as essential. Advocates of sex education in the home in the United States often cite need based on the proliferation of sexual activity by younger children or the abundance of sexual misinformation that is available—even though parents admit this observation is made intuitively and not from research reflecting sexual attitudes and behaviors. Although sex education in the home is wide reaching and can apply to adults and children, the phrase is often interpreted as meaning sex education from parents to children. Other than parents, children and adults have many other options for sex education in the home: traditional media outlets such as television or print publications; new media outlets such as Internet sites or Web pages; talk between friends and family members; and even observation of romantic or sexual activity. Adults often educate themselves and each other through literature or disclosure of sexual needs or desires to partners.

Parents and guardians often cite concerns about misinformation and child safety as key reasons for initiating conversations about sex. Women report being expected to facilitate such talks more than men, in part because men usually handle such talks with males and women usually discuss these issue with other females. When an exception is made, it is usually the mother who will discuss sex with her sons. There are many reasons for parents to talk about sex with their children. For women, the reasons include the onset of menstruation, a first boyfriend, and becoming a teenager. For men, the occasions may include discovery of pornography, a first girlfriend, or becoming a teenager. Talks may occur with younger children after they inquire about where babies come from or after they see adults engaged in sexual acts. Many times, though, these conversations are less direct, filled with elements of myth or fantasy, or provide simplified forms of information.

Sex Education in the Home: Conservative and Liberal Approaches

Labeling parent-child sex education approaches as conservative or liberal often distorts or unfairly and artificially dichotomizes the attitudes and beliefs most parents carry about sex and its role in their culture. Often, too, most guides for parents simplify sex education information into conservative or liberal categories. Conservative literature often points out the need for traditional values in sex education in the face of liberal school systems and sex-saturated media outlets. Similarly, liberal literature frequently points out the need for honest discussions about sex in the face of school systems that have been co-opted by insufficient and ineffective conservative approaches and media outlets that are saturated with

unhealthy messages about sex. Each form of literature often carries recurring themes about the importance of sexual education.

Conservative literature tends to encourage dialog between parents and children about sex, often suggesting religious faith be a part of these conversations. To this end, parents are encouraged to tell their children to consult them before engaging in sexual activity. Abstinence also is encouraged, as birth control and other contraceptives are never fully protective. Like conservative literature, liberal-facing materials often encourage an open dialog. Instead of a focus on faith, there is a concentration on feelings. Discussion of various forms of birth control and contraceptives also is encouraged, as is affirmation of sexual feelings and desires being a normal part of life. Liberal literature also is more likely to encourage parents to acknowledge that experimenting with sexual activity is likely and encourages communication about knowing one's limits and responsibilities.

Despite most literature about parent–child sex education being aimed at a conservative or liberal audience, many studies demonstrate general apathy toward the causes being advanced by such literature. Additionally, critics and sex educators cite limitations to both approaches, including lack of recognition of the full spectrum of sexuality. While neither the conservative nor the liberal literature tends to examine same-sex feelings and attractions, the possibility of same-sex attraction being validated or encouraged in public schools is often listed as a reason conservative parents should consider talking about sex with their children. Both liberal and conservative approaches also encourage parents to act as role models, noting that conversations about sexual responsibility will only hold with children if they see their parents modeling sexual responsibility as well. A lot of literature also highlights the idea that sexual conversations between parents and children may be awkward, but research suggests such claims may be overstated.

Mechanisms for Sex Education in the Home

When it comes to parents talking about sex with children, a variety of aides and options are available to facilitate discussion. While most people report not using any of these mechanisms, many parents do. These materials are readily available and can be purchased through Internet outlets. Two particular tools for sex education discussions that continue to increase in popularity are children's storybooks aimed at introducing children to sexualized bodies and reproductive sex acts and virginity rings or pledges aimed at young women.

Storybooks such as Peter Mayle's *Where Did I Come From?* have been around for decades and use playful illustrations and colorful comparisons to help children understand sex and sexuality in frank but sensitive terms. For instance, in the case of Mayle's book, an orgasm is compared to a sneeze from the genitals; sex is compared to jumping rope; and sperm and ova are turned into characters to explain how they function. Some of these books contain candid drawings of the various body parts, while others describe sexual processes and help children to understand how their own bodies will grow and change over time—as will their attitudes about boys or girls. The emergence of such books have placed women in a more central role as sex educators, since women tend to read storybooks to children more than men.

Another tool for facilitating sex education discussions are virginity rings or pledges. The pledges are often prewritten contracts that can be purchased online or through many religious organizations that teens or preteens are asked to sign. These pledges usually acknowledge a commitment to religion, parents, and self-respect. A ring is often worn by the signer as a reminder of their promise; if the child engages in a sexual act, then the ring should be removed. Ideally, though, the ring will remain until marriage. Typically, young women are asked to sign these contracts, sometimes in conjunction with a dance or purity ball, where many young women all sign at once and celebrate the occasion with their fathers as their dates. This is not exclusive to women; some young men sign these pledges and wear the rings as well.

Despite tools of all kinds being used to help facilitate talks, most parents report they discuss sex with their children based on unexpected incidents, such as a sudden graphic representation of sexuality on a television program, or after being discovered by their child while engaging in sexual activity with a partner. The biggest regret many parents report is a defensive or stern tone related to sexuality. Many also regret orally attacking a child about his or her behavior when they find evidence that may suggest engagement or consideration of sexual activity.

Adult Education

Of course, adults educate each other about sex in the home, too. While this can happen in conversation at parties or in casual conversations with friends, sex partners also will educate each other about sex—usually in conjunction with their own sexual needs or desires. Sometimes a partner will confide that sex has become routine, and so a video or description of different sexual positions, games, or toys can be used to add spice to a sexual relationship.

Sex education also comes in the form of sexual practice. When engaging a new sexual partner, one not only begins a learning process about how to please that individual but likely will learn new tricks or techniques that, if enjoyed, can be shared with future partners. This form of active education may be especially true if partners are engaging in a new form of sex not yet experienced; one partner may teach another how to perform oral or anal sex; how to use a certain toy; or even how to engage in a particular fantasy. Although sex education is often thought of as something that occurs at a given point in one's life, for most individuals it is something that will continue for as long as he or she is sexually active. Women, in particular, become more open to learning about their own sexual thoughts, feelings, and desires as they mature and social inhibitions are shed.

See Also: Contraception, Religious Approaches to; Contraception Methods; Heterosexism; Pornography/Erotica; Purity Balls; Sex Education, Comprehensive.

Further Readings

Altman, Dennis. *Global Sex*. Chicago: University of Chicago Press, 2002.

Bailey, Kristen, ed. *Sex Education*. Farmington Hills, MI: Greenhaven Press, 2004.

Bleakly, Amy, et al. "Public Opinion on Sex Education in U.S. Schools." *Archives of Pediatrics and Adolescent Medicine*, v.160/11 (2006).

Luker, Kristen. *When Sex Goes to School: Warring Views on Sex—and Sex Education—Since the Sixties*. New York: W. W. Norton, 2006.

Mayle, Peter. *Where Did I Come From?* New York: Little, Brown, 1984.

Jimmie Manning
Northern Kentucky University

Sex Offenders, Female

Until recently, little was known about female sex offenders in the United States; today, the literature is nascent but growing. The primary reason for the lack of knowledge about female sex offenders is that their offenses go largely unreported. Increasing awareness regarding this population stems from highly publicized cases in which young female teachers have engaged in sexual relations with students. These cases do not represent the majority and may perpetuate myths about a subject in which researchers still have much to learn.

Female-perpetrated sex crimes are relatively rare, though this phenomenon may be skewed. Sex offenses are among the most underreported of all crimes, and female-perpetrated sex crimes may be reported less often than those committed by males. Nevertheless, official criminal justice statistics suggest that less than 10 percent of sex crimes are committed by women. However, one recent study suggests that upwards of 20 percent of all sexual abuse events are committed by women. One to 6 percent of arrests and 2 percent of those incarcerated for sex crimes are women. Victimization surveys, which seek to address the limitations of official statistics, suggest that over 60 percent of female and 27 percent of male victims report sexual victimization by a female.

While the National Crime Victimization Survey reports that female-perpetrated offenses account for 6 percent of offenses in which the offender acted alone, 40 percent of offenses involving multiple offenders included a woman. These statistics are similar to those found in other societies as well. Official statistics from the United States are similar to those in Australia, the United Kingdom, and Canada; approximately 6 percent of cases known to Australian authorities were perpetrated by female sex offenders. In other parts of the world, the percentage of female sex offenders known to authorities is much lower. In 2008, only 1 percent of all accused sex offenders in South Africa were women.

Need for Information and Understanding

Because there is a dearth of information available, it is difficult to assess whether official statistics account for a reflection of reality or simply a lack of understanding about sexual abuse by women. If it is true that female-perpetrated offenses are more prevalent than statis-

tics suggest, many factors may be at play. For instance, women are seen as nurturing caregivers, simply unable to harm a child. Conversely, the shame and guilt associated with abuse by a female may be so great that victims choose not to report. Unfortunately, female perpetrated sex crimes are often not seen as criminal because of the belief that male victims would not become aroused if they were not willing participants. This narrow belief suggests that women only commit sex crimes against adult males and does not account for the broad spectrum of abuse that might occur.

Professional biases might also account for the lack of information. Law enforcement officials are often trained with the assumption that men are offenders and women are victims. This may affect the ways in which law enforcement agencies react to allegations of sexual abuse committed by women. The extent to which harm is caused may be minimized, the seriousness of the offense may be undermined, or the allegation itself may be seen as unfounded.

Societal views about gender stereotypes also affect the medical field. When an allegation of abuse is reported to medical personnel, it is possible that the individual might assume the offender is male. If this information is voluntarily provided, the abuse is often seen as less harmful.

Common Characteristics

Researchers acknowledge some common characteristics of this population as a whole. These women tend to have a history of victimization and abuse, mental health and substance abuse issues, and difficulties maintaining intimate relationships. Female sex offenders tend to commit incestuous offenses and often report having been the victim of incest as children themselves.

Women who commit sexual abuse may have longer offense histories because they are thought to begin abusing at a young age and because their acts rarely become known to the authorities. Often, their behaviors are seen as normal caretaking behaviors. These characteristics do not suggest that all female sex offenders are alike. In fact, there is much heterogeneity within the population. Three typologies have been created, but they are not mutually exclusive, nor do they account for all female sex offenders.

Teacher/Lover. These women often report marital discord or relationship issues with age-mates. They often suffer from cognitive distortions or thoughts that neutralize the potential harm they cause. For instance, many of these women believe that they are teaching the victim about sexuality or romance and therefore do not consider the behavior abuse.

Predisposed. Women in this category tend to experience deviant sexual fantasies, have histories of sexual abuse, and have a tendency to abuse their own children. They often suffer from psychological problems.

Male-Coerced. Individuals in this category often report feeling powerless and fear being alone. Thus, they often end up in male-dominated relationships, report various forms of abuse at the hands of their spouse, and often the male partner begins abusing children first before coercing the woman to engage in the abusive acts as well.

In part because of the heterogeneity within this population and partially because of the dearth of research on female sexual offending, assessment of risk and treatment protocols are lacking around the globe. Though assessment tools have been validated on both adult and adolescent female sex offenders, nothing is said about the etiology of sexual deviancy in this population. Though gender-specific treatment programs are not common, the Center for Sex Offender Management suggests that the trend in gender-responsive treatment protocols is growing. For instance, programs serving the female sex-offending population are reporting that they are more likely to address prior victimization and trauma, intimacy skills, and family reunification. Yet, as of late 2009, no accredited treatment programs for female sex offenders existed in the United Kingdom. Due to cultural attitudes about the extent to which people believe women can abuse, it is extremely difficult to ascertain estimates of sexual abuse by women worldwide. Unfortunately, this hinders the facilitation of treatment and assessment protocols around the globe.

See Also: Megan's Law; Perpetrators, Female; Rape, Incidence of; Rape, Legal Definitions of; Rape, Prosecution Rates of; Sex Offenders, Male; Stereotypes of Women.

Further Readings

Center for Sex Offender Management. *Female Sex Offenders.* Washington, DC: U.S. Department of Justice, 2007.

Denov, M. *Perspectives on Female Sex Offending: A Culture of Denial.* Hampshire, UK: Ashgate Publishing, 2004.

Dowden, C. and D. Andrews. "What Works for Female Offenders: A Meta-Analytic Review." *Crime and Delinquency*, v.45 (1999).

Hunt, L. "Females Who Sexually Abuse in Organizations Working With Children: Characteristics, International, and Australian Prevalence Rates: Implications for Child Protection." *Child Wise* (2006).

Oliver, B. E. "Preventing Female-Perpetrated Sexual Abuse." *Trauma, Violence, and Abuse*, v.8 (2007).

Vandiver, D. and G. Kercher. "Offender and Victim Characteristics of Registered Female Sexual Offenders in Texas." *Sexual Abuse: A Journal of Research and Treatment*, v.16 (2004).

Alissa R. Ackerman
University of California, Merced

Sex Offenders, Male

Since the end of the 20th century, public attention regarding sex crimes has increased dramatically. The impetus for this increase was a collection of highly publicized cases in which young children were abducted, raped, or even murdered by someone with whom they were not acquainted. This entry will provide information regarding the types of sex offenders, legislation aimed at preventing new sex crimes, treatment, and myths about the sex offender population

Male sex offenders constitute a heterogeneous group of individuals whose offenses range from noncontact crimes such as exhibitionism or viewing child pornography, to contact offenses including child molestation, sexual assault, and rape. Regardless of the offense, sex offenders commit crimes for various reasons, many for nonsexual reasons. In recent years, researchers have come to understand more about the etiology of offending behavior, suggesting that many male sex offenders exhibit poor social skills and low self-esteem. In addition, researchers have created typologies to classify offenders based on common characteristics. Typologies are important because they aid in identifying people who may be predisposed to offending and to ascertain what treatment might be effective and for whom.

Rapists

Many rapists have a negative view of women. They often identify with a hypermasculine role as well. Most rapists are classified into four distinct categories: sexual, sadistic, power, and opportunistic rapists. Most experts agree that the majority of rapes are more based on nonsexual needs than sexual ones.

Statutory rape occurs when an individual over the age of consent engages in sexual activity with someone who is a minor. The age of consent varies considerably around the world. In some countries, the age of consent is as young as 12, while in others it may be as high as 20. The global average age of consent is 16. Statutory rape laws raise interesting questions about the fine line between rape and consent. When a 16-year-old engages in sexual relations with a 17-year-old who is above the age of consent, did the older of the two take advantage of the younger?

Romeo and Juliet laws have simplified the issue. These laws serve to reduce or eliminate the criminal penalties associated with sexual relations when the only issue is the legal inability to form consent. These laws generally apply when there is a limited age difference between the two parties and the younger party is over the age of 14.

Child Molesters

Many child molesters exhibit similar characteristics to rapists. They often have low self-esteem and feelings of vulnerability and may have difficulties with adult relationships. A premise in regards to a typology involves the fixated-regressed continuum. Fixated offenders are thought to have a sexual attraction to children and suffer from what is known as a paraphilia, or persistent and intense sexually arousing fantasies or urges that involve children, or nonconsenting people, or nonhuman items and often involves suffering or humiliation. Pedophilia is the persistent and intense attraction to prepubertal children, and ephebophilia is an attraction postpubescent adolescents. Fixated offenders typically exhibit paraphilic behaviors beginning in adolescence, and many have a high rate of recidivism. Only a small minority of child molesters suffer from pedophilia, but pedophilic behavior, when committed by a fixated child molester, tends to occur over long periods of time. In contrast, the majority of child molesters are regressed, meaning their primary sexual attraction is to age-mates, but their offenses stem from environmental stressors. Often their offending behavior does not begin until adulthood and tends to manifest itself with children to whom they have access. These individuals are less likely to reoffend, once treated.

Child Pornography and Child Prostitution

With the increased popularity of the Internet, access to pornography has become effortless. In the United States, possession, purchase, distribution, and production of child pornography are all illegal. Most Internet-based child pornography originates from Websites hosted around the globe, making it increasingly difficult to police. However, in 2008, a global cyber-policing effort, spanning five countries and three continents, uncovered one of the largest child pornography rings to date. In a secret chat room, offenders were trading images of over 400,000 children. From this global raid, 22 individuals were arrested worldwide, and 20 children were rescued from dangerous situations. As evidenced by this global effort, child pornography is a worldwide issue, and as the Internet grows, law enforcement strategies will revolutionize the way such issues are handled.

Child prostitution has also become a national and international concern. Research on this subject is still lacking, but in the United States alone, it is estimated that upwards of 300,000 children are at risk of becoming exploited for child prostitution. Though seen as a social problem in the United States, in other parts of the world, sex trafficking and child sex tourism make the issue of child prostitution a pandemic.

Though the number of child prostitutes varies and is difficult to estimate, estimates from the United Nations Children's Fund (UNICEF), the International Labour Organization (ILO), and other research shows that the numbers are quite high. For instance, in Cambodia, approximately one-third of all prostitutes are under the age of 18, while in Thailand about 40 percent of all prostitutes are children. In Peru, approximately 500,000 children are child prostitutes, and in Brazil there are estimates of child prostitution that range from as low as 250,000 to as high as 2 million. It is estimated that 1 million children per year worldwide are drawn into the sex tourism industry. Usually, the patrons of the child sex tourism industry are men who travel specifically to engage in sexual activity with minors. These men come from all income brackets, and most originate from North America and western Europe. International efforts to stop the child prostitution industry have been unsuccessful. While some countries have written legislation making these acts illegal, they are often unenforced, especially when the perpetrator is from a foreign country. There is some evidence to suggest that law enforcement officials, corrupted by the industry, procure children for prostitution and often protect the brothels and pimps for whom these children work. The United States has passed legislation targeting sex tourists when it can be proven that the individual had the intent to engage in sexual acts with minors while traveling abroad.

Noncontact Offenses

Voyeurism and exhibitionism are common noncontact acts most often committed by men. Voyeurism is the act of watching or spying on someone without their consent and when they have a reasonable expectation of privacy, whether during undressing, bathing, or engaging in sexual activity. Although research suggests that voyeuristic acts can be traced back to biblical times, it is only in recent years that legislation specifically targeting this behavior has been passed. Canadian legislation passed a law criminalizing voyeurism in 2005. Nonconsensual voyeurism became illegal in the United Kingdom in 2004, and the U.S. federal government passed the Video Voyeurism Prevention Act of 2004, although many U.S. states had unlawful surveillance statutes long before this time. It is difficult to estimate the prevalence and incidence of voyeurism, mostly because it is often unknown to victims.

Exhibitionism

Exhibitionism is the showing of one's genitals or private parts to a person or people who do not consent. While it is extremely difficult to estimate the number of exhibitionists, some researchers suggest that it is one of the most common sexual offenses. Interestingly, outside of North America and western Europe, it appears that exhibitionism is extremely rare, if nonexistent. However, research has yet to determine why this is the case.

Myths About Male Sex Offenders

It is often believed that sex offenders have a very high recidivism rate. This myth often provides the justification for blanket community-based policies. However, researchers estimate that the average re-offense rate for another sex offense is less than 20 percent over five years and is lower than typical recidivism rates for non–sex offenders. Because sex offenders are not all the same, recidivism rates differ depending on the sample one studies. A recent meta-analysis found that rapists had a higher re-offense rate (19 percent) when compared with child molesters (13 percent) after five years. Recidivism rates also vary by victim characteristics. One study found that individuals with extra-familial male victims have a higher re-offense rate (35 percent) than for incest offenders (9 percent). In addition, many people believe that sex crimes are increasing each year, but in actuality the rate of known rapes has decreased slightly each year since the early 1990s.

It is often thought that sex offenders only commit sex crimes, but this is often not the case. In fact, research suggests that sex offenders are generalists in their criminal behavior; this would include sexually based and other crimes. For instance, a national study found that 12 percent of incarcerated rapists had previous sex crimes on their record, whereas 61 percent had a conviction for another type of felony.

Community Protection Laws

Regardless of the many myths surrounding this population, policies have been in place since the early 1990s that aim to protect communities from sex offenders. These laws were initially designed to target dangerous, repeat offenders, but over time the number and scope of individuals mandated to abide by such policies has dramatically increased. It is important to note that community protection laws in the United States differ significantly from those in use in other countries. While many countries utilize sex offender registries for law enforcement purposes, the United States is the only country known to emphasize community notification.

Registration laws require registered sex offenders to report their address and other demographic information to local and/or state law enforcement. Community notification laws were created after citizens argued that registration was not enough to protect children. As such, state and local law enforcement agencies are required to provide notification to the public when certain sex offenders move into or reside in a neighborhood. Passive notification includes the Internet sex offender registries that are available online for every state. Active notification requires officials to notify communities, whether via the newspaper, knocking door-to-door, sending out letters, or placing flyers in the community.

Recent legislation also includes the use of residency restrictions that deny sex offenders from living within a certain distance from places where children congregate. These sites may include schools, parks, daycare centers, malls, churches, and even school bus stops. Distances vary from 500 feet to 2,500 feet. Many sex offenders are also mandated to global positioning system (GPS) tracking allowing officials to know their whereabouts at all times. These community protection laws are rightfully justified but cost millions of dollars to enforce. Despite the well-intentioned goals of this type of legislation, there is mixed empirical evidence to suggest that it reduces recidivism.

Treatment

Sex offenders who attend and complete community-based treatment are less likely to re-offend than individuals who do not. Today's treatments include cognitive-behavioral and relapse-prevention techniques, but effectiveness depends on factors such as type of sex offender, type of treatment, and the community agencies involved in the effort. Individuals who drop out of treatment are at an increased likelihood of offending.

Research on this population is nascent but growing. From what researchers have learned over the last two decades is that, while some sex offenders are extremely dangerous, the majority are not likely to reoffend, especially when provided with community-based treatment. Current legislation is intended to assist in the prevention effort, but results on effectiveness are mixed. The field of research is still growing, but it has come a long way in understanding the etiology of offending behavior.

See Also: Megan's Law; Rape, Incidence of; Rape, Legal Definitions of; Rape, Prosecution Rates of; Sex Offenders, Female.

Further Readings

Association for the Treatment of Sexual Abusers. "Reducing Sexual Abuse through Treatment and Intervention With Abusers." Beaverton, OR: Policy and Position Statement, 1996.
Center for Sex Offender Management. "Myths and Facts about Sex Offenders." http://www.csom.org/pubs /mythsfacts.html (accessed July 2010).
Greenfeld, L. "Sex Offenses and Offenders: An Analysis of Data on Rape and Sexual Assault." Washington, DC: U.S. Department of Justice, Bureau of Justice Statistics, 1997.
Hanson, R. et al. "Predicting Relapse: A Meta-Analysis of Sexual Offender Recidivism Studies." *Journal of Consulting and Clinical Psychology*, v.66 (1998).
U.S. Federal Bureau of Investigation. "Human Trafficking— FBI Initiatives." http://www.fbi.gov/hq/cid/civilrights /trafficking_initiatives.htm (accessed July 2010).

Alissa R. Ackerman
University of California, Merced

Sex Workers

Sex workers are individuals associated with the multibillion-dollar sex industry that encompasses live sex shows, sex shops, strip clubs, escort services, phone sex, sex tourism, massage parlors, exotic dancing, prostitution, and pornography.

The sex industry is a malleable and changing sector that is influenced by political, economic, cultural, and geographic contexts. Sex work occurs in a wide range of venues that represent different activities and relationships, with differing degrees of danger, coercion, and consent. Therefore, a simplistic definition of sex work as an activity of selling sex in exchange for money, drugs, or other agreed-upon commodities fails to represent its complexity.

The language used in reference to sex work varies and reflects larger societal discourses. Sex work has been described as a health issue, a sin, female oppression, exploitation, domestic violence, a choice, a crime, a lethal form of violence against women, a human rights violation, and a form of employment. Sex workers operate globally; however, because activities related to sex work are outlawed in many countries, accurate figures on numbers of individuals involved, income, types of activities, and migration patterns are imprecise. Despite the visibility of one segment of sex workers (prostitutes, who are street workers), the majority is largely an invisible, nonhomogenous, marginalized population. The literature on sex work allots disproportional attention to some actors such a prostitutes and less to customers, managers, or transgendered workers.

Sex Work Discourses

The subject of sex work and sex workers is contested and diverse because the issues related to sex work and sex workers are represented by ideological and conceptual differences that shape the competing discourses. The oppression/abolitionist discourse represents sex work as a form of violence against women and the abusive exercise of men's power over women that is characteristic of patriarchal societies. Proponents contend that genuine consent is never given for engaging in sex work because sex workers are coerced by "third parties" who exploit them for personal financial gain.

Women advocates who hold this perspective object to the term *sex work* because it serves to mask the harassment, exploitation, and brutality that characterizes the relationships in this context. For this group, the term *sex work* implies vocational choice that misrepresents an essentially oppressive relationship as an employer–employee relationship; therefore, they oppose decriminalization of sex work. Advocates argue that although legal support of sex work might normalize the "sale of sex," it would neither reduce the trauma and stigma faced by sex workers nor legitimize women in the sex trade.

For example, they point out that in countries where prostitution is legal, contempt for women in the sex industry remains evident and acceptance of sex work does not translate to inclusion and respect of sex workers. Furthermore, by co-modifying and exploiting women and children, decriminalization would provide an enabling environment for traffickers. Their advocacy agenda supports the penalization of third parties as an important step in the abolition of the sex industry.

Sex workers demonstrating for better working conditions at the 2009 Marcha Gay in Mexico City. Despite the visibility of prostitutes who are street workers, the majority of sex workers are largely invisible, nonhomogenous and marginalized.

Libertarian and sex workers themselves coined the terms *sex work* and *sex workers* to redefine the selling of sexual services from a psychological or social characteristic of women to a form of employment for men and women. Representing sex work as a form of employment is a necessary beginning step in advocating for human and labor rights of sex workers at a local, national, and global level. When the selling of sexual services is considered work, then those involved are empowered to articulate their needs within the legitimate context of workplace rights. Viewed from the perspective of agency, sex workers in various countries have created organizations that fight for human rights and challenge stigmatization and discriminatory laws.

Because this group views sex work as a means of making a living, they support the decriminalization of sex work and argue that the selling of sexual services is not significantly different from the selling of, for example, legal or health services. The positioning of sex work as a contract for service, as inevitable, and as an exercise of free will by women in search of a vocation has resulted in many societies globally decriminalizing prostitution. Numerous arguments in support of the legalization of prostitution are offered in the literature. Criminalization drives prostitution underground and limits the ability of women to establish safe places to procure and to provide services. Decriminalization, on the other hand, facilitates societal control of human immunodeficiency virus (HIV) and provides safer working conditions with reduced police harassment and diminished stigma associated with women in prostitution. However, both the oppressive/abolitionist and libertarian discourse are unidimensional and fall short of representing the complexity of sex work. Sex workers operate in varying structural conditions, encounter a range of working conditions, and have various experiences in relation to satisfaction, subordination, and personal agency.

Why Individuals Engage in Sex Work

Historically, social and psychological theorists focused on discovering why women engage in sex work. Much of the work has been done in the area of prostitution, which is generally understood to be an abnormality precipitated by dysfunctional childhood environments. Key antecedents for women entering prostitution were broadly explored in 1980s, when female sex workers were described as possessing a psychological paralysis produced by past circumstances that resulted in immobility, victimization, and feelings of hopelessness. These antecedents include poverty, childhood physical and sexual abuse, race, ethnicity, and lack of sustainable options. The racialization of prostitution is evident in indigenous First Nations women in Canada, Karen women in Thailand, and Mayan women in Mexico. Nevertheless, causal links among these factors have not been verified as necessary or sufficient reasons for females entering the sex trade. Unanswered questions remain, for it is noted that many others exposed to similar life circumstances do not engage in prostitution-related behaviors.

Increasingly, sex work has developed a transnational character. Many women enter the sex trade willingly as migrant sex workers. Due to cultural, social, and employment barriers in their home countries, sex workers choose to travel globally to improve their economic status. For some, engaging in sex work offers escape from oppressive, poverty-defined home environments and an opportunity to support family members in their home countries. However, some advocates of sex workers question whether individuals freely choose sex work, because when economic opportunities within a home country are limited, transnational sex work is not a choice based on credible options but an alternative that is measured against other oppressive alternatives. Another aspect of migrant sex work is trafficking. Trafficked sex workers are individuals who are transported for profit, without their consent, and kept in sex work and/or other forms of labor by threats, blackmail, or abuse. Although reliable statistics on this group are impossible to obtain, trafficking is widely considered to be a modern-day form of slavery that is a human rights violation.

Advocacy

Although female sex workers are often portrayed as the "othered women" who live outside societal prescriptions of acceptable reproductive and family roles, contemporary feminists guard against denouncing sex workers because it imposes an ethnocentric bias on circumstances that are foreign to most middle-class Western feminists. Instead, advocates call for strategies that ensure safety and human rights. Attention directed to sex workers has historically been oriented toward health or social problems associated with sex work. Women with intense and high exposure to their clients are at high risk for rape and physical assault. Health issues include their susceptibility to HIV and other sexually transmitted diseases. Also, women in prostitution report a profound sense of worthlessness and experience psychological symptoms such as dissociation, post-traumatic stress disorder, depression, anxiety, flashbacks, numbing, and irritability. Fear of arrest and social contempt are factors in these women's reluctance to seek shelter and medical help.

Women who attempt to exit sex work face numerous barriers. These include a lack of emergency services such as shelters and detoxification facilities, as well as a dearth of long-term supports such as safe long-term housing, addiction recovery centers, vocational training, peer support, outreach, and treatment for debilitating mental health issues. Women who are visible minorities frequently encounter a paucity of culturally sensitive advocacy services. Migrant sex workers face additional barriers related to immigration laws. However, regardless of the perspective, there is consensus that sex workers are an "at-risk" population who should minimally be guaranteed full human rights and supported with employment and vocational training that offers viable alternatives.

See Also: Prostitution, Legal; Reproductive and Sexual Health Rights; Trafficking, Women and Children.

Further Readings

Bloch, A. "Victims of Trafficking or Entrepreneurial Women? Narratives of Post-Soviet Entertainers in Turkey." *Canadian Woman Studies*, v.22/4 (2003).

Bowen, R. *From the Curb: Sex Workers Perspectives on Violence and Domestic Trafficking.* Vancouver: British Columbia Coalition on Experiential Women, 2006.

Raphael, J. *Listening to Olivia: Violence, Poverty, and Prostitution.* Lebanon, NH: Northeastern University Press, 2004.

Trepanier, M. "Trafficking in Women for Purposes of Sexual Exploitation: A Matter of Consent?" *Canadian Woman Studies*, v.22/4 (2003).

Weitzer, R. "Sociology of Sex Work." *Annual Review of Sociology*, v.35 (2009).

Constance Anne Barlow
Janki Shankar
University of Calgary

Sexting

As a consequence of advances in mobile technologies, people were provided the ability to send text messages via cellular telephones. As mobile technologies continued to evolve, the "texting" of images and video became readily available as well. While most messages are benign, the act of sending sexually explicit messages, images, or videos via cellular telephone has been dubbed "sexting." The practice can be dangerous because the images are explicit and sent in real time. New technologies present opportunities to disseminate widely one's private conversations or images, a practice in which the original party has no control.

Although sexting is legal among consenting adults, the behavior among teenagers has become a significant concern. In some instances, sexting is seen as high-tech flirting, whereas in other, more disturbing scenarios, the purpose is unequivocally to harass and bully others. In either case, parents, school administrators, and law enforcement are concerned, and multiple cases have resulted in the charging of teenagers under child pornography statutes. The bringing of formal charges has stirred considerable debate over the most appropriate way to handle the issue. In 2009, the American Civil Liberties Union filed a lawsuit against a Pennsylvania district attorney arguing that child pornography laws were now being utilized to prosecute the individuals they were designed to protect.

In at least three states, prosecutors have charged teens for sexting. In Pennsylvania, six students were charged after three female students sent nude images to three male students. In Ohio, a female student was adjudicated an "unruly child" after texting a nude image of herself to her former boyfriend who then circulated the image around school after an argument. An Indiana teen was charged with a felony after sending an image of his genitals to female classmates. Many are concerned that the problem has progressed beyond the control of adults. However, others are not convinced.

While it has been suggested that one in five high school students has sent an explicit photo, one researcher believes these claims are out of proportion. As part of the Digital Youth Report survey, C. J. Pascoe interviewed 80 teens, and stated that her findings did not equal what many others believe.

Regardless of the actual amount of sexting that occurs, some school administrators and lawmakers believe that legislation has not caught up with advances in technology, and many do not believe that the act of consensual sexting should result in the teens having the label *sex offender* placed on them. Efforts to streamline the two have begun, and numerous states have initiated changes in legal statutes to decriminalize the use of sexting among teens. In 2009, Vermont, Ohio, and Utah began changing legislation to decriminalize consensual texting among teens.

See Also: Adolescence; Crime Victims, Female; Megan's Law; Pedophilia Online; Pornography, Portrayal of Women in; Pornography Produced by Women; Reproductive and Sexual Health Rights.

Further Readings

American Civil Liberties Union. "ACLU Sues Wyoming County D.A. for Threatening Teenage Girls With Child Pornography Charges Over Photos Of Themselves." http://www.aclu.org/technology-and-liberty/aclu -sues-wyoming-county-da-threatening-teenage-girls -child-pornography-charg (accessed January 2010).

Associated Press, "Utah Lawmakers OK Bill on 'Sexting.'" http://www.ksl.com/?nid=148&sid=5823252 (accessed January 2010).

Irvine, Martha. "Porn Charges for 'Sexting' Stir Debate." Associated Press. http://www.msnbc.msn.com/id /29017808 (accessed January 2010).

The National Campaign to Prevent Teen and Unplanned Pregnancy and CosmoGirl.com. "Sex and Tech: Results From a Survey of Teens and Young Adults." http://www .thenationalcampaign.org/sextech/PDF/SexTech _Summary.pdf (accessed January 2010).

Alissa R. Ackerman
University of California

Sexual Harassment

Sexual harassment is now understood as a social problem embedded in notions of intimidation and power between individuals in the workplace. These defining characteristics properly frame sexual harassment outside of any discussion of innocent misunderstanding, misplaced expressions of attraction, or simple gender differences.

In the earliest articulations of sexual harassment, before a definitive legal standard was set in the mid-1980s, incidents of sexual harassment were most often described in terms of the power differences attributed to males and females in the public sphere of the labor market as well as the domestic sphere of home and hearth. Within this theoretical frame, sexual harassment most often becomes an issue whenever a woman's work is adversely impacted by employers, co-workers, or even subordinates who inappropriately regard her as an object of sexual attention rather than a colleague in the workplace.

The study of sexual harassment from a social science or humanities standpoint tends to differ from the legal standpoint because of these particular details. The issues of accountability and personal agency differ across these fields, and the consequences under the law are much more concrete in application, certainly, than the more philosophical-oriented discourses often found in purely academic literature and research. Nonetheless, sexual harassment continues to be largely defined and understood as an issue of discrimination of men toward women, and under the law, it is, more often than not, interpreted using male experience as a reference.

Over the years, however, sexual harassment has come to be more properly understood as a twisted implementation of power directed against an individual regardless of gender or sexuality, thus making it clear that sexual harassment occurs whenever inappropriately sexual conduct complained of is sufficiently "severe, pervasive, and unwelcome" in nature as it occurs in the workplace or under the auspices of a relationship governed by workplace dynamics, as was articulated in the landmark case *Meritor v. Vinson* in 1986.

Sexual Harassment in Law and Public Policy

On a national level, the public debates surrounding political celebrities such as former Senator Robert Packwood, former U.S. President William J. Clinton, and current presiding U.S. Supreme Court Justice Clarence Thomas shed light on what constitutes sexual harassment in the workplace, or at least which behaviors are not considered appropriate for the workplace and could lead someone to be sanctioned for such behavior. Sexual harassment in the workplace is a specific form of sex discrimination that specifically violates Title VII of the Civil Rights Act of 1964. Claims of sexual harassment in schools must be asserted under Title IX of the Education Amendments of 1972. The U.S. Supreme Court has ruled that schools have an obligation under Title IX to prevent and address harassment against students, whether perpetrated by peers or by employees of the school system.

In those instances where the plight of female sexual harassment victims has been purposefully given consideration, the focus has quite often been on the issues of credibility and consent on the part of the female victim rather than a pointed examination of the behavior of male offenders and the institutions that have been socially constructed, such that they may be said to foster incidents of sexual harassment.

This is why so much of the research and writing on this subject uses the language of individuals having been "targeted" for sexual harassment. This language emphasizes both the unequal power dynamics inherent in sexual harassment as well as the purposeful nature of the offense. Thus, the overriding theme in most of the literature to be found on sexual harassment shares the common theme that sexual harassment is behavior that is unwelcome or unsolicited, sexual in nature, and is deliberate or repeated.

The "Reasonable Woman" Standard

One question that has arisen on this issue is whether we should focus on the woman's view or that of the alleged male offender in cases assessing complaints of sexual harassment. This is called the "reasonable woman" standard, as set forth by the Ninth Circuit Court in the case *Ellison v. Brady* in 1991. This standard advances the argument that sexual harassment can only be accurately understood from a woman's perspective, which is necessarily different from a man's perception of how this behavior is actually experienced, moving attention away from any defense asserting how well intentioned or innocuous the behavior at issue was.

The "reasonable woman" standard has been criticized for several reasons, one of which is that there is no universal understanding of a woman's experience and, therefore, this standard cannot be fairly applied in all cases of sexual harassment.

In *Meritor Savings Bank v. Vinson*, the Supreme Court of the United States outlined two circumstances when sexual harassment may be legally recognized. The first is called "quid pro quo" sexual harassment. This involves a grant or denial of benefits rendered based upon an employee's response to unwelcome sexual advances, requests for sexual favors, and so forth. To successfully make this claim, a woman who has been sexually harassed must be able to demonstrate a substantive connection between some type of negative occupational result and her refusal to submit to a supervisor's sexual advances.

Hostile or Abusive Working Environments

The second circumstance that may give rise to a claim of sexual harassment is an employee's contention that "discrimination based upon sex has created a hostile or abusive working environment," as stated in *Meritor*. As such, sexual harassment can be perpetrated by either coworkers or supervisors, because to commit this type of harassment, the actor need have no greater power in the workplace than the victim. Donald Petersen and Douglas Massengill have explained that there is no direct threat by a supervisor that the victim will lose a position, pay, or benefits in a hostile environment harassment claim. *Meritor* is most celebrated, then, for the Court's ruling regarding hostile environment sexual harassment. This landmark case shifted the burden to respondents accused of sexual harassment having to explain their behavior without forcing complainants to provide tangible evidence beyond the complaint of having their working environment tainted to such an extent that he or she was unable to properly perform his or her duties of employment.

This change in the standard of proof would seem to have been made with an understanding that occurrences of sexual harassment are, more often than not, a subjective assessment of events because the behavior at issue is most likely to occur in circumstances in which there may be few witnesses to the incident(s) except the perpetrator and the victim and individuals may differ as to how one should interpret the events at issue. The Court's ruling was quite specific in articulating the standard of workplace dynamics that were unacceptable, therefore successfully shifting the focus back to how individuals are to behave toward one another in the workplace, eschewing the personal relationships of the respondents at issue.

This case also presented a clearly articulated standard of behavior for employers to enforce and effectively implement to avoid being held liable for the behavior of their employees under the auspices of their employment contracts. Legal doctrine since 1990 has further clarified the standards articulated in *Meritor* by finding employers liable for the action of coworkers that result in hostile environment working conditions for both female and male workers (*Faragher v. City of Boca Raton*, 524 U.S. 775 in 1998; *Burlington Industries, Inc. v. Ellerth*, 524 U.S. 742 in 1998, and *Oncale v. Sundowner Offshore Services, Inc.* 523 U.S. 75 in 1998).

More recently in 2002, the Ninth Circuit case of *Rene v. MGM Grand Hotel, Inc.*, considered the issue of same-sex claims of sexual harassment predicated on the basis of sexuality. Medina Rene claimed that he had been sexually harassed by male coworkers because he was gay. Although this case was summarily dismissed by a district court judge, the Ninth Circuit Court of Appeals reversed this decision, ruling that "Title VII forbids offensive touching (a physical assault of a sexual nature) whether the attack is performed by members of the same sex or by members of the opposite sex." This court also held, however, that "a person's sexual orientation is irrelevant to the analysis." The U.S. Supreme Court chose not to consider this case in 2002.

Sexual Harassment in Academic Research

Most existing research on sexual harassment in the labor market focuses largely upon gender and power dynamics as they manifest themselves within the workplace. The elements of gender, class, race, age, marital status, and occupation emerge as particularly relevant to any serious study of sexual harassment in the labor market as well.

One explanation for sexual harassment behaviors posits that such incidents are extreme expressions of gender dominance in the workplace. This explanation for sexual harassment is based upon gender socialization that characterizes men as aggressive or dominant and women who are expected to be submissive or nonassertive as agents in the workplace. According to this perspective, sexual harassment is about power—gaining power or retaining power over subordinates by those in positions of authority. Moreover, this theoretical framework highlights the means by which men in privileged positions have reinforced their privilege and, as Irene Padavic and James Orcutt

have argued, "maintained dominance over women at work and in society more generally." In short, sexual harassment is intended as a pejorative check on women's agency in the workplace.

The second explanation for sexual harassment one will find in much of the research and writing on this topic utilizes the theoretical framework of sex-role spillover. This explanation, first articulated by Barbara Gutek, advances the theory that a woman is perceived only in relation to her socially prescribed gender role in whatever occupation she may be pursuing, particularly in the face of male-gendered occupational norms. The sex-role spillover explanation of sexual harassment locates the main crux of this social problem in the carryover into the workplace of gender-based, and therefore female-subordinating, expectations. In this context, men perceive women solely in terms of their gendered status in society and, therefore, experience resentment because women are perceived as violating the public sphere dominated by men, having wrongfully left their proper role in the domestic sphere.

One manifestation of this ideological stance is occupational segregation, that is, women are relegated to occupations that accentuate their ascribed status as caretakers in society. This theoretical explanation for sexual harassment behaviors is most applicable to the hostile environment harassment scenario because it highlights the ways in which the actual performance of a woman's job is made more difficult by the very occupational beliefs and practice we have sanctioned as acceptable organizational practices and policies, which arguably exist apart from the workers themselves. Each of these cases provide evidence that women who are in male-dominated professions are most likely to be targeted for sexual harassment because they have most encroached upon the public sphere (in comparison to those women in traditionally female occupations in the public sphere) that has, heretofore, been dominated by men and constructed with the values and identity politics of male values in mind.

The current literature on sexual harassment that takes place within specific organizations and differing workplace environments seeks to answer questions related to institutional forces that may foster or inhibit incidents of sexual harassment. Several studies also seek to identify those factors endemic to organizational structure that may perpetuate conditions which allow sexual harassment behaviors to flourish;

for example, the gendered nature of particular jobs or the workplace setting overall.

Survey studies of sexual harassment are largely based upon scenarios described to students and/or employees that seek to ascertain what scenarios, in their collective opinion, constitute sexual harassment. Studies such as this have established that (1) women are more apt to be sensitive to and distinguish acts of sexual harassment from mere gender discrimination than men, (2) women are likely to identify more serious forms of sexual harassment than men, and (3) that both of these seem to be the case regardless of age.

Sexual harassment continues to be a social problem that receives prolific treatment in the legal arena and in scholarly studies of the workplace. There is still much to be learned about sexual harassment as we seek to find ways to curtail its occurrence in the workplace, in schools, and in public policy considerations. We should continue to ensure that academics and lawyers continue to work in concert as we seek to understand all of the facets which both foster discourage the targeting of persons for sexual harassment.

See Also: Bullying in the Workplace; Sex Offenders, Male; Sexual Orientation–Based Legal Discrimination: Outside United States; Sexual Orientation–Based Legal Discrimination: United States.

Further Readings

Baird, Carol L., et al. "Gender Influence on Perceptions of Hostile Environment Sexual Harassment." *Psychology Reports*, v.77 (1995).

Burlington Industries, Inc. v. Ellerth, 524 U.S. 742 (1998).

Davis v. Monroe County Board of Education, 67 U.S.L.W. 4329 (1999).

Ellison v. Brady, 924 F.2d 872 (9th Cir. 1991).

Faragher v. City of Boca Raton, 524 U.S. 775 (1998).

Flax, J. *The American Dream in Black and White: The Clarence Thomas Hearings.* Ithaca, NY: Cornell University Press, 1998.

Gebser v. Lago Vista Independent School District, 524 U.S. 274 (1998).

Gutek, Barbara A. *Sex and the Workplace.* Hoboken, NJ: Jossey-Bass, 1985.

Harris v. Forklift Systems, Inc., 510 U.S. 17 (1993).

Henson v. Dundee, 682 F.2d 897 (1982).

Jones v. Clinton. U.S. District Court, Arkansas, Western Division (1997).

Juliano, Ann C. "Did She Ask for It: The 'Unwelcome' Requirement in Sexual Harassment Cases." *Cornell Law Review*, v.77 (1992).

Kohlman, Marla H. "Spotlight: Anita Hill, Feminist Praxis Today and Yesterday." In Karen O'Connor, ed., *Gender and Women's Leadership: A Reference Handbook*, Thousand Oaks, CA: Sage, 2010.

MacKinnon, Catharine A. and Reva B. Siegel. *Directions in Sexual Harassment Law*. New Haven, CT: Yale University Press, 2004.

Meritor Savings Bank, FSB v. Vinson, 477 U.S. 57 (1986).

MGM Grand Hotel, LLC v. Medina Rene, 538 U.S. 922 (2003).

Oncale v. Sundowner Offshore Services, Inc. 523 U.S. 75 (1998).

Padavic, Irene, and James D. Orcutt. "Perceptions of Sexual Harassment in the Florida Legal System." *Gender & Society* (October 1997).

Paludi, M. and C. A. Paludi, Jr. *Academic and Workplace Sexual Harassment*. Westport, CT: Praeger, 2003.

Petersen, D. and D. Massengill. "Same Sex Sexual Harassment: Is It Actionable Under the Civil Rights Act?" *Journal of Individual Employment Rights*, v.5.2 (1996).

Rene v. MGM Grand Hotel Inc, 305 F.3d 1061 (2002).

Stockdale, Margaret S. "What We Know and What We Need to Learn About Sexual Harassment." In Margaret Stockdale, ed., *Sexual Harassment in the Workplace*. Thousand Oaks, CA: Sage, 1996.

Marla H. Kohlman
Kenyon College

Sexual Orientation

Sexual orientation typically describes an individual's emotional and/or physical attraction to others with respect to sex or gender. Generally accepted to refer to an individual's exclusive attraction to men, women, or both, academic studies often reflect that sexual orientation is better represented as a dynamic continuum in which individuals may be attracted to a particular person in a given situation regardless of gender. Women who date and/or have sex exclusively with other women often identify as "lesbian," although sometimes the more general "gay" is used. Women who are attracted to both men and women consider themselves "bisexual," although they may also identify themselves as straight or lesbian, depending on the situation.

Ideas regarding female sexual orientation vary around the world. There's also a greater acceptance for women's various sexual identities. Still, scores of conservative activists stand in staunch opposition to rights based on sexual orientation, especially in Western cultures where ideas of sexuality are more open to debate. Many cultural critics and feminist scholars contend attacks made on alternative sexualities are based on gender biases toward women. Because discrimination regarding nonheterosexual identity is often viewed as a form of social control over women and their sexuality—or, in the case of men, a form of control aimed at keeping them from behaving in a womanly manner—some sex researchers have recently advanced arguments that women's sexual experiences and desires are key to understanding sexual orientation from a scientific perspective.

The History of the Idea of "Sexual Orientation"

When the term *sexual orientation* was first coined in an anonymous German pamphlet in 1869, it referred to a particular type of man who was oriented toward sex with other men. Although homosexuality existed prior to the argument presented in the pamphlet, it was not widely held that "homosexual" was an identity category similar to race or sex. Instead, same-sex activity was either not conceived of at all or was seen as something any person was capable, depending on the culture. The term *lesbian* is believed to have originated in 1890, but not as an identity category. It was, rather, an adjective for a type of erotic stimulation in which some women engaged. By the 1920s, the word became commonly used as an identity category, especially in Western cultures.

This reconceptualization of homosexuality was largely accepted by mental health communities in Europe and the United States and was processed as a mental disorder for men. Women's sexuality was largely ignored, as females were not seen as having any kind of sexual orientation—even though gender identity disorders, conceived of as biological females unnaturally behaving as men, were recognized. The idea of female sexuality began to change in the 1920s in many parts of the world, and notions that women have sexual orientations, whether they are negatively or positively accepted, continue to advance today.

While a variety of cultural events around the world have continued to advance the rights of non-straight individuals, perhaps one of the most significant advances in sexual identity understanding came when the American Psychological Association removed homosexuality from its list of disorders in 1973. This action was encouraged, in part, by studies from Dr. Alfred Kinsey demonstrating that same-sex sexual behavior was more common than previously believed. Dr. Kinsey's findings had worldwide implications and mild effects on public policy in the United States, which is still viewed by many European countries as old-fashioned in its sexual beliefs.

Women and Sexual Orientation Around the World

Cultural perceptions of women and their sexual orientations—if women are considered by a culture to have a sexual orientation at all—continue to vary. For example, in many Middle Eastern countries, homosexual acts by men are considered crimes punishable by death. In comparison, people in these cultures are largely unaware that lesbianism exists and often have a hard time conceptualizing the notion of two women living together and being life partners. Still, this can vary widely by country. For instance, in Pakistan, women are allowed to have intimate relationships with other women so long as they don't intrude upon their wifely duties; women are expected to take a husband.

In some African nations, such as Nigeria, Kenya, and Cameroon, women are allowed to marry other women, but it is understood that one of the women in the relationship will take on a masculine role. In other African countries, such as Lesotho, same-sex sexual behavior is not seen as sexual at all since a penis is not involved. While sexual orientation in some African nations result in violence against lesbian women, including rape, other countries on the continent are quite progressive on the subject and accepting of the women. In fact, the South African government was the first country in the world to acknowledge sexual orientation as a protected classification.

In most Asian countries, homosexuality is strongly discouraged and is often hidden, even where it is legal. Homosexuality, though, is seen largely as a male construct, with India and China both particularly resistant to the idea that women may have nonheterosexual leanings. Japan, however, has acknowledged lesbianism on a social level since the 1920s. Many citizens in Japan and India, though, believe sexual orientation to be a symptom of Western imperialism. Japanese feminist movements often debate the necessity or obligation of including sexual orientation as part of their mission. Attitudes and perceptions toward women's sexual orientation in South America vary widely across the continent, although some cultures acknowledge dual genders that may lead to dual sexual attractions.

Western Cultures and Conceptions of Sexual Orientation

Historians and social scientists tend to agree that the meaning of "sexual orientation" seems to be in flux in Western cultures. Social and political movements aimed at sexual equality continue to represent sexual orientation as a fixed-identity category. In stark contrast, scholars are generating research findings suggesting sexual orientation, especially for women, is not a simple matter. Queer activists advance similar arguments about sexual relativity and fluidity, even if they are not always based upon the same evidence generated by scientists.

Still, all three groups would likely agree that sexual orientation is a social construct used to make sense of other people than it is a true representation of attraction, desire, and relational tendencies. Some advocates for gay, lesbian, bisexual, and transgender (GLBT) rights argue this is a dangerous stance, especially since conservative movements that seek to prevent same-sex relational rights posit that homosexuality is a choice and against religious doctrine. Cultural critics have noted that similar arguments derived from religious doctrine have been used to justify racism and sexism.

The current debate that continues in Western cultures is viewed as important to sexual orientation worldwide, since Western countries are seen as driving movements regarding sexual orientation. In many Third World countries, notions of diverse sexualities are introduced through activists or philanthropists visiting their nations.

Western countries generate virtually all research about sexual orientation and gender identity, influencing social and political forces in other cultures. Feminist scholars have argued that too much of this research is male focused and that it does not address the antiwoman biases that accompany rejection of nonheterosexual orientations. The scholars believe that the topic of female sexual desire has been and continues to be stifled, minimized, confused, or understudied. These contentions play out in many cultural practices, including "lesbian chic"—the idea that two women having physical relations is stimulating to heterosexual men—or "heteroflexible assumption"—masculine ideas that women can be turned straight or that lesbians, more so than gay male behavior, is temporary or the result of emotional angst. Cultural critics largely agree, however, that the next few decades will likely see many prejudices and assumptions fade as acceptance of diverse sexual orientations becomes more prominent worldwide.

See Also: Bisexuality; Coming Out; "Femininity," Social Construction of; Gay and Lesbian Advocacy; Heterosexuality; Lesbians.

Further Readings
Altman, D. *Global Sex*. Chicago: University of Chicago Press, 2002.
Diamond, L. M. *Sexual Fluidity: Understanding Women's Love and Desire*. Cambridge, MA: Harvard, 2008.
Drushel, B. and K. German, eds. *Queer Identities/Political Realities*. Newcastle, UK: Cambridge, 2009
Garnets, L. D. and D. C. Kimmel, eds. *Psychological Perspectives on Lesbian, Gay, and Bisexual Experiences*, 2nd Ed. New York: Columbia University, 2003.
Miller, N. *Out of the Past: Gay and Lesbian History From 1869 to the Present*. New York: Advocate, 2008.

Jimmie Manning
Northern Kentucky University

Sexual Orientation: Scientific Theories of Causation

Although causal theories of sexual orientation generally fall into two categories, biological/genetic and social/environmental, sexual orientation, as a complex, multidimensional construct, cannot be explained fully by either alone. Most theories are constrained by their operational definitions of sexual orientation (e.g., self-identification, sexual attraction, and/or sexual activity); evidence that sexual orientation is fluid, especially for women; and their emphasis on explaining homosexuality rather than heterosexuality, often grouping homosexuality and bisexuality together. Although women's sexual orientation has been the focus of scholarship, theories tend to focus on men's sexual orientation.

Genetic Theories

There are some interesting genetic theories about sexual orientation. These include homosexual men report more brothers who are homosexual than do heterosexual men and homosexual women report more sisters who are homosexual than do heterosexual women. Moreover, homosexual relatives of homosexual men and women tend to be from the maternal side, suggesting that homosexuality is X-chromosome linked, and some research reports greater maternal-line fecundity for homosexual than heterosexual men. Twin studies report sexual orientation concordance rates of 20–60 percent; concordance rates for monozygotic twins reared separately are similar to those for monozygotic twins raised together.

Biological theories highlight the relationship between prenatal hormones like androgens on early sexual differentiation of the brain and later sex-typed behavior such as gender nonconformity and homosexual orientation. Specifically, high prenatal androgen exposure is thought to be associated with homosexuality in women and heterosexuality in men, whereas low androgen exposure is associated with homosexuality in men and heterosexuality in women. Possibly the most studied are people with Congenital Adrenal Hyperplasia (CAH), which involves excessive prenatal testosterone production and consequent genital masculinization in genetic females. Longitudinal research demonstrates that girls with CAH display more male-typical toy preferences, play, and behaviors than non-CAH girls. One review of 18 studies from 1968 to 2007 found that homosexual and bisexual orientations were greater in women with CAH compared to non-CAH control groups, although most CAH women identified themselves as heterosexual. When orientation was specified as erotic imagery and sexual activity, greater homosexual and bisexual erotic imagery was evidenced

in CAH compared to non-CAH women. Other conditions investigated include Androgen Insensitivity Syndrome and 5α-Reductase Deficiency.

Parental Influence

Prenatal androgen influence on sexual orientation also has been investigated indirectly by testing for differences on physiological markers associated with prenatal androgen exposure. Markers include 2D:4D finger-length ratios, handedness, dermatoglyphics, autoacoustic emissions, and waist-to-hip ratios. For example, although ethnicity, height, method of measurement, and hand are important moderating factors, generally speaking, homosexual Caucasian women tend to show smaller right-hand 2D:4D ratios (typical of heterosexual men) than their heterosexual counterparts, and homosexual Caucasian men tend to display larger 2D:4D ratios (typical of heterosexual women) than their heterosexual counterparts.

A review of 20 studies found that both homosexual men and women display higher rates of nonrighthandedness than heterosexual men and women, respectively, although the relationship appears stronger in women than in men. Moreover, homosexual men show higher rates of nonrighthandedness and extreme righthandedness than heterosexual men. This relationship is complicated by recent evidence of an interaction between handedness and the fraternal birth order effect (i.e., homosexual men tend to report a larger number of older brothers than do heterosexual men). Here, nonrighthandedness and homosexual orientation appears restricted to men with no or few older brothers, whereas the presence of older brothers increases the odds of homosexual orientation predominantly among men with moderate righthandedness.

Explanations include the role of androgen receptor gene deficiencies associated with men's nonrighthandedness and the maternal immune system on homosexual orientation. According to this theory, the mother's immune system enacts a reaction against male-typical differentiation of the fetus's brain, specifically, the hypothalamus, which increases homosexual orientation for each successive male fetus. Early postmortem studies demonstrate smaller interstitial nucleus of the anterior hypothalamus in homosexual than heterosexual men, a site animal research suggests is important in sexual behavior.

Social and Environmental Theories

Social/environmental theories of sexual orientation range from psychoanalytic to social learning in nature. Dr. Sigmund Freud believed that all humans were bisexual to start but early experiences with parents influenced later homosexual or heterosexual orientation, primarily because of a domineering mother or an absent dominant father. More contemporary advocates emphasize external stressors, inadequate parenting, or same-sex role modeling as causes of homosexual orientation, although there is little evidence to supports this view. There also is little evidence that parental sexual orientation influences a child's preferences.

Learning theories stress rewards and reinforcement for early same-sex sexual encounters, especially at the time when sexual exploration occurs. More contemporary social theorists stress the role of gender nonconformity as a significant predictor of adult homosexual orientation, which has been linked to genetic and biological factors, as noted above. Daryl Bem's Exotic Becomes Erotic theory suggests that biological factors such as prenatal hormones influence childhood temperament rather than sexual orientation and that temperament leads to conforming or nonconforming gender behavior.

Gender-conforming children feel differently from opposite sex peers, and gender-nonconforming children feel differently from same-sex peers, which generates significant arousal that later becomes erotic in nature. Retrospective research demonstrates that homosexual men and women report feeling differently from same-sex peers in childhood, and personality research suggests varying degrees of gender nonconformity among homosexual and bisexual people. However, this inversion hypothesis is rejected by other social environmental theories, especially those explaining women's sexual orientation. Here researchers opt for a multiple-pathways perspective, drawing attention to the exclusivity of gender and sexuality, the indirect role of biology, the influence of higher education on homosexual experiences, lifespan changes, and sociocultural forces that determine how women's sexuality is experienced.

See Also: Bisexuality; Coming Out; "Femininity," Social Construction of; Gay and Lesbian Advocacy; Heterosexuality; Lesbians; Sexual Orientation.

Further Readings

Bem, Daryl. "Exotic Becomes Erotic: A Developmental Theory of Sexual Orientation." *Psychological Review*, v.103/2 (1996).

Ellis, Lee and Ashley Ames. "Neurohormonal Functioning and Sexual Orientation: A Theory of Homosexuality-Heterosexuality." *Psychological Bulletin*, v.101/2 (1987).

Peplau, Leticia and Linda Garnets. "A New Paradigm for Understanding Women's Sexuality and Sexual Orientation." *Journal of Social Issues*, v.56/2 (2000).

C. Werhun
University of Winnipeg

Sexual Orientation and Race

Sexual orientation and race are social identities that matter. Both identities often influence perceptions of who a person is and what a person does or should do. Both can motivate discrimination from others, and both are contextual. For example, a woman may pass as straight in one place and time, bisexual in another, and as a lesbian in another; Hispanic in one context, Native American in another, and Caucasian in another.

Sexual orientation and race also intersect in complex and indefinite ways. For instance, "gay" is sometimes referred to as a "white" label denoting sexual orientation. One reason for this denotation is that, in the United States, "gay marriage" and economic equality are often positioned as the most pressing issues for all same-sex desiring persons. However, these are often the most pressing issues for privileged, often white, gay persons. Consequently, other issues are overshadowed and disregarded because of the focus on marriage and economic equality—issues like racism, religion, homophobia, immigration, and homelessness.

A White Label

Another reason gay is sometimes considered a white label is that for many white people, sexual orientation is contingent upon object choice—for example, a man intimate with another man must be gay; with a woman, straight; and with men and women, bisexual. However, members of other races, particularly African American, Hispanic, and Middle Eastern populations, treat sexual orientation as not stemming from object choice but rather the position played in an intimate sexual encounter. For instance, a man who sexually penetrates a man is not necessarily gay (or homosexual), particularly because the man assumes an active, dominant role. However, the man being penetrated may be considered gay, because he assumes a passive, feminized role. Among these races, the dominant and masculine "penetrator" is, or could easily identify as, heterosexual. What makes this view of sexual orientation and race fascinating is that a man's self-identification of sexual orientation—"I am heterosexual"—can be conceived of differently by persons of different races based on his intimate acts with others (e.g., for some races, the penetrator is gay because of object choice; for other races, the penetrator is heterosexual because of role played). In this example, there are also devaluing assumptions about sex and gender as gayness is marked by passivity, femininity, and weakness, whereas the penetrator is "safe" from such ascriptions by being masculine and dominant.

Coming Out

Coming out of the closet—disclosing a same-sex sexual orientation—can function differently depending on race as well. Coming out often happens when a person says, "I am gay or a lesbian," when a person engages in intimate affairs with another person of the same sex, or when a person assumes a particular position in a sexual act. However, the statement "I will never get married [to someone of the other sex]" might indicate, for others, that the person possesses same-sex desire, for example, a woman who says "I will never get married" can indicate, for others, that she is a lesbian. And such assessment may be tied to race: it seems that white women—the founders of feminism—have created social spaces in which they can live free of being attached to men. However, women of other races (e.g., Hispanic, Middle Eastern) may still be perceived as being tied to men and the institution of marriage, not only out of religious and cultural obligation but also because feminism is predominantly a white philosophy and movement.

The Afro-Latino phenomenon of "machismo" illustrates ways in which sexual orientation and race can intersect as well. This phenomenon stems from racial and ethnic contexts that position men as the undisputed authorities of familial units, as the ones who make decisions, serve as the sole financial contributors, and exert authority over other family members. These men must also be heterosexual—that is, able to love, marry, protect, and/or procreate with someone of the opposite sex. A man who does not demonstrate such traits or who does not find persons of the opposite sex attractive may thus be marked as weak and inferior. Consequently, same sex–desiring men who reside in such Afro-Latino contexts may have different experiences of sexual orientation than men who do not come from similar situations.

The machismo phenomenon implicates women as well. In Afro-Latino contexts, women may be relegated to a necessary-but-secondary role in a family. They may not have a legitimate voice in decision making, be able to work outside the home, or be able to refuse servicing men. Additionally, women—should they be unable to marry a man or demonstrate maternal characteristics (e.g., childrearing)—may be evaluated as selfish by choosing to not contribute to family lineage or inferior by not being able to establish a relationship with a man.

See Also: Bisexuality; Coming Out; Critical Race Feminism; "Femininity," Social Construction of; Gay and Lesbian Advocacy; Heterosexuality; Lesbians; Sexual Orientation; Sexual Orientation–Based Legal Discrimination: United States; Sexual Orientation–Based Social Discrimination: United States.

Further Readings

Asencio, M., ed. *Latina/o Sexualities: Probing Powers, Passions, Practices, and Policies*. New Brunswick, NJ: Rutgers University Press, 2010.

Battle, J. and S. L. Barnes, eds. *Black Sexualities: Probing Powers, Passions, Practices, and Policies*. New Brunswick, NJ: Rutgers University Press, 2010.

Hawley, J. C., ed. *Postcolonial, Queer: Theoretical Intersections*. Albany: State University of New York Press, 2001.

Lester, T., ed. *Gender Nonconformity, Race, and Sexuality*. Madison: University of Wisconsin Press, 2002.

Yoshino, K. *Covering: The Hidden Assault on Our Civil Rights*. New York: Random House, 2006.

Tony E. Adams
Gerardo Moreno
Northeastern Illinois University

Sexual Orientation–Based Legal Discrimination: Outside United States

The discriminations faced by homosexuals and bisexuals in many member countries of the European Union (EU) are highlighted by the Council of Europe and other organizations. A turning point in the fight against discriminations happened in 1997, based on sexual orientation in Europe, due to the fact that, thanks to the amendments to the EC Treaty, this ground of discrimination was introduced in the EU-binding legislation (specifically the Council Directive 2000/78/EC of November 27, 2000, establishing a general framework for equal treatment in employment and occupation).

The implementation of this Directive in the 27 member states should grant minimum standards of protection against direct and indirect discriminations based on sexual orientation. In implementing the above-mentioned directive, member states went, in many cases, beyond the areas of employment, banning discriminations also in the access to public goods and services, housing, and social benefits. Nonetheless, a recent study on homophobia and discrimination on grounds of sexual orientation, accomplished by the European Union Fundamental Rights Agency following the request from the European Parliament, elicits that still many differences occur in treatment and protection by the law for homosexuals and bisexuals. For example, due to the fact that same-sex couples are still excluded from having marriage rights in many EU member states, unequal treatment of same-sex couples often occurs.

This discrimination urges the EU institutions to clarify the situation regarding the rights and benefits provided for spouses and partners under the 2004/38/EC Free Movement Directive of April 29, 2004, on the right of citizens of the European Union and their family members to move and reside freely within the territory of the Member States; the 2003/86/EC Family Reunification Directive of September 22, 2003, on the right to family reunification; and the 2004/83/EC Qualification Directive of April 29, 2004, on minimum standards for the qualification and status of third-country nationals, stateless persons as refugees, or as persons who otherwise need international protection and the content of the protection granted.

In spite of the harmonization of EU antidiscrimination laws in all member states, the freedom of expression of homosexuals is still restricted in some countries, where gay marches were not authorized by politicians, as happened in Poland in the early 21st century. In non-EU-eastern European and Balkan countries, the situation of sexual orientation–based legal discrimination is very controversial and could be ameliorated by the entry into the European Union, because antidiscrimination laws are a key element of the *acquis communautaire.* Homosexuality has gradually become legal since the years after the fall of the Berlin Wall in 1989, and, where existing, so-called sodomy laws have been abolished (e.g., Russia). Same-sex marriages are banned in all these countries. In some of them (Bosnia and Herzegovina, Georgia, Macedonia, Montenegro, and Serbia) some discriminations based on sexual orientation have started being punished by governments.

Africa

In Africa, there are very different legislations across countries. In most African states, homosexual acts are illegal and punished with imprisonment, while only a few of the remaining ones do not discriminate toward homosexuality and consider it legal. For example, in 1996 South Africa passed the first constitution in the world protecting sexual orientation and, in 2005 marriage rights were extended to same-sex couples. Moreover all antihomosexual discriminations are explicitly banned in South Africa, Mozambique, Réunion, and Mauritius. In South Africa and in Réunion, homosexuals are also allowed to serve in the military.

On the contrary, almost in the same period, the Nigerian government discriminated against both same-sex marriage and any form of advocacy of gays and lesbians, making the situation of homosexuals' defenders very critical. In addition, in North Africa there has been an increasing criminalization of homosexuality over the last several years. It is worth noting that male homosexuality is sometimes the only punished case or, at least, it is punished harsher than the female one or a different evidence system is applied. Nongovernmental organizations point out that discriminations in these countries happen in almost every field of life, and harassment by the police is also worrying. Even if penalties are harsher in those countries where a restricted version of the Shari`a is enforced (up to 14 years of prison and even death penalty and lashes), in many states the discriminatory laws are secular and have colonial origins. The same remarks can be made for the Middle East states as well, for example, Saudi Arabia, Iran, Yemen, and the United Arab Emirates, where homosexual acts can still be punished with the death penalty.

Asia

In south Asia, India and Nepal do not consider homosexuality as a crime anymore, respectively since 2009 and 2007. Additionally, the Nepalese Supreme Court extended discrimination laws to homosexuals.

In east Asia, with the exception of North Korea, homosexuality is legal, but antidiscrimination laws are nonexisistent. An attempt to introduce sexual orientation among the protected discrimination grounds failed in South Korea in 2007 under the pressure of the Protestant church.

The Americas

In most parts of Central and South America, homosexuality is legal. In some states only male homosexuality is punished, as, for example, is the case in Jamaica and Belize. Even if same-sex marriages are banned in almost all countries, a more tolerant attitude is slowly coming into being. This happened, for example, in Uruguay, which was the first Latin American country to recognize same-sex relationships by law at the national level in 2008. Many states (e.g., Chile, Ecuador, Mexico, Peru, Uruguay) have introduced national sexual orientation–based antidiscrimination laws.

The quick overview provided above can offer an understanding of the current situation regarding same-sex–based legal discrimination. It leads to the conclusion that in many countries, homosexuality is still considered illegal and punished harshly in instances where so-called sodomy laws persist and public order regulations are (mis)used for prosecuting homosexuals. This is particularly the case for male homosexuality. Regarding female homosexuality, a side effect of these legislations is the practice of forced marriages. When examining the legislations of the rest of the countries, where same-sex orientation is not criminalized and they do not have explicitly legal–based discriminations, only a minority of them has enforced pieces of law banning direct and indirect

discriminations. It goes without saying that this gap makes it extremely difficult to enforce equality and to effectively tackle discriminations based on sexual orientation.

See Also: Sexual Harassment; Sexual Orientation–Based Legal Discrimination: United States; Sexual Orientation–Based Social Discrimination: Outside United States; Sexual Orientation–Based Social Discrimination: United States.

Further Readings

European Union Fundamental Rights Agency. "Homophobia and Discrimination on Grounds of Sexual Orientation in the EU Member States Part I - Legal Analysis, 2008. http://fra.europa.eu/fraWebsite /research/publications/publications_per_year/2008/pub _cr_homophobia_0608_en.htm (accessed June 2010).

Human Rights Watch. "Together, Apart. Organizing around Sexual Orientation and Gender Identity Worldwide." 2009. http://www.hrw.org/en/reports /2009/06/10/together-apart (accessed June 2010).

Barbara Giovanna Bello
University of Milano

Sexual Orientation–Based Legal Discrimination: United States

Since the late 19th century, American federal and state governments, the U.S. Army and U.S. Navy, psychiatrists, and social conservatives have attempted to restrain same-sex desire, known pejoratively as sodomy and homosexuality. Homosexual, lesbian, gay, bisexual, and transgender (LGBT) individuals were oftentimes under investigation by police, psychiatrists, and courts. Only late in the 20th century did supportive communities overturn harmful labels and challenge the legal punishments and social stigmas imposed by unsupportive heterosexuals.

In early-20th-century Times Square in New York City, working- and middle-class men nurtured short-term sexual relationships, but their intimacy was threatened when the mayor and councilors ordered police to arrest men caught in same-sex liaisons. The encounters were considered sodomy and were illegal in the state. Although culprits were rarely convicted, gays faced loss of employment and emotional ties to their families if their names appeared in the newspaper.

Psychiatrists researched same-sex sexuality, and from 1880 to 1920, homosexuality was diagnosed as gender inversion—those who acted on homosexual impulses were deemed deficient in their understanding of gender norms. Gender inversion gave way to a discourse of homosexuality as a mental illness in the 1920s; psychiatrists listed it as a disorder until 1973.

Sodomy had been illegal in the Army and Navy since 1889, but before World War II, only a handful of convictions had been handed down—the military had to convene a court martial in cases of suspected sodomy, and the accused were innocent until proven guilty. From 1943 until the end of World War II, however, soldiers caught or suspected of homosexuality were sent immediately to military hospitals, were dishonorably discharged, and lost their veterans' benefits—47,000 personnel were discharged in this manner.

In the 1950s Cold War political climate, the federal government considered homosexuals vulnerable to blackmail and involvement with communists. Similar to what the military had done in the 1940s, the federal government terminated suspected homosexual civil servants. The police waited in notable gay meeting places or cruising areas in cities to arrest individuals engaged in same-sex activity, and although a charge for cruising rarely went to trial or was convicted, it did result in an arrest record, which could lead to dismissal from employment, eviction by unsympathetic superintendents, and severance of emotional ties to family and friends.

In the 1960s, the police and mafia controlled gay bars and restaurants through a system of bribes and payoffs. These spaces were thus vulnerable to raids, especially during elections, when politicians seeking election or reelection ordered these ghettos "cleaned up" as part of a larger agenda of "getting tough on crime and criminal behavior." As with being arrested in the park, an arrest in a gay bar endangered one's career and family ties. Resistance to state sanctions was steadily growing, however, culminating in the June 28, 1969, raid on the Stonewall Inn in New York City. The raid triggered organized resistance from patrons and led to an unprecedented number of public displays of solidarity in the following year.

Support Through Activism

In the aftermath of Stonewall, LGBT individuals forged activist ties, working to decriminalize sodomy in state laws, pass laws prohibiting discrimination in housing and employment, and lobby for investigation of police forces and liquor authorities. The justice system, however, resisted attempts by lesbians and gays litigating in divorce proceedings to seek custody and visitation rights, and in 1977, the first public rumblings of resistance to LGBT activism occurred after the passage of Miami's Gay Rights Ordinance. Singer Anita Bryant entered antigay activism with her "Save the Children" campaign, designed with the immediate purpose of repealing the statute and, in the long term, preserving the nuclear, Christian, and heterosexual family.

She found support from Jerry Falwell's recently formed Moral Majority, whose members considered lesbian and gay rights activists and feminists to be moral threats. Evangelical Christian author and psychologist James Dobson established Focus on the Family and the Family Research Council in 1977 and 1983, respectively, to monitor and report on policy options for "nuclear, Christian families." Bryant, Falwell, and Dobson thought of homosexuality as sexual behavior only and not deserving of legal protection. Whereas lesbians and gays and their feminist allies believed in a sexual revolution liberating Americans from fixed gender roles and sexual identities, their opponents believed that such propositions hurt children.

Republicans looked increasingly to Evangelical Christians for support, and Bryant, Falwell, and Dobson contributed to successful campaigns to repeal gay rights ordinances. The defeat of Jimmy Carter's Democrats in 1980 resulted in a new era of social conservatism. In response, lesbians and gays concentrated on accessing benefits enjoyed by heterosexual couples, such as renter's succession rights, hospital visitation rights, and healthcare benefits. The human immunodeficiency virus and acquired immune deficiency syndrome (HIV/AIDS) crisis, coupled with an average 7,000 reported incidents of homophobic violence per year, underlined the need for such rights.

Changing the Political and Social Climate

The election of Bill Clinton's Democrats in 1992 failed to substantially change the political and social climate. Instead of lifting the ban on lesbians and gays in the military, the Democrats adopted a compromise, "Don't

Ask, Don't Tell," policy. Court rulings in Hawaii and Alaska in favor of marriage equality were stalled by the passage in Congress of the 1996 Defense of Marriage Act. At the state level, however, Vermont, Maryland, Alaska, Oregon, California, Illinois, Pennsylvania, and Washington overturned previous bans on second-parent adoptions by lesbian and gay couples.

Despite a Republican government in Washington, D.C., civil unions or marriage equality was achieved in Vermont in 2000 (civil unions) and 2009 (marriage); Massachusetts in 2004 (marriage); New Jersey (civil unions), California (marriage), and Connecticut (repeal on ban of same-sex marriage) in 2008; Maine in 2009 (marriage); and the District of Columbia (marriage) and Hawaii (civil unions) in 2010. The States of Maryland, New York, and Rhode Island recognize as married those with licenses from outside of their respective jurisdictions.

However, the challenges to equality for lesbians, gays, bisexuals, and transgender people under the laws of the United States remain. In the 2008 presidential election, voters in California narrowly repealed same-sex marriage, and on November 3, 2009, voters in Maine repealed same-sex marriage in a referendum by a vote of 300,848 to 267,828. The District of Columbia is the only jurisdiction prohibiting a parent's sexual orientation from being a consideration in a child custody case, and the state of Minnesota is the only jurisdiction prohibiting discrimination on the basis of gender identity. Thirty-eight states allow dismissal from employment because of sexual orientation or gender identity, 42 states have laws defining marriage as between one man and one woman, and 30 state legislatures have amended their constitutions to prohibit same-sex marriage. Seven states prohibit second-parent adoption for same-sex couples. Opponents to LGBT equality insist that children raised by same-sex couples would not learn acceptable gender roles and believe that decisions on marriage and adoption rights should be made through referenda or votes in state legislatures. Moderates prefer civil unions or "everything-but"-type legislation. Often, opponents believe that lesbians and gays do not aspire to long-term, committed relationships.

Lesbians and gays were an invisible minority in American society that came to be noticed by police and psychiatrists early in the 20th century. Despite attempts by psychiatrists and the various agents of the American governments to restrain same-sex desire, those who became part of a homosexual minority struggled to define themselves as members acceptable to the heterosexual majority. As medical theories of illness gave way to acceptance of homosexuality as a normal variation of human sexuality, social conservatives resisted what they considered to be an assault on Christian families in the United States. As governmental objection to same-sex relationships is easing, the socially conservative Christian forces strive to restrict LGBT equality by depicting homosexuality as a choice and a curable illness. Such fallacies have slowed but not ended the path to sexual equality in the United States.

See Also: Heterosexism; Homophobia; Homosexuality, Religious Attitudes Toward; Same-Sex Marriage.

Further Readings

Bérubé, A. *Coming Out Under Fire: The History of Gay Men and Women in World War Two*. New York: Free Press, 1990.

Cahill, S. *Same-Sex Marriage in the United States: Focus on the Facts: Post-2004 Election Edition*. Toronto: Lexington Books, 2004.

Cahill, S. and S. Tobias. *Policy Issues Affecting Lesbian, Gay, Bisexual, and Transgender Families*. Ann Arbor: University of Michigan Press, 2007.

D'Emilio, J. *Sexual Politics, Sexual Communities: The Making of a Homosexual Minority in the United States, 1940–1970*. Chicago: University of Chicago Press, 1983.

Moats, D. *Civil Wars: A Battle for Gay Marriage*. Toronto, Canada: Harcourt, 2004.

Wolfson, E. *Why Marriage Matters: America, Equality, and Gay People's Right to Marry*. Toronto, Canada: Simon & Schuster, 2004.

Jonathan Anuik
Lakehead University, Orillia

Sexual Orientation–Based Social Discrimination: Outside United States

Social discrimination can be defined as unfavorable treatment of individuals or groups on arbitrary grounds related to gender, age, race, religion, sexual orientation, or disability. Excluded individuals and communities thereby suffer distinct disadvantages by comparison with the rest of the population.

Documented Violations

The following violations based on sexual orientation have been documented in all parts of the world: a violation of right to education because of an unsafe climate created by peers or educators in schools; violence, bullying, or harassment in private and public life; torture or cruel, inhuman, or degrading treatment in the course of police activity; arbitrary arrest of individuals suspected of having a homo/bisexual identity; violation of the right to a fair trial because of the prejudices of judges and other law enforcement officials; violation of rights to free expression and free association because of a homophobic climate in which the people discriminated against live; restrictions on the right to practice religion; the prohibition of the right to work; refusal of the right to social security, assistance, and benefits; denial of the right to physical and mental health services because of the prejudices of some medical practitioners; a lack of adequate training for healthcare personnel regarding sexual orientation issues or the general assumption that patients are heterosexuals; and the prevention of the right to equal access to goods, housing, and other facilities.

A joint International Gay, Lesbian, Bisexual, Transgender and Queer Youth and Student Organization (IGLYO) and ILGA-Europe project confirms that young LGBT people are particularly discriminated against. Research by Stonewall also demonstrates that women are more likely to experience lower economic well-being than men as a result of lower pensions and fewer opportunities to access education, employment, and training. This is exacerbated in the case of women who live together. LGBT persons also may risk multiple discrimination on two or more grounds: access to key social benefits, such as employment, healthcare, education, and housing; and social marginalization and social exclusion.

International and European Instruments on Sexual-Orientation Discrimination

International and European human rights law has been slow to provide protection from discrimination on the basis of sexual orientation. Several European Union (EU) laws offer protection from discrimination

based on sexual orientation. The European Parliament (EP) passed several (nonbinding) resolutions on sexual orientation, the first, adopted in 1984, calling for an end to work-related discrimination on the basis of sexual orientation. On May 1, 1999, the provision in Article 13 of the Treaty of Amsterdam introduced the first international treaty, which explicitly refers to discrimination on the ground of sexual orientation. This was further strengthened with the passage of the Charter of Fundamental Rights of the EU Article 21. EU institutions have acknowledged that social exclusion occurs in a variety of fields and that it is not limited to employment (European Council 2002, 14164/1/02 REV 1). However, EU policies have tended to focus mainly on employment-related and income-related exclusion. There is limited attention given to the interaction between exclusion and discrimination in education and health. In 2000, the European Commission adopted the Employment Equality Directive 2000/78, establishing equal protection against discrimination based on various grounds, including sexual orientation in employment.

EU law regards discrimination against transgender persons as a form of sex discrimination. This principle was established by the Court of Justice in 1996, where it was held that the dismissal of an individual following gender reassignment was unlawful discrimination on the grounds of sex (Case C-13/94, P v S and Cornwall County Council [1996] ECR I-2143). Gender-identity discrimination is the term now generally used to describe discrimination against transgender persons. Social inclusion was put on the European Social Policy Agenda at the Nice European Council in December 2000. The fight against poverty and social exclusion was introduced to the EU agenda as one of the central elements of the Lisbon Strategy launched at the European Council in March 2000. However, little attention has been paid to the exclusion that LGBT people experience in the context of European social policy and, in particular, the EU social inclusion strategies.

Nondiscrimination and equality are fundamental components of the United Nations (UN) instruments. However, the UN has long been silent on this issue. Some progress has been made. In its 1994 decision in *Toonen v. Australia*, the UN Human Rights Committee (HRC) held that the references to "sex" in Articles 2 and 26 of the International Covenant on Civil and

Political Rights should be taken to include sexual orientation. With this case, the Human Rights Committee created a precedent within the UN human rights system in addressing discrimination against lesbians, gays, and bisexuals.

The International Covenant on Economic Social and Cultural Rights prohibited discrimination for "race, color, sex, language, religion, political or other opinion, national or social origin, property, birth or other status." In its General Comment No. 20 on Non Discrimination in Economic, Social and Cultural Rights (art. 2, para. 2), adopted in May 2009, the UN Committee on Economic, Social and Cultural Rights prohibition list includes sexual orientation and gender identity. The committee states that "other status," as recited in article 2(2), includes sexual orientation within its definition.

The International Labour Organization (ILO) does not itself prohibit discrimination on the basis of sexual orientation but permits state parties to add additional grounds. In May 2007, the ILO issued a major report "Equality at Work: Tackling the Challenges," under the follow-up to the ILO Declaration on Fundamental Principles and Rights at Work, which was adopted in 1998. For the first time, the ILO specifically addressed discrimination on the basis of sexual orientation, both in its press release and, more fully, in the report itself. The report's wording was cautious and descriptive.

National Legislation and the Situation in Practice

Although in a large number of states around the world, LGBT persons are not protected under antidiscrimination legislation, EU member states have made many commitments to combating discrimination on the ground of sexual orientation within the EU.

However, informal controls are the hardest to change, since even after legal barriers are removed, mistrust and bias continue to exist. Even though in EU member states that recognize the rights of LGBT persons, such people are denied in practice basic civil, political, social, and economic rights. A survey by the EU Agency for Fundamental Rights (FRA) in 2007 shows that 18 out of 27 EU member states already provide quite comprehensive protection against discrimination on grounds of sexual orientation. However, the social situation remains worrying. A joint IGLYO

and ILGA-Europe project of 2007 shows that LGBT people continue to face discrimination and exclusion across Europe in all spheres of life. Some EU member states establish public agencies to investigate sexual orientation–based discrimination, and some of them can initiate legal action for the benefit of the victim.

See Also: Sexual Orientation; Sexual Orientation–Based Social Discrimination: United States; Sexual Orientation–Based Violence: Outside United States; Sexual Orientation–Based Violence: United States.

Further Readings

Committee on Legal Affairs and Human Rights. "Discrimination on the Basis of Sexual Orientation and Gender Identity." http://assembly.coe.int /Documents/WorkingDocs/Doc09/EDOC12099.pdf (accessed July 2010).

Dymski, G. A. "Poverty and Social Discrimination: A Spatial Keynesian Approach." 2004. http://www.econ omiaetecnologia.ufpr.br/textos_discussao/texto_para _discussao_ano_2004_texto_02.pdf (accessed July 2010).

Stonewall. "Social Exclusion." www.stonewall.org.uk/ what_we_do/research_and_policy/2880.asp (accessed July 2010).

Kadriye Bakirci
Istanbul Technical University

Sexual Orientation–Based Social Discrimination: United States

Discrimination based on sexual orientation is typically understood as acts that harm lesbian women or gay men. These acts or behavior often involve gay and lesbian people being treated differently because of their sexual orientation. Social discrimination includes double standards of treatment, when gay or lesbian people are treated worse than heterosexual people. In these cases, lesbian women and gay men would not have confronted discrimination if they were heterosexual. Moreover, these discriminatory acts often stem from prejudice, or negative ideas, about lesbian women and gay men. Social discrimi-

A rainbow-colored banner with the phrase "All Are Welcome" shows an acceptance of homosexuality at this church.

nation, which can occur in many settings, differs from legal discrimination to the extent that it is not part of U.S. law. Nevertheless, social discrimination can have significant effects on lesbian women and gay men.

Discrimination in the Workforce

Most scholars have examined sexual orientation–based discrimination in the workforce. In the United States, federal law prohibits employment discrimination based on characteristics such as race, religion, gender, and national origin, but not based on sexual orientation. Thus, it is legal to fire someone for being gay or lesbian in many U.S. states. As of 2010, 29 states do not have statutes forbidding employers from firing an employee because of his or her sexual orientation. As a result, some gay and lesbian people decide to keep their sexuality hidden out of fear that they may be fired or denied promotion. Some stud-

ies suggest that gay and lesbian people tend to be the most satisfied with their jobs when they are allowed to be open about their sexuality; that is, when they do not feel they have to conceal it from others.

Discrimination against gay and lesbian people in the workforce can also occur at the time of hiring. Some studies indicate that lesbian women and gay men are less likely than heterosexual people to be hired for certain jobs. Furthermore, some of these studies suggest that lesbian women and gay men are less likely than their heterosexual counterparts to be promoted. As a result, in some occupations gay and lesbian people make, on average, less money than heterosexual people. These income differences vary considerably based on the occupation, but lesbian women and gay men generally tend to make less than their heterosexual counterparts. Thus, the workplace discrimination confronting gay and lesbian people often has detrimental effects, possibly including forms of harassment, in which gay and lesbian people confront a hostile work environment.

Workplace harassment can take on many forms, but it generally involves behavior that makes it more difficult for gay and lesbian people to enjoy being at work. This behavior, which can be perpetrated by coworkers as well as superiors, often leads gay and lesbian people to quit their jobs and move to a more accommodating workplace. Verbal harassment of gay and lesbian people sometimes involves homophobic language such as the words *fag* or *dyke*. Many gay and lesbian people consider these words offensive verbal attacks on their sexual orientation. Other lesbian women and gay men have used these words as a way of reclaiming them to reduce their power.

Although discrimination against gay and lesbian people has most frequently been examined in the workforce, it occurs in other settings as well. Many gay and lesbian people face rejection from their families on "coming out"; that is, when they tell others of their sexual orientation. In these situations, family members sometimes respond by rejecting the gay or lesbian person's identity, either by verbally attacking the gay or lesbian person or by refusing to acknowledge their sexual identity. In some cases, parents have told their gay or lesbian children to leave the home. These forms of discrimination have resulted in relatively high rates of homelessness among gay and lesbian youth.

Discrimination in the Military

Recently, discrimination against lesbian women and gay men in the military has received a considerable amount of attention. Throughout American history, military service personnel have been removed from duty for identifying themselves as gay or lesbian. Considerable attention has also been devoted to violence against lesbian women and gay men. These forms of violence are often now considered a "hate crime," as they are motivated by prejudice or "hate." Matthew Shepard, a gay man from Wyoming who was murdered in 1996, is the most well-known incident of hate crime, but other gay and lesbian people have also experienced violence because of their sexual orientation. Many studies, for example, suggest that gay and lesbian youth are more likely to be bullied than heterosexual adolescents. Discrimination against gay and lesbian people can have lasting psychological effects. When a gay or lesbian person is fired, for example, they may suffer not only a loss of income but also a loss of self-worth. In other cases these psychological effects may be short-lived, as some lesbian women and gay men are able to recover from the discrimination they confront.

Defining the Discriminatory Behavior

In most cases, acts of discrimination against lesbian women and gay men are perpetrated by people who identify as heterosexual. At times, discrimination based on sexual orientation can occur against people who identify as heterosexual. In these cases, a person who identifies as heterosexual may be mistakenly perceived as gay or lesbian and then experience discrimination as a result. Most typically, however, discrimination based on sexual orientation involves a heterosexual person discriminating against a gay or lesbian person. It involves, in other words, a heterosexual person treating lesbian women or gay men as inferior to heterosexual people.

Scholars have generally defined sexual orientation–based discrimination as behavior that is intentionally designed to harm gay or lesbian people. In these cases, discrimination involves the actions of one person or a group of people who cause harm to a gay or lesbian person. Other scholars, however, have tried to define discrimination more broadly. These scholars have argued that discrimination against gay and lesbian people exists at the societal, rather than the individual, level. A societal-based understanding

of discrimination means that heterosexual people are granted privileges based on their sexual orientation, whereas gay and lesbian people are disadvantaged based on theirs. For instance, in the United States, gay and lesbian people are not granted the same rights as heterosexual people with regard to adoption, marriage, and hospital visitations. Discrimination, in other words, is institutionalized—it is built into the organization of society. Scholars who have defined discrimination in societal terms have used the terms *heterosexism*, *heterocentrism*, and *heteronormativity*. These three terms have slightly different meanings, but all three signify a society in which heterosexuality is constructed as ideal. These understandings of discrimination contend that U.S. society establishes heterosexuality as normal and homosexuality as immoral and unnatural.

Gender Differences in Discriminatory Behavior

Scholars exploring sexual orientation–based discrimination have also outlined important gender differences. These scholars argue that lesbian women experience different forms of discrimination than gay men. That is, lesbian women confront forms of discrimination unique to their position in society. For instance, lesbian women are often more likely than gay men to confront forms of sexual harassment in the workforce or to be passed over for a job promotion. Moreover, lesbian women also sometimes face discrimination based on their gender. Discrimination against gay men, in contrast, often reinforces the cultural devaluation of femininity. In other words, gay men frequently experience discrimination when they are perceived as feminine. In this sense, sexual orientation–based discrimination encourages men to perform gender in traditionally masculine ways.

Discrimination has also been shown to vary considerably based on race and social class. Gay and lesbian people who are black or Latino, for instance, may confront forms of discrimination that their white counterparts do not. Social class further complicates this picture, as middle-class gay and lesbian people do not face many of the challenges confronting poor lesbian women and gay men.

In the United States, some attempts have been made to address discrimination against lesbian women and gay men. For instance, to address workplace discrimination based on sexual orientation, the

Employment Non-Discrimination Act has been introduced in the U.S. Congress. This law would broaden employment protections for gay and lesbian people by banning sexual orientation-based discrimination at the national level.

See Also: Bullying in the Workplace; Coming Out; Hate Crimes; Heterosexism; Homophobia; Homosexuality, Religious Attitudes Toward; Lesbians; LGBTQ; Sexual Harassment; Sexual Orientation; Sexual Orientation–Based Legal Discrimination: United States; Sexual Orientation–Based Violence: United States.

Further Readings

Badgett, M. and V. Lee. *Money, Myths, and Change: The Economic Lives of Lesbians and Gay Men*. Chicago: University of Chicago Press, 1997.

Croteau, J. M. "Research on the Work Experiences of Lesbian, Gay, and Bisexual People: An Integrative Review of Methodology and Findings." *Journal of Vocational Behavior*, v.48/2 (1996).

Herek, G. M. "Hate Crimes and Stigma-Related Experiences Among Sexual Minority Adults in the United States: Prevalence Estimates From a National Probability Sample." *Journal of Interpersonal Violence*, v.24/1 (2009).

Levine, M. P. and R. Leonard. "Discrimination Against Lesbians in the Work Force," *Signs*, v.4/1 (1984).

Doug Meyer
Graduate Center of the City University of New York

Sexual Orientation–Based Violence: Outside United States

Under international law, all human beings are born free and equal in dignity and rights. Yet lesbian, gay, bisexual, and transgender (LGBT) people still face deep-rooted prejudice and widespread discrimination and violence.

The range of violence or abuse is limitless and includes women being raped to "cure" their lesbianism, sometimes at the behest of their parents; individuals prosecuted because their private and consensual relationship is deemed to be a social danger; loss of custody of their children; individuals beaten by police; individuals assaulted and sometimes killed on the street; regular subjection to verbal abuse; bullying at school and in the workplace; denial of employment, housing, or health services; denied of access to the armed forces; denial of asylum when they do manage to flee abuse; individuals raped and otherwise tortured in detention; individuals threatened for campaigning for their human rights; individuals driven to suicide; and individuals executed by the state.

An article published by the Integrated Regional Information Networks in 2005 stated among other things that honor killings by Iraqis against a gay family member are common and that the killers are given some legal protection. The reports published by Human Rights Watch in 2009 and the U.S. State Department in 2010 detail torture of men accused of being gay in Iraq. The reports published by the International Lesbian and Gay Association in 2007 and the U.S. State Department in 2010 found that eight countries today still retain capital punishment for homosexuality: Iran, Mauritania, Saudi Arabia, Sudan, United Arab Emirates, Yemen, Nigeria, and Uganda. All are predominantly Muslim countries.

A survey published in 2009 by the European Union Agency for Fundamental Rights shows that LGBT persons experience discrimination and homophobic and transphobic bullying and harassment across the European Union. There are several accounts of attacks on LGBT venues in a number of member states, from criminal damage to premises of LGBT nongovernmental organizations or community sites to harassment or assaults on LGBT persons at venues.

A report prepared by the Committee on Legal Affairs and Human Rights of the Council of Europe in 2009 shows that homophobic and transphobic attitudes are deeply rooted in most Council of Europe member states, with the consequence that LGBT people, as well as human rights defenders working for the rights of LGBT persons, face strong prejudice, hostility, and widespread discrimination all over Europe.

Serious Consequences for the Young

Homophobia and transphobia have particularly serious consequences for young LGBT people. There is evidence that LBT women are particularly affected by some forms of gender-based violence, such as rape, sexual violence and harassment, and forced marriages. The Agency for Fundamental Rights survey reveals that lesbian and bisexual women are more likely than gay or bisexual men to experience assault within private settings. Homophobic or transphobic hate crimes and hate speeches affect LGBT persons in various ways. Violence and discrimination affects health and can affect social inclusion and economic well-being. The fear of homophobia and transphobia also contributes to the "invisibility" of LGBT persons in many social settings. Many transgender people barely, if at all, participate in social and public life, and many others who do participate are so traumatized and frightened by the hostility they face that they are unable to live their life in peace and dignity. Their image in the media, curricula, and arts is made up of misconceptions, ignorance, and lack of knowledge.

Violence against LGBT individuals may occur either at the hands of individuals or groups or as part of state enforcement of laws targeting people who are perceived to violate heteronormative rules and who contravene perceived protocols of gender and sexual behavior. Behind much of the discrimination and violence faced by LGBT people is lack of knowledge and understanding about sexual orientation, strong prejudices, and a refusal by some leading politicians, opinion leaders, and religious leaders to accept that LGBT people are entitled to the same human rights as other humans. This underpins a high degree of homophobic and transphobic discourse in the public sphere and gives legitimacy to those state actors—police, prison officers, public prosecutors, judiciary, local authority officials, and even ombudspersons—who fail to uphold, or who even attack, the rights of LGBT people. Hate speech in the media and Internet is also of particular concern. Underreporting and nonreporting of crime is a major problem with regard to the LGBT community, and therefore there is a significant lack of data on sexual orientation–based crimes. Victims of hate crimes, driven by homophobia or transphobia, often face cultural or social obstacles to the reporting of attacks and threats.

International and European Instruments on Sexual Orientation–Based Violence

International and European organizations emphasize the universality of human rights and fundamental freedoms. However, until very recently, no legal protection on the basis of sexual orientation could be found at the international level. Notwithstanding the mass execution of homosexuals during World War II, there is virtually no mention of this victim group in the judgment of the International Military Tribunal at Nuremberg. Nor did homosexuals find protection in the 1948 United Nations Convention on the Prevention and Punishment of the Crime of Genocide; the United Nations Convention Against Torture and Other Cruel, Inhuman, or Degrading Treatment or Punishment (1984); or the Rome Statute of the International Criminal Court (1998).

Since April 1993, the United Nations High Commissioner for Refugees has recognized in several advisory opinions that gays and lesbians qualify as members of a "particular social group" for the purposes of the 1951 convention and the 1967 Protocol Relating to the Status of Refugees. In its publication "Protecting Refugees," the United Nations High Commissioner for Refugees states: "Homosexuals may be eligible for refugee status on the basis of persecution because of their membership of a particular social group. It is the policy of the [United Nations High Commissioner for Refugees] that persons facing attack, inhuman treatment, or serious discrimination because of their homosexuality, and whose governments are unable or unwilling to protect them, should be recognized as refugees."

National Legislation

The legal position of homosexuals varies significantly from country to country, from constitutionally entrenched freedom, to discrimination on the basis of sexual orientation, to laws that make homosexual acts punishable by death. Nonetheless, a clear trend exists within human rights law toward greater protection of homosexuals as a group.

The International Lesbian and Gay Association's research found that 78 countries, mostly in Africa and Asia, continue to consider male-to-male relationships illegal. Female-to-female relationships are not illegal in 44 of these countries. In contrast, in a large number of Council of Europe member states, although homosexuality is not illegal, LGBT persons are not protected under antidiscrimination or hate-crime legislation. In addition, LGBT persons sometimes experience a lack of appropriate protection from law enforcement officials. A European Union Agency for

Fundamental Rights (FRA) study shows that 18 of 27 European Union member states already provide quite comprehensive protection against discrimination and harassment on grounds of sexual orientation. The social situation, however, is worrying. In recent years, a series of events in European Union member states, such as banning pride marches, hate speeches from politicians, and intolerant statements by religious leaders, have sent alarming signals and sparked new debate about the extent of homophobia and discrimination against LGBT persons in the European Union.

See Also: Coming Out; Hate Crimes; Sexual Harassment; Sexual Orientation; Sexual Orientation–Based Legal Discrimination: Outside United States; Sexual Orientation–Based Violence: United States.

Further Readings
Council of Europe. "Discrimination on the Basis of Sexual Orientation and Gender Identity." Report of the Committee on Legal Affairs and Human Rights, 2009. http://assembly.coe.int/Main.asp?link=/Documents /WorkingDocs/Doc09/EDOC12087.htm (accessed April 2010).
European Union Agency for Fundamental Rights (FRA). "Homophobia and Discrimination on Grounds of Sexual Orientation and Gender Identity in the EU." http://www.fra.europa.eu/fraWebsite/attachments/ FRA_hdgso_report-part2_en.pdf (accessed April 2010).
Gontek, Ines. "Sexual Violence Against Lesbian Women in South Africa." Master's Thesis in African Studies, Cologne, 2007. http://ilga.org/ilga/static/images/ oldsite/SexualViolenceAgainstLesbianWomeninSouth AfricabyInesGontek.pdf (accessed April 2010).
Human Rights Watch. "They Want Us Exterminated." http://www.hrw.org/en/node/85049/section/3 (accessed April 2010).
Ottosson, D. "State-Sponsored Homophobia: A World Survey of Laws Prohibiting Same Sex Activity Between Consenting Adults." http://ilga.org/statehomophobia /State_sponsored_homophobia_ILGA_07.pdf (accessed April 2010).
PinkPaper.com. "U.S. State Dept. Reports on LGBT Life in Nearly Every Nation." http://news.pinkpaper.com/ NewsStory.aspx?id=2620 (accessed June 2010).

Kadriye Bakirci
Istanbul Technical University

Sexual Orientation–Based Violence: United States

Sexual orientation–based violence against lesbians and bisexual women is perpetrated on interpersonal, institutional, and cultural levels. The pervasiveness of violence targeting lesbians and bisexual women reflects the ideological nature of hate-based violence more generally. In expressions of hate violence or discrimination, the perpetrator targets members of marginalized communities in order to uphold their interpretations of social norms. Lesbians and bisexual women have traditionally been positioned as a threat to heterosexuality, a cornerstone of traditional society. This leaves them personally open to harm and with less access to prevention efforts or direct services meant to address violence in mainstream situations.

Mainstream society's normalization of heterosexuality has required that any other form of sexual orientation be labeled as different and less than. Cultural institutions responsible for reproducing heterosexuality as the norm have created a variety of labels to describe the sociocultural derision of lesbians and bisexual women including: sinful, broken, abnormal, sick, childish, a phase, a lifestyle, and dangerous to the family, society, and children. Such acts of marginalization separate out lesbians and bisexual women and leave them open to harm simultaneously based in and justified through this stigmatization.

Bullying and Violence

The violence against lesbians and bisexual women is inclusive of violence against women more generally, upholding the argument that heterosexism, homophobia, and biphobia are deeply connected to misogyny, the hatred of women. Heterosexism is the maintenance of heterosexuality as the normative and singularly desirable form of sexuality. Homopbobia is the irrational fear of lesbians and gay men that frames them as a threat to heterosexuality. Biphobia is the irrational fear of people who are not solely attracted to members of the opposite sex. Thus, while sexual assault is more prevalent against women than men, lesbians and bisexual women face both a greater risk of sexual assault as women and homophobic, biphobic, and/or heterosexist revictimization as well.

Violence against lesbians and bisexual women often begins early and continues across their lifespan. The dread of the potential for one's daughter to be lesbian or bisexual is enough for family members to heavily monitor any gender or sexuality nonconformity. Intrafamilial violence takes many forms for lesbian and bisexual women, especially for those who are either gender nonconforming or who come out at an early age. Intrafamilial violence toward lesbians and bisexual women takes on many forms, from ridicule and disowning a child to sexual assault aimed at "fixing" her, to kicking her out of the home. For girls who do not subscribe to the lessons of enculturation, there is also a range of socially supported encouragements to conform, from stigmatization to reprimands to forceful correction of behaviors and desires.

Young girls who transgress the boundaries of heterosexuality face extreme pressure to conform when they are bullied in school settings. Bullying is a form of hostility targeting an individual deemed less than or socially deviant by their peers. For example, it is a way to reinforce both gender and sexuality norms. This phenomena is also extending into the workplace, where adults target coworkers in much the same fashion as schoolyard bullies. In states without equal protection in employment, even the rumors that a woman is a lesbian or bisexual may be enough to lead to termination.

Intimate Partner Violence (IPV) is a pattern of behavior in which one partner exerts power and control in order to maintain dominance in a relationship. The myriad tactics used by abusers reflect the power dynamics of each individual situation. Such tactics include physical harm; verbal, emotional, and economic abuse; threats regarding immigration, parental and HIV status, and pet abuse, as well as any of the forms of identity-based discrimination prevalent in society. For lesbians and bisexual women, these are compounded by the potential for discrimination outside the violent relationship.

If a woman is forced to keep her sexual orientation private for fear of losing a job, a home, or friends and family, the resulting isolation makes it virtually impossible for her to speak about any same-sex relationship with those most able to provide support. When there are few to no witnesses to violence or no one to check in with, abusers have an easier time perpetrating violence. In states where there are

no protections for lesbians or bisexual woman with children, states may award sole or primary custody to the other parent or relative based on the assessment that a lesbian or bisexual woman is an unfit parent due to her sexual orientation. In situations where the police are called, the assessment of IPV is often not correctly made, leaving the victim open to further harm.

Sexual Assault

Sexual assault is any unwanted sexual act that a person is forced to either perform or receive. Though sexual assault is rightfully framed as violence in the form of power and control, many of the state legal definitions of sexual assault set the parameters using gendered terms realted to men harming women. Many of the mainstream victim's services were designed with little to no regard to the experiences of a woman sexually assaulted by another woman. For many lesbians and bisexual women who experience sexual assault by another woman, it is often within the context of domestic violence, when sexual assault is used as a form of power and control.

Lesbian and bisexual women also face sexual assault by men. Some experience these attacks while in dating or marital relationships with men. Others may experience such violence in attacks meant to "cure them" or "change them."

Interpersonal violence such as domestic violence and sexual assault are rarely spoken about either within lesbian and bisexual communities or in the mainstream. For lesbian and bisexual women, societal marginalization is so significant that to bring interpersonal violence into the open for many feels like potentially exposing the lesbian and bisexual communities to even further stigmatization. Underreporting makes it difficult to assess the prevalence of such violence.

Seeking Help

When lesbian and bisexual survivors of violence do try to access victims services, they are often met with responses that revictimize them. There are numerous points at which this revictimization can occur in the process of seeking services. Outreach may not be designed to attract lesbian or bisexual women to services. Intake forms may not reflect the lives or experiences of these women. Well-intentioned but culturally insensitive victims assistance providers sometimes ask inappropriate questions or make harmful assumptions. Occasionally some service providers also intentionally harm lesbian or bisexual survivors of violence when they try to force their homophobic, biphobic, or heterosexist views on survivors by, for instance, blaming a survivor's sexual orientation for the violence rather than locating the responsibility in the acts of the perpetrator. If a survivor lodges a complaint based on the unfair treatment, they may further risk not receiving services through being falsely accused of noncompliance or being difficult to serve.

Another site of institutional violence toward lesbian and bisexual women survivors of violence is the structural inequalities inherent within the heterosexist construction of options for victims of violence. For instance, most law enforcement officials are not adequately trained to assess for intimate partner violence between two women. Most domestic violence counselors and advocates are not able to make the determination of who is the primary aggressor in an IPV situation.

The most extreme expression of violence experienced by lesbians or bisexual women is murder. Murders of lesbians or bisexual women, as with other hate motivated murders, are often extraordinarily violent, involve more than one attacker, and quite often are preceded by sexual assault. The "overkill" is said to be the expression of an attacker's desire to erase the entire existence of his or her victim. It is an attacker's way of sending a message of hate to entire communities.

Over the last 30 years, with the strengthening of the lesbian, gay, bisexual, transgender, and queer (LGBTQ) antiviolence movement, there have been shifts in cultural attitudes. The passage of the Matthew Shepard and James Byrd Jr. Hate Crimes Act in 2009 expanded protections to LGBTQ victims of violence. Yet several state-sanctioned obstacles to safety remain. The Federal Defense of Marriage Act (DOMA) and state-specific DOMAs prevent same gender marriage, which means that over 1,000 rights are withheld from same-gender couples who wish to marry. Many of these rights serve as protection from a variety of forms of discrimination and oppression. The "Don't Ask, Don't Tell" regulation in the armed forces has kept lesbian and bisexual women from speaking about their relationships and thus from accessing potentially vital support services. With such state-sanctioned and enforced discrimination, it becomes that much more difficult overall to establish the sociocultural argument that lesbians and bisexual women have the right to be safe and deserve access to services in times of need.

See Also: Bullying in the Workplace; Sexual Harassment; Sexual Orientation–Based Social Discrimination: Outside United States; Sexual Orientation–Based Social Discrimination: United States.

Further Readings

Billies, Michelle, et al. "Naming Our Reality: Low-Income LGBT People Documenting Violence, Discrimination and Assertions of Justice." *Feminism & Psychology*, v.19 (2009).

Girschick, Lori B. *Woman-to-Woman Sexual Violence.* Lebanon, NH: Northeastern University Press, 2002.

Hardesty, Jennifer L., et al. "Lesbian/Bisexual Mothers and Intimate Partner Violence: Help Seeking in the Context of Social and Legal Vulnerability." *Violence Against Women* (December 2009).

Patzel, Brenda. "What Blocked Heterosexual Women and Lesbians in Leaving Their Abusive Relationships." *Journal of the American Psychiatric Nurses Association*, v.12 (2006).

Todahl, Jeffrey L., et al. "Sexual Assault Support Services and Community Systems: Understanding Critical Issues and Needs in the LGBTQ Community." *Violence Against Women*, v.15 (2009).

Kim Fountain
Independent Scholar

Sexually Transmitted Infections

More commonly known as sexually transmitted diseases (STDs), sexually transmitted infections (STIs) carry a heavy burden of disease for women. The World Health Organization (WHO) recommends that the term *STI* replace the term *STD*, as it better reflects the asymptomatic nature of most infections.

Genital human papillomavirus (HPV) is the most common STI, with more than 40 types that can affect the skin of the genitals. Most do not develop symptoms, and untreated HPV in women can cause cervical cancer, genital warts, and cancers of the vulva, vagina, and anus. HPV is transmitted through vaginal and anal sexual contact. Preventing HPV-related diseases includes regular cervical cancer screenings and pap exams. There is also now a vaccine for girls aged 11 through 26 years to reduce the risk of developing certain types of HPV and cervical cancers. There is no such vaccine for men yet.

Gonorrhea is the second most common STI in the United States. Chlamydia and gonorrhea commonly co-occur but are separate infections. Also known as "silent" STIs because a majority of women never experience symptoms, both gonorrhea and chlamydia can cause painful urination and pain during sexual activity; bleeding between periods; itching of the genital area; a foul odor; and white, yellow, or green discharge. They are often mistaken for a vaginal infection. Symptoms usually appear one to three weeks after infection. In 2008, the rates for women were 119.4 compared with men at 103.0 cases per 100,000. Among all women in 2008, those aged 15 to 24 years had the highest rates. Both chlamydia and gonorrhea, if left untreated, can lead to pelvic inflammatory disease (PID), which can later lead to serious health problems for women such as tubal infertility, ectopic pregnancy, and chronic pelvic pain. One million women develop PID annually.

Caused by two different viruses (HSV-1, which often causes sores around the mouth and lips, and HSV-2 which causes genital sores), the herpes simplex virus (HSV; genital herpes) is untreatable but manageable. Often appearing as one or more sores on or around the genitals or rectum, the blisters break open, leaving painful open sores may take two weeks to a month to heal and often lay dormant until another cyclical outbreak. Symptoms can also be flulike and include swollen glands and feverishness. HSV is transmitted from these open sores and from skin that does not appear to have a sore, but most people are unaware of their infection. Genital HSV-2 is almost two times more common in women than men.

Syphilis

Syphilis in the primary stage is marked by the presence of one or more sores, which appear between 10 and 90 days after contact but are often pain-

less. Lasting three to six weeks, the sore will often heal without treatment. The second stage of syphilis is characterized by skin rash mucous membrane lesions, fever, sore throat, and swollen lymph glands, among other symptoms. Without treatment, syphilis can progress to a dormant phase (where no signs or symptoms are present), and later a tertiary stage. About 15 percent of people progress into the third phase, where syphilis damage can happen to major internal organs, including the brain, and can lead to paralysis, numbness, gradual blindness, dementia, and even death.

Untreated STIs that lead to PID cause an estimated 100,000 (1 in 10) women to become infertile every year. PID occurs when bacteria move upward from a woman's vagina or cervix to her reproductive organs. Sexually active women (with multiple sexual partners) of childbearing age are at risk, and women younger than 25 years are more likely to develop PID than those older than 25 years.

The most lethal STI is human immunodeficiency virus (HIV), and poverty is a significant risk factor for infection and inadequate treatment. HIV is transmitted in bodily fluids like blood, semen, and vaginal fluids and by sharing needles. People infected with HIV are vulnerable to other infections. HIV disproportionately affects minority women. Between 1999 and 2002, 71.8 percent of all women with HIV were African American. In addition, studies have found that the presence of STIs facilitate the transmission of HIV. Most STIs are often treated with a single dose or multiple doses of antibiotics; however, some strains of gonorrhea are now becoming resistant to antibiotics. STIs such as syphilis can be successfully treated with antibiotics only in early stages, and viruses such as HSV, HPV, and HIV cannot be cured.

Complications in Pregnancy

Pregnancy can be complicated by most STIs and can be passed to infants through vaginal delivery. This is rare for HPV but more common with gonorrhea, chlamydia, HSV, and syphilis. Pregnant women with HIV can take a combination of drugs that are designed to prevent transmission to a fetus. STIs such as HIV and syphilis can cross the placenta and infect an unborn baby, and infants can contract gonorrhea, chlamydia, and HSV as they pass through the birth canal. HIV is unique in that a child can also be infected after birth through breastfeeding. STIs can lead to early labor and uterine infections after delivery, low birth weight, neonatal sepsis, blindness, deafness, stillbirth, and other conditions.

Throughout the world, women are plagued by STIs. In 1999, WHO estimates that 340 million new cases of curable STIs were reported (syphilis, gonorrhea, trichomoniasis, and chlamydia) in adults 15 to 49 years of age. In developing countries, STIs and associated complications are among the top five disease categories for which adults seek healthcare, WHO reports that in women of childbearing age, STIs (excluding HIV) are second only to maternal factors as causes of disease and death.

Global prevalence estimates of curable STIs in 1999 are highest for persons in south and southeastern Asia at 48 million, followed by those in sub-Saharan Africa, at 32 million. Women, on average, become infected at rates higher than men. For example, chlamydia was estimated to affect 50 million women in 1999 compared with 48 million men; 23.96 million of these women were in south and southeastern Asia, and only 8.24 million were in sub-Saharan Africa. Gonorrhea affected a total of 33.65 million women in 1999 compared with 28.70 million men; 15.09 million of these women were in south and southeastern Asia.

Syphilis affected 6.47 million women in 1999, the lowest rate of a curable STI, yet only 5.29 million men were affected; again, the highest percentage of women by region were in south and southeastern Asia. Although rates of new cases of syphilis are lower in other regions, WHO states that incidence rates are reaching epidemic levels in eastern Europe and central Asia. A new health program is being implemented to reduce the number of children born with congenital syphilis, as rates are rising for nearly every country in the European Union, WHO states, indicating that pregnant women are not sufficiently screened and tested.

Women at a Higher Risk

For every measured curable STI, except trichomoniasis, women had higher rates of infection than men, and women in south and southeastern Asia had higher rates than women in sub-Saharan Africa, WHO reports. This regional trend is reversed for HIV rates in 2005; the highest incidence for HIV was in Africa, at 1,935 per 100,000 persons, and 246 per 100,000 per-

sons in southeastern Asia. Higher prevalence rates of HIV were also seen in Africa (21,721 per 100,000) than in southeastern Asia (3,274 per 100,000).

All women, including pregnant women, should be regularly tested by a healthcare professional for STIs and HIV. Reducing the risk of contracting an STI and HIV includes safer sex practices and minimizing the number of sexual partners.

See Also: Health, Mental and Physical; Infertility, Incidence of; Infertility, Treatments for; Pregnancy.

Further Readings
Centers for Disease Control and Prevention. "Sexually Transmitted Diseases." http://www.cdc.gov/std (accessed November 2009).

Committee on Prevention and Control of Sexually Transmitted Diseases, Institute of Medicine. *The Hidden Epidemic: Confronting Sexually Transmitted Diseases.* Washington, DC: National Academies Press, 1997.

Holmes, King, et al. *Sexually Transmitted Diseases.* New York: McGraw Hill, 2007.

World Health Organization Department of HIV/AIDS. "Global Prevalence and Incidence of Selected Curable Sexually Transmitted Infections." http://www.who.int/docstore/hiv/GRSTI/000.htm (accessed May 2010).

Valerie R. Stackman
Howard University

Seychelles

Seychelles is a small, 283-square-mile island nation in the Indian Ocean, which became independent of Great Britain in 1976. The population of 87,476 (as of July 2009) includes French, African, Indian Chinese, and Arab citizens, reflecting the Seychelles' location between African and Asia and its lack of an indigenous population. The island nation has served as a transit point for trade from at least the 16th century. Roman Catholicism is the predominant religion, accounting for 82.3 percent of the population, with Anglicans the next largest religion represented, at 6.4 percent. Seychelles enjoys a high standard of living, with a per capita gross domestic product of $19,400 in 2009 (61st highest in the world and among the highest in Africa). Life expectancies are 68.33 years for men and 77.85 for women. The nation has a high debt load, which may imperil the government's ability to continue to provide its many services.

Officially, women are equal to men in Seychelles, including in employment and inheritance. However, human rights investigations have revealed that domestic violence against women and children is a continuing problem: laws prohibit domestic abuse, but police rarely intervene unless a weapon is involved, and often cases are dismissed in court or the perpetrator receives a light sentence. Rape of girls under age 15 also is reported as a problem not sufficiently dealt with by legal authorities. Prostitution is illegal, but prostitutes generally are not subject to arrest unless other crimes are involved. Seychelles instituted free public education in 1981, and currently the literacy rate is 92.3 percent for women and 91.4 percent for men. About 90 percent of women are in the labor force, similar to the male percentage. Ten women served in the 24-seat national assembly as of 2007, and two served in the cabinet. Seychelles has had only three presidents since independence, none of them female.

By tradition, Seychelles has a matriarchal society, and single mothers are the norm. The fertility rate is 1.93 children per woman, and infant mortality is 12.3 deaths per 1,000 live births, among the lowest in Africa. Abortion is legal to save the mother's life or to preserve her mental and physical health, and in cases of rape or fetal impairment.

See Also: Government, Women in; Roman Catholic Church; Single Mothers.

Further Readings

Scarr, Deryck. *Seychelles Since 1770: History of a Slave and Post-Slavery Society.* Trenton, NJ: Africa World Press, 2000.

United Nations Statistics Divisions. "UNdata: A World of Information: Gender Info." http://data.un.org/Explorer.aspx?d=GenderStat (accessed February 2010).

United States Department of State. "2007 Country Reports on Human Rights Practices: Seychelles." http://www.state.gov/g/drl/rls/hrrpt/2007/100502.htm (accessed June 2010).

Sarah Boslaugh
Washington University School of Medicine

Shari`a Law

The term *Shari`a* is usually translated as "Islamic law." However, it encompasses a broad range of issues, from daily worship practice to humanity's relationship with the divine to family and criminal law. Shari'a is drawn from several sources. The Qur'an is the primary legal source, and the *Sunnah,* the example set by the prophet Muhammad, is secondary. There is also a centuries-long tradition of Islamic legal interpretation and scholarship. Today, many Muslim women live in countries that make provisions for Islamic law or Islamic courts within the legal system. In most cases, states that provide for Islamic law in some capacity do so only for family-law matters for Muslims. In recent decades, many states have enacted reforms to address gender inequities in the law.

In countries where Islamic courts handle disputes among Muslims, women often bring the majority of cases forward. Usually, these claims involve family matters like marital disputes and divorce claims. Many types of divorce are permitted in Islamic law. Divorce by male unilateral repudiation, which in classical law does not need the approval of the wife or a legal authority, is well known, but women may seek divorce in court on various grounds, which differ according to legal school. Ethnographic research in places like Kenya, Zanzibar, and Yemen shows that women are often successful in winning their claims in court.

In the 7th century, the advent of Islam brought many new legal rights for women. Polygyny was restricted, and women could inherit property and initiate divorce. However, in light of modern standards, classical Islamic law has notable inequities. For example, men inherit a greater share of property than their sisters, can marry up to four wives, and can divorce with greater ease than women. Since the mid-20th century, many states have taken measures to remedy such inequities to reflect modern values. Reforms have often aimed at equalizing men's and women's rights in divorce, and with the advent of formalized legal codes, men's right to divorce through unilateral repudiation has often been restricted. Legal reform in Morocco, Tunisia, and Malaysia, for example, required all divorces to take place in the courts. Several countries have aimed to restrict polygyny in an effort to enhance gender justice, and Tunisia abolished the practice entirely, arguing that although it may have been con-

marriage, but another states that no man could possibly treat multiple wives equitably. Earlier modernist scholars made similar arguments about polygymy.

See Also: Islam; Islamic Feminism; Progressive Muslims (U.S.); Secularity Law, France.

Further Readings

An-Na'im, A. *Islamic Family Law in a Changing World: A Global Resource Book.* London: Zed Books, 2003.

Esposito, J. L. and N. J. DeLong-Bas. *Women in Muslim Family Law.* Syracuse, NY: Syracuse University Press, 2003.

Mir-Hosseini, Z. *Marriage on Trial: A Study of Islamic Family Law, Iran and Morocco Compared.* London: I. B. Tauris, 2000.

Stiles, E. *An Islamic Court in Context: An Ethnographic Study of Judicial Reasoning.* New York: Palgrave Macmillan, 2009.

Welchman, L., ed. *Women's Rights and Islamic Family Law.* London: Zed Books, 2004.

Erin Stiles
University of Nevada, Reno

The Qur'an is the primary source for Islamic law, and the examples set by the prophet Muhammad are secondary.

sidered acceptable at one point in Islamic history, the practice was not appropriate in the modern period.

In recent years, scholars and feminist organizations have campaigned for greater gender equity through the framework of Islam. Scholars have argued that the Islamic sacred sources stress gender equity, and activists have used this as a foundation to struggle for public policy ensuring women's rights. For example, Sisters in Islam, a Malaysian organization promoting Muslim women's rights, has recently argued that restricting polygyny is religiously correct. Although according to most interpretations of Islamic law, Muslim men may marry up to four wives, the organization interprets verses of the Qur'an that deal with polygyny (4:3 and 4:129) as discouraging the practice: One verse requires equal treatment of wives in a polygynous

Shepard, Judy

American gay rights activist Judy Shepard is the mother of Matthew Shepard, the 21-year-old gay college student whose 1998 murder captured national attention and energized debate on hate crimes legislation. Shepard and her husband, Dennis, created the Matthew Shepard Foundation in their son's memory, but she has been the face and the voice of the organization, serving as its executive director from 1999 to 2009. She continues to serve as board president and to travel across the United States speaking passionately of the need for social justice and acceptance of diversity.

From Homemaker to Activist

Born Judy Peck in Glenrock, Wyoming, in 1952, Shepard was the daughter of the town postmaster and a post office senior clerk. While a student at the University of Wyoming in Laramie, she met Dennis Shepard. The young woman who planned to be a teacher and the oil rigger married and moved to Casper, Wyoming, where Dennis had a job with the Occupational Safety and Health Administration. Matthew, the first of two sons, was born to the Shepards in 1976. Seventeen years later, Dennis Shepard's work as a safety engineer for Aramco took the family to Saudi Arabia. Shepard and her husband were still in Saudi Arabia five years later when the call came with the news that Matthew had been beaten, tied to a fence, and left for dead near Laramie. Less than a week later, Matt was dead, and Shepard's transformation from quiet homemaker to gay rights activist had begun.

Matthew Shepard was not the first victim of anti-gay violence, but the combination of his youth, the brutality of his murder, and the ordinariness of his family galvanized public sentiment. Memorials were held across the country, and contributions poured in to help cover medical costs. The Shepards used the contributions as seed money for the Matthew Shepard Foundation. Shepard began making speeches, calling for hate crime legislation to be extended to include sexual orientation. Soon the self-described introvert was making as many as 50 speeches a year, eventually racking up 250,000 frequent-flier miles annually as she spoke to crowds about her son's death and his life, as well as about the need for social acceptance and legal protection for gays and lesbians.

Five times Congress approved a bill providing for that protection, and each time the proposed legislation was defeated. After a decade as a crusader, Shepard published her memoir, *The Meaning of Matthew*, in September 2009. In the book, Shepard recounted in straightforward fashion her family's life, the unimaginable horror of Matt's murder, and her years of activism. On October 22, 2009, Congress passed the Matthew Shepard and James Byrd, Jr. Hate Crimes Prevention Act, which extended hate-crime status to include a victim's actual or perceived gender, sexual orientation or identity, or disability. President Barack Obama signed the bill into law on October 28, 2009.

See Also: Gay and Lesbian Advocacy; Hate Crimes; Sexual Orientation–Based Violence: United States.

Further Readings

Haygood, Will. "Honor Thy Son: Out of Tragedy, Judy Shepard Became Mother of a Movement." *The Washington Post* (July 13, 2003).

Loffreda, Beth. *Losing Matt Shepard*. New York: Columbia University Press, 2001.

Shepard, Judy. *The Meaning of Matthew: My Son's Murder in Laramie and a World Transformed*. New York: Hudson Street Press, 2009.

Wylene Rholetter
Auburn University

Shiva, Vandana

Vandana Shiva is a feminist environmentalist and philosopher of science whose work combines scientific and economic research with the principles of grassroots activism and social justice movements to resolve environmental problems at the local and global levels. Born November 5, 1952, in Dehradun, India, to a farmer mother with a love for nature and a forest conservationist father, Shiva demonstrated an early concern for environmental activism and social justice. During the 1970s, she participated in the Chipko movement—a nonviolent struggle by female peasants in India to prevent the cutting of trees and reclaim their traditional forest rights.

After receiving a B.S. in physics, Shiva pursued a master's degree in philosophy at the University of Guelph, Ontario, Canada, and then completed her doctoral degree in quantum theory physics at the University of Western Ontario in 1979. When her sister, a physician, informed her of the health effects of nuclear radiation on lifeforms, she began to question why her science education had not exposed her to such knowledge, prompting her eventual critiques and analyses of the worldview and assumptions of mainstream science. She later went on to undertake research in science, technology, and environmental policy at the Indian Institute of Science and the Indian Institute of Management in Bangalore.

Preservation of All Lifeforms

The author of more than 300 papers in scientific and technical journals, Shiva has also written several books, including *Soil Not Oil* (2008), *Earth Democracy* (2005), *Water Wars* (2002), *Stolen Harvest: The Hijacking of the Global Food Supply* (2000), *Biopiracy: The Plunder of Nature and Knowledge* (1997), *Monocultures* of the Mind: Perspectives on Biodiversity and Biotechnology (1993), and Staying Alive: Women, Ecology and Development (1988). In these works, she argues for the wisdom of many traditional practices in agriculture. She also promotes the ideals of partnership and cooperation and believes that other definitions of freedom, knowledge, and progress are needed to liberate both women and the environment from the restrictive definitions held by Western cultures since the Enlightenment period. She asserts that women's liberation will not take place unless there is a simultaneous struggle to preserve and liberate all lifeforms on earth from the dominant patriarchal and capitalist structures.

In her mission to put her ideas into practice, Shiva founded the Research Foundation for Science, Technology, and Ecology in 1982. Nine years later, she started Navdanya ("nine seeds"), a farm and organization whose mission is to save seeds, protect indigenous knowledge, and promote diversity while empowering women and children. With the creation of Bija Vidyapeeth ("Seed University"), an organic farm and center for holistic living, Shiva inaugurated a series of month-long courses to disseminate knowledge and initiate dialogue about holistic living. Through her assistance to grassroots organizations of the Green movement in Africa, Asia, Latin America, Ireland, Switzerland, and Austria with campaigns against genetic engineering, she has also contributed intellectual and activist support to contemporary essential debates about intellectual property rights, biodiversity, biotechnology, bioethics, and genetic engineering.

Awarded the Right Livelihood Award (more commonly known as the "Alternative Nobel Prize") in 1993 and the Global 500 Award of the United Nations Environment Program, Shiva is one of the leaders of the International Forum on Globalization and the ecology advisor to several organizations, including the Third World Network and the Asia Pacific People's Environment Network. She also serves on the boards of many organizations, such as the World Future Council and Slow Food International. Through her efforts to create a new paradigm for scientific research and to work in novel ways with communities, Shiva has had a profound effect on contemporary environmentalist thought and action.

See Also: Ecofeminism; Environmental Activism, Grassroots; Environmental Issues, Women and; Environmental Justice; Navdanya; Women's Environment and Development Organization.

Further Readings

Mies, Maria and Vandana Shiva. Ecofeminism. London: Zed Books, 1993.

Shiva, Vandana. Biopiracy: The Plunder of Nature and Knowledge. Cambridge, MA: South End, 1997.

Shiva, Vandana, ed. Close to Home: Women Reconnect Ecology, Health and Development Worldwide. Philadelphia, PA: New Society, 1994.

Shiva, Vandana. Earth Democracy: Justice, Sustainability, and Peace. Cambridge, MA: South End, 2005.

Shiva, Vandana, ed. Manifestos on the Future of Food and Seed. Cambridge, MA: South End, 2007.

Shiva, Vandana. Monocultures of the Mind: Perspectives on Biodiversity and Biotechnology. London: Zed Books; Penang: Third World Network,1993.

Shiva, Vandana. Soil Not Oil. Cambridge, MA: South End, 2008.

Shiva, Vandana. Staying Alive: Women, Ecology and Development. London: Zed Books, 1988.

Shiva, Vandana. Stolen Harvest: The Hijacking of the Global Food Supply. Cambridge, MA: South End, 2000.

Shiva, Vandana. Water Wars: Privatization, Pollution and Profit. Cambridge, MA : South End, 2002.

Shiva, Vandana and Ingunn Moser, eds. Biopolitics: A Feminist and Ecological Reader on Biotechnology. London: Zed Books, 1995.

Danielle Roth-Johnson
University of Nevada, Las Vegas

Shoemaker, Carolyn

Carolyn Shoemaker is an observational planetary astronomer who has discovered more than 30 comets and 800 asteroids, more than any other astronomer. She received wide recognition and media attention in 1993 after she codiscovered a comet that would impact Jupiter in July 1994. Shoemaker's discovery allowed both amateur and professional astronomers to witness the event, providing important insight into what would happen if a comet hit Earth. The Jupiter comet was named Shoemaker-Levy 9 after Shoemaker and her husband, astronomer and geologist Gene

Carolyn Shoemaker at the 18-inch Schmidt at Palomar Observatory in a 1986 photo taken by her husband, Gene.

mother of three children. Carolyn had accompanied her husband on many research trips and helped him as a field assistant for his work mapping and analyzing impact craters. After her children were grown, Shoemaker began working with her husband at the California Institute of Technology (CalTech). She used a stereoscope to review photographs of the night sky, looking for comets and Earth-approaching asteroids, spending as many as 100 hours to find one comet. The couple moved to Arizona, where Gene Shoemaker founded the USGS Center for Astrogeology and his wife worked as a visiting scientist. Gene Shoemaker was killed in a car accident in 1997 while the couple was on a research trip together in Australia; since then, Shoemaker has continued her astronomical observations for USGS.

Shoemaker was awarded an honorary doctorate in science from Northern Arizona University in 1990. She was named a Cloos Scholar of earth and planetary sciences at Johns Hopkins University in 1990. In 1996, she received an Exceptional Achievement Medal from the National Aeronautics and Space Administration (NASA); that same year Shoemaker was named both a Woman of Distinction by the National Association for Women in Education and a Distinguished Alumna of California State University, Chico. For her collaborations with her husband, she was corecipient of the Rittenhouse Medal of the Rittenhouse Astronomical Society in 1988 and the James Craig Watson Medal for astronomy from the National Academy of Science in 1998.

See Also: Astronomy, Women in; Science, Women in; Science Education for Girls; Women's Studies.

Further Readings

Levy, David H. *Impact Jupiter: The Crash of Comet Shoemaker-Levy 9.* New York: Basic Books, 1995.
U.S. Geological Survey. "Carolyn Shoemaker." Astrogeology Science Center. http://astrogeology.usgs .gov/About/People/CarolynShoemaker (accessed June 2010).
The Woman Astronomer. "Carolyn Shoemaker: The Comet Hunter." http://www.womanastronomer.com /carolyn_shoemaker.htm (accessed (June 2010).

Tiffany K. Wayne
Independent Scholar

Shoemaker, and their colleague, amateur astronomer David Levy. Since 1980, Shoemaker has been a visiting scientist at the U.S. Geological Survey's (USGS) Center for Astrogeology in Flagstaff, Arizona, where her husband was founding director. She has conducted regular observations at Palomar Observatory in California and is a research professor at Northern Arizona University in Flagstaff. Shoemaker's career achievements are all the more remarkable because she does not hold an advanced degree in astronomy and came to the field only later in life after raising a family.

Carolyn Jean Spellmann Shoemaker was born June 24, 1929, in Gallup, New Mexico. She received a bachelor's degree from Chico State College in California in 1949 and a master's degree in history and political science in 1950. She was a schoolteacher and then, after marrying Gene Shoemaker in 1951, a stay-at-home

Shooting Sports, Women in

Sports shooting arose from target practice, which was developed to hone hunting, self-defense, and military skills. Similar to the evolution of many sports, shooting was seen as a masculine activity, thus making it difficult for women to initially participate. Yet women have proven themselves to be outstanding shooters since the late 1800s, as past newspaper accounts have documented. Today, women around the globe excel in all levels of competition, including the Olympic games.

Women first participated in the Olympics in 1968, competing alongside men in open events. At the 1976 Olympic Games, American Margaret Thompson Murdock became the first female shooter to win an Olympic medal, the silver, in the 50m rifle 3 position event, and in 1992, Chinese shooter Shan Zhang won the gold in International Skeet. This was the last year women competed against men. By 1996, all shooting events had become segregated, and rules for the women's events were changed, making it impossible to compare their scores with those of men.

The Impact of Religious Beliefs

Some women are prohibited from participating because of the national religious beliefs held by their home countries. The first Islamic Countries Women Sport Games were organized in 1993 to accommodate Islamic restrictions on body and hair covering for women, which prevented Islamic women athletes from participating in the Olympics. Men could attend the awards ceremonies, but the competitions themselves were women only, which allowed women to wear the gear necessary for full mobility during competition. Even although the outfit was less an issue for shooters because they could easily remain concealed, it was not until 1996 that Iran, a Muslim country, allowed its female citizens to participate in the Olympics. Lida Fariman was Iran's female shooting representative that year.

Similar to other Olympic athletes, female shooters may be supported by their family, community, government, and national sports organizations, and/or through commercial endorsements. Star shooters are given resources with hopes they will bring home medals for their country. For example, American Kimberly Rhode was supported by her family, her local gun club, commercial endorsements, and USA Shooting, the governing body for Olympic shooting sports; in 1996, at age 17 years, she won a gold in Double Trap. The People's Republic of China has a 60-year history of supporting its athletes; at the 2008 games, Chinese female shooters brought home gold medals in three of the six shooting matches: Wenjun Guo (10m air pistol), Ying Chen (25m pistol), and Li Du (50m rifle 3 positions). Du also won a gold medal in the 10m air pistol in 2004.

Although still not a popular sport with most women, shooting is one of the few sports in which women can compete equally with men in many types of competitions. This is because shooting requires talent, skill, and mental acuity more than muscles. Evidence of this can be seen among military women, who demonstrate outstanding firearm skills and may be placed on coed shooting teams. This was the case for American Spc. Liana Bombardier, member of the U.S. Army Marksmanship Unit. Bombardier won the Service Rifle National Long Range Rifle Championship in 2003—a first for women in the competition's 100-year history.

For shooters as well as other female athletes participating in traditionally male sports, prejudice remains. Issues of masculinity and homosexuality, along with social, cultural, and religious values, continue to play a role in encouraging or denying female shooters competitive opportunities. Whether competing with a shotgun, handgun, or rifle, competitive women shooters face formidable expenses: a quality firearm, ammunition, a place to practice, and thousands of hours of practice time are minimum requirements. In those countries where female shooters have found support, they have succeeded.

See Also: Cowboy Action Shooting; "Femininity," Social Construction of; Gender, Defined; "Masculinity," Social Construction of; Olympics, Summer; Olympics, Winter; Rhode, Kim; Sports, Women in; Title IX.

Further Readings

Birrell, S. and C. L. Cole. *Women, Sport, and Culture.* Champaign, IL: Human Kinetics, 1994.

Hargreaves, Jennifer. *Heroines of Sport: The Politics of Difference and Identity.* New York: Routledge, 2000.

Hargreaves, Jennifer. *Sporting Females: Critical Issues in the History and Sociology of Women's Sports.* New York: Routledge, 1994.

Hartmann-Tews, I. and G. Pfister. *Sport and Women: Social Issues in International Perspective.* New York: Routledge, 2003.

Pagán, Paula J. Randall. "Woman Wins National Rifle Championship," *Soldier* (November 2003).

USA Shooting. http://www.usashooting.org (accessed July 2010).

Nancy Floyd
Georgia State University

Showalter, Elaine

Elaine Showalter, professor emeritus at Princeton University, revolutionized the field of feminist literary theory with the publication of *A Literature of Their Own: British Women Novelists from Brontë to Lessing* (1978), "Toward a Feminist Poetics" (1979), and "Feminist Criticism in the Wilderness" (1981), among other seminal texts. With *Feminist Poetics*, she established the field of gynocriticism—a mode of literary theory that seeks to examine women as writers by interrogating the history, themes, genres, structures, and other features of literature by women.

Education and Career

Elaine Cottler was born in 1941 in Boston, Massachusetts. Her father worked in the wool business and her mother was a housewife. Her parents disowned her when she married English Showalter in 1962. The Showalters have two children: Michael Showalter and Vinca Showalter LaFleur. Showalter earned her bachelor's degree from Bryn Mawr College, a master's degree from Brandeis University, and a Ph.D. from the University of California, Davis in 1970. In her essay "Twenty Years on: 'A Literature of Their Own' Revisited," Showalter recounts receiving her Ph.D. the same month that she gave birth to her second child. She began teaching at Princeton University in 1984 and retired in 2003. Her Ph.D. thesis, *The Double Critical Standard*, formed the basis of *A Literature of Their Own*, her foundational extension and reworking of the feminist literary theory set up in Virginia Woolf's *A Room of One's Own* (1929).

As Showalter imagined it, gynocriticism functions as an attempt to create a female framework for analyzing women's literature rooted in female experience and liberated from male literary history. She explains in "Toward a Feminist Poetics" that studying stereotypes of women, sexism in male-authored literary criticism, and the limitations of women's roles in literary history only reinscribes these inequalities and neglects the lived experience of women writers, readers, and subjects. Her project engendered a tremendous interest in recovery work and led to the canonization of many forgotten female authors.

Moreover, gynocriticism provided a much-needed corollary to the images of women criticism typical of Mary Ellmann and Kate Millet. Showalter's writing, along with Ellen Moer's *Literary Women* (1976), helped identify clear trends and trajectories in women's literary history; they also opened up and enriched the study of women's lives and experiences by suggesting ways of dismantling literary and cultural hierarchies. However, gynocritics' emphasis on biological essentialism led many feminist literary theorists (notably Toril Moi) to critique it; Margaret J. M. Ezell also exposed many of the sedimented biases toward 19th-century literature in Showalter's work as well as in Sandra Gilbert and Susan Gubar's roughly contemporaneous study *The Madwoman in the Attic* (1979).

Some of Showalter's other major works of feminist literary theory include *The Female Malady: Women, Madness, and English Culture, 1830–1980* (1985), *Sexual Anarchy: Gender and Culture at the Fin-de-Siècle* (1990), *Sister's Choice: Tradition and Change in American Women's Writing* (1991), *Hystories: Hysterical Epidemics and Modern Media* (1997), and *Inventing Herself: Claiming a Feminist Intellectual Heritage* (2001). She has also written academic novels and articles for popular publications, ranging from the *Guardian* and the *Nation* to *People* magazine.

See Also: Feminism, American; Feminism on College Campuses; Working Mothers.

Further Readings
Allen, Carolyn J. "Feminist(s) Reading: A Response to Elaine Showalter." *Writing and Sexual Difference.* Chicago: University of Chicago Press, 1982.

Jacobus, Mary. "Reading Woman (Reading)." *Feminisms: An Anthology of Literary Theory and Criticism.* New Brunswick, NJ: Rutgers University Press, 1997.

Showalter, Elaine. *A Jury of Her Peers: Celebrating American Women Writers From Anne Bradstreet to Annie Proulx.* New York: Vintage, 2010.

Showalter, Elaine. "Twenty Years On: 'A Literature of Their Own Revisited." *Novel: A Forum on Fiction,* v.31/3 (1998).

Emily Bowles
Lawrence University

Sierra Leone

Sierra Leone is a small country located on the West African coast that is home to approximately 6 million people and is continually ranked as one of the poorest countries in the world. In 2002, Sierra Leone emerged from a 10-year civil war that ravaged the country and resulted in over half of the population being displaced. Over 80 percent of all refugees were women and children. From 1991 to 2002, Sierra Leone was embroiled in bloody civil war, which greatly affected the lives of the nation's women. Throughout the war, women were abducted, were victims of sexual violence, and were forced into conscription. Between 50,000 and 64,000 women were victims of sexual violence, such as rape and sexual slavery, and many were forced into unwanted marriages. When returning to society, former refugees and soldiers lacked basic healthcare, education, food, shelter, and clothing.

Before the outbreak of civil war in Sierra Leone, women were viewed as second-class citizens in the eyes of the law and social norms. Polygamy is practiced in many parts of Sierra Leone, which can cause conflict within the family and expose women to increased risks of sexually transmitted diseases and human immunodeficiency virus and acquired immune deficiency syndrome (HIV/AIDS). Genital mutilation is also practiced in Sierra Leone.

Women in urban areas of Sierra Leone have been making strides in education and political reform, but

This primary school was completely destroyed during Sierra Leone's 10-year civil war. Rebel soldiers used it as a base and training ground, and used its books and wooden furnishings as fuel for fires.

the uneven distribution of schools has caused this movement to grow slowly. Most schools are located in the south and in urban areas, leaving women in rural settings uneducated. There has been an emphasis on the education of women in Sierra Leone by local governments, the United Nations (UN), and associated organizations. After the war, hundreds of nongovernmental organizations emerged to institute rehabilitation and reintegration projects. Many of these projects targeted young women with the intention of improving their economic and emotional status and increasing their knowledge of health and reproductive issues.

In an effort to create peace and stability in Sierra Leone, UN peacekeeping forces have had a large presence in the country; as a result, there has been an increase in prostitution. Women working as prostitutes are often faced with sexual violence, the spread of HIV/AIDS, and lack of proper reproductive healthcare. Large-scale efforts to protect women from physical and sexual violence have proved fruitful over the past few years. In 2007, after efforts made by woman's groups, three "gender bills" were made into law. The Domestic Violence Act, the Registration of Customary Marriage and Divorce Act, and the Devolution of Estates Act offer women in Sierra Leone the protection of the law, which was not available previously.

See Also: Domestic Violence; Female Genital Surgery; Geographical Distribution; Rape in Conflict Zones; Reproductive and Sexual Health Rights.

Further Readings

Coulter, Chris. *Bush Wives and Girl Soldiers: Women's Lives Through War and Peace in Sierra Leone*. Ithaca, NY: Cornell University Press, 2009.

Lamin, Sylvester Amara. *Women and Development in Sierra Leone*. Baltimore, MD: Publish America, 2007.

McKay, Susan and Dyan Mazurana. *Where Are the Girls? Girls in Fighting Forces in Northern Uganda, Sierra Leone and Mozambique: Their Lives During and After the War*. Montreal, Canada: Rights & Democracy, 2004.

Steady, Filomina Chioma. *Women and Collective Action in Africa: Development, Democratization, and Empowerment, With Special Focus on Sierra Leone*. Basingstoke, UK: Palgrave MacMillan, 2006.

Meggan A. Houlihan
Ball State University

Sigurðardóttir, Jóhanna

Jóhanna Sigurðardóttir (Icelandic), or Johanna Sigurdardottir (as generally printed in the English press), became prime minister of Iceland in 2009—the first woman to hold that position in the country's history and the world's first openly homosexual head of state. Iceland's longest-serving member of parliament, Sigurðardóttir brought three decades of legislative experience to her new position, along with a reputation for championing social issues such as gender equality and rights for the disabled and elderly. A member of the Social Democratic Alliance party, she won support across the political spectrum. Polls gave her a 73 percent approval rate at a time when Iceland was in the midst of an economic meltdown and government ministers were scorned as contributors to the crisis.

Sigurðardóttir was born in Reykjavik in 1942. She worked as a flight attendant for what is now Icelandair and became involved with trade unions early in her professional life, serving as president of the Board of the Icelandic Cabin Crew Association in 1966 and 1969 and as president of the Board of Svölurnar, Association of Former Stewardesses, in 1975. She married Torvaldur Johannesson, a banker, in 1970, and the couple had two sons, born in 1972 and 1977. She and Johannesson divorced, and in 2002, she wed Jonina Leosdottir, a writer, in a civil ceremony. Although the international press headlined Sigurðardóttir's sexual orientation, it is a nonissue in Iceland, which decriminalized gay sex in 1940 and made same-sex marriages legal in 1996, one of the first countries to do so.

An Impressive Political Career

First elected to parliament in 1978, Sigurðardóttir was reelected eight times. She served as minister of Social Affairs and Social Security four times between 1994 and 2009. Her refusal to use the official limousine and driver provided to all ministers set the tone for her service. She is credited with pushing through policies that widened housing opportunities for Iceland's poor and strengthened the social welfare system. When her bid to become leader of the Social Democratic Party in 1994 failed, she briefly formed her own party but returned to the Social Democrats in 2000 and rejoined the government as social affairs minister in 2007, where she remained until 2009. Her persistence in pushing for the rights of the less privileged earned her the sobriquet "Saint Johanna."

When Iceland's conservative-led government collapsed in 2008 in the wake of a failed banking system, double-digit unemployment, and rising public anger with elected officials, the new coalition government of Social Democrats and Left-Greens named Sigurðardóttir as acting prime minister. In April elections, her coalition won a strong mandate, and she was sworn in as prime minister on February 1, 2009. Promising to return to Iceland's social welfare roots, Sigurðardóttir announced a plan to replace the central bank's directors and to pursue membership in the European Union.

The latter goal is not without controversy because of the history of disputes with the United Kingdom, a European Union member, concerning fishing rights and territorial waters, but Sigurðardóttir was not swayed in her commitment to European Union membership as Iceland's best hope for economic recovery.

She has also acted on her belief in an egalitarian government. Arguing that women were "untainted" by the errors of former leadership, she set up a government that is 50 percent female. *Forbes* named her to its 100 Most Powerful Women list for 2009. Her formidable strength on national and international issues suggests the title is well earned.

See Also: Flight Attendants; Iceland; Heads of State, Female; Representation of Women in Government, International.

Further Readings

Books LLC. *Icelandic Women in Politics: Vigdís Finnbogadóttir, Jóhanna Sigurðardóttir, Valgerður Sverrisdóttir, Þorgerður Katrín Gunnarsdóttir.* Books LLC, 2010.

Byers, David. "Johanna Sigurdardottir, World's First Openly Gay Leader, to Take Power in Iceland." *Times Online* (January 29, 2009). http://www.timesonline .co.uk/tol/news/world/europe/article5610520.ece (accessed August 2010).

McDonald, Alyssa. "Gordon Brown Went Beyond What Was Justified." *New Statesman.* http://www.newstates man.com/europe/2010/01/gordon-brown-iceland -interview (accessed July 2010).

Wylene Rholetter
Auburn University

Sikhism

Sikhism is a monotheistic religion established primarily in the 15th century in the Punjab region of southern Asia and has approximately 25 million followers worldwide. The term *Sikh* originates from the Sanskrit words *Sisya* and *Siksa,* meaning "disciple" or "learner" and "instruction," respectively. Punjabi and Gurmukhi are the primary languages used in Sikhism and by the Sikh people.

Pillars of Practice and Scripture

Sikhism has three foundational pillars: Naam Japna, Vand Chakna, and Kirat Karni. Naam Japna is the recitation of God's name through meditation or singing hymns from the Guru Granth Sahib, the Sikh Holy Scripture. Vand Chakna is the concept of sharing with others, including a mandatory donation of 10 percent of one's earnings. This concept is further practiced in Sikh Gurdwara's, the place of worship, where a free kitchen is open to all. Working hard and truthfully is the idea of the third pillar, Kirat Karni. Additionally, Sikhism teaches equality among all of humanity, preaches overall truthful living, demands social justice, and denounces superstitions and blind rituals.

The Guru Granth Sahib is a collection of religious teachings in the form of hymns or *shabads,* prayers, and poems, describing the ethereal qualities of God and the importance of remembrance. The Guru Granth Sahib consists of 1,430 pages composed by six of the 10 Sikh Gurus, as well as numerous saints and poets from various religions whose views were deemed consistent with the Gurus' message. The open acceptance of a non-Sikh's work into the Holy Scripture was a social breakthrough at its time. This scripture even incorporated words of the lowest social caste, the untouchables, thereby raising them to the level of saints and denouncing the caste system. The Guru Granth Sahib is the written embodiment of the 10 Gurus and is thus considered the final Guru of the Sikhs.

Once a Sikh is ready to fully embrace the teachings of the Guru Granth Sahib, he or she will participate in the Sikh version of the baptism ceremony, known as Amrit Sanchar. A Sikh is required to wear five articles, known as the Five Kakkars. These include *Kesh,* unshorn hair; *Kara,* a steel bracelet; *Kanga,* a small comb; *Kirpan,* a dagger (that is legally required in the United States to be less than four inches long); and *Kachera,* a specially designed undergarment. All these guidelines are outlined in the Sikh Rehat Maryada, a more recently compiled code of conduct of the principles taught by the Gurus. The democratic nature of Sikhism is seen in the ability of Sikhs to create their code of conduct, in that religious rules can made or changed by the Sikhs as long as they do not go against the teaching of the Guru Granth Sahib.

Position and Achievements of Sikh Women

"From woman, man is born;

Within woman, man is conceived; to woman he is engaged and married.

Woman becomes his friend; through woman, the future generations come.

When his woman dies, he seeks another woman; to woman he is bound.

So why call her bad? From her, kings are born.

From woman, woman is born; without woman, there would be no one at all."

(Sri Guru Granth Sahib Ji [SGGSJ], p. 473)

Guru Nanak Dev Ji, the first of the 10 Sikh Gurus, taught his disciples the importance of equality among race, ethnicity, age, and gender. As can be seen in the above quotation, women are to be held in equally high stature as men in Sikhism, as women are the means by which men exist and all of humanity continues. Salvation within Sikhism is defined as achieving spiritual enlightenment, in which the soul is merged with the light of God. "In all beings is the Lord pervasive, the Lord pervades all forms male and female" (SGGSJ, p. 605).

Thus, it can be seen that this enlightenment is not only for a man, but a woman can achieve this highest form of salvation as well.

There are numerous examples of Sikhism's emphasis on women's equality. However, women are not always equally treated in society, due to strong cultural norms within Sikh households. Women are often overly protected and men given more free reign, due to what is thought to be the vulnerability of women. Another example of this inequality is the reported cases of infanticide in the highly Sikh-populated Punjab region of India. Though prohibited by the teachings of Sikhism, female infanticide is prominent in that region.

A Sikh preacher addressing an audience in the Golden Temple, the most sacred shrine of the Sikhs, in Amritsar, India.

When looking at high-level Sikh leaders, very few if any women have infiltrated the ranks within the religious hierarchy despite being involved in lower-level processes, such as voting. Women are equals when attending services, performing hymns, and even leading congregations. However, the religious-governing bodies have tended to be dominantly male.

Today, we are seeing numerous Sikh women gain ground in various fields, from politics to sports, science, and even music. In 1999, Jagir Sekhon was elected to be mayor of the London Borough of Greenwich, making her the first woman Sikh mayor in Britain; Balwinder Kaur Bhatia and Harpreet Kaur Gill were the first Sikh women to represent India in the 1980 Moscow Olympics; Dr. Kalpana Chawla was the first Indian woman to go into space; and Snatam Kaur Khalsa is a New Age Grammy Award nominee for her spiritual music. On a smaller scale, Sikh women have become a facet of American society, impacting lives by their work in medicine, engineering, law, and much more.

If applied correctly, the teachings of Sikhism promote complete equality between men and women in all aspects of life, from day-to-day differences to salvation. Unfortunately, all too often, these teachings are overshadowed by cultural and societal norms leading to inequality and sexism among Sikh's. Sikh women today are strengthening themselves and their presence by using Sikhism's religious teachings of equality to make an impact in the world.

See Also: India; Pakistan; Religion, Women in; Religious Fundamentalism, Cross-Cultural Context of.

Further Readings

Cole, W. Owen. *Understanding Sikhism (Understanding Faith).* Edinburgh, UK: Dunedin Academic Press, 2004.

Samra, Mandeep Kaur. *Modern Sikh Historiography.* Anand Parbat, Delhi, India: K. K. Publication, 2004.

Virdi, Manprit Kaur. "Silence: Resistance or Acquiescence? Sikh Women's Perspectives on Canadian Law." *Socio-Legal Studies, Master's Research Paper.* Toronto: York University, 2010.

Mandeep Kaur
University of Texas, Austin
Jasmeet Kaur
Independent Scholar
Parminder Singh
Centers for Disease Control and Prevention

Singapore

Singapore is a small island nation-state with a population of close to 5 million people. It is a former British colony that gained its independence in 1965. Singapore is a multiethnic and multireligious society: the three major ethnic groups are Chinese (75 percent), Malay (13 percent), and Indians (9 percent). The country has four official languages: English, Mandarin Chinese, Malay, and Tamil. English is the language of administration and commerce and is widely spoken all over the island. Commonly described as one of the "Asian Tigers" or "Little Dragons," Singapore is among the Asian "miracle economies" that transformed from "Third World" to "First World" in 30 years. It has one of the highest gross domestic products in the world, and its major industries are electronics, financial services, petroleum refining, and pharmaceutical manufacturing. State power is extremely strong, and the government has been controlled by the People's Action Party since gaining its independence from Britain.

At first glance, Singaporean women appear to enjoy a high level of autonomy, independence, and state protection. This level of protection comes from the groundbreaking Women's Charter, a bill passed in 1961 that legalized important civil and social rights for the nation's women. The Woman's Charter outlawed polygamy and legally allowed women to own property, stand for public office, conduct business in their own names, and participate in all forms of social, economic and political activity.

Singaporean women receive high levels of education and form 42.1 percent of all economically active residents. All women receive at least 10 years of mandatory education, and Singaporean women comprise 53.1 percent of university graduates. The nation's women are strongly encouraged to participate in the country's workforce. Since the 1970s, the government has made several attempts to entice mothers to return to work after they have given birth.

Discrimination in the Home

Despite advances in education, government, and business, Singaporean women still face discrimination at home. In this society there is the persistent belief in traditional family values, which position men as the head of the household. While possessing the same legal and political rights as men, Singaporean women still generally continue to believe that their primary responsibility is in the home rather than in their careers.

This domestic image of women accounts for the lack of women in powerful positions, both within the government and in important civil and corporate bodies. There are no full female ministers in the Singapore parliament. Women's issues are only represented in the "Women's Desk," a subsidiary of the Family Policy Unit within the government's Ministry of Community Development, Youth and Sports. In the private sector, only 27.5 percent of people in managerial and executive positions in the country are women. At the top level, only 14.7 percent of women are chief executive officers, managing directors, or director generals.

In addition, because tradition holds that men should be the head of the household, 61 percent of women choose to remain economically inactive to fulfill the role of housewife/homemaker. Women also consistently earn less than men, and less than half of the top income bracket earners are women. Older women between the ages of 55 and 64 find it much more difficult to find employment than men.

However, this scenario is rapidly changing. In 2006, 23.4 percent of parliament members were women, a large improvement over the 16.13 percent in the previous parliament. The Singapore government also is actively creating policies to ameliorate the conditions of life for older women. This situation is likely to further improve as Singaporean women become more educated and as the state begins to shift its policies to include more women in positions of power.

See Also: Equal Pay; Gender Roles, Cross-Cultural; Government, Women in; United Kingdom.

Further Readings

Heng, Geraldine. "State Fatherhood: The Politics of Nationalism, Sexuality and Race in Singapore." In Andrew Parker, et al., eds., *Nationalisms and Sexualities*. London: Routledge, 1991.

Holden, Philip. "A Man and an Island: Gender and Nation in Lee Kuan Yew's *The Singapore Story*." *Biography*, v.24/2 (2001).

Trocki, Carl. *Singapore: Wealth, Power and the Culture of Control*. London: Routledge, 2006.

Adeline Koh
Independent Scholar

Single Mothers

A number of different terms have been used to refer to households where only one parent, usually the mother, cares for dependent children: unmarried mothers, lone mothers, single mothers, one-parent families. "Lone parent" usually implies living alone without a partner but with dependent children. "Single parent" is more suggestive of marital status, that is, never married. Among one-parent families, the term *lone mother* today still constitutes a central factor, both for historical and sociodemographic reasons. First, the one-parent figure has historically coincided with that of the "unmarried mother." The considerable numerical disproportion between "lone" mothers and fathers in favor of the former should also not be forgotten. This may be explained by multiple factors: the tendency to give custody to the mother in case of separation or divorce; the higher death rate among men; the higher rate of second marriages among divorced men than women; the tendency of children born outside wedlock to live with their mothers.

The families composed of one parent do not, however, constitute a static reality: we may rather speak of plural experiences, historically molded and co-located at the crossing of complex, contrasting trends that are worth illustrating and commenting upon.

Difficulty of Simply Defining Lone Parents

Lone parents are generally defined in the research as families consisting of one parent, who is not a cohabitant, who is either living alone or with others, and who has dependent children. Although grouped together under a "single" definition, these families in reality vary greatly, due to the different existential and relational forms that may create them: widowhood, procreation outside wedlock, separation in fact, legal separation, or divorce.

Similarly, there is a great variability in the factors that may bring about the end of the condition of single parenthood: for example, marriage, cohabitation, children gaining independence, or children leaving the family nucleus. With this variety of transitions around the condition of single parenthood, a standard international definition does not exist to define this figure with precision.

In particular, there are three aspects that create ambiguity in pinpointing a criterion enabling the clear definition and thus facilitating the quantification of the phenomenon in a comparative view:

- the marital status of the parent (bachelor/spinster, married, separated, or divorced);
- the composition of the family: the presence or absence of a member of the family of origin, of a relative, of a partner. This variety strongly

questions the very concept of single parenthood (ie., may a parent actually exist "alone?").

- the definition of a "dependent" child (until what age may a child actually be considered dependent on the family of origin?).

The strong differences existing between the various national differences make the data sources highly heterogeneous and often difficult to compare.

Differences in Lone Mother Households

A second observation: lone mothers are often presented as a homogeneous group, sharing similar disadvantages and existing as a group distinct from other women and from two-parent households. This conflation facilitates the social construction of lone motherhood as a social problem. Lone mothers are still constructed as deficit families in social and educational policies. They are positioned within a discourse that places lone-mother families as a threat to the moral order.

And yet, lone-parent families are increasingly diversifying today, and the variations in age and generation, gender, ethnic group, and sexual orientation must not be underestimated. A transition is in fact taking place between the old lone parenthood, due to widowhood, to the new lone parenthood, stemming from the voluntary conclusion of the family union and from births outside wedlock. This transition reveals interesting aspects for both the social sciences and for social policies. Lone parents belonging to different groups are necessarily bearers of diversified needs: if lone widowed and probably elderly mothers, living with adult children, may pose a problem of dependence on their children, the problem arising from divorced or unmarried mothers is closely linked to the burden of family responsibilities and dependence of young children.

The experience of lone parents may, moreover, take on very different meanings according to the point in the life course at which it occurs. Young lone mothers, for example, embody significant contradictions, mixing the needs of adult life and those of adolescence. They accelerate and, at the same time, overlap the events that accompany the transition into adult life. They have considerably anticipated the reproductive function: motherhood precedes the completion of their education, their entry into the labor market and the estab-lishment of an autonomous household. This "wrong" sequence of events is the cause of their vulnerability.

As far as gender is concerned, while lone mothers are more numerous than lone fathers, on the other hand the number of lone fathers is constantly increasing. The past 15 years have seen a marked increase in the number of lone fathers in the United States and in the interest shown to this population by social science researchers. In 2000, 11 percent (approximately 179,000) of lone parents were men in the United Kingdom. In Germany, the percentage of lone fathers increased from 13.6 percent of all lone parents in 1991 to 19.5 percent in the year 2000.

Being lone mothers and fathers also appear to be experiences that may vary greatly from one culture to another and from one ethnic group to another. This is because the individual perception of this condition, its duration, and the form of help and support networks activated, for lone mothers in particular, may vary considerably.

But the spaces of everyday living questioned by the growing presence and diversification of one-parent families and households do not end here. We are speaking of the changes that have profoundly affected traditional gender balances and that have at the same time influenced the composition of one-parent families and households. We also mean the increasingly complex crossings between lone parenthood, changes in gender identity, and plurality of sexual desire and orientation that have further diversified the reality of these families: nonheterosexual, transgender, and transsexual lone parents. It should be acknowledged that research on lesbian and gay parents and their children, though no longer new, is still limited in extent.

Extended Families and Social Isolation

A further significant point for reflection is found in the idea that the parent is truly, actually "alone." While on the one hand, common sense suggests that the lone mother or father lives only with her/his children, lone parenthood turns out to be a much more complex condition. These nuclei may benefit from the presence of a member of the family of origin, a relative, or a partner. In other words, lone mothers and fathers may form a family as such and be part of an extended family—for example, that of the family of origin—living with friends/acquaintances, and so on.

Studies on teenage lone mothers carried out in Italy show that this group—although very small in number—cannot be considered as homogeneous regarding its needs. On the contrary, we may hypothesize its polarization, in terms of the variable "distance" from the family, into two segments with strongly differentiated needs. On the one hand are women who live with their family, with a high degree of protection and help; on the other hand are young women who cannot rely on any family support, for example, lone migrant mothers.

Research studies carried out in France reveal that, in the case of some communities (e.g., central African, Caribbean) the word *monoparentalité* is highly unsuitable. They are often extended families, in which the generations live together and tend to mix (the mother helping the daughter, the elder brothers and sisters taking care of the younger ones), and in which—also due to the frequently poor financial means—the networks of family, relatives, and friends may be active in enabling the lone mother to work. Community membership may, on the other hand, also bring negative effects to bear on the life courses of lone parents. There are also forms of concealed mono-parenthood in some cultures where being a lone mother is considered blameworthy and a stigma. This situation may often be kept hidden from the eyes and opinions of others.

Rather than of "lone" mothers and fathers, therefore, we may speak of forms of social isolation—the absence of contacts with other people in everyday life—which may affect some of these families.

Economic Disadvantages Considered

A further, important common factor in international statistics is that one-parent families constitute a disadvantaged group in terms of financial, personal, and time resources. These nuclei equally reveal a greater dependence on the welfare systems (which is generally seen in a longer duration of the periods when making use of social benefits). However, the discursive construction of the "single mother on welfare" does not match reality. Lone mothers do not constitute a disadvantaged group in themselves; that is, there is no causal relationship or inevitable association between the condition of lone parenthood and the condition of poverty. As far as the mothers are concerned, their disproportionate vulnerability to deprivation stems from the interaction between economic disadvantages and gender inequalities in the labor market, in the family and care section, and in the welfare systems.

The biographies of lone mothers are in fact closely intertwined with a complex interacting of factors that, starting from the low recognition of women's unpaid work in the nonmonetary economy, reach the limits deriving from the gender division of work, the assumption by social policies of women's dependence on their male partner and the lack of women's income following widowhood, separation or divorce, as well as due to the failures and delays on the part of divorced husbands in contributing financially to the upkeep of their former wives.

Regarding lone fathers, we must mention the growing financial difficulties encountered after separation or divorce in coping with their obligation to maintain their former wives and children. The problem linked to the high costs of renting and the lack of public-funded housing should also not be forgotten, in that it may considerably affect the quality of their lives. Lastly, the transition into lone fatherhood also has to be dealt with. A study in the United Kingdom by Gingerbread on 115 lone fathers shows that the main support during the transition into lone fatherhood came from their children's grandparents and friends and neighbors. Twenty-two percent said that no one had supported them. The main support they would have liked was a group or individual to talk to, to counter their social isolation and the pressure of sole responsibility for their children.

For these reasons also, the children in one-parent families do not seem to be very numerous. For example, Italian data relating to 2003 show that, in the majority of cases, there is only one child (68.2 per cent), while there are few with three or more children. The situation is very different for couples with children: 45.1 percent have one child and 43.8 percent have two.

The reasons for this difference may be due to various factors: in the case of unmarried mothers, they probably tend not to repeat the difficult experience of bringing up children outside a couple relationship, while in the case or separated or divorced persons, the existence of a more conflicting couple relationship and a shorter period of living together is likely to have influenced this decision. The number of children in families with one parent is also affected by the factor of the parents' age. Widowed mothers, generally older, have a larger number of children than others, because they are likely to have concluded their procreative capacity before the death of their husband.

See Also: "Femininity," Social Construction of; Gender, Defined; Gender Roles, Cross-Cultural; Stereotypes of Women.

Further Readings

Daguerre, Anne and Corinne Nativel, eds. *When Children Become Parents. Welfare State Responses to Teenage Pregnancy*. Bristol, UK: The Policy Press, 2006.

Duncan, Simon and Rosalind Edwards, eds. *Single Mothers in International Context: Mothers or Workers?* London: UCL Press, 1997.

Edin, Kathryn and Laura Lein. *Making Ends Meet: How Single Mothers Survive Welfare and Low-Wage Work*. New York: Russell Sage Foundation, 1997.

Ford, Reuben and Jane Millar, eds. *Private Lives and Public Responses: Lone Parenthood and Future Policy*. London: Policy Studies Institute, 1998.

Kiernan, Kathleen, et al. *Lone Mothers in Twentieth Century Britain: From Footnote to Front Page*. Oxford, UK: Oxford University Press, 1998.

Klett-Davies, Martina. *Going it Alone? Lone Motherhood in Late Modernity*. Aldershot, UK: Ashgate, 2007.

Standing, K. "Lone Mothers and 'Parental' Involvement: A Contradiction in Policy?" *Journal of Social Policy*, v.28/3 (1999).

Elisabetta Ruspini
University of Milano-Bicocca

Single-Sex Education

Single-sex schools have been utilized throughout history for very different purposes. For example, so-called first-generation single-sex schools came to existence as male-only institutions expressly because males were thought to be the sex that was capable and deserving of education. Eventually, all-female academies were born to prove that women, too, were capable of learning and also deserved a share of societal attention in the education sphere.

However, it was not until the advent of the Common School Movement, started by Horace Mann in the 1830s, that students of the working class and poor were deemed fit for education. During this time, public schools became coeducational—not for any philosophical reason, but due to efficiency and budgetary concerns stemming from the numerical growth of willing students. Single-sex schools continued, mostly in the form of private, oftentimes parochial institutions.

In modern times, so-called second-generation single-sex schools have reinvented themselves as a medium for affirmative action and a remedy to social disadvantage. For example, Detroit and Milwaukee school districts attempted to establish single-sex academies for boys of African heritage yet met rigorous resistance. Attempts to establish single-sex schools for girls were also met with threats of litigation from civil rights groups. The most famous case was the Young Women's Leadership School (YWLS) in New York City.

Besides being a focus of recent popular culture, single-sex schooling has received legitimacy in the policy environment with changes to Title IX in conjunction with the No Child Left Behind Act (NCLB). After Republican Senator Kay Bailey Hutchison of Texas introduced the amendment to NCLB, schools offering gender-separate classrooms have increased from four in 1998 to 228 in 2006, with 44 of those schools entirely single sex. While political will reflects support for expanding parental school choice, current policy discourse continues to assume balkanized positions between those believing single-sex schools are a violation of civil rights and those purporting that such schools are a remedy to a multitude of problems youths face in urban society.

Effects of Single-Sex Schooling

To date, none of the exhaustive reviews of the literature have turned up a significant body of evidence demonstrating negative effects of single-sex schooling. A limited number of studies indicate mixed or ambiguous results. Research citing positive effects indicates encouraging changes in attitude, self-esteem, academic engagement, higher achievement, and greater gender equity. Overall, findings are especially convincing for low-income and working-class students and particularly persuasive concerning African American and Hispanic students.

For example, girls who attend single-sex schools experience higher levels of self-esteem and confidence. This is an important consideration because a feeling of confidence is a variable cited most often in predicting female mathematics achievement. While more research is needed to ascertain possible cause-effect relationships, there is a general consensus that girls in single-sex schools prefer math and physics and perceive them as less masculine than their co-educated peers. Similarly, boys from single-sex environments exhibited stronger preferences for music and art when compared with other boys in coeducational environments.

Studies also show that girls who attend single-sex schools are provided more opportunities to serve in leadership positions in their schools, whereas in coed environments, girls might be members of clubs, but the boys take the leadership roles. Overall, girls who attended single-sex schools evidenced more open attitudes and exhibited more flexible behaviors when it came to gender characteristics.

Both boys and girls who attend single-sex schooling options experience a school culture strongly geared toward academic achievement and as such, spend significantly more time on homework than students who attend coed schools. Studies of adult women who attended all-girls' schools growing up indicate higher academic aspirations and attendance at more selective universities than might be predicted by their high school grades and achievement test scores. In addition, these young adult women were more apt to be politically engaged on their college campuses and have plans to attend graduate school. A sustained effect of single-sex secondary education was the less-stereotypic opinions women have of gender roles into their adult lives.

Single-sex schools seem to promote more collaborative environments as well as higher levels of order and calm. Male and female students in single-sex environments consistently report higher levels of confidence and peace than those in coed settings. Additional research is needed to further explore the school or classroom-level characteristics that seem to promote a more orderly, caring milieu. It may be that the practices that materialize in a single-sex school can be transferrable to a coed setting.

There is still much to learn about single-sex schooling. Overall, the majority of research literature recommends that the limited research results—positive, negative, or ambiguous—be utilized for developing a future research agenda rather than as definitive evidence that unequivocally endorses increasing single-sex options in the public sector.

See Also: Educational Opportunities/Access; No Child Left Behind; Science Education for Girls; Title IX.

Further Readings

Datnow, Amanda and Lea Hubbard. *Gender in Policy and Practice: Perspectives on Single-Sex and Coeducational Schooling.* New York: Routledge, 2002.

Salomone, Rosemary C. *Same, Different, Equal: Rethinking Single-Sex Schooling.* New Haven, CT: Yale University Press, 2003.

Shmurak, Carole B. *Voices of Hope: Adolescent Girls at Single Sex and Coeducational Schools.* New York: Peter Lang, 1998.

Katherine Cumings Mansfield
University of Texas at Austin

"Singletons"/Single by Choice

The terms *singleton* and *single by choice* reflect the move in recent decades toward singleness as a positive social identity, particularly for women. Wider economic and social changes in recent decades have led to diversity in partnership practices and increasing numbers of people experiencing periods of singleness. These changes also give rise to the possibility of claiming singleness as chosen. Academic research on singleness suggests this may not be experienced unequivocally as a clear-cut choice, and in part this is a result of the ongoing stigmatization of singleness. The single-by-choice movement campaigns against discrimination and for equal rights for single people.

The term *singleton* reflects the move in recent decades toward a positive identity for single people, particularly women. It was popularized in the novel *Bridget Jones' Diary*, which was part of increasing attention being paid to single women in popular culture from the mid-1990s (e.g., *Sex and the City*, which was first broadcast on HBO in 1998). A *Time* cover story in 2000 referred to the increasing numbers and visibility of single women as "a major societal shift." The meanings of singleness vary in relation to specific time and place, reflecting wider social changes such as the delay and decline in marriage. Defined as unmarried (never-married, divorced, and widowed), "single" includes those in cohabiting relationships as well as single parents.

According to U.S. Census Bureau statistics, 43 percent of all adult U.S. residents in 2009 were unmarried. "Single by choice" refers to those who do not wish to be in a romantic relationship. Although historical research demonstrates that remaining single is by no means new, the ability to claim this status as chosen is situated in particular contemporary circumstances. Economic and social transformations of the 20th century, alongside political movements that challenge traditional sexual and domestic relations, have contributed to changes in the status of women and provided both the material means and a cultural context in which choosing singleness is, for some women, a possibility.

Undesirable Status

Recent academic studies on the meanings of singleness for women, however, find that this remains a tensional location, with women equivocal about claiming singleness as chosen. In part this is because of the dominant cultural narrative of the centrality of marriage and family. Long-standing stereotypes of singleness present this as an undesirable status, for which single women are to be pitied: choosing singleness challenges dominant heteronormative discourses that privilege marriage and/or coupledom. Backlash responses are evident in the depiction of single women as selfish careerists or commitment-phobics who risk loneliness and isolation in old age, as well as in political concerns over the societal consequences of the demise of the traditional nuclear family.

Bella de Paulo has coined the term *singlism* to capture the ongoing stereotyping and discrimination experienced by single people, with access to various legal rights and benefits dependent on marital status. The emergence of a single-by-choice movement, illustrated by various campaigning groups and activities (e.g., the American Association of Single People, as well as Unmarried and Single Americans Week) is a political response to singlism. The concept of single by choice reflects a political moment of contestation over the basis on which individuals are afforded rights and recognition in respect of their partnership status. Increasing diversity in personal relationships may lead in the longer term to an undermining of partnership status as a category of difference and the basis on which individuals are afforded such rights.

See Also: Childlessness as Choice; Heterosexism; Marriage; Partner Rights; Same-Sex Marriage.

Further Readings

De Paulo, Bella. *Singled Out: How Singles Are Stereotyped, Stigmatized, and Ignored, and Still Live Happily Ever After.* New York: St. Martin's, 2006.

Reynolds, Jill. *The Single Woman: A Discursive Investigation.* New York: Routledge, 2008.

Simpson, Roona. *Contemporary Spinsterhood in Britain: Gender, Partnership Status and Social Change,* Saarbrücken, Germany: VDM, 2009.

U.S. Census Bureau. "Unmarried and Single Americans Week 2009." http://www.census.gov/Press-Release /www/releases/archives/facts_for_features_special _editions/014004.html (accessed November 2009)

Who Needs a Husband?" *Time* (August 28, 2000). http:// www.time.com/time/magazine/0,9263,7601000828,00 .html (accessed November 2009).

R. Simpson
University of Edinburgh

Sirleaf, Ellen Johnson

Ellen Johnson Sirleaf (1938–) was elected Liberia's first woman president in November 2005, the first democratically elected and currently serving woman to head any African nation. As president, Sirleaf recalls in her memoir, no one expected her to win; the odds were long. But this was not the first time Liberia's "Iron Lady" would overcome the odds. As her biography attests, her route to the presidency included many odds-defying moments, including her upbringing, education, and an adult life filled with fear, arrest, and exile. Yet, she ran for office "to bring motherly sensitivity and emotion to the presidency," according to an interview with the BBC. As a result,

U.S. Deputy Secretary of Defense Gordon England with Liberian President Ellen Johnson Sirleaf in 2007.

Shirleaf represents two extremes, which enable a remarkable understanding of Liberian culture to which she devotes her presidency.

As a child, Sirleaf's father was taken in as a ward by an American family of settlers working in Monrovia, the capital of Liberia. Though Sirleaf's lineage can be traced to the Gola chief in the village of Julejuah, this dual-family background embodies many of the struggles that the Republic of Liberia experienced in embracing its own independence.

As a ward for the McGrity family, Carney Johnson, as he was known, experienced the benefits of education and employment that would not have been available to him in the home village. He apprenticed with a practicing lawyer, was introduced to the world of politics, developed a successful law practice, and served in the Liberian legislature, the first indigenous man to be elected to the Liberian House of Representatives.

Sirleaf's mother was a light-skinned woman of German and African descent, born in a farming village in Liberia. Taken in by the Charles Dunbar family, a prominent family with political and economic connections, Sirleaf's mother was afforded great educational opportunities, even studying abroad for a year. When Sirleaf was a child, her mother opened a school in which Sirleaf was educated. Her mother was a traveling Presbyterian minister.

As a child of a lawyer and political official, teacher and minister, she became the beneficiary of a childhood that prepared her well for adult challenges. She had a unique connection to her indigenous roots as well as the opportunities that education and political awareness provided. As she explains in her memoir, she draws strengths from both worlds.

Sirleaf's education includes a degree in accounting and a master's degree in public administration from Harvard University. A rather unconventional route for an African woman, she did experience the dangers of a traditional life as well. She married James Sirleaf when she was only 17, living under his controlling and abusive hand, and quickly had four sons before seeking a divorce.

Political Career

Sirleaf's political life started as head of a division at the Treasury Department after returning to Liberia in 1965. Her efforts to challenge corruption and financial mismanagement started at this time and continued during her leadership as Liberia's minister of finance in 1979 in the William Tolbert administration. However, in the 1980 military coup in which Samuel Doe seized power, Tolbert and members of his cabinet were assassinated; Sirleaf narrowly escaped danger and went into exile in Kenya, where she served as director of Citibank in Nairobi and later in the World Bank. In 1984, when Doe unbanned political parties and declared himself leader, Sirleaf returned to Liberia to campaign against him in the 1985 elections; she was arrested and served nearly a year in jail before being exiled once again.

During the 1990s, Sirleaf served as assistant secretary general of the United Nations. In 1997. she returned to Liberia to seek election against Charles Taylor, a man whose rebellion she at one time supported, but received only 10 percent of the vote to his 75 percent in a field of 14 candidates. While international observers declared the election fair, Sirleaf's life was threatened, and she was charged with treason for contesting him. By 2003, Taylor handed over the presidency to his deputy, accused of inciting violence and unrest. Opposing groups signed a peace accord, and a transitional government was put in place, with Sirleaf serving as head of the Government Reform Commission.

Sirleaf was finally elected president of Liberia in 2005 after a runoff election with her closest challenger. In her inaugural address, she paid homage to her "illiterate grandmothers" while she pledged a "fundamental break with the past." The many contradictions of her life's journey would culminate in a "new era of democracy," during which she pledged economic renewal, an end to corruption, and reconciliation for the country.

See Also: Liberia; Representation of Women; Representation of Women in Government, International.

Further Readings

BBC News. "Profile: Liberia's 'Iron Lady.'" (November, 23 2005). http://news.bbc.co.uk/2/hi/africa/4395978.stm (accessed November 2009).

Sirleaf, Ellen Johnson. *This Child Will Be Great: Memoir of a Remarkable Life by Africa's First Woman President.* New York: HarperCollins, 2009.

Sirleaf, Ellen Johnson and Elisabeth Rehn. *Progress of the World's Women 2002 Volume One: Women, War, Peace: The Independent Experts' Assessment on the Impact of Armed Conflict on Women and Women's Role in Peace-Building.* New York: United Nations Development Fund for Women, 2003.

Kristina Horn Sheeler
Indiana University Purdue University Indianapolis

Slasher Movies

A group of horror films known as slasher movies usually foreground a psychopathic, mass murderer who threatens, stalks, and finally kills his victims in a gruesome, terrifying way, using such weapons as knives, machetes, chainsaws, and razors, hence the term *slasher.*

With precursors including the 1960 Alfred Hitchcock film *Psycho* and Michael Powell's *Peeping Tom,* the slasher escapes easy classification/definition, since it encompasses and incorporates elements from—as well as overlaps with and influences—numerous other film genres: rape-and-revenge; exploitation; Italian films of the 1960s and 1970s by Dario Argento and Mario Bava; pornography and "torture porn"; splatter; and supernatural horror, since slashers often feature a villain who resurrects, is immortal, and/or is undead.

Evolution of the American Type

Classic American slashers such as *The Texas Chainsaw Massacre* (Tobe Hooper), *Halloween* (John Carpenter), *Friday the 13th* (Sean Cunningham), and *A Nightmare on Elm Street* (Wes Craven) are franchises that have inspired numerous sequels and remakes, each featuring the same killer. These works have also successfully crossed over into adaptations for television, books, video games, and graphic novels.

In slasher films, the killer's victims are generally—but not exclusively—female, often groups of adolescents or college students who are away from parental or adult supervision on a university campus or in an isolated setting, such as a summer camp or a country house in a rural location. Killers are usually males; iconic examples of slasher villains are Leatherface (*The Texas Chainsaw Massacre*), Freddy Krueger (*A Nightmare on Elm Street*), and Michael Myers (*Halloween*)—all of whom have become major pop culture figures—although there are some notable exceptions. In the first film of the *Friday the 13th* series, the killer is Pamela Sue Voorhees, mother of protagonist Jason, who, after his mother's murder, subsequently becomes the mass murderer in the following films in this series.

The slasher reached its zenith in the 1970s and early 1980s, with blockbuster films such as *The Texas Chainsaw Massacre* (1974), *Halloween* (1978), and *Friday the 13th* (1980) and their subsequent sequels, as well as other popular slasher films of this era. The American slasher film generally declined in terms of popularity in the mid-1980s, although it saw a revival in the mid-1990s with Wes Craven's *Scream* film cycle starting in 1996, which inaugurated successful slasher franchises throughout the 1990s and 2000s, culminating in the "torture porn" slasher franchises such as *Saw* (2004, James Wan), *Hostel* (2005, Eli Roth), and their sequels, as well as other cinematic variations upon them.

Critics and the "Final Girl"

Critics, academics, and film theorists have analyzed the slasher film, considering how it represents, objectifies, and/or victimizes its female characters, as well as female spectatorship of slasher films, as in the work of Isabel Cristina Pinedo. Carol J. Clover's concept of the "Final Girl" is a cornerstone of slasher movie criticism. According to Clover, the Final Girl is the last remaining female (a girl or young woman) who overtakes the killer. Unlike the killer's other female victims, the final girl is usually a tomboy, bookworm, and/or virgin; she may have a personal connection to the killer; and she often has a gender-neutral and/or masculine name. Yet in her fight against the killer, she takes on elements of his monstrosity—which most likely were already present within her—by using his own weapon to vanquish him. For Clover, slasher spectatorship blurs boundaries of gender and subject positions, from male villain to the final girl, thereby raising important questions about the slasher film's vexed relationship to feminism and its constructions of gender.

See Also: Dating Violence; Menstruation; Pornography/Erotica; Pornography, Portrayal of Women in; Self-Defense, Armed; Self-Defense, Unarmed; Stereotypes of Women; Third Wave.

Further Readings

Baumgartner, Holly Lynn and Roger Davis, eds. *Hosting the Monster*. Amsterdam and New York: Rodopi, 2008.

Clover, Carol J. "Her Body, Himself: Gender in the Slasher Film." *Representations*, v.20 (1987).

Cowan, G. and M. O'Brien. "Gender and Survival vs. Death in Slasher Films: A Content Analysis." *Sex Roles: A Journal of Research*, v.23/3,4 (1990).

Creed, Barbara. *The Monstrous-Feminine: Film, Feminism, Psychoanalysis*. London: Routledge, 1993.

Duggan, Lisa. *Sapphic Slashers: Sex, Violence and American Modernity*. Durham, NC: Duke University Press, 2000.

Gill, Pat. "The Monstrous Years: Teens, Slasher Films, and the Family." *Journal of Film and Video*, v.54/4 (2002).

Pinedo, Isabel Cristina. *Recreational Terror: Women and the Pleasures of Horror Film Viewing*. Albany: State University of New York Press, 1997.

Rockoff, Adam. *Going to Pieces: The Rise and Fall of the Slasher Film, 1978 to 1986*. Jefferson, NC: McFarland & Company, 2002.

Schneider, Steven Jay and Daniel Shaw, eds. *Dark Thoughts: Philosophic Reflections on Cinematic Horror*. Lanham, MD: Scarecrow Press, 2003.

Wyrick, Laura. "Horror at Century's End: Where Have All the Slashers Gone?" *Pacific Coast Philology*, v.33/2 (1998).

Marcelline Block
Princeton University

Slovakia

Slovak Republic (SK) represents a parliamentary democracy of the central European region, with a population of 5.4 million and Bratislava as the capital. The nation was created in 1918 as Czechoslovakia. Women suffrage was enacted in 1920. After World War II, the country became a part of the Communist Bloc. As the women's movement was subject to control by the Communist Party, the second wave of feminism never took place. Transition to democracy occurred in 1989. In 1993, Czechoslovakia peacefully split into the Czech Republic and the Slovak Republic, respectively. In 2004, SK joined the European Union.

A nun in Bratislava, Slovakia. The current Slovak women's movement is influenced by the Catholic Church.

The current Slovak women's movement is influenced by the Catholic Church and is represented mainly by few nongovernmental organizations.

Women rights have a high standard that is required for all European Union (EU) members by the common EU law. In 2004, the broad Discrimination Act was enacted. However, instances of discrimination against women still occur, mainly due to gender, sexuality, age, and ethnicity (i.e., Roma minority).

The most serious form of discrimination in the SK was the coerced sterilization of Roma women. The Communist regime took a systematic approach to the sterilization throughout the 20-year period of 1970 to 1990. After 1990, sterilizations became rare and concerned cases of uninformed women who signed approval documents for the procedure without being aware of the consequences of their acts.

Motherhood rights of Slovak women are still not fully protected. In 2009, the Abortion Act was amended and required all applications be reported to the authorities, including women's personal details.

Households typically depend on incomes of both partners. Perception of childcare as the domain of women is strong in the countryside, and employers are unwilling to hire women with children. There is a commonly accepted perception that men are the main economic provider. The proportion of unemployed mothers is increasing. Every third woman with three or more children is currently unemployed, the highest percentage in the EU. Part-time job arrangements are similarly underdeveloped in Slovakia. In 2008, only 4.2 percent of women and 1.4 percent of men had part-time jobs. The gender pay gap is 23.6 percent.

Women represent 19.3 percent of all members of the parliament. In presidential elections, woman candidates generally receive strong voter support, although, without success so far.

See Also: Fertility; Part-Time Work; Roma "Gypsy" Women; Roman Catholic Church.

Further Readings

Henderson, K. *Slovakia: The Escape From Invisibility.* London: Routledge, 2002.

Kirschbaum, S. J. *A History of Slovakia: The Struggle for Survival.* New York: Palgrave Macmillan, 2005.

Slovak National Centre for Human Rights: "Report on the Observance of Human Rights Including the Observance of the Principle of Equal Treatment in the Slovak Republic 2008." http://www.snslp.sk (accessed November 2009).

Petra Zářecká
Masaryk Univerzity, Czech Republic

Slovenia

Despite the fact that women's equality is commonly accepted in the Republic of Slovenia (RS), inequality persists. In 2001, a referendum was presented to voters that asked them to decide if a single woman should have the right to medically assisted conception. Following a heated public debate that exposed lingering prejudices and stereotypes, the referendum failed. The majority determined that single women need a man's active participation in conception and that a single woman cannot provide a proper upbringing for her child. Despite these feelings, currently about one-half of all children in the RS are born to unmarried mothers.

Women account for more than half of Slovenia's 2 million people, and their average life expectancy exceeds men's by seven years, to 82 years, and they represent nearly half of the country's active population. More than 90 percent of women are employed full time. Women's participation in the workforce has become a traditional value in this region. All periodic attempts aimed at returning women to the home, which are backed by some political parties as well as the Catholic Church in Slovenia, have been futile.

Women's intensive participation in the Slovenian labor market is connected to their education level. Women in the RS have a somewhat higher average level of education than men; among the EU countries, the RS ranks first, with 94 percent of women aged 20 to 24 who have finished at least secondary school. Women constitute a majority among students at Slovenian universities. Nevertheless, Slovenian education is characterized by an exceptionally high gender polarization in the choice of students' studies; women show a strong preference for the humanities and social sciences and much less for science and technology. This also is reflected in strong gender polarization of the occupational structure. The RS is characterized by a comparatively high degree of feminization in education, healthcare, social services, and judicial administration. Women dominate in service industries such as trade, catering, tourism, and financial intermediation. They also formed the major labor force in the processing industry; however, most of this sectors' enterprises have been shut down in the past decade, leaving their strictly specialized and poorly educated workers unemployed.

The areas least accessible to RS women are concentrated in social and political power. The cases of women who have succeeded in attaining top managerial positions are extremely rare. There are other occupations in which women are faced with these "glass ceilings," even those in which women represent the majority of employees. Within different levels of state politics, women have comparatively fewer opportunities now than in the era of socialism. The Slovenian Parliament is one of few with a small number of female representatives, only 13 percent. No improvement is expected. Following the municipal elections of 2006, only seven of 210 mayors in the RS are women. In the RS, women continue to be the ones doing most of the unpaid household work and taking sick leaves to take care of family members. Compared with their male colleagues, women are paid less for their work. The average difference in earnings is 8 percent; the differences, however, tend to increase with better paying and professionally more challenging employment. In the Slovenian language, the word *poverty* is a feminine gender noun; the risk-of-poverty rate is greater in women than in men. It is older, single, inactive, and unemployed women in particular that face the greatest risk.

See Also: Gender Quotas in Government; Household Division of Labor; Poverty, "Feminization" of; Professions, by Gender.

Further Readings

Cox, John K. *Slovenia: Evolving Loyalties.* London: Routledge, 2009.

Luthar, Oto, ed. *The Land Between: A History of Slovenia.* New York: Peter Lang, 2008.

Statistical Office of the Republic of Slovenia. http://www .stat.si/doc/pub/dejstva_zenske_moski_en.pdf "Men and Women in the RS," (accessed December 2009).

Sabina Žnidaršič Žagar
University of Primorska, Koper

"Snowflake Babies"

"Snowflake babies" is the term used by some groups, such as Nightlight Christian Adoptions, which coined the term to refer to embryos that are frozen in liquid nitrogen that remain unused after the process of in vitro fertilization (IVF), and are then donated or put up for "embryo adoption" to select heterosexual couples.

These frozen embryos are known as snowflake babies for two reasons. First, those using this term understand that from the moment of fertilization, like snowflakes, no two embryos are alike. And second, using the term *babies*, they understand personhood as beginning at the moment of fertilization. The status of embryos, however, is a highly contentious issue and one of significant social and reproductive consequence to women for the 21st century.

IVF is a procedure used by couples experiencing infertility or by same-sex couples wanting a child. In IVF, eggs are surgically removed from ovaries and mixed with or injected with sperm for fertilization in laboratories. While multiple eggs are removed for IVF, not all of the fertilized eggs, or embryos, are used in the procedure to implant them into the uterus. To prevent the gestation of multiple fetuses during one pregnancy, the number of embryos implanted into a womb depends on the age and health of the woman and the health of the fertilized eggs, or embryos.

Disadvantages and Failures

Not all of these embryos are healthy. It is the healthiest embryos, sometimes referred to as the "prettiest" embryos, that are transferred to the uterus, usually between days two and six after fertilization. These embryos are composed of approximately between four cells and 100 cells. When it is decided that the remaining frozen embryos are no longer wanted by those from whom they have been retrieved, organizations such as Nightlight Christian Adoption, using language of adoption for embryos, try to arrange for "adoption" by select couples.

While such adoptions are encouraged by these organizations, it is important to note that, especially for couples experiencing infertility, using leftover embryos from couples who themselves have compromised fertility does not provide the best chance of achieving a good pregnancy outcome.

Practical and ethical concerns over both IVF and embryo adoption procedures are being debated. There are already hundreds of thousands of embryos that remain frozen in tanks and that require monitoring and storage expenses. While some of these embryos are under the active control of their genetic originators, others are left unused, many not viable or optimal for their intended use. Options for frozen embryos include keeping them frozen, destroying them, donating them for stem cell or other research, or donating them for implantation—each of which has practical, legal, social, and moral consequences in need of careful consideration.

See Also: Abortion, Ethical Issues of; Adoption; Lesbian Adoption; Pregnancy; Pro-Life Movement; Reproductive and Sexual Health Rights; Suleman, Nadya "Octomom."

Further Readings

Brakman, Sarah-Vaughan and Darlene Fozard Weaver, eds. *The Ethics of Embryo Adoption and the Catholic Tradition: Moral Arguments, Economic Reality and Social Analysis.* The Netherlands: Springer, 2007.

Cahn, Naomi. *Test Tube Families: Why the Fertility Market needs Legal Regulation.* New York: New York University Press, 2009.

Horsey, Kirsty and Hazel Biggs, eds. *Human Fertilisation and embryology: Reproducing Regulation.* London: Routledge,, 2007.

Ontario Ministry of Health and Long-Term Care, Medical Advisory Secretariat. "In Vitro Fertilization and Multiple Pregnancies: Health Technology Policy Assessment." Ontario: Ontario Medical Advisory Secretariat, 2006. https://ozone.scholarsportal.info/bitstream/1873 /420/1/269307.pdf (accessed November 2009).

Deborah Davidson
York University, Canada

Soap Operas, Cross-Culturally Considered

Even though soap operas are typically considered a women's genre, soap operas are often watched and enjoyed by both men and women around the world. Soap opera as a genre was created for radio during the 1930s in the United States. Soap and detergent companies such as Procter and Gamble, Colgate-Palmolive, and Lever Brothers sponsored these early radio programs. Since then, soap operas gradually became one of the most profitable, influential, and successful programming in U.S. broadcasting history and are also a popular genre around the world.

Most of these early shows were aired everyday for 15 minutes. These early soap operas mainly targeted housewives and focused on the issues of family, love, and relationships. Furthermore, they usually centered on a primary family and followed its everyday affairs and issues. Because of their continuous nature, these shows often ended with a climax to invite or encourage the audience to tune in and listen to the next episode.

In the United States in the 1950s, daily soap operas successfully transferred from radio to television. *Guiding Light*, which originated in radio, made its way to television in 1952. Most of the longest-running daytime soap operas, such as *Guiding Light* (CBS), *As the World Turns* (CBS), and *Another World* (NBC), were created by the legendary Irna Phillips in the 1950s and 1960s. Other widely popular shows (*Search for Tomorrow*, *The Edge of Night*, *The Secret Story*, and *Love of Life*) were created in the 1950s.

Due to the success of early soap operas, several other daytime series were created in the 1960s to attract audiences from different cultural and economic backgrounds. *The Doctors* and *General Hospital* (ABC), centered in fictional hospitals, were created, and *Day of Our Lives* (NBC), *Another World* (NBC), *One Life to Live* (ABC) and others made their first appearances. ABC's *One Life to Live* (*OLTL*), created by Agnes Nixon, one of Irna Philips's protégées, focused on the issues of class and introduced nontraditional (ethnically and racially diverse) characters. Prior to *OLTL*, soap operas mainly focused on upper-middle-class and upper-class families and their elegant and complicated lives.

Current Issues and Society

Some of the most popular U.S. soap operas were created in the 1970s. Nixon created the widely acclaimed *All My Children* in 1970 for ABC. Another Phillips protégée, William J. Bell, who also wrote for *Another World* and *Days of Our Lives* for several years, created his first show, *The Young and the Restless*, in

1973. In addition, *Ryan's Hope* (ABC), another widely acclaimed show, was created. These newer shows reflected some of the societal dynamics of the 1970s and portrayed characters that reflected on cultural issues like alcoholism, rape, abortion, racial tension, interracial relationships, and women's roles in society. Acclaimed characters, such as Julie Horton (*Days of Our Lives)* and Erica Kane (*All My Children*), represented the changing role of women in U.S. society. They were independent and successful in a predominantly male world. Bell's *The Young and the Restless* extensively focused on a younger cast and followed their complex lives.

Most of these shows were 30-minute episodes but were able to tell multiple interrelated stories about the lives of their characters. Due to their open-ended nature, they often created suspenseful climaxes to attract their audiences. Several other shows, such as *Santa Barbara, Capitol, Loving, The Bold and the Beautiful, Generations,* and *Port Charles*, were created during the 1980s and 1990s to reflect current trends and contemporary issues.

As a genre, soap operas also appeared in other countries in different formats. In Mexico and Latin American countries, they are known as telenovelas. These shows, unlike their U.S. counterparts, often air once or twice a week. They differ from U.S. shows in that respect but also mainly focus on families and romantic relationships, crime, and contemporary societal issues. Daytime series are also popular in European countries, such as the United Kingdom, the Netherlands, Germany, and Ireland, as well as in Australia, New Zealand, and other parts of the world. Both U.S. soap operas and telenovelas are widely popular in other parts of the world and are considered profitable cultural exports.

Female Characters in Soap Operas

Until the 1970s, women were often portrayed in traditional roles, such as housewives, nurses, and secretaries. During 1970s and 1980s, more independent and successful female characters were created. Clearly, soap operas were influenced by the changing societal roles of women and the feminist movement. Starting in the 1980s, daytime series incorporated female doctors, lawyers, and businesspeople. Still, some of the female representations remained problematic, and women often faced violence or physical abuse. Story lines have focused on the psychological outcome of domestic abuse, rape, hostile workplaces, and women's health issues such as breast cancer awareness and acquired immune deficiency syndrome (AIDS). Ethnically and racially diverse strong female characters were also introduced to the shows. Recently, soap operas worldwide have introduced the subject of same-sex relationships and issues of homosexuality.

See Also: Celebrity Women; Gender, Defined; Gender Roles, Cross-Cultural.

Further Readings:

Mateliski, Marilyn J. *Soap Operas Worldwide: Cultural and Serial Realities.* Jefferson, NC: McFardland & Company, 1998.

Nochimson, Martha. *No End to Her: Soap Opera and the Female Subject.* Berkeley: University of California Press, 1993.

Simon, Ron, et al. *Worlds Without End: The Art and History of the Soap Opera.* New York: Harry Abrams, 1997.

Ahmet Atay
University of Louisville

Soccer, Children's

Although soccer dates back to Greek and Roman times, it was not until the 1800s that soccer was introduced to the United States. From what was then commonly known as a boys' or men's college sport, soccer now sees no gender boundaries. Children's soccer, better known as "youth soccer," gained momentum both recreationally and competitively in the 1990s. The growing popularity of the sport in the United States is credited to the 1994 FIFA Men's World Cup and the 1999 and 2003 FIFA Women's World Cups, which were all held in the United States.

Today, youth soccer is considered one of the most popular sports for boys and girls in America. Children's soccer is both an outdoor and indoor sport. This relatively low-cost sport requires players to pay a registration fee, and purchase shin guards, a ball, soccer cleats, socks, and a uniform. The United States

Youth Soccer Association, the largest member of the United States Soccer Federation, currently has more than 3 million players registered between the ages of 5 and 19. The American Youth Soccer Organization boasts more than 650,000 players; the Soccer Association for Youth registers over 150,000 players.

In addition to these major youth soccer groups, there are many other organizations that support youth soccer, such as the YMCA, CYO, and local parks and recreation leagues. From kicking the ball around during recess to playing on organized soccer teams, millions of children between the ages of 4 and 19 play youth soccer each week.

Youth soccer not only includes millions of players, but there are also large numbers of coaches and parents who dedicate their time to the development of young players. From coaching children on the field to fund-raising to working the concession stand, to cheering on athletes on the field, parents and coaches volunteer their time to nurture children into well-rounded athletes.

Children's soccer is also a family-oriented sport. Many soccer families can be seen with their soccer decals on their vehicles, toting their outdoor chairs around and sharing a meal purchased at the concession stand. In is not uncommon to see parents sporting their "Soccer Mom" or "Soccer Dad" sweatshirts around on game day.

From Preschool to Tomorrow's Pros

Youth soccer in the United States ranges from recreational soccer to competitive travel soccer. With their short hems down to their ankles and their shin guards up to their knees, children in the younger age groups (4 to 6 years) are often accompanied on the field by their coaches. At this young age, players often need to be coached as to which direction to kick the ball on the field. Young soccer players can often be seen picking daisies on the game field or sighting high-flying objects like birds or planes during active game time. It is at this stage that young players first begin to develop their focus on the game. The intention of recreational soccer is to introduce the players to a fun form of exercise, the development of teamwork, and a positive, sports-minded attitude.

As children grow older and begin to refine their ball skills and strategic play (positioning, attack, defense and ball possession, etc.), the game of soccer becomes more competitive. From the middle school ages, many children go on to play high school soccer. What used to be a male-dominated sport has become one of the most popular high school sports for young women. Today over 40 percent of soccer players are female.

With millions of children playing soccer in recreational and competitive soccer, youth soccer in the United States continues to be a strong foundation for the future of high school, collegiate, amateur, and professional soccer.

See Also: Soccer, Professional; Soccer Moms; Sports, Women in.

Further Readings

Litterer, Dave. "Women's Soccer History in the USA: An Overview." *The American Soccer History Archives.* http://homepages.sover.net/~spectrum/womensover view.html (accessed December 2009).
Soccer Association for Youth, USA. http://www.saysoccer .org (accessed July 2010).
U.S. Youth Soccer. *US Youth Soccer Website.* http://www .usyouthsoccer.org/index.html (accessed July 2010).

Christine Pease-Hernandez
Slippery Rock University

Soccer, Professional

Traditionally, soccer has always been identified as the "world's game" because of its universal popularity, recognition, and access. Pettus tells us that soccer is also known as the "people's game" because it is the only game that can be commonly found in a large arena being watched by thousands of cheering fans, as well as on local parks and recreation fields being played by 5-year-old children.

Although men's soccer teams have received a tremendous amount of media attention, accessibility, and continual growth, the rise in popularity of women's soccer is only a few decades old. Not until the success of the 1999 U.S. women's soccer team, with players like Mia Hamm and Brandy Chastain, did women's soccer become recognizable and acknowledged in the male-dominated soccer world.

The Early Years and the Inception of Women's Soccer

In 1918, the Committee on Women's Athletics was charged with establishing the rules for many of the emerging popular sports for women. In reality, the committee was responsible for modifying the rules of the men's game to ensure that the rules of the women's game maintained a certain level of propriety and that women would not look like warriors while playing soccer. At the competitive level, men's soccer has always had a reputation for being an aggressive and fast sport. In fact, there is some evidence suggesting that soccer, or a game very similar to soccer, was used in Ancient Greek and Roman times to prepare young warriors for battle and military training.

In the end, the committee determined that playing time for the women's game should be shortened and the length and width of the field should be reduced in size, so that the women did not have to run as far and for as long. The controlling male influence feared that soccer, along with any other form of prolonged physical activity for women, would pose as a safety risk and health hazard for women. Beyond the physical concerns and unfounded safety risks, a concern also existed that the emotional stressors of participation and competition would prove to be overwhelming for women, ultimately causing them to collapse. Of course, we now know that these claims are false, and that physical activity, on the soccer field or otherwise, is a beneficial endeavor for women in many realms.

The Move to the Suburbs

The late 1950s saw the rise of suburban living. On arrival in the suburbs, people found open fields and space to play sports. The 1950s also experienced a major increase in the organization of youth sport, and soccer leagues were formed throughout many communities. In the 1960s the American Youth Soccer Organization was established to determine rules and standards for participation for boy and girl players. Girls were provided with opportunities to play in community leagues with rules that encouraged a less aggressive style of play, and the girls' game was shorter in duration than the boys' game. At this time, there was not a future for girls' soccer much beyond the community leagues, even though the boys who participated in organized community leagues could look forward to playing in high school and beyond.

It was not until the passage of Title IX, an educational reform act demanding equitable resources and opportunities regardless of gender, did opportunities for girls and women to participate in soccer beyond their community field increase.

Title IX and the Growth of Women's Soccer at the Collegiate Level

Title IX was a major piece of legislation passed in 1972 that opened many doors for girls and women in the many sport and physical activity arenas. Five years after the passage of Title IX, opportunities for women in soccer at the collegiate level increased, and community programs continued to grow. Interestingly, women's soccer at the collegiate level found its initial home at Ivy League colleges and universities, which created some questions about which girls were playing soccer in the United States and how accessible the "people's game" actually was. Today, girls make up 40 percent of the soccer players in the United States and the quintessential "soccer mom," in her minivan full of young soccer players, continues to dominate the cultural landscape of youth soccer.

The Significant Impact of One Man

Anson Dorrance, a former men's soccer player at the University of North Carolina, Chapel Hill (UNC-CH), took over as the coach of the women's team at UNC-CH and began to shape his team and, unknowingly, the overall game of soccer for girls and women. Dorrance became aware that he was going to have to recreate the "culture" of performance expectations for his female athletes by breaking down socially accepted stereotypical gender expectations of how women were supposed to perform on the field as athletes. Dorrance knew that girls and women in sport and physical activity settings were historically encouraged to be less competitive and less physical in their styles of play.

Through years of work and advocacy and the establishment of a women's championship game for collegiate soccer players with the National Collegiate Athletic Association, Dorrance's coaching efforts have manifested into a sport space for women that is respected and admired by many. The UNC-CH women's team was one of the first competitive soccer programs at the collegiate level and continues to set the performance standard for all other collegiate soc-

The German Potsdam women's team, winners of the Union of European Football Association's Women's Cup Final in 2005.

Further Readings

Hargreaves, J. "Olympic Women: A Struggle for Recognition." *Women and Sports in the United States: A Documentary Reader*. Lebanon, NH: Northeastern University Press, 2007.

Markovits, A. S. and S. L. Hellerman. "Women's Soccer in the United States: Yet Another American 'Exceptionalism.'" *Soccer and Society*, v.4/2 (2003).

Pettus, E. "From the Suburbs to the Sports Arenas." *Nike Is a Goddess*. New York: Atlantic Monthly, 1998.

Shugart, Helene A. "She Shoots, She Scores: Mediated Constructions of Contemporary Female Athletes in Coverage of the 1999 U.S. Women's Soccer Team." *Western Journal of Communication*, v.67/1 (2000).

Sokolove, M. *Warrior Girls*. New York: Simon and Schuster Paperbacks, 2008.

Donna Duffy
University of North Carolina, Greensboro

cer programs, as well as creating a culture of soccer superiority that young girls continue to admire.

One Defining Game, and History Was Made

In 1999, the U.S. Women's Soccer team, also known as the "Girls of Summer," defeated China to win the World Cup in front of 78,481 spectators—the largest crowd to ever watch a women's soccer game. In addition, it was one of the first times that girls and boys, women and men, arrived at a women's soccer match carrying signs and banners and covered in paint spelling out the women's soccer players' names and jersey numbers.

The women of the 1999 World Cup women's soccer team became the most significant and recognizable role models for young female soccer players, and they provided a different sport perspective for these young athletes. No longer were young female athletes looking at professional male athletes as the "standard." Many argue that this game solidified the notion that girls and women can successfully compete at the highest level and created national enthusiasm for both soccer and, more important, girls and women as creditable athletes and as important role models for female athletes.

See Also: Soccer, Children's; Soccer Moms; Sports, Women in; Title IX.

Soccer Moms

The term *soccer mom* generally refers to a married, middle-class suburban women with children. Literally, a soccer mom is viewed as driving her children to and from their soccer games in her minivan. Metaphorically, a soccer mom is a woman who is devoted first and foremost to her family's needs and, as a result, puts her children's desires and activities above her own, even if she also has a job. In the early 1980s, the term *soccer mom* was used by mothers who were raising money for their children's soccer team.

However, the term gained media prominence in Susan Casey's 1995 Democratic campaign for the Denver City Council. When Casey was asked about the term after it became introduced a year later in the 1996 presidential campaign between Bill Clinton and Bob Dole, she insisted that she meant no gender stereotype. Rather, Casey was simply trying to describe her dual responsibilities as an accomplished woman and mother and to suggest she could manage both. By 1996, however, soccer mom became the term Republican strategists used to describe what was believed to be a primary swing vote in the presidential campaign. Republican strategists, in fact, believed that part of the reason why soccer moms needed to be reached was because they were just too busy, too "harried," with working and mothering to have time to pay attention to politics. Thus, then and now, the primary description of soccer moms is stressed women who are attempting to juggle both their domestic and professional responsibilities.

The soccer mom was also a very important political shift from the news discourse of Year of the Woman that dominated the 1992 presidential political campaign to "women as mothers" that dominated the 1996 presidential campaign. In fact, this change between the presidential campaigns shifted media from discussing women as political power wielders (as in Year of the Woman) to discussing women as a group of swing voters defined primarily by their family and mothering obligations. In other words, there was an important shift from seeing women as accomplished public women and mothers to primarily as mothers, regardless of their professional lives/roles. As a result, this shift also suggests a soccer mom is unquestionably a mother first, with all other roles as secondary. Consequently, the soccer mom worked to obscure and diminish women's public success in the service of seeing them most importantly as private women, whose primary work was as mothers in the home, even if a woman actually had a job.

Political Weight and Power

As soccer mom has become a staple of the contemporary lexicon, it continues to be considered a voting demographic, and the term emerges periodically in political campaigns and discussions both in local and national campaigns. While soccer moms were primarily considered Democrats in the late 1990s and early 2000s, today, more and more soccer moms are associated with Evangelical Christianity and are considered to be both more conservative and Republican. Soccer mom has also become a label for a consumer group that is often targeted in advertising campaigns, particularly for both SUVs and minivans.

As such, soccer mom has become a label promoted and used by advertisers to sell products, and consequently, the label has become entrenched in an ideology of consumerism that equates mothering with consumption and conflates personal choices with product consumption and lifestyle choices. Finally, in some media coverage, the term *soccer mom* has taken on negative connotations. Specifi-

cally, soccer moms are often accused of forcing their children to attend too many after-school activities or play on too many sports teams, while they are also seen as hyperparenting or overparenting their children instead of allowing them to "just be children" or enjoy their childhood.

See Also: Childcare; Christianity; "Security Moms"; Work/Life Balance.

Further Readings

Peskowitz, Miriam. *The Truth behind the Mommy Wars: Who Decides what Makes a Good Mother.* Emeryville, CA: Seal Press, 2005.

Vavrus, Mary Douglas. "From Women of the Year to 'Soccer Moms': The Case of the Incredible Shrinking Women." *Political Communication*, v.17 (2000).

D. Lynn O'Brien Hallstein
Boston University

Social Justice Activism

Social justice activism involves individual or group action that is intended to achieve economic, environmental, political, or social change. There are two primary beliefs that relate to and support social justice activism. The first is that some groups suffer disadvantages as a consequence of their gender, race, class, sexual orientation, (dis)ability, language, age, nationality, or religion. The second belief is that individuals or groups can be agents of change and can challenge or disrupt barriers that deny equitable opportunities and circumstances for all to thrive and achieve in a world free from oppression.

Feminism is rooted in women's social justice activism, as women have been integral to social justice movements throughout history and around the globe. They have campaigned for the legal rights of women, while also promoting sexuality and reproductive freedoms. Furthermore, 21st-century feminist activism has focused on economic, professional, and educational equity, including women's rights to achieve political power at all levels.

Middle-class white women from Western Europe and North America led early feminist movements, which primarily focused on gender equity for white women. This focal point created enough tensions between both white women and black women that it catalyzed the development of black feminism.

Black feminism recognizes that gender, race, and class oppression are inextricably linked. Women's movements that endeavor to challenge or disrupt gender and/or class oppression yet ignore race can end up discriminating through racial bias. Be that as it may, feminist social justice activism in the 21st century not only has focused on the issues that appear to limit or oppress white women; it also has concentrated on being inclusive of other marginalized identities, including race, class, gender, and ethnic backgrounds.

Moreover, in the 21st century, activists of marginalized identities outside Western Europe and North America, including former European colonies in Africa, the Caribbean, southeast Asia, and parts of Latin America, have participated increasingly in women's social justice activism. Additionally, women around the globe have formed cross-racial partnerships that move beyond racial and ethnic barriers to accommodate intersections of collective identities that foster resistance to patriarchal forms of power and domination.

For example, STITCH is a network of U.S. women working with Central American women to advocate for fair wages and just treatment in the workplace in Central America. Likewise, Women for Women International is a global women's movement that works toward eliminating gender inequities and economic, political, and social injustice.

On March 8, 2010, the centennial anniversary of International Women's Day, Women for Women International sponsored a campaign, Join Me on the Bridge, where thousands of women around the globe stood united in an unprecedented manner to honor the resilience of women survivors of war, genocide, massive rape and torture, and displacement. Together, women across the globe connected banners of fabric on which they painted their visions for a peaceful, prosperous future, free from war.

Consciousness-Raising Activism

Social justice activists characteristically use a repertoire of protest strategies to expose and resist oppression. Despite the fact that strategies and tactics have changed over time and location, based upon resources, the level of support, and other issues, activism in women's sociopolitical movements in the 21st century continues to be associated with the development of a social justice consciousness.

Feminists pedagogy began with the telling of women's individual stories of "making the personal political." Consequently, consciousness-raising activism and widespread education is frequently the first step that feminist activists take toward social change.

Women activists have written books, journal articles, pieces in magazines, and newspapers, and they have produced visual art, films, and music to expose oppression and to educate the masses. They have relied heavily on the media and other communication technologies to educate and organize individuals and groups to take action. In some respects, media and communication technologies have made many forms of social justice activism much easier to initiate. Feminists have used Websites, YouTube, blogging, Facebook, and podcasting to raise awareness. The Internet, in particular, has served as a tremendous outreach tool, connecting women and others across the globe. Democracy in Action is an organization that backs social justice agendas by offering small and medium-sized nonprofit organizations access to online organizing engines. Similarly, the Independent Media supports the global social justice movement by providing (on its Website) up-to-the minute reports, photographs, and audio and video footage of global social justice challenges.

In the 21st century, consciousness raising remains a key strategy toward social change among feminist social justice activists. Through consciousness raising, people learn more than the fact that there is injustice in the world. They learn about various forms of social injustice—where it is, how it happens, what makes the situation(s) unjust, and who is advantaged and who is disadvantaged. Social justice activists may identify strategies or tactics upon which they and other social justice activists might reflect and use to challenge and disrupt the injustices that some groups suffer as a consequence of being dominated by those who have political, economic, and social power.

Economic Activism

Women activists have frequently used their spending power in struggles for social, economic, and political change. Activists have supported those companies and businesses that promote a just global economy.

On the other hand, activists have boycotted companies and organizations to raise awareness about the influence of business practices on employees, neighborhoods, and the planet.

A boycott is a form of social justice activism in which individuals voluntarily abstain from using, purchasing, or doing business with an individual or organization as an expression of political protest. Whether activists are protesting the inequitable treatment of women at a retail chain (e.g., Walmart's exclusion of contraceptive coverage in insurance plans and its gender discriminations in pay, promotion, and compensation) or mobilizing against sweatshops, boycotts can help raise awareness in communities and can help get the attention of the company or business being targeted.

Likewise, labor unions, at times, have acted collectively against economic social injustices, with strikes playing a significant role in social justice activism. In the 21st century, teacher strikes in the United States continue to be a major strategy that unions use to obtain higher wages and benefits for teachers, who are disproportionately women employees. Through collective economic action, based upon the businesses we as consumer activists choose to support and those we chose to avoid, we are empowered to create a just global economy that ensures that all workers are paid equitably and are treated with respect.

Environmental Activism

Women, even more so than men, tend to have great concern for the environment. Consequently, women have played important roles in environmental forms of social justice activism. Winona LaDuke (Anishinaab) for example, is an internationally renowned environmental activist who began speaking out about these issues at an early age, addressing the United Nations at the age of 18. In the 21st century, LaDuke continues to devote herself to Native American and environmental concerns, as well as political and women's issues. Similarly, Rita Arditti helped to found the Women's Community Cancer Project, whose mission was to raise awareness concerning environmental exposures that contributed to cancer in women. Connecting her feminist, environmentalist, and biology backgrounds, Arditti criticized the medical world for being male-dominated and influenced by major chemical producers.

Rachel's Network is a 21st-century environmental activist organization that builds coalitions among women who are concerned about the environment, health, and women's empowerment. Named in honor of author and scientist Rachel Carson, Rachel's Network draws attention to pressing environmental issues while promoting women as impassioned leaders and agents of change dedicated to the stewardship of the earth.

In the 21st century, women's environmental social justice activism has been largely recognized in a few key areas, particularly in green consumerism and in local government. Green consumerism concerns the intentional purchase of products and services that consumers feel do not contribute to the destruction of the planet. This may entail minimal harm to or exploitation of human beings, animals, and the natural environment.

Art- and Craft-Themed Forms of Social Justice Activism

Art- and Craft-themed forms of social justice activism are prominent today. These forms include photography, video, installation, painting, printmaking, sculpture, fiber, and metals. An exhibition titled "A Complex Weave: Women and Identity in Contemporary Art" highlights 16 female, first- and second-generation contemporary artists, who make the personal political through an assortment of art forms that highlight various facets of oppression related to their gender and identity (e.g., race, ethnicity, class, national origin, or sexual orientation).

Many feminists are reclaiming traditionally feminized arts-related activities, such as knitting, sewing, quilting, and other crafts as forms of activism. Through this reclamation, contemporary women who identify themselves as feminists strive to embrace domestic arts to highlight traditionally female-dominated art forms that have been marginalized and undervalued.

A common form of art- and craft-themed activism is the "knit-in," where knitters take possession of a public space and knit, while involved in the act of protest. That public space could be a bus, a park, or a public building, among others. Activists, such as the Penn State Knitivism Club at Pennsylvania State University, have used the knit-in to highlight the genocide in Darfur; bring attention to lesbian, gay, bisexual and transgender rights in Uganda; and raise awareness of sexual violence.

Craftivism, similar to knitivism, is a 21st-century addition to the arts and crafts lexicon in which craft is joined with activism. While acts of resistance or protest are expressed through crafts and other creative endeavors, craftivism is also centered on ideals of environmentalism and sustainability. When purchasing new materials, many craftivists select products that are green or fairly traded, such as homespun yarns and organic fabrics. Especially common within the movement is the use of thrifted, vintage, and repurposed materials and products, so as to promote reuse and minimize waste.

Social Justice Activism: What It Has Accomplished

In the 21st century, there is greater awareness of social injustice. Moreover, in many cases (through social justice activism) there are more government policies and laws that prohibit various forms of social injustice, such as sexual harassment, discrimination in pay, promotion and compensation, and discrimination on the basis of sexual orientation.

Whereas women's social justice activism has profoundly shaped the political, economic, and social landscape around the globe, contemporary feminism has moved beyond being simply a "women's movement"; it has become a social justice movement in which men and women activists, in many cases, employ strategies of resistance that challenge oppression and enable social justice to flourish. In the 21st century, men and women representing all identities and backgrounds are engaged in social justice activism as planners, organizers, teachers, researchers, advocates, and foremost players, supporting or opposing feminism, homosexuality, women's reproductive rights, legalized abortion, and antiracism.

While social, political, and economic circumstances for many of the oppressed have improved, oppression in its multiple forms is still pervasive throughout the world. Given the gravity of societal injustice and the energetically changing social justice activism around the globe, this has increasingly warranted the formation of coalitions and alliances between various organizations, communities, and countries, including Haiti, China, Korea, the United States, Rwanda, and other African countries. Moreover, the continuing transformation of social injustice and its contemporary manifestations, from forced child labor to racial disparities in healthcare, will necessitate evolving social justice strategies and partnerships among those who confront and challenge systemic oppression, in all its forms, to create more just societies.

See Also: CODEPINK; Ecofeminism; Granny Peace Brigade; LaDuke, Winona; Nongovernmental Organizations Worldwide; Peace Movement; Plumwood, Val; Rachel's Network; Social Justice Theory; Transnational Feminist Networks; Womanism; Women in Black; Women's International League for Peace and Freedom.

Further Readings
Barndt, Deborah. *Wild Fire: Art as Activism.* New York: Sumach Press, 2006

Bumgardner, Jennifer, Amy Richards, and Winona LaDuke. *Grassroots: A Field Guide for Feminist Activism.* New York: Farrar, Straus & Giroux, 2004.

Dell, Pamela. *Protecting the Planet: Environmental Activism (Green Generation).* Mankato, MN: Compass Point Books, 2010.

Ferree, Myra and Aili Tripp. *Global Feminism: Transnational Women's Activism, Organizing, and Human Rights.* New York: New York University Press, 2006.

Glickman, Lawrence B. *Buying Power: A History of Consumer Activism in America.* Chicago: University of Chicago Press, 2009.

Leafgren, Sheri, Brian D. Schultz, Michael P. O'Malley, and Larry Johnston. *The Articulation of Curriculum and Pedagogy for a Just Society: Advocacy, Artistry, and Activism.* Troy, NY: Educator's International Press, 2007.

Seidman, Gay W. *Beyond the Boycott: Labor Rights, Human Rights, and Transnational Activism.* New York: Russell Sage Foundation Publications, 2009.

Wanda B. Knight
The Pennsylvania State University

Social Justice Theory

Social justice theory addresses the oppressions that arise from the many "-isms" of institutionalized prejudice. The 21st century's ideals of social justice challenge the social and political contexts of the

20th century, situating being female in the broader construction of multidimensional and intersecting identities. As a conceptual framework, social justice theory recognizes lived experiences, identity politics, and hierarchies of oppression as legitimate sources of knowledge. Moreover, social justice theory allows the combination of theory and practice to create praxis, resulting in the ontological necessity for solutions to injustice. However, in this age of instant communications and globalization, multiple ontologies arise with disagreement over what is just for whom. A single unifying theory of social justice, applicable throughout the world, remains elusive.

Modern Justice Approaches

Theories of justice in the last century were rooted in hegemonic tradition. This century looks beyond these traditional social, political, and cultural visualizations of justice by asking us to consider the question, Justice for whom? Social justice impels more than an equal distribution of goods or a balancing of rights and wrongs. Modern justice approaches must take into account the multidimensional and intersecting identities of individuals to end oppression. Therefore, justice may be different for different people, depending on their particular position in the public sphere and on their geographical sphere.

Multiple dimensions of identities intersect and create identity politics that require recognition of the many ways a person experiences the social, political, and cultural justice of the world. Social justice theory accounts for institutionalized oppression allowed and experienced for being other than a member of the dominant social group. Sexism, racism, classism, ableism, ageism, heterosexism, and anti-Semitism are only a few of the many institutionalized forms of oppression that social justice theory analyzes through identity politics. Moreover, lived experiences serve as a critique for hierarchies of oppression that promote one form of institutionalized prejudice over another. Oppression can be experienced as one or many identities.

Social justice theory includes the practice of social justice. This combination of theory and practice together is known as *praxis*. Praxis can manifest in many forms of resistance to injustice. Feminist pedagogy rooted in the academy, and social justice movements rooted in the community, are examples of this combination of theory and practice to promote and achieve social justice.

Feminist pedagogy recognizes lived experience as a valid source of knowledge. Dominant social groups have long controlled the ideas of truth and fairness that lead to justice, but by allowing everyone a voice, and listening to those voices, knowledge and alternate paradigms of truth and fairness leading to alternate theories of justice are created. The implication of alternate sources of knowledge is a rewritten history and future in which everyone can recognize themselves represented or missing in the social, political, and cultural arenas of justice.

Injustice Resistance Movements

Coalitions of resistance to injustice are found in modern social movements including but not limited to the women's, civil rights, human rights, women's health, reproductive justice, and environmental justice movements. These movements and the many activist groups and individuals associated with them share the methodological assumption of identity politics and work toward solutions to ending the many forms of oppression.

In the last century, women's rights, civil rights, and human rights movements were concerned with particular inequalities of voting, representation, and access to justice. Women achieved the right to vote with the passage of the Nineteenth Amendment to the Constitution of the United States of America in 1920, but in the 21st century, that right is still denied to women around the globe. Activists also achieved great success in the United States with the passage of the Civil Rights Act of 1964. However, ethnic and indigenous oppressions continue within, across, and beyond those borders. Moreover, human rights movements continue to work toward realizing the mandate of the 1948 United Nations Universal Declaration of Human Rights in the courts and communities of the world. The women's health, reproductive justice, and environmental justice movements work toward a social justice that includes human rights and civil rights concerns but expands the idea of justice to the environment around and within our bodies.

Global Theory

Globally, social justice theory is the realm of debate over what is just for whom, where. Multiple ontologies for social justice may be necessary to cease social, political, and cultural oppressions throughout the world. Modern communications systems and economic globalization continuously redefine identity politics and compel a reimaging of what is right and wrong, fair and true, or just and unjust.

See Also: Chicana Feminism; Critical Race Feminism; Ecofeminism; Environmental Justice; Feminism, American; Feminist Jurisprudence; Global Feminism; Iranian Feminism; Islamic Feminism; Social Justice Activism; Women's Studies.

Further Readings

Adams, Maurianne, et al. *Readings for Diversity and Social Justice,* 2nd ed. New York: Routledge, 2010.

Capeheart, Loretta. *Social Justice: Theories, Issues, and Movements (Critical Issues in Crime and Society).* Brunswick, NJ: Rutgers University Press, 2007.

Fraser, Nancy. *Scales of Justice: Reimagining Political Space in a Globalizing World (New Directions in Critical Theory).* New York: Columbia University Press, 2009.

Shell Gosztyla
State University of New York, Albany

Solomon, Suniti

Suniti Solomon is an Indian microbiologist who diagnosed that country's first case of human immunodeficiency virus (HIV) in 1986. She founded the nonprofit YR Gaitonde Centre for AIDS Research and Education in 1993, which offers HIV and sex education, counseling and testing services, and outpatient and inpatient services for over 12,500 persons living with HIV. Solomon has published extensively on HIV epidemiology and has participated in international conferences on the subject. Retired from her duties as a professor at Chennei Medical College in India, she continues her work with HIV patients as doctor, researcher, and counselor.

The only girl among eight children born into a Chennai-based Maharashtrian Hindu family in the leather trade, Solomon first became interested in medicine when a health officer visited the Gaitondes home to administer the smallpox vaccine.

She received an M.D. in microbiology from Madras (now Chennei) Medical College, where she met her husband, a cardiac surgeon. For nearly 10 years, the Solomons traveled in Britain, the United States, and Australia, where Suniti continued her training. The couple returned to India in 1973 and began work in a government-run hospital. Solomon was on the faculty of Madras Medical College when she became interested in tracking the acquired immune deficiency syndrome (AIDS) virus in India. Because the lack of an openly gay community in India made it impossible to replicate studies that had first identified the virus in the United States, Solomon and one of her graduate students checked blood samples from 100 female sex workers in Madras. Six of them tested positive, and Solomon had found her life's work.

Initial Denial and Failure to React

For seven years, she could refer her HIV patients only to the Tambaram Sanatorium, built in 1928 as a refuge for patients with tuberculosis. With no concerted efforts to educate the public about the disease, cases of AIDS began to increase. Today, according to the World Health Organization, an estimated 5.13 million people in India are HIV-positive or are afflicted by AIDS—the second-largest population after South Africa. In 1993, Solomon renovated a building that the United States had built to house lepers and founded the YRG Centre for AIDS Research and Education, which is dedicated to using education, counseling, and testing to raise HIV awareness. Later, a virology laboratory and a 26-bed inpatient facility were added. The number of patients cared for at the clinic has increased tenfold since 1993. With the help of drugs that have become less expensive and more readily available, patients are living longer, but the problems that confront them are no less disturbing in a country where the stigma against HIV patients is still strong.

Solomon also has become increasingly committed to gender issues as they relate to HIV. The percentage of Indian women in the affected population has grown from 10 percent in the 1990s to 50 percent. Solomon argues that although long-term goals of empowering women must be met, addressing the immediate need for information and healthcare for women in a culture that denies them access to such services without the permission and financial support of men is crucial to halting what she calls the "feminization of

AIDS." Solomon currently serves as the president of the AIDS Society of India.

See Also: HIV/AIDS: Africa; HIV/AIDS: Asia; HIV/AIDS: Europe; HIV/AIDS: North America; HIV/AIDS: Oceania; India; Physicians, Female.

Further Readings

Chandrasekaran, Anupama. "Freedom to Live With HIV: Suniti Solomon." http://www.livemint.com/2009/08/14210824/Freedom-to-live-with-HIV--Sun.html?h=B (accessed April 2010).

Narain, Jai P., ed. *AIDS in Asia: The Challenge Continues.* Thousand Oaks, CA: Sage, 2004.

YRG Care. "Dr. Suniti Solomon." http://www.yrgcare.org/overview/dr.suniti.htm (accessed March 2010).

Wylene Rholetter
Auburn University

Solomon Islands

The Solomon Islands archipelago consists of more than 900 islands. There are 10 provinces, including Honiara, the capital city. The majority of Solomon Islanders are Melanesian. On gaining independence from Britain in 1978, Solomon Islands inherited the Westminster system of government. "Customary law," known as *kastom*, which varies across the archipelago, is a recognized source of law under the constitution. The Christian churches are also extremely important in Solomon Islands societies.

Women's roles in the family, tribe, community, and church are highly regarded and respected. These roles also were important in their roles as mediators and peacemakers in conflict. More recently, an assessment of women in employment showed that more women are now working in the public and private sector.

Despite these gains, a key emerging issue for women is their exclusion from decision-making processes. There are no women members of Parliament, only five women in provincial governments, five women permanent secretaries and some women directors of divisions within the public service. When linked to the broader socioeconomic context of development, weak management systems and mechanisms, and high levels of violence against women, the need to empower rural women and to provide policy and legislative reform at the national government level exists. Solomon Islands women face significant challenges in acquiring substantive gender equality.

Women's challenges are framed by the demands of globalization, capitalism, and modernization, which have created significant social change in the past decade. Conflict accompanies social change, particularly between the norms created by modern human rights discourse and the norms of *kastom*, tradition, and Christianity. The need to support women as they adapt to the cash economy and, at the same time, for broader society to adapt to women's changing social roles is increasing, but significant problems are evolving as a consequence. There is a need for an increased engagement of local women with expertise and experience to influence and drive social change and to make informed decisions about the creation of social change that is locally appropriate. It is clear that the country is in need of supporting changes that will advance the status of women, but such changes need to be couched within legal frameworks that will ensure change of attitudes toward women as equal citizens. Although Solomon Islands women's development paths will evolve at their own pace and with their own version of progress, there are concerns, nonetheless, about the quality of women's lives in the communities while they wait for their government to more effectively represent their interests and their rights as citizens.

See Also: Christianity; Equal Pay; Indigenous Women's Issues; Representation of Women in Government, International.

Further Readings

Central Intelligence Agency. "The World Factbook: Solomon Islands." https://www.cia.gov/library/publications/the-world-factbook/geos/bp.html (accessed July 2010).

Glenn, R. W. *Counterinsurgency in a Test Tube: Analyzing the Success of the Regional Assistance Mission to Solomon Islands.* Santa Monica, CA: RAND, 2007.

U.S. Department of State. "Solomon Islands." http://www.state.gov/r/pa/ei/bgn/2799.htm (accessed July 2010).

Ruth Basi Afia Maetala
Ministry for Women, Youth, and Children Affairs

Somalia

In 1960, British Somaliland merged with Italian Somaliland to create Somalia. The decades after that were generally filled with turmoil, and in 1991 the clans of northern Somalia created the Republic of Somalia, which is located in East Africa along the shores of the Gulf of Aden and the Indian Ocean. The new republic was subsequently plagued with internal strife, border disputes, and famine. Somalia, which is not recognized by other countries, is the fourth-poorest country in the world, with a per capita income of only $600 and a poverty rate of 71 percent. More than 70 percent of the workforce is engaged in agriculture, and 37 percent of the population is urbanized.

Early in the 21st century, some stability was restored as a result of a national plan to establish a representative government under a new constitution. Eighty-five percent of the population is Somali, and all Somalis are Sunni Muslim. Somalia has a large nomadic population, as well as large groups of refugees who relocate to avoid famine and clan warfare. The women in these groups are particularly vulnerable to discrimination and violence. Patriarchy is practiced according to Somali-styled Islamic law, which devalues women, who are required by law to wear the veil. Major problems include violence against women, systemic discrimination of women, and the prevalence of female genital mutilation. Women's rights groups actively promote equal rights and greater female political participation.

Marriage and Women's Rights

A married woman is considered the property of her husband and his tribe. Early marriages are arranged by either parents or tribal chiefs. At times, girls have been sold in marriage to ensure family safety. Polygamy is common. Women have few rights in divorce cases, but they may be awarded custody of girls younger than 15 years and boys younger than 10 years. Honor and revenge killings are common. In cases of wrongful death, a woman's life is considered only half as valuable as that of a man. Female inheritance is limited to half that of male heirs. In the past, few women owned property because of the practice of passing land from father to son, but this has changed in response to a rise in the number of woman-headed households.

Amid political and economic turmoil, large numbers of women have been forced in the role of breadwinners. This new role has led to a redefinition of the roles of Muslim women. They have formed study groups to educate themselves by reading the Qur'an and determining its application to their lives in the 21st century. This new insight led to a campaign to end the universal practice of infibulation, a form of female genital mutilation.

Women in Politics

The quota system requires that women fill 12 percent of parliamentary seats, yet in 2008, there were only 23 women in the 275-seat Parliament, and the only woman in the cabinet was the minister for Gender and Family Affairs. A female held that same position in the Somaliland government, in which two women sat in Parliament. For the first time, two women also sat in the Puntland Parliament.

Somalia ranks sixth in the world in infant mortality (109.19 deaths per 1,000 live births). Female infants (99.79 deaths per 1,000 live births) have a considerable advantage over males (118.31 deaths per 1,000 live births). That advantage continues into adulthood, resulting in a female life expectancy of 51.53 years and a male life expectancy of 47.78 years. However, there is little difference in the median ages for women (17.6 years) and men (17.5 years). With a fertility rate of 6.52 children per woman, Somalia ranks fourth in the world in fertility. Somalis have a 0.5 percent human immunodeficiency virus and acquired immune deficiency syndrome (HIV/AIDS) adult prevalence rate and a high risk of contracting bacterial and protozoal diarrhea, hepatitis A and E, typhoid fever, dengue fever, malaria, Rift Valley fever, schistosomiasis, and rabies. Educational levels and literacy are extremely low for both men (49 percent) and women (25.8 percent).

Violence against women is a pervasive problem, and the fact that there is no national judiciary means that justice is unevenly applied. Women are raped by police, members of the military, and rival clans. Rape laws are not generally enforced, and there are no laws against domestic violence or spousal rape. Rape victims are considered "impure," and families may try to mitigate social disgrace by turning to tribal chiefs to negotiate settlements with perpetrators. Although illegal, prostitution is prevalent.

See Also: Domestic Violence; Female Genital Mutilation; Geographical Distribution; HIV/AIDS: Africa; Honor Killings; Rape, Cross-Culturally Defined.

Further Readings

AFROL News. "Somalia." http://www.afrol.com/Cat egories/Women/profiles/somalia_women.htm (accessed February 2010).

Breneman, Anne R. and Rebecca A. Mbuh. *Women in the New Millennium: The Global Revolution.* Lanham, MD: Hamilton Books, 2006.

Central Intelligence Agency. "Somalia." https://www.cia .gov/library/publications/the-world-factbook/geos /so.html (accessed February 2010).

McGown, R. "Somalia: Redefining Social Roles: The Extraordinary Strength of Somali Women." *Women and Environments International Magazine*, v.58/59 (2003).

Social Institutions and Gender Index. "Gender Equality and Social Institutions in Somalia." http://genderindex .org/country/somalia (accessed February 2010).

U.S. Department of State. "2008 Human Rights Report: Somalia." http://www.state.gov/g/drl/rls/hrrpt/2008 /af/119024.htm (accessed March 2010).

Elizabeth Rholetter Purdy
Independent Scholar

Annika Sörenstam plays the 2008 LPGA Championship, prior to announcing it would be her final season on the LPGA Tour.

Sörenstam, Annika

Annika Sörenstam is one of the greatest female athletes in history and the most successful and famous woman golfer in 21st-century history. Before she retired from professional golf in December 2008, Sörenstam won 72 Ladies Professional Golf Association (LPGA) tournaments and 17 European tournaments—a total of 89 golf tournament wins around the world. Based on her talent and success, Sörenstam is the first player in LPGA history to cross the $20 million threshold of career earnings, and in 2001, her score of 59 in an official LPGA tournament was and still is the lowest score in female golf history. Her fame as a woman golfer parallels the fame of male golfers Arnold Palmer, Jack Nicklaus, and Tiger Woods.

Born in Stockholm, Sweden, on October 9, 1970, to Gunilla and Tom Sörenstam, Sörenstam was a natural athlete, who started playing golf at age 12. In 1987, she became a member of the Swedish National Golf Team, and in 1990 she played golf as a freshman at the University of Arizona. The following year, Sörenstam won seven collegiate titles and was the first non-American to win the NCAA U.S. National Golf Championship. In 1992, after winning the World Amateur championship, she became a professional golfer.

During the next 16 years, Sörenstam rewrote the LPGA and Ladies European record books, and her success has improved women's golf. Sörenstam's dominance, talent, and determination in the sport enabled her to set a multitude of scoring records and earn 10 Major wins from 1995 to 2006. She won a record eight Player of the Year awards; six Vare trophies (awarded to the LPGA player with the lowest average strokes per round for the season); and three Associated Press Female Athlete of the Year awards in 2003, 2004, and 2005. She also earned one-third of all LPGA records.

In 2003, not only was Sörenstam inducted into the World Golf Hall of Fame based on her tremendous LPGA win record, but she also made international headlines when she played in the Colonial Golf Tournament in Fort Worth, Texas, becoming the first woman since Babe Zaharias qualified for the 1945 Los Angeles Open to play against men in a PGA event.

As an elite athlete, Sörenstam successfully transitioned from professional golfer to entrepreneur the last few years of her career. In April 2007, she opened her Annika Academy golf instruction and training center near Orlando, Florida. In addition to helping others improve their golf abilities, she continues to design golf courses around the world. On a personal note, Sörenstam and her husband, Mike McGee, had a baby girl named Ava on September 1, 2009. Sörenstam's dedication, strong work ethic, mental toughness, competitive spirit, and near flawless golf technique have made her a hero for men and women around the globe.

See Also: Business, Women in; Golf; Sports, Women in.

Further Readings

Annika Sorenstam. "About." http://www.annikasorenstam .com/about.htm (accessed June 2010).

Savage, Jeff. *Annika Sörenstam.* Minneapolis, MN: First Avenue Editions, 2005.

Sörenstam, Annika. *Golf Annika's Way: How I Elevated My Game to Be the Best—and How You Can Too.* New York: Gotham Books, 2007.

Yvonne Doll
U. S. Army Command and General Staff College

Sotomayor, Sonia

Associate Justice of the Supreme Court of the United States of America Sonia Sotomayor is a woman of many "firsts." In 1992, at the age of 38 years, Sotomayor became the first American of Puerto Rican descent to be appointed to the federal bench in New York State, when she was commissioned as a judge in the U.S. District Court for the Southern District of New York. The youngest judge in the court and the first Puerto Rican woman to sit as a judge in a U.S. federal court, she served there until 1998, when she was confirmed to occupy a seat on the U.S. Court of Appeals for the Second Circuit. Sotomayor was the first Latina to serve on that court, hearing appeals in more than 3,000 cases and writing approximately 380 majority opinions in her 10 years on the appellate bench. President Barack Obama nominated Sotomayor to serve on the U.S. Supreme Court on May 26, 2009. Following partisan hearings before the Senate Judiciary Committee, she was confirmed with a vote of 68–31 on August 6, 2009, by the full Senate. Sotomayor became the first Hispanic and the third woman to serve on the U.S. Supreme Court when she was sworn in on August 8, 2009.

Education and Career Beginnings

Sotomayor was born in Bronx, New York, on June 25, 1954, to Puerto Rican immigrant parents, Juan Sotomayor and Celina Baez Sotomayor. Spanish was her first language. She lived in the Bronx housing projects, was diagnosed with type 1 diabetes at age 8 years, and mourned the death of her father at age 9 years. Raised as a Catholic, she attended highly regarded Cardinal Spellman High School in the Bronx, where she was active in student government, participated on the forensics team, and graduated as valedictorian of her class.

Sotomayor earned her B.A. summa cum laude from Princeton University in 1976. Elected to Phi Beta Kappa, she also won the M. Taylor Pyne Prize—the top honor that Princeton awards undergraduate students. Entering Yale Law School in the fall of 1976, Sotomayor distinguished herself as an editor of the *Yale Law Journal* and also as managing editor of the student-sponsored journal *Yale Studies in World Public Order.* She was granted her J.D. in 1979 and was admitted to the New York Bar the following year. Sotomayor married Kevin Noonan in 1976; the couple divorced in 1983. They had no children.

During her Supreme Court confirmation hearings, Sotomayor was repeatedly called to explain a remark that she made in a 2001 lecture she delivered at the University of California–Berkeley. In that address, she spoke about the ways in which gender and national origin might make a difference in how judges rule. She quoted a comment, attributed to Justice Sandra Day O'Connor, that "a wise old man and a wise old woman will reach the same conclusion in deciding cases" and then referenced herself, remarking that although she might not fully agree with the statement, "I would hope that a wise Latina woman with the richness of her experiences would more often than not reach a better conclusion than a white male who hasn't lived that life." Sotomayor's comments were criticized as evidence of liberal, racially biased attitudes that she might bring to bear on the Supreme Court. She took great care to distance herself from the remark and others like it, asserting, "I do not believe that any ethnic, racial or gender group has an advantage in sound judgment." The "wise Latina" statement was merely "a rhetorical flourish that fell flat," she argued, and she assured her detractors that she would rule based on the law, not on racial bias.

High-Profile Cases

Sotomayor rendered several high-profile rulings before her Supreme Court appointment. In March 1995, in *Silverman v. Major League Baseball Player Relations Committee, Inc.,* she issued the ruling that ended the 1994 baseball strike. In that same year, in *Dow Jones v. Department of Justice,* she supported the *Wall Street Journal*'s bid to obtain and print a photocopy of the last note left by Deputy White House Counsel Vince Foster before his suicide. In a 2002 abortion-related decision, in *Center for Reproductive Law and Policy v. Bush,* Sotomayor ruled for the Bush administration's practice of withholding public funds from nongovernmental organizations that perform or promote abortion in foreign countries.

A 2008 employment discrimination case heard in the Second Circuit, *Ricci v. DeStefano,* occasioned a controversial ruling in which Sotomayor voted with the majority in a ruling that allowed the city of New Haven to discard the results from a test for firefighters because no African Americans had scored high enough on the exam to qualify for promotion. The ruling was later overturned by the Supreme Court in 2009 in a 5–4 decision, stating that certain New Haven white firefighters had been victims of racial discrimination when their promotions were denied as a result of the test's invalidation.

See Also: Attorneys, Female; Ginsburg, Ruth Bader; Judges, Female; O'Connor, Sandra Day.

Further Readings

Center for Reproductive Law and Policy v. Bush, 304 F. 3d 183 (Second Circuit 2002).

Dow Jones v. Department of Justice, 880 F. Supp. 145 (S.D.N.Y. 1995).

Ricci v. DeStefano, 530 F. 3d 87 (Second Circuit; June 9, 2008; per curiam).

Silverman v. Major League Baseball Player Relations Committee, Inc., 880 F. Supp. 246 (S.D.N.Y. 1995).

Sotomayor, Sonia. "A Latina Judge's Voice." (Judge Mario G. Olmos Memorial Lecture), in "Raising the Bar: Latino and Latina Presence in the Judiciary and the Struggle for Representation." *Berkeley La Raza Law Journal* (Spring 2002).

"Sotomayor's Notable Court Opinions and Articles." *New York Times* (July 10, 2009).

Supreme Court of the United States. "Biographies of Current Justices." http://www.supremecourtus.gov (accessed July 2010).

Mary L. Kahl
State University of New York, New Paltz

South Africa

The Republic of South Africa is a country located on the southern extremity of the continent of Africa. The country is bordered by Namibia, Botswana, Zimbabwe, and Mozambique, and has Lesotho, a small, mountainous country, landlocked within its borders. South Africa has a lengthy coastline fringed by both the warm Indian Ocean and the cold South Atlantic Ocean, and although the climate is generally temperate, temperature varies throughout the country.

South Africa is home to more than 50 million people and is recognized for its diversity of language, culture, and religion (earning it the nickname of "The Rainbow Nation") but also for its tumultuous political past. Following nearly 300 years of colonial rule, the policy of apartheid, which determined rights and privileges to all citizens based on racial classification, was endorsed by the ruling white minority from 1948 until 1994.

This policy relegated all individuals who were classified as non-white to the status of second-class citizen. Embodied within the policy of apartheid was the ideology of segregation, referred to as separate development, which meant that access to public transport, state schools, hospitals, residential and public facilities, and indeed even cemeteries was defined on the basis of race. Women classified as black or African faced a double-pronged oppression: By virtue of race and gender, African women were subjugated and denied access to urban areas in which their husbands frequently worked as migrant laborers, and they were regularly denied access to employment on the grounds of both race and gender.

Despite the demise of apartheid and the remodeled South African constitution of 1996 being heralded as one of the most democratic and progressive constitutions in the world, in that it recognizes 11 official languages and provides legal protection for women from rape, domestic violence, and discrimination, momentous changes in the nation's legislation have not brought about significant changes to the majority of South Africa's population. Notwithstanding cultural and linguistic heterogeneity, patriarchy is a dominant cultural standard throughout South Africa, and although in the contemporary era the gendered status quo has theoretically been leveled, many women still face widespread discrimination, persecution, and violence. Shared cultural norms of many groupings within South Africa specify that women belong to the lineage into which she has married, and practices such as "bridewealth" (the payment of cattle, or in the contemporary era other material commodities, from the family of the groom to the family of the bride) and "levirate" (a man's wife being required to marry her deceased husband's brother) ensure continued control over women and their fertility.

The Impact of HIV/AIDS

In South Africa, the dawn of democracy coincided with the rise of human immunodeficiency virus and acquired immune deficiency syndrome (HIV/AIDS). South Africa presently has the highest absolute number of people living with HIV of any nation in the

Young women from the Zulu tribe in South Africa. The country is called "The Rainbow Nation" because of the diversity of language, culture, and religion represented by the more than 50 million people living there.

world, and approximately 25 percent of all pregnant women are infected with HIV. HIV/AIDS rates are showing no sign of abating, and the local epidemic has placed insurmountable care challenges on the shoulders of women. In South Africa, as is typical in the entire sub-Saharan African region, HIV/AIDS is a gendered disease, with women more likely to contract the disease than their male counterparts as a result of their biological makeup, coupled with sociocultural and economic vulnerability. The growing number of orphaned and vulnerable children in need of care as traditional prime-age caregivers succumb to the disease has thrown the effectiveness of the extended family safety net as the first line of defense against the disease into question.

In accordance with the National AIDS Plan of 1994, male condoms were distributed en masse in the 1990s in an attempt to curb the spread of the disease, but this wide-scale distribution did not amount to mass usage. As women's vulnerability increased against the backdrop of the nearly 40 percent unemployment rate and the increasing HIV/AIDS rate of the country, new gender-sensitive protection schemes are being sought, such as the introduction of the female condom and microbicides. At the same time, women are rising to the challenge and devising localized community initiatives and support networks in an attempt to meet the increasing care challenges placed on them in the era of HIV/AIDS.

See Also: Childcare; Foster Mothers; Gender Roles, Cross-Cultural; HIV/AIDS: Africa; Migrant Workers.

Further Readings

Campbell, J. "Women in South Africa: International Violence and HIV/AIDS: Intersections and Prevention." *Journal of Black Studies*, v.35/4 (2005).

Crewe, M. "Reflections on the South African HIV/AIDS Epidemic." *Society and Transition*, v.33/3 (2002).

De la Porte, S. "Redefining Childcare in the Context of AIDS: The Extended Family Revisited." *Agenda*, v.75/2 (2008).

Kingdon, G. and J. Knight. "Unemployment in South Africa: The Nature of the Beast." *World Development*, v.32/3 (2004).

Susan de la Porte
University of KwaZulu-Natal, South Africa

South Korea

The Republic of Korea, which borders both the Sea of Japan and the Yellow Sea, broke away from the northern section of the country after what is now known as North Korea became communist in the wake of World War II. With the help of the United States and the United Nations, South Korea managed to fend off communist encroachment in the early 1950s and established a path of democracy and economic prosperity. By the early 21st century, 81 percent of the population had become urbanized, and South Korea had become one of the 20 largest economies in the world, with a per capita income of $27,700. Nevertheless, 15 percent of the population lived in poverty, and a disproportionate number were women and children.

Although the number of women in the labor force has continued to expand, many female workers are relegated to entry-level jobs. South Korean society is heavily traditional, and women face entrenched discrimination in both their personal and public lives. Other problems of major concern are rape, violence against women, and human trafficking.

Korean society is highly homogeneous, with the only significant minority group being 20,000 Chinese. There is more diversity in religion, with Christians (26.3 percent) and Buddhists (23.2 percent) dominating. Korean is the official language, but most Koreans also learn English at the middle and high school levels.

The Ministry of Gender Equality, which was established in 2001, has been charged with protecting women's rights. This agency has engaged in campaigns to raise public awareness of women's issues, ranging from gender equality to violence against women. Nevertheless, a report issued by the United Nations Development Programme reveals that South Korea has been losing ground on the Gender Empowerment Index, dropping from 68th in the world in 2007 to 72nd in 2008. Divorce carries considerable stigma in South Korea, but Family Law reforms instituted in 1989 recognized the rights of divorced women to maintain property interests and greater contact with their children. A 2005 ruling by the Supreme Court held that married women had the same property rights as males and daughters had equal inheritance rights as sons.

Reproductive rights are strongly debated in South Korea, and feminists argue that abortion rights have

On average, South Korean women attend school for 15 years, have 1.21 children, and live to an average age of 82.

been based on government efforts to control population growth, with access becoming more widespread whenever the government attempts to curtail growth and becoming more restricted when growth is encouraged.

Education and Politics

South Korea has an infant mortality rate of 4.02 deaths per 1,000 live births for female infants and 4.49 deaths per 1,000 live births for male infants. The female advantage continues throughout life, with women having a life expectancy of 82.22 years compared with 74.45 years for men. South Korean women give birth to an average of 1.21 children each. The median age for women is 38.5 years compared with 36 years for men. Men have a considerable advantage over women in the realm of education, with a school life expectancy of 18 years for men as opposed to only 15 years

for women. As a result, most men are literate (99.2 percent), but only 96.6 percent of women older than 15 years are able to read and write.

Because of the legal requirement that political parties generate a proportional slate that is 50 percent female and a geographical slate that is 30 percent female, women are regularly elected to office. In 2008, there were 41 females in the 299-seat National Assembly. Two of 13 justices on the supreme court and two of 15 cabinet ministers were female. Efforts to address the needs of women led to the passage of the Sexual Equality Employment Act of 1999, which was followed by an upsurge in the number of gender discrimination and sexual harassment cases reported to authorities.

Violence and Sexual Harassment

In 1998, in response to rising incidences of domestic violence, the national legislature passed the Prevention of Domestic Violence and Victim Protection Act. Yet almost a third of married women become victims of domestic violence. Some shelters are government subsidized, and the government has increased support for victims. Although rape is illegal, there are no specific laws dealing with spousal rape.

Sexual harassment is also a widespread problem, and the Korea Institute for Health and Social Affairs and the Korean Institute of Criminology report that 17.9 percent of women become victims of some sort of sexual crime in their lifetimes. However, most of these crimes go unreported because of the social stigma attached to sex crimes. During World War II, scores of Korean women were forced into prostitution to satisfy the sexual appetites of Japanese soldiers. Today, those "comfort women" receive allowances of $387 from the Korean government. Despite efforts to control it, prostitution is still widespread, particularly in the capital city of Seoul. In 2008, the government passed the Act on the Prevention of the Sex Trade and Protection of Victims Thereof in an effort to deal with the growing problems of trafficking and sexual tourism.

In recent years, there has been considerable talk of Korean unification. A study released in 2001 by Younghee Kim and Youngah Change predicted that in the case of unification, women would be particularly vulnerable to contradictory views on women's rights in the areas of abortion, adultery, and head-of-family recognitions because of North Korea's more restrictive positions on the rights of women.

See Also: Abortion Laws, International; Domestic Violence; North Korea; Prostitution; Sexual Harassment.

Further Readings

Central Intelligence Agency. "The World Factbook: Korea, South." https://www.cia.gov/library/publications/the-world-factbook/geos/ks.html (accessed April 2010).

Kim, Younghee and Youngah Chang. "Laws Related to Women in Preparation for Unification of North and South Korea." *Korean Women Today*, v.67/7 (2001).

Kim, Youngok and Huynjoo Min. "The Polarization of the South Korean Female Labor Market." *Women's Studies Forum*, v.23/41–47 (2007).

Online Women in Politics. "Women's Rights in Korea." (2001). http://www.onlinewomeninpolitics.org/women sit/kr-w-sit.pdf (accessed April 2010).

U.S. State Department. "2008 Human Rights Report: Republic of Korea." http://www.state.gov/g/drl/rls /hrrpt/2008/eap/119044.htm (accessed April 2010).

Elizabeth Rholetter Purdy
Independent Scholar

Southern Baptist Convention

Although Baptists have been in America since colonial days, it was not until 1845 that a group of males from what would become the Confederate States organized the Southern Baptist Convention (SBC) in Augusta, Georgia. They split from other Baptists over cultural issues, most notably slavery, and subsequently grew to become the largest protestant Christian denomination in the United States composed of some 42,000 churches and over 16 million members in local congregations. The Southern Baptist Convention is both more and less than a religious denomination: more in that it represents the bureaucratic agencies, staff, and media of the denomination and less in that Baptist doctrine bestows autonomy on the local church. Recent annual meetings of the SBC have been marred by very public doctrinal disagreements over the inerrancy of the Bible and position statements on marriage, the family, and women in the ministry. Voting members at these annual meetings are official "Messengers," most of them pastors, who represent "friendly cooperating" congregations.

The Southern Baptist Faith and Message

The essence of Southern Baptist doctrine is contained in its "Faith and Message" (F&M), first written in 1925 and revised in 1963 and 2000. According to the SBC Website, this is the only "consensus statement" of doctrinal beliefs approved by the SBC. The latest revisions were the work of a 15-member committee composed of 10 white males, two white females, one Asian, one African American, and one Hispanic, a diverse committee in comparison with those of the past.

Faith and Message consists of 18 articles, ranging from affirmation of the Bible as God's inerrant truth to the last, and newest, on the family. Each article is followed by scriptural references suggesting biblical support. The 2000 revisions to the F&M reflect the culmination of what has become known as a "fundamentalist takeover" or a "conservative resurgence" that began in the late 1970s and was virtually completed over the next 20 years. Fundamentalist leaders replaced liberal or moderate agency heads and trustees of affiliated colleges, universities, and seminaries with those in concurrence on the major issues of the conservative movement, beginning with the inerrancy of the Bible.

The Southern Baptist Convention and Women

Not until 1918 could women serve as Messengers, and not until 1929 were they allowed to address the Convention. However, women's progress toward equality in the SBC was interrupted by the conservative resurgence. Three F&M articles are particularly revealing of the roles of women in the SBC. Revised article VI on the church states that, "the office of pastor is limited to men as qualified by Scripture." While local churches may choose to ordain women, few will defy the SBC by "calling" them as senior pastors, leaving them to serve as missionaries, assistant pastors, ministers of youth or education, or chaplains in various institutions. Article XV on the Christian and the Social Order was revised to affirm the sanctity of all human life, ". . . from conception to natural death." Article VXIII on the Family, new in the 2000 F&M,

proclaims, "Marriage is the uniting of one man and one woman," and then seemingly affirms the equality of husband and wife—but not without qualification.

The husband and wife are of equal worth before God, since both are created in God's image. A husband is to love his wife as Christ loved the church. He has the God-given responsibility to provide for, to protect, and to lead his family. A wife is to submit herself graciously to the servant leadership of her husband even as the church willingly submits to the headship of Christ. The scriptural citation in support of this statement is in the New Testament book of Ephesians, chapter 5 and, although not cited, is followed closely by an admonition for servants to obey their masters. Some SBC agency employees were asked to sign a statement affirming their support of the revised F&M, in some cases creating divisions within families and exacerbating divisions within the SBC.

The Future for Southern Baptists

The increasing politicalization of the SBC and the heavy-handed conservative takeover of agencies, institutions, and resources have not been without costs. Growth has slowed as churches struggle to win new converts and to diversify their aging, white, and middle-class congregations. The Baptist Alliance formed in 1987 and the Cooperative Baptist Fellowship formed in 1991 have claimed some churches and individuals with their more moderate positions on the Bible and on social issues.

See Also: Christianity; Fundamentalist Christianity; Marriage; Ministry, Protestant; Religion, Women in Religious Fundamentalism, Cross-Cultural Context of.

Further Readings

Ammerman, Nancy T. *Baptist Battles: Social Change and Religious Conflict in the Southern Baptist Convention.* New Brunswick, NJ: Rutgers University Press, 1995.

Cline, Austin. "Southern Baptist and the Role of Women." (1998). http://atheism.about.com/od/baptistssouthern baptists/a/baptistwomen.htm (accessed October 2009).

Fletcher, Jesse C. *The Southern Baptist Convention: A Sesquicentennial History*. Nashville, TN: Broadman and Holman, 1994.

Leonard, Bill. "When the Denominational Center Doesn't Hold: The Southern Baptist Experience." *The Christian Century* (September 22, 1993).

Southern Baptist Convention. Official Website of the Southern Baptist Convention. http://sbc.net (accessed October 2009).

Joyce E. Williams
Texas Woman's University

Spain

In 1983, the Institute of Woman (*Instituto de la Mujer*) was created to promote gender equality. There are many associations—public and private feminist associations, organizations and independent groups that constitute a rich feminist movement—working to improve the position of women in Spain and to combat discrimination in the country in the wake of its move into democracy in 1978.

Spain is home to 46 million people, 49.5 percent of whom are men and 50.5 percent are women. Life expectancy is 77.6 years for men and 84.1 years for women. Citizens age 85 and older are twice as likely to be women. Approximately 29 percent of households consist of two members, 24.6 percent are composed of four people, and 5.9 percent have more than five members. Women have an average of 1.4 children, a rising number, and enter motherhood at 29.3 years on average. Abortion, legal since 1985 and now under revision, is 11.5 per thousand women and continuously growing.

A Ministry of Equality (*Ministerio de Igualdad*) has recently been created to pass public policies on gender equality and to ensure gender mainstreaming in all areas of social, economic, and political affairs, with very promising perspectives. It is still soon to evaluate the impact that those and other state actions are having on Spanish women. Several new laws have been approved to guarantee gender equality, such as *Ley Orgánica 3/2007 Para la Igualdad Efectiva ee Mujeres y Hombres*, *Plan Estratégico Para la Igualdad de Oportunidades Entre Mujeres y Hombres* (2008-2010), and *Ley Orgánica 1/2004 de Medidas de Protección Integral Contra la Violencia de Género*. The later, aimed at eliminating violence based on gender, has been one of the most important legislative advances in contemporary Spain, despite the many challenges yet to face.

According to the *Observatory on Violence Against Women,* that law and other institutional measures have not reduced the number of female deaths, and the number of claims continues to grow. Women commit fewer crimes than men. Nine out of 100 convicted people are women, and only 7.7 percent of prisoners are women.

Regarding education, 48.5 percent of enrolled pupils in compulsory education are girls, but this rate increases to 51.5 percent in secondary school and/or vocational training. The enrolment of women in college is 54 percent, 62.6 percent in adult education (2006–07). Even though 48.7 percent of women win awards and successfully complete their studies, they don't necessarily get jobs. Women teachers represent 62.4 percent of all teachers, but only 36.9 percent are college professors. Female professors represent just 14.4 percent of the teaching staff in colleges and universities, of which only 12 percent have been awarded an honorary doctorate. At the Royal Academies of Science, Language, Arts, and so on, only 6.4 percent of members are women.

Women's access to employment was higher than men's between 2002 and 2007, yet the female employment rate continues to be 55.4 percent compared to men's at 71.9 percent. The annual salary for women was 83.2 percent of male wages before taxes in 2006. The global economic crisis has had an impact on both men and women. However, women occupy more part-time jobs to help meet a family's needs, and 94 percent of women leave their jobs and become homemakers, mostly due to childcare constraints.

The healthcare system in Spain covers all citizens and instances. The presence of women in politics, power, and decision making has improved considerably in recent years. Women occupy 36.3 percent of the seats in Parliament and 28 percent in the Senate. On the national level of government, half are female ministers in the national Parliament, but only 32 percent of senators are women. Six out of 10 judges are female, although just 7.9 percent become *magistradas* (judges of highest court). Spain ranks 16 out of 179 in the Human Development Index, being the Gender-Related Development Index (GDI) of 11 (among a total of 136 countries).

See Also: Domestic Violence; Educational Opportunities/Access; Representation of Women.

Further Readings

Instituto de la Mujer (España, 2009). http://www.inmujer .migualdad.es/MUJER/mujeres/igualdad/index.htm (accessed November 2009).

Morant, I. *Historia de las Mujeres en España y América Latina.* Valencia, Spain: Ediciones Cátedra, 2006.

Twomey, L. *Women in Contemporary Culture: Roles and Identities in France and Spain.* Bristol, UK: Intellect Books, 2003.

Amalia Morales Villena
University of Granada

Sports, Women in

Historically, sport and physical activity were positioned as masculine undertakings designed to demonstrate the virility of the participants in an effort to determine the worthiness of a man as a provider, protector, and warrior. Women were not allowed to watch the events, let alone compete in the events. As social and political changes surfaced in the European nations and early America during the 19th century, women began to test the boundaries of sport and physical activity participation, eventually gaining access and opportunity.

Women and the Ancient Olympic Games

During the first Olympic Games in 776 B.C.E., women were not allowed to participate in or attend the Olympic Games. Women were deemed a distraction for the male participants, and therefore were prevented from any participation or spectatorship in the games. However, as a result of the success and popularity of the 776 B.C.E. games, the Heraea Games were created in the 6th century B.C.E., in honor of the Greek goddess Hera, as an athletic event specifically for women. Like the male events, the Heraea Games consisted of track-and-field type sports. In order to compete in the events, female participants were required to dress like men. Interestingly, males were not allowed to watch the female athletes compete. In the ancient world, there was a fear and long-held belief that if a male watched a female compete in athletic events, the male may perceive the female's athletic prowess as unattractive, resulting in fewer marriages and consequently fewer children born to carry on Greek values and beliefs.

It was not until 1900, when the Olympic Games were held in Paris, France, that women began to compete with men in the Olympic Games. Nineteen women representing various nations were among the first Olympic female competitors in the 1900 games, including Helen de Pourtales from Switzerland, who competed in yachting; Elvira Guerra from France, who competed in equestrianism; Charlotte Cooper from Great Britain, who competed in tennis; and Margaret Abbott from the United States, who competed in golf. Interestingly, Abbott was the first American female to earn a medal in the Olympic Games in golf, typically identified in 1900 as a male-dominated sport.

Before Title IX: A Shift in Attitudes

Gaining access and creating opportunities for girls and women in physical activity and sporting settings became a figurative "race" for equality. As women began to advocate for the institutionalization of their rights and freedoms in the athletics world, as well as other parts of their lives, they were faced with oppressive and biased attitudes that continued to act as barriers to their participation. Prior to 1870, organized sport and physical activity opportunities for women were simply recreational in nature. In theory, these recreational opportunities were noncompetitive, unorganized, and without specific rules and guidelines. However, it is believed that women infused a competitive spirit into their physical efforts, as a result of natural instinct.

In the mid-1800s and early 1900s, women began to form their own clubs and organize competitions among each other. Women's teams organized informal "play days" with other local universities, sororities, and groups. Interestingly, the female players on each team were responsible for organizing the entire event. Support from organized athletic sectors was nonexistent. These competitions were not widely

There was a time when women were not allowed to watch sporting events, much less compete in them. In the mid-1800s and early 1900s, women began to form their own clubs and organize competitions among each other.

recognized, because the competitions were intramural in nature and because women as athletes were disregarded as unimportant and unattractive.

Gaining Momentum

Throughout the women's suffrage movement, women challenged the general beliefs and attitudes regarding women's capabilities not only on the field but in the classroom, in the workplace, and in governmental institutions. Through actions and words, women demanded the same freedoms and opportunities that were afforded to men and boys. Through years of hard work, advocacy, and sacrifice, women gained access. In 1920, the Nineteenth Amendment passed, giving U.S. women the right to vote and become a part of the governmental system, which afforded women a voice and some degree of power to influence the decisions that were made on a broad level that impacted their lives.

This first wave of feminism impacted women's access to sport and physical activity. As a result, women made moderate strides in gaining further access to resources and opportunities related to their sport and physical activity experience, especially for women attending college. Women who attended college in the early 1900s were generally from wealthy, positioned families. The sports that were popular at the time were defined by the upper class and consequently reflected their values and traditions. Early forms of sport and physical activity were positioned based on socioeconomic status. Generally speaking, sport and physical activity for women were individual in nature and included horseback riding, yachting, croquet, tennis, and swimming. As women sought more opportunities, they were allowed limited access to local clubs, primarily attended by men. During their club time, women were not allowed to participate with the men and were provided with certain times on various days when they could participate in sports and physical activities.

Sport and Physical Activity as a Health Hazard?

A belief began to emerge that participation in sport and physical activity was hazardous to a women's health. It was once believed that women should conserve their energy and that it should only be expended on necessary household chores and child rearing. In addition, a belief from the ancient Olympic games remained steadfast: it was thought watching women participate in sport and physical activity was unattractive. It was believed that participation in sport and physical activity could impact a woman's ability have and carry a baby to full term. Dr. Edward Clarke published *Sex in Education; A Fair Chance for Girls* in 1874, in which he continued to question women's aptitude for physical activity. Clarke believed that physical exertion and brain activity must be limited at the onset of menstruation. Regardless of the type of sport, women were encouraged not to exert themselves; women's sports and physical activity were positioned by society as meant for enjoyment and recreation only. Today, we understand that there are many physical and environmental factors that contribute to a women's daily energy level and that a healthy approach to physical activity is a requisite to living a long, healthy life.

The Impact of Title IX on Access and Opportunity

As a part of the civil rights movement, women experienced feminism on a larger scale and began to move toward greater equality in many aspects of their lives. In 1972, Title IX, an educational reform act that mandated equal access for all minority groups, including women, was passed. In essence, the bill legislated that any organization or institution that received federal monies was required to adhere to new governmental policies that required equal access and resources for all groups of people, and that no person could be discriminated against or denied access based on their race or gender. While Title IX experienced some significant "growing pains" as it was applied and adopted, Title IX did allow women and girls more access and opportunities in the sport and physical activity arena, as well as the broader educational realm.

A report by the Women's Sports Foundation (WSF) published in June of 2007 indicated that female participation levels in collegiate sports experienced steady growth in the 1990s and has leveled off in the 2000s. Data collected by the WSF indicated that participation in intercollegiate activities increased by 25,000 athletes from 1995 to 1996. Since the passage of Title IX in 1972, it is well documented that women and girls have experienced greater access to sport and physical activity opportunities. Unfortunately, women and girls are still faced with various institutions and organizations failing to completely comply with and adhere to Title IX, which results in continuous challenges.

It can be argued that Title IX has been the most significant piece of legislation for American women and girls since the passage of the Nineteenth Amendment. As the historic impact of Title IX continues to be understood and responsibility applied, women and girls should continue to advocate for their equal rights and access to resources. A close examination of sport and physical activity trends indicates that women and girls still face barriers as they continue to seek equal access and opportunities. However, if history does repeat itself, it is clear that women will continue to gain momentum and not only advocate for their own rights and greater access, but they will also continue to pave the way for future generations of female athletes.

See Also: Basketball, College; Boxing; Coaches, Female; Figure Skating; Gender Roles, Cross-Cultural; Golf; Gymnastics; Olympics, Summer; Olympics, Winter; Little League; Running/Marathon; Soccer, Children's; Soccer, Professional; Swimming; Tennis; Title IX; Women's National Basketball Association.

Further Readings

Acosta, R. V. and L. J. Carpenter. "Women in Sport." In Donald Chu, Jeffrey O. Segrave, and Beverly J. Becker, eds., *Sport and Higher Education*. Champaign, IL: Human Kinetics, 1985.

Bell, R. "The History of Women in Sport Prior to Title IX." *The Sport Journal*, v.10/2 (2007).

Clarke, E. *Sex Education; or, a Fair Chance for Girls*. Boston: James R. Osgood and Company, 1874.

Hult, J. S. "The Story of Women's Athletics: Manipulating a Dream 1890–1985." In D. M. Costa and S. R. Guthrie, eds., *Women and Sport: Interdisciplinary Perspectives*. Champaign, IL: Human Kinetics, 1994.

Hultstrand, B. J. "The Growth of Collegiate Women's Sports: The 1960s." *The Journal of Physical Education, Recreation, and Dance*, v.64/3 (1993).

Ladda, S. "The National Association for Girls and Women in Sport: 110 Years of Social Justice and Change." *The Journal of Physical Education, Recreation, and Dance*, v.80/7 (2009).

Motley, M and M. Lavine. "Century Marathon: a Race for Equality in Girls' and Women's Sports." *The Journal of Physical Education, Recreation & Dance*, v.72/6 (2001).

Donna Duffy
University of North Carolina, Greensboro

Sports Announcers, Female

When Lesley Visser took over the color commentator duties in the fourth quarter of a preseason National Football League (NFL) game between the Miami Dolphins and New Orleans Saints, the longtime female sports announcer made history. No woman had ever been given the color announcing job before in an NFL game, making Visser's November 3, 2009, appearance special.

Although Visser's achievement was lauded among women's groups, female sports announcers face multiple obstacles in earning opportunities and respect in sports broadcasting, especially in mainstream men's sports coverage of football, basketball, and baseball.

Stereotypes Permeate Decision Making

Women are largely denied the opportunity to work in the broadcast booth for men's sports, where announcers give play-by-play commentary and "color" analysis. They also face cultural stereotypes that position them as lacking the knowledge and credibility to speak authoritatively to an audience about a game. The structural barriers work in harmony with negative cultural attitudes to preserve a status quo in which women are marginalized and devalued in sports and sports-related professions, including sports announcing.

Ongoing demographic research published by The Institute for Diversity and Ethics in Sport at the University of Central Florida has shown the extent to which women are excluded from this profession. For example, in 2008, women occupied 3 percent of all NFL sports broadcasting positions, the same number as in 1996. In the 2008–09 season, women made up 8 percent of National Basketball Association (NBA) announcers and just 2 percent of those on TV during 2008 Major League Baseball (MLB) broadcasts. Further, in the 2008 Summer Olympics, NBC employed just one female play-by-play announcer, Andrea Joyce—and she covered rhythmic gymnastics, a sport open only to female competition.

Scholars argue that one reason women do not receive opportunities in this and other sports-related professions is the stereotype that women are not naturally suited for sports. In many Western cultures, sports are positioned as something that comes "natural" to boys and men, and thus often viewed as a male domain; women, on the other hand, are seen as outsiders. This is troublesome in televised sports, where a play-by-play announcer describes the action and a color commentator explains certain plays and strategies. Both jobs require an authoritative presence; if women are perceived as lacking competence, those making hiring decisions may decide women are not capable of doing the job and audience members may question the validity of their commentary.

Struggling to Advance From the Sidelines

When women do appear on television as part of a men's sports broadcast, they nearly always work as sideline reporters, covering softer, off-the-field news, which in many ways replicates women's "outsider status" in the context of sports. Well-known personalities such as ESPN's Erin Andrews, Fox Sports' Andrea Kremer, and CBS's Visser have all made careers at this position. Although sideline reporters are a visible part of the broadcast, scholars argue that they are not central to the production's success, giving the job a lower-status connotation. Further, most female sideline announcers must meet unwritten rules about Western standards of youthful beauty and sex appeal, making the position more about aesthetics and less about reporting acumen.

Some scholars argue that women may be left out from high-profile positions because they are not getting the necessary training at smaller TV stations to prepare them for a leap to national and regional broadcasts. Demographic information substantiates that claim; according to the Radio Television and Digital News Association's 2008 edition of an ongoing census of women in sports broadcasting at local TV stations, women made up just 8 percent of local TV sports anchor positions and about 19 percent of sports reporters.

There are women, however, who are challenging the status quo. Pam Ward has provided play-by-play for select college American football games for ESPN since 2000, and Beth Mowins received a similar opportunity from ESPN in 2005. Suzyn Waldman is the color analyst on the YES Network for New York Yankees baseball games. Ward has also called the play-by-play for the Women's National Basketball Association games, and it is when women's sports are broadcast on television that women may have the best opportunity to move from the sideline to the prestigious broadcast booth. Still, in a society where patriarchal ideology positions men and men's sports as superior, working in women's sports is viewed as a kind of second-class status, and it remains to be seen what the future holds for women in this profession.

See Also: Gender Roles, Cross-Cultural; Sports, Women in; Stereotypes of Women; Visser, Leslie; Women's National Basketball Association.

Further Readings

Etling, Laurence and Raymond Young. "Sexism and the Authoritativeness of Female Sportscasters." *Communication Research Reports*, v.24/2 (2007).

Finder, Chuck. "The Big Picture: Ward Does Play-by-Play as Well as Boys." *Pittsburgh Post-Gazette.* (November 7, 2002). http://www.awsmonline.org/newsletters/newsletters_winter03.pdf (Accessed November 2009).

Papper, Bob. "2008 Women and Minorities Survey." *Radio Television Digital News Association.* http://www.rtdna.org/pages/media_items/the-face-of-the-work force1472.php (Accessed November 2009).

Skerski, Jamie. "From Sideline to Centerfold: The Sexual Commodification of Female Sportscasters." In Tom Reichert and Jaqueline Lambiase, eds., *Sex in Consumer Culture: The Erotic Content of Media and Marketing.* London: Routledge, 2005.

Erin Whiteside
Penn State University

Sports Illustrated Swimsuit Edition

In 1964, the popular men's sport magazine, *Sports Illustrated* (SI), published its first *Sports Illustrated* Swimsuit Issue (SISI). Each subsequent year, the magazine has dedicated an issue featuring beachwear rather than sports news. Although the first SISIs primarily focused on fashion and contained mostly travel and tourism advertisements, over the years the issue became less and less about fashion and travel and focused more on the sexual appeal of the models sporting the swimsuits in exotic locations. The SISI's targeted consumers consist predominately of heterosexual males. The SISI is extremely popular and usually outsells regular issues of SI. There are varying opinions on the merit of the issue, as fans classify it as art and critics consider it a form of pornography. In addition, the overall message of the issue implies that it is just for fun and celebrates the expression "boys will be boys."

The SISI has been slow to incorporate diverse ethnicities of featured swimsuit models. For instance, it was not until 1990 that a women with very dark skin was selected to model for the special issue. Since 2001, the SISI has incorporated advanced photography techniques and swimsuit designs that go beyond conventional standards. Many of the models sport body paint only rather than a fabric bathing suit. Body paint can be misleading, because it encourages the viewer to consume the images as they would art; however, researchers have argued that when women are body painted, they become predominately objects and experience higher levels of sexualization.

Sexualization and the Advertiser

The swimsuit models in the SISI represent varying degrees of sexualization. For example, if the model wears a very revealing bathing suit, typically her body positioning and pose are not sexually suggestive. However, if a model wears a bathing suit that is more modest and not as revealing, she is positioned in ways that heighten her sex appeal.

The advertisements that are commonly found throughout the SISI elevate the sex appeal and sexualization of the issue. Specifically, advertisements contain subliminal messages about sexual activity and how to achieve improved sexual experiences. The most commonly advertised products in the SISI are condoms, alcohol, and automobiles.

SI generally does not focus or cover women's sport in depth, except during the Winter and Summer Olympics. Furthermore, few elite female athletes have been selected for the cover of the SISI. Those athletes who have appeared, including Anna Kournikova and Venus Williams, have been photographed and captured in highly sexualized poses, further raising questions about the trivialization of women athletes and women's sport. Moreover, elite male athletes' wives and professional cheerleaders have been more frequently featured in the SISI than elite women athletes. Overall, critics argue that the SISI is more about sexy models than sport. In 2007, SI revised its subscription policies, and subscribers can now opt out of receiving the SISI.

The SISI remains very popular, however, and interested consumers can purchase a DVD of the making of a particular issue. To keep up with the Internet age and maintain a high profile among a Web-based society, the SISI has put significant effort into the design of its Website. The Website provides opportunities for consumers to watch videos, order swimsuit calendars, visit the SISI Hall of Fame, get to know the models better, and even receive swimsuit applications on their smart phones.

See Also: Advertising, Portrayal of Women in; Pornography, Portrayal of Women in; Sports, Women in.

Further Readings

Creedon, Pamela J. *Women, Media and Sport: Challenging Gender Values.* Thousand Oaks, CA: Sage, 1994.

Davis, Laurel R. *The Swimsuit Issue and Sport: Hegemonic Masculinity in Sports Illustrated.* Albany: State University of New York Press, 1997.

Sports Illustrated Swimsuit Issue. http://www.sports illustrated.cnn.com/vault/swimsuit/home/index.htm (accessed November 2009).

C. Weaving
St. Francis Xavier University

Sports Officials, Female

Despite the recent advancement of some female sports officials to the ranks of the professional leagues and amateur world championships, female sports officials still lag behind their male counterparts in terms of numbers and opportunities for advancement. Advocates of gender equity in sports anticipated that an increase in the number of school-sponsored teams and increased participation opportunities for women at all levels of sport would result in increased job opportunities for female coaches, athletic administrators, and sport officials. While job opportunities did increase at all levels of sports with the passage of Title IX legislation in 1972, most of those positions were filled by males.

Prior to 1972, girls' and women's sports were primarily coached, administered, and officiated by women. As early as the 1920s, the Committee on Women's Athletics (CWA) wrote and administered the rules of sport for girls and women. After 1972, with the demise of the Association for Intercollegiate Athletics for Women (AIAW), CWA's successor, and the takeover of women's sports by the National Collegiate Athletic Association (NCAA), female administrators, coaches, and officials were often relegated to secondary roles in women's sports.

For most sports, officials and referees officiating is a part-time job or even volunteer work that is generally undertaken in addition to their primary career. Thus, the number of sports officials at various levels is difficult to determine, as well as the number that have advanced to the highest ranks. A report by the NCAA on gender equity in college coaching and administration indicated that while 88 percent of the 1,127 female officials who responded to the gender equity survey were satisfied with their positions, 35 percent were dissatisfied with their opportunities for advancement. Furthermore, time (28 percent) and family (25 percent) commitments were cited by female officials as the most commonly perceived barriers to female representation in intercollegiate athletics officiating.

Female Officials Who Overcame Gender Barriers

Notwithstanding these perceived barriers and the lack of gender equity efforts in officiating, some women have advanced to the highest levels of officiating. For example, Marcy Weston served as an AIAW and NCAA official for 20 years (1964–84), was the NCAA secretary-rules editor for the Women's Basketball Committee (1985–98), and was the NCAA national coordinator of women's basketball officiating from 1984 until 2005. She also became the chair of the National Association of Sports Officials (NASO) board of directors. The association awarded her its highest achievement award, the Gold Whistle, in 2008. Weston's successor as NCAA national coordinator is Mary Struckoff. Struckoff previously coached, was a high school athletic administrator, and officiated at the high school and collegiate levels.

Other females who have broken the gender barrier in sports officiating in the last several decades include Pam Postema and Ria Cortesio. Postema umpired for six years in the Triple AAA Pacific Coast League, worked Major League Baseball (MLB) spring-training games in 1988, and then was released by minor-league baseball following the 1989 season. She filed a federal sex discrimination lawsuit against baseball that was settled out of court. In 2007, Cortesio became the first female since Postema to officiate a MLB spring-training game. Later that year, after umpiring for nine seasons in the Double A minor leagues, Cortesio was released by minor-league baseball. Currently there are no female umpires in professional baseball.

Gwen Adair was the first women to referee a world title fight. On June 5, 1998, she officiated a junior middleweight match between Pedro Ortega and Luis Campas at Auditorio Municipal in Tijuana. She refereed more than 100 amateur boxing bouts and earned her professional license in 1980. Adair refereed for 20 years and is currently a boxing judge. She has been inducted into the World Boxing Hall of Fame, the California Boxing Hall of Fame, and the California Boxers Association Hall of Fame.

Perhaps the female officials who have received the most media attention in the past decade are Violet Palmer and Dee Kantner. These women were the first females to officiate regular season games at the highest level of a men's professional sport league. In 1997, the National Basketball Association (NBA) hired Palmer and Kantner as full-time NBA referees. Palmer, who previously officiated at various levels of women's basketball, also became the first female to officiate an NBA playoff game in 2006. She is still an NBA official and in 2009 was named the coordinator of women's collegiate basketball officials for the West Coast Conference. Kantner, who also refereed women's collegiate basketball before becoming an NBA referee, was fired by the NBA in 2002. Kantner is currently supervisor of officials for the Women's National Basketball Association (WNBA).

The Next Generation

These women and other female officials have paved a path for the next generation of female officials. In the past several years, female officials have begun breaking barriers at the highest levels of amateur, collegiate, and professional sport leagues. Sarah Thomas became the first female official in NCAA Division 1A football in 2007. She then became the first female to be part of an officiating crew for a postseason bowl game between Marshall University and Ohio University in 2009. Also in 2009, Kim Winslow became the first female to referee an Ultimate Fighting Championship mixed martial arts bout. Amy Fearn became the first female to referee an English Football League men's professional soccer match in 2010. Leah Wrazidlo is a top ice hockey official in USA Hockey's Officiating Development program. In 2009, she officiated several men's junior hockey games and has worked at several International Ice Hockey Federation (IIHF) Women's World Championships. She was also chosen by the IIHF to officiate women's hockey games at the 2010 Winter Olympics.

See Also: Basketball, College; Sports, Women in; Title IX; Women's National Basketball Association.

Further Readings

Lieber, Jill. "NBA's Only Female Ref Doesn't Back Down." *USA Today* (November 7, 2005). http://www.usatoday .com/sports/basketball/nba/2005-11-07-palmer_x.htm (accessed February 2010)

National Collegiate Athletic Association (NCAA). "Gender Equity in College Coaching and Administration." Indianapolis, IN: NCAA, 2009.

Reid, Cathy. "Recruiting Female Officials." Australian Sports Commission. http://www.ausport.gov.au/sports officialmag/roles_and_responsibilities/recruiting _female_officials (accessed June 2010).

Corinne M. Daprano
University of Dayton

Sri Lanka

Sri Lanka is an island nation off the coast of India in the Indian Ocean. The nation has been subject to outbreaks of civil warfare since the 1980s and has about 460,000 internally displaced people. The population of about 21 million is primarily Sinhalese (73.8 percent), with 8.5 percent Tamil.

Buddhism is the predominant religion (69.1 percent), with minorities including Muslims (7.6 percent), Hindus (7.1 percent), and Christians (6.2 percent). Per capita gross domestic product was $4,500 in 2009 and is unequally distributed—the Gini index measurement of the inequality of income stands at 49, the 28th highest in the world, with 23 percent of the population living below the poverty line. In 2009,

the World Economic Forum rated Sri Lanka as 16th highest (i.e., most equal) out of 134 countries in terms of gender equality. On a scale where one indicates perfect equality and zero means inequality, Sri Lanka got a score of 0.740 overall, with subscores of 0.960 for health and survival (1st in the world), 0.930 for educational attainment (68th in the world), 0.594 on economic participation and opportunity (99th), and 0.169 on political empowerment (6th).

The literacy rate is lower for women than it is for men, 89 percent versus 93 percent, but women outnumber men in current school enrollment at both the primary and secondary levels. Women are less likely to be in the labor force than men, 46 percent versus 79 percent), and earn about 72 percent of what men do for comparable work. However, women hold a disproportionate number of professional and technical positions relative to their labor force participation. Women held only 6 percent of seats in Parliament and a similar percentage of ministerial positions in 2009, but a woman has served as head of state: Chandrika Kumaratunga was the president of Sri Lanka from 1994 to 2005.

Sri Lanka is a source and destination for human trafficking of women and children for sexual exploitation and involuntary servitude as well as internal forced labor. Save the Children ranks Sri Lanka 54th on its Mothers' Index, 51st on its Women's Index, and 63rd on its Children's Index. Infant mortality is 18.57 per 1,000 live births.

See Also: Buddhism; Heads of State, Female; Poverty; Trafficking, Women and Children.

Further Readings

Central Intelligence Agency. "The World Factbook: Sri Lanka." https://www.cia.gov/library/publications /the-world-factbook/geos/ce.html (accessed February 2010).

United Nations Statistics Divisions. UNdata: A World of Information: Gender Info. http://data.un.org/Explorer .aspx?d=GenderStat (accessed February 2010).

Winslow, Deborah and Michael D. Woost, eds. *Economy, Culture, and Civil War in Sri Lanka*. Bloomington: Indiana University Press, 2004.

Sarah Boslaugh
Washington University School of Medicine

Starhawk

Starhawk, whose birth name is Miriam Simos, is an American Wiccan, writer, teacher, ecofeminist, and social justice activist. Starhawk was born on June 17, 1951, in St. Paul, Minnesota. She holds a B.A. in fine arts from the University of California, Los Angeles, and an M.A. in psychology from Antioch West University. She lives part time in San Francisco in a collective house and part time in the woods of Sonoma County, California.

From the publication of her first book in 1979, *The Spiral Dance: A Rebirth of the Ancient Religion of the Great Goddess*, Starhawk has been central to the revival of earth-based spirituality and Goddess religion. Today, she is a leading voice of the neo-pagan movement.

In *The Spiral Dance*, Starhawk explores the historical growth, suppression, and 20th-century reemergence of the ancient Goddess-worshipping religion, Wicca. Next, she outlines the three pillars of her thealogy (a feminist approach to theism), which are that Goddess is immanent in the world; what affects one of us affects all of us; and Goddess religion is lived in community. Together, these thealogical imperatives require compassion, continuous striving for justice, and focus on common struggles rather than individual salvation. A large portion of the book is devoted to the practice of Wicca.

The Role of Wicca in Social Change and Justice

In subsequent work, Starhawk has emphasized the role of social change in Wicca with a particular emphasis on feminist transformation of patriarchal power over individuals, institutions, and policies. Consistent with many feminist theorists, Starhawk decries "power over" and urges the embrace of "power-with." Ultimately, she calls for a transformative understanding of the social constructions "male" and "female."

For more than three decades, Starhawk has traveled internationally to speak, teach, and advocate for and about Wicca, respect for and care of the Earth, feminist action, nonviolence, antiglobalization, and other social justice issues. The foundation of Starhawk's appeal as a teacher and guide are her prolific and varied output of materials about the meaning of a Wiccan life—including 11 books; a blog called *Dirt Worship*; contributions to films such as *Signs Out of Time* on the work of renowned scholar of Goddess cultures Marija Gimbutas; Wiccan songs and chants; contributions to spiritual and political conversations on Beliefnet and *Newsweek*'s blog, *On Faith*; and a call to action for the women's peace organization.

Starhawk is also a cofounder of Reclaiming, an activist branch of modern Paganism, and a coteacher for Earth Activist Trainings, which are intensive seminars on permaculture design, political organizing, and Earth-based spirituality.

Starhawk's work has been translated into 11 languages and has won several awards, such as the 1988 Media Alliance Meritorious Achievement Award for nonfiction for *Truth or Dare: Encounters with Power, Authority, and Mystery*; the 1994 Lambda award for Best Gay and Lesbian Science Fiction for her novel *The Fifth Sacred Thing*; the 2003 Nautilus Award for distinguished literary contributions to spiritual growth, conscious living, and positive social change for *Webs of Power: Notes From the Global Uprising*; and the 2010 Silver Nautilus Award for *The Last Wild Witch*, a children's book. Starhawk's archives are maintained at the library of the Graduate Theological Union in Berkeley, California.

See Also: Ecofeminism; "Femininity," Social Construction of; Feminist Theology; Religion, Women in; Wicca/Goddess Spirituality.

Further Readings

Starhawk. *The Earth Path: Grounding Your Spirit in the Rhythms of Nature*. San Francisco: HarperSanFrancisco, 2004.

Starhawk. *The Last Wild Witch*. Portland, OR: Mother Tongue Ink, 2009.

Starhawk. *The Spiral Dance: A Rebirth of the Ancient Religion of the Great Goddess*. San Francisco: HarperSanFrancisco, 1979.

Starhawk. *Truth or Dare: Encounters With Power, Authority, and Mystery*. San Francisco: Harper SanFrancisco, 1988.

Starhawk. *Webs of Power: Notes From the Global Uprising*. Victoria, BC: New Society Publishers, 2002.

Starhawk, et al. *Circle Round: Raising Children in the Goddess Tradition*. New York: Bantam, 1998.

Sue Thomas
Pacific Institute for Research and Evaluation

Staša Zajović, Stanislava

A long-standing activist, Staša Zajović was born in 1953 in Niksic, Yugoslavia. She holds a degree in Romance languages from the University of Belgrade and is fluent in Italian, Spanish, and English. Since her student days, she has been a civil rights activist and heavily involved in the first feminist initiatives in the former Yugoslavia. In 1991, inspired by the Women in Black of Israel and Palestine, Staša Zajović established and cofounded Women in Black in Belgrade. Since this time, she has continued to be a strong feminist and antimilitarist voice in Serbia. She is an initiator, organizer, or active participant in all antiwar actions, performances, peace marches, and other street actions undertaken by the Women in Black against war, nationalism, militarism, and fundamentalism. In cooperation with like-minded organizations, she has also participated in numerous antimilitarist, peace and feminist demonstrations, campaigns, networks, coalitions, conferences, meetings and seminars. As a coordinator of Women in Black in Belgrade, she has organized weekly peace vigils in Belgrade and across Serbia and Montenegro. Dressed in black and silent, Women in Black condemned the war and the crimes committed in the interest of Serbian nation.

Coordinator for Many Causes

Staša Zajović is the author of numerous articles, essays, and papers in local, regional, and international media and various other publications on women and war, politics, reproductive rights, nationalism, and antimilitarism. Throughout the years, she has organized many educational activities focused on women's human rights, women's peace politics, interethnic and intercultural solidarity, women and power, and women and antimilitarism. She is the initiator and coordinator of various educational programs, such as the Traveling Women's Peace Workshops on Power and Otherness Education for Democracy, Law in our Everyday Life (Street Law), and Transitional Justice—A Feminist Approach. She initiated several women's network groups, such as the Women's Peace Network, The Coalition for a Secular State, The International Network of Women's Solidarity against War/International Women in Black Network, and the Network of Conscientious Objectors and Anti-militarism in Serbia. Her guiding principles are the need for truth and justice for crimes committed in "our name" and solidarity with people around the world who are interested in promoting nonviolence, civil society, and peace. She supports and encourages civil disobedience as a core human right and freedom and believes that justice is "too important to be left to politicians because it depends on each of us." Staša Zajović is also dedicated to building a culture of responsibility for war, and punishment of war crimes is one of her core aims. She wants to see the government in Serbia be held responsible for its actions and accountable to its people. Together with Women in Black, Staša Zajović is constantly under threat and is often attacked by the hooligans and extreme nationalists in her country.

Staša Zajović has been nominated for and won a range of prizes and awards. Among these are the Millennium Peace Prize, Honorary Citizenship of Tutin, and nomination for the Nobel Peace Prize as part of the 1,000 Women for the Nobel Peace Prize campaign in 2005.

See Also: Peace Movement; Women in Black; Women's International League for Peace and Freedom.

Further Readings

Women Living Under Muslim Laws. "Serbia: The Harassment of Women in Black Belgrade Continues." http://www.wluml.org/node/90 (accessed June 2010).

Zajović, Staša. "Birth, Nationalism, and War." http://www.hartford-hwp.com/archives/62/039.html (accessed June 2010).

Zajović, Staša. "Bratunac: Yet Another Site of the Crimes Committed in Our Name." *Secularism s a Women's Issue.* http://www.siawi.org/article383.html (accessed June 2010).

Olivera Simic
University of Melbourne

Stay-at-Home Mothers

The concept of stay-at-home motherhood is largely a 20th- and 21st-century construct. Historians argue that the beginning of stay-at-home motherhood dates back to the 1920s and 1930s. Today, external idealized expectations, financial concerns, and women's own desires can lead to feelings of guilt over whether they choose to devote themselves to full-time motherhood or combine mothering with working outside of the home.

Such conflicts for mothers, both personally and politically, distract from the continued public/private dichotomy and the dual burden of work and care that many contemporary mothers, whether staying at home or in paid work, continue to struggle with. In such conflicting circumstances, women are striking (sometimes poor) bargains to meet dual demands of work and home.

The Stay-at-Home Ideal

By the 1940s, many mothers suffered the same pressures as mothers today in terms of both the double bind and the double shift. At this time, many women of child-bearing age were well educated and/or equipped with skills relevant to the workplace, but they were also living in a culture where it was considered best for mothers to stay at home with their children. Mothers who worked outside of the home often, as do working mothers today, cited financial necessity as the reason for undertaking paid labor, saying that they would stay a home if they could.

The child-rearing manuals of the 20th century that became popular from the 1950s onward emphasized the "good" or "ideal" mother as the one who was responsible and devoted and who put her children before anything else, including her own sexual and intellectual identity. The first responsibility of this good and ideal mother was to her child(ren), and she was expected to be grateful for her lot and to find motherhood completely fulfilling. Childcare manuals were presented as scientific tracts, written by officials in various levels of government and members of the medical, nursing, and psychological professions—people whose knowledge of children was (and is) frequently based on a professional, rather than a parental, relationship.

Although different countries have had their particularly influential experts, mothers were increasingly spoken to by experts from an orthodoxy that stressed the mother's responsibility for the psychological well-being of the child. For example, pediatricians such as Benjamin Spock and social psychologists such as Penelope Leach all have argued that consistent nurture by a single primary caregiver

is absolutely crucial. Daycare centers, preschools, spouses, and babysitters may help out, but they are incidental to the bond the child really needs with an individual adult—usually the biological mother.

The portrayal of so-called "good" and "bad" mothers in the media also helps to define appropriate behavior and appropriate feelings surrounding this experience. One example of a so-called bad mother is the mother who "selfishly" puts the interest of her own careers before the care of her children and her male partner: Stay-at-home mothers are, in addition to the care of their children, expected to provide both emotional and physical support to men to enable them to fulfill their role as breadwinners, which involves working outside of the home and supporting one's family financially. Thus, just as the concept and expectations of the stay-at-home mother are built on gender stereotypes, so are the concept and expectations of the male breadwinner role that complements it. Therefore, fathers who challenge the norm face similar negative sanctions to mothers who do likewise.

The media frequently feature famous/celebrity mothers, with a variety of supermodels, pop singers, actors, footballers, politician's wives, and other celebrities attracting attention. Many of the articles focus on the time mothers give to their children, and these women are often held up as good and "not-so-good" examples of motherhood to others. One of the most famous women of the late 20th century—Princess Diana—was celebrated worldwide for being a devoted mother, and although she was not a stay-at-home mother as such, she did have more to do with her two sons' upbringing than many, if not all, previous British royal mothers. She chose their schools and clothes and planned their outings while negotiating her public duties around their timetables. To many, the Princess of Wales was a role model who was admired for her beauty and her high-profile charity work, not least her involvement in acquired immune deficiency syndrome (AIDS) issues and the international campaign against landmines. However, her mothering role was perhaps most admired, and she has been described as "a mother before all else."

Challenging Expectations

Since the 1970s and the rise of Second Wave Feminism, women have questioned their roles as wives and mothers. In the 1970s and 1980s, feminists argued that the home was a site of oppression for women. As women often earn less than men, when a couple do decide that one of them should stay home to care for their children or to care for dependent elderly relatives, it is usually the women who leave paid work outside of the home. This can trap women into financial dependency and into feeling they have less right to spend the family income. In support of this, there is evidence that women put their own needs last behind other members of the family, and when money is short, it is women who go without food, clothes, and other necessities.

Thus, mothering at home has formed part of, rather than been a challenge to or subversion of, traditional Western family ideology. The dominance of this ideology has been eroded in many Western countries in recent years, but a residual and powerful idea remains that mothers will still stay at home to care for their children, especially in the preschool years, to provide "intensive mothering" for their children. Today, the home is perhaps more usefully viewed as a site of conflict rather than of oppression—conflict between parents over the sexual division of labor, between paid and unpaid work, between mothers at home and mothers at work, and between a bipolar political agenda and policies. Above all, however, there is conflict within for many women: between notions of selfhood and motherhood and of good and bad mothering, complete with accompanying anxiety and guilt.

Such conflict is often played out in the public domain in various guises internationally. For example, in the United Kingdom, there are public debates about the worthiness of different groups of mothers staying at home, such as "government-funded" teenage mothers versus wealthy, upper-middle-class, older "yummy mummies." There are the "mommy wars" that rage in the United States between working moms and stay-at-home moms (and as such, maternal vs paid child care), and there is the persistence of mothering at home in Australia, where approximately 50 percent of mothers stay at home with preschool children. In Sweden, there is the take-up of maternal (and paternal) leave (i.e., the state enables mothers to stay at home). In Asia, there are the "new Victorians"—comprising an increasing idealization of mothers at home in countries such as Singapore and Hong Kong along class lines: the leisured mother at home assisted by a (foreign worker) maid. Overall, worldwide, although 40 years ago stay-at-home mothers were the norm, today they are the exception, and there are now fewer stay-at-home mothers than ever. Arguably, at least women now have a choice, but rising house prices and financial instability worldwide erode the choice for many, and rising childcare costs make it too expensive for some to undertake paid labor.

See Also: Childcare; Domestic Workers; Equal Pay; Focus on the Family; Homeschooling; Stereotypes of Women; Working Mothers.

Further Readings

Arnup, K. K. *Education for Motherhood: Advice for Mothers in Twentieth-Century Canada.* Toronto: Toronto University Press, 1994.

Bock, G. and P. Thane. *Maternity and Gender Politics: Women and the Rise of the European Welfare States, 1880s-1950s.* London: Routledge, 1994.

Dr. Spock. http://www.drspock.com/home/0,1454,,00 .html (accessed December 2008).

Focus on Families. http://www.statistics.gov.uk/focuson /families (accessed June 2010).

Freeman, T. "Loving Fathers or Deadbeat Dads? The Crisis of Fatherhood in Popular Culture." S. Earle and G. Letherby, eds., *Gender, Identity and Reproduction: Social Perspectives.* Basingstoke, UK: Palgrave, 2003.

Groskrop, V. "Is This the End of the Stay-at-Home Mother?" *The Guardian* (May, 26, 2008).

Hays, S. *The Cultural Contradictions of Motherhood.* New Haven, CT: Yale University Press, 1996.

Marshall, H. "Childcare and Parenting Manuals." In A. Phoenix, et al., eds. *Motherhood: Meanings, Practices and Ideologies.* London: Sage, 1991.

Reid Boyd, E. "'Being There': Mothers Who Stay at Home, Gender and Time." *Women's Studies International Forum,* v.25/4 (2002).

Woodard, K. "Representations of Motherhood." In S. Earle and G. Letherby, eds. *Gender, Identity and Reproduction: Social Perspectives.* Basingstoke, UK: Palgrave, 2003.

Elizabeth Reid Boyd
Edith Cowan University
Gayle Letherby
University of Plymouth

Steinem, Gloria

For many Americans in the 1970s and 1980s, Gloria Steinem was the public face of feminism. A journalist and political activist, she is best known as the founding editor of *Ms.* magazine—a position she held from 1972 until 1987. For over 40 years, she has lent her energies to innumerable initiatives on behalf of women's rights and social justice.

Born March 25, 1934, into a middle-class but downwardly mobile family in Toledo, Ohio, Steinem grew up under difficult circumstances. After her parents divorced when she was 11 years old, she found herself charged with caring for her mother, who suffered from bouts of mental illness. The experience of living alone with her mother in impoverished conditions—at times, their home was infested with rats—profoundly affected Steinem. As she later explained, "At home it felt dangerous. I felt safer outside."

Steinem attended Smith College, where she majored in political science and graduated magna cum laude. During her senior year, she became engaged, and her life seemed poised to follow the typical course of a 1950s coed. Instead, however, Steinem abruptly broke off the relationship and made plans to travel to India on a fellowship. Waiting for her visa to clear in London, she discovered she was pregnant; with the reluctant help of a doctor, she managed to obtain an abortion. Steinem then went on to India, where she studied and traveled for over a year, gaining exposure to the ideas of Mahatma Gandhi. She has described her time in India as a turning point in her life—a time when she acquired a heightened awareness of discrimination and inequality.

After returning to the United States in 1958, Steinem began working for the Independent Research Service, a nonprofit educational foundation that encouraged young Americans to participate in International Communist Youth Festivals to help counter Soviet-backed propaganda. Funded by the Central Intelligence Agency, the program was part of the government's attempt to fight communism through cultural means. At the time, Steinem did not perceive the link to the agency as problematic, but the connection would return to haunt her.

In 1960, Steinem moved to New York and began forging her way as a freelance writer. She acquired a reputation as a glamorous girl-about-town, but she

American feminist and journalist Gloria Steinem at a 1972 news conference for the Women's Action Alliance.

initially struggled to land serious assignments. In 1968, her writing took a more political turn when she cofounded and became a columnist for *New York* magazine. By then, Steinem had become involved with a number of left-wing protest movements and political campaigns. Among many other activities, she marched with Women Strike for Peace, lent her support to Cesar Chavez's campaign on behalf of migrant farm workers, and championed George McGovern's presidential campaigns.

Steinem was actually somewhat slow to warm to the cause of feminism. As a self-supporting woman concerned with issues of poverty and racism, she found little to embrace in Betty Friedan's 1963 manifesto, *The Feminine Mystique*, which focused on the plight of suburban housewives. In 1969, however, Steinem experienced an emotional epiphany when she attended a speakout on abortion sponsored by a radical feminist group, the Redstockings. Soon thereafter, she wrote her first explicitly feminist column, "After Black Power, Women's Liberation."

Throughout the 1970s, Steinem engaged in a whirlwind of feminist activity. She frequently delivered talks on women's issues, always insisting that she be paired with an African American woman speaker. (Dorothy Pitman Hughes, Florynce Kennedy, and Margaret Sloan all shared the stage with her.) In 1971, she helped to convene the National Women's Political Caucus, an organization committed to increasing the number of women who hold political office. The following year, Steinem cofounded *Ms.* magazine, a publication that played a critical role in helping feminism reach a more mainstream audience. She also established the Ms. Foundation for Women, which has supported such initiatives as the Take Our Daughters to Work Program.

Surrounded by Controversy

Despite her tireless efforts and personal generosity, Steinem proved a controversial figure within feminist ranks. The more experienced Friedan resented how the media—dazzled by Steinem's photogenic image—anointed her the leader of the feminist movement (*Newsweek*, for instance, featured Steinem on its cover as early as 1971, before she had much of a track record as a feminist), and many younger, more radical feminists suspected her of diluting the movement's radical essence. In 1975, members of the Redstockings revived the issue of Steinem's connection to the Central Intelligence Agency and essentially accused her of being a government agent. In truth, what Steinem really infiltrated was mainstream culture. "Because of her beauty," the communications scholar Susan Douglas has argued, she could "smuggle radical critiques of the status of women into mainstream discourse and gradually get them accepted." In 1983, a collection of Steinem's articles, *Outrageous Acts and Everyday Rebellions*, became a best seller.

As feminism faltered in the 1980s, Steinem experienced personal and health difficulties that led her to become more introspective. In 1992, she published *Revolution From Within: A Book of Self-Esteem*, which many reviewers criticized as a retreat from social activism and a regrettable foray into pop psychology. In the 1990s, she also drew criticism for her credulous support of recovered memory therapy—a movement that many psychologists and psychiatrists have questioned.

In 2000, Steinem drew headlines when, at age 66 years, she married David Bale, a South African entrepreneur and political activist. (Bale died only three years later.) Though Steinem had in the past denounced the institution of marriage, she convincingly defended herself from charges of capitulation: "If I had married when I was supposed to get married, I would have lost my name, my legal residence, my credit rating, many of my civil rights. That's not true anymore. It's possible to make an equal marriage." Steinem herself deserves a sizable share of the credit for those changes. As of 2010 and in her 70s, she remains a powerful advocate for women and the dispossessed.

See Also: Feminism, American; Feminist Publishing; Journalists, Print Media; *Ms.* Magazine.

Further Readings

Heilbrun, Carolyn G. *The Education of a Woman: The Life of Gloria Steinem.* New York: Ballantine Books, 1996.

Ladensohn Stern, S. *Gloria Steinem: Her Passions, Politics, and Mystique.* Secaucus, NJ: Carol Publishing, 1997.

Steinem, Gloria. *Moving Beyond Words: Age, Rage, Sex, Power, Money, Muscles: Breaking the Boundries of Gender.* New York: Touchstone, 1995.

Steinem, Gloria. *Outrageous Acts and Everyday Rebellions*, 2nd Ed. New York: Holt, 1995.

Steinem, Gloria. *Revolution From Within: A Book of Self-Esteem.* Boston: Little, Brown and Company, 1993.

Rebecca Jo Plant
University of California, San Diego

STEM Coalition

Formed in 1999, the Science, Technology, Engineering, and Mathematics (STEM) Education Coalition advocates for financial and political support of STEM programs at all educational levels. STEM education is seen as a vital component for sustaining scientific and technical innovation, economic and community development, and global competitiveness. Increasing diversity in STEM fields for women and minorities is essential to these goals.

Coalition Activities

The STEM Education Coalition supports policies that increase federal funding for STEM programs. The coalition has more than 1,200 members and includes individuals, universities, professional societies, community organizations, and the private sector. The STEM Coalition is cochaired by the American Chemical Society and the National Science Teachers Association. The STEM Education Coalition recognizes that STEM education programs in the United States are not keeping pace internationally. The coalition identifies several areas for improving STEM education in the United States, including increased funding for teacher professional development, improving the technological infrastructure in schools, supporting after-school programs, funding research and development, and building partnerships between the public and private sector.

In the past few years, the STEM Educational Coalition has been influential in ensuring that every major education law included provisions for supporting STEM education. For example, in 2008, the Higher Education Opportunity Act (Public Law 110-315) included funding for STEM teacher professional development, scholarships for students to obtain STEM degrees, and outreach efforts that engage minority youth in hands-on STEM learning. The No Child Left Behind Act (Public Law 107-110), passed in 2002 and reauthorized in 2007, provides increased funding for educational technology.

Gender and STEM Education

In recent years, much of the economic growth in the United States has come from the science and engineering sector, yet women and minorities continue to be underrepresented in these fields. STEM educators have identified a "leaky" pipeline that contributes to the underrepresentation of women in STEM fields. In middle school, studies suggest that there is an achievement gap between girls and boys on math and science test scores. At the high school level, girls are less likely to enroll in advanced math and science courses, which are the prerequisites for pursuing STEM degrees in college. At the college level, female students make up only 20 percent of engineering undergraduate degrees and 17 percent of computer science degrees. According to the U.S. National Science Foundation, women comprise only 24 percent of jobs in the technical workforce. The coalition supports gender equity by lobbying for increased funding for STEM educational initiatives, such as after-school programs that increase girls' interest in STEM careers. Additionally, several member organizations conduct specific activities related to gender equality.

See Also: Education, Women in; Engineering, Women in; Mathematics, Women in; No Child Left Behind; Physics, Women in; Science, Women in; Science Education for Girls.

Further Readings

Burke, Ronald J. and Mary C. Mattis, eds. *Women and Minorities in Science, Technology, Engineering, and Mathematics: Upping the Numbers.* Northhampton, MA: Edward Elgar, 2007.

Williams, Mary F. and Carolyn J. Emerson. *Becoming Leaders: A Practical Handbook for Women in Engineering, Science, and Technology.* Reston, VA: American Society of Civil Engineers, 2008.

Wilson, Steven H., ed. *Science, Engineering and Technology in the United States.* New York: Nova Science Publishers, 2009.

Carolyn Cunningham
Independent Scholar

Stereotypes of Women

Stereotypes may be described as the result of cognitive procedures leading to the process of categorization, one of the most important tools our mind has to organize knowledge and deal with the complexity of reality. At the same time, however, stereotypes are the expression of values and are used to express a general idea of a certain social group, as if this agreement were preexistent, regardless of the stereotype. Stereotypes freeze the characteristics of a social group and block its potential for development during an interaction or narration. Stereotypes therefore offer a false simplicity of reality, since they condense a large amount of information and connotations. To be truly valid, they need to collect a wide consensus, and hence, once they are stated, they become the expression of the values of a society. It is through stereotypes that we obtain our understanding of a particular social group. For these reasons, the analysis of gender stereotypes provides invaluable data to understand what we expect from women and men and what we mean by "female" and "male" behaviors.

Gender Stereotypes

Gender stereotypes (stereotypes of women and of men) are shared hypersimplified images or representations of reality that influence collective thinking by filling with specific contents the convictions and ideas of a determinate social group regarding men and women and the relationships between them. Among these, we find "Men are better at repairing/maintaining things in the home; women are better at housework"; "Little boys are stronger and livelier than little girls"; "Boys do not cry."

Men and women are also perceived as complementary; that is, biologically destined to an eternal relation of attraction ("What is a woman without a man?; And a man without a woman?"; "Women and men reciprocally complete each other"; "Men are naturally attracted by women; women are naturally attracted by men"). Furthermore, bodily features are synonymous with differences in skills and aptitudes. Hence the idea of the "naturalness" of a system of gender relations marked by an unequal distribution of material and symbolic resources. And so we have women who are "good at" caring work, and "rational," "dynamic," and "stronger" men who successfully devote themselves to economic activities and supporting their families.

The social construction of fatherhood and motherhood is also outlined, sustained, and strengthened by many commonplaces: "Children must stay with their mother"; "Women are made to be wives and mothers"; "Women are fulfilled when they become mothers, men in supporting their family"; "Fathers are not very suited to caring activities."

It can be easily understood that these stereotypes have driven female and male apart and often set them against each other. This rigid conception of the man-woman relation has also created an often very burdensome constraint—for both sexes. A key example is that the rejection of femininity continues to constitute one of the main organizers of hegemonic masculinity. Whatever race, social class, age, ethnic group, or sexual orientation one belongs to, being a man means above all "not being a woman." Antifemininity (together with

the principle of the "natural" subordination of female to male) is at the heart of the contemporary and historical idea of masculinity, so much so that virility is described more in negative terms (what a man is not) than in positive ones (what he is). We also mention a continuing ambivalence toward women in positions of power and authority: women have been limited by gender-coded lines drawn between their roles in the public and private sphere, in the home and the polis.

This dichotomy—historically constructed around male and female biological features—also ensured the conditions for the development and survival of industrial society, characterized by standardized life courses and families with a single, stable wage earner, where the salary of the male breadwinner was assimilated to a family wage. Talcott Parsons clearly theorized the separation of roles between women and men and the differentiation of the sexual roles in the family. Mother and father are representatives and bearers, for their children, of two distinct, complementary codes. The husband-father is the instrumental leader, assigned with the management of social relations and the financial support of the family and its members; he is the figure who indicates limits and duties, who exercises authority, who favors the interiorization of the rules of social living. The wife-mother instead has the role of expressive leadership centered on internal relations within the family and its affective function. She is the parent with the task of ensuring the immediate satisfaction of children's needs, tending to yield to their demands. For structural-functionalists, the biological-sexual difference essentially corresponds to a difference in aptitude that reserves different specific scopes to men and women, functional to the maintenance of order and equilibrium in society. And the family is interpreted as a functional necessity, because without it, the human species would die out.

Stereotypes and Socialization

The stereotypes of men and women, closely interrelated to the social construction of gender identity, are conveyed with the concurrence of all the agencies of socialization: family, schools, peer groups, organizations, the media, and the workplace.

The process of acquiring gender identity (the recognition of the social implications accompanying the belonging to one of the two biological sexes) already begins before birth. The little boy/girl already exists in the parents' imaginary, when they wonder which sex it will be, whether it will look like its mother or father, what it will be when "it grows up." Knowing that the child in the womb is a girl or a boy offers parents, relatives, brothers and sisters, and friends the chance to choose the most suitable colors for its layette, furniture, and furnishings and to buy "suitable" toys. The established rules are rarely broken, and the implicit social rules are generally respected. All of us must have had to buy a present for an expected baby: who opted for a pink dress or a doll for a boy? How many of us have sought to question the culturally shared gender identity (what we think is "right," "suitable," "appropriate" for a boy or a girl) through "unsuitable" actions, attitudes, and gifts?

After the birth, parents and relatives are concerned to dress the baby in such a way as to make its gender belonging clear, since they do not want to be constantly asked whether the baby is a boy or a girl. This question arises spontaneously in case of ambiguity, in order to better guide our verbal and nonverbal communication. As soon as the child's gender is clear, it will be treated differently according to whether it is a boy or a girl: the child will respond to these stimuli with different feelings and by behaving differently.

The school system is also not exempt from stereotypes linked to femininity and masculinity. While schooling seems to be based on a pedagogy that is defined as "neutral," in reality, it distinguishes between "feminine" and "masculine" aptitudes and skills. In line with the models characterizing the other agencies of socialization, the institutional training system today still demands of young women demonstrations of "femininity" and compliancy and offers young men a strong training, oriented to autonomy and the development of technical, logical, and rational skills. The prevalent forms of learning in school educational and professional training systems are still essentially constructed to highlight traditional values and behaviors linked to feminine and masculine roles.

This tendency becomes particularly evident when dealing with scientific knowledge and access to the new technologies, which constitute an essential requisite for finding a good job. Regarding the choice of a school, pupils at agrarian, industrial, nautical, and aeronautical technical and professional institutes are mainly male, while those specializing in business, tourism, and social services mainly tend to be girls,

as do those at classical and language lyceums and in teacher training. This might surprise us if we think of the introduction of the same, shared courses for boys and girls (that ought to provide them with the same experiences and the same objectives).

Stereotypes and Choices

Gender stereotypes also play a highly important role in the field of professional choices and collocations. Various studies on young people and families regarding choices made at the end of secondary school clearly show the differing parental influence regarding the planning for the future of sons and daughters and, in particular, the working and professional strategies. Girls are given more space in the dimension of "expressive" motivations; the instrumental aspect prevails, however, for boys. The analysis of some interviews highlights that the factors considered important for women's work are "fulfillment" and "individual interests," while "earning" and "financial stability" are mentioned above all by the parents of boys.

In reality, while the emphasis placed on individual self-fulfillment for girls may be seen as a sign of open-mindedness, we may also consider that it tends to repropose a model of female identity that is at least partly traditional. We may hypothesize that girls are "free" from having to produce much income not so much because it is not useful, or not important, but in that it is taken for granted that theirs will be the "second" income in the family, complementing the "real" earnings produced by male work.

We may ask the following question: how many and what changes have taken place in time within the culturally constructed meanings of sexual differences? Various research studies carried out in very different local contexts show a significant continuity in time of the use of stereotypes linked to sexual belonging. Men continue to be perceived as strong, rational, logical, and independent; women are specularly described as dependent, calm, ready to listen and show affection, and good at caring work.

The separation between masculinity-production and femininity-reproduction also seems to be very clear: women can carry out caring work better than men. The conviction also arises that the nature of human gender is characterized by essential differences: what is man is not woman, and vice versa. Lastly, while it is true that men and women are distinguished by what concerns personal characteristics, interpersonal relations, and intellectual inclinations, on the other hand, some changes are emerging. We are speaking of the growing complexity of the significants linked to "being a woman," a trend that seems to reflect the intense process of diversification in female identities (as in the growing inclusion of women in the job market and their considerable investment in education) and that is not perceivable in the case of men, an identity perceived as more stable in time.

Younger Generational Thinking

Some studies show that among the younger generations, something is changing between the two genders, although at different speeds. While some very traditional stereotypes ("it is right that the man should be the boss in the home") are not frequently shared, others continue to have a strong appeal (for example, seeing the man as the wage earner or the connection between motherhood and women's self-fulfillment), although with interesting differences between boys and girls. Young men are more attached to traditional values (such as the family) and, at the same time, continue to be imprisoned in the model of "work at all costs" (the man "must" work), showing a more limited planning capacity than their female peers.

Women instead show a greater distancing from stereotyped perceptions and also growing expectations linked to an image of autonomy and everyday and professional independence. These tendencies are definitely linked to the strong increase in women's education, but at the same time, the greater freedom and creativity regarding expectations of a professional future are available for girls also because a social image of women's work still seems to be widespread, considering it as secondary compared to that of men. Although a considerable number of young women today seem to identify with gender-relational models based on emancipation and sharing of responsibilities, motherhood—and the social recognition linked to the production of this event in a life course—continues to occupy an important place in the trajectories of their identity construction.

See Also: Antifeminism; "Femininity," Social Construction of; Gender, Defined; Gender Roles, Cross-Cultural; "Masculinity," Social Construction of; Toys, Gender-Stereotypic.

Further Readings
Broverman, I. K., et al. "Sex Roles Stereotypes: A Current Appraisal." *Journal of Social Issues*, v.28/2 (1972).
Dyer, R. *The Matter of Images. Essays on Representation.* London: Routledge, 1993.
Garlick, B., et al, eds. *Stereotypes of Women in Power: Historical Perspectives and Revisionist Views.* New York: Greenwood Press, 1992.
Ruspini, E., ed. *Changing Femininities, Changing Masculinities. Social Change, Gender Identities and Sexual Orientations.* Sociological Research Online, v.12/1 (2007). http://www.socresonline.org.uk/12/1/contents-html (accessed June 2010).
Williams, J. E. and D. L. Best. *Measuring Sex Stereotypes: A Multinational Study.* Newbury Park, CA: Sage, 1990.

Elisabetta Ruspini
University of Milano, Bicocca

Sterilization, Involuntary

Sterilization refers to the permanent interference of the ability of an individual to reproduce, most often through surgical methods. Sterilization is considered involuntary when an individual is either unable to provide consent, has been denied the opportunity to provide consent, or has been deceived or coerced into providing consent. Many countries throughout the world have a history of forced or involuntary sterilization programs. Currently, mentally retarded individuals continue to be legally sterilized without consent.

Modern methods for female sterilization include tubal ligation, hysteroscopic sterilization and hysterectomy. Both tubal ligation and hysteroscopic sterilization methods entail closing off the fallopian tubes to prevent eggs from traveling to the uterus. Though considered permanent sterilization, in some cases, the procedures can be reversed. Hysterectomy refers to the surgical removal of the uterus. It is irreversible and, generally, not used for contraceptive purposes.

For much of the 20th century, interest in involuntary sterilization was for eugenic purposes. Eugenicists believed that physical disabilities, mental defects and social ills such as poverty, promiscuity, criminality, and drug or alcohol abuse were hereditary. Those with these genetic predispositions were believed unfit to reproduce, and sterilization was touted as a means to humanely eliminate social problems from society. Involuntary sterilization was argued to benefit society as a whole by reducing the economic and social drain caused by undesirable populations.

By the 1930s, eugenics programs were adopted by as many as 30 U.S. states and by countries around the world, including Canada, Sweden, the United Kingdom, Germany, and China. Evidence reveals that, most often, victims of these sterilization programs were poor and women from minority groups. After World War II brought attention to the eugenics practices of Nazi Germany, public support for forced sterilization programs waned. With the exception of China, most countries abandoned wide-scale sterilization programs by the 1970s.

Despite abandonment of formal programs, practices of involuntary sterilization continue. Recent reports highlight the forced sterilization of poor and indigenous women in Peru and Brazil in the late 1990s as well as Roma women in the Czech Republic and human immunodeficiency virus (HIV)-positive women in Namibia.

Much of the concern surrounding involuntary sterilization today focuses on issues of "informed consent." Generally, there are three requirements for informed consent: the decision for sterilization must be voluntary, the decision for the procedure must be made by a woman who is intellectually competent, and it must be made with complete knowledge and understanding of the facts, including alternative options.

Determining if consent is voluntary or coerced is complicated. In some cases, coercion may be blatant (e.g., a physician refusing to deliver a baby or perform an abortion unless the woman consents to sterilization). In other cases, coercion may be more subtle. There is evidence to suggest that healthcare providers

China's one-child policy forbids couples from having more than one child. In 2002, China outlawed the use of physical force to make a woman submit to an abortion or sterilization, but it is not strictly enforced.

vary the kinds and amount of information they provide, as well as the quality of services offered, based on the social characteristics (e.g., race, class, age, type of insurance, etc.) of their patients. Qualitatively different interactions between healthcare providers and patients may explain why, in the United States, for example, African American women and women with public or no health insurance are more likely to undergo sterilization than white women or women with private insurance.

Taking Advantage of the Vulnerable

An additional form of coercion, inducement, also may exist. Inducement exists when a vulnerable person is offered an incentive to effect a decision that would not be offered if she were in a more defensible postion. For example, in California, Florida, Illinois, and Minnesota, community groups such as Project Prevention post billboards in poor, minority areas offering cash to women who obtain long-term birth control or sterilization. Economically vulnerable women may be susceptible to such inducements. Additionally, residing in a jurisdiction eager to prosecute women whose children are born drug-exposed also may make sterilization increasingly attractive for those suffering from addictions.

For the mentally retarded, involuntary sterilization continues to be legal. In the United States, most states have safeguards, such as a judicial review, in place to ensure that sterilization of the mentally retarded is not abused. Before an individual can be sterilized, it must be demonstrated that sterilization is necessary, that it would serve the best interests of the mentally retarded person, and that less intrusive forms of contraception are unacceptable.

Similar to programs in the past, involuntary sterilization of the mentally retarded is not without controversy. Debates center on how best to determine the capacity or competence of the mentally retarded and on how much the guardian or caretakers' needs should be taken into consideration. With regard to capacity, mental retardation itself does not constitute incompetence, and the functional capacities of an individual may vary from one task to the next. Answering questions of how to measure capacity and who is in the best position to measure such capacity (e.g., parents/guardians, physicians, and judges) often proves challenging. In addition, tensions may arise when what is considered the best interest of the mentally retarded person differs from the interests of the caretaker or guardian. In jurisdictions without safeguards in place to reduce the abuse of sterilization, differing interest of parents or guardians and the mentally retarded individual are of paramount concern.

See Also: HIV/AIDS: Africa; Poverty; Reproductive and Sexual Health Rights; Sterilization, Voluntary.

Further Readings

Brantlinger, Ellen. *Sterilization of People With Mental Disabilities: Issues, Perspectives, and Cases.* Westport, CT: Auburn House Publishing, 1995.

Diekema, Douglas. "Involuntary Sterilization of Persons With Mental Retardation: An Ethnical Analysis." *Mental Retardation and Developmental Disabilities Research Reviews*, v.9 (2003).

Reilly, Phillip. *The Surgical Solution: A History of Involuntary Sterilization in the United States.* Baltimore, MD: Johns Hopkins University Press, 1991.

Elyshia Aseltine
University of Texas at Austin

Sterilization, Voluntary

Voluntary sterilization is one of the most cost-effective methods of family planning. These methods include occlusion of the Fallopian tubes in women or the vas deference in men. Rates of sterilizations are influenced by several external factors, such as geographical area and accessibility of the procedure.

It is important that anybody who accepts this permanent method of birth control makes a voluntary and informed decision. Comprehensive counseling includes that clients should understand that these methods are permanent. Consent should be signed by the client only. Other family-planning methods, including long-acting reversible contraception, should be discussed. Long-acting reversible contraception is a method that requires administration less than once per cycle. These methods include intrauterine copper devices, levonorgestrel-intrauterine systems, progestogen-only injectable contraceptives, progestogen-only subdermal implants, and combined hormonal vaginal ring. Long-acting reversible contraception methods combine reversibility with high effectiveness, as they do not rely exclusively on compliance or correct use. These methods should be considered an option if the client had previous menstrual abnormalities that were well managed on contraceptives. It is important to discuss male sterilizations, which are more effective than female sterilizations, and with fewer complications. Sterilization does not prevent sexually transmitted infections, including human immunodeficiency virus (HIV). The client needs to make a voluntary choice and has the right to change his or her mind any time before the procedure.

A medical history and clinical examination should be performed to decide which procedure would best fit the specific client. World Health Organization medical eligibility criteria should be used to determine eligibility in medical conditions. The client should be advised to continue her current method of contraception until her first menstruation after the procedure, and in the case of transcervical procedures, to continue for three months, until tubal occlusion is confirmed.

Procedures

Interval tubal sterilizations can be done any time during the menstrual cycle or postpartum within the first 48 hours or after six weeks. The choice of a laparotomy or laparoscopy depends on the facility where the procedure will be done, as well as the equipment available and experience of the surgeon.

Laparoscopy

The laparoscopic method is the preferred method for interval sterilizations. It requires special equipment and skills and can be done in a day theater using local or general anesthesia. Minor complications are less common than with laparotomy. Carbon dioxide is most commonly used to insufflate the peritoneal cavity through a Veress needle, but nitrous oxide may be better when using local anesthesia. Different methods to occlude the tubes include coagulation, silastic rings, or mechanical clips.

Unipolar coagulation can be associated with serious complications including bowel injury. Bipolar coagulation is associated with less complication but is less effective and has a higher incidence of ectopic pregnancies. Silastic ring applications results in more

technical difficulties and a bigger area of the Fallopian tube undergoing sclerosis. Minimal tubal damage is caused by mechanical clips.

Laparotomy

Sterilizations can be done during a caesarean section, postpartum, or as an interval method. A minilaparotomy, which is less invasive, is usually done. The incision in the skin is about 4 cm in size, and a uterine elevator is used in the interval period for easier access to the tubes. Several methods to occlude the tubes are described. In the Viennese method, the tube is tied at two places about 1 cm apart with an absorbable suture. Plain or chromic catgut should not be used because of the risk of adhesion formation. The tube is divided between the two ligations. The Pomeroy technique, Parkland's Hospital method, and Irving method are variations on this operation. A small segment of tube is removed when using the Parkland's Hospital method. In the Irving method, the proximal end of the divided tube is buried in the posterior aspect of the uterus, and the distal end of the divided tube is buried in the broad ligament. Care is taken to prevent any hemorrhage. The Viennese method has a very low failure rate and destroys only a small section of both tubes—this improves the chances of later tubal reanastomosis, if ever necessary.

Transcervical Procedures

These procedures are done in an office setting without any anesthesia. It requires special equipment and skills. The advantage is these procedures can be performed on women with high risk to anesthesia and expected difficult procedures. Several methods such as electrocoagulation and cryoagulation were abandoned earlier because of their high failure rates and serious complications. Chemical agents have been tested but are not widely used because of concerns of efficacy and possible carcinogenic effects. Several methods using mechanical occlusive material with hysteroscopy, which is very promising, have been developed lately.

Male Sterilization

Vasectomy is a simple operation that can be performed under local analgesia as an outpatient procedure. Morbidity of the operation is low. Vasectomy is not immediately effective because spermatozoa may remain in the epididymis for some time. The patient must rely on other methods of contraception until azoospermia has been confirmed on two occasions. Vasectomy has no effect on sexual performance or testicular function.

See Also: Caesarean Section, Rates of; Childlessness as Choice; Pregnancy; Sterilization, Involuntary.

Further Readings

Dowbiggin, Ian R. *The Sterilization Movement and Global Fertility in the Twentieth Century*. New York: Oxford University Press, 2008.

Kluchin, Rebecca M. *Fit to Be Tied: Sterilization and Reproductive Rights in America, 1950–1980 (Critical Issues in Health and Medicine)*. New Brunswick, NJ: Rutgers University Press, 2009.

Schoen, Johanna. *Choice and Coercion: Birth Control, Sterilization, and Abortion in Public Health and Welfare (Gender and American Culture)*. Chapel Hill: North Carolina University Press, 2005.

Petrus Steyn
Stellenbosch University

Steroid Use

Anabolic steroids are derivatives of the hormone testosterone. Scientists at the University of Chicago isolated testosterone in 1927 from bull testicles, and by 1935, Yugoslavian researchers had discovered how to produce synthetic testosterone. Many physicians in the 1930s promoted the use of synthetic testosterone to restore youth in older men and reinvigorate the body. Today, physicians prescribe steroids to stimulate muscle growth, bone development, and appetite, particularly among patients suffering from cancer and acquired immune deficiency syndrome (AIDS).

Doctors also prescribe steroids to stimulate male sex characteristics and puberty in boys. Steroid use is also common among healthy men and women for cosmetic purposes to build muscles or decrease body fat. However, in addition to producing anabolic effects, prolonged high doses of testosterone produce unwanted androgenic effects including acne, increased body hair growth, and long-term effects such as liver damage, high cholesterol, high blood pressure, and changes to the left ventricle of the heart. In women, steroid use causes irregular menstrual cycles, deepened voices, and enlargement of the clitoris.

Most people associate steroid use with bodybuilders attempting to sculpt a muscular physique and athletes who use performance-enhancing drugs to achieve superior athletic performances. The earliest recorded steroid use by athletes at the Olympic Games was at the 1952 Olympics in Helsinki, where athletes from the Soviet Union, competing for the first time since Russia participated in the 1912 games, dominated the weightlifting events. Two years later, a Russian physician allegedly revealed the team had used steroids in Helsinki. Steroid use was prevalent in the heavy sports by 1968. When the International Olympic Committee (IOC) appointed a medical commission in 1967, one of the committee's first tasks was to address the use of steroids in sport. A ban on steroid use ensued, but scientists did not discover a reliable test for steroid detection until 1973.

Women Athletes and Steroid Use

Two of the biggest doping scandals in sport involve women athletes. A program of systemic, state-sponsored doping in East Germany, in effect between 1972 and 1989, facilitated athletic success in many women's sports. Officials and coaches of the German Democratic Republic's sports schools administered steroids in tablet form to athletes as young as 10 years old, telling children the pills were vitamins, and conducted experiments to determine optimal doses for facilitating athletic performance. Many young women consumed high doses of the steroid oral-Turinabol unbeknown to their parents.

Evidence released after the collapse of the communist German state revealed that East German athletes, in addition to athletes from the Soviet Union and Eastern bloc countries, consumed large doses of steroids, despite none of the athletes producing positive drug tests in competition. East Germany developed tests to detect steroids and routinely tested its athletes before competitions; athletes testing positive withdrew from events rather than risk detection.

Widespread steroid use reappeared in the 1990s when, fueled by a topical testosterone known as dehydrotestosterone (DHT), Chinese athletes skyrocketed to success in the women's swimming and athletics events. Despite the women's extremely muscular builds, Chinese coaches claimed their athletes' success was due to rigorous training and the use of traditional Chinese herbs. However, numerous positive tests for DHT uncovered an extensive doping network motivated by coaches' and clubs' desire to win prize money and endorsement contracts.

Another prominent steroid scandal in women's sports involved American sprinter Marion Jones. Following her success winning five medals at the Olympic Games in 2000, Jones secured multiple sponsorship and endorsement deals. Although she denied using steroids throughout her career, evidence obtained in the BALCO investigations linked Jones to steroids. She eventually acknowledged her steroid use; served a prison sentence for perjury; and, at the IOC's insistence, returned her Olympic medals. Even though many people still associate steroids with masculinity and male athletes, steroid use remains a problem in women's sports.

See Also: Body Image; Olympics, Summer; Sports, Women in; Swimming.

Further Readings

Beamish, Rob and Ian Ritchie. *Fastest, Highest, Strongest: A Critique of High-Performance Sport*. New York: Routledge, 2006.

Roberts, Paul K. *Steroid Use and Abuse (Drug Transit and Distribution, Interception and Control Series)*. Hauppauge, NY: Nova Biomedical Books, 2009.

Roleff, Tamara L. *Steroid Abuse (Hot Topics)*. Farmington Hills, MI: Lucent Books, 2010.

Sarah Teetzel
University of Manitoba

Stewart, Martha

Caterer, author, lifestyle expert, Martha Stewart has been all of the above and more. She is one of the most successful and controversial female entrepreneurs of the 21st century. Born in 1941, Martha Kostyra spent most of her childhood in Nutley, New Jersey. An excellent student, she was one of the first women in her high school to take advanced mathematics. Stewart was involved in several extracurricular activities and was credited with planning one of the best proms in Nutley High School history.

Schooling and Early History

Throughout high school, Stewart worked part-time jobs to save for college. This eventually led her to a career in modeling in New York City. Her all-American looks even earned her a spot in an early Lifebuoy soap commercial. Her hard work paid off, and with a partial scholarship, Stewart began attending Barnard College in 1959.

At the age of 19, Stewart met law student Andy Stewart. The two were married, and she left school to work full time as a model to support Andy's last years at Yale. In 1961, she was chosen as one of *Glamour* magazine's 10 best-dressed girls.

In 1963, she and Andy traveled to Europe, a trip that she credits with expanding her world view of art, architecture, and history. It inspired her to return to Barnard to study those subjects. Her exposure to European cuisine and love of cooking motivated her to test every one of Julia Child's recipes.

After graduating from Barnard, Stewart set her sights in a new direction. She chose Wall Street, passed her brokerage exam, and became a stockbroker. Between 1968 and 1971, a time when women were still working to expand career opportunities, Stewart was commanding a six-figure salary. Although Stewart enjoyed this work, she had not forgotten her love of food, art, and the finer things. She and Andy purchased a run-down farmhouse in Westport, Connecticut, and the experience of rehabilitating that home inspired her to perfect the art of entertaining.

Taking the Publishing World by Storm

Stewart began catering in 1975 and eventually landed her first publishing contract for the book *Entertaining*. One of the most expensive cookbooks to be published at that time, it made Martha Stewart a household name. She established herself as an authority on catering, cooking, entertaining, and hosted her first PBS special in 1986 called *Holiday Entertaining with Martha Stewart*.

Although both men and women follow her, not everyone agrees with her signature phrase, "It's a good thing." She is often criticized for her over-the-top approach to entertaining, once referred to as "Marie Antoinette, dressed as a milk maid." Her response to accusations of being out of touch with everyday people was to became a Kmart spokesperson in 1987.

Negative Publicity

Shortly thereafter she experienced a messy public divorce. Stewart launched her first of many magazines, *Martha Stewart Living*, one of the most profitable starts in magazine history. This led to her syndicated television show in 1993, and in 1995 she bought back her magazine from Time Warner and founded Martha Stewart Living Omnimedia (MSLO). On October 19, 1999, Stewart rang the opening bell on Wall Street as MSLO went public. Naturally, she catered the entire affair to celebrate the valuing of her empire at nearly $2 billion. In 2001, Stewart was named the third most powerful woman in America by the *Ladies Home Journal*.

In 2004, Stewart was convicted of lying to investigators about a stock sale and served five months in prison. Immediately after her release she began a comeback campaign to rehabilitate her image and her business, and by 2006 she appeared to achieve both with the company's return to profitability. Julia Child once said she admired Stewart because Stewart was a self-made woman. Stewart's ambition, determination, and success have certainly earned her a position as a significant woman in American history.

See Also: Celebrity Women; Crafting Industry; Entrepreneurs; Journalists, Print Media; Reality Television.

Further Readings

Allen, Lloyd. *Being Martha: The Inside Story of Martha Stewart and Her Amazing Life.* Hoboken, NJ: Wiley, 2006.

Byron, Christopher M. *Martha Inc.: The Incredible Story of Martha Stewart Living Omnimedia.* Hoboken, NJ: Wiley, 2002.

Martha Stewart Living Omnimedia. "Martha Stewart Official Website." http://www.marthastewart.com (accessed November 1, 2009).

Meachum, V. *Martha Stewart: Successful Business Woman.* Berkeley Heights, NJ: Enslow Publishers, 1998.

Erika Cornelius Smith
Purdue University

Studio Arts, Women in

The start of gender discrimination cannot be pinpointed, but the unequal application of resources and opportunities between men and women seemingly has permeated human society from the time the sexes were defined. Women were considered the weaker of the two sexes, and it was once widely thought that women were less capable than men of producing intelligent—let alone brilliant—works of art. Even when women were sparingly admitted to arts fellowships, the idea of the "woman artist" was somewhat oxymoronic. Women were presumed to be better in domestic arts, and studio arts were deemed the realm of men.

A studio is an artist's workroom. An *atelier* (French for "studio") today refers to a collective in which artists learn and improve under the guidance of a teacher who mentors them to higher levels of skill. (Sometimes the term is used to describe a house of fashion design. Earlier connotations of the word referred to an artist and his assistants, who together produced art under the chief artist's name.) Studio art, then, is work produced in studios or ateliers—drawings, paintings, prints, sculptures, photographs, film, digital images, texts and performance, glass and metal works, and sound. The term excludes artistic works created in other settings, such as classrooms or factories.

Most colleges and universities that offer degrees in studio arts offer the studio experience (a place where you work alone and daily on your art), guidance in preparing a portfolio, attention to exposing one's work to juries and other reviewers, and often some art history, but academic art departments expect that majors sample several of the art forms named above, seldom allowing a concentration in just one. The atelier experience does not offer a degree but, instead, allows the student to concentrate on developing skills in a single art form.

Why Focus on Women's Studio Arts?

To be able to do or view women's art required activism. Compared with the opportunities available to men to practice, teach, and obtain funding for arts and art histories, women's opportunities were severely restricted. Women make up just over one-half of all visual artists and 53 percent of degree-holders of art, yet men dominate U.S. art departments (holding 80 percent of the positions), female artists earn a third of male artists' earnings, and grants for arts activities are overwhelmingly offered to men (73 percent). Of the curated exhibits in art museums, 85 percent are devoted to men's art—women's work is displayed in only 15 percent of these, and minority women's in .003 percent. Of works actually acquired by museums, only 4 percent of these are women's artistic creations.

Activists have long used both protest and philanthropy in creative and unrelenting ways to address the long-term imbalance in the recognition of and support for men's and women's arts. Organizations were formed to address this inequity through activism and philanthropy. Arguably the oldest and more prominent of these organization is The Pen and Brush Club, organized in the late 1800s by sister painters Janet and Mary Lewis to promote women painters and sculptors (as well as writers, composers, and performers).

Founded by artists in 1971, the Women In the Arts Foundation has used protest, documentation of discrimination, and testimony in Washington, D.C., to fight for greater equality for women artists (the organization's founding documents are housed in the Smithsonian Institution). The Women's Caucus for Art came together in 1972 under the leadership of Ann Sutherland Harris—an art historian who founded this strongly feminist organization fighting for gender equality in the arts. The D.C.-based National Museum of Women in the Arts is dedicated solely to recognizing the work of women artists through exhibitions, educational programs, and a library/research center, and it produces *Women in the Arts* magazine—the only U.S. magazine exclusively promoting women's achievements in visual, literary, and performing arts.

What Sources Educate About Women's Art and Women Artists?

There is neither an agreed-on women's artistic canon nor a single historical trajectory of women's arts that can be pointed to as the established register of uniquely important literary, two-dimensional, or three-dimensional arts created by women. Yes, women toil at art, but women artists as a rule do not collectively dialogue to unify their work into a tradition or body of singular "women's arts." The women's/feminist movement sparked both activism and scholarship on women artists, and the rise of Internet access has made the Web a place for organizing and disseminating collected material.

Thus, notable efforts to codify a body of women's studio arts contributions and place searchable databases on publicly accessible Internet sites deserve recognition. One such effort is the Women Artists Archives National Directory, whose Rutgers University organizers have created databases on archived papers and data on women who have been actively producing art at least since 1945. They hold no archives themselves but collect information on archives, committing those data to three databases: a repository of organizations working on women's arts, a collections database describing the archival source material held about particular artists or artists' organizations, and the entity database, a collection of basic information about artists and their personal and professional histories. As of the writing of this article, however, the site reports a failure to be able to updated as a result of cuts to the budget. The Varo Registry of Women Artists (began in 1996 and named for surrealist female painter Remedios Varo) provides Web pages for participating artists' images and personal statements. Another group providing online resources is the Women in the Arts Foundation.

The most prominent academic journal focusing on women's art is *n.paradoxa*, and it does so in a global and feminist fashion. As for physical sites, the Washington, D.C.–based National Museum of Women in the Arts reports being "the only museum in the world dedicated exclusively to recognizing the contributions of women artists." Begun in the 1960s by collectors Wilhelmina and Wallace Holladay, the museum maintains Clara, a directory of female artists, and holds archives on the women artists listed in the Clara database.

Some argue that in the 1970s and 1980s, women made great strides in the art world, but others, such as the Guerrilla Girls, an organization of feminist arts activists, might argue that progress is far from sufficient. Since 1985, their campaign has used street theater, posters, and other humorous and visible modes of focusing attention on sex biases in the arts.

From Where Has Women's Art Come? Where Is It Going?

In times gone by, the rare successful woman in studio arts had close connections to sufficiently prominent others in the art world or to the Christian church (predominantly, nuns). For example, 16th- and 17th-century artists Catharina van Hemessen, Marietta Robusti Tintoretto, Lavinia Fontana, and Teresa del Po learned from or were apprenticed to their artist fathers, and when history speaks of Camille Claudel (lover to Rodin) and Sofonisba Anguissola (court painter to King Phillip of Spain), it tends to focus on their colorful lives but not their talents as artists in their own right, nor their significant contributions to the world of art. During the Renaissance, the rise of humanism (belief in the dignity of all people) was the likely cause of increased freedom of women to pursue studio arts, although women were not in equal measure welcome to pursue careers as artists (rather than craftswomen).

With the rise of academies for the training and promotion of artists, women's exclusion was calculable. In the Renaissance and Baroque periods, women were rarely accepted into academies compared with men; women were not welcome to paint nudes, as the models were mainly male, and painting nudes is considered even today a crucial part of training. Thus, female artists' self-portraits are important records in the history of women's art, for they show the artists using themselves as models, portraying their female selves as educated figures and not detached muses, and depicting the female nude as more than an object meant for subjugation by men's sexual eye. More opportunities for women opened in the late 19th century, as evidenced by the opening of Female School of England's Royal College of the Art and the 1876 Philadelphia Centennial Exposition, which overwhelmingly displayed art made by men but had a Women's Pavilion displaying art from 1,500 women's artists in 13 countries.

In the 20th century, women's art and artists became more widely known still. For example, photographers Dorothea Lange and Annie Leibovitz became well-known for capturing the American social landscape (albeit from quite different vantage points). However, the quest for equality in women's work in the arts has a Western (i.e., North American and European) bias, largely ignoring all but the most popular women artists of color (such as Frida Kahlo, Faith Ringgold, and Kara Walker), who have reached acclaim sufficient enough to have their work displayed in iconic galleries open to the public. The November 2001 conference "Women Artists at the Millennium" gave rise to a book of the same name, and it exemplifies one of the more recent attempts to redress the inequalities that give rise to the underrecognition of artists who continue to fill varied categories of "other."

See Also: Art Criticism: Gender Issues; Arts, Women in the (21st Century Overview); Chicago, Judy; *Dinner Party, The* (Judy Chicago); Fiber Arts, Women in; Guerrilla Girls; Holzer, Jenny; Kngwarreye, Emily; Leibovitz, Annie; Photography, Women in; Walker, Kara.

Further Readings

Armstrong, Carol and Catherine de Zegher. *Women Artists at the Millennium*. Boston: MIT Press, 2006.

Barlow, Margaret. *Women Artists*. New York: New York Universe, 2008.

Chadwick, Whitney. *Women, Art, and Society*. London: Thames & Hudson, 2007.

Frostig, Karen and Kathy A. Halamka. *Blaze: Discourse on Art, Women and Feminism*. Newcastle upon Tyne, UK: Cambridge Scholars, 2009.

The Guerrilla Girls. *The Guerrilla Girls' Bedside Companion to the History of Western Art*. New York: Penguin, 1998.

Reckitt, Helena and Peggy Phelan. *Art and Feminism*. London: Phaidon, 2006.

Rosen, Randy, et al. *Making Their Mark: Women Artists Move Into the Mainstream, 1970–1985*. New York: Abbeville Press, 1989.

Showalter, Elaine. *A Jury of Her Peers: Celebrating American Women Writers From Ann Bradstreet to Annie Proulx*. New York: Vintage, 2010.

Vilna Bashi Treitler
Baruch College

Sudan

In the 21st century, Sudan has become the most politically troublesome spot in the world, and human rights abuses there are well documented. After attaining independence from Britain in 1956, two separate civil wars erupted over domination of the south by northern Muslim Arabs. Together, war, famine, and human rights abuses have cost the lives of more than 2 million people. The situation has reached crisis status in western Darfur, where a separate conflict has displaced

USAID-supported vocational classes in Sudan gave women the skills to earn income as seamstresses.

200,000 and left 400,000 dead. Even though per capita income rose to $2,300 in 2009, economic health was threatened by inefficient infrastructures and an unemployment rate of 18.7 percent. Sixty percent of the labor force is engaged in agriculture, much of which is subsistence farming. Forty percent of the population lives below the poverty line. Less than half (43 percent) of Sudanese live in urban areas. More than half the population is black, but there is a large Arab minority (39 percent). Seventy percent of the population is Sunni Muslim, and one-fourth of Sudanese adhere to indigenous beliefs. The 5 percent who are Christian live mostly in southern Sudan and Khartoum.

Sudanese law is based on Shari'a law, which mandates a subservient position for women. Girls are considered less valuable than boys from birth. Despite the fact that the constitution grants equal rights to women, it has no relation to actual practice. In addition to systemic discrimination, major problems for Sudanese women include enslavement, violence, and female genital mutilation. In 2008, women filled approximately 70 of 450 seats in the National Assembly, and three women sat in the cabinet.

Human Rights Abuses

Sudanese women are segregated from men in daily life. To travel, females need permission from husbands or male guardians. Women have no right to own property, and widows receive only an eighth of their late husbands' estates. One-third of the remainder is allotted to daughters, and two-thirds to sons. Some groups allow men to take wives on a trial basis, lasting up to four years. If a man chooses not to continue the marriage after that, he simply returns his wife to her family. He is required to pay a set sum for children born during the marriage. Women abandoned in this way are free to marry again without stigma. Mothers have almost no legal rights, and divorced mothers maintain child custody only until girls turn 8 years old and boys turn 6 years old. Arranging marriages for young girls is still common. Women can only marry non-Muslim men if they convert to Islam. Since 1991, women employed in government offices and all female teachers and students are bound by Islamic dress codes that require them to be entirely covered except for face, hands, and feet.

The Sudan ranks 14th in the world in infant mortality, with a rate of 82.43 deaths per 1,000 live births. Female infants (82.37 deaths per 1,000 live births) have only a slight advantage over male infants (82.48 deaths per 1,000 live births).

The survival advantage is greater for adult women, who have a life expectancy of 52.4 years compared with 50.49 years for men. The median age of 19.2 years for women is somewhat higher than that of men (18.9 years). Sudanese women have a total fertility rate of 4.48 children. The Sudanese have a very high risk of contracting bacterial and protozoal diarrhea, hepatitis A and E, typhoid fever, malaria, dengue fever, African trypanosomiasis, schistosomiasis, meningococcal meningitis, and rabies. Avian flu has also been identified. Female educational opportunities are limited, and barely half of those women older than 15 years can read and write; however, 71.8 percent of men are literate.

Although prohibited, female genital mutilation is still common, and Sudan uses the severe Pharaonic type of female genital mutilation, which is generally performed on girls between the ages of 4 and 7 years. More than 90 percent of girls in the north have been subjected to this procedure. Health problems resulting from the practice, which is often conducted under unsanitary conditions by ill-trained paramedical personnel, include urinary problems, infections, and death.

Human rights reports document the enslavement of women and children in Darfur, where Popular Defense Forces under the command of Sudan's president are committing daily atrocities. Women are regularly gang raped and tortured. The international community, including the American Anti-Slavery Group, is heavily involved in the effort to help these women. The Swiss-based Christian Solidarity International human rights organization has purchased many women and returned them to their homes, but scores of women remain unaccounted for.

Domestic violence and rape are major concerns, but no specific laws protect women from violence. Women who file charges against attackers are often accused of lying. Unmarried pregnant women who state they have been raped are subject to arrest and charges of adultery, which is a capital offense. In parts of southern Sudan, rape is considered socially acceptable, but families may demand payment if pregnancy results. Spousal rape is not illegal. Sexual harassment is not against the law, but harassers may be charged with gross indecency. Prostitution is a growing problem.

See Also: Domestic Violence; Female Genital Surgery, Geographical Distribution; Female Genital Surgery, Types of; Islam; Rape in Conflict Zones; Representation of Women in Government, International.

Further Readings

Central Intelligence Agency. "The World Factbook: Sudan." https://www.cia.gov/library/publications/the -world-factbook/geos/su.html (accessed June 2010).

Hanson, Jessica and Anna Stanley. "Slavery, Violence Against Women Continue Worldwide." *National NOW Times*, v.33/1 (2001).

Social Institutions and Gender Index. "Gender Equality and Social Institutions in Sudan." http://genderindex .org/country/sudan (accessed June 2010).

Tripp, Aili Mari, et al. *African Women's Movements: Changing Political Landscapes.* New York: Cambridge University Press, 2009.

U.S. Department of State. "2008 Human Rights Report: Sudan." http://www.state.gov/g/drl/rls/hrrpt/2008 /af/119026.htm (accessed June 2010).

Elizabeth Rholetter Purdy
Independent Scholar

Suicide and Race

Suicide and suicide attempts are intentional self-harm. Individuals who think about and plan suicide are at risk for completing suicide. Women have much lower rates of completed suicide but are eight times more likely to attempt suicide than men. Suicide deaths and attempts vary among groups of women according to their race and ethnicity; mortality from self-inflicted harm is highest among American Indian, Alaskan Native and white women and lowest among black, Hispanic and Asian/Pacific Islander women. Strategies to reduce risk are most effective if they provide culturally appropriate interventions to the needs of a particular group.

American Indian/Alaskan Native Women (Non-Hispanic)

The U.S. government recognizes 564 Native American tribes, each with a unique culture. American Indian and Alaskan Native women have a suicide rate of 15.1 per 100,000, the highest among U.S. women. Suicide is among the top 10 leading causes of death for five age groups of American Indians and Alaskan Natives. It is a leading cause of death for girls ages 10 to 14 and young women ages 15 to 24; in both age groups, suffocation is the leading cause. For women ages 35 to 44, suicide is the fifth-leading cause of death, primarily from poisoning. Many deaths also result from firearms. Young Indian women have suicide rates two or three times higher than women in the general population. American Indian/Alaskan Native women face high rates of unemployment, alcohol and substance abuse, and domestic violence. Further, mental and physical health facilities available on reservations may lack the resources to address the individual and community needs that result in high levels of suicide.

Asian American and Pacific Islander Women (Non-Hispanic)

Asian and Pacific Islanders are a diverse group. Some have been in the United States for generations, while others are recent immigrants. The suicide rate for women in this group is 5.7 per 100,000. Self-inflicted harm is among the top 10 leading causes of death for all age groups between 10 and 64 years with suffocation the most common method used. This is the only racial/ethnic group in which drowning is a leading cause of suicide. Asian American women born in the United States report higher suicide ideation and attempts than the general population. In this group, women ages 18 to 34 are the most vulnerable to thinking about and planning suicide.

Black Women (Non-Hispanic)

The suicide death rate for black women, including African American and Caribbean females, is 5.0 per 100,000 in the United States. For women 10 to 34 in this group, suicide is among the top 10 causes of death. Among older black women, most suicides result from firearms, with handguns used four times more often than rifles or shotguns. Risk has been relatively low for black youth in the United States, but the rate has risen dramatically in recent years. African American girls are more likely to attempt suicide than Caribbean girls.

Suicide risk for African American women may be reduced by strong extended family ties and by religious beliefs, but few studies exist to validate this hypothesis.

Hispanic and White Women (Non-Hispanic)

Women who identify themselves as Hispanic represent many different countries. Hispanic women in the United States have a suicide rate of 4.9 per 100,000, the lowest rate among the groups included in U.S. statistics. Suicide is among the top 10 causes of death for females ages 10 to 44, with suffocation, poisoning, and firearms the leading means of self-inflicted harm.

Hispanic girls are more likely to have thought about or attempted suicide than other girls of the same age. They may be torn between the conflicting demands of their parents and American culture with few acceptable resources to help them meet their mental health needs.

Among white women, the suicide rate is 13.9 per 100,000 and is a significant cause of death in several age groups. For white girls 10 to 14, suicide is the third-leading cause of death, with suffocation accounting for almost three-fourths of the total. For young women 15 to 24, suicide is the second-leading cause of death; suffocation, firearms, and poisoning comprise nearly all these cases. For women 25 to 64, poisoning, firearms, and suffocation are responsible for high death rates. In the majority of cases of firearm and poisoning deaths, the specific means are unspecified.

The largest increase in suicide deaths in recent years has been among white women 45 to 54.

International Statistics and Responses

Globally, suicide rates vary by race and ethnicity. Indigenous populations often have higher suicide rates than the rest of the population; this is evident in both Canada and Australia. Whites in most countries have about twice the suicide rate of other races. Suicide rates are highest in eastern European countries and lowest in Latin America. Little reliable research exists on ethnic variations in less developed countries. In almost all parts of the world women attempt suicide more than men, but men are more likely to complete suicide. Suicide-prevention strategies must take cultural characteristics, such as language, history and heritage, and religion, into account to adequately reach a target population. Because suicide is often a result of mental health problems, especially depression, accessible and affordable resources that individuals trust must be available. Limiting access to firearms also will reduce risk for women contemplating suicide.

See Also: Suicide Bombers, Female; Suicide Methods; Suicide Rates.

Further Readings

Carr, Alan. *Depression and Attempted Suicide in Adolescents.* Hoboken, NJ: Wiley-Blackwell, 2002.

Krug, Etienne G., Linda L. Dahlberg, James A. Mercy, and Zwi, Anthony, & Lozana. "World Report on Violence and Health." Chapter 7. Geneva: World Health Organization, 2002.

National Center for Injury Prevention and Control. http://webappa.cdc.gov/sasweb/ncipc/leadcaus10.html (accessed July 2010).

Rebecca Reviere
Howard University

Suicide Bombers, Female

Terrorist groups have used suicide bombers to carry out deadly attacks against their targets of choice for many years. The use of female suicide bombers is a fairly recent phenomenon. The first known terrorist attack by a female bomber occurred in Lebanon on April 9, 1985, when Sana'a Mehaydali, a 16-year-old member of the Syrian Social Nationalist Party (SSNP), drove a bomb-laden truck into an Israeli Defense Force convoy, killing two Israeli soldiers. Since then, several other terrorist groups have used female bombers to carry out suicide missions. Some of these groups include the Liberation Tigers of Tamil Eelam (LTTE), the Kurdistan Workers Party (PKK), Chechen rebels, Al Aqsa Martyrs, Palestinian Islamic Jihad (PIJ), and, most recently, Hamas.

The use of female bombers has been growing internationally, and female bombers have carried out attacks in Sri Lanka, Chechnya, Israel, Lebanon, and Turkey. The most prolific user of female bombers has been the LTTE, a group that has used female bombers in roughly one-third of its 200 attacks.

Suicide bombing is a lucrative tactic used by many terrorist groups because, although it is a low-cost operation that does not require significant investment, it may result in mass casualties and extensive physical damage to infrastructure. Furthermore, since the bomber is expected to die as a result of the attack, there is little risk that he or she will be interrogated and will surrender information that could endanger the organization. Also, terrorism, and especially suicide terrorism, has serious psychological effects on the general public that could influence desired policy changes or, at the very least, increase awareness for a particular cause.

Traditionally, most terrorist groups used only males for suicide bombing missions. In fact, some religious leaders even opposed the use of females. For example, Sheikh Ahmed Yassin, the spiritual leader of Hamas, publicly opposed the use of females in suicide bombings in 2002 and suggested that women should play only a supporting role in terrorist activities.

In recent years, however, terrorist groups have been more inclined to use females as bombers. In 2004, Yassin acknowledged that some terrorist missions required the use of females for strategic reasons since women were able to obtain easier access to potential targets. Therefore, the use of women for suicide bombing missions may be due to their ability to circumvent security measures that tend to focus on males.

The Advancement of Women

Today, female suicide bombers are considered psychologically and physically as capable as men to carry out their assigned missions. Similar to their male counterparts, women have driven bomb-laden vehicles, carried bomber "bags," and strapped massive explosives on their bodies. Women have even carried explosives in prosthetic devices that mimic the look of a pregnant stomach.

Terrorist groups have realized that the tactical use of females has resulted in some important strategic advantages. In addition to obtaining easier access to targets, female bombers seem to garner more media attention and exposure, resulting in an enhanced psychological effect. Furthermore, allowing women to participate increases the total number of potential combatants and enlarges the pool of possible recruits. In addition, the use of female bombers tends to encourage recruitment and increase male participation in suicide attacks. In a sense, the use of females appeals to men's sense of chivalry and desire to protect females from violence by volunteering to serve in their place.

Since the use of women is a relatively new phenomenon, there only have been a small number of female bombers to date. In fact, female bombers account for only about 15 percent of suicide attacks worldwide. Because of the small numbers of female bombers and the the fact that suicide attackers die means that there is little data available to help explain who becomes a bomber and why.

Enough is known, however, to discredit the stereotypical notion that all suicide bombers are poor, uneducated, self-destructive sociopaths. Rather, female bombers seem to come from a wide range of backgrounds and cultures. Some are widows and others have never been married; some are unemployed and others are professionals; some are poor and others are middle class.

Despite the considerable limitations on what is known about female bombers, one fact is clear: female bombers, much like their male counterparts, tend to be young. On average, female suicide bombers are between 21 and 23. Sixteen-year-old Sana'a Mehaydali was the youngest known female bomber, and 37-year-old Shagir Karima Mahmud, a member of SSNP, is believed to be the oldest.

The recruitment methods used to select women for suicide missions seem to be similar to the methods used to recruit men. Many suicide bombers, both male and female, have experienced the loss of family members or close friends, and recruiters take advantage of their grief, anger, and thirst for revenge. Recruiters use systematic indoctrination to transform youthful innocence and enthusiasm into a sense of commitment to the group's particular cause. Beyond religious and patriotic motivations, suicide bombers often receive large sums of money and enhance their family's social status and their personal reputation. While many women willingly choose to participate in suicide bombing missions for those reasons, some may be used by terrorist groups unwittingly. There have been reports of terrorist groups using mentally challenged women for some attacks in Iraq.

See Also: Conflict Zones; Perpetrators, Female; Religious Fundamentalisms, Cross-Cultural Context of; Terrorists, Female.

Further Readings

Bloom, Mia. "Mother. Daughter. Sister. Bomber." *Bulletin of the Atomic Scientists*, v.61/6 2005.

Kronin, Audrey K. "Terrorists and Suicide Attacks." *Congressional Research Service Report for Congress* (2003). http://thebulletin.metapress.com/content/t52xq81673464kj5/061006015-SD01.pdf (accessed January 2010).

Zedalis, Debra D. "Female Suicide Bombers." Carlisle, PA: United States Army War College, Strategic Studies Institute, 2004. http://www.strategicstudiesinstitute.army.mil/pdffiles/PUB408.pdf (accessed January 2010).

Julie Ahmad Siddique
City University of New York Graduate Center

Suicide Methods

Approximately 30,000 individuals in the United States commit suicide every year, and over half a million attempt suicide. Many more think about it. Globally, about 1 million people kill themselves yearly. Men are at least four times as likely to die from suicide as women, yet women attempt suicide significantly more often than men.

The methods that individuals use to kill or to attempt to kill themselves vary according to availability and familiarity, acceptability, and intention. Women typically use less violent methods than men unless they are intent on death. Women in the United States, and in most parts of the world, are most likely to die from self-inflicted harm from poisons, hanging, and firearms. American men are most likely to die from gunshots.

Since suicidal individuals often act on impulse, methods that are harder to find and to use present lower risk. Prevention strategies depend on targeting individual decision making and understanding the means of self-inflicted harm. Having valid data is an important step in the solution.

Poison and Firearms

The 10 categories of self-poisoning include painkillers, tranquilizers, narcotics, alcohol, gases, organic solvents, and pesticides. Women have ready access to drugs and, since many drugs are slower acting, have a chance to reconsider their choice to die. Further, they are easy to use and relatively nonviolent. Women in the United States and Europe use poisons more than other means to attempt or complete suicide. In both cases, drug overdoses are most likely responsible for death, but the type of drug is usually unspecified on the death certificate.

Carbon monoxide poisoning is more common in industrialized countries and is usually a result of breathing fumes from a running car in a small, sealed space. Carbon monoxide poisoning in Hong Kong has increased from burning charcoal in an enclosed space. Pesticide poisoning is more common for women in Asian countries and in rural areas.

Guns are a main cause of violent death in the United States, several other countries in the Americas, and in some European countries. They are a significant cause of suicide death for women in the United States, and black women are at particular risk. Individuals usually shoot themselves in the head or the chest.

Firearm suicide is more frequent in countries where firearms are common in private households. When guns are available, individuals have access to a lethal and quick method of inflicting harm; this is especially problematic if the suicide attempt is impulsive. Of all types of firearms, handguns are responsible for the largest number of suicide deaths.

Hanging, Strangulation, and Suffocation

Women in the United States and around the world have high rates of suicide by suffocation, particularly hanging and suffocation with a plastic bag. Among girls ages 10 to 14 years, hanging is the most common means of suicide. Asian/Pacific Islander and American Indian/Alaskan Natives are most likely to die by suffocation among ethnic groups in the United States. Hanging is used when no other means is available; it requires some preparation and determination and is a violent way to die. The proportion of hangings typically decreases as either pesticide suicide or firearm suicide increases.

Other Categories

Other methods of suicide are less common. Drowning and submersion, for example, are more frequent in areas with ready access to water, such as coastal regions. Drowning as a method of suicide is rare among American women. It is only among Asian/Pacific Islander women that drowning is a significant cause of death. Death by explosive materials has increased. The wars in the Middle East have spawned a rash of suicide bombers, some of whom are women. Women move more easily through checkpoints and markets and can camouflage the explosive with bulky clothing or false pregnancies.

Self-immolation (death by fire) is found more often in India, perhaps as a legacy from the early practice of *sati* and the availability of kerosene for cooking. Sharp objects are used more often in suicide attempts than in completed suicide. Cutting one's wrists is in this category. Deadly single-vehicle, single-occupant crashes are more common for men than women. Classifying these deaths is problematic; it is often unclear if the death was intentional or accidental.

Jumping from high places such as buildings, cliffs, and bridges is rare in the United States. It is more common in areas with many tall buildings, such as Hong Kong. Deaths can occur when someone jumps or lies in front of a moving object. Individuals may drive a car onto the track and wait for the train. These suicides are more common in areas with developed

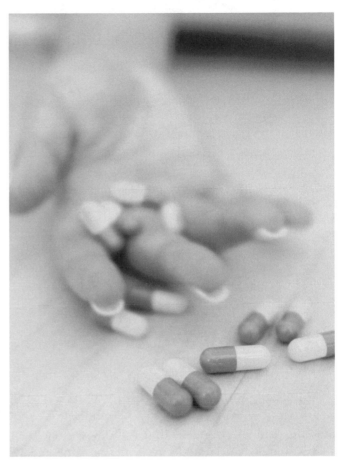

Women attempt suicide significantly more often than men, with drugs being an accessible, relatively nonviolent method.

train or subway systems. The method of suicide can also be left unspecified on the death certificate.

Prevention and Reporting

Suicide is a preventable form of death. Successful prevention strategies target the individual, such as developing suicide hotlines, and the specific means of suicide, such as installing tall fences around high bridges.

Suicide methods are categorized by *The International Classification of Disease—10th Edition*. Many deaths, however, are not coded as suicides because of the stigma; the suicide rate is probably much higher than reported. Some methods, such as shooting and hanging, are reported more accurately than others. Monitoring suicide rates and methods is crucial for developing strategies for prevention.

See Also: Honor Suicides; Suicide and Race; Suicide Bombers, Female; Suicide Rates; Suttee.

Further Readings

Ajdacid-Gross, V., M. G. Weiss, M. Ring, U. Hepp, M. Bopp, F. Gutzwiller, and W. Rössler. "Methods of Suicide: International Suicide Patterns Derived From the WHO Mortality Data Base." *Bulletin of the World Health Organization*, v.86/9 (2008).

Granello, Paul F. and Juhnke, Gerald A. *Case Studies in Suicide: Experiences of Mental Heath Professionals.* Upper Saddle River, NJ: Prentice Hall, 2009.

Stone, Geo. *Suicide and Attempted Suicide: Methods and Consequences.* New York: Carroll & Graf, 2001.

Rebecca Reviere
Howard University

Suicide Rates

Every year, nearly 1 million people globally die from self-inflicted harm. It is the 13th-leading cause of death worldwide. Between 10 to 20 million attempt suicide, and many more think about ending their lives. Suicide and suicide attempts are not equally distributed across the population; rates vary across many dimensions.

These substantial variations reflect differences in acceptability of suicide, availability of methods, and community norms. Suicide has an impact far beyond the individual death; families, friends, and communities suffer. In most countries, women have lower suicide mortality rates but more suicide attempts than men.

Gender Differences

In the United States, men outnumber women in suicide deaths four to one, but women attempt suicide at least 10 times more often. Suicide is the seventh-leading cause of death for men in the United States and the 16th for women. Women in China, especially rural areas, have suicide rates equal to men.

Women and men typically differ in their approach to suicide. Men use more lethal means, mainly firearms; women are more likely to die by hanging/suffocation or to use poisons, particularly drugs in the United States and Europe. An overdose gives an individual time to reconsider and is often considered a cry for help rather than a serious attempt. However, when women intend to kill themselves, they do, usually with firearms in the United States.

It is unclear why women have lower suicide completions. Their higher levels of seeking help or their concern for their loved ones and the needs of their children may be protective. Globally, risk increases with age; in general, elderly men have the highest rates of suicide. The suicide rate among young people is increasing at a faster pace than among the elderly, but experts argue that this may indicate more accurate reporting. There has been a sharp increase in suicide among American girls ages 10 to 19 and among black youth. Women in the United States are most at risk for suicide death between the ages of 35 and 54.

Other Factors

Race and ethnicity also impact suicide, although data on minority women are slim. In the United States, suicide rates among black, Asian American, and Hispanic women are lower than among white and American Indian/Alaskan Native women. Globally, indigenous populations have relatively high rates of suicide. Married people are less likely to die by suicide than those who are single, divorced, or widowed. Having young children in the home and being pregnant are protective forces. The exception is the increased suicide risk among women with postpartum depression. Interpersonal crises, however, or a family history of suicide increase risk for later suicide.

Psychiatric illness is a major risk factor for suicide. Major affective, anxiety, substance abuse, and psychotic disorders predispose women to think about, attempt, and carry out suicide.

Individuals with serious depression are particularly vulnerable to suicide. Paradoxically, women have higher rates of major depression than men yet kill themselves at lower rates. Women who are clinically depressed, however, are more likely to die from suicide than women in the general population. Depression that is more severe and more chronic is related to higher suicide risk in both women and men. The feelings of hopelessness associated with depression make other solutions to perceived problems unimaginable. Risk increases when the depressive episode begins to set in or to lift. Previous attempts are a major risk factor for later suicide.

Alcohol and drug abuse are related to increased risk of suicide. Women who are alcoholic are significantly more likely to attempt suicide than nonalcoholic women. The exact relationship between the substance use and death is not always clear. An individual may drink to excess to make suicide easier, or increased depression resulting from alcohol use may be to blame. Countries in the Soviet bloc have higher-than-average rates of alcohol-related suicides.

Individuals who have experienced traumatic events such as job loss and economic problems, loss of a spouse, or imprisonment may be overwhelmed with depression and isolation. Ending one's life might seem the only solution. Evidence suggests that differences in brain chemistry may also be different for those who complete suicide. Individuals who have been diagnosed with a chronic illness, such as cancer, human immunodeficiency virus and acquired immune deficiency syndrome (HIV/AIDS), or tuberculosis or who have uncontrolled pain are at risk for suicide. Physician-assisted suicide for terminally ill individuals is legal only in the Netherlands and Oregon and only under certain conditions.

Research in several countries, including the United States, has established links between domestic violence and suicide attempts for women. Estimates suggest that from 26 to 40 percent of all victims attempt suicide. Heightened stress from physical, sexual, and psychological abuse leads to mental health problems that are linked to suicide risk.

More highly educated women are more likely to kill themselves than women with less education. Women physicians, for example, both in the United States and Finland, have higher suicide mortality than women in other professions or in the general population. Suicide rates are similar for female and male physicians.

Country/Community

Risk of death by self-inflicted harm varies by country and community. Reported suicide rates are higher in eastern European countries and lower in predominantly Catholic and Muslim countries. Asia accounts for 60 percent of the world's suicides. Reliable data are not available for suicide rates in Africa. Culture also plays a role in suicide acceptability. Whether suicide is seen as a sin, a taboo, a pathway to glory, or a rational alternative to one's problems influences the decision to end one's life. Rates are also related to religious beliefs.

Some areas have relatively high suicide rates; slums, areas with high numbers of migrants, commu-nities facing natural disasters, and agricultural communities with recent crop failures are examples.

In regions with political violence, suicide bombers may be revered, and increasingly, women are recruited or forced into this decision. Those who volunteer for these missions are radicalized but not mentally ill.

Theory and Validity of Reporting

Émile Durkheim was the first to study suicide statistically; he discovered that patterns were not random through a population and developed his theoretical classification scheme. He proposed four categories of suicide: (1) individuals were overly integrated into a group and thus willing to sacrifice for the group (altruistic suicide), (2) individuals were isolated from the group with no sense of belonging (egoistic suicide), (3) individuals were faced with rapid social change (anomic suicide), and (4) individuals were in overly repressive environments (fatalistic suicide).

Suicide rates are calculated by dividing the number of suicide deaths in a population by 100,000. The accuracy of these statistics varies, particularly in countries with poorly developed vital registration systems. Stigmatization and cultural attitudes toward suicide may influence reporting, and suicide may be deliberately miscoded on a death certificate. Making international comparisons is problematic. Quality data are important for prevention efforts.

See Also: Suicide and Race; Suicide Bombers, Female; Suicide Methods.

Further Readings

Bertolote, José Manuoel and Alexandra Fleischman. "A Global Perspective in the Epidemiology of Suicide." *Suicidology*, v.7/2 (2002).

Chaudron, Linda H. and Eric D. Caine. "Suicide Among Women: A Critical Review." *Journal of the American Medical Women's Association*, v.59/2 (2004).

Durkheim, Émile. *Suicide.* New York: Free Press, 1951.

World Health Organization (WHO). "Suicide Prevention: Emerging From the Darkness." Geneva: WHO, 2003. http://www.searo.who.int/en/Section1174/Section1199/Section1567/Section1824.htm (accessed October 2010).

Rebecca Reviere
Howard University

Suleman, Nadya "Octomom"

Known throughout the United States as the "Octomom," Nadya Suleman came to international attention after delivering octuplets. Early news of her pregnancy and delivery was heralded as a medical miracle. Soon, however, fierce public outrage surfaced and ethical debates began when it was discovered that Suleman already had six children and was unmarried, unemployed and receiving public assistance.

Suleman was born in California as an only child to parents Edward and Angela Doud. She married young and soon separated from her husband after being unable to conceive a child. While working as a technician in a psychiatric hospital, Suleman saved her money, often working double shifts, to pay for expensive in vitro fertilization (IVF) treatments. During a riot at the hospital, Suleman was hurt and suffered a lower-back injury. She received disability payments for the sustained injury, which she also used to finance her IVF treatments.

In 2001, she received her first IVF treatment from Dr. Michael Kamrava and gave birth to her first child. Between 2002 and 2006 she had five more children through in vitro fertilization, including a set of twins, for a total of six children. In 2008, she had her final IVF treatment, hoping for one more child. She was implanted with her final six embryos and each survived, with two splitting into twins, for a total of eight children. All 14 of Suleman's children share the same donor, a friend who remains unnamed. Upon learning that Dr. Kamrava knowingly implanted more than the recommended number of embryos with full knowledge of Suleman's situation, many in the medical community called for an investigation into his practice and tougher IVF laws.

The controversy surrounding Suleman's decision to continue having children was heightened by her television appearances. She stated that her longing for a large family was to fill a void she felt in her own life. Much of the public has decried her decision as selfish, considering one of her children has autism, she was receiving federal food stamps and the student loan money she was using to supplement her income had ended. Suleman has defended her decision to intentionally become a single mother to a large brood, often stating that children are gifts from God and her remaining embryos deserved a chance at life. She intends to continue pursuing her master's degree in psychology and viewed receiving food stamps as a temporary resource. She continued to assert that she is a loving mother to her children and would be able to provide for them emotionally and eventually financially.

Suleman was offered and accepted a reality television contract, produced by European production company Eyeworks. American networks were hesitant to produce the show due to her damaged public image. While Suleman has been demonized in mainstream American media, there also have been calls to help her and celebrate the miracle of the octuplets' birth, as they are the longest surviving octuplets in the world. She has received help from her family, community, and church, and she accepts donations on behalf of the children via her Website.

See Also: Celebrity Women; Infertility, Treatments for; Reality Television; Reproductive and Sexual Health Rights; Single Mothers.

Further Readings
Johnston, Josephine. "Judging Octomom. (Ethics of In Vitro Fertilization)." *The Hastings Center Report* (March 11, 2010).

Otto, Sheila and Winifred J. Ellenchild Pinch. "Ethical Dimensions in the Case of the 'Octomom': Two Perspectives." *Pediatric Nursing* (January 9, 2010).

The Responsibility Report. "Octomom. The Mother of Responsibility?" http://www.responsibilityproject .com/blog/octomom-the-mother-of-irresponsibility -/?src=keyword_s=ggl_K=Octuplets_C=Parenting _G=OctupletMom_Octuplet_M=Broad#fbid=Z4rg7 snLjIP (accessed August 2010).

Leesha M. Thrower
Northern Kentucky University

Supermodels

Supermodels are extremely well-paid fashion models who usually also hold celebrity status in Western culture. They often are successful high-fashion models who then gain more mainstream popularity through commercial modeling including makeup campaigns and cover shoots for fashion magazines. Most supermodels can be recognized by their first names.

Many people can be credited with coining the term *supermodel*. Similarly, there is no agreement as to who the first supermodel was; those frequently considered here are Twiggy, Gia Carangi, and Lisa Fonssagrives. Janice Dickenson claims to have coined the term and by that definition, a hybrid of "superman" and "model," she claims also to be the first supermodel. Fonssagrives was featured on more than 200 covers of *Vogue* throughout her career, which led to the magazine's prominence in creating future supermodels.

In the 1980s, couture houses began signing exclusive modeling contracts, and thus models were endorsing products with their names as well as appearances. By the 1990s, supermodels became prominent media figures alongside other media superstars. Supermodels appeared on talk shows, were cited in celebrity gossip magazines, were featured in blockbuster movies, and were romantically involved with film stars. With this mainstream popularity, their wages grew. Linda Evangelista is famously quoted as having said that she "did not wake up for less than $10,000 a day." Though many models were referred to as supermodels in the 1990s, including but not limited to Christie Brinkley, Helena Christensen, and Elle Macpherson, only the "big six" were officially recognized as such by the fashion world: Claudia Schiffer, Cindy Crawford, Kate Moss, Linda Evangelista, Naomi Campbell, and Christy Turlington.

In the late 1990s, possibly due the fact that supermodels had been dominating the face of advertising, popular singers, actors, and other entertainers began to replace supermodels on magazine covers and in ad campaigns. In the early 2000s, models like Tyra Banks and Heidi Klum took to reality television shows—widely popular *America's Next Top Model* and *Project Runway*, respectively—as chances for "super" status in the modeling world were fewer. *America's Next Top Model* often features a "supermodel," seemingly earning this title here through designer campaigns and cover presences, as a guest judge in the last segment of the show. Prominent designer Karl Lagerfeld has described both shows as trashy, despite being a photographer on the French version of *America's Next Top Model* and noting that the show has yet to produce any supermodels.

Presently, few companies employ or assist in creating supermodels; one exception, however, is Victoria's Secret. The lingerie company's Angels line employs high-profile models with multiyear, multimillion-dollar contracts. Besides Banks and Klum, other Angels are Alessandra Ambrosia, Adriana Lima, Doutzen Kroes, Miranda Kerr, Marisa Miller, and Gisele Bündchen, who has been the highest-paid model since 2005.

Criticism

The image of the supermodel has been criticized for conforming to a Western beauty standard, encouraging an unhealthy body image, ageism, and racism, which in part may also be a factor in the demise of the supermodels from the 1990s who were largely born in North America. Prominent models who have emerged since 2000 have largely come from non-English-speaking countries. Supermodel Kate Moss is probably most famous and notorious for her slender figure and party lifestyle. Unlike the other supermodels of her time—like Crawford, Schiffer, and Campbell, who were known for their height and curvy figures—Moss, who started modeling at 14, popularized the "waif" figure as Twiggy had when she was modeling in her teens in the 1960s.

Though many models exhibit unattainably thin figures for the average woman, Moss receives mass amounts of criticism for normalizing unhealthy eating habits, like those associated with anorexia. Recently, she is reported as living by the phrase *nothing tastes as good as being thin/skinny feels*, once again drawing attention to her potential dangerous influence.

See Also: Advertising, Aimed at Women; Advertising, Portrayal of Women in; Banks, Tyra; Body Image; Celebrity Women; Diet and Weight Control; Eating Disorders; Representation of Women; Stereotypes of Women.

Further Readings

Dickinson, Janice. *No Lifeguard on Duty: The Accidental Life of the World's First Supermodel.* New York: Harper Collins, 2002.

Halperin, Ian. *Beautiful and Bad: Inside the Dazzling and Deadly World of Supermodels.* New York: Kensington, 2001.

Halperin, Ian. *Shut Up and Smile: Supermodels and the Dark Side.* London: Mainstream Publishing, 2000.

Mary Shearman
Simon Fraser University

Suriname

Considered a Caribbean country, Suriname is actually located in South America. A former Dutch colony, Suriname declared itself an independent republic in 1975 and in 1991 democratically elected its first president. Its population of 493,000 is multiethnic and multicultural; however, 70 percent of the population lives below the poverty line. Legally, women in Suriname have equal access to education, employment, and property, yet traditional social customs often prevent women from taking full advantage of their rights. Sex trafficking is a significant problem for Suriname, which further compromises women's rights and status.

With its many ethnicities and cultural influences, some Suriname cultures are matrifocal, while others are patriarchal. In some areas, custom has families marrying off their daughters at age 15, which prevents the girl from finishing her education. While a free education is open to all, girls who live in the cities have a much greater chance of going to school. About 85 percent of urban children attend school, but only 50 percent of rural children have the opportunity.

Discrimination and Violence Against Women

In the workforce, women experience wage and employment discrimination. Women earn less than men for the same jobs, and 60 percent of women work in traditionally feminine jobs, such as administrative and secretarial work. Nongovernmental organizations (NGOs) such as the National Women's Movement and Women's Business Group have tried to help women develop their own businesses to further women's economic opportunities.

Violence and sexual abuse is a major issue for women. There are no domestic violence laws. The NGO Stop Violence Against Women reports that violence against women is a common problem, and the organization is working to develop networks with police and local communities to address the needs of the victims and arrest the perpetrators. A 2003 Trafficking in Persons Report explained that sex trafficking goes largely ignored by the government, which makes Suriname a popular destination for sex traffickers. Both Suriname women and migrant women are victims of the sex trade. Poverty forces families to sell their children into the trade, or send them to work

Suriname's Foreign Affairs Minister Lygia Kraag-Keteldijk (right) is welcomed by her Brazilian counterpart Celso Amorim.

in the cities, where they are promised a real job but are kidnapped and forced into prostitution.

See Also: Domestic Violence; Poverty; Trafficking, Women and Children; Sex Workers.

Further Readings

Mohammed, P. and C. Shepherd, eds. "Gender in Caribbean Development." Papers presented at the Inaugural Seminar of the University of the West Indies Women and Development Studies Project. Kingston, Jamaica: University Press of the West Indies, 2002.

Momsen, J. *Women and Change in the Caribbean.* Bloomington: Indiana University Press, 1993.

Sedoc-Dahlberg, B., ed. *The Dutch Caribbean: Prospects for Democracy.* London: Gordon and Breach, 1990.

Monica D. Fitzgerald
Saint Mary's College of California

Suttee

Suttee is epistemologically the feminine of *sat,* or true, and hence it is a generic term for a chaste woman; *sati* is the more popular spelling. The term has come to denote the custom of widow immolation on her husband's funeral pyre, by force or by her own volition. The custom was begun by the Aryans when they settled in northern India. With the advent of the Mughals, the custom became more popular when, in order to save their honor, the war widows of the Rajput families performed collective immolation—suttee (also known as *jauhar*).

There were norms laid down for the ritual, and in *Yallajeeyam,* one finds instructions about the methods and practitioners of the custom. What began as a means to save their honor came to be used as an instrument by the patriarchs to get rid of the possible claimants of the property left behind by their husbands. It is notable that this ritual was performed more frequently in the royal and elite families than by the poor. Property, social honor, and acute apathy to widows were considerations that seem to have played an important role in instigating the suttee incidences. These issues were more relevant among the landed gentry, as the poor had nothing to safeguard. Also, since submission and surrender have been hailed as women's virtues in these patriarchal societies, the women who performed suttee were deified by the community. *Devlis*, or honor stones, were inscribed to mark their glory.

Medhatithi and Banabhatta criticized this custom severely and likened it to suicide, which is considered a sin and hence forbidden by the Vedas. In 1812, after the self-immolation of his sister-in-law, Raja Ram Mohan Roy started agitation against this custom. In 1829, the practice came to be formally banned in William Bentinck's regime in the Bengal Presidency lands. Rajasthan followed suit when in 1846 Jaipur banned the practice. Nepal continued to practice *suttee* until the 20th century, and the Indonesian island of Bali enter-

tained this practice until the beginning of 20th century, when eventually the Dutch colonial rule banned it.

Stray incidents of suttee have been reported even after the 1987 commission of the Sati (prevention) Act, when Roop Kanwar's immolation invited a lot of hue and cry. As late as 2008, a 75-year-old woman performed suttee in Chattisgarh in Raipur district. It takes a long time to change mindsets, and these rare incidents, despite strong legislation, are a result of engendered beliefs. However, it needs to be mentioned that *Manusmriti,* which is the ancient law book of the Aryans, does not propagate suttee at all. It was because of the various distorted situations that such distortions crept into the tradition. Selfishness, lust, and the desire to control seem to be the reasons behind suttee.

See Also: Hinduism; India; Suicide and Race; Suicide Methods; Suicide Rates.

Further Readings

Datta, Vishwa Nath. *Sati: A Historical, Social and Philosophical Enquiry Into the Hindu Rite of Widow Burning.* Silsden, UK: Riverdale, 1988.

Hawley, John Stratton. *Sati, the Blessing and the Curse: The Burning of Wives in India.* Oxford, UK: Oxford University Press, 1994.

Major, Andrea, ed. *Sati: A Historical Anthology.* Oxford, UK: Oxford University Press, 2007.

Asha Choubey
M.J.P. Rohilkhand University

Suu Kyi, Aung San

Born on June 19, 1945, in Rangoon, Burma (today known as Myanmar), Aung San Suu Kyi, one of the world's most prominent female politicians, is Burma's pro-democracy leader. General secretary of the opposition party, the National League for Democracy (NLD), she represents the fight for human rights and freedom for Burma's people.

At the age of 2, Suu Kyi's father, commander of the Burma Independence Army, was assassinated. Subsequently, Suu Kyi, the third child in her family, lived with her mother, Daw Khin Kyi, who became a prominent public figure, and her two older brothers.

A Theravada Buddhist, Suu Kyi was educated in English Catholic schools in Burma and later received a degree in politics in India. In 1972, she married Michael Aris, an expert in Tibetan and Himalayan studies, who she met at Oxford University while earning a B.A. in philosophy, politics, and economics followed by a Ph.D. at the School of Oriental and African Studies at the University of London in 1985. Aris, with whom Suu Kyi had two sons, died from prostate cancer in London in 1999.

Political Life

In 1998, the violent military suppression of popular demonstrations following the resignation of General Ne Win, Burma's military dictator since 1962, led Suu Kyi to the front line of Burma's political stage. On August 15, Suu Kyi sent an open letter to the government requesting multiparty elections, following which, on August 26, she made a public address to a mass audience calling for democratic government. Shortly after, Suu Kyi became general secretary of the newly formed NLD. In defiance of a state ban on

Famous Buddhist monk Thamanya Sayadaw with Daw Aung San Suu Kyi after her release from her first house arrest.

political gatherings of more than four people, Suu Kyi pursued a speech-making tour throughout Burma.

From January to July 1989, Suu Kyi continued campaigning. On February 17, the military junta issued an official prohibition against Suu Kyi's standing for election, and Suu Kyi was placed under house arrest on July 20. Despite detention, on May 27, 1990, Suu Kyi was elected prime minister as leader of the winning NLD, which won 82 percent of the votes and 394 of 492 seats. Her detention prevented her from assuming office.

Over the past 20 years, Suu Kyi has been placed under house arrest multiple times, with many international figures including United Nations (UN) Secretary-General Ban Ki-moon and several governments, appealing for her release. She has made brief public appearances and engaged in meetings with UN diplomats. The trespass of an American man, John William Yettaw, onto her property in May 2009 led to the trial of Suu Kyi and her two maids in August 2009 and a sentence of another 18 months of house arrest.

Even while detained, she remained a global figure in the fight for human rights, authoring over 10 books and receiving multiple awards, including the Nobel Peace Prize in 1991. She issued public statements, including the keynote address to the NGO Forum at the Fourth World Conference on Women in Beijing in 1995. In November 2010, Suu Kyi was released from house arrest after 15 straight years, drawing a cheering crowd of thousands. She spoke to supporters, saying that "People must work in unison. Only then can we achieve our goal."

See Also: Heads of State, Female; Human Rights Campaign; Myanmar; Representation of Women in Government, International.

Further Readings

Suu Kyi, Aung San. *Voice of Hope: Conversations.* New York: Seven Stories Press, 1997.

Suu Kyi, Aung San, with introduction by Michael Aris, ed. *Freedom From Fear and Other Writing,* 2nd ed. New York: Penguin, 1995.

Wintle, Justin. *Perfect Hostage: A Life of Aung San Suu Kyi, Burma's Prisoner of Conscience.* New York: Skyhorse Publishing, 2008.

Ramona Vijeyarasa
University of New South Wales

Swaziland

A small, landlocked kingdom in Southern Africa, between Mozambique and South Africa, Swaziland has a population of 1.18 million. It is a developing economy, based on manufacturing, agriculture, and service industries. About 75 percent of the population lives on subsistence farming, and 60 percent makes less than $1.25 a day. Women head one-third of Swazi households. The population is 60 percent Christian, 30 percent indigenous religions, and 10 percent Muslim.

Swaziland's national adult human immunodeficiency virus (HIV) prevalence is more than 40 percent (nearly 50 percent among young women). Together with Botswana and Lesotho, Swaziland is intimately tied to South Africa's mining economy; these four countries show the highest HIV prevalence in the world. The National Emergency Response Council on human immunodeficiency virus and acquired immune deficiency syndrome (HIV/AIDS) in 2004 estimated that over 60,000 children have lost parents, giving rise to child-headed households—more than 15,000 without a living adult, and with children as young as 8 years old caring for their siblings. The growing effect of HIV/AIDS on families, and young women particularly, has continued to grow.

On a positive note, Swaziland holds the second-lowest rate of teenage births worldwide (closely followed by industrialized countries such as Switzerland and the Netherlands) and has recently approved (in April 2009) free primary education in public schools for all children. The literacy rate for women between 15 and 24 years of age is 89 percent (87 percent for men). Regarding political representation, only 11 women were in Parliament in 2004 (as opposed to three in 1995).

Recent amendments to the Constitution of Swaziland provide equal legal rights to men and women and grant married women several rights, such as to own property, to hold a passport, to open a bank account, or to ask for a bank loan. Women previously could only do that with their husband's permission, as they were legally considered minors. Nevertheless, Swazi women are for the most part under the permanent guardianship of their husband, with no independent right to manage property or to keep custody of children that commonly belong to the father. Part of the problem is that married women do not own land; instead, they obtain usufruct rights through marriage in Swaziland, as in several African countries. Thus, a dual system allows the coexistence of customary law and civil laws, greatly undermining gender equality—especially in cases of violence against women or marital abuse. Customary law largely determines rural people's lives—those of women in particular—which is an enormous challenge for social transformation toward gender equity.

Gender Equality Public Policies

Women's organizations, nongovernmental organizations, and gender activists such as the Swaziland Action Group Against Abuse and Hlobisile Dlamini-Shongwe fight violence against women with numerous campaigns and actions. According to the *National Survey on Violence Experienced by Female Children and Youths in Swaziland*, conducted by the government, United Nations agencies, and nongovernmental organizations, nearly half (48.2 percent precisely) of Swazi women experienced some form of sexual violence between infancy and age 24 years.

Swaziland's membership in the Southern Africa Development Community has favored reform. Within the community's gender machinery, it is worth mentioning the Southern African Research and Development Centre, the Gender Unit, and the Gender Advisory Team, all of which were created in the 1990s to develop gender equality public policies and to promote research and actions on gender issues in coordination with major international development agencies, such as the United Nations Development Fund for Women. Along the same lines, support for the Platform for Women's Land and Water Rights in Southern Africa led the Southern Africa Development Community in setting up a land desk to advocate for national land policies that protect women's interests and rights.

See Also: Children's Rights; HIV/AIDS: Africa; Representation of Women in Government, International.

Further Readings

Aphane, Mary-Joyce D. "Multiple Jeopardy: Domestic Violence and Women's Search for Justice in Swaziland." Mbabane, Swaziland: Women and Law in Southern Africa, 2001.

Buseh, Aaron G., et al. "Cultural and Gender Issues Related to HIV/AIDS Prevention in Rural Swaziland:

A Focus Group Analysis." *Health Care for Women International*, v.23/2 (2009).

Hlanze, Zakhe and Lolo Mkhabela. *Beyond Inequalities: Women in Swaziland*. Harare: Southern African Research and Development Centre, Women in Development Southern Africa Awareness–University of Western Cape, 1998.

Soledad Vieitez-Cerdeño
University of Granada

Sweatshops

The "sweatshop" concept, which originated during the Industrial Revolution in 19th-century England, refers to a workplace where workers were employed for piecework under a subcontracting system. In this system, business owners had no contracts with the sweatshop workers individually. Instead, they hired middlemen to manage workers and workshops on their behalf. The middlemen, whose contracts were based on the piecework factory workers performed, pressured workers to make their productivity rates as high as possible.

The subcontracting system also enabled middlemen to earn more by maximizing the margin between what they received for contracts and what they paid workers. The lower the workers' wages, the greater the profits for middlemen. Thus, profits were derived from the "sweat" of workers exploited by business owners represented by middlemen who invested as little money as possible in labor.

Sweatshop laborers were the weakest members of their society, coming from the most desperate and vulnerable classes. They were often children and women who had no bargaining power for living wages. Sweatshop workers were forced to work excessively long shifts for minimal wages. They endured hazardous conditions, often without safety protections or any knowledge of the danger. This inhumane treatment of factory labor was a central principle of sweatshops, which were geared to maximizing profits at the workers' expense.

Globalization and Women

In contrast to how sweatshops emerged in response to demands for cheap labor during the Industrial Revolution, today's sweatshops are consequences of globalization. Free-trade agreements are key factors in globalized relationships between developed countries such as the United States, Canada, and Japan and various developing nations. These agreements lifted or lowered barriers such as taxes, labor laws, and environmental restrictions, which contributed to expansion of market access and foreign investment.

The North American Free Trade Agreement (NAFTA) between the United States and Mexico was ratified to increase trade through the development of export-oriented industry in Mexico. On one hand, NAFTA helped reduce chronically high unemployment in Mexico. Newly developed export processing zones (EPXs) such as *maquiladoras* attracted multinational corporations (MNCs), creating sweatshop employment for local citizens. On the other hand, NAFTA failed to address wage standards, safety regulations, and health concerns that affect factory workers. While trade agreements brought economic growth and market expansion, they also fostered global exploitation of sweatshop workers, especially women.

Similar to their 19th-century counterparts, contemporary sweatshop workers are employed under subcontracting systems instead of being directly hired by corporations. According to a 2007 study, approximately 60 percent of factory workers in Mexico's electronics industry were employed by temporary agencies. As more women were brought into the global economy as cheap labor, sweatshops became predominately female. Women are considered more suitable than men are for repetitive tasks, such as sewing garment pieces and assembling small parts, because of their presumed "feminine qualities" of patience, dexterity, and obedience.

Young, uneducated women with little or no knowledge about basic rights for workers or working experiences are especially preferred. They were less likely to unionize or challenge the company for better treatment. Consequently, young female workers tend to be victimized by profit-oriented corporate strategies such as violations of human rights and safety standards. Most victims of industrial disasters such as fires and factory explosions are young female workers. An industrial fire that occurred in a toy factory in Thailand in 1993 was one of the worst industrial disasters in capitalist history, causing 188 deaths and 469 causalities. Most of the dead were rural

Hazardous working conditions such as unsafe equipment, toxic chemicals, poor ventilation, high noise levels, strong fumes, polluted air, high production quotas, and long periods of machine-paced repetitive motion lead to a wide range of health problems.

women who came to the city in search of jobs, some as young as 13 years of age.

Special Pressures on Young Women

Some exploitative, discriminative practices are gendered and specifically target female workers. Even though young women are recruited, pregnant women are excluded from being hired. Pregnancy discrimination takes various forms: pregnancy testing for job applicants, sporadic pregnancy monitoring through humiliating means, and forced resignation when discovered to be pregnant. Women are vulnerable to sexual harassment by factory managers or supervisors, who use sex to intimidate and punish female subordinates. Sexual abuse and violence, including propositions and rape, are common in gendered power relationships.

Hazardous working conditions such as unsafe equipment, toxic chemicals, poor ventilation, high noise levels, strong fumes, polluted air, high pro-duction quotas, and long periods of machine-paced repetitive motion lead to a wide range of health problems. Reproductive health problems are gender specific. These include irregular menstruation, premature pregnancies and miscarriages; and babies born with birth defects, disabilities, or low birth weights. Long-term effects of exposure to hazardous workplaces are also serious concerns. When factory workers demand higher wages and better working conditions, MNCs that own sweatshops shift production to other countries or regions. Nike, for example, first moved production from the United States to Taiwan and South Korea, and later to Indonesia, Vietnam, and China in pursuit of the lowest production costs.

Sweatshops are not unique to developing counties. They also operate in industrial countries like the United States. According to the Department of Labor, half the factories in the U.S. garment industry failed to follow basic labor laws. Violation of labor laws lead to exploitation of factory workers, which resembles conditions for sweatshop workers in developing countries. Similar to the identities of sweatshop workers in developing countries, most garment factory workers in the United States are women. Many of these young and uneducated women are recent immigrants, some are undocumented workers, primarily Asians and Latinas. They tend to lack English language skills, knowledge of their rights as workers, and resources to protect themselves from exploitation.

See Also: Environmental Issues, Women and; Global Feminism; Health Insurance Issues; Human Rights Campaign; Management Styles, Gender Theories; Maquiladoras; Migrant Workers; Sexual Harassment; Unions.

Further Readings
Abell, Hilary. "Endangering Women's Health for Profit: Health and Safety in Mexico's Maquiladoras." *Development in Practice*, v.9/5 (1999).
Foo, Lora Jo and Nikki Fortunato Bas. "Free Trade's Looming Threat to the World's Garment Workers." *Sweatshop Watch* (October 30, 2003). http://digitalcommons.ilr.cornell.edu/cgi/viewcontent.cgi?article=1000&context=globaldocs (accessed June 2010).
Greider, William. "These Dark Satanic Mills." In David M. Newman and Jodi O'Brien, eds., *Sociology: Exploring the Architecture of Everyday Life*, 5th ed. Thousand Oaks, CA: Pine Forge Press, 2004.
Paterson, Kent. "Temping Down Labor Rights: The Manpowerization of Mexico." Corpwatch (January 6, 2010). http://www.corpwatch.org/article.php?id=15496 (accessed June 2010).
Webster University. "Woman and Global Human Rights: Women and Sweatshops." http://www.webster.edu/~woolflm/sweatshops.html (accessed June 2010).

Ayako Mizumura
University of Kansas

Sweden

Formerly a major military power, Sweden opted for neutrality in both World Wars. With a healthy economy and no need for a post-war military build-up, Sweden was able to focus on building an extensive social welfare system. By the early 21st century, only 15 percent of the population lived in rural areas, and 1 percent of the Gross National Product was derived from agriculture. Despite a recession that began late in 2008 and a 9.3 unemployment rate, Sweden ranks 27th in the world in per capita income ($36,800) and is seventh on the United Nations Development Programme list of countries with very high human development.

Sweden's indigenous population consists of Swedes with Finnish or Sami minorities. From a religious perspective, Sweden is largely Lutheran, 87 percent. Women's rights started early in Sweden, in the 18th century, but it was not until 1919 that Swedish women regained the right to vote in national elections. By that time, women were already playing a significant role in party politics.

The first women took their seats in Sweden's Parliament following the 1921 elections. As the 20th century progressed, equality for women became an inherent part of life in this northern European country, and Sweden became known as one of the most female-friendly nations in the world, charging the equal opportunity ombudsman with monitoring women's rights. Despite its progressive stance on women's rights, Sweden, like virtually every other country in the world, has a problem with domestic violence and human trafficking. Sweden has one of the lowest infant mortality rates (2.75 deaths per 1,000 live births) in the world. Female life expectancy is 83.26 for females and 79.59 years for males. The median age for females is 42.6 years. Women have a fertility rate of 1.67 children. Sweden, which has a 99 percent literacy rate for both males and females, ranks 21st in the world in educational spending, and girls stay in school longer than boys, 17 years versus 15 years.

After decades of steadily gaining in representation, women experienced a sharp decline in the 1990s. The Support Stockings, a feminist group composed of women from all fields, responded by opening public debate on women in politics. After the 1994 elections, women accounted for half of all government positions. By the beginning of the 21st century, Sweden had the highest percentage of women in Parliament in the world, 43 percent, and half of cabinet ministers were female. In 2007, women filled 165 of 349 seats parliamentary seats and 10 of 22 cabinet seats.

As a result of its gender equality policies, Sweden topped the list in the 2007 Global Gender Gap Report.

At that time, 79 percent of Swedish women worked outside the home. Relative wage equity exists in Sweden, but many women work only part time. Sweden has instituted a generous family leave policy that allows both mothers and fathers to take a year's leave at 80 percent of their salaries. Additionally, parents with school-age children may opt for six-hour workdays. Sweden also provides tax support for mothers who stay at home with their children.

To cope with violence against women, the government strictly enforces all rape laws, including those dealing with spousal rape. Punishment is more severe for repeat offenders and for those in close relationships with their victims. The government provides extensive support for victims, including providing new identities and homes to keep them away from their abusers. Funding for domestic violence services is shared by national and local governments. In 2004, some legislators developed the idea of funding programs for victims by levying taxes on all males. Sweden also has a problem with trafficking. Some women are forcibly brought into the country, and others are trafficked through Sweden into Asian countries.

See Also: Domestic Violence; Infant Mortality; Trafficking, Women and Children; United Nations Development Fund for Women.

Further Readings

Biswas, Ranjita. "Sweden: His and Hers: The Swedish Balance." *Women's Feature Service* (January 5, 2009).

Breneman, Anne R. and Rebecca A. Mbuh. *Women in the New Millennium: The Global Revolution.* Lanham, MD: Hamilton Books, 2006.

Central Intelligence Agency. "The World Factbook: Sweden." https://www.cia.gov/library/publications/the -world-factbook/geos/sw.html (accessed June 2010).

Douglas, Carol Anne and Palmer Gibbs. "Sweden: Lawmakers Propose Tax on Men." *off our backs,* v.34/11–12 (November–December 2004).

Smith, Beverley. "Public Recognition for Women's Unpaid Labor." *WIN News,* v.29/2 (Spring 2003).

U.S. Department of State. "2008 Human Rights Report: Sweden." http://www.state.gov/g/drl/rls/hrrpt/2008 /eur/119107.htm (accessed June 2010).

Elizabeth Rholetter Purdy
Independent Scholar

Sweet Honey in the Rock

Sweet Honey in the Rock is an a cappella ensemble of African American women based in Washington, D.C. The group's musical and vocal repertoire encompasses many genres, including African American spirituals, congregational songs, gospels, blues, hymns, lullabies, and chants, as well as the more modern sounds of jazz, hip-hop, rap, and reggae. Thematically, Sweet Honey addresses issues relating to the worldwide struggle for justice, working against racism, war, and homophobia and for the rights of women, children, and differently abled persons.

Sweet Honey was founded in 1973 by Bernice Johnson Reagon as an ensemble that included Reagon, Carol Maillard, Louise Robinson, and Mie. The first song Reagon taught the group was one she had heard growing up in southwest Georgia, based on a passage in Psalm 81:16 about honey emerging from rocks to reward the faithful. When Reagon heard the quartet's harmonized chorus, she named the group accordingly.

Approximately 25 different women have sung with the group since it started, but its founding principles of activism, education, and social change have remained constant. From its initial four singers, the group expanded to five, and then added a sixth—a sign language interpreter—in 1980 to facilitate communication with members of the deaf community. Reagon served as the group's artistic director and chief composer/arranger until her retirement in 2004.

The group's achievements are remarkable, considering that initially its members held full-time jobs and sang part time. For instance, Reagon worked with the Smithsonian Institution in various capacities for 25 years, serving as researcher for the Festival of American Folklife, director of the Program in African American Culture, and curator in the National Museum of American History's Division of Community Life.

She became a distinguished professor of history at American University in 1993 and also taught at Spelman College. Maillard is an actress who has performed professionally on and off Broadway, in Hollywood films, and on television programs. Robinson left Sweet Honey for a career in the theater and then founded another a cappella quintet, Street Sounds, before returning to Sweet Honey in 2004. Ysaye Maria Barnwell, who joined the group in 1979, holds a doctorate in speech pathology and is a composer in her

Sweet Honey in the Rock live at Ravinia in July 2006. The group's musical and vocal repertoire encompasses many genres including African American spirituals, congregational songs, and chants, as well as the more modern sounds of jazz, hip hop, and rap.

own right. Aisha Kahlil (joining in 1981) and her sister, Nitanju Bolade Casel (joining in 1985), have had extensive careers in African dance, choreography, and jazz improvisation.

Sweet Honey has performed on six continents around the world, averaging 40–50 concerts per year. Since its founding, the group has released some 25 LPs, CDs, and DVDs, receiving two Grammy Awards for its work. Album titles—such as *Go in Grace, Raise Your Voice, The Women Gather, Freedom Song, Sacred Ground, Still on the Journey, All for Freedom, Feel Something Drawing Me On,* and *We All . . . Everyone of Us*—confirm the group's commitment to issues of justice and freedom for all.

See Also: Arts, Women in the; Black Churches; Ecofeminism; Hip Hop; LGBTQ.

Further Readings

Barnwell, Ysaye Maria, ed. *Continuum: The First Songbook of Sweet Honey in the Rock.* Southwest Harbor, ME: Contemporary A Cappella, 1999.

Pérez, Marvette. "Interview With Bernice Johnson Reagon." *Radical History Review,* no.68 (1997).

Reagon, Bernice Johnson, ed. *We Who Believe in Freedom: Sweet Honey in the Rock—Still on the Journey.* New York: Anchor Books, 1993.

Sweet Honey in the Rock. http://www.sweethoney.com (accessed November 2009).

James I. Deutsch
Smithsonian Institution

Swimming

The Fédération Internationale de Natation (FINA) organizes and regulates swimming races in the freestyle, backstroke, breaststroke, butterfly, and individual medley events, as well as competitions in diving, synchronized swimming, water polo, and open-water swimming. Since 1908, FINA has recognized and verified world records, established and modified the rules for each discipline, and organized the aquatics events at the Olympic Games and FINA world championships. Women have accomplished many feats in the sport of swimming but have faced many challenges as well.

Bathing emerged as a popular leisure activity in the early 1800s to enhance cleanliness and good health. Consequently, cities and private clubs built numerous baths and indoor pools, and swimming became an acceptable recreational pursuit for women in most areas of the world. Strict rules and social norms separated women and men at public swimming facilities because mixed bathing contravened acceptable standards of behavior. In many countries, public swimming facilities remained segregated by sex until the 1950s. The cycling craze of the 1890s facilitated the growth and acceptance of women's swimming. The invention of the safety bicycle enabled women to travel to the water to swim without their husbands and families, which led to dress reform, greater independence, and an increased number of recreational activities for women.

Competitive Sport

Competitive swimming emerged as a sport in the mid-1800s, but women, often the unmarried daughters of swimming instructors, did not begin entering swimming races until the 1870s. Prior to this time, women's roles in swimming involved passively watching and supporting the male competitors. Carnivals known as swimming galas, where participants demonstrated "scientific swimming" techniques, were popular at the end of the 19th century. Combining swimming, dance, and gymnastics, swimming galas were considered less rigorous and physically demanding than competitive swimming and, therefore, more appropriate for women to participate.

In 1907, Annette Kellerman of Australia performed "water ballets" throughout the United States in a glass tank filled with water, and many spectators found her sleeveless and legless attire controversial. At that time women's swimming costumes were designed to preserve women's modesty, not facilitate ease of movement through the water. Charlotte Epstein, considered the mother of American swimming, fought for bathing suit reform as well as the addition of women's water polo events and longer swimming races equal to the men's distances. Advo-

cates from the National Women's Life Saving League campaigned for women to be permitted to swim without stockings. The popularity of sunbathing in the 1920s, the rationing of fabrics during World War II, and the introduction of the bikini in Paris ultimately led to relaxed social expectations regarding women's swimming attire. The size of swimsuits reappeared as an issue of contention in 2008 after swimmers wearing full-body, highly engineered bathing suits that increase swimmers' buoyancy and reduce their drag through the water set numerous world records. As of 2010, competitive swimsuits must not extend beyond the neck, shoulders, and ankles and cannot be more than 1mm thick.

Olympic Games

The Olympics included women's swimming events for the first time at the 1912 Olympic Games in Stockholm. Men competed in swimming events at the first modern Olympic Games in 1896 and at each Olympic Games thereafter. FINA did not achieve gender parity in the number of men's and women's events included on the swimming program at the Olympic Games until 1996 in Atlanta. The swimming events at the 2008 Olympic Games in Beijing included 17 women's and 17 men's events in the pool; however, the women competed in the 800m freestyle while the men compete in the 1,500m freestyle. In Beijing, swimmers competed in women's and men's 10km open water swimming events for the first time. At the 2008 Paralympic Games, the swimming program included 11 women's events, 12 men's events, and four relays for competitors in several classifications.

For most of the 20th century, swimmers from Australia and the United States dominated the women's swimming events at the Olympic Games and FINA world championships. However, in the 1970s and 1980s, women from East Germany achieved unsurpassed success in the pool, and athletes from China dominated women's swimming in the 1990s. While none of the East German swimmers tested positive for banned substances, files made public after the reunification of Germany show that swimmers were systematically given anabolic steroids without their consent. A large number of positive drug tests from female Chinese swimmers in the 1990s led to China's suspension from the 1995 Pan Pacific swimming competition. FINA's subsequent investigation concluded that doping in women's swimming in China stemmed from the economic opportunities created by success rather than a system of state-controlled doping.

Several women made significant contributions to swimming and are well known throughout the world. American Gertrude Ederle was the first woman to swim across the English Channel. Her time of 14 hours and 39 minutes in 1928 broke the men's record by almost two hours and demonstrated that women's bodies could handle long-distance swimming. Other well-known swimmers include Australian Dawn Fraser, East German Kristin Otto, and American Dara Torres. Fraser won three consecutive gold medals in the 100m freestyle at the Olympic Games in 1956, 1960, and 1964 and held the world record in the event from 1956 until 1972. Otto won six gold medals in 1988 at the Olympic Games, but her remarkable feat is now thought to have been fueled by the East German doping program. In 2008, Torres competed in her fifth Olympic Games and, at 41 years old, became the oldest woman to win an Olympic swimming medal.

See Also: Olympics, Summer; Sports, Women in; Steroid Use; Torres, Dara.

Further Readings

Colwin, C. M. *Breakthrough Swimming*. Champaign, IL: Human Kinetics, 2002.

Silver, M. *Golden Girl: How Natalie Coughlin Fought Back, Challenged Conventional Wisdom, and Became America's Olympic Champion*. Emmaus, PA: Rodale, 2006.

Torres, D. and E. Weil. *Age Is Just a Number: Achieve Your Dreams at Any Stage in Your Life*. New York: Broadway Press, 2010.

Sarah Teetzel
University of Manitoba

Switzerland

Switzerland is a landlocked country in central Europe sharing borders with France, Germany, Austria, and Italy. Swiss citizens enjoy a high standard of living with a 2009 per capita gross domestic product of $41,600

(18th highest in the world) and low unemployment of 3.7 percent. Literacy is nearly universal for both men and women, and life expectancy is the 10th highest in the world at 78.03 years for men and 83.83 years for women. The country is multicultural, with four national languages, and the population is primarily German (65 percent), with the largest minorities French (18 percent) and Italian (10 percent). The population is mostly Roman Catholic (41.8 percent), Protestant (35.3 percent), and Muslim (4.3 percent).

Women in Switzerland only received the right to vote in 1971 and the country is in some ways caught between a culture that dictates traditional sex roles and a modern world in which they are less relevant. Currently, the World Economic Forum rates Switzerland as one of the most gender equal in the world. On a scale from zero (inequality) to one (total equality), Switzerland had an overall score of 0.743, 13th highest in the world in 2009. In educational attainment, Switzerland scored 0.979 (88th highest in the world). In health and survival, the country scored 0.978 (59th); in economic participation, 0.685 (48th); and in political empowerment, 0.169 (12th).

Women in the Labor Force

Seventy-five percent of Swiss women are in the labor force, as compared to 87 percent of men. Women's income overall is about 66 percent that of men. Women constitute 29 percent of Switzerland's Parliament members and 43 percent of government ministerial positions. Ruth Dreifuss was the first woman elected President of the Confederation (head of state) in 1999. Other women prominent in Swiss government include Eveline Widmer-Schlumpf, since 2007 head of the Department of Justice; Doris Leuthard, since 2006 head of Economic Affairs; and Micheline Calmy-Rey, since 2002 head of Foreign Affairs.

Swiss women enjoy a high level of support for maternity childcare and gynecological concerns, although less than that provided by some other northern European countries. Maternity leave pays 80 percent of salary for 98 days, and family allowances are paid to parents with children, generally up to age 16 or 19. The level of support and age qualifications is set by each canton or territory. However, childcare is a problem, as it is handled separately by each canton and the number of places is generally considered insufficient.

Abortion is available on demand, and 82 percent of Swiss women have reported using contraceptives. All births are attended by skilled health personnel, and the infant and maternal mortality ratios are low at four per 1,000 live births and five per 100,000 live births, respectively. Save the Children ranks Switzerland 14th out of 43 More Developed Countries on its Mothers' Index, 16th on its Woman's Index and 17th on its Children's Index.

See Also: Childcare; Equal Pay; Infant Mortality; Government, Women in; Maternal Mortality; Parental Leave; Representation of Women in Government, International.

Further Readings

Central Intelligence Agency. "The World Factbook: Switzerland." https://www.cia.gov/library/publications/the-world-factbook/geos/sz.html (accessed June 2010).

History of Switzerland. "The Long Way to Women's Right to Vote in Switzerland." http://history-switzerland.geschichte-schweiz.ch/chronology-womens-right-vote-switzerland.html (accessed June 2010).

U.S. Department of State. "2005 Country Report on Human Rights Practices in Switzerland." http://www.state.gov/g/drl/rls/hrrpt/2005/61678.htm (accessed June 2010).

Sarah Boslaugh
Washington University School of Medicine

Syria

Syria is a Middle Eastern country that shares borders with Turkey, Iraq, Jordan, Israel, and Lebanon, as well as with a Mediterranean Sea coastline. The population of approximately 21.8 million is primarily Arab (90.3 percent) and Muslim (74 percent Sunni Muslim, 16 percent other Muslim). The legal system is based on French and Ottoman civil law, while the family court system is based on Islamic law. In 2009, Syria increased the punishment to men convicted of "honor killing" of female relatives suspected of illicit sexual behavior.

The World Economic Forum rates Syria as one of the most unequal countries in the world with regard to gender. On the Gender Gap Index, which ranks countries on a scale of zero (unequal) to one (equal), Syria received an overall score of 0.607, ranking it 121st out of 134 surveyed countries. On health and survival, Syria scored 0.976 (68th in the world) and on educational attainment Syria received a 0.931 (105th). In addition, on economic participation and opportunity, Syria scored 0.461 (120th), and on political empowerment it received a 0.060 (116th).

Only 22 percent of Syrian women are in the labor force, as opposed to 80 percent of Syrian men. Women earn an average of 68 percent of what men receive for comparable work. Women constitute about 15 percent of Syrian professional and technical workers and 40 percent of legislators, senior officials, and managers. Women hold 12 percent of the seats in the nation's parliament and about 6 percent of ministerial positions. Literacy is lower for women (73.6 percent) than for men (86 percent), although currently most girls, 92 percent, attend elementary school.

Save the Children ranks Syria near the bottom of Tier II or Less Developed Countries on issues relating to women and children's health and welfare. In 2009, Syria ranked 58th out of 75 countries on the Mothers' Index, 62nd on the Women's Index, and 55th on the Children's Index. Syria has a total fertility rate of 3.12 children per woman, and 93 percent of births are attended by skilled personnel. More than half of married Syrian women report using contraceptives. Infant and maternal mortality are both high at 12 per 1,000 live births and 130 per 100,000 live births, respectively. Maternity leave is provided for 50 days at 70 percent of wages.

Syria's population includes about 305,000 internally displaced persons from the Golan Heights, 1.0 to 1.4 million Iraqi refugees, and about 500,000 Palestinian refugees. Syria is a Tier 3 country regarding human trafficking, meaning that the government has not made significant efforts to deal with the problem. Syria is both a destination and transition country for women and children trafficked for forced labor and sexual exploitation, and legal foreign workers within Syria have been forced into conditions of involuntary servitude.

See Also: Contraception Methods; Honor Killings; Honor Suicides; Islam; Representation of Women in Government, International; Shari`a Law; Trafficking, Women and Children.

Further Readings

Central Intelligence Agency. "The World Factbook: Syria." https://www.cia.gov/library/publications/the-world -factbook/geos/sy.html (accessed June 2010).

Lawson, Fred. *Demystifying Syria (SOAS Middle East Issues Series).* London: Saqi Books, 2010.

Leverett, Flynt. *Inheriting Syria: Bashar's Trial by Fire.* Washington, DC: Brookings Institution Press, 2005.

Rubin, Barry. *The Truth About Syria.* New York: Palgrave Macmillan, 2008.

Sinjab, Lina. "Honour Crime Fear of Syria Women." *BBC News* (October 12, 2007). http://news.bbc.co.uk/2/hi /middle_east/7042249.stm

Sarah Boslaugh
Washington University School of Medicine

T

Tajikistan

The central Asian republic of Tajikistan has had a diverse history. Despite conflicts designed to prevent a Bolshevik takeover of central Asia after 1917, the Soviets gained control in 1925. Four years later, they established the Tajik SSR. A five-year civil war broke out in 1991 with the dissolution of the Soviet Union. While most former Soviet republics have become economically vulnerable, Tajikistan is the poorest among them with a per capita income of only $1,800. Sixty percent of the population lives below the poverty line.

Nearly 80 percent of the population is Tajikand, and 85 percent of Tajikistanis are Sunni Muslims. Since the post-Soviet return to traditionalism, there has been little separation of church and state. Even though women have a constitutional right to equality, in practice, they are not treated equally. Female status continues to fall, leaving women vulnerable to a variety of ills including poverty, exploitation and abuse. Despite their dependence on males, many women have become single mothers resulting from abandonment, or because male heads-of-household were killed in the civil war.

Women in Tajikistan Society

By some estimates, 90 percent of all Tajikistani husbands have more than one wife. Women are extremely vulnerable to societal factors that allow human trafficking and girls as young as 13 years old are forced to marry. Women's groups report that as many as 70 percent of wives are abused by their husbands and in-laws. Because women are economically dependent, they have limited opportunities for escape. Consequently, there is a high rate of suicide among abused women. Due to a tradition of arranged marriages, even women of high social standing have little say in whom they marry; often, they have only brief contact with potential spouses. Many marriages are informal agreements, leaving wives without legal protection. Except in the case of a legally married first wife, wives in polygamous marriages have no legal rights at all.

There is only limited access to employment in Tajikistan, and at least half of the labor force works outside the country. Wives are allowed to work only when their husbands agree. Nearly 75 percent of the population continues to live in rural areas, although only 23 percent of the workforce is employed in agriculture. The median age for Tajikistani females is 22.4 years. With an infant mortality rate of 35.91 deaths per 1,000 live births, females have a considerably higher survival rate than male infants, whose mortality is 45.9 deaths per 1,000 live births. That advantage continues into adulthood, and females have a life expectancy of 68.52 years compared to 62.29 years for males. Tajikistani women have a fertility rate of 2.99 children per woman.

Tajikistan ranks 132nd in the world in educational spending. The female literacy rate is 99.2 percent only slightly lower than the 99.5 percent of males. Girls

Shaodat Sharipova and her six children received emergency heating from a USAID-backed effort in Tajikistan.

goes to school for only 10 years compared to 12 years for boys, and few women pursue higher education.

See Also: Domestic Violence; Polygamy, Cross-Cultural; United Nations Development Fund for Women.

Further Readings

Central Intelligence Agency. "The World Factbook: Tajikistan." http://www.cia.gov/library/publications/the -world-factbook/geos/ti.html (accessed February 2010).

Oates, Lauryn. "Tajikistan: A Fundamental Concern." *Herizons,* v.21/1 (Summer 2007).

Organisation for Economic Co-operation and Development. "Gender Equality and Social Institutions in Tajikistan." http://genderindex.org/country/tajikistan (accessed February 2010).

Elizabeth Rholetter Purdy
Independent Scholar

Take Back the Night

Take Back the Night marches are a centerpiece of college and university-based feminist organizing in the contemporary United States. Growing out of 1970s national and transnational activism supporting greater inclusion of women in all aspects of society and seeking greater attention to the violence women face at the hands of family, associates, and strangers, this often annual event combines direct action tactics with support and education.

History

While U.S. women have long been involved in public protests in support of feminist as well as other goals, the late 1960s and 1970s saw an increase in specifically feminist organizing. One strand of this activism focused on sexual assault and the sexual exploitation of women in the pornography industry. Maria Bevacqua traces the concept of Take Back the Night to a pamphlet titled *Stop Rape* published in 1971 by Women Against Rape (WAR) in Detroit, Michigan. A few years later, a prominent anthology called *Take Back the Night* dedicated to "the thousands of women in this country and abroad who recognize the hatefulness and harmfulness of pornography, and who are organizing to stop it now" emerged chronicling the movement. For its editor Laura Lederer and many other 1970s organizers, taking back the night meant demanding that women be safe not only from sexual assault but also from prostitution and other forms of sex work that they linked to violence against women.

In 1976, a group called Women Against Violence in Pornography and the Media (WAVPM) was formed. The San Francisco–based group's first action was a march down Broadway, a recognized porn strip, to protest pornography and live sex shows. Six hundred women attended the march. Marches continued throughout the early 1980s, eventually moving from the impoverished Tenderloin district to North Beach, an area attracting a wealthier clientele.

In 1978, they sponsored a conference called "Feminist Perspectives on Pornography," including a Take Back the Night March sometimes described as the first. However, archival documents identify marches in Boston, Denver, Philadelphia, and London in October 1978, prior to WAVPM's November 18, 1978, event. Bevacqua also identifies a 1977 memorial speech called "Take Back the Night" given by Anne Pride at a march sponsored by the Pittsburgh Alliance Against Rape. These events may have been modeled after international protests that began in Belgium in 1976 during the International Tribunal on Crimes

Against Women. Since 1977, events called Take Back the Night or Reclaim the Night have been held in the United Kingdom, Australia, India, Italy, Germany, Canada, and the United States.

Like other institutions stemming from the women's liberation movement including consciousness-raising groups, music festivals, rape crisis centers, and feminist bookstores, Take Back the Night was designed to provide a place for women to speak the truths of their lives in a culture privileging male perspectives and experiences. Central aspects of Take Back the Night marches include a nighttime procession temporarily taking streets often unsafe for women, speak-out sessions, speakers and musicians addressing violence against women, information about services, and on-sight support for those in need.

Other U.S. marches during the 1970s also targeted sexual violence and sometimes addressed other forms of social exclusion. On April 28, 1979, in response to the murders of 11 black women in the Boston area, between 400 and 500 people, mostly women, marched from Boston Common to then-mayor Kevin White's home in Mount Vernon Square. The event was organized by a coalition including the Combahee River Collective and other women of color organizations and emphasized the confluence of racism and sexism much more than most early Take Back the Night marches in the United States.

Contemporary Marches

Continued concerns about sexual assault influence many university groups and a few communities to organize annual Take Back the Night marches in the United States. April is Sexual Assault Awareness Month for many schools and organizations and marches often occur as one part of the month's programming. Take Back the Night marches ideally provide a forum for translating private emotions of grief and rage into a collective, political response.

Controversies about inclusion are endemic to Take Back the Night. Concerns about gender are particularly salient due to Take Back the Night's roots in the 1970s and 1980s movement for women's rights. However, as observed by many scholars and activists, race and gender cannot be separated. Writing about Reclaim the Night marches in the United Kingdom, for example, Kum-Kum Bhavnani and Margaret Coulson describe demonstrations moving through black neighborhoods, insinuating that they are the loci of violence while demanding greater police presence, a request that ignores histories of police brutality against people of color. Racism positions women from different backgrounds in different relationships to social power and discussions of violence against women that do not address other forms of violence do not adequately challenge social structures that affect many women (and people of other genders).

Justifying the exclusion of some people (in this case, men) is always interwoven with intentional and unintentional exclusions of others (in this case, transgendered people and people of color). The exclusion of men is also based on a binary understanding of gender in which men perpetrate violence and women experience it. This framework ignores the experiences of transgender people, men survivors of sexual violence, women perpetrators, and people in same-sex relationships. Contemporary marches grapple with how to best connect to Take Back the Night's history while addressing the needs of current survivors. Many are inclusive of transgender people and most have spaces where men are welcome. However, questions about inclusion continue to structure conversations about this now annual event.

See Also: Dating Violence; Rape Crisis Centers; Social Justice Activism; Violence Against Women Act.

Further Readings

Bevacqua, Maria. *Rape on the Public Agenda: Feminism and the Politics of Sexual Assault.* Lebanon, NH: Northeastern University Press, 2000.

Bhavnani, Kum-Kum and Margaret Coulson, "Transforming Socialist Feminism: The Challenge of Racism." In Kum-Kum Bhavnani, ed., *Feminism and "Race."* Oxford UK: Oxford University Press, 2001.

Lederer, Laura, ed. *Take Back the Night: Women on Pornography.* New York: Willliam Morrow, 1980.

Take Back the Night. "A History of Take Back the Night." http://www.takebackthenight.org/history.html (accessed November 2009).

Vance, Carole S., ed. *Pleasure and Danger: Exploring Female Sexuality.* London: Routledge, 1984.

Elizabeth G. Currans
College of William and Mary

Taliban

Taliban originally designated the militant Islamic movement that opposed the mujahideen warring factions involved in the civil war that followed the retreat of the Soviet army from Afghanistan in 1989. Since their gradual and ongoing overthrow from late 2001 forward, the term describes a loose alliance of insurgents who have been continuously fighting against Afghan government forces and their Western allies. Despite formal differences and compromises with modernity that include the use of advanced technology and the integration of global capitalism, all groups covered by the term *Taliban* are united in their defense of personal patriarchal privilege and a uniquely repressive attitude toward women.

Taleb (plural *Taliban*) is an Arabic word meaning pupil/student of Islam and the eponymous movement indeed originated in madrassas (religious schools) in Pakistan, where hundreds of thousands of destitute orphans from refugee camps in Pakistan were given rudimentary board and lodging and schooled in rigorous Saudi Wahhabi Islam as well as extreme anti-Western propaganda. These institutions were funded by Saudi Arabia with the support of Pakistan's pro-Fundamentalist premier, Zia Ul-Haq, both allies of the United States in their fight against the Soviet Union in Afghanistan. The religious and political indoctrination including extreme misogyny paved the way for the Fundamentalist movement that was to control Afghanistan; these students in the madrassas were ideal candidates for recruitment by Al-Qaeda.

Initial Acceptance

Motivated less by political power than by a desire to rid the country of the anarchy, violence, and lawlessness engendered by competing warlords, the Taliban, basing themselves on Fundamentalist Qur'anic principles, were well received by Afghan populations exhausted by war and strife. These had been alarmed by the Communist attempts at gender equality and so were relieved by the Taliban's reactionary views on women. As a Pashtun movement, the Taliban were welcomed in Pashtun areas at a time when this community (over 40 percent of the total population) had been ousted from power for the first time in Afghan history by the feuding warlords. After having gained control of Kandahar (1994), Herat (1995), and then Kabul (1996), with financial assistance coming from Osama bin Laden, they declared the Islamic Emirate of Afghanistan, occupying 95 percent of the country, save part of the northeast.

During their reign, the Taliban promoted an unique form of ultrapuritanical Political Islam, strongly influenced by Saudi Fundamentalism and harsh Pashtun customary law. Music, dancing, films, images, photographs, Western fashions, and alcohol were made illegal. The cult of local saints, folk practices, and women's regional costumes were banned, as was the cultivation of opium poppies and the sale of the resin. Ethnic cleansing against the Hazaras was instituted. Punishments took the form of public amputations and executions (by shooting or stoning), all of which sent shock waves through Afghan society, which had hitherto practiced its own folk version of Islam.

Pre-Islamic works of art were destroyed as idols, hence the notorious dynamiting of the Bamyan Buddhas and the wholesale destruction of artifacts in the Kabul Museum. Women were completely excluded from public space, from the workplace to the school and even hospitals if men were present. The application of what became a veritable gender apartheid was in the hands of the Department of the Promotion of Virtue and the Prevention of Vice, whose zealots policed women's activities: in hospital wards, in private homes where secret literacy classes were held, in the street where the sound of a woman's heel hitting the pavement was enough to bring the whip down. One result of this policy is that a whole generation of Afghans—boys and girls—was deprived of schooling and basic healthcare, because both primary school teachers and nurses (as well as many often Soviet-trained doctors) were female.

The Taliban were overthrown by American military action, in retaliation for the destruction of the Twin Towers of the World Trade Center in New York City on September 11, 2001. Nevertheless, Taliban-inspired insurgency remains powerful, supported by counterparts in Pakistan and the North-West frontier Province (NWFP), financed by Al-Qaeda and drug trafficking. These neo-Taliban present themselves as the legitimate face of "true" Afghanistan in the face of foreign occupation, the defenders of Holy Islam on a permanent jihad (holy war) against Western unbelievers. For this reason, they defend poppy cultivation to support Afghan rural communities' opposition to U.S. antinarcotics policies. Many of their commanders are directly involved and partake in the globalized drug economy. Likewise, they use modern technology and the media, Websites, videos, even songs for propaganda purposes.

Despite promises to build schools for girls, the level of health and education remains abysmal in the areas they dominate, where about 98 percent of women remain illiterate. The neo-Taliban are impeding polio vaccination and other medical care in the provinces under their control, something that is also happening in Taliban areas in Pakistan. Nevertheless, these insurgents are not united; internal strife over narcotics and smuggling, the degree of opportunistic compromise with the government, shifts of alliances with Al-Qaeda, ISI local warlords or U.S. and NATO forces cannot be solved by mullahs, even though the Qur'an is remodeled at will to fit the most extreme situations, including suicide bombers, a concept abhorrent to Afghan mentality.

Even if the Taliban edicts have disappeared, severe discrimination against women has remained as a guarantee of ruthless male domination. This is what unites all the strains of neo-Taliban and most of their rural opponents. Customary practice, presented as Qur'anic law, ensures that women never even get the rights Islam entitles them to, that is to say, a share of inheritance and a minimal say in their lives. In this country, which remains 80 percent rural, marriages are routinely arranged and often forced on girls under 16; extreme violence against women goes unpunished. Maternal and infant mortality figures have barely changed since the fall of the Taliban government.

See Also: Afghanistan; Islam; Wahhabism.

Further Readings

Porter, Patrick. *Military Orientalism, Eastern War Through Western Eyes.* London: Hurst, 2009.

Rashid, Ahmed. *Taliban, Militant Islam, Oil and Fundamentalism in Central Asia.* New Haven, CT: Yale University Press, 2001.

Skaine, Rosemarie. *The Women of Afghanistan Under the Taliban.* Jefferson, NC: McFarland & Company, 2001.

Carol Mann
University of London

Tamang, Stella

Stella Tamang is well known as an innovative activist for women, indigenous populations, and religious minorities, both in her native Nepal and internationally. Her work to promote both social justice and peace has animated ideals and values with practical and applied principals. Through her work as an educator she has developed programs that combine education and practical skill building as a means of overcoming poverty and social dependence. Tamang's promotion of peace emphasizes the importance of women's voices in changing attitudes toward violence. As an activist for peace, justice, and nonviolence, Tamang started Milijuli Nepal and the International Fellowship of Reconciliation, which is based in the Netherlands. She was recognized as one of the 1000 Peace-Women who were jointly nominated for the Nobel Peace prize in 2005.

Stella Tamang was born in Nepal in 1948. She is a member of the indigenous Lama community, and as a Buddhist in a nation that was, until 2008, a Hindu kingdom, Tamang understood the political implications of minority status. Her parents migrated to Burma in search of work when she was a child, affording her an opportunity to study and learn English. These events were key to Tamang's own academic achievement as the first woman in her community to study at university. Through her advantages, she recognized the need for literacy and education as a means to social and political equality. This is particularly important in Nepal, where poverty and years of civil war have kept half a million children out of school—more than 60 percent of them girls. In 2001, the overall literacy rate for women was 42.5 percent compared with 65.1 percent for men.

Education and Career

Tamang began her career as an educator by developing schools for disadvantaged children in her own community. Her first school continues nearly 40 years later as a low-fee secondary school with about 900 students. Designed to meet a different need, the Bikalpa Gyan Kendra (alternative learning center) employs a philosophy Tamang calls "learn and earn" to combat the exploitation of indigenous Tamang girls in the sweatshop-based carpet industry in Kathmandu. Young women are taught skills they can take back to their villages, providing practical economic opportunities and maintaining their dignity and independence while preserving Tamang culture. The residential school program includes sustainable agriculture, market gardening, traditional handicrafts, and basic business skills.

Tamang is the founder of a number of organizations in Nepal that seek to unify indigenous women who have been politically marginalized. In a nation that denies many women legal access to land, Tamang's work ensures they have a voice not only in national women's movements but also in decision making at the national level. Tamang is a strong advocate for indigenous peoples worldwide, taking a leadership and organizational role in many committees and international meetings within the United Nations (UN) and beyond. Most notably she has taken a leadership role in the Commission of the Status of Women, organized by the United Nations Permanent Forum on Indigenous Issues at the UN. She is also founder and chairperson of the South Asia Indigenous Women's Forum (2002), providing a forum in which indigenous women from all over Asia can work together to lobby and advocate at national, regional, and international levels.

Tamang is married to an advocate for indigenous rights in Nepal and has three children, one of whom is a peace activist.

See Also: Alternative Education; Education, Women in; Nepal; Sweatshops.

Further Readings

Dhakal, Sanjaya. "Nepalese Women Under the Shadow of Domestic Violence." *Lancet*, v.371 (2008).

"Nepal's Overburdened Women." *Economist*, v.358/39 (2001).

Peace Women Across the Globe. "Stella Tamang." http:// www.1000peacewomen.org/eng/friedensfrauen_bio graphien_gefunden.php?WomenID=196 (accessed March 2010).

United Nations Permanent Forum on Indigenous Peoples. "Indigenous Women Today: At Risk and a Force for Change." http://www.unclef.com/hr/indigenousforum /women.html (accessed March 2010).

Jill Allison
Memorial University of Newfoundland

Tanzania

Tanzania, a sub-Saharan, east African country, has a total population of 41 million. Women make up roughly 52 percent of the population and have an average life expectancy of 53 years of age. The acquired immune deficiency syndrome (AIDS) epidemic in Tanzania affects life expectancy and infant mortality, resulting in lower population growth.

Women account for 80 percent of the labor in rural areas and 60 percent of the food production, yet 60 percent of women live in poverty. Women farm small plots, sell produce, and provide the basic needs (food, clothing, and medical care) for their families. However, rural African women rarely have rights to their husband's income and are often expected to pay for incidentals (such as children's school fees and uniforms) on their own.

Many women do not have reproductive rights (i.e., decision making with regard to family planning and birth control). Women also often have migrant spouses who form second families and return home infected with human immunodeficiency virus (HIV). Domestic violence between intimate partners is also a primary concern among many African-ethnic women and has been shown to have a correlation with lower rates of education among women.

Women have limited access to education, and this accessibility is often determined by where they live (rural versus urban areas), their socioeconomic status (rich versus poor), and the effect of speaking standardized versus unofficial languages, resulting in a 62 percent literacy rate for women.

Often when girls have accessibility to education, family instances of HIV/AIDS may require them to stay home and care for their ailing parents or siblings, work to offset family debt and provide income for sustenance, or divert funds to medical bills resulting from the disease. In addition, girls are shown to be three times more likely to contract HIV and are more often coerced into engaging in sexual intercourse with older men—oftentimes teachers. Teenage pregnancy among girls is also a factor of inequality, as well as discrimination and harassment. In some instances, girls are expelled from school if they are pregnant. In other circumstances, it has been reported that girls are seen as a barrier to education or as a distraction.

Advances in Tanzanian education include practices to expand opportunities for women in primary and secondary schools.

politics and economics. More women are involved in co-op farms and encouraging others to embrace "self-reliance," and women are also able to join the National Servicemen Corps, which provides intensive training enabling women to serve in nation-building efforts.

See Also: Convention on the Elimination of All Forms of Discrimination Against Women; Educational Opportunities/Access; HIV/AIDS: Africa; Rural Women.

Further Readings

Evans, R. *Poverty, HIV, and Barriers to Education: Street Children's Experiences in Tanzania.* Oxford, UK: Oxford University Press, 2002.

Mbilinyi, M. *Searching for Utopia: The Politics of Gender and Education in Tanzania. Women and Education in Sub-Saharan Africa.* Boulder, CO: Lynne Rienner, 1998.

Stamback, A. *Education Is My Husband: Marriage, Gender and Reproduction in Northern Tanzania. Women and Education in Sub-Saharan Africa.* Boulder, CO: Lynne Rienner, 1998.

Stromquist, N. "Women and Illiteracy: The Interplay of Gender Subordination and Poverty." *Comparative Education Review*, v.34/1 (1990).

Jennifer Jaffer
Independent Scholar

Education and Poltics

Notable advances in education include current practices to further expand educational opportunities throughout Tanzania, both at a grassroots level and at formal primary and secondary schools. There is also an effort being made to differentiate needs and delivery methods between urban versus rural training opportunities, providing focus on business, economics, and health. Some of the projects underway include school rehabilitation, teacher improvement, and gender sensitization workshops aiming for increased support of girls in school.

Women play a more prominent role in the development of government policy and formation of organizations focused on women's issues. The country's leaders are taking action and are including women in decision making by guaranteeing that a set percentage of seats in both local government and parliament will be held by women, resulting in the concerted effort to encourage women to play a more assertive role in

Te Kanawa, Dame Kiri

Kiri Te Kanawa is an internationally acclaimed lyric soprano of Maori descent. She was still in her teens when she began winning vocal competitions in her native New Zealand and in neighboring Australia. In the nearly four decades since her 1971 debut, she has appeared in many of opera's most coveted roles, entertaining audiences in Paris, Milan, Salzburg, and Vienna, as well as appearing regularly at London's Covent Garden and New York's Metropolitan Opera. She also has a long history as soloist with renowned orchestras and substantial success as a recording artist. More recently, she has devoted the greater part of her time to mentoring a new generation of opera stars.

Born in 1944 to an unmarried Anglo mother and a married Maori father, Te Kanawa was adopted at birth by Nell and Tom Te Kanawa of Gisborne, New

Zealand. Her ambitious mother recognized Te Kanawa's musical gift and had her singing—mostly show tunes—from an early age. In 1956, the family moved to Auckland so that Te Kanawa could study at St. Mary's Girls' School. She was 19 years old when she won second place in New Zealand's Mobil Song Quest. Fame came suddenly when she recorded her country's first gold album. At age 21 years, she claimed first prize in the Mobil contest and earned a scholarship to study at the London Opera Centre.

In London, she studied with Vera Rozsa—her first operatic training. Her singing of Elena in *La donna del lago* at the Camden Festival in 1969 brought her recognition as a promising talent, and her debut in a major role at Covent Garden as Mozart's Countess Almaviva in *The Marriage of Figaro* soon followed. She moved from success to success, debuting at the Metropolitan Opera as Desdemona in Verdi's *Otello*. The vibrancy of her voice and her undeniable physical beauty and stage presence led to her performances in some of opera's most glamorous soprano roles: Marschallin in Richard Strauss's *Der Rosenkavalier*, Marguerite in Gounod's *Faust*, and Amelia in Verdi's *Simon Boccanegra*. Perhaps her most famous role, and one she identifies as a favorite, is Donna Elvira in Mozart's *Don Giovanni*. Throughout the 1970s and 1980s, she was one of the world's leading sopranos.

Crossover Successes

Te Kanawa's fame has never been limited to opera houses. In 1981, she sang at the wedding of the Prince of Wales to Lady Diana Spencer before one of the largest live television audiences for any singer in history. A year later she was made a Dame Commander of the British Empire. Crossover success followed with albums of Kern, Gershwin, Porter, and Berlin, plus the world premiere of Paul McCartney's Liverpool Oratorio. She gave open-air concerts; released albums of classical music, Broadway musicals and Maori songs; and advertised Rolex watches. Millions of moviegoers heard her sing Puccini's *O Mio Babbino Caro* over the credits of the Merchant-Ivory film *A Room With a View*.

Continued Success

In the late 1990s, everything changed. Te Kanawa married Desmond Park in 1967. The couple adopted two children in the 1970s, and he became her manager in the 1980s. In 1997, their 30-year marriage ended amid scandal. Her response was to distance herself from opera and turn her attention to recitals and solo concerts. She also developed an interest in helping younger singers. She has raised large sums for her own Kiri Te Kanawa Foundation to help New Zealand singers, and she teaches and mentors young singers at the Metropolitan's Young Artist Development Program and the Solti/Te Kanawa Accademia di Bel Canto in Italy.

See Also: Adoption; Classical Music, Women in; Mentoring; New Zealand.

Further Readings
Fingleton, David. *Kiri Te Kanawa: A Biography.* New York: Atheneum, 1983.
Singer, Barry. "The Good Life." *Opera News*, v.69/5 (2004).
Taylor, James C. "Kiri Te Kanawa Emerges With a Song in Her Heart." *Los Angeles Times* (June 14, 2009). http://articles.latimes.com/2009/jun/14/entertainment/ca-kiri14/2 (accessed April 2010).

Wylene Rholetter
Auburn University

Teachers' Unions

Collective action taken by workers in a particular industry to achieve common goals is at the heart of the unionization process. However, before a union can exist, there must be an industry for which to advocate. This was not always the case. The notion of free public schooling in the United States is as commonplace today as it was controversial over 150 years ago. At the beginning of the country, education was for the elite, not the masses. Women and minorities were systematically denied educational access, and when opportunities were available, they were not equitable. This created an additional barrier for women and minorities to overcome before being allowed to advance in and admitted to not only teachers' unions but into the profession itself.

These issues were compounded on a global scale. In Belgium, during the onset of the 20th century, the International Committee of National Federations of Teachers in Public Secondary Schools was formed.

While teachers faced similar discrimination struggles worldwide, some of the unions in the United States were hesitant to merge with international unions they felt could be influenced by communistic government control. International unions struggled with the large amount of teacher issues. Finally, the largest group to form, Education International (EI), was given birth in 1993, by the merging of two groups: International Federation of Free Teachers' Unions and World Confederation of Organizations of the Teaching Professions. The EI expects that those entering its union have female representation, as one of the organization's aims is "to give particular attention to developing the leadership role and involvement of women in society."

In the United States, the state of Massachusetts was the first to form school laws, institute qualifications for teachers, and expand school infrastructure via the auspices of a newly established board of education in 1837. According to Charles Kerchner and Julia Koppich, as teacher organizations were established, they supported an industrial-style form of union advocacy with emphasis on the separateness of labor and management, on adversarial relationships, and on protection of teachers.

Although female teachers have dominated the elementary school levels since the late 1800s and constitute nearly half of the high school teaching staffs across the country today, women systematically were not afforded opportunities for advancement in the teaching profession; many were denied educational opportunities, entrance into the more "elite" secondary and postsecondary employment pool when qualified, and admittance into some unions once established in the profession. Union messages seemed well suited to the plight of the early female teacher as her rate of pay was disproportionately lower than her male counterparts, her marital status kept her from acquiring work, and she faced rudimentary sanitary conditions and crowded classrooms on a daily basis.

Currently, two of the largest and most prominent educational organizations in the United States are the National Education Association (NEA), founded in 1857 (formerly the National Teachers Association, NTA), and the American Federation of Teachers (AFT), founded in 1916. Each organization targeted distinct groups of teachers. While the NEA drew mostly from rural areas, the AFT primarily drew membership from urban city centers. AFT, unlike the NEA, directly affiliated itself with the Association of Federated Labor (AFL) and the labor movement. While the American Federation of Teachers came about during a time of global labor movements, the National Education Association by comparison was more conservative in its approach and focused on its development as a professional organization with special attention to educational research.

Women were initially denied full entrance into the NEA (allowing two "honorary" female members during its founding), but the organization was nonetheless slightly ahead of the bureaucratic curve of the U.S. government. For example, prior to the Nineteenth Amendment in 1920, the NEA elected its first female president, Ella Flagg Young, in 1910. While AFT had female founders and organizers—most notably Margaret Haley—from its inception, a female president would not be elected until the 1930s. In 1997, Sandra Feldman became the second female president and the 15th overall AFT president. She resigned in 2004 for health reasons and died in 2005. Her legacy is a testament to previous organizers.

It was not until collective bargaining rights were acquired by the United Federation of Teachers (UFT) in New York that teachers' unions were catapulted into major prominence. Through it all, women have been a cornerstone of leadership in these endeavors, but unlike the labor market of the 1960s and 1970s, women now have additional options in their career pursuits.

Current Union Issues

Today, issues of charter schools and teacher tenure/ seniority are at the forefront of work related issues for teachers and professors. During a July 2009 AFT conference, where EI general secretary Fred van Leeuwen was in attendance, one of the hot topics discussed by AFT president Weingarten was the need for collaboration among professionals for overall school improvement. President Randi Weingarten believes charter and public schools should be held to the same accountability standard and stated, "[these schools] should not be pitted against each other." Other areas of concern are tenure practices at secondary and postsecondary institutions, where women do not often garner the same tenure percentage levels as their male counterparts. Each union (national or international) has its hands full, as creating effective change over large areas with varying political climates proves difficult. The collective action dilemma continues, but now people can organize on a global scale more readily with the advent of modern technology.

See Also: Education, Women in; Educational Administrators, College and University; Educational Administrators, Elementary and High School; Unions.

Further Readings

American Federation of Teachers. http://www.aft.org (accessed April 2010).

Education International. "About Us." http://www.ei-ie.org /en/aboutus (accessed April 2010).

Kerchner, Charles Taylor and Julia Koppich. "Negotiating What Matters Most: Collective Bargaining and Student Achievement." *American Journal of Education*, v.113/3 (2007).

Malin, Martin H. and Charles Taylor Kerchner. "Charter Schools and Collective Bargaining: Compatible Marriage or Illegitimate Relationship?" *Harvard Journal of Law & Public Policy*, v.30/3 (2007).

National Education Agency. http://www.nea.org (accessed April 2010).

Sonia Adriana Noyola
Del Mar College

Team Owners, Female

With a few notable exceptions that include New York Mets owner Joan Payson and Cincinnati Reds majority owner Marge Schott, women have historically been absent from the world of sports-team ownership. After a failed attempt to keep the Giants baseball team in New York in 1957, Payson became the cofounder and majority owner of the New York Mets. She was the first female in American history to buy a sports franchise for a major-league team. When Schott purchased a minority share in the Cincinnati Reds in 1984, it was only the second time in history that a female had been approved as a franchise owner. Because the world of sports has long been dominated by males, women have also been shut out of positions as presidents and general managers.

Generally, women who have become involved in sports-team ownership have done so as a result of family connections. Georgia Frontiere, for instance, became the owner of the Los Angeles Rams as a result of the death of her husband, Carroll Rosenbloom. Likewise, Joan Kroc inherited the San Diego Padres from her husband, Ray Kroc, the man who built McDonald's into a fast-food empire. Other women who entered the field through their relationships with particular males were Violet Bidwell of the Chicago Cardinals, Grace Comiskey of the Chicago White Sox, and Jackie Autry of the California Angels.

It is not only women who have worked to break down barriers in the business of sports-team ownership. National Basketball Association (NBA) commissioner David Stern, who exerted pressure for the formation of women's sports leagues, believes the inclusion of women at all levels of various sports is important to attracting women consumers to the field of sports.

Women's Sports Teams a Key Factor

As a rule, it is predictably women's sports that have proved most welcoming to female team owners. In 2005, Shelia Johnson, a spa owner who cofounded the Black Entertainment Network (BET) with her ex-husband Robert Johnson (who owned the Charlotte Bobcats), became the first female to own a Women's National Basketball Association (WNBA) team. As a member of a group of financial backers known as Lincoln Holdings LLC, which purchased the WNBA's Washington Mystics, Johnson also became the first African American woman in history to become part owner of three professional sports teams, since Lincoln Holdings also owns the National Hockey League's Washington Capitals and has a minority interest in the NBA Washington Wizards. Johnson is most actively involved with the Mystics, serving as team president, managing partner, and governor. She sees her involvement as a major gain for African American women and believes that her participation will open doors for other African American women interested in owning sports teams.

After Johnson entered the field, Michelle Williams, a member of the singing group Destiny's Child, bought a minority share in the Chicago Sky. Elsewhere, four Seattle businesswomen took over the WNBA's Storm in an effort to keep the franchise in Seattle after that city's men's basketball franchise had moved to Oklahoma City.

Two years after her husband Garry died of cancer in 2007, Atlanta businesswoman Kathy Betty decided to buy the Atlanta Dream, the local WNBA team. She announced that her move was motivated by both her interest in sports and her desire to provide the young people of Atlanta, particularly young women, with positive role models. She believes that encouraging woman-to-woman networking is necessary in teaching women to become more aware of their power to influence the business world. Betty's interest in basketball has long been evident through her support of Georgia Tech's basketball program.

While still a definite minority in the field of sports-team ownership, women have become more of a presence in the 21st century. Denise DeBartolo York owns the San Francisco 49ers with her husband John, but it took a lawsuit against her brother Edward to win that status. Kathy Goodman and Carla Christofferson own the Los Angeles Sparks, a WNBA team. When the Rickets family, consisting of a sister and three brothers, bought the Chicago Cubs, Laura Rickets became the first openly gay sports-team owner in American history. Women in countries other than the United States have also become involved in the business of sports-team ownership. In India, Priety Zinta, the adopted daughter of Shandar-Amrohi and the granddaughter of movie mogul Kamaal Amrohi, is co-owner of the King XI Punjab, an Indian Premier League cricket team. Zinta is best known for her participation in the Hindu-language film industry commonly referred to as "Bollywood."

See Also: Business, Women in; Philanthropists, Female; Sports, Women in; Sports Announcers, Female; Sports Officials, Female; Widows; Women's National Basketball Association.

Further Readings

Carter, Ivan. "BET's Sheila Johnson Becomes Part Owner, President of Mystics." *Washington Post* (May 25, 2005). http://www.washingtonpost.com/wp-dyn/content /article/2005/05/24/AR2005052400946.html (accessed July 2010).

Swartz, Kristi E. "Atlanta Businesswoman Kathy Betty to Buy WNBA Team." *The Atlanta Journal-Constitution* (October 29, 2009). http://www.ajc.com/sports/atlanta -business-woman-kathy-betty-177579.html (accessed April 2010).

Weiner, Evan. "Women Owners Slowly Gaining Traction." *New York Sun* (June 13, 2008). http://www.nysun.com /sports/women-owners-slowly-gaining-traction /79969 (accessed July 2010).

Elizabeth Rholetter Purdy
Independent Scholar

Teen Pregnancy

Also referred to as adolescent pregnancy, teen pregnancy is generally defined as a teen woman conceiving before the age of 20. The bulk of research looking at rates of teen pregnancy examines information from the 20th century forward, and although cross-national comparisons remain difficult to make, national data are often separated between "developed" and "developing" countries. Additional variables included, if available, are race and ethnicity, educational level of the pregnant teen, economic level of the pregnant teen, her living situation (e.g., living with the child's biological father and/or her biological parent or parents), access to sex education and contraception, and access to healthcare and sources of nutrition. Two major concerns stand out in the research: teen pregnancy as a social problem and the health of pregnant adolescents and their children.

Statistics on Teen Pregnancy

Similar to most issues that emphasize rates, figures, and statistics, data for teen pregnancy rates across the globe are difficult to obtain. Each nation determines which demographic information it collects, not all hospitals maintain records, and many academic studies rely upon self-reported information. Importantly, a distinction exists between the teen pregnancy "rate" and teen pregnancy "births," since, depending upon the nation in question, end-of-pregnancy rates may be as high as one in two. Pregnancy ends through various means, including abortion (legal or illegal) and miscarriage, physical abuse, lack of nutrition, and unknown biological reasons. Reliability of the data proves an additional challenge to researchers who study the impact of adolescent pregnancy and the overall health of teen woman and their children. A glance at the research shows that reports vary greatly, reporting either significant differences or little to no differences in maternal and infant health of women giving birth before age 20 compared to women giving birth after 20.

Regardless of the challenges in calculating teen pregnancy birth rates, researchers have established an early-21st-century world average for adolescents of 65 births for every 1,000 women giving birth. Rates range as low as five or less in Japan and Switzerland, to under 45 in Turkey and 50 in the United States, to a regional average of 140 in sub-Saharan Africa.

Meta-analyses can often point out potential biases in the data sources, methods, and comparisons. After careful consideration of the multiple studies, the World Health Organization developed a reading of the concerns commonly said to face pregnant teens and their children. Hypertension, though often studied, does not appear to increase in women under 20 any more than women over 20, and while anemia rates vary throughout the world, these rates more likely vary due to sources of nutrition rather than pregnancy. Malaria, human immunodeficiency virus (HIV), and iodine deficiency continue to be great threats in many regions of the globe, not only to pregnant teens but also to their children. Importantly, these three issues threaten the bulk of the population in particular areas and are not specific to teen pregnancy, although a lack of proper levels of iodine in teens can lead to decreased brain development in the fetus. Preterm births, low-birthweight-babies, and infant mortality do appear to be higher in the adolescent birth population, but the latter two may stem more from preterm births, as women over 20 who have preterm births also have higher rates of low birth weight and infant mortality than do their counterparts.

Maternal death is higher among pregnant teens, particularly in developing nations where overall maternity care is somewhat low or difficult to acquire.

Unintended teen pregnancy in the United States is a persistent social issue for society as a whole. The United States has the highest rate of pregnant underage girls, followed by Hungary, New Zealand, and the United Kingdom.

Unsafe abortions may also contribute to the high rate of maternal death in teens, afraid or unsure of how to inquire about safe abortions, if available. Studies do confirm high rates of physical and sexual abuse of teen mothers, before, during, and after conception and birth, and rates of physical abuse and neglect are often high in the children of teen mothers.

A Social Problem?

Teen pregnancy rates in most developed nations have been declining overall since the 1950s, with contemporary rates lower than 1950s rates. Between 1975 and 1995, some developed nations, including the United States and Great Britain, declared teen pregnancy as one of the major issues facing their societies. Even in the 1990s, when politicians raised concerns, many did, and still do, question the validity of notions such as "epidemics" of teen pregnancy, not simply because of the historically low rates. Concerns stem instead from social morality that deems young women as unfit mothers or of discriminatory practices due to the overrepresentation of women of color and immigrant women in the statistics.

Regardless of developed or developing nation status, most countries continue to encourage marriage before the birth of a child. In cultures where young women are married soon after menarche (the age of first menstruation), the age of first marriage and first pregnancy likely occur to an adolescent woman. Although it remains impossible to note all countries, India, Bangladesh, and Niger often encourage young women to marry close to the age of 15 when menarche occurs, thus contributing to the high rate of births among teen mothers. In developed nations, where the rate of marriage has increased over the last 50 years in individuals in their mid- to late 20s, many still raise concerns about the high rate of teen births, even as these nations' understandings of acceptable familial structures continue to shift toward unmarried cohabitation and single parenting. This acceptance, however, does not seem to extend to women who are under the age of 20 when they deliver children, even as the United States, for example, sees approximately half of all births to unmarried women.

Globally, subcommunities within each nation that have higher rates of immigrants, minority racial or ethnic populations, poverty or low socioeconomic status, and little educational experience lead to higher rates of teen pregnancy. This confluence of rates has created a great deal of commentary for many decades. In welfare states, researchers attempt to determine the cost savings of delaying pregnancy until after the age of 20. Communities attempt to discern how raising the standard of living could reduce the cycle of teen pregnancies within communities, even though other studies suggest that daughters of teen mothers show a decrease in the cycle. Others argue that majority populations demonstrate a fearfulness based upon discrimination when they decry teen pregnancy because of the high rate of racial and ethnic minority women who are teens and pregnant. Amid these arguments, it is known that raising the level of safety; access to safe and reliable contraceptives, sex education, and healthcare; and access to educational opportunities would certainly improve the standard of living for the community, even if they do not decrease the rate of teen births.

Additional discussions about teen pregnancy in the 21st century include increased length of adolescence (with some statistics using 10–19 as the age group designation), decreased age for puberty and menarche in girls across the world, and increased numbers of teens within the general population (with recent figures in the United States, for example, higher than during the post–World War II "baby boom"). In conjunction with increases in HIV infection and sexually transmitted infection (STI) rates, many advocate increased access to holistic sexual education and contraception, with some arguing that decreased rates of teen pregnancy in areas such as the Netherlands and France indicate a direct link between honest and thorough sexual education combined with contraception access and decreased teen pregnancy rates. Studies remain mixed on the latter argument, however, suggesting that cultural beliefs about sexuality, economic and educational levels, and young women's desire to be mothers play as big of a role as sex education and contraception.

See Also: Adolescence; Marriage; Pregnancy; Sex Education, Cross-Culturally Compared; Single Mothers.

Further Readings

Daguerre, Anne and Corinne Nativel, eds. *When Children Become Parents: Welfare State Responses to Teenage Pregnancy.* Bristol, UK: The Policy Press, 2006.

Hamilton, B. E., J. A. Martin, and S. J. Ventura. "Births: Preliminary Data for 2008." *National Vital Statistics Reports*, v.58/16 (2010).

Lee, Yookyong. "Early Motherhood and Harsh Parenting: The Role of Human, Social, and Cultural Capital." *Child Abuse & Neglect*, v.33 (2009).

Moore, Ann M., Kofi Awusabo-Asare, Nyovani Madise, Johannes John-Langba, and Akwasi Kumi-Kyereme. "Coerced First Sex Among Adolescent Girls in Sub-Saharan Africa: Prevalence and Context." *African Journal of Reproductive Health*, v.11/3 (2007).

Samandari, Ghazaleh and Ilene S. Speizer. "Adolescent Sexual Behavior and Reproductive Outcomes in Central America: Trends over the Past Two Decades." *International Perspectives on Sexual and Reproductive Health*, v.36/1 (2010).

Save the Children. "State of the World's Mothers 2004." http://www.savethechildren.org/publications/mothers /2004/SOWM_2004_final.pdf (accessed August 2010).

Singh, Susheela, Jacqueline E. Darroch, and Jennifer J. Frost. "Socioeconomic Disadvantage and Adolescent Women's Sexual and Reproductive Behavior: The Case of Five Developed Countries." *Family Planning Perspectives*, v.33/6 (2001).

World Health Organization (WHO). "Adolescent Pregnancy: Issues in Adolescent Health and Development." Geneva: WHO, 2004. http://libdoc.who .int/publications/2004/9241591455_eng.pdf (accessed August 2010).

Rita Jones
Lehigh University

Tennis

Tennis is a sport that is played either between two players (singles) or two teams of two players (doubles). Tennis is an Olympic sport and has players at all levels of society and at all ages around the world. It is a popular spectator sport with a global audience.

The game as we know it dates back to 16th-century France. It spread to Europe, becoming popular in England in the 19th century, before spreading around the world. In 1884, women competed alongside men at Wimbledon. During the 1920s, women's tennis emerged as a popular spectator sport; French player Suzanne Lenglen is credited for popularizing tennis, as she was the first to reveal her calves and forearms, instead of wearing the concealing garments that were more conventional at the time.

In 1970, U.S. player Billie Jean King, with eight others, formed the Virginia Slims Tennis Circuit. In 1973, King founded the Women's Tennis Association (WTA), and that year Wimbledon and the US Open offered equal prize money to men and women for the first time. Lucrative television contracts coupled with high-end sponsorship has pushed the prize money and earnings of women tennis players to the tens of millions.

Sony Ericsson became the tour's worldwide title sponsor in 2005. This $88 million, six-year deal was the largest and most comprehensive sponsorship in the history of tennis and of women's tennis. The tour includes 2,200 players representing 96 nations and competing for over $86 million at 53 events in 33 countries and four Grand Slam tournaments: the Australian Open, Roland Garros, Wimbledon, and the US Open. There are five tiers of WTA events, and Futures tournaments organized by the International Tennis Federation (ITF) form the lower levels.

A Progressive Sport Still Wrestles Image Concerns

Sport has been an area that has traditionally excluded women, limiting their ability to participate. However, tennis is stereotypically represented as a sport for women. Most sports have distinct competitions for both men and women, but in few instances is the parallel staging of events as explicit as it is in tennis. The competition within both gender classes typically attracts much attention; still, commentators contend of women's tennis that "it is a different game." The most notable organizational difference between a Grand Slam tennis game for men and women is that in the former it takes three winning sets, as opposed to two, to win the match.

When compared to the coverage given to women in other sports, tennis fares well. For example, the US Open Women's final for the last years of the 1990s received higher television ratings in the United States than that of the men. Examinations of global media on sports reveal that women tended to not only be underrepresented but trivialized, stereotyped, devalued, and marginalized. For example, a 2000 study in the United

Kingdom found that only 5.9 percent of sports media coverage focused on women's sport, and one-third of that coverage was devoted to tennis player Anna Kournikova, even though she had never won a tournament on the professional women's circuit.

The institutional and cultural practices of tennis have historically promoted images of a racialized femininity, constitutive of the middle-class standard of white, heterosexual womanhood embodied in the likes of Chris Evert or Maria Sharapova. There appears to be a "panic" in tennis when women's bodies do not conform to these conventions. For example, Chris Evert, describing the athletic ability of sisters Venus and Serena Williams said that it was difficult for the "women who aren't Amazons" to compete with them. Martina Navratilova's muscular athletic body challenged normative ideas of acceptable femininity in sport. Commentators also noted that her unpopularity was because, since 1978, Navratilova has been an "out" lesbian.

Other famous female players of the U.S. Open era include Margaret Court, Monica Seles, Justine Henin, Evonne Goolagong-Crawley, Hana Mandlikova, Aranxta Sanchez-Vicario, Virginia Wade, Jennifer Capriati, Tracy Austin, Mary Peirce, Svetlana Kuznetsova, and Kim Clijsters. Chinese tennis player Zheng Jie, Venus Williams (U.S.), Tatiana Golovion (France) and Vera Zvoraneva (Russia) have been named as Promoters of Gender Equality, as part of the Sony Ericsson WTA Tour's partnership with the United Nations Educational, Scientific and Cultural Organization (UNESCO). The program also has a fund for women and leadership; it offers mentoring, scholarships, and fellowships for women and girls. The program draws from the history of the WTA and its players in their quest for gender equality and emerged from discussions following the tour's season-ending tournament in Madrid in 2005.

See Also: Gender Roles, Cross-Cultural; *Sports Illustrated* Swimsuit Edition; Sports, Women in; Williams, Venus and Serena.

Further Readings

Douglas, Delia D. "Venus, Serena, and the Women's Tennis Association: When and Where 'Race' Enters." *Sociology of Sport Journal*, v.22/3 (2005).

Forman, Pamela J. and Darcy C. Plymire. "Amelie Mauresmo's Muscles: The Lesbian Heroic in Women's Professional Tennis." *Women's Studies Quarterly*, v.33/1–2 (2002).

King, Billie Jean and Starr, Cynthia. *We Have Come a Long Way: The Story of Women's Tennis*. New York: McGraw-Hill, 1998.

Danai S. Mupotsa
Monash University

Terrorists, Female

Female terrorism is the threat or use of force against civilians in order to create a climate of fear and advance a political agenda. Political violence targeting noncombatant populations occurs in civil wars, revolutionary wars, nationalistic wars, armed resistance, guerrilla warfare, and peasant wars. Terrorism is described as a form of "asymmetric warfare." Guerrilla organizations employ terrorist tactics but limit the targets of their attacks to military and government personnel.

In recent years, female terrorism has become synonymous with civilian-directed suicide attacks conducted by women. This terrorism-suicide bombing linkage obfuscates the fact that most female terrorism has involved women and girls witnessing or directly participating in terrorist acts such as torture, murder, kidnapping, hijacking, rape, physical/psychological deprivation, destruction of community infrastructure (e.g., cropland, water systems, roadways, humanitarian efforts, health clinics), mutilation, human sacrifice, drug use, and cannibalism.

Inside the "Typical Recruit"

There is no single profile for a female terrorist. Female terrorists originate from a vast list of ethnicities and races; they can be secular or religious, fanatical or unemotional, single or married, childless or mothers, girls or women, educated or uneducated, from poverty or from wealth.

Most female suicide bombers are socially functional and lack suicidal tendencies. Women become involved in terrorism for political and non-political reasons, including (1) exposure to war, or living under occupation; (2) experience of trauma, such as the murder, torture, or kidnapping of another person;

(3) exposure to and purposely seeking out radical organizations; (4) internal desire for meaning in the face of lived chaos; (5) religious adherence to a violent ideology; (6) participation in nationalist groups; (7) network links to terrorist organizations through marriage or family; (8) suicide bomber friend or relative; and (9) personal crisis such as childlessness, lack of employment or education (due to war), or the loss of a beloved.

Some young women and girls enter militant groups because of an ideological orientation to the cause; to get out of poverty, to gain food and shelter, or to attain otherwise unavailable educational, employment, or personal opportunities; to earn valuable skills; to break free of an oppressive family dynamic that may include sexual abuse or imbalanced domestic responsibilities; to obtain protection; to reunite with family; to increase confidence and experience through intelligence gathering, propagandizing, or liaison work; or even to seek adventure in an environment perceived to be free of gender-based strictures.

Tamil Tiger female militants in Sri Lanka, for example, seek to defend Tamil life and their communities from perceived transgressors and to die a purposeful death. Naxalite women in West Bengal seek to dismantle India's caste-based society, implement land reforms for the poor, and enfranchise the poor. The so-called Black Widows of Chechnya perpetrated their attacks because agency in militancy assuaged them of their feelings of powerlessness. Women in al-Qaeda and white supremacist operations are often introduced to terrorist networks through their marriages to radical men. A high percentage of young women and girls involved with terrorism and militancy do not participate willingly. Many are "recruited" through physical force, abduction, being born into the militant organization (born of an abducted mother), seized by another group, or gang-pressed.

Psychological trauma after a loss can make women vulnerable to the influence of militant organizations which sell "martyrdom" as a way to overcome grief, survivor guilt, and feelings of disempowerment. Radical groups provide straightforward solutions to emotional pain and a strong sense of purpose through intelligible ideological positions. Experiences of camaraderie (brother/sisterhood), self-empowerment (arming oneself), promises of paradise, the possibility of great glory, and concrete answers amid overwhelming turmoil can justify revenge, militant activity, and/or self-sacrifice.

Real and Propagandized Effects of Female Bombers

Female suicide bombers are highly useful for organizations seeking tactical advantage: stories of female martyrs inspire potential operatives, elicit global media attention, and cause greater unease in victim populations, compared to male counterparts.

Although there were many female suicide bombings in the 1980s, the contemporary debate on female suicide bombings was sparked primarily by the bombings of Hawa Barayev in June 2000 in Chechnya that killed 27 Russian special forces operatives, and Wafa Idris in January 2002 in an Israeli shopping district. Not only did Barayev and Idris receive the backing and logistical support to carry out their acts from religiously based resistance movements (the Chechen rebels and al-Aqsa Brigades, respectively), but after an initial period of hesitation, Islamic jurists gave them first tacit and later overt support through *fatwas* (edicts) claiming their legitimacy as martyrs of Islam. The *fatwa* endorsement of Barayev effectively sanctified suicide bombings, which has had the concomitant effect of perpetuating cycles of feminine violence.

"Contagion theory" is used to better understand the popularization of suicide bombings as an ideal path to martyrdom. Public approval is critical to the continued use of female suicide bombers. For example, there was widespread condemnation of the suicide bombing by Reem al-Riyashi, because she was a mother of two small children.

Public discourse on female terrorists tends to accentuate only certain elements of their reality. The narratives are often reductionist. Some narratives benefit militant recruitment of women and include idealizations about the female terrorists' profound beauty, purity, intelligence, heroism, and piety. Other narratives define women terrorists as social outcasts, defective socially or personally, suspicious, manipulated, exploited, undisciplined, bored, naive, a family burden, masculine tough, or having been forcibly recruited.

Feminist accounts sometimes position the female warrior as a new form of liberated actor who uses aggression to achieve equality. Most of the frames that employ gender clichés (that separate the feminine and their violence or that claim the feminine violator is liberated), and are used to describe or justify women's involvement in terrorism, potentially undermine the real political grievances and political agency of feminine violence. In fact, gender stereotypes about the apparent "softness" of women are utilized by radical women to avoid detection at security checkpoints and deliver maximum damage.

Mixed Messages for Martyrs

The female terrorist is often a side note within literature on terrorism. Despite the temporary symbolic value of militant women to radical causes, and the ritual celebration of their acts within organizations, most female terrorists are treated like second-class soldiers and martyrs. Female terrorists complicate the world but are downplayed because armed women violate traditional gender order (war is treated as a man's game) or because the idea of killer women leads to sensationalism or condemnation; women's violence in isolated events appears to lack consistency and persistence; women have not pierced through power hierarchies of militant organizations; and male decision making appears to control female militant activity.

Scholars predict that militant organizations will continue to employ white converts to Islam and young girls and pregnant women as suicide bombers, tandem bombings (simultaneously or sequentially), and multiple targets. The use of pregnant women sends a profound statement of determination but could result in public backlash over the destruction of an innocent child.

See Also: Combat, Women in; "Femininity," Social Construction of; Guerrilla Fighters, Female; Suicide Bombers, Female; Wars of National Liberation, Women in.

Further Readings

Alison, Miranda. "Women as Agents of Political Violence: Gendering Security." *Security Dialogue*, v.35/4 (2004).

Berko, A. *On the Way to Heaven: the World of Female and Male Suicide Bombers and Their Dispatchers*. Tel Aviv, Israel: Yediot Ahronot Books and Hemed Books, 2004.

Ness, Cindy D. *Female Terrorism and Militancy: Agency, Utility, and Organization*. London: Routledge, 2008.

Melissa Finn
York University

Thailand

Due to deindustrialization, globalization, and emerging transnational networks, women in Thailand have experienced recent shifts in identity, as well as altered relations to family and work in the public sphere. In particular, the feminization of migration (both internal and external) has had an enormous impact on the social position of women in Thai society. Migratory transformations have primarily occurred in informal sectors, such as domestic labor, the sex industry, factory labor, and other forms of informal labor such as the selling of food and clothing, and have increased women's autonomy by fostering their participation in waged work.

Although male migrants from China and their Sino-Thai children are often credited with Thailand's increased economic development, Ara Wilson has shown that women constitute the backbone of a vast range of global-local marketplaces and Thai industries. Thai women share a considerable amount of power in business and in politics, however, they are disadvantaged relative to Thai men. For example, although women secured equal voting rights in 1933 and 300,000 more women than men voted in 1995, women nonetheless make up only a small percentage of Thailand's elected officials. And although women's participation in village councils has increased in the 21st century, women's overall participation and inclusion remains low relative to men's.

Given Thailand's accession to the United Nations Convention on the Elimination of All Forms of Discrimination Against Women (CEDAW) and ratification of the 1975 International Labour Organization's Convention on Equality of Opportunity for Women Workers, Thai women are somewhat protected by labor laws, particularly in the case of maternity leave and equal pay for men and women. However, employers of unskilled or semiskilled laborers frequently ignore or circumvent these requirements. Further, employers' tendency to construct women as well suited to menial tasks also creates a system in which women have less access to high-skilled, higher-paying positions in a range of industries.

Sex Workers and Mainstream Concerns

The country's sex industry has been at the center of contentious debates originating both within and outside of Thailand, in which sex workers are positioned as either exploited victims or as agents who rationally and freely choose their work. Recently, however, numerous scholars have complicated this dichotomy, noting the larger systemic and global dynamics that impact and are impacted by Thai sex workers. In fact, sex tourism, often credited for the spike in prostitution in Thailand, makes up a relatively small portion of the larger Thai sex industry. Although Thailand has a global reputation for sexual labor, the majority of Thai women have no connection whatsoever to this industry. Often stigmatized and characterized as transmitters of human immunodeficiency virus and acquired immune deficiency syndrome (HIV/AIDS), women who do work in Thailand's sex industry have nonetheless benefitted from increased access to free condoms and clients' compliance with condom use.

Thailand has a middle-aged population (15–64 years: 70.3 percent; 65 years and over: 8.5 percent; median age for male: 32 years; median age for female: 33.7 years) of approximately 65.5 million, with the total fertility rate at 1.64 children born to every woman. In response to Thai women's need for affordable access to safe abortions and other reproductive health services, nongovernmental organizations such as the Women's Health and Reproductive Rights Foundation of Thailand have recently emerged.

See Also: Business, Women in; Convention on the Elimination of All Forms of Discrimination Against Women; Economics, Women in; Government, Women in; Migrant Workers; Reproductive and Sexual Health Rights; Sex Workers; Traffic in Women and Children.

Further Readings

Central Intelligence Agency. "The World Factbook: Thailand." http://www.cia.gov/library/publications/the -world-factbook/geos/th.html (accessed June 2010).

Mills, Mary Beth. *Thai Women in the Global Labor Force: Consuming Desires, Contested Selves.* Brunswick, NJ: Rutgers University Press, 1999.

Wilson, Ara. *The Intimate Economies of Bangkok: Tomboys, Tycoons, and Avon Ladies in the Global City.* Berkeley: University of California Press, 2004.

Danielle Antoinette Hidalgo
Tracy Royce
University of California, Santa Barbara

Thatcher, Margaret

Political leader Margaret Hilda Thatcher (neé Roberts, born October 13, 1925) was the first woman to lead a major Western democracy. The British prime minister between 1979 and 1990, Thatcher won three successive general elections as leader of the Conservative Party. An intensely controversial figure in Britain, she is renowned for her right-leaning reforms of United Kingdom (UK) economic and foreign policy. During her time in office, she achieved a high international profile, being associated in particular with the Ronald Reagan administration.

Thatcher had a profound and lasting impact on British politics. Many critics claim that her economic policies were socially divisive and extremely destructive to core institutions and national infrastructure. Conversely, her proponents argue that Thatcher's trade union reforms, privatization and deregulation agenda, and her tough stance on tax and spending provided the foundation for a period of unparalleled economic prosperity in Britain toward the end of the 20th century.

Reform and Policy Agendas

Although she was the first female political leader of a Western democracy, Thatcher did not perceive herself as a feminist. She neither actively advanced the political careers of female colleagues nor did she pursue a markedly female-friendly policy agenda. By occupying the most powerful position in Britain for over a decade, Thatcher changed perceptions and expectations of the role women might play in the public sphere.

She was married to wealthy businessman Denis Thatcher from 1951 until his death in 2003. They had two children, twins Carol and Mark. Remarkably, for the era, as the mother of young children, she continued to train and then work as a tax lawyer, relying on a nanny for childcare. Despite her personal experiences, Thatcher did not seek reforms in family-friendly or work-life reconciliation policy when she was in government.

The daughter of a grocer and town councilor in Grantham, a small town in England, Thatcher attended a local state school and then Somerville College at the University of Oxford (1943–47). As a university student, she read chemistry and became politically active, later getting elected president of the

Former Prime Minister Margaret Thatcher remained an intensely controversial figure in Britain long after her term ended.

Conservative Association. In her mid 20s, Thatcher twice ran for election unsuccessfully. In 1959 things changed and she was elected to Parliament. That election began a 30 year career of representing the constituency of Finchley, in north London.

In 1975, Thatcher was elected leader of the Conservative Party and thus head of the opposition. This achievement gave Thatcher the unique distinction of being the first woman to lead a Western political party, and it launched a national and international career. Between 1959 and 1975, Thatcher held various government posts, the most notable of these was Education Secretary. It was during this time that she earned the moniker *Thatcher the Milk Snatcher* for her policy to stop free milk for school children.

Early on in her premiership, Thatcher faced the challenges of recession and high unemployment. Influenced by Keynesian economic thinking, she instigated reforms collectively referred to as "Thatcherism." She pursued a policy of economic liberalization, which extended to the selling and opening up to competition of state assets.

Political Career as "Iron Lady"

Nicknamed the "Iron Lady" by the Soviets, a moniker to which she took much pleasure, Thatcher worked with the Reagan administration during the last years of the Cold War. After the dissolution of the Soviet Union, her "Thatcherite" ideas proved influential in the reconstruction of post-communist central and eastern Europe. Other events of note during her terms in office included the Falklands War in 1982; the year-long miner's strike in 1984–85; the introduction of the Community Charge or "poll tax"; and the introduction of a national curriculum in schools. Thatcher narrowly survived an assassination attempt by the Irish Republican Army (IRA) in 1984.

Pushed from power by her own party in 1990, Thatcher was made a member of the Upper Chamber of Parliament, the House of Lords in 1992, and granted the title Baroness Thatcher. She retired from public life in 2002.

See Also: Clinton, Hillary Rodham; Heads of State, Female; Political Ideologies; United Kingdom.

Further Readings

Campbell, John. *Margaret Thatcher: Grocer's Daughter to Iron Lady*, London: Vintage, 2009.

The Margaret Thatcher Foundation, http://www .margaretthatcher.org (accessed December 2009).

Thatcher, Margaret. *The Downing Street Years: Memoirs of the Premiership*. London: HarperCollins, 1993.

Vinen, Richard. *Thatcher's Britain: The Politics and Social Upheaval of the 1980s*. London: Simon & Schuster UK, 2009.

Alison Smith Koslowski
University of Edinburgh

Third Wave

The term *third wave feminism*, coined in the early 1990s, is a term for a dynamic, sometimes contentious, body of thinking and activism within contemporary feminism. It defies easy definition, including even in terms of when to mark the origin of third wave ideas. In general, however, third wave feminism is viewed as the "next wave of feminism" that followed second wave feminism. Although there is an origins dispute, there is no doubt that from the early 1990s to the present, the third wave has become a global, more diverse inquiry into social systems of sex, race, and gender inequality and differences than occurred during second wave feminism.

Even though there is no single approach, three core strands of early third wave thinking/activism—postfeminism, power feminism, and Girlie feminism—are often included under the label third wave feminism and remain important today. Among the three strands, core sensibilities exist, even if various methods and ways of thinking are used. First, third wave feminists take the achievement of the second for granted in the sense that most (but not all) third wavers were raised after the successes of second wave feminism and, as a result, tend to assume women's equity and emphasize and organize around diversity, multiplicity, and contradiction. Indeed, third wave feminism celebrates difference in terms of identity construction, in which signifiers such as race and binary gender are rejected in favor of ambiguity and multiple subject positions.

Third wavers are also committed to a politics of difference rather than commonality, such that they embrace contradiction so that apparently inconsistent political viewpoints coexist in the name of third wave feminism. As a result, and unlike much second wave politics, third wave feminists organize around differences or diversity among women rather than via a unified concept of women. Today, primarily under the rubric of "intersectional analyses," much third wave feminism continues to develop ways of thinking that recognize the intersection of various multiple, shifting bases of oppression, primarily around race, class, gender, sexuality, and (dis)ability, and aim to create coalition politics based on interlocking—yet always shifting and changing—forms of oppression and axes of identity.

Beginnings

Initially, the early 1990s was considered the beginning of the third wave. However, recent academic work suggests that third wave ideas began to appear in writings and discussions focused on the intersections of feminism and racism in the mid-1980s, primarily by women of color. These early writings called for a "new subjectivity" or feminist "voice"

that honored race in response to the overwhelming focus on white women's issues in much of the media-represented second wave feminism and the failure to attend to race by many white second wave feminists. This focus was articulated initially by some of the key activists in the second wave: Cherrie Moraga, Gloria Anzaldúa, bell hooks, Chela Dadoval, Audre Lorde, Maxine Hong Kingston, and other feminists of color. Focusing on race continued, mostly in academic circles, until the Anita Hill and Clarence Thomas hearings.

The Hill–Thomas hearings, conducted by the U.S. Senate Judiciary Committee to investigate professor Anita Hill's allegations of sexual harassment by Thomas, was televised live in October 1991. Although the hearings had no legal significance and Thomas was eventually confirmed, many mark the hearings as the symbolic beginning of a new discussion of gender inequity and sexual harassment in America, which continued long after the hearing was over in both academic and popular circles. As a result, 1991 is often credited with initiating a new conversation—a third wave conversation—about feminism and feminist ideas in both popular and academic circles.

There is little dispute that by 1992 the term *third wave feminism* came into the public consciousness, or at least that of the political left, when Rebecca Walker, daughter of Alice Walker, founded the Third Wave Direct Action Corporation in 1992 with Shannon Liss. This organization became the Third Wave Foundation in 1998. The nonprofit institution cultivated young women's leadership.

At the same time, key third wave texts—including one that Walker edited—were written in the early 1990s and are now recognized as central to the development of third wave feminism. Thus, there is no dispute that, in the early 1990s, feminism resurfaced both within media and academic circles, and many women, especially young women, became reengaged with a new kind of feminism.

By 1995, two key third wave intellectual explorations were published: Rebecca Walker's *To Be Real: Telling the Truth and Changing the Face of Feminism* and Barbara Findlen's *Listen Up: Voices From the Next Generation of Feminists*. In these works, the mostly young authors reveal that the feminism they articulate is organized around a new set of issues and indicate a real shift in emphasis, concern, and demands among women who had grown up within second wave feminism's successes. Walker, for example, explicitly argues she and the authors of *To Be Real* are expanding what constitutes feminism and feminist practices. Even though both Walker and Findlen's texts emphasize their differences from the second wave, they do not reject feminism outright and, in fact, embrace a feminist understanding grounded in generational continuity—a continuity based on the notion of a "next generation" emerging.

Moreover, even though many early third wavers eschew theory, the focus of the authors is postmodernist, in that third wavers privilege diversity over commonality, the individual over the collective, and difference over similarity, and they explore everyday forms of power instead of the large-scale structural power that was the primary focus of the second wave. As a consequence, feminist academics now view 1991–95 as the early phase of third wave feminism and place Walker and Findlen's text as a foundational text of that phase. Equally important, recent academic scholarship on the third wave suggests that subsequent anthologies repeat the framework of the 1995 collections in their focus on differences over commonality and individuality over the collective, whereas cross-generational dialogue has become more common.

The early phase of third wave feminism also saw the development of three additional strands of thinking and activism—postfeminism, power feminism, and Girlie feminism—that also continue to be important to contemporary thinking. In terms of postfeminism, the early phase was marked by debate about whether or not the terms *third wave* and *postfeminism* were synonymous.

Contemporary scholars now recognize that part of the debate stems from the contradictory uses of the term *postfeminism*. Indeed, some scholars then and now use it to mean "after" feminism, as a way to signal the end of the particular era and tactics associated with second wave feminism, whereas others—particularly the media—use the term to indicate the "death" of feminism, or that feminism is no longer necessary because of the successes of second wave feminism. Some of this definitional confusion continues today; however, some academic feminists, particularly outside of the United States, argue that "postfeminism" can and should be employed as a term that indicates

continuity and connection between second wave and contemporary feminisms in the same way that the equally contentious terms "postmodern" and "poststructuralism" are used to indicate, simultaneously, both a connection to and ongoing development of a body of intellectual ideas over the last 40 years.

Power Feminism

In addition to postfeminism, both "power feminism" and "victim feminism" emerged under the rubric of third wave feminism. Naomi Wolf coined both terms in her 1993 book *Fire With Fire: The New Female Power and How It Will Change the 21st Century*. Primarily critiquing academic writing, Wolf argued that it was time to move away from what she argued was the "victim" feminism of the second wave—feminism that focused exclusively or too much on the victimization women face in their personal and professional lives. Rather than be victims, Wolf claims that women as a group do hold significant social power—in part because of the stereotypes of women being less violent, gentler, and so on. Thus, she argues for a form of "power feminism" that would motivate women, especially younger women, to claim their individual power and achieve as much as men within current social and political structures. Contemporary work continues to debate and explore the ideas and politics of power feminism for the contemporary context.

Girlie Feminism

Yet another strand of early third wave feminism that continues to be important today is "girl power feminism" or "Girlie feminism." By the early and mid-1990s, both scholars and the media began to discuss how the successes of second wave feminism were affecting girls' lives. In particular, as both focused on girls doing better at school, girls as "sassy" and unafraid, and girls as more confident, the idea of "girl power" emerged. As young women began to embrace the idea of girl power, a celebratory and optimistic form of third wave feminism developed.

Girlie feminism has some similarities with power feminism in that it centers on the idea of young women doing whatever they want, as long as it is done with a fierce, optimistic attitude. In addition, Girlie feminism intersects feminism with feminine culture, focusing particularly on rebelling against the idea that, as women do not want to be exploited sexually, they are not sexual, and the belief that girls and power do not mix. Thus, Girlie feminism reclaims models of heterosexual power relations as pleasurable, rather than demeaning, and embraces standard tropes of feminine sexuality. As with the other early strands of third wave feminism, Girlie feminism continues to be important in the contemporary context.

Intersectionality

A more recent development in third wave feminism is intersectional analysis. Intersectionality explores how race, sex, (non)ability, and class intersect rather than work as discrete or separate categories that are sometimes (or not) added onto gender. Third wave intersectional analysis is sometimes viewed as a new standpoint or location for critique by contemporary feminism, whereas others employ intersectionality as "gender maneuvering," in which there is a deliberate attempt to challenge and play with the ways that gender is thought to organize people's lives and activities.

As a result, intersectional analyses see various components of identity as interdependent and codeterminative rather than additive and discrete. Moreover, because much of the early work on third wave feminism was critiqued for being too individualistic and unconcerned politically, contemporary work focuses on coalitional politics built around intersectional identities.

Today, many third wavers recognize that identities are complicated and are constantly shifting and changing within different contexts and intersections; however, when used critically and reflectively, a coalitional politics can emerge. Thus, as with the past, third wave feminism today is neither monolithic nor a single-issue feminism, and it continues to be known for its debates and controversies rather than consensus.

See Also: Critical Race Feminism; Feminism, American; Feminism on College Campuses; Feminists for Life; Global Feminism; Transnational Feminist Networks.

Further Readings

Baumgardner, Jennifer and Amy Richards. *Mainfesta: Young Women, Feminism, and the Future.* New York: Farrar, Straus, and Giroux, 2000.

Dicker, Rory and Alison Piepmeier, eds. *Catching a Wave: Reclaiming Feminism for the 21st Century.* Lebanon, NH: Northeastern University Press, 2003.

Henry, Astrid. *Not My Mother's Sister: Generational Conflict and Third-Wave Feminism.* Bloomington: Indiana University Press, 2004.

Heywood, Leslie. *The Women's Movement Today: An Encyclopedia of Third-Wave Feminism.* Westport, CT: Greenwood Press, 2006.

Heywood, Leslie and Jennifer Drake, eds. *Third Wave Agenda: Being Feminist, Doing Feminism.* Minneapolis: University of Minnesota Press, 1997.

Wolf, Naomi. *Fire With Fire: The New Female Power and How It Will Change the 21st Century.* New York: Random House, 1993.

D. Lynn O'Brien Hallstein
Boston University

Thomas, Helen

Reporter Helen Thomas covered 10 presidents and nearly 75 years of what she calls Washington's "kitchen sink" beat. The former dean, and doyenne, of the White House press corps, whose seniority allowed her to end presidential press conferences with "Thank you, Mr. President" until the George W. Bush administration rescinded that honor, is also the author of several books and was a newspaper columnist for Hearst Newspapers since stepping down as White House bureau chief for United Press International in 2000. Thomas retired on June 7, 2010.

Born in Winchester, Kentucky, on August 4, 1920, Thomas was the seventh of nine surviving children. Her father had immigrated to Kentucky in 1892 from a part of Syria now known as Lebanon, followed by her mother, as his bride, in 1902. In 1924, the Thomas family followed relatives to Detroit, where Thomas's father bought a grocery store. Thomas attended public schools in Detroit and graduated from Wayne State University in 1942 with a bachelor's degree in English. Shortly after graduation, she traveled to Washington, D.C., to visit a cousin and decided to stay.

She took her first journalism job as a copy girl, earning $17.50 a week at the *Washington Daily News*. A few months into the job, she was assigned local stories as a cub reporter, until her Detroit roots, which had led her to join a union and then participate in a strike, got her fired. The United Press quickly hired

Thomas to write wire stories and start her days at 5:30 a.m. Thomas continued working the "dawn patrol" until, in 1955, she convinced her bosses she deserved the beat that today defines her: Washington and the White House.

Thomas was president of the National Woman's Press Club in 1959–60 and became the first woman officer of the National Press Club in 1971, after the club had excluded women for 90 years, when she became financial secretary. Also in 1971, Thomas married her competition—Associated Press reporter Douglas Cornell. About five years into their marriage, Cornell developed Alzheimer's disease; he died in 1982. In 1974, United Press International promoted Thomas to White House Bureau Chief—a position she held until stepping down in 2000 to protest the acquisition of UPI by News World Communications, the "media arm" of Sun Myung Moon's Unification Church. Since then, Thomas has covered the White House as a columnist for Hearst Newspapers. She has written several books about press and politics, a memoir, and a children's book.

Thomas has been honored with journalism awards from Ohio University, the University of Texas, Columbia University, and Wayne State University. In addition, Thomas has received lifetime achievement awards from the International Women's Media Foundation and the Society of Professional Journalists. She has received the William Allen White Journalism Award, the National Press Club Fourth Estate Award, and the Bob Considine Award. Brown University, George Washington University, Michigan State University, and St. Bonaventure University have recognized Thomas with honorary doctorates.

See Also: Lebanon; Journalists, Print Media; Syria.

Further Readings

Helen Thomas. http://www.helenthomas.org (accessed June 2010).

Thomas, Helen. *Front Row at the White House: My Life and Times.* New York: Scribner, 1999.

Thomas, Helen. *Thanks for the Memories, Mr. President: Wit and Wisdom From the Front Row at the White House.* New York: Scribner, 2002.

Carolyn Edy
University of North Carolina

Tibetan Women's Association

The Tibetan Women's Association (TWA) was established in Lhasa on March 12, 1959. After the Chinese Communist Party took political control of Tibet, the TWA followed the Dalai Lama to India and was not reinstated until September 10, 1984.

As of 2010, the TWA was the exiled Tibetan community's second-largest nongovernmental organization. Its headquarters are located in Dharamsala, India, and it has more than 30 offices throughout India and numerous overseas branches in, for example, New York, London, Quebec, Ontario, Vancouver, Minnesota, Colorado, Kathmandu, Zurich, Victoria, Calgary, Pokhara, Tashiling, Phokhara Tashi, and Palhkiel. The TWA handles issues of Tibetan religion, cultural self-identity, social welfare, political pursuits, educational needs, ecological protection of the natural environment, human rights, women's rights, and so on.

Tibetan feminist activism is interlocked with the well-known issues of Tibetan human rights. Birth control policies, sterilization, abortion, and sex workers in Tibet, for example, concern the TWA. On March 9, 2009, the president of the TWA, B. Tsering, had a meeting with Taiwanese feminists and discussed the lack of protection for Tibetan women who were pregnant for the second time and protection for their children. Although the Chinese communist government claimed there would be no punishment for non-Han women's second-time pregnancies, many Tibetan women who are pregnant for the second time are actually compelled to have an abortion, even in the fifth or seventh month of their pregnancy. In addition, more and more women in current Tibet have become sex workers, which lowers Tibetan women's social status overall and hinders Tibetan women's empowerment.

Because of Tibet's unique background, the TWA is different from most feminist activist organizations that wrestle with a male-centeredness that tortures women within the same society. The TWA's current goal is not internal battles against Tibetan men but collaborative projects with Tibetan men's organizations to fight against Chinese communist power. For instance, it joined the boycott against the Chinese governmental organization of the Olympics in 2008—its target being the Chinese central administration, not sports. Most exiled Tibetans regard Chinese communists as invaders and request Tibetan independence, and the TWA struggles for both Tibetans' own nation state and gender egalitarianism.

The TWA's counterpart is Tibetan fulian (Tibetan Branch of the All-China Women's Federation) in terms of attitudes toward Chinese communist domination. Contrary to the TWA, the Tibetan fulian praises communist contributions and disagrees with exiled Tibetans on their pursuit of Tibet's independence, although its responsibility is also Tibetan women's welfare and rights.

See Also: China; Contraception Methods; India; Nepal; Sex Workers.

Further Readings

Butler, A. *Feminism, Nationalism, and Exile Tibetan Women*. New Delhi: Kali for Women, 2003.

Ezung, E. *Women in Exile: Tibetan Women Refugees' Experiences in India*. New Delhi: WISCOMP, 2005.

"NGO Alternative Report on Tibetan Women: The Status of Tibetan Women, 1995–2000." Dharamsala: Tibetan Women's Association, 2000.

Tsering, T. *The Road to Beijing: The Tibetan Women's Association Campaign Strategies for the United Nations Fourth World Conference on Women*. Dharamsala: Tibetan Women's Association, 1995.

"Violence and Discrimination Against Tibetan Women." San Francisco: Tibet Justice Center, 1998.

Ya-chen Chen
Clark University

Title IX

Title IX, part of the 1972 Education Amendments Act, is a United States law that prohibits gender discrimination in "any education program or activity receiving Federal financial assistance." In 1988, Congress affirmed that it applies to entire institutions, not only to specific programs that receive funding. Women and girls have made dramatic gains as a result of Title IX, but those gains have not created equality, nor have they been uncontested. Title IX was designed to remedy gaps in the 1964 Civil Rights Act, which exempted education from gender equity guarantees, but its farthest reaching impact has been on sports.

Although women's athletic opportunities likely would have increased in the wake of the women's movement, Title IX greatly facilitated that expansion. In 1971, 7 percent of high school athletes were female, fewer than 30,000 women played college sports, and their institutions allocated only 2 percent of athletic budgets to them. Female athletes confronted stereotypes that sports desexed them, and they were expected to subdue competitiveness in favor of feminine grace.

By 2008, 41 percent of high school athletes were girls. In 2005, 166,728 women played college sports, and they received 35 percent of athletic budgets. These numbers represent a tremendous expansion of opportunity but not equity. Two out of every three dollars spent on college sports still go to men, and women's participation falls short of proportional representation at college and high school levels.

In 1979, the U.S. Department of Health, Education, and Welfare established athletics compliance guidelines known today as the "three-prong test." Educational institutions must demonstrate one of the following: that male and female athletic participation is proportional to the student body; a history of program expansion for the underrepresented sex; or that the underrepresented students' interests are fully met by the school's offerings (since 2002, controversial student-interest surveys are permitted to gauge interest). Schools that fail to comply face lawsuits and complaints filed with the federal government.

Controversies

A major controversy surrounds how institutions achieve proportional representation, the most common compliance measure. The National Collegiate Athletic Association initially saw proportionality as attainable, because when Title IX took effect, men far outnumbered women in colleges. Today, women make up over half of college students; proportionality is harder to achieve without deeper changes. Critics argue that Title IX takes away men's opportunities. Particularly when low-profile sports such as wrestling and gymnastics are cut, critics blame the creation of new women's sports. The reality is more complicated. Most college sports are non-revenue producing, so women's teams mean more pressure on athletic budgets.

Pitting men's minor sports against women's sports, however, encourages the stereotype that sports really are men's domain and that women are less entitled to play. It also diverts criticism away from football programs in which budgets have ballooned since the 1970s. Football is often protected by the myth that it produces revenue for institutions, but only one in five football programs recuperates its costs. Americans have yet to fully confront the question of where expensive commercial football programs fit into the educational missions of colleges and universities.

As women's sports grew in funding and prestige, women lost some control over their programs. Athletic associations run by and for women folded, and the overall percentage of female coaches and administrators in women's sports decreased as men sought these jobs. Moreover, racial equity issues are often overlooked in celebrating Title IX. Commonly added sports such as soccer, water polo, and lacrosse, due to their popularity in suburban high schools, tend to draw mainly white women. Finally, like men's sports, women's sports increasingly focus on specialization and commercial market success, a phenomenon that increases sports' profiles but diminishes the role of athletics as a tool to teach students of all levels.

Beyond Sports

Title IX applies to all educational programs, including science, mathematics, and technology. Due in part to Title IX, the gender gap in these fields has been closing since the 1970s. In 2008, a National Science Foundation study showed no gender gap in math standardized test scores for girls and boys. Still, women's participation in these fields lags behind men's. Similarly, advances in high school vocational and community college career-training programs have been limited. Title IX has created institutional awareness and procedures for preventing and punishing sexual harassment. Because sexual harassment can deprive students of educational opportunity, the Supreme Court ruled in 1992 that students can seek monetary damages from their institutions if they fail to take reasonable measures to protect them from sexual harassment. Title IX has also improved women's educational employment conditions, leading to an overall growth of women in academia and to a near leveling of salaries in K–12 education. Girls and women have made significant gains under Title IX, but gender inequity in education remains. The law has legitimized women's claims to full access, but that will come only with increased institutional and national enforcement.

See Also: Mathematics, Women in; Science, Women in; Science Education for Girls; Sexual Harassment; Sports, Women in.

Further Readings

American Association of University Women. "Title IX Athletic Statistics." http://www.aauw.org/act/laf/library/athleticStatistics.cfm (accessed July 2010).

Carpenter, L. J. and R. V. Acosta. *Title IX*. Champaign, IL: Human Kinetics, 2005.

Festle, M. J. *Playing Nice: Politics and Apologies in Women's Sports*. New York: Columbia University Press, 1996.

National Coalition for Women and Girls in Education. "Title IX at 35: Beyond the Headlines." Washington, DC: National Coalition for Women and Girls in Education, 2008.

Suggs, W. *A Place on the Team: The Triumph and Tragedy of Title IX*. Princeton, NJ: Princeton University Press, 2005.

Ware, S. *Title IX: A Brief History With Documents*. New York: Bedford/St. Martin's, 2007.

Jennifer Helgren
University of the Pacific

Togo

Togo is a west African country with a small coastline (56 kilometers, on the Gulf of Guinea) and shares land borders with Benin, Burkina Faso, and Ghana. Per capita Gross Domestic Product of Togo is $900—among the lowest in the world—and 32 percent of the population lives below the poverty line. Togo's population of about 6 million is almost entirely African (99 percent), with small minorities of Europeans and Syrian-Lebanese. Most follow indigenous beliefs (51 percent), with 29 percent Christians and 20 percent Muslims.

Togo is the site of many human rights violations, including restrictions on the press and on freedom of assembly, unprosecuted rape and domestic violence against women, sexual harassment (including harassment of female students), trafficking in persons, female genital mutilation (outlawed but estimated to be practiced on about 6 percent of girls), forced labor, and discrimination against women. Although the law prohibits discrimination on the basis of gender and the current government has taken steps to address these problems, serious concerns remain.

Women dominate commerce and market activity in urban areas, but in rural areas they have few economic opportunities. A husband may control his wife's earnings and restrict her right to work, and under traditional law, women have no rights to maintenance after divorce or inheritance in the case of their husband's death. Education is free and compulsory, but only about 41 percent of girls finish primary school and 9 percent finish secondary school; female literacy is estimated at 46.9 percent.

Togo provides a poor standard of healthcare and social services for most of its citizens. Life expectancy is 57.4 years for men and 61.99 years for women and, coupled with a high population growth rate (2.754 percent—20th highest in the world), results in an extremely young population (median age, 18.7 years). Infant mortality is high, at 56.84 per 1,000 live births, as is total fertility, at 4.79 children per woman. An estimated 3.3 percent of adults are infected with human immunodeficiency virus and acquired immune deficiency syndrome (HIV/AIDS)—more than half of them women. The international organization Save the Children rates Togo low on many measures relating to the health and welfare of women and children: overall, Togo ranked 25th among 40 Tier III or Least Developed Countries on the Mothers' Index, 29th on the Women's Index, and 16th on the Children's Index.

See Also: Female Genital Surgery, Terminology and Critiques of; Poverty; Traffic in Women and Children.

Further Readings

United Nations Statistics Divisions. "UNdata: A World of Information: Gender Info." http://data.un.org/Explorer .aspx?d=GenderStat (accessed February 2010).

U.S. Department of State. "2008 Human Rights Report: Togo." http://www.state.gov/g/drl/rls/hrrpt/2008 /af/119029.htm (accessed February 2009).

Sarah Boslaugh
Washington University

Tonga

Unlike other Pacific Islands, the kingdom of Tonga is a constitutional monarchy. Following a period of membership in the Polynesian kingdom, Tonga became a British protectorate in 1900 and joined the Commonwealth of Nations in 1970. In the 21st century, three-fourths of this archipelago of islands still lives in rural areas, and agriculture generates a fourth of the gross national product.

With a per capita income of only $4,600, nearly a fourth of the population lives in poverty. Many women have to work more than one job to support their families. In this highly traditional society, women have low status. Suffrage is universal for anyone 21 and over, but only a few women have managed to defy tradition and achieve positions of leadership.

Most women who have done so have connections to Tongan nobility. Tongan inheritance laws favor males, and even an illegitimate male child is allowed to inherit rather than a widow or daughter. A widow who inherits must cede all claims to her inheritance if she remarries or has sexual intercourse.

Tonga is heavily dependent on foreign aid and on remittances from Tongans who work abroad. Young people are particularly susceptible to the 13 percent unemployment rate. Tonga ranks 99th on the United Nations list of countries with very high human development. The islands are divided ethnically between Polynesians and Europeans, and the religious orientation tends to be Christian.

The median age for females is 22.8 years. Tonga's infant mortality rate is 11.58 deaths per 1,000 live births. Women have a longer life expectancy than males, living to an average 74.41 years compared to 68.18 years for men. Tonga ranks 112th in the world in fertility, and women give birth to 2.25 children on the average. Literacy is nearly equal for women and men, with a rate 99 percent. Both females and males receive approximately 13 years of schooling.

Domestic Violence and Sexual Harassment

There have been reports of rising rates of rape in Tonga, but there are no laws against spousal rape. Domestic violence also is on the rise, but most cases go unreported. Abused women can turn to the National Center for Women and Children and the Free Wesleyan Church for help. Neither prostitution nor sexual harassment is illegal in Tonga.

Women's rights groups are active in Tonga, and they work closely with organizations from other Pacific islands, but Tongan women don't feel they receive essential support from their own government. Following the 1995 World Conference on Women in Beijing, the government created a women's unit within the prime minister's office. In 2003, Tonga adopted a National Policy on Gender and Development, which was designed to guarantee equal wages and improve the lives of Tongan females.

See Also: Domestic Violence; Property Rights; United Nations Development Fund for Women.

Further Readings

Central Intelligence Agency. "The World Factbook: Tonga." https://www.cia.gov/library/publications/the-world-factbook/geos/tn.html (accessed June 2010).

Henry, Alice. "Women's Work." *off our backs*, v.22/3 (March 31, 1981).

United States Department of State. "2008 Human Rights Report: Tonga." http://www.state.gov/g/drl/rls/hrrpt/2008/eap/119060.htm (accessed June 2010).

"Women's Fight for Economic Justice: A Critical Look at UN and Government Goals, Conventions and Policies: The Case of Tonga." *IWTC Women's Globalnet*, v.281 (August 30, 2005).

Elizabeth Rholetter Purdy
Independent Scholar

Torres, Dara

Dara Torres is a world-renowned athlete who has been described as the fastest and oldest woman in American swimming. In 2008, 41-year-old Torres distinguished herself by competing successfully at the Beijing Olympics, 24 years and one child after her initial Olympic appearance. In doing so, she shattered the age barrier in a field dominated by youth, and inspired older athletes to return to competition.

Torres is best known as a record-setting Olympic champion swimmer. Born in the United States in 1967, Torres began competing internationally at age 14 and won her first Olympic gold medal three years later. She earned 28 National Collegiate Athletics Association All-American swimming awards, the maximum possible, as an athlete at the University of Florida, where she also completed a degree in Communication.

She is the first American swimmer to compete in five Olympic games, winning medals in each competition. With four gold, four silver, and four bronze medals, Torres also shares the record for the most Olympic medals won by a female swimmer. Over the course of her lengthy career, she has set numerous American and Olympic records, including a world record for the 50-meter freestyle. In 2009, she won the national title in this event for the 10th time since 1982.

Outside the Pool

Torres has complemented her athletic career with professional activities outside the pool. In 2009, she published a self-help book based on her success in challenging the age barrier, *Age Is Just a Number: Achieve Your Dreams at Any Stage in Your Life*. As a fashion model, she has walked the runway and appeared in magazines. In 1994, she became the first athlete to be included in the *Sports Illustrated* swimsuit issue, challenging the conventional physical beauty standards promoted by the influential publication. She has also worked as a television commentator for national networks including ABC, Fox, ESPN, TNT, and the Discovery Channel.

Torres has emerged as a role model not only for her athletic prowess and longevity but also for her ability to persevere in the face of adversity and conventional barriers. Over the course of her career, Torres overcame an eating disorder, the loss of her father to cancer, the demands of single motherhood, and two divorces to reemerge as a world-class swimmer.

She has demonstrated that middle age may present new challenges for athletes, but it does not prevent them from competing successfully against the inexperience of youth. Torres's professional and personal life experiences reflect the multiple roles women are expected to play in contemporary Western society as well as the importance of questioning gender, age, and beauty norms.

See Also: Aging, Attitudes Toward; Olympics, Summer; Sports, Women in; Swimming.

Further Readings

Mullen, P. H., Jr. *Gold in the Water: The True Story of Ordinary Men and Their Extraordinary Dream of Olympic Glory*. New York: Thomas Dunne, 2001.

Premier Management Group. "Dara Torres." http://www .DaraTorres.com (accessed June 2010).

Torres, Dara with Elizabeth Weil. *Age Is Just a Number: Achieve Your Dreams at Any Stage in Your Life*. New York: Broadway Books, 2009.

USA Swimming. "Dara Torres Profile." http://www.usa swimming.org/DesktopModules/BioViewManaged .aspx?personid=10e6c9c4-0e67-465f-be5f-051652fe33 0c&TabId=1453&Mid=6519 (accessed June 2010).

Judith R. Halasz
State University of New York, New Paltz

Toxic Waste, as Women's Issue

Toxic waste, also called hazardous waste, may take many forms, from nuclear radiation to air, wind, ground, and water pollution, and is caused by the careless use or accidental spills of toxic chemicals. These and other forms of waste often result in the destruction of our forests and waterways and pollute the atmosphere and soil. Toxic waste began as a byproduct of the commercial and manufacturing activities of industrialization but has since expanded and is now a problem among other industries as well, including medical, agricultural, and military industries. Toxic waste is often hazardous to the environment and human health and can increase mortality and morbidities for those who are exposed.

Rachel Carson's book, *Silent Spring*, published in 1962, spawned new concerns for how environmental degradation may affect our health and well-being. Carson, a scientist, writer, and ecologist, wrote *Silent Spring* to inform the public about the potential lasting harmful effects of the haphazard use of synthetic chemicals on humans, animals, and our environment. She stressed the importance of diversification of plant and animal species as a way to avoid overuse of pesticides and advocated strongly for people's right to know about environmental contamination. During the 1970s and 1980s, many industries advanced their use and production of hazardous chemicals but often failed to ensure public safety.

Specifically, nuclear accidents at the Three Mile Island power station in Pennsylvania in 1979 and at a Chernobyl power station in the Ukraine in 1986 released massive amounts of radioactivity into the environment. These events increased fear about the dangers of nuclear power, and people living in the aftermath of these disasters face social, psychological, health, and economic problems. Daily life for women living near Chernobyl changed drastically after the incident as a result of food contamination and concerns for their children's health. Although long-term effects from exposure are still being investigated, there has been a significant increase in thyroid cancer among children.

In another incident, the transnational American company Union Carbide set up a pesticide-producing plant in Bhopal, India, in 1970. An explosion at the plant on December 3, 1984, killed thousands of people in ghastly ways within a few hours and has killed approximately 20,000 people since then as a result of their exposure to the toxins. The local water and soil are still so heavily contaminated with lead, mercury, and organochlorines that birth defects, reproductive disorders, and other disabilities continue to affect each generation. Women continue to experience severe reproductive health problems, including menstrual irregularities, miscarriage, premature menopause, increased rates of cervical cancer, and pelvic inflammatory disease, among others.

Long-Term Exposures

Although these events were all catastrophic accidents, there also exists a history of less prominent, long-term exposures that have been revealed as a result of activist pressure and investigations. For example, the Stringfellow Acid Pits were designated by the state of California in 1955 as a disposal site for toxic chemicals from corporations across California. In 1978, the pits became flooded from heavy rains, and the existing dam was not expected to be able to hold up, so the state approved the release of 1 million gallons of contaminated water into the surrounding communities, and children playing in the giant puddles were directly exposed to the polluted waters. A variety of health-related effects associated with exposures from this waste site are still being researched.

A similar catastrophe occurred in Love Canal, a blue-collar neighborhood near Niagara Falls, New York. A mile-long area, originally made into a canal trench, was purchased by a chemical company that used it as a waste dump and then later sold it for $1 to the city of Niagara Falls. In 1954, a school was built on the site. Almost 25 years later, Lois Gibbs, a resident of Love Canal, became concerned with her children's health.

On further investigation, Gibbs discovered that her neighbors were experiencing an extraordinarily high incidence of miscarriages, reproductive cancers, still-births, birth defects, and other rare diseases. Gibbs believed that there was a direct link between the toxic waste site and the health problems experienced by her own family and neighbors. State authorities dismissed her complaints, so Gibbs organized the women in her community to demand relocation. The New York State Health Department finally began to investigate and subsequently discovered that chemicals had exuded into the soil and groundwater.

Woman's Role in Toxic Waste Events

These events and others were brought to light through the work of women who lived in these communities and became activists when the health of their families was at stake. Toxic waste is a women's issue in the context of women's socially and culturally defined roles as mothers and subsistence workers. Across the globe, taking care of family is still primarily women's work, and thus, when toxic waste becomes a human health threat, women are often the first to notice and the first to mobilize. The same roles that lead women to become concerned with toxic waste also put women at higher risk for dangerous exposures because women often work more intimately with toxic substances. Overexposure to occupational chemical hazards is often the result of weak enforcement of lax safety regulations that include lack of protective gear and proper cleaning facilities, inability to read and/or understand labels on the chemical containers, and reuse of the chemical containers for storing food and water.

Traditionally, environmentalism has been viewed in the United States as a white, middle-class issue; however, environmental degradation is very much a class and race issue because waste sites are often relegated to poor, minority communities. Furthermore, Indian reservations in the United States are particularly vulnerable because they do not have stringent

environmental regulations, and because of the high poverty levels on the reservations, leaders can be bribed to accept toxic waste on their land.

Toxic waste activism is often community based and commonly grows out of women's subjective experiences within their communities. Governmental resistance, and the increasing demands for scientific research to investigate the health effects of exposure to toxic waste, keep toxic waste at the forefront of women's issues in the 21st century.

See Also: Brockovich, Erin; Cancer, Environmental Factors and; Ecofeminism; Environmental Activism, Grassroots; Environmental Justice; Gibbs, Lois; Rachel's Network; Women's Environment and Development Organization.

Further Readings

Carson, R. *Silent Spring.* Boston: Mariner, 1962.

Colborn, T., et al. *Our Stolen Future: Are We Threatening Our Fertility, Intelligence, and Survival? A Scientific Detective Story.* New York: Plume, 1997.

Krauss, C. "Blue-Collar Women and Toxic-Waste Protests: The Process of Politicization." In Richard Hofrichter, ed., *Toxic Struggles: The Theory and Practice of Environmental Justice.* Salt Lake City: University of Utah Press, 2002.

Sarangi, S. "The Bhopal Aftermath: Generations of Women Affected." In Miriam Jacobs and Barbara Dinham, eds., *Silent Invaders: Pesticides, Livelihoods and Women's Health.* London: Zed Books, 2003.

Schettler, T., et al. *Generations at Risk: Reproductive Health and the Environment.* Cambridge, MA: MIT Press, 1999.

Seager, J. *Earth Follies: Coming to Feminist Terms With the Global Environmental Crisis.* London: Routledge, 1994.

Erica H. Anstey
University of South Florida

Toys, Gender-Stereotypic

The distinctions we use to separate men from women, and the qualities that go into what we call "masculine" and "feminine," are arbitrary and culturally defined. Gender roles are perpetuated and learned through gender socialization, and toys may be considered a type of gender socializing agent. Socialization connects the different generations to one another. Socialization constitutes the set of processes through which the values, norms, and practical know-how of a society are handed down from generation to generation. It is the expression of the value system characterizing the various societies and plays a role of great importance in the formation of identity and of male and female roles. On it depends the success of the transformation process of the biological characteristics into behaviors appropriate to them; from "nature" in "conformity and adaptation."

By gender, we in fact mean the process of social construction of the biological characteristics (sex). Definition, representation, and motivation of appropriate behaviors are connected with the social expectations linked to the status of a man or a woman. The process of gender differentiation is supported and made legitimate by the whole system of values of each society and by all the agencies of socialization: family, school system, peer groups, means of communication and working, associative, religious, and political experiences.

Shaping the Young

Younger and older boys and girls are encouraged to behave in different ways. They learn to walk, speak, and act in the prescribed way for their gender according to the expectations of the social groups and culture they belong to. Insufficiently compliant behavior is generally more tolerated in little boys, while little girls are expected to behave more "gently" from the early years of their lives. Boys are in fact considered physically and verbally more aggressive, physically stronger and risk seeking. Masculinity places emphasis on personal fulfilment achieved through qualities such as independence, willingness to risk, and daring. Little girls, on the other hand, are perceived as weaker, gentler, and more inclined to listen and perform care work.

These perceptions are reflected in the parents' behaviors, when, for example, they seek to give differentiated toys as presents. Model cars, trains, planes, soldiers, construction games for boys; dolls to dress and undress, soft toys, toy kitchens, and little dollhouse sets for the girls. Parents themselves will encourage sons and daughters to take part in activities connoted by specific gender characteristics. Boys are more likely than girls to be given tasks concerning repairs and maintenance in the home and the acquisi-

tion of skills outside the home environment; girls are more called on to collaborate in cleaning tasks, washing, and preparing meals.

Gender socialization, through toys, teaches and reinforces stereotypical gender roles: "Boys are better at math"; "Boys can run faster than girls"; "Boys invent things, girls use the things boys invent"; "Boys fix things, girls need things fixed." It is widely accepted that toys for boys tend to be cars, trains, action games, and toys that focus on respect for their physical abilities. Girls' toys are associated with physical attractiveness, nurturance, and domestic skill. The toys rated as most likely to be educational and to develop children's physical, cognitive, artistic, and other skills are typically rated as neutral or moderately masculine.

A second key point: people might think that toys are more androgynous these days. But go into any toy shop and you will find separate aisles, and even separate floors, for girls and boys. Toy stores divide toys into "boys" and "girls" sections; furthermore, toy packaging exhibits significant color differences. The store aisles contain plenty of pinks, yellow, whites, lavenders, reds and pastels for girls; conversely, the boys' aisles have an array of blue, the most popular "boy" color, as well as green, red, black, gray, and brown. Also, inventory may reveal sexism. Female sections are usually much bigger than the male side, possibly feeding into the stereotype that women seek more material objects then men. Gender-neutral toys seem an exception rather than a rule.

While toys are gender stereotyped for all age groups, there seems to be more flexibility in the gender stereotyping of toys for infants and toddlers.

Differences by Age Cohort

A study designed to compare how 5- to 13-year-old children's leisure activity preferences (participants consisted of 120 children, 60 boys and 60 girls from a private school in Nebraska) revealed that sex was a significant factor in determining toy category selection. Boys preferred manipulative toys, vehicles, and action figures, which tend to encourage manipulation, construction, and active exploration. In contrast, girls preferred dolls, stuffed animals, and educational toys, which tend to encourage the development of verbal rather than visual-spatial skills.

A second study carried out in Italy at the national level, shows that the preferences expressed by boys and girls for the different types of games highlight uniformity but also singularity and differences that tend to widen as the children grow. Children aged from 3 to 5 years prefer traditional toys: dolls for the girls (88.4 percent), toy cars and trains for the boys (73.5 percent), although both share a love for construction games, puzzles, and drawing, games involving movement and the manipulation of materials such as plasticine.

With the passing of years, interest increases for games of movement, especially with girls. Between 6 and 10 years, gender differences reemerge: 70.6 percent of girls continue to love drawing; among their male peers this preference falls to 47.5 percent. Moreover, 71.6 percent of boys like playing football and, again among the boys, video games are popular (65.2 percent). The same data reveal that 23.7 percent of girls aged 3 to 5 and 27.1 percent of those aged 6 to 10 prefer role games (e.g., mothers and daughters, sellers and customers), while the percentages for boys of the same age are 10.8 percent and 11.4 percent.

Lastly, 43.6 percent of girls between the ages of 3 and 5 and over a third of those in the 6 to 10 age group play at miming household tasks, as compared with 13.9 percent (age three to five) and 8.6 percent (6 to 10 years) among boys. Technology continues to be a "male" territory: already in the 3 to 5 age group the boys who love playing with video games and computers account for two-and-a-half times the number of girls (25.6 percent against 10.4 percent). Between the ages of 6 and 10, the use of computer games rises decisively, involving 65.2 percent of boys and 38.7 percent of girls.

Play Patterns and Social Skills
Several studies have looked at the way in which girls and boys play with toys and why. One of the key things that makes a child play with a gender-stereotypical toy is the way they have seen adults interacting with the same toys. Boys and girls are probably guided toward a certain type of game by the same attitudes shown by their parents and relatives, who have in mind (and have in their turn been socialized by) precise gender models, which sons and daughters have to match up to.

Through the ceaseless alternation of daily interactions, in which gender differentiation appears, and in reactions to the adoption of behaviors considered more or less appropriate to sexual identity, adults hand down the same system of roles, values, and rules handed down to them, which their children have to respect in order to be socially accepted. These values find confirmation in the peer group with which children compare themselves; they have also received them from their grandparents, parents, and relatives, and in their own turn demand them to be respected. Due to the stereotypical activities based on gender that society expects children to abide by through the toys they choose, boys and girls become limited only to their own gender, not allowing them to explore different roles. Play with gender-stereotyped toys may indeed foster differential social and cognitive skills in boys and girls. Girls restricted to traditionally girlie toys run the risk of growing up believing that appearance, nurturing, and domestic skills are more important than anything else in life. Boys, on the other hand, if they play solely with boys' toys like soldiers and competitive games, could grow up with the gender conditioning that aggression, violence, and competition are both fun and not to be condemned.

Thus, from an educational development perspective, it is widely accepted that both boys and girls will benefit from playing with a wide variety of different toys and games, whether they are traditional boys' toys or girls' toys.

See Also: Barbie Dolls; Bratz Dolls; "Femininity," Social Construction of; Gender, Defined; Gender Roles, Cross-Cultural; "Masculinity," Social Construction of; Stereotypes of Women.

Further Readings
Campenni, C. Estelle. "Gender Stereotyping of Children's Toys: A Comparison of Parents and Nonparents." *Sex Roles*, v.40/1–2 (1999).

Cherney, Isabelle D. "Gender-Linked Differences in the Toys, Television Shows, Computer Games, and Outdoor Activities of 5 to 13-Year-Old Children." *Sex Roles*, v.54/9–10 (2006).

Idle, Tracey, et al. "Gender Role Socialization in Toy Play Situations: Mothers and Fathers With Their Daughters and Sons." *Sex Roles*, v.28/11 (1993).

Owen Blakemore, Judith E., Sheri A. Berenbaum, and Lynn S. Liben. *Gender Development.* London: Psychology Press, 2008.

Elisabetta Ruspini
University of Milano, Bicocca

Track and Field, Women in

Like they have in many other sports, women have made a strong showing in the area of track and field—definitely over the past century, and even more so since 2000. Though women have carved a significant place for themselves and their talents on the track, in the jumping pits, and while throwing a shot or discus, some female track-and-field athletes struggle with self-perception, use techniques similar to male athletes to alter their bodies, and sometimes face difficult and hurtful accusations about their gender because they behave or look like men.

Scholars and researchers find the discussion about women, gender, and track especially interesting since men and women are both associated with the sport (in comparison to sports like basketball or ice skating, which are most closely identified with men and women, respectively). Though women in track and field are often viewed as "masculine," and they face pressures common to male athletes, women have continued to flourish in the sport.

Body Image, Reshaping Actions, and Controversy

In "Exploring Women Track and Field Athletes' Meanings of Muscularity," Amber D. Mosewich worked with eight women while probing the women's perceptions of themselves and their varying degrees of muscularity. Mosewich observed that these women found themselves confronted with the stereotypical expectations associated with the female body, one that is slender and agile, rather than muscular and strong, like those of the athletes involved in Mosewich's study. Men, who are encouraged to be muscular and robust—especially as athletes—do not face the same questions and concerns about self-image and self-acceptance as female track-and-field athletes whose bodies do not align with the stereotypical representation of women.

Scholars have also recently examined how female track-and-field athletes, like their male counterparts, use various supplements to control body weight, muscle, and tone. The report "Enhancing Appearance and Sports Performance: Are Female Collegiate Athletes Behaving More Like Males?" by Susan M. Muller, Teena R. Gorrow, and Sidney R. Schneider, examines how women athletes, including those in track and field, do indeed use supplements and specific behav-

iors to mold their bodies into top form, a trend most often associated with male athletes. Muller, Gorrow, and Schneider assert that many contemporary athletes do not simply participate in a sport because they enjoy it but because they desire fame, whether from securing a contract with a professional team or product endorsements.

According to the study, only 42.4 percent of men took dietary supplements to improve their bodies and performance, but over twice as many women (99.1 percent) engaged in this behavior. Only 9.6 percent of men in the study took supplements specifically used to lower their amount of body fat, whereas over three times as many women (33.8 percent) turned to supplements to decrease their body fat. These statistics imply that women feel more concerned with losing body fat, and quickly, than their male counterparts.

A controversy that has recently rocked women's professional track and field concerns Caster Semenya, a female athlete from South Africa. As Ariel Levy examines in her feature "Either/Or," published by the *New Yorker*, fans and officials alike have questioned Semenya's true gender. She has the genitalia of a woman, but, according to medical reports, does not have a uterus or ovaries; some doctors claim she has testes that never descended. In turn, Semenya has more testosterone than her fellow athletes, which, as Levy says, provides her with an obvious advantage. Doctors and officials have waged very political debates about Semenya's gender.

Semenya's situation remains noteworthy because of the discussions it has generated, focused on gender, determining gender, and what traits make a person—undeniably—either a woman or a man. Semenya's case, even more significantly, has raised questions about protecting athletes' human rights, which were sorely violated in Semenya's case.

Media Bias of a Subtle Form

When asked which sports most television viewers prefer to watch, many say male sports since they appear faster paced and more aggressive than female sports; the same holds true for track, but several scholars believe they have discovered why viewers find women's track-and-field events less entertaining than the men's. In the article "'Naturally' Less Exciting? Visual Production of Men's and Women's Track and Field Coverage During the 2004 Olympics," Jennifer Greer,

Marie Hardin, and Casey Homan argue that, because of the way in which the competition between the female and male competitors is presented, viewers' perceptions are influenced to believe the men's events are more stimulating to watch.

The authors observed that men's track-and-field events vary the camera angles, types of shots, and even special effects much more frequently than in the coverage of the women's track-and-field events, thus portraying the men's events as more engaging and exciting. The choices made by the media, as noted by Greer, Hardin, and Homan, raise important questions about the representation of women's sports—track, in particular—especially in the medium of television.

International female track-and-field athletes proved themselves in various recent competitions, most notably the Olympics held in Sydney (2000), Athens (2004), and Beijing (2008). Gold medal winners in Sydney include Pauline Davis-Thompson (Bahamas), Cathy Freeman (Australia), Maria de Lurdes Mutola (Mozambique), Nouria Mérah-Benida (Algeria), Gabriela Szabo (Romania), Derartu Tulu (Ethiopia), Olga Shishigina (Kazakhstan), Irina Privalova (Russia), Liping Wang (China), Naoko Takahashi (Japan), Heike Drechsler (Germany), Yelena Yelsina (Russia), Tereza Marinova (Bulgaria), Stacy Dragila (United States), Yanina Karolchik (Belarus), Ellina Zvereva (Belarus), Trine Hattestad (Norway), Kamilla Skolimowska (Poland), and Denise Lewis (Great Britain).

The following women won gold medals in the 2004 Athens Summer Olympics: Yulia Nesterenko (Belarus), Veronica Campbell (Jamaica), Tonique Williams-Darling (Bahamas), Kelly Holmes (Great Britain), Meseret Defar (Ethiopia), Xing Huina (China), Joanna Hayes (United States), Fani Halkia (Greece), Mizuki Noguchi (Japan), Athanasia Tsoumeleka (Greece), Yelena Slesarenko (Russia), Yelena Isinbayeva (Russia), Françoise Mbango Etone (Cameroon), Yumileidi Cumbá (Cuba), Natalya Sadova (Russia), Olga Kuzenkova (Russia), Osleidys Menéndez (Cuba), and Carolina Klüft (Sweden).

Beijing female track and field gold winners were Shelly-Ann Fraser (Jamaica), Veronica Campbell-Brown (Jamaica), Christine Ohuruogu (Great Britain), Pamela Jelimo (Kenya), Nancy Jebet Lagat (Kenya), Tirunesh Dibaba (Ethiopia), Dawn Harper (United States), Melanie Walker (Jamaica), Gulnara Galkina-Samitova (Russia), Constantina Diță-

Tomescu (Romania), Olga Kaniskina (Russia), Tia Hellebaut (Belgium), Yelena Isinbayeva (Russia), Maurren Maggi (Brazil), Françoise Mbango Etone (Cameroon), Valerie Vili (New Zealand), Stephanie Brown Trafton (United States), Aksana Miankova (Belarus), Barbora Špotáková (Czech Republic), and Natalya Dobrynska (Ukraine).

See Also: American Girl Dolls; "Masculinity," Social Construction of; Running/Marathons; Steroid Use; Sports, Women in; Title IX.

Further Readings
Greer, Jennifer D., Marie Hardin, and Casey Homan. "'Naturally' Less Exciting? Visual Production of Men's and Women's Track and Field Coverage During the 2004 Olympics." *Journal of Broadcasting & Electronic Media*, v.53/2 (June 2009).
Levy, Ariel. "Either/Or." *The New Yorker*, v.85/39 (November 30, 2009).
Mosewich, Amber D. "Exploring Women Track and Field Athletes' Meanings of Maculinity." *Journal of Applied Sport Psychology*, v.21/1 (2009).
Muller, Susan M., Teena R. Gorrow, and Sidney R. Schneider. "Enhancing Appearance and Sports Performance: Are Female Collegiate Athletes Behaving More Like Males?" *Journal of American College Health*, v.57/5 (2009).
Tricard, Louis Mead. *American Women's Track and Field, 1980-2000: A History*. Jefferson, NC: McFarland, 2007.

Karley Adney
University of Wisconsin, Marathon County

Trafficking, Women and Children

Human trafficking constitutes a form of modern-day slavery and one of the most severe forms of human rights abuses in the 21st century. It is one of the fastest growing forms of international crime and poses a significant threat to the safety and well-being of individuals throughout the world. Trafficking refers to the transfer, relocation, or transportation of human beings for the purposes of economic gain or other forms of exploitation and through the use of threat, coercion, fraud, abduction, or deception. It is typically done for purposes of sexual exploitation, forced labor and domestic servitude. Trafficking is a phenomenon associated with increasing globalization and is perpetuated by the ever-present global inequalities of gender, race, and economics. Trafficking victims are denied their basic human rights and are often kept locked up and isolated, thus restricting their opportunities for escape. Victims who are trafficked into sex work are at high risk for violence as well as human immunodeficiency virus and acquired immune deficiency syndrome (HIV/AIDS) and other sexually transmitted diseases.

As with most forms of criminal activity, it is difficult to collect accurate data about human trafficking. However, advocacy organizations and governments alike assert that the overwhelming majority of individuals who are trafficked are women and children—including both female and male children—and it is estimated that approximately half of all individuals trafficked each year are under the age of 18. Data indicates that internationally between 1 and 2 million individuals are newly trafficked each year, while millions more remain captive within the trafficking system. In addition, tens of thousands of individuals are trafficked domestically each year, including from one state to another or from a rural area to an urban one (or vice versa) within the same state.

Victims who disobey their captors are often beaten, tortured, or even killed. Recent years have witnessed increased efforts by governments, nongovernmental organizations (NGOs) and media sources to combat trafficking. However, there remain significant challenges not only in respect to raising awareness about this problem but also in prosecuting traffickers and assisting victims.

A Global Problem

Trafficking is most often a means of securing individuals for participation in various types of forced labor. It may be carried out by small networks of individuals, with each one responsible for a different aspect of the process of luring or abducting a victim, transporting them, or overseeing them once they arrive at their final destination. However, trafficking is most often carried out as part of organized crime activities. It is one of the largest criminal industries in the world, ranking third behind arms dealing and the drug trade, and generates billions of dollars in profits each year. Human trafficking is a global phenomenon and impacts nearly every country in the world—wealthy and impoverished, small and large, democracies and republics, and even monarchies. Internationally, there are distinct geographic patterns that emerge in regard to both the origins of trafficked individuals and their destinations. Victims of international trafficking are most often lured or taken from poor nations or conflict zones (referred to as "source" countries) and then pass through other "transit" countries before reaching their final destination.

At present, the most common origins of trafficked individuals include Asia, Bangladesh, China, India, Pakistan, Russia, eastern Europe (particularly Belarus, Lithuania, Romania, Ukraine, and Moldova), Mexico, parts of South America (especially Brazil and Colombia), and the Caribbean. Victims may be sent nearly anywhere in the world. However, known trafficking routes demonstrate that primary destinations for trafficked individuals tend to be industrialized, relatively prosperous nations, including those in Western Europe, Asia, the Middle East, and North America (particularly the United States).

Trafficking of Children

Children constitute a significant portion of trafficking victims. Trafficking has been defined as a form of child abuse and a clear violation of children's rights under international doctrines such as the United Nations Convention on the Rights of the Child. Governments and NGOs have reported that although the majority of child victims are adolescents, even infants and toddlers are regularly trafficked. The majority of child victims are trafficked into sex work. Indeed, the HIV/AIDS pandemic has helped create a global demand for child sex workers, particularly as many believe them to be "pure" and free from the disease. It has become increasingly apparent that children are also trafficked via the international adoption system.

While developing nations serve as the primary source countries for child victims who enter this system, Western Europe and North America serve as the primary destinations. Other trafficked children are forced to provide cheap labor for various services and industries (especially domestic and agricultural work as well as mining) or forced to serve as child soldiers during times of war. There have been documented cases of child victims being sold as brides and others being used as human sacrifices. Traffickers frequently prey upon poverty-stricken and war-torn areas and may obtain child victims in a number of ways. Parents who are living in abject poverty might simply sell their child to traffickers to obtain much-needed income. Children who are living on the streets or in orphanages may be abducted or lured by the promise of toys, food, money, new parents, or a stable home.

Efforts to Combat Trafficking

In recent years, there have been increased efforts to combat trafficking. International entities such as the United Nations, the Organization of American States, and the European Union have been vocal opponents of trafficking and have provided forums where member states can share information about trafficking, including as it pertains to trafficking patterns, the prevalence of trafficking, and strategies for combating this problem both domestically and internationally. Individual countries have overwhelmingly supported such efforts, and by 2008, 80 percent of countries throughout the world had passed their own antitrafficking legislation. Many states have passed similar legislation. In addition, NGOs and media sources have helped raise awareness about trafficking of adults and children alike. NGOs have been especially active in antitrafficking efforts.

In addition to disseminating information about the problems associated with human trafficking, promoting antitrafficking legislation, and setting up hotlines for reporting cases of trafficking, they also have been at the forefront of victim services. Such services have included identifying and rescuing victims, supplying them with basic necessities including food and shelter, providing healthcare and counseling, offering legal assistance, helping them obtain social service benefits, and job training/rehabilitation.

Despite these gains, there is a lot left to do to eradicate human trafficking. First, while awareness campaigns have been somewhat effective, they tend to equate human trafficking with sexual exploitation and forced sex work. While it is true that many victims are trafficked for the sex trade, many others are forced to work as domestic servants or in agriculture, mining and factories. Thus, awareness campaigns must expand their scope. Second, while it is common for victims who are forced into sex work to be arrested

and prosecuted under antiprostitution laws, arrest and prosecution rates for traffickers remain alarmingly low. Traffickers who are convicted often receive only minimal fines or jail terms. Third, efforts must be expanded to provide support and services for trafficking victims.

While many countries and states have agreed to such services and support them in principle, few have devoted the resources necessary to establish and maintain appropriate and timely assistance for trafficking victims. Finally, and most significantly, it is imperative to combat the ideologies and inequalities that give rise to trafficking in the first place.

See Also: Adoption; Child Abuse, Perpetrators of; Child Abuse, Victims of; Child Labor; Convention on the Rights of the Child; Prostitution, Legal; Rape, Incidence of; Sex Workers; Sexually Transmitted Infections; United Nations Development Fund for Women.

Further Readings
Academy for Educational Development. "Human Trafficking.org: A Web Resource for Combating Human Trafficking." http://www.humantrafficking.org (accessed June 2010).
Ebbe, Obi N. I. and Dilip K. Das. *Global Trafficking in Women and Children*. Boca Raton, FL: Taylor & Francis Group, 2008.
Hynes, H. P. and J. G. Raymond. "Put in Harm's Way: The Neglected Health Consequences of Sex Trafficking in the United States." In J. Silliman and A. Battacharjee, eds. *Policing the National Body: Race, Gender, and Criminalization*. Cambridge, MA: South End Press, 2002.
Kara, Siddarth Ashok. *Sex Trafficking: Inside the Business of Modern Slavery*. New York: Columbia University Press, 2008.
King, Gilbert. *Woman, Child for Sale: The New Slave Trade in the 21st Century*. New York: Chamberlain Brothers, 2004.
The Project to End Human Trafficking. http://www.end humantrafficking.org (accessed June 2010).
Strategic Global Initiatives. "Stop Child Trafficking Now." http://www.sctnow.org (accessed June 2010).
Zhang, Sheldon S. *Smuggling and Trafficking in Human Beings: All Roads Lead to America*. Westport, CT: Praeger, 2007.

J. Duquaine-Watson
University of Texas at Dallas

Transgender

There are two strands of meaning associated with the term *transgender*. The first describes a person interested in acquiring some or many of the physical characters of the opposite sex without necessarily questioning his/her biological genitals. These people desire to express in behaviors and in interpersonal relations their feelings apart from their anatomical structure and without planning the physical alteration of their body.

The term also takes on a second, more generic meaning, and this may lead to some confusion. It may describe individuals who show a different behavior from what is often considered socially appropriate for their gender. In other words, it refers to all identities or practices that cross over, cut across, move between, and combine socially constructed sex/gender boundaries. Crossdressers and drag kings and queens are included as transgender people just as intersex persons are sometimes also transsexuals. Transgender people experience the many nuances separating the "ideal" models of man and woman in their everyday lives.

The term *crossdresser*, which has taken the place of the unsuitable word *transvestite*, is generally associated with a person who feels an affinity and interest in some female or male prerogatives, such as gestural expressiveness and clothing. These persons may change their bodies by removing body hair and/or taking hormones; they do not change their sexual characteristics because they wish to "appear" to be women or men. In the past, the adoption of male clothes by women, for example, was a way to enjoy all those privileges, rights, and freedoms, which men could exclusively access. On the other hand, it was not only women in men's clothes who attracted the attention of medical doctors and researchers but also men who assumed feminine attitudes, clothes, and desires. While cases of individuals willing to live their entire lives in a guise opposite to that of their own gender were already frequent in modern times, the phenomenon seems to have increased at the turn of the 19th and 20th centuries. This was a historic moment marked by rapid changes brought about by industrialization and urbanization, coupled with the start of the consumer society.

Examples of this include drag queens, men who make use of showy female clothes; and drag kings, females who dress up in male clothes. The message

Dr. Camille Cabral, a transgender activist at a demonstration for transgender people in Paris, October 1, 2005.

drag kings and queens convey may be very complex. They are men and women who, by transforming their bodies as a form of art and as part of an artistic performance, take over the rules determining masculine and feminine and put them on show, performing them. Through their shows, they deconstruct the genders, mix them and confuse the boundaries, showing what genders really are: undefined and constantly changing.

Transgender Characteristics

Intersex persons display mixed sexual and reproductive characteristics. Within intersexuality a distinction should be made between the cases concerning primary sexuality and those related instead to secondary sexual characteristics. Primary sexual characteristics refer to the type of gonads and genital structures (ovaries or testicles); secondary sexual characteristics refer to the bodily and physiological differences. Intersexuality regarding the primary sexual characteristics is called hermaphrodism, while intersexuality depending on secondary sexual characteristics is called pseudo-hermaphrodism.

It is extremely rare for an individual to have both testicles and ovaries present. Cases of male and female pseudo-hermaphrodism are more common and are conditions marked by a physical appearance typical of the "opposite" sex, whose features appear normal. Male pseudo-hermaphrodism, for example, is when a genetically male man has external genitals and secondary sexual characters that are ambiguous or female. For this reason pseudo-hermaphrodism may be the cause of erroneous gender attribution of sex at birth.

Medial Technology

Although the anomaly has been known from ancient times, hermaphrodites were not taken into consideration by medicine for a long time. The development of medical technology changed the situation. The gender clarification progress made by surgery generated many problems for intersex people, who were increasingly forced to undergo operations for gender correction. The criteria chosen were strongly "genital" based: if a person had grown up as a girl, with breasts and other secondary female sexual features, but also had two testicles, she was consequently coopted into the male ranks.

Intersexuality is not a sexual disorder, however. It refers, instead, to individuals born in an "intermediary" sex compared to what is culturally considered necessary to socially construct men and women. Moreover, the various degrees of intersexuality are not an illness or a deformity; they are simple bodily variations.

Discrimination and Intolerance

Transgender or transsexual people have to cope with many discriminatory processes. Social institutions are often intolerant of gender diversity. Many areas of social and economic life—such as the right to motherhood or fatherhood—should be reviewed to ensure full citizens' rights for nonheterosexual people and to reduce the power of heteronormativity. In many countries, heterosexuality and marriage have long been protected by law and given access to various rights under social security. Also, there has been a general lack of attention, and a lack of comparative research, to the complex intersection between forms of social disadvantage such as gender and sexual orientation. These obstacles have profound impacts on homosexual, bisexual, transgender, and transsexual people's lives.

See Also: Bisexuality; Coming Out; Drag Kings; "Femininity," Social Construction of; Gender, Defined; Gender Reassignment Surgery; Heterosexism; Heterosexuality; Homophobia; LGBTQ; "Masculinity," Social Construction of; Sexual Orientation.

Further Readings

Halberstam, J. "Mackdaddy, Superfly, Rapper: Gender, Race, and Masculinity in the Drag King Scene." *Social Text* (1997).

Hines, S. *Transforming Gender. Transgender Practices of Identity, Intimacy and Care.* Bristol: The Policy Press, 2007.

Hird, M. "Gender's Nature: Intersexuals, Transsexuals and the 'Sex'/'Gender' Binary." *Feminist Theory.* v.1/3, 2000.

Roen, K. "But We Have To Do Something: Surgical Correction of Atypical Genitalia." *Body and Society,* v.14 (2008).

Ruspini, Elisabetta, ed. "Changing Femininities, Changing Masculinities. Social Change, Gender Identities and Sexual Orientations." *Sociological Research Online,* v.12/1 (2007).

Elisabetta Ruspini
University of Milano, Bicocca

Transnational Feminist Networks

A transnational feminist network (TFN) brings together women from three or more countries around a specific set of grievances and goals, such as women's human rights, health, or economic justice. As fluid and nonhierarchical structures that span local and global spaces, such networks are connected to globalization processes and engage extensively in cyberactivism. Four types of contemporary TFNs are discussed: those that target the neoliberal economic policy agenda; those that focus on the danger of fundamentalisms and insist on women's human rights, especially in the Muslim world; women's peace groups that target conflict, war, and empire; and networks engaging in feminist humanitarianism and international solidarity.

Globalization is a multidimensional process entailing economic, political, cultural, and geographic aspects, in which the mobility of capital, peoples, discourses, and organizations takes on an increasingly transnational or global character. TFNs are both a response to "globalization-from-above" (neoliberal capitalism, the increasing power of institutions of global governance, growing inequalities, and persistent poverty) and a contributor to "globalization-from-below" (a more people-oriented form that would institutionalize economic justice, peace, and human rights). The growth of TFNs was assisted by the United Nations Decade for Women (1976–85) and by the revolution in information and computer technologies, both of which allowed transnational feminist activists to mobilize and engage with the world of public policy.

Transnational feminist organizing and advocacy had appeared in the 1980s, but it was not until the mid-1990s that it came to the attention of feminist scholars. Preparations for the United Nations Fourth World Conference on Women, to take place in Beijing in September 1995, gave resources to existing women's groups and provided the impetus for the formation of new ones.

The Road to Transnational Feminism

Women's groups have been working together across borders since the early 20th century. In midcentury, however, their discourses, priorities, and strategies diverged sharply, reflecting ideological differences as well as the economic gulf between rich countries and the developing or postcolonial world. In the 1970s, feminist groups encompassed liberal, radical, Marxist, and socialist ideologies, and these political differences constituted one form of division within feminism. The Cold War cast a shadow on feminist solidarity in the form of the east–west divide. Many First World feminists saw legal equality and reproductive rights as key feminist demands and goals, whereas many Third World feminists emphasized underdevelopment, colonialism, and imperialism as obstacles to women's advancement. Disagreements came to the fore at the beginning of the first and second United Nations world conferences on women, which took place in Mexico City in 1975 and in Copenhagen in 1980, respectively.

A shift began to take place in the mid-1980s, during preparations for the third United Nations world conference on women, which was held in Nairobi, Kenya, in 1985. What enabled this shift were three critical economic and political developments both within states and regions and at the global level. First was the transition from Keynesian economics, with its emphasis on government intervention for full employment and citizen welfare, to neoliberal economics, with its emphasis on free markets, privatization, and trade and financial liberalization, along with a new international division of labor that relied heavily on (cheap) female labor. The second factor was the decline of the welfare state in the global north and the developmental state in the global south, which placed a heavy burden on women's reproductive or domestic roles. The third factor was the emergence of various forms of fundamentalist and right-wing religious movements that threatened women's autonomy and human rights.

The new economic and political realities led to a convergence of feminist perspectives: for many northern feminists, economic issues and development policy became increasingly important, and for many southern feminists, increased attention was now directed to women's legal status, autonomy, and rights. This was accompanied by the formation of a number of TFNs that brought together women from global north and global south alike to respond to economic pressures and patriarchal movements. Many of the women who formed or joined the TFNs were scholar-activists involved in the women-and-development research community. The networks they created in the 1980s, such as DAWN, WIDE, and Women Living Under Muslim Laws, engaged in policy-oriented research, advocacy, and lobbying around economic justice and women's human rights.

With support from United Nations agencies and Western-based foundations, more TFNs were formed in the years preceding and following the United Nations Fourth World Conference on Women. By this time, TFNs had formed a broad agenda that included a critique of unjust economic policies, as well as an insistence on women's full citizenship, reproductive rights, bodily integrity, and autonomy, no matter what the cultural context. This agenda is inscribed in the Beijing Conference Declaration and Platform for Action, with frames that resonate globally and are adopted by women's groups throughout the world: women's human rights, gender justice, gender equality, an end to the feminization of poverty, and an end to violence against women.

Feminism Against Neoliberalism

In the latter part of the 1990s, alarmed by the global reach of neoliberalism, feminist scholar-activists began addressing issues of globalization and the new global trade agenda. TFNs such as DAWN, WIDE, the Women's Environment and Development Organization, the Marche Mondiale, and others participated in the critique of neoliberalism, arguing that new rules of global free trade undermined national laws protecting workers and the environment. Transnational feminists also argued that employment losses and dislocations brought about by new international trade agreements would be disproportionately borne by women.

Feminism Against Fundamentalisms

When Islamist movements demanded stricter application of Islamic laws and norms, the implications for women were especially significant: women would be veiled in public, and in the family they would be placed under the authority of male kin or husbands. In response, antifundamentalist feminist networks were formed by expatriate Iranian and South Asian women residing in Europe and the United States. These included Women Living Under Muslim Laws, the Sisterhood is Global Institute, and the Women's Learning Partnership. Established in 1984 by a group of women from Muslim-majority countries, Women Living Under Muslim Laws has become a well-known international solidarity network with publications, exchanges, and an Alert for Action system.

Feminism Against War and Imperialism

One of the world's oldest peace organizations, and indeed the oldest TFN, is the Women's International League for Peace and Freedom, founded in 1915 by 1,300 women activists from Europe and North America opposed to what became known as World War I. Late-20th-century globalization was accompanied by a new wave of conflicts in Afghanistan, Bosnia, and central Africa involving serious women's human rights violations. Women's groups responded by forming new networks such as Women in Black, Medica Mondiale, Women Waging Peace, and Women for Women International. These organizations underscored the spe-

cific vulnerability of women and girls during wartime, the pervasive nature of sexual abuse, and the need to include women's voices in peace negotiations. In addition, they produced research to show that women's groups had been effective in peace building in Northern Ireland, as well as in Bosnia and central Africa.

In the new century, wars in Afghanistan and Iraq galvanized women across the globe to support existing peace organizations and/or build new ones. In 2002, another group to emerge from this context was U.S.-based Code Pink: Women for Peace. Its mission statement identifies it as "a women-initiated grassroots peace and social justice movement working to end the war in Iraq, stop new wars, and redirect our resources into healthcare, education and other life-affirming activities." In 2007, six women Nobel Peace Prize winners formed the Nobel Women's Initiative, with a view toward ending militarism and conflicts and bringing about peace and stability in the Middle East and elsewhere.

Feminist Humanitarianism

Although almost all TFNs may be regarded as internationalist and solidaristic, inasmuch as they are concerned about the plight of "sisters" across borders and boundaries of nationality, religion, and class, not all engage in humanitarianism as operational work. Feminist humanitarianism consists of moral support and material assistance for those in conflict zones or repressive states and is characteristic of MADRE, Medica Mondiale Kosovo, Women for Women International, and Code Pink. During a 2004 visit to Iraq, Code Pink took $650,000 in medical supplies and other aid for the Fallujah refugees who were forced from their homes when the Americans destroyed their city. Though ignored by the U.S. media, the mission garnered enormous attention from Al-Jazeera, Al-Arabiyya, and Dubai and Iranian television, which witnessed an example of American compassion.

MADRE began its work in the early 1980s, during the war in Nicaragua, when the United States sponsored the conservative Contra rebels. Partnering with sister organizations in Cuba, Nicaragua, El Salvador, Palestine, Sudan, Iraq, and Haiti, among other countries, MADRE has consistently provided aid for women and children. Working in partnership to provide emergency aid to displaced women and families in Darfur, it sent about $500,00 worth of clothing and bedding to small refugee camps in 2005. MADRE has worked with its feminist partner the Organization of Women's Freedom in Iraq to address the problem of "honor killings" that spiked after the invasion. MADRE also has supported the creation of women's shelters for victims of domestic and community violence in Baghdad, Kirkuk, Erbil, and Nasariyeh, run largely by volunteers from the Organization of Women's Freedom in Iraq.

Strategies and Achievements

Similar to other transnational social movements, TFNs create, activate, or join global networks to mobilize pressure outside states. Working alone or in coalitions, TFNs mobilize pressure outside states via e-petitions, action alerts, and appeals; acts of civil disobedience; other forms of public protest; and sometimes direct action. Second, TFNs participate in multilateral and intergovernmental political arenas. They observe and address United Nations departments, and they consult United Nations agencies and regional commissions. By taking part in and submitting documents to intergovernmental organization meetings, and by preparing background papers, briefing papers, and reports, the TFNs increase expertise on issues. By lobbying delegates, they raise awareness and cultivate supporters. The purpose of such interaction is to raise new issues, such as gender and trade, women's human rights, and violence against women in war zones, with a view toward influencing policy.

Third, TFNs act and agitate within borders and vis-à-vis states to enhance public awareness and participation. They work with labor and progressive religious groups, the media, and human rights groups on social policy, humanitarian, development, and militarization issues. They link with local partners, take part in local coalitions, and provoke or take part in public protests. Fourth, TFNs network with each other in a sustained process of internetworking and Internet-working. As such, their virtual advocacy or cyberactivism spans local, national, regional, and transnational terrains.

Policy successes have followed from their activism. TFN lobbying led to the insertion of important items in the final Vienna Declaration of the 1993 Conference on Human Rights, such as the assertion that violence against women was an abuse of human rights and attention to the harmful effects of certain traditional or customary practices, cultural prejudice,

and religious extremisms. The declaration also stated that human rights abuses of women in situations of armed conflict—including systematic rape, sexual slavery, and forced pregnancy—were violations of the fundamental principles of international human rights and humanitarian law. TFNs working on conflict and peace also inspired United Nations work on women, peace, and security. In October 2000, the United Nations Security Council issued Resolution 1325, calling on governments (as well as the United Nations Security Council itself) to include women in negotiations and settlements with respect to conflict resolution and peace building.

TFN advocacy has influenced intergovernmental organizations and the World Bank. Gender budgets, gender audits, gender mainstreaming, and gender equality are mechanisms and frames promoted by TFNs that now have been adopted by multilateral agencies, international nongovernmental organizations, and even governments.

Transnational feminism is characterized by a critique of social and gender inequalities and a set of strategies to enhance women's rights within the family and society. The strategies involve networks engaged in research, lobbying, and advocacy, as well as public protest and cross-border humanitarianism and solidarity, for women's human rights and gender equality. The Internet has facilitated feminist advocacy and solidarity campaigns, helping women connect and share information, plan and coordinate activities more rapidly, and mobilize effectively and extensively.

See Also: Association for Women's Rights in Development; Global Feminism; MADRE; Nongovernmental Organizations Worldwide; Peace Movement; United Nations Conferences on Women; Women's International League for Peace and Freedom.

Further Readings

Antrobus, Peggy. "Bringing Grassroots Women's Needs to the International Arena." *Development*, v.3/65–67 (1996).
Enloe, C. *Globalization and Militarism: Feminists Make the Link*. Lanham, MD: Rowman & Littlefield, 2007.
Ferree, Myra Marx and Aili Marie Tripp, eds. *Global Feminism: Transnational Women's Activism, Organizing, and Human Rights*. New York: New York University Press, 2006.

Helie-Lucas, M. "Women Living Under Muslim Laws." In J. Kerr, ed., *Ours by Right: Women's Rights as Human Rights*. London: Zed Books/Ottawa: North–South Institute, 1993.

Keck, Margaret and Kathryn Sikkink. *Activists Beyond Borders: Advocacy Networks in International Politics*. Ithaca, NY: Cornell University Press, 1998.

Lycklama À Nijeholt, et al., eds. *Women's Movements and Public Policy in Europe, Latin America, and the Caribbean*. London: Garland, 1998.

Moghadam, V., ed. *From Patriarchy to Empowerment: Women's Participation, Movements, and Rights in the Middle East, North Africa, and South Asia*. Syracuse, NY: Syracuse University Press, 2007.

Moghadam, V. *Globalization and Social Movements: Islamism, Feminism, and the Global Justice Movement*. Lanham, MD: Rowman & Littlefield, 2009.

Moghadam, V. *Globalizing Women: Transnational Feminist Networks*. Baltimore, MD: Johns Hopkins University Press, 2005.

Naples, N. and M. Desai, eds. *Women's Activism and Globalization*. London: Routledge, 2002.

Wichterich, C. *The Globalized Woman: Notes From a Future of Inequality*. London: Zed Books, 1999.

Valentine M. Moghadam
Purdue University

Transsexuality

The (somewhat criticized and challenged) terms *gender dysphoria* or *gender identity disorder* indicate a sense of inappropriateness about one's assigned sexual body and the associated gender role.

On the one hand, it is a state of discomfort and malaise regarding the biological sex, giving rise to a feeling of inadequacy and extraneousness. On the other hand, it also means experiencing extraneousness regarding the gender identity allotted to one's sex. By gender identity, we mean the sexual perception of oneself and of one's behavior, acquired through personal and collective experience, which makes individuals able to relate to others (as bearers of a recognizable, clear, and shared gender identity). In other words, it is the recognition of the implications of one's belonging to a sex in terms of development of attitudes, behaviors, and desires that more or less conform to cultural and social expectations.

The lack of harmony may be understandable if we think that the concept of "normality" lies in the matching of sexual characteristics and gender identity; in the "staticness" of gender; and in the polarization between two genders (male and female), considered the only "natural" categories. Gender identity is usually perceived as a stable characteristic that will not encounter changes in time. The relationship between sexual characteristics and gender has historically developed within a schema considered natural, permanent, and compulsory, according to consolidated models and predefined life destinies.

The most evident outcome of the widening of the space between gender and sex is transsexuality, the sign of a discrepancy between gender identity and anatomic sex, with the consequent need and desire to draw as close as possible to the body to which one "feels" one belongs. While the transgender person does not desire to permanently modify his/her body, the transsexual seeks a correction to physical forms, to adapt them to the gender identity they feel is their own. Transsexuality may therefore be defined as a phase of change, a transition—the way taken to reach the "opposite" sex, the state of transition from one gender to the other. It may also represent a way of living one's gender identity, a feeling of "having always known" that it may persist throughout an entire life or be "discovered" only in adulthood. The "ultimate" outcome of this process is the surgical operation for the reconstruction of a physical morphology enabling the harmonization of the body with the perception of one's gender identity. An individual of the male sex may undertake an approach toward the female sex, or an individual of the female sex may proceed toward the male pole. We, in fact, speak of MtF (male-to-female) and FtM (female-to-male) transsexuals, two acronyms used to indicate the departure and arrival point and to underline the transition (from-to).

According to some, however, transsexuals do not change sex because the chromosomes remain the same and it is not possible to guarantee the reproductive function. It would therefore be more correct to speak of a gender change (i.e., a transformation of men to women and women to men).

The term *transsexual* recently entered official lexis—first, in the strictly scientific and academic one, to later become, in the last few decades, common usage—by replacing the inadequate term *transvestite*. The term was introduced by the American psychologist David Cauldwell in the late 1940s and was taken up by the American sexologist and gerontologist Henry Benjamin to describe the persons undertaking a process to adapt their physical body to the perception they have of themselves through hormone, aesthetic, and surgical treatment. No precise terminology existed previously to describe the transition from one sex to the other, and transsexuals were frequently "mistaken" for homosexuals by scholars of psychology and psychiatry. Clinical environments finally became aware of the problem with the impetus exercised by the considerable increase in requests for sexual reassignment surgery, increasing from the late 1950s. In the wake of the first operations and the sensation they aroused, the first centers for the study of transsexuality were established in the United States in the 1970s.

Transsexuality is a complex, many-sided, multiform condition. One may enter transsexuality for very different reasons, at different moments in one's life course. There are transitions that start, proceed differently in various directions (MtF or FtM), stop, start up again, and may be concluded with a surgical sexual reassignment. There are persons who recognize themselves in the transition and enhance the thousand and one nuances found in the transition from one gender to the other. They are thus not only individuals "trapped" in the wrong body but those that combine the concepts of male and female in new, original ways, experimenting nomadisms, hybridizations, and contaminations between being "men" and "women."

Transsexuality is also socially constructed: by medico-psychiatric discourses, expert opinions, fears and stereotypes, and the absence of educational and training strategies. The significance we attribute to changes in the body is far more important than the changes that are actually produced. The sex change has often assumed exaggerated proportions in the public imaginary: the fantasies and fears aroused by this process—often perceived as wrong, incomprehensible, and unnecessary, in that it is applied to "healthy" bodies—conceal the meaning of this change, the richness of this experience, and the teaching that may stem from it.

See Also: "Femininity," Social Construction of; Gender, Defined; Gender Reassignment Surgery; Gender Roles, Cross-Cultural; Homophobia; "Masculinity," Social Construction of; Sexual Orientation; Transgender.

Further Readings

Denny, Dallas. *Gender Dysphoria: A Guide to Research.* London: Routledge, 1994.

Garfinkel, Harold. *Studies in Ethnomethodology.* Englewood Cliffs, NJ: Prentice Hall, 1967.

Hausman, Bernice Louise. *Changing Sex: Transsexualism, Technology and the Idea of Gender.* Durham, NC: Duke University Press, 1995.

Prosser, Jay. *Second Skins: The Body Narratives of Transexuality.* New York: Columbia University Press, 1998.

Elisabetta Ruspini
University of Milano, Bicocca

Trinidad and Tobago

Trinidad and Tobago, an island nation in the Caribbean Sea, is among the most prosperous Caribbean countries with a per capita gross domestic product (GDP) of $23,300 in 2009. The largest ethnic groups in Trinidad's population of about 1.2 million are South Asian Indians (40 percent) and Africans (37.5 percent), while the principal religious groups are Roman Catholic (26 percent) and Hindu (22.5 percent). The World Economic Forum rates Trinidad and Tobago as one of the most equal countries in the world with regard to gender. On a scale from 0 (inequality) to 1 (percent equality), overall Trinidad's score was 0.73 and ranks 19th out of 134 countries. On education, Trinidad scored 0.99 (58th), on health and survival 0.98 (1st), on economic participation and opportunity 0.59 (44th), and on political empowerment 0.17 (27).

Literacy is almost universal (98 percent for women), education is free through the tertiary level, and more than 50 percent of tertiary students are female, although women constitute only one-third of the professors at that level (versus a majority of teachers at the primary and secondary levels). Sixty percent of women are in the labor force, and women make up over 50 percent of the professional and technical workers. However, women earn only about 67 percent of what men do for comparable work. Women hold 27 percent of the seats in Parliament and hold 36 percent of the ministerial positions. Notable women in Trinidad's politics include Karen Nunez-Tesheira (Minister of Finance), Hazel Manning (Minister of Local Government), Esther Le Gendre (Minister of Education), and Christine Kangaloo (Ministry of Science, Technology, and Tertiary Education).

Women are entitled to 13 weeks of maternity leave at 100 percent of wages for the first month and 50 percent thereafter. All births are attended by trained personnel, and prenatal care is nearly universal. The infant mortality rate is 33 per 1,000 live births, and the maternal mortality ratio is 45 per 100,000 live births. Save the Children rates Trinidad in the midrange of Tier II or less developed countries on factors relating to maternal and child health and welfare: 33rd out of 75 countries on its Mothers' Index, 38th on its Women's Index, and 37th on its Children's Index.

See Also: Government, Women in; Parental Leave; Roman Catholic Church.

Further Readings

Hausman, R., et al. "The Global Gender Gap Report 2009." Geneva: World Economic Forum, 2009. http://www.we forum.org/en/Communities/Women%20Leaders%20 and%20Gender%20Parity/GenderGapNetwork/index .htm (accessed February 2010).

Lewis, L. *The Culture of Gender and Sexuality in the Caribbean*. Gainesville: University Press of Florida, 2003.

Save the Children. "State of the World's Mothers 2009: Investing in the Early Years." http://www.savethe children.org/publications/?WT.mc_id=1109_hp_hd _pub (accessed February 2009).

Sarah Boslaugh
Washington University

Trotta, Margarethe von

Margarethe von Trotta is one of the world's leading film directors, who won the Venice Film Festival Award for "Best Director" for her film *Marianne and Juliane* in 1981 and has been honored by film festivals in New York, Boston, Vancouver, Rome, Paris, and other cities. In the early years of her career, she was also an award-winning screen actress who starred in major films, most notably in Volker Schlondorff's *Coup de Grace*.

Von Trotta's film *Rosenstrasse* (2002) was premiered at the Venice Film Festival and was widely discussed during its run in New York City the following year. Among von Trotta's other films are *The Lost Honor of Katarina Blum* (co-directed with Schlondorff) and *Rosa Luxemburg*, for which Barbara Sukowa won "Best Actress" at the Cannes Film Festival in 1985.

Born in Berlin in 1942, von Trotta is the most important woman director to emerge from the New German Cinema. Her first solo feature was *The Second Awakening of Christa Klages* (1977), though von Trotta hit her stride only with the films that followed in rapid succession over the next several years, from *Sisters* to *Sheer Madness* and—her masterpiece— *Marianne and Juliane*.

Themes and Fullness of Characters

Though a number of her films have much to do with politics, and others work upon a much more intimate, even domestic canvas, von Trotta has always been deeply engaged with the psychology and the struggles of women: as wives, friends, sisters, activists, journalists, lovers. The films are marked by a scalding intensity and ask haunting questions about betrayal, dependence, and violence. Without question a German filmmaker operating from a complicated sense of what it means to be German in the wake of the Nazi period, von Trotta is also invested in the broadest human questions of guilt and identity.

Though admirers have described her as a feminist filmmaker, von Trotta has rejected the epithet, arguing that her films have no ideological agenda and that her interests are too various to be accommodated in a narrow conception of her work. Often, in fact, her male characters, though clearly of secondary importance, are richly complicated and appealing, their motives by no means reducible to the rage for power or control.

Alert to the myriad ways in which human beings manage to hurt one another and, often in the same motion, to destroy themselves, von Trotta refuses to portray women simply as helpless victims or to suggest that every aspect of human relations can be explained by "patriarchy." Even where her women are enmeshed in struggle and given over to suffering or sacrifice, she typically accords to them an extraordinary thoughtfulness. Those who are too weak or neurotic to survive are typically juxtaposed with other women who are distinguished by their brilliance and durability.

Von Trotta has identified Ingmar Bergman as her "favorite filmmaker," and there is no question that her work commands the kind of serious attention few other directors deserve. In every one of her films, we feel that matters of the utmost importance have been engaged by an artist who is uncompromising and who handles her material—the personal and the political—with an extraordinary combination of tenderness and delicacy but with no trace of sentimentality. The enormous power of von Trotta's films has much to do with the director's sheer intelligence and craft but also with her insistence upon shaping encounters of piercing concreteness while refusing to pretend that we will ever fully understand what matters most to us as human beings.

See Also: Film Directors, Female: Europe; Film Directors, Female: International; Film Production, Women in; Germany; Terrorists, Female;

Further Readings

Andac, B. "Senses of Cinema: Margarethe von Trotta." November 2002. http://archive.sensesofcinema.com /contents/directors/02/von_trotta.html (accessed July 2010).

Berardinelli, James. "The Promise (Review)." In *Reel Views 2*. Boston: Justin, Charles & Co., 2005.

European Graduate School. "Margarethe von Trotta: Biography." http://www.egs.edu/faculty/margarethe -von-trotta/biography (accessed July 2010).

Robert Boyers
Skidmore College

Tunisia

Tunisia is commonly considered a leading country in both the Arab and Muslim worlds, as far as women's rights are concerned. Thanks to the policy initiated by Habib Bourguiba, the militant leader who played a major role in the struggle for the country's independence and ruled over it for 30 years (1956–87), women in Tunisia now enjoy the same schooling and work opportunities as men. Under favorable laws, they have been granted the chance to live an active and emancipated life. Government institutions and organizations have been created to help them progress in their career and personal life.

Promising Statistical Changes

In the field of education, 99 percent of 6-year-old girls went to school in 2007. Compared to 32 percent of the total secondary school population in 1975–76, the rate of female students in 2006–07 was 53 percent. In 2004–05, the rate of female students in higher education reached 59 percent. These rates explain the high rate of female employment, which was as high as 25 percent of the total active population in 2007. Women are particularly active in the field of education, as they represented, for instance, 40 percent of university staff in 2007, compared to 22 percent in 1991–92. In 2007, there was a woman minister and five women secretaries of state.

Various sociological and political forces account for such rates. Women's rights in Tunisia were reinforced by Bourguiba's "Code of Personal Status" (1957), which included a number of revolutionary laws breaking with some Muslim laws and customs. One such legislation is the prohibition of polygamy and the redefinition of the contractual nature of marriage and the equal rights of both partners. The code also set a minimum age for marriage and made the bride's consent compulsory. The condition of women in Tunisia continued to improve in the post-1987 period, which corresponds to president Ben Ali's rule, known as the Change. Ben Ali's government enhanced women's rights through the creation of a number of institutions, such as the Ministry of Women, Family, Childhood and the Elderly Affairs (created in 1992 under the name Ministry of Women and Family Affairs); the National Women and Family Council; and Women's Research, Study, Documentation and Information Centre. A number of associations were also created to ensure women's welfare, like the National Union of Tunisian Women.

In the field of health, Tunisian women benefit from special health programs. Since the 1960s, the government reinforced a family-planning policy and tried to combat maternal and child mortality; it created health centers to promote family health and offer a wide range of preventive and therapeutic measures to women. Both maternal and child mortality rates have declined in most parts of the country except in the Western regions. Infant mortality rates (under 1 year of age) declined from 41 percent in 1990 to 18 percent in 2007. Under-5 child mortality rates equally declined from 52 percent in 1990 to 21 percent in 2007. The neonatal mortality rate was 13 percent in 2004.

The maternal mortality rate is 70 per 100,000. Thanks to the family planning policy, more and more women use contraceptive measures, so that the lifetime births per woman are 1.9. Tunisia has today an annual population growth of 1.09 percent; it is thus far below other northern African countries like Algeria and Morocco.

Despite the huge progress Tunisia has made on the level of legislation and social improvement, Tunisian women still suffer from persistent gender inequalities caused by a number of cultural factors like social status, traditionalism, and patriarchy. Gender equality is largely maintained by women's access to education and their urban mode of life. In this respect, rural women are far more discriminated against, exploited as underpaid labor hands and curbed in the traditional role of submissive housewives and childbearers.

In both rural and urban areas, there is also a large gap between political effort to reform laws on the one hand and the static, sexist, and patriarchal mentality on the other hand. Women lose ground in the field of gender equality since the mentality of judges and police officers have not changed in line with the newer legislation, and they remain largely cooped up in a patriarchal mindset while applying the laws. For instance, domestic violence is still largely tolerated as a private family problem in spite of the existence of a harsh law making it punishable through a two-year imprisonment and a fine. Inheritance laws are still subject to Islamic Shari`a rules and compel female inheritors to receive half the amount of their male counterparts.

Women in Tunisia today face two opposed and co-existing currents: a modernizing current that made huge steps in the direction of gender equality and a traditionalist current fed by fundamentalist ideologies and pulling women and society back toward sexism, discrimination, and gender inequality.

See Also: Algeria; Arab Feminism; Islam; Government, Women in; Marriage; Maternal Mortality; Morocco; Rural Women; Shari`a Law; Working Mothers.

Further Readings

Nordhagen, E. M. "Tunisia Gender Profile." Afrol News. (June 2000). http://www.afrol.com/features/13250 (accessed May 2010).

Pace, E. "Habib Bourguiba, Independence Champion and President of Tunisia, Dies at 96." *New York Times.* (April 7, 2000). http://www.nytimes.com/2000/04/07/world /habib-bourguiba-independence-champion-and-pres ident-of-tunisia-dies-at-96.html (accessed July 2010).

United Nations Children's International Emergency Fund "Tunisia: Background." http://www.unicef.org/info bycountry/Tunisia.html (accessed July 2010).

Lamia Tayeb
Higher Institute of Human Sciences

Turkey

The Republic of Turkey is a Eurasian country established in 1923 as the successor state to the Ottoman Empire. Under the leadership of Mustafa Kemal Ataturk, the country underwent a modernization and Westernization project with various social, legal, and political reforms. Women obtained the right to vote and to be elected in municipal elections in 1930 and in parliamentary elections in 1934. Approximately 70–75 percent of the population is Turkish, 18 percent is Kurdish, and 7–12 percent belong to other ethnic groups. The official language is Turkish, and the most widely spoken minority language is Kurdish. As to religion, 99.8 percent of the population is registered as Muslim, whereas 0.2 percent is registered as Christian or Jewish. The secularist heritage of the country represented by the army and the rise of political Islam rendered the female body a major field for this contest of power, as reflected in the headscarf ban.

Gender Equality

Gender equality is protected by law in Turkey, but sexual orientation and transgender equality are not protected. Turkey signed the Convention on the Elimination of All Forms of Discrimination against Women in

1986. Despite recent advancements in the constitution, the civil code, the criminal code, and the labor act, the implementation and realization of women's rights has been a challenge. Besides, there are laws and regulations that discriminate on the basis of gender. Political customs and patriarchal family structure also prevent women from enjoying their rights as equal citizens.

Despite the long history of women's political participation, the ratio of women in the national parliament in 2010 is 9.1 percent. Tansu Çiller was Turkey's first female prime minister between the years 1993 and 1996, but the country has never had a female president. There are currently no female governors, and only 16 of 155 ambassadors are female. Female life expectancy is 74.19 years, and the median age of women is 28.4 years. The fertility rate of women in Turkey is 2.1. The infant mortality rate has decreased from 44.2 per 1,000 live births in 2003 to 25.78 per 1,000 live births in 2010. Violence against women, particularly domestic violence and violence in the name of honor, is still a pressing issue. The problem of violence is intensified by the absence of adequate support mechanisms.

Turkey ranks 102nd in the world in educational expenditures. The literacy rate in the country is 88.1 percent, and there is a significant difference between male literacy at 96 percent and female literacy at 80.4 percent. Since boys' education is attributed more importance and girls' domestic labor is desired, more girls quit elementary school than boys.

Turkey is a middle-income country, ranking 98th in world income, with a per capita income of $11,200. The Gender Related Development Index of Turkey is 0.763, and it ranked 79th of 157 countries in 2009. Sixty-nine percent of the population in Turkey live in urban areas. The gap between female and male employment rates has risen since the mid-1990s. Current labor force participation rate is 71.3 percent for men and 24.8 percent for women. Share of women in wage employment in nonagricultural sectors is only 19.9.

See Also: Domestic Violence; Financial Independence of Women; Honor Killings; Representation of Women in Government, International; Veil.

Further Readings

Central Intelligence Agency. "The World Factbook: Turkey." https://www.cia.gov/library/publications/the -world-factbook/geos/tu.html (accessed June 2010).

Turkish Republic Prime Ministry Directory General on the Status of Women. "National Research on Violence Against Women in Turkey 2008." http://www.ksgm.gov .tr//tdvaw/Statistics.htm (accessed May 2010).

Turkish Statistical Institute. "Census of Population; Social and Economic Characteristics of Population." http:// www.turkstat.gov.tr/Kitap.do?KT_ID=11&metod =AnaKategori (accessed June 2010).

United Nations Development Programme. "UNDP Turkey and Gender in Development." http://www.undp.org.tr /Gozlem2.aspx?WebSayfaNo=86 (accessed May 2010).

Rustem Ertug Altinay
New York University

Turkmenistan

A former member of the Soviet Union, Turkmenistan is located in central Asia along the Caspian Sea. Since independence was declared in 2001, the country has been struggling with a 60 percent unemployment rate, but further development of oil and gas reserves is eventually expected to improve the $6,700 per capita income. Almost half of the workforce is engaged in agriculture, mostly in cotton production. Roughly half the population lives in urban areas. At present, nearly a third of Turkmens live below the poverty line, and government corruption depletes what resources are available. In this homogeneous society, 85 percent of the population identify themselves as Turkmens. Because 89 percent of the populous is Muslim, this politically authoritarian country has a highly traditional culture in which a woman's status is essentially defined by reproduction. The government exercises strict control over the dissemination of information concerning the status of women. Although the constitution guarantees gender equality, in reality women have no legal right to protest discriminatory treatment.

When the Soviet Union gained controlled of central Asia in the 1920s, it launched a campaign of *raskreposhchenie zhenshchin* to free women from those restrictions and bring them into the agricultural and industrial workforce. Reform efforts included preventing arranged marriages in which young girls were basically sold into marital slavery,

To counter Turkmenistan's high level of road fatalities, youth are trained on responsible driving, road safety, and first aid.

the veiling and seclusion of women, polygyny, and limiting educational opportunities for females. The campaign met with violent resistance. After the dissolution of the Soviet Union, religious and cultural traditionalism again determined the proper roles for women. The length of compulsory education for girls was dropped from 11 years to 9, and many girls began marrying at the legal age of 16. In rural areas, many of those marriages were arranged by parents who forced their daughters into marriage.

According to social indicators, the median age for women in Turkmenistan is 24.8 years. The country ranks 58th in the world in infant mortality, with 45.36 deaths per 1,000 live births. Females have a life expectancy of 70.95 years compared to 64.94 years for males.

Turkmenistan has a fertility rate of 2.22 children per female. Female literacy is 98.3 percent compared to 99.3 percent for males. In 2005, 94 percent of females 15 years and over were in the workforce. However, they were generally limited to fields such as education and healthcare, which are considered suitable to women. The limited data that is available indicates that women are discriminated against in both hiring and wages. Women received the right to vote and stand for election in 1926, but no women were elected to parliament until 1990. By 2005, only 5 percent of legislators were female.

Violence against women also continues to flourish, and women have little recourse against such actions. Turkmen law guarantees women the right to own and inherit property, but male rights predominate. Women are often forbidden from traveling outside the country, and movement within Turkmenistan also may be limited. When outside their homes, women are often subjected to security checks.

See Also: Domestic Violence; Marriages, Arranged; United Nations Development Fund for Women.

Further Readings
Blackwell, Carole. *Tradition and Society in Turkmenistan: Gender, Oral Culture, and Song.* Richmond, VA: Curzon Press, 2001.
Central Intelligence Agency. "The World Factbook: Turkmenistan." https://www.cia.gov/library /publications/the-world-factbook/geos/tx.html (accessed June 2010).
Keller, S. "Trapped between State and Society: Women's Liberation and Islam in Soviet Uzbekistan, 1926–1941." *Journal of Women's History,* v.10/1 (Spring 1998).
NAM Institute for the Empowerment of Women. "Turkmenistan." http://www.niew.gov.my/niew/index .php?option=com_docman&task=cat_view&gid=52 &Itemid+60&lang=en (accessed February 2010).
Social Institutions and Gender Index. "Gender Equality and Social Institutions in Turkmenistan." http://gender index.org/country/turkmenistan (accessed June 2010).

Elizabeth Rholetter Purdy
Independent Scholar

Tuvalu

Tuvalu has come to epitomize the approaching catastrophe of worldwide climate change and sea-level rise. Although the island nation has a population of just under 12,000, Tuvalu has become a "poster child" for encroaching environmental disaster, a case that has been well documented through films and newspaper, magazine, and journal articles.

The nation is an island group made up of nine coral atolls in the South Pacific Ocean, about half way between Hawaii and Australia. Tuvalu means "eight standing islands," and refers to eight islands that have supported the population for at least several hundred years. These islands are Funafuti, Nanumaga, Nanumea, Niutao, Nui, Nukufetau, Nukulaelae, and Vaitupu. Altogether, Tuvalu is composed of nine atolls and reef islands, and has a land area of just 26 square kilometers and a population of 11,600 people. It is an isolated and culturally distinct nation that gained independence in 1978 from the British and has been a member of the United Nations since 2000.

Tuvalu natives are 96 percent Polynesian and 4 percent Micronesian. The median age of men in Tuvalu is 22.4 years and 26.0 years for women. Women have a higher life expectancy rate than men, with women living to an average of 66.5 years versus men at 62.3 years. The fertility rate in Tuvalu is 3.14 children born per woman. Tuvalu has an infant mortality rate of 38.6 deaths per 1,000 live births for males and 32.22 deaths per 1,000 live births for females. Men and women both attend school for an average of 11 years. The country has poor soil and is highly dependent upon imported food and fuel. Subsistence farming and fishing are the primary sources of income. Approximately 15 percent of adult males work abroad on merchant ships, and their remittances contributed nearly $2 million to the economy in 2007.

Economic and Environmental Shocks

Since independence, Tuvalu has been characterized by its vulnerability to environmental and economic shocks, even though the government has engaged in sound and innovative policies, and the country has displayed enduring social stability. Therefore, Tuvalu has taken a leadership role in discussions of global climate change, seeking to raise public awareness through speeches at the United Nations, leadership in regional organizations, and high-profile participation in global policy conferences. Tuvaluan leaders demand that the world acknowledges the sustainability challenges that Tuvalu faces, the effect of global climate change, accept responsibility for the rising sea levels and altered weather patterns that Tuvalu is experiencing, and that worldwide leaders take steps to act. Sustainability challenges in Tuvalu include managing the pressure on biophysical and social systems from population growth, high population density, changing aspirations, and internal migration to the main administrative center on Funafuti.

Climate change is likely to interact in complex ways with other socioecological imperatives in Tuvalu. In its summary of research into climate change impacts, the Intergovernmental Panel on Climate Change indicates that small island states such as Tuvalu are likely to face exacerbated coastal erosion and land loss, increased flooding, increased soil salinization and saltwater intrusion into groundwater, increased frequency of coral bleaching in reef systems, and other impacts on biophysical systems. If climate change trends continue, Tuvalu could become uninhabitable within the next half century, perhaps the first nation of environmental (climate) refugees.

While media has portrayed Tuvalu as an appealing victim of global warming, it should be noted that the men and women of Tuvalu have played an active and resilient role in ensuring the future economic and environmental sustainability of their nation.

See Also: Climate Change as a Women's Issue; Fertility; Infant Mortality.

Further Readings

Allen, F. "Will Tuvalu Disappear Beneath the Sea? Global Warming Threatens to Swamp a Small Island Nation." *Smithsonian*, v.35 (2004).

Barnett, J. "Titanic States? Impacts and Responses to Climate Change in the Pacific Islands." *Journal of International Affairs*, v.59 (2005).

Pollock, E., producer/director. "Tuvalu: That Sinking Feeling." PBS Frontline/World Rough Cut. (2005). http://www.pbs.org/frontlineworld/rough/2005/12 /tuvalu_that_sin_1.html (accessed July 2010).

Dara Nix-Stevenson
University of North Carolina at Greensboro

"Two-Spirit"

Cross-cultural comparative studies have shown that genders, sexes, and sexualities are not always fixed into binary categories such as femininity and masculinity, female and male, or homosexuality and heterosexuality. In Native American cultures, both historically and presently, more than two gender, sex, and sexuality categories are marked and institutionalized. Two-spirit is a contemporary designation for Native Americans who are transgender, intersex, lesbian, gay, or bisexual, and has served to replace the term *berdache*, which was primarily used by anthropologists to describe gender variant and nonheterosexual people and practices within Native American cultures.

The term *two-spirit* was coined in 1990 at the third annual spiritual gathering of Native American lesbian and gay peoples, which took place near Winnipeg, the capital and largest city of Manitoba, Canada. Two-spirit indicates the presence of both a feminine and masculine spirit within one body and may be used to refer to traditions wherein multiple gender, sex, and sexuality categories are institutionalized within Native American tribal cultures. The English phrase two-spirit is not meant to be translated into Native American languages; to do so may change its common meaning.

The decision by Native Americans to use the label *two-spirit* was deliberate, with a clear intention to maintain cultural continuity with past native cultures and to distance themselves from non-native lesbians and gays. Two-spirit is a generic term for Native Americans who are not heterosexual or who are ambivalent in terms of gender or sex, although not all Native Americans who identify as "transgender," "intersex," "lesbian," "gay," or "bisexual" also identify with the two-spirit label, and some reject the term altogether.

Two-spirit people have been previously termed *berdache* by social scientists in the disciplines of anthropology, history, sexology, sociology, and psychology, and by other writers on the subjects of sexuality and gender. The earliest use of the term *berdache* dates back to the 1700s, when such individuals were condemned. The word *berdache* originally came from the Persian *bardaj*, and spread to Italian, via the Arabs,

as *bardasso* and to Spanish as *bardaxa* or *bardaje* by the early 1500s. At about the same time the word *bardache* appeared in French and referred to the passive homosexual partner. The term has also been translated as "kept boy" or "male prostitute." With this etymology, the term *berdache* has been generally established as derogatory, insulting, and inappropriate.

Berdache has been used in anthropological writings not to refer to "kept boys" or "male prostitutes," but to describe what was perceived as cross-dressing, homosexuality, intersexuality, and transgenderism, as institutions that were viewed positively in Native American cultures. This sometimes idealized or romanticized view of purportedly positively sanctioned Native American gender or sexual categories do not fit the experiences of many contemporary transgender, intersex, lesbian, gay, or bisexual Native Americans who have had to leave their reservations or communities because of persistent transphobia and homophobia.

See Also: Coming Out; Gay and Lesbian Advocacy; Gender, Defined; Gender Roles; Homophobia; Intersex; Sexual Orientation–Based Social Discrimination: Outside United States; Sexual Orientation–Based Social Discrimination: United States; Transgender.

Further Readings

Dancing to Eagle Spirit Society—Two Spirited People. "The Way of the Two Spirited People." http://www .dancingtoeaglespiritsociety.org/twospirit.php (accessed March 2010).

Jacobs, Sue-Ellen, Wesley Thomas, and Sabine Lang, eds. *Two-Spirit People: Native American Gender Identity, Sexuality, and Spirituality.* Urbana: University of Illinois Press, 1997.

Cathy Borck
City University of New York